Hellenic Studies 2

Labored in Papyrus Leaves:
Perspectives on an Epigram Collection
Attributed to Posidippus (P.Mil.Vogl. VIII 309)

Labored in Papyrus Leaves:
Perspectives on an Epigram Collection
Attributed to Posidippus (P.Mil.Vogl. VIII 309)

Edited by Benjamin Acosta-Hughes,
Elizabeth Kosmetatou, and Manuel Baumbach

Center for Hellenic Studies
Trustees for Harvard University
Washington, D.C.
Distributed by Harvard University Press
Cambridge, Massachusetts, and London, England
2004

Labored in Papyrus Leaves: Perspectives on an Epigram Collection Attributed to Posidippus (P.Mil.Vogl. VIII 309),
edited by Benjamin Acosta-Hughes, Elizabeth Kosmetatou, and Manuel Baumbach
Copyright © 2004 Center for Hellenic Studies, Trustees for Harvard University
All Rights Reserved.
Published by Center for Hellenic Studies, Trustees for Harvard University, Washington, D.C.
Distributed by Harvard University Press, Cambridge, Massachusetts and London, England
Production editors: Jennifer Reilly and Ivy Livingston
Production: Ivy Livingston
Cover design and illustration: Michael Horsley
Printed in Baltimore, MD by Victor Graphics

Editorial Team
Senior Advisers: W. Robert Connor, Gloria Ferrari Pinney, Albert Henrichs, James O'Donnell, Bernd Seidensticker
Editorial Board: Gregory Nagy (Chair), Christopher Blackwell, Casey Dué, Mary Ebbott, Anne Mahoney, Leonard Muellner, Ross Scaife
Managing Editor: Gregory Nagy
Executive Editors: Casey Dué, Mary Ebbott
Production Editors: M. Zoie Lafis, Ivy Livingston, Jennifer Reilly
Web Producer: Mark Tomasko

Library of Congress Cataloging-in-Publication Data:
Labored in papyrus leaves: perspectives on an epigram collection attributed to Posidippus (P.Mil.Vogl. VIII 309) / edited by Benjamin Acosta-Hughes, Elizabeth Kosmetatou, and Manuel Baumbach.
    p. cm. — (Hellenic Studies ; 2)
Includes bibliographical references and index.
ISBN 0-674-01105-8 (alk. paper)
1. Posidippus, of Pella, b. ca. 310 B.C.—Epigrams. 2. Posidippus, of Pella, b. ca. 310 B.C.—Authorship. 3. Posidippus, of Pella, b. ca. 310 B.C.—Manuscripts.
4. Epigrams, Greek—History and criticism. 5. Manuscripts, Greek (Papyri)
I. Acosta-Hughes, Benjamin. II. Kosmetatou, Elizabeth. III. Baumbach, Manuel.
IV. Title. V. Series.
PA4399.P15L33 2003
888'.0102—dc22   2003018580
23456789

For the Directors and Fellows of the CHS 2001–2002
with gratitude and affection

TABLE OF CONTENTS

Preface

G. Nagy ix

Abbreviations x

Editors' Note xiii

Introduction

B. Acosta-Hughes, E. Kosmetatou, M. Baumbach 1

1. S. Stephens and D. Obbink, *The Manuscript* 9

2. D. Obbink, *Posidippus on Papyri Then and Now* 16

3. D. Sider, *Posidippus Old and New* 29

4. B. Acosta-Hughes, *Alexandrian Posidippus: On Rereading the GP Epigrams in Light of P.Mil.Vogl. VIII 309* 42

5. G. Nagy, *Homeric Echoes in Posidippus* 57

6. A. Sens, *Doricisms in the New and Old Posidippus* 65

7. K. Gutzwiller, *A New Hellenistic Poetry Book: P.Mil.Vogl. VIII 309* 84

8. R. Hunter, *Notes on the* Lithika *of Posidippus* 94

9. M. Smith, *Elusive Stones: Reading Posidippus'* Lithika *through Technical Writing on Stones* 105

10. D. Schur, *A Garland of Stones: Hellenistic* Lithika *as Reflections on Poetic Transformations* 118

11. M. Baumbach and K. Trampedach, *"Winged Words": Poetry and Divination in Posidippus'* Oiônoskopika 123

12. S. Stephens, *For You, Arsinoe . . .* 161

13. B. Dignas, *Posidippus and the Mysteries:* Epitymbia *Read by the Ancient Historian* 177

Table of Contents

14. E. Kosmetatou, *Vision and Visibility: Art Historical Theory Paints a Portrait of New Leadership in Posidippus'* Andriantopoiika 187

15. M. Fantuzzi, *The Structure of the* Hippika *in P.Mil.Vogl. VIII 309* 212

16. E. Kosmetatou, *Constructing Legitimacy: The Ptolemaic* Familiengruppe *as a Means for Self-Definition in Posidippus'* Hippika 225

17. N. Papalexandrou, *Reading as Seeing: P.Mil.Vogl. VIII 309 and Greek Art* 247

18. R. Thomas, *"Drownded in the Tide": The* Nauagika *and Some "Problems" in Augustan Poetry* 259

19. P. Bing, *Posidippus'* Iamatika 276

20. D. Obbink, 'Tropoi' *(Posidippus AB 102–103)* 292

Afterword
    G. Hoffman, *An Archeologist's Perspective on the Milan Papyrus* 302

Concordance 309

Bibliography 313

Figures . . . . after page 344

Contributors 349

Indexes 353

PREFACE

Gregory Nagy

Harvard University's Center for Hellenic Studies, located in the city of Washington, D.C., brings together a variety of research and teaching interests centering on Hellenic civilization in the widest sense of the term "Hellenic," encompassing the evolution of the Greek language and its culture as a central point of contact for all the different civilizations of the ancient Mediterranean world.

Labored in Papyrus Leaves, edited by Benjamin Acosta-Hughes, Elizabeth Kosmetatou, and Manuel Baumbach, is part of a new monograph series, "Hellenic Studies." The title of the series reflects the humanistic breadth of the enterprise.

The present collection of contributions exemplifies the diversity and the topicality of the series. The editors, who were also the prime organizers of the original colloquium that brought together the contributors, have integrated a wide variety of approaches and interests in focusing on the new Posidippus Papyrus. A careful reading of this monograph leads to a deeper understanding of the "state of the art" in confronting the inherent problems of poetics and authorship in Hellenistic poetry.

ABBREVIATIONS

AB	Austin, C. and Bastianini, G., eds. *Posidippi Pellaei Quae Supersunt Omnia*. Milan, 2002.
AP	*Palatine Anthology.*
APl	*Planudean Anthology.*
BG	Bastianini, G. and Gallazzi, C. (eds.), con la collaborazione di C. Austin, *Posidippo di Pella: Epigrammi* (P.Mil.Vogl. VIII 309). Papiri dell' Università degli Studi di Milano, 8. Milan, 2001.
BKT	*Berliner Klassikertexte.* Berlin, 1904–1939.
CA	Powell, J. U., ed. *Collectanea Alexandrina*. Oxford, 1925.
CEG	Hansen, P. A., ed. *Carmina epigraphica Graeca saeculorum VII–V a. Chr.* Berlin, 1983.
CEG2	Hansen, P. A., ed. *Carmina epigraphica Graeca saeculi IV a. Chr.* Berlin, 1989.
CGF	Kaibel, G., ed. *Comicorum Graecorum fragmenta*. Berlin, 1899.
EG	Page, D. L., ed. *Epigrammata Graeca*. Oxford, 1975.
FdD	*Fouilles de Delphes.*
FGE	Page, D. L., ed. *Further Greek Epigrams*. Cambridge, 1981.
FGrHist	Jacoby, F., ed. *Die Fragmente der Griechischen Historiker.* Berlin 1923-1930. Leiden 1940–1998.
GLP	Page, D. L., ed. *Greek Literary Papyri I.* Cambridge, Mass., 1942.
Gow	Gow, A. S. F., ed. *Theocritus.* 2 vols. 2nd ed. Cambridge, 1952.
GP	Gow, A. S. F. and Page, D. L., eds. *The Greek Anthology: Hellenistic Epigrams*. 2 vols. Cambridge, 1965.
GP *Garland*	Gow, A. S. F. and Page, D. L., eds. *The Greek Anthology: The Garland of Philip.* 2 vols. Cambridge, 1968.

GV	Peek, W., ed. *Griechische Vers-Inschriften I: Grab-Epigramme.* Berlin, 1955.
ID	*Inscriptions de Délos*
IG	*Inscriptiones Graecae*
I. Metr. Egypt	Bernand, Etienne, ed. *Inscriptions métriques de l'Egypte gréco-romaine. Recherches sur la poésie épigrammatique des Grecs en Egypte.* Annales littéraires de l'Université de Besançon 98. Paris 1969.
MMA 1908	*Metropolitan Museum of Art: Catalogue of the Collection of Casts.* New York, 1908.
MW	Merkelbach, R. and West, M. L., eds. *Hesiodi fragmenta selecta.* 3rd ed. Oxford, 1990.
OCT	*Oxford Classical Texts*
OGIS	Dittenberger, W., ed. *Orientis Graeci Inscriptiones Selectae.* 2 vols. Leipzig 1903–5.
P.Berol.	*Papyrus Berolinensis*
PCG	Kassel, R. and Austin, C., eds. *Poetae comici Graeci.* Vols. 2–5, 7. Berlin, 1983.
P.Mil.Vogl.	Papiri dell' Università degli Studi di Milano. Milan 1961–2001.
P.FirminDidot	Papyrus from the Firmin-Didot Collection (cf. P. Louvre).
Pf.	Pfeiffer, R., ed. *Callimachus.* 2 vols. Oxford, 1949–51.
PLF	Lobel, E. and Page, D., eds. *Poetarum Lesbiorum fragmenta.* Oxford, 1955.
P.Lille	Papyrus grecs (Institut Papyrologique de l'Université de Lille).
P.London.Lit.	Milne, H. J. M., ed. *Catalogue of the Literary Papyri in the British Museum.* London 1927.
P.Louvre	Papyri in the Département des Antiquités Égyptiennes— Département des Antiquités Grecques, Étrusques et Romaines.
PMG	Page, D. L., ed. *Poetae melici Graeci.* Oxford, 1962.
PMGF	Davies, M., ed. *Poetarum melicorum Graecorum Fragmenta* I. Oxford, 1991.

Abbreviations

P.Oxy.	*The Oxyrhynchus Papyri.* London, 1898.
PSI	*Pubblicazioni della Società Italiana per la ricerca dei papiri greci e latini in Egitto.*
P.Petrie	*The Flinders Petrie Papyri.* Dublin 1891–1905.
P.Tebt.	*The Tebtunis Papyri.* London 1902–1976.
RE	Pauly, A., Wissowa, G., and Kroll, W., eds. *Real-Encyclopädie der klassischen Altertumswissenschaft.* Stuttgart, 1893–1978.
SB	Preisigke, F., ed. *Sammelbuch griechischer Urkinden aus Aegypten.* Strasbourg, 1915.
SEG	*Supplementum Epigraphicum Graecum.*
SH	Lloyd-Jones, H., and Parsons, P., eds. *Supplementum Hellenisticum.* Berlin, 1983.
SVF	Arnim, H. von, ed. *Stoicorum veterum fragmenta.* 3 vols. Leipzig, 1903–1921.
W	West, M. L., ed. *Iambi et Elegi Graeci ante Alexandrum cantati.* 2 vols. 2nd ed. Oxford, 1989.

All references to Posidippus follow the *editio minor* unless otherwise noted. All references to the *Hellenistic Epigrams* by Gow-Page are to Posidippus unless otherwise noted.

EDITORS' NOTE

In reproducing the text(s) of the new epigrams preserved by P.Mil.Vogl. VIII 309 the editors have chosen to retain the lunate sigma and iota adscript of the papyrus. Given that the text(s) of these epigrams is still undergoing substantial revision through new reading and supplementation at the time this volume goes to press, we felt it best to represent the poems on the printed page as they are preserved in the papyrus. For all other Greek texts, including the earlier known epigrams of Posidippus, we have followed the conventions of standard editions. For the most part we have preferred to use Latinized spellings in transliterating Greek names, and in translation of Greek text.

In the interest of uniformity all epigrams attributed to Posidippus are given with the numeration of the 2002 Austin/Bastianini edition (the *editio minor*); where individual contributors cite a different text, they note this. The pre-Milan epigrams are given with both AB and GP (or *SH*) numbers.

Translations given in individual articles are the authors' own unless otherwise noted.

INTRODUCTION

Shut not your doors to me proud libraries,
For that which was lacking on all your well-fill'd shelves, yet
   needed most,
I bring,
Forth from the war emerging, a book I have made,
The words of my book nothing, the drift of it every thing,
A book separate, not link'd with the rest nor felt by the intellect,
But you ye untold latencies will thrill to every page.

            Walt Whitman, *Leaves of Grass*, 1855

There are many ways of presenting a new book, and Walt Whitman has chosen a provocative one. His book, *Leaves of Grass*, seemingly looking for a place in the canon of established books, i.e. in the libraries, is different as it contains a secret, which cannot be intellectually perceived: the secret of poetry and its power, which goes beyond words and unfolds itself only in the act of reading. In this case *Labored in Papyrus Leaves* contains no such secret. By presenting a variety of perspectives on an epigram collection attributed to the third-century BCE poet Posidippus of Pella it hopes to attract, inspire, and accompany readers, who are looking for it in another "new" poetry book—the third-century BCE epigram collection preserved by P.Mil.Vogl. VIII 309.

    The loss of the greater part of Greek literature from antiquity is one of the enduring sorrows for all those who find themselves drawn to the voices of this cultural past. For all the careful and painstaking labor of those who work in the areas of classical antiquity to delineate a lost world, and for all the intellectual effort of their audience(s) to imagine such a world, this effort must necessarily be, at least in part, in vain. For the reality of this loss is constantly, and frustratingly, present. Hence the joy we feel at the appearance of a new text, somehow miraculously preserved, is the greater. The last few decades have seen several new poetic texts that have greatly enhanced our knowledge of Archilochus, Stesichorus, Simonides, and Callimachus.[1] In the early autumn of 2001 a truly substantial collection of

---

[1] The so-called "First Cologne Epode" (1996a West) was first edited by Merkelbach and West 1974. The "Lille Stesichorus" (*PMGF* 22b) consists of several papyrus fragments; the longest of these,

1

Introduction

Hellenistic epigrams, some 112 poems attributed to Posidippus of Pella (ca. 315–250 BCE), was first made available to scholars and to the general public. Edited in exemplary fashion by G. Bastianini and C. Gallazzi, with the collaboration of C. Austin, these epigrams appeared in the lavish edition *Posidippo di Pella—Epigrammi* (P.Mil.Vogl. VIII 309), the eighth volume of the papyrological series *Papyri dell'Università degli Studi di Milano*. A second edition of this text, which also included the entire literary tradition associated with Posidippus, was published a year later by C. Austin and G. Bastianini with Italian and English translations in a convenient small volume that a wide audience of specialists and non-specialists alike will cherish.

The concept of putting together *Labored in Papyrus Leaves* was born at the Harvard Center for Hellenic Studies (CHS) in Washington, D.C. during an extraordinary fruitful conference on the poet Posidippus entitled Ἐν βύβλοις πεπονημένη: *On Reading A New Epigram Collection*. It was the culmination of a happy collaboration between the 2001–2002 Junior Fellows that was conceived and concluded during the better part of their year at the Center. It had already been clear from the moment the *editio princeps* appeared that this collection was not only going to increase enormously our knowledge of Hellenistic epigram, but was also going to be of great importance for the understanding of ancient poetry collections, the early book roll, and the aesthetics of organizing texts. As soon as the new epigram collection arrived at the CHS, the Fellows realized that this new text afforded a very unusual opportunity for collegial interaction and interdisciplinary dialogue. Only two of these epigrams were previously known in Byzantine sources: the scholar John Tzetzes attributes one (AB 15) to Posidippus, and one (AB 65) is included under Posidippus' name in the *Planudean Anthology*. A few of the epigrams were published by the editors in a preliminary edition,[2] and some significant scholarly work had already treated some of the unpublished epigrams. Yet the majority of these short poems were essentially unknown: there existed no extensive tradition of scholarship to inform, or prejudice, the reader's initial encounter with the texts. At the same time, a collection that included poems on gemstones and statuary, poems honoring contemporary historical figures, among them three Ptolemaic queens, poignant poems that figure definitions of happiness, bereave-

....

P.Lille 76, was edited first by Ancher in Meiller 1976, and again by Parsons 1977. Cf. Bremer, van Erp Taalman Kip, and Slings 1987:24–61 ("First Cologne Epode"), 128–74 ("Lille Stesichorus"). The collected "New Simonides" fragments are conveniently available, with English translation, in Boeddeker and Sider 2001:13–29. The same papyrus that gave us the "Lille Stesichorus" is also the source of a large part of the extant opening to Callimachus *Aetia* 3, the *Victory of Berenice* (*SH* 254–269).

[2] Bastianini and Gallazzi 1993a, 1993b.

2

ment, and loss, and poems that were clearly a nexus of allusions to earlier and contemporary Greek literature, provided a very special space for the varied scholarly trajectories of the Fellows to come together. Whether art historical, archaeological, historical, philosophical or literary, each area of interest in the ancient world could view, and react to, a new cultural monument.

With encouragement and generous support of the directors and staff of the CHS, the Fellows decided to organize a round-table discussion of these new texts. As initially conceived, the round-table was to consist of the Fellows themselves and an equal number of invited participants: experts in papyrology, Hellenistic poetry, Greek epigram, and Latin literature. Each participant in the round-table was invited to choose a poem or selection of poems on which to speak. In the process of selection, there was surprisingly little overlap: when the participants met on April 19–20, 2002, all nine transmitted categories of epigrams collected in the new papyrus were represented by at least one speaker, some by several.[3] In preparation for the conference, the Fellows met weekly to read together and discuss each epigram category represented in the papyrus roll, each from his or her point of view. It consequently became clear that it was also desirable that the panels be organized to follow the collection in sequence. The resulting program, which is reflected in this volume, represents a confluence of these two trajectories. In the end, the conference brought together twenty-three speakers from different academic backgrounds and fields in order to approach the new epigram collection from a variety of perspectives. Thus art historians, archaeologists, philologists, papyrologists, ancient historians, epigraphists, as well as specialists in comparative literature and ancient politics entered an interdisciplinary dialogue on the new epigram collection, which turned out to be an intellectually deeply rewarding experience.

This interdisciplinary approach seemed to be most natural as in a way the 'object' of the conference, Hellenistic epigram, can also be called an interdisciplinary genre: it enters into a deliberate and constant dialogue with other literary, epigraphical, or archaeological sources. In the Hellenistic era, this technique aimed at engaging the reader into an entangling relationship with the poet and his work by offering limited information and often ambiguous clues. By challenging intellect and scholarly erudition at the same time, epigrammatists invited their audiences to participate in a process of supplementation through which they reconstructed stories and solved riddles. In short, they supplied the context from which literary epigram had been severed. A variety of different perspectives is therefore necessary in order to understand the complexity of the epigrams and to participate in an interactive reading that P. Bing has well defined as "Ergänzungsspiel".[4]

---

[3] For the program, see http://www.chs.harvard.edu/classicsat/.
[4] See Bing 1995.

Similarly, the perfect modern reader of Hellenistic epigram would be a learned reader, who combines the knowledge of different fields at the intersection of which participants to the CHS conference engaged in a kind of *Ergänzungsspiel* themselves by combining their collective expertise in discussions. Eager to share the results of this fruitful encounter with a wider public, we now present twenty papers that will hopefully invite readers to widen this *Ergänzungsspiel* by entering into a discussion on Posidippus' extraordinary poetry book.

Aware that this unique moment might prove fleeting, the directors of the CHS resolved at the conclusion of the round-table to continue the "reading" of the new epigrams beyond the conference itself and the publication of its proceedings. And so the electronic Posidippus issue of Classics@ came to life, which should be understood as an integral part of the CHS Posidippus project. The Classics@ issue has a two-fold purpose. First it provides a venue for continually updating the text of the new epigrams with recent conjectures and new readings, thus maintaining an ongoing textual discourse on the poems. As Hunter has convincingly argued, more editions of the "new" Posidippus are bound to follow until a definitive text is established, and this is already evident in the number of proposed restorations that are due to appear in print.[5] In this respect the electronic medium, which allows easy and frequent updates, is the only way that a version of the "new" Posidippus can always be current. Second, the CHS Posidippus website will constitute a clearinghouse for information on scholarship on the text, in the form of translations, an updated bibliography, links to conference sites, and information on forthcoming publications.[6]

The collection of papers in this volume includes discussions on general aspects of the work, such as transmission, style, and language, which are then contextualized following a comparison with the "old" Posidippus. In the second part of the volume, all individual sections of the papyrus are discussed and presented from different perspectives. This section constitutes a collection of the voices and perspectives of those who took part in the CHS colloquium. The reader is thus offered a critical overview of the entire work through an interdisciplinary approach. Hoffman's afterword summarizes the main ideas presented by the individual authors.

Although this volume is not primarily concerned with questions of authorship or editorship, none of which affect proposed approaches, the attribution of all epigrams to the Pellaean poet seems to be supported by most contributors on the basis of the following considerations:[7]

[5] Hunter 2002:24.
[6] See http://www.chs.harvard.edu/classicsat/.
[7] For a discussion of authorship see also Hunter 2002:25.

1. As stated above, two epigrams are already known as poems of Posidippus, one from the *Planudean Anthology* and one from Tzetzes. No modern arguments against these specific attributions have been based on sound premises and conclusions.[8]

2. Ongoing analysis of the epigrams, their dialect, vocabulary, and stichometrics seems to support the original editors' attribution.[9]

3. As many papers in this volume show, there is a careful structure within the individual sections of the papyrus, as well as in the entire book, including linguistic links within and between epigrams and sections. This consideration suggests that the collection was carefully planned and put together, possibly by the author himself, although the participation of an outside editor cannot be excluded at the current state of the evidence.[10]

H. Lloyd-Jones has put forward the strongest objections to the attribution of the book to Posidippus during a panel discussion at the American Philological Association in Philadelphia (2002) and in his review of the *editio princeps*.[11] His main arguments rest on his opinion that some of the epigrams are uneven and of poor quality, especially when compared to the "old" Posidippus, as well as on the old dispute on the authorship of a work entitled *Soros* which some attribute to this poet, but which others associate with a collaborative effort of Posidippus, Asclepiades, and Hedylus.[12]

The importance of the Milan papyrus for scholars of the ancient world will be enduring in the years to come, as its publication has enormous implications for future scholarship. Old and new questions on the literary traditions in the collection will arise. Influences between texts from various periods will be explored in the scholarly struggle to reconstruct the intertextual network to which Posidippus belongs. In this regard, work on Posidippus' influence on Latin literature has just begun, more is to follow, and this will prove a particularly fruitful endeavour.[13] The "new" Posidippus as a product of its time, associated with Ptolemaic self-definition will occupy historians of ancient politics for many years to come. Last, but not least, studies on Posidippus are now coming of age, and they will certainly also stimulate renewed interest in epigram and ancient anthologies.

In introducing this volume and delineating the importance of its contents for the study of Hellenistic epigram, it is worth taking note that this genre has itself

---

[8] See Albrecht 1996:80–81,86,105–106.

[9] On dialect, see Sens (this volume) and some discussion in Hunter 2002:25. On the stichometrics of the collection, see Fantuzzi 2002.

[10] Cf. Gutzwiller (this volume) and Hunter 2002:25.

[11] Lloyd-Jones 2002.

[12] On a discussion of *Soros,* see Gutzwiller 1998:152–157 and Nagy (this volume).

[13] See Hutchinson 2002; Magnelli 2002.

only recently acquired its current position in the study of ancient texts. In all truth, the publication of the Milan papyrus has contributed significantly to a trend in scholarship that began to take form a few years earlier. This was in part due to an increased appreciation of Hellenistic poetry generally, both for its own artistic value and its intertextual response to earlier Greek poetry, and in part to an increased awareness of the multifaceted complexity of Hellenistic epigram itself.[14] The biennial Hellenistic Poetry Workshops sponsored by the University of Groningen (Neth.) have done much to bring scholars working in the area of Hellenistic poetry together, and to provide a venue for scholarly exchange. The series *Hellenistica Groningana*, the published results of these workshops, has been an especially effective medium for the dissemination of current work on Hellenistic poetry, including epigram.[15] With the publication of K. Gutzwiller's *Poetic Garlands: Hellenistic Epigrams in Context*, the study of epigram and of epigram collection attained a new level of importance in the world of classical scholarship. Complementing important studies by P. Bing and L. Rossi on the evolution of epigram from inscribed verse form to book to anthology, *Poetic Garlands* has greatly contributed to the research on individual epigram authors, on the poetic function of epigram in an era that saw it appropriate characteristics of other genres, on the relationship of ecphrastic epigram and art object, and on the aesthetics of order in poetry collection.

As the present volume goes to press, the future of scholarship on the Hellenistic epigram could not look brighter. Important new work on epigram has appeared in several studies, including L. Rossi's monograph on the epigrams attributed to Theocritus, M. Fantuzzi's study of epigram in his large-scale work on Hellenistic poetry co-authored with R. Hunter, and D. Sider's edition and commentary of the epigrams of Philodemus. New commentaries are in progress on the epigrams of Asclepiades and Meleager (by A. Sens and K. Gutzwiller respectively) and a new study of selected Hellenistic epigrams (by P. Bing) in the Cambridge Greek and Latin Texts series is eagerly awaited. The study of Hellenistic epigram has come a long way indeed from the days when these gems were relegated to commentaries on Roman elegy or dismissed as emblematic of a decadent era of Greek cultural belatedness.

This past year has been tremendously rewarding for all participants in the CHS Posidippus project. For our part, as editors, we would like to acknowledge all those who supported and encouraged us in our endeavour. First, we thank the Directors, Gregory Nagy and Douglas Frame, for funding and organizing this conference, for

---

[14] Seminal recent works in Hellenistic epigram include that of Bing 1988, 1995, 1998, and Walsh 1990, 1991.

[15] Several volumes of the series include work on epigram: the fifth volume in the series is devoted entirely to Hellenistic epigram.

ntrusting us with this project, and for cheering us all the way. The staff of the CHS ontributed greatly to its success, especially Adam Briscoe, Sylvia Henderson, and Richard Louis. Jill Robbins made sure that all our interlibrary loans arrived promptly. Colleagues shared their knowledge and expertise, offered their encouragement, and often provided us with their own newly published work. We particularly thank Silvia Barbantani, Guido Bastianini, Luigi Bravi, Willy Clarysse, Violetta de Angelis, Gian Luigi Forti, Claudio Gallazzi, Antonella Karlson, Mary Lefkowitz, Maria Lauretta Moioli, Valeria Passerini, Brunilde Ridgway, Guido chepens, and Dorothy J. Thompson. The University of Milan, in particular Professor Violetta de Angelis, the *LED Edizioni*, in particular Dr. Valeria Passerini, the Greek Archaeological Service, the Greek Archaeological Fund, the German Institute in Athens, Dumbarton Oaks, and the Library of Congress provided permissions for the publication of photographs. The editing of a complex manuscript would never have happened so quickly and efficiently without Zoie Lafis, Ivy Livingston, Jake MacPhail, Uche Nwamara, and especially Leonard Muellner. Words cannot express our deep gratitude to Jennifer Reilly for her help with both the organization of the conference and the production of this book.

Finally, we would like to salute the inspiration that was provided by the 2001–2002 Fellows of the CHS who made this a particularly fruitful and unforgettable sabbatical year. Our heartfelt thanks go to the Senior Fellows who elected the specific group, and so provided the opportunity for us to engage in this collegial endeavour. To our dear colleagues and friends, then, this volume is affectionately dedicated for a wonderful year. Let their names appear below for one last time together:

Benjamin Acosta-Hughes, Manuel Baumbach, Hans Beck, Sylvia Berryman, Beate Dignas, Myriam Hecquet-Devienne, Gail Hoffman, Sean Kelsey, Elizabeth Cosmetatou, Nassos Papalexandrou, David Schur, Jan Szeif, and Kai Trampedach.

1

The Manuscript[1]
Posidippus on Papyrus

Susan Stephens
Stanford University

Dirk Obbink
University of Oxford

Posidippus is no stranger to papyrus. The mentions of Posidippus in finds of Hellenistic epigrams exceed that of all other epigrammatists, the majority of whom are known from Roman papyri that reflect the ordering of Meleager's *Garland*. Apart from P.Mil.Vogl. VIII 309,[2] there are five poems of Posidippus that have been found on papyrus, four of which are otherwise unknown:

i.   P.Petrie II 49a (= P.Lond.Lit. 60 = AB 114 = *SH* 961), the so-called Epithalamium for Arsinoe. Now only the foot of a column of a third-century BCE papyrus roll that derives from papyrus cartonnage discovered in the Fayum (Gurob). On back of the roll, the title σύμμεικτα ἐπιγράμματα is written (and again the other way up), together with the name Ποσειδίππου.[3]

ii. P.Louvre 7172 (*P.Firmin-Didot*), containing AB 115-116 (= 11–12 GP = Page, *GLP* 104a–b). Written before 161 BCE, opisthographic papyrus roll, consisting of poems written by the orphaned sons of a Macedonian

---

[1] Our references to the *Epigrams* (and *Elegy* in the case of the poem on Old Age) of Posidippus are to the numeration of the *editio minor* of Austin and Bastianini (= AB).

[2] *Ed. pr.*; commentary, analysis of readings, plates: BG.

[3] Plate in Lasserre 1959:224, 227; Fraser 1972:1.607 and 2.858n403 reports autopsy of the papyrus by T. C. Skeat that failed to find any trace of names of other epigrammatists in addition to Posidippus' on this papyrus as suggested by Lasserre and reported e.g. by Gow-Page in *HE* comm. (introd. to Posidippus). Presumably the title was copied from the collection from which the writer copied the poem itself.

mercenary in the Memphite Sarapeum.[4] The roll includes excerpts from comedy and tragedy as well. The name Ποσειδίππου and the title ἐπιγράμματα are given as heading to the texts of two otherwise unknown epigrams—one (AB 115 = 11 GP) on the dedication of the lighthouse by Sostratus of Cnidos:

Ποσιδίππου ἐπιγράμματα
Ἑλλήνων σωτῆρα, Φάρου σκοπόν, ὦ ἄνα Προτεῦ, | Σώστρατος ἔστησεν Δεξιφάνους Κνίδιος· οὐ γὰρ ἐν Αἰγύπτωι σκοπαὶ οὔρεος οἳ ἐπὶ νήσων κτλ.

The other epigram (AB 116 = 12 GP) refers to the shrine of Arsinoe-Aphrodite at Cape Zephyrium by Callicrates of Samos. AB 119 of the Milan roll concerns the same dedication by the same Callicrates; the text of this epigram is preserved by Athen. VII 318d (ἔγραψε δὲ καὶ Ποσείδιππος).[5]

iii. P.Berol. 14283 (AB 118 = SH 705), a waxed wooden tablet from the first century CE. This is a long elegiac poem on the poet's old age, his poetry and his statue set up in the square in Pella. Posidippus' name together with the place-name are mentioned in the poem.

iv. P.Freib. 4 (AB 65 = 18 GP = SH 973). This is a papyrus sheet of the first century BCE with a text of the Lysippus epigram, preceded by another by Theodorides (first century BCE), likewise on a statue. No author is named, but the epigram on Lysippus (also known to Himerius Or. XLVIII 14 with a variant reading and no author's name) is given by AP XVI (Planudean Appendix) 119 with the ascription Ποσειδίππου.

v. P.Tebt. I 3 (AB 117 = 24 GP, from a first-century BCE papyrus roll). Names of poets survive from what seems to have been a collection, but they are all broken: - - -]ιππου might be Posidippus. There are only ends of several lines, but the poet seems to praise a friend for his taste or skill in poetry.

---

[4] For the Egyptian context: Thompson 1987:105–121; Thompson 1988:261. The title and author, together with the text of the epigrams, contain numerous copying errors and orthographical idiosyncracies characteristic of the level of competence of the writer.

[5] Bing 1998:21–43 argues that Posidippus' epigram records the dedication not of the lighthouse per se but of the statue of Zeus Soter which stood atop it. The new AB 110.1 εἴαρος ἡ Ζεφυρ- may derive from such a context, and the dedications in AB 37–38 may refer to this same temple: cf. 37.8 ναοπόλο[υ.

What We Can Deduce From the Milan Roll

In addition to these—all of them informally written texts[6]—we now have P.Mil.Vogl. VIII 309, a papyrus roll recovered from a section of mummy cartonnage forming a chest piece or pectoral.[7] It now measures 19.6 x 152.8 cm. and contains 16 columns and 606 lines of text. The text has numerous errors, many of which appear to have been left uncorrected, though there are a fair number of corrected errors, either made by the original scribe, by a reader, or a second hand. There is no sign of a diorthotes; but the practice of Ptolemaic copying suggests somewhat greater tolerance for orthographic variation and the kind of errors that a reader can correct for himself.

We can identify four stages in the life of this papyrus:

1. The original manuscript written along the fibers of a roll, containing epigrams, and written in a hand that likely belongs to the later part of the third century (ca. 230–200 BCE). The hand is that of a professional scribe, so this is not a privately made copy.

2. Subsequently, the original protocollon—the sheet attached at the opening of the roll to strengthen it—was replaced, either because the opening was somehow damaged or for another reason.

3. A text containing mythological material of some kind was written on the back of the roll.[8] This text can be dated by comparanda to the early second century and the hand is documentary in style (which makes the dating somewhat more secure). It is in four columns extending 72.5 cm. It is written upside down with respect to the text of the epigrams and covers an area running from cols. 6–13. From the fact that this second text only occupies the center of the roll, we can infer that the two sides were in simultaneous use. If not, we should expect that the roll would have simply been cut down to the necessary size for the new text.

4. Finally, at some point around or after 176 BCE, the papyrus was sent to a recycling center and formed into the pectoral from which it was recovered. The papyrus itself had a useful life, we may infer, of at least 30 years (giving a low date for the initial writing) to 176, very possibly much longer—50 or more years.

The habit of recycling paper, whether it contained a literary text or a document, seems to have been a common practice during the Ptolemaic period. The Lille Callimachus (third century BCE), for example, came from a mummy mask

---

[6] That is to say, they consist of copies of publicly circulating epigrams made by private individuals, and are not to be confused with informally composed and recorded poems: cf. Wissmann 2002:215–230.

[7] From the Fayum, according to the antiquities dealer who acquired and sold the papyrus. For illustrations of the cartonnage pectoral and accompanying head-piece (both subsequently destroyed in the process of extricating the papyrus layers), see Bastianini and Gallazzi 1993.

[8] To be published by C. Gallazzi.

and chest piece, found in Magdola (1901-1902).[9] The Milan cartonnage almos certainly came from one of the necropoleis in the region of the Fayum—an area t the south and west of Alexandria in which in the third century a large number c Ptolemaic veterans were settled. This would provide a plausible context in whic such a roll might have been read, though nothing about where it might have bee written. Unfortunately, there is no consistent relationship between a Greek literar text found in this way and the documents discovered with it.[10] It may hav belonged to whomever the documentary texts belonged; it may just as easily hav found its way to the recycling center via an independent route. There is at least on other cartonnage find that includes material from Alexandria as well as locall written documents, so the Milan epigrams might have been a text disseminate from the center. But equally they could have been copied locally. In the Tebtuni collection in Berkeley (P.Tebt. I 1–2), for example, there is a lyric anthology copie next to and in the same hand as a royal decree of Euergetes II (118 BCE). This i the hand of a professional scribe. There is also the example of the brothers living i the Serapeum at Memphis in 160 BCE who copied, along with other literar extracts, two dedicatory poems of Posidippus (*P.Firmin-Didot*). They also include on the same roll a bread account and a private letter.[11] Their hand, however, is no professional. Still, these two examples serve to indicate a context in which a anthology of epigrams might have been copied, read, and later recycled.

For evidence of anthologies of epigram in this period, two other papyri ar relevant:

1.　The first is an Oxyrhynchus papyrus (P.Oxy. 3724) of the late first centur CE. It contains a list of seventy-five incipits written in a documentary hand, whicl should indicate that it was a privately made copy. Twenty-seven of the incipits hav been identified as belonging to Philodemus and there are good reasons to think tha all of them belonged to that author. If so, we have an incipit list organized t produce a selected edition of epigrams of Philodemus. It should be noted that thes incipits are occasionally reversed, some crossed out, with occasional ticks in th margin—all of which suggests a process of reorganizing.

2.　The second is an unpublished Vienna papyrus (P.Vindob. G 40611), als from cartonnage and found with documents datable to the last third of the thir century BCE.[12] It consists of five fragments from a roll measuring 17 cm x 70 cn

---

[9] Meillier 1976:261-26, 345–346; Parsons and Kassel 1977; Livrea 1979; *SH* 254–269.

[10] See van Minnen 1998 for a list of papyrus texts and the context of their finds.

[11] Lewis 1986:69–87; Thompson 1987:113, 116; Thompson 1988:261; Gutzwiller 1998:22–23. Se also Acosta-Hughes, Nagy, Obbink, and Sider (this volume).

[12] It is described in Harrauer 1981; *CPR* XVIII p. 1; Cameron 1993; Gutzwiller 1998, 23–24. Th papyrus, to be published by B. Krämer and P. J. Parsons, is illustrated and discussed in Göock

and contains incipits from over 200 epigrams. Only one of the incipits has so far been identified—and not to everybody's satisfaction—as from Asclepiades (*AP* XII 4b). It bears the title τὰ ἐπιζητούμενα τῶν ἐπιγραμμάτων ἐν τῆι α′ (= 1st) βύβλωι. Each incipit is accompanied by a number, e.g., 4, 8, 10, that is, presumably, the numbers of lines of the epigram to which the incipit belongs. At the bottom of col. 1 is the notation (εἰσι) κ′ στίχοι πη′, that is there are 20 lines, 88 verses. Col. 2 has the same notation as col. 1, col. 3 has (εἰσι) κδ′ στίχοι ρ′ (= 24 lines, 100). The total for book one is given as 83 incipits and 344 lines. Other identifiable numbers indicate that the Vienna epigrams like the Milan will have had mainly four and six line epigrams, with a few longer poems, though one poem of 21 in the Vienna cannot have been an epigram. In both we have mainly four and six line epigrams, with a few longer poems. These numbers are typical.

The Milan papyrus has two features relevant for understanding it as a literary manuscript: the repair of the opening of the roll and the stichometrics found throughout. Specifically:

1. The opening of the roll as it stands seems to have been damaged or cut in some way and its original cover sheet replaced with another, which is rather narrower and attached not by overlapping the left edge (which is the usual practice) but by being fastened underneath. The editors assume that the roll is complete and that we have the original opening. They infer this from the fact that they read the category heading [λιθι]κά—in the top margin. They also point to the fact that the stichometric number for this section is correct for the actual lines still extant, thus guaranteeing that the section is complete. We cannot read the letters they claim to see, which in any case would be rather high in the margin, not in line with the top of the subsequent columns. The anomaly in the placement of this heading (if it is there) in combination with the recut left margin raises the question of whether we in fact have the original beginning of the roll. William Johnson has argued that line 1 of col. i is in fact an addition in the upper margin of col. i, written by a second hand (after the original beginning of the roll was detached) in order to make col. i begin with a complete poem.[13] According to him it is written noticeably above the level of the first lines of the subsequent columns in the roll. An examination of the papyrus, however, reveals that the graphic typology and ink of the hand that wrote line 1 of col. i differs little, if at all, from the text of the rest of the roll: its differences are certainly not sufficient to establish the presence of another writer at work.

....

2002:18, who argues for a connection between the verse-counts marked by numbers in the margin before the epigram-incipits of the Vienna papyrus and Callimachus' cataloguing of poetry in his *Pinakes*.

[13] Johnson in Gutzwiller 2004 (forthcoming).

In addition, the level of line 1 of col. i does not appear to be significantly different from that of the first lines of the subsequent columns: the disparity is caused by the necessity of straightening out in Photoshop the angle at which fr. 1 of col. i (containing line 1) appears in the volume of plates accompanying P.Mil.Vogl. VIII 309 in order to effect a comparison with the level of the first line of the subsequent columns.

It would be quite easy in principle to cut off one or more of the opening columns (perhaps another full section) and attach a new protocollon. But if the scribe numbered the sections as he copied, then this could only happen if the beginning of the category—λιθικά—coincided with the top of a column (if not the title). Otherwise the stichometrics, which appear to have been written by the original hand, would need to have been added after the fact. Either scenario is possible, but there is a greater likelihood that the scribe would have totaled as he went. The lack of title at the opening cannot be used as evidence of anything in particular. Literary texts in antiquity regularly bore end-titles not initial titles, though occasionally we have evidence of titles added at a roll's beginning or on the outside of the protocollon at right angles to the text.[14] Should we not expect, if we have the original beginning, some kind of dedicatory poem? We initially thought that the opening poems, now fragmentary, of the *Lithika* would have contained the necessary dedicatory information. But there are reasons to doubt this, given what we can see of the poems.[15]

2. There are two separate stichometric systems on this papyrus. The first is a total of lines (M = 40) entered at the foot of col. 1. If the scribe wished to have a total of the number of lines copied (and from the presence of this number, presumably he did), all he needed to do was multiply this number by the total number of columns in the completed text to arrive at a sufficiently accurate count. There is, however, a second set of numbers used in conjunction with a point placed at every tenth line of each section. (The points begin with a new section and are not cumulative for the whole papyrus.) The stichometrics occur at the end of each section and provide a total for that section. The numbers are not cumulative, which is the normal practice, so their purpose is not to provide a simple count of the whole, but must perform some other function. (In fact adding up these individual numbers to reach a total for the whole would be quite tedious.) Why section totals? We can think of three possibilities:

---

[14] On the placement of titles in general, see Albino 1962–1963:219–34; Cockle 1987:219–222; Fredouille and Deléani 1997; Hengel 1984; Luppe 1977:89–99; Nachmanson 1941; Oliver 1951:232–61; Schmalzriedt 1970. On titles and *agrapha* at the beginnings of rolls, see Bastianini 1996:25–27.

[15] See Hunter (this volume), who argues that the *Lithika* may have commenced from Zeus.

(a)   for balance
(b)   for control
(c)   for extraction from another longer roll (or rolls).

With respect to balance: if you were constructing a roll of some 600+ lines in total, jotting down the number of lines in a section would allow you, as you progressed, to think about balancing long against short sections without having to look over the whole section. The Milan text has section lengths of respectively 126, 40, 38, 116, 50, 98, 26, 32, and 32 before it breaks off. While this suggests a certain amount of variation of section size, the sizes are not varied exactly, nor would this degree of variation be particularly difficult to achieve. For this reason we are inclined to discount this explanation.

The use of such numbers as a control is more likely—the totals close the sections and would serve to guarantee completeness in comparison with an exemplar also so numbered or for a corrector or a future copyist. It is worth considering these numbers as a method of control in a particular environment. If the Milan papyrus was a collection produced from an incipit list like that of the Vienna papyrus we can imagine the scribe who produced a new roll based on such an incipit list would first keep his running totals (hence the dots at every tenth line), then set out the final count of each section to indicate to himself or his employer that all of the poems marked for extraction had been found.

There is, of course, a fourth possibility—that the numbers were already in the exemplar and were simply copied in by the scribe as if it were an integral part of the text. But this would only push back the explanation a generation; it does not explain their original function. While the incipit lists we have from Oxyrhynchus and Vienna are presumably locally produced for a private collection, it is worth considering whether an author or editor organizing an epigram collection would have proceeded much differently. Do we imagine him to be producing an autograph and laboriously copying out his poems in the order he wanted them? Or is it more likely that he indicated his own preferences via such an incipit list and gave it to his scribe to copy?

2

Posidippus On Papyri Then and Now

Dirk Obbink
University of Oxford

In order to contextualize the new epigrams of Posidippus,[1] I must take you from the Fayum—the large agricultural oasis south of Cairo where the Milan roll was found—across the desert to the Northeast to Saqqara, just south of the pyramids at Giza. From there comes the painted limestone stele, now in the Cairo Museum (SI 685; *I. Metr. Egypt* 112). Its painted inscription, datable by its letter shapes, advertizes the services of a Greek oracle-seller, Kres (or perhaps: 'a Cretan') who has enterprisingly set up shop outside the precinct of the nearby Memphite Serapeum, itself an oneirotic oracular shrine of an institutional type. Apart from depicting a Greek temple (steps to a raised floor, roof and columns with Egyptianizing Caryatids), and altar with approaching bull (perhaps recalling the Apis bulls, entombed in their huge sarcophagi in the underground sanctuary nearby), it bears a metrical epigram of anonymous composition, addressing the passerby, with a practical purpose—in light of which we might hesitate to call it poetry, but verse and an epigram it remains:

ἐνύπνια κρίνω τοῦ θεοῦ πρόσταγμα ἔχων
τυχ᾽ ἀγαθᾶι· Κρής ἐστιν ὁ κρίνων τάδε.

I interpret dreams at the god's command,

Good luck! It is Kres who gives interpretations here.

An apposite epigram appears in the Milan roll, from the section subtitled οἰωνοσκοπικά, 'divination from bird signs', similarly advertising the divinatory services of one Damon (AB 34):

---

[1] References to the *Epigrams* of Posidippus are to the numeration of the *editio minor* of Austin and Bastianini (= AB).

16

ἐκ τούτου ⟨τοῦ⟩ πάντα περισκέπτοιο κολωνοῦ
Δάμων Τελμησσεὺς ἐκ πατέρων ἀγαθὸς
οἰωνοσκοπίας τεκμαίρεται· ἀλλ᾽ ἴτε φήμην
καὶ Διὸς οἰωνοὺς ὧδ᾽ ἀναπευσόμε[νοι.

From this hill which commands a panoramic view
Damon of Telmessus of good paternal stock
makes his predictions from bird signs. But do come along
to consult here the prophetic voice and omens of Zeus.

One wonders whether this epigram is to be read as serving a purely practical
purpose, similar to the advertisement of Kres from Saqqara given above. Or is the
panoramic view, for example, provided by the vantage point described in the
epigram of Posidippus on Damon designed to complement artfully the far-sighted-
ness of Zeus' prophecies that it advertises? Both epigrams are localized by their
respective texts by deictic pronouns (τάδε in the epigram of Kres, and ἐκ τούτου
τοῦ κολωνοῦ in Posidippus AB 34), and individuated by objectively naming a
professional practitioner. Both have an ostensibly practical purpose—and in that
sense are occasional—unambitiously monumentalizing, perhaps, within the
circumscribed contexts of their respective advertizers' lives and occupations. In both
we are briefly allowed a private glimpse into the business life of a private diviner, at
once mundane and mysterious, practical and portentous.

The topic of divination itself lends these verses a sub-literary cast: the entire
section of οἰωνοσκοπικά constitutes virtually a verse manual on divination from
bird signs in miniature, though each can be read as an individual epigram and some
are paired. A good comparison here is afforded by the collection of horoscopic
epigrams in elegiacs by Anubion,[2] which includes some written for famous figures
of history or myth (Oedipus, Philip of Macedon) or professions, e.g. the orator. The
theme of divination occurs elsewhere in the new Posidippus epigrams. AB 36
describes the dedication of a statue to Arsinoe, upon receipt of a command from
her in a dream to do so. AB 33 is a grave epigram that describes the death of the
deceased as ironically and tragically determined by acting on an erroneous interpretation of a dream. AB 40 describes a temple thesauros in the shape of a statue
through whose mouth money is received by a priestess in return for an oracle
response. The epigrams of the Milan roll that depict individuals (most of them

---

[2] P.Oxy. 4503–7 with Callimachean metrical preferences: e.g. 4504 ii 16-18 (horoscope of Oedipus);
4505 fr. 26-10 (of a good orator μ]ύθων τε ῥητῆρα ταχὺν πρη[στῆρα φέροντα; cf.
Posidippus, AB 27.5–6 (col. v 4–5) φήνη παῖδ᾽ ἀγαγοῦσα καὶ ἐν θώκοις ἀγορητὴν | ἡδυεπῆ
θήσει, 'a vulture as a child's omen will make him a sweet-speaking orator').

17

women) as participants in the mysteries might also be cited in this connection (A 43–4, 46, 58). Book XI of the *Palatine Anthology* contains a section of relate poems on astrologers and diviners, many of them skoptic. Theocritus *Idyll* 2 wit its epigrammatic refrain might be also compared in this connection. AB 34 c Damon [no. 2] instantiates what can only be an epigrammatic sub-genre that would characterize as sub-literary and occasional in its content if not in its comp sition, perhaps with literary aspirations, insofar as it seems to aspire to conformi to a type, but admits of significant variation: i.e. not a copy or metaphrastic versic but another example of its class.

Of course drawing attention to such sub-literary and occasional aspects of th poems is hardly tantamount to proving that they were actually set up for display the manner of the epigram of Kres at Saqqara, or even composed expressly for su a purpose. But the deictic function of the pronoun is sufficient to establish at lea the fiction of its display or purpose and so its occasionality. And while I do thir that many (perhaps as many as half) of the new epigrams could have been plausib inscribed in some medium or context (and it is hard to think how some, e.g. A 61, could have been destined for any other use), even in the one instance where th appears certainly to have been the case, transmission of the poem can be seen have occurred by scribal means: i.e. through copying from a manuscript rather tha from the monumentally inscribed version.

The conclusion necessitated then is that monumentality is not a necessar condition for occasionality in these poems, but only a sufficient condition. It highly unlikely that many (if any) of the epigrams of Posidippus owe their surviv (as opposed to their composition) to their inscription on stone or any oth medium than papyrus. So far from the scenario envisaged in the following quot tion from Charlotte Bronte:

> The place was large enough to afford half an hour's strolling without the
> monotony of treading continually the same path; and for those who
> love to peruse the annals of graveyards, here was variety of inscription
> enough to occupy the attention for double or treble that space of time.
> Hither people of many kindreds, tongues and nations had brought their
> dead for interment; and here on the pages of stone, of marble and of
> brass were written names, dates, last tributes of pomp or love in
> English, in French, in German, in Latin . . . Every tribe and kindred
> mourned after its own fashion; and how soundless was the mourning of
> all.[3]

[3] Charlotte Bronte, *The Professor*. That the passage could be taken as reflecting a scenario plausible
the ancient world may be inferred from its use since the nineteenth century (and it is still so use

Here curious readers consult epitaphs in a graveyard like an historical library. Bing has argued that only exceptionally were texts on stone read and cited in antiquity.[4] He concludes (with some justification) that, in general, monumental verse inscriptions were not read, at least not in the same way as books, i.e. as repositories of literary texts. Those like Craterus and Polemon of Ilium, who went around collecting the texts of monumental inscriptions for transmission in book form, seem to have been few and far between. Fraser[5] adduces the interesting argument that the 'publication of epigrams in roll form explains how such pieces written by poets in one part of the Greek world were imitated in other parts, for it is not likely that isolated short poems would have traveled in the same way that complete rolls did,' while inscriptions on stone, of course, do not move at all. This would have been a decisive development: collections of epigrams are not present in the fourth century, but exist by the time of Posidippus. Thus the epigram became divorced from its lapidary context, which in turn facilitated the enlargement of and alteration of the genre's scope. The burden of proof lies on the shoulders of those who would claim that any of the epigrams that purport to be inscribed on an object were actually so inscribed, to show that they were ever actually cited from such a source.

So let us turn to Posidippus, at least insofar as he was known on papyrus before the Milan roll came to light, and an epigram independently attested in connection with its inscription on a monument. It derives from the same location at Saqqara, where in the Memphite Serapeum a large archive of papers comprising a temple archive (one them bearing a pair of epigrams by Posidippus) were recovered by archaeologists in the late nineteenth century.

The papyrus is P.Louvre 7172 (*P.Firmin-Didot*), containing AB 115–16 (= 12, 14 GP = Page, *GLP* 104a–b).[6] Written before 161 BC, on an opisthographic papyrus roll, it consists of poems written by the orphaned sons of a Macedonian mercenary in the Memphite Sarapeum.[7] The roll includes excerpts from comedy

---

for turning into Latin and Greek in British schools: see Archer-Hind and Hicks 1920:148, which gives a sample Latin version: *Locus in tantum patebat ut semihoram ibi obambulare posses nec tuis semper insistendo vestigiis taedio affici: quod si cui studium esset rerum gestarum memoriam qualem sepulcra praeberent pernoscendi, tanta inerat ibi elogiorum varietas ut duplex quoque vel triplex temporis spatium posset haec legendo traducere, illuc enim suos genere natione lingua diversi alii aliunde convexerant sepeliendos, et nomina annosque cum supremis quoque amoris vel ambitionis testimoniis, Anglice Gallice Germanice vel etiam Latine scripta in tabulas aereas marmoreas lapideas incidenda curaverant. mortuos sibi quaeque gens, cognatio quaeque suo more lugebant, quanto omnes in illo luctu silentio!*

[4] Bing 2002a:38–66.

[5] Fraser 1972:I 608.

[6] Discussed as no. (ii) above in Stephens-Obbink, 'The Manuscript' (in this volume).

[7] For the Egyptian context: Thompson 1987:105–121; Thompson 1988:261. The title and author, together with the text of the epigrams, contain numerous copying errors and orthographical idiosyncracies characteristic of the level of competence of the writer and consistent

and tragedy as well. The name Ποσειδίππου and the title ἐπιγράμματα, together with the beginning of the first epigram inset as an incipit-title, are given as a heading[8] to the texts of two otherwise unknown epigrams—one (AB 116 = 12 GP) on the dedication of the lighthouse by Sostratus of Cnidos, and another (AB 117 = 24 GP) on the shrine of Arsinoe-Aphrodite at Cape Zephyrium by Callicrates of Samos:

Ποσιδίππου ἐπιγράμματα

Ἑλλήνων σωτῆρα, Φάρου σκοπόν, ὦ ἄνα Προτεῦ, / Σώστρατος ἔστησεν Δεξιφάνους Κνίδι'ος'·
οὐ γὰρ ἐν Αἰγύπτωι σκοπαὶ οὔρεος οἷ' ἐπὶ νήσων,
ἀλλὰ χαμαὶ χηλὴ ναύλοχος ἐκτέταται.
τοῦ χάριν εὐθεῖάν τε καὶ ὄρθιον αἰθέρα τέμνειν
πύργος ὅδ' ἀπλάτων φαίνετ' ἀπὸ σταδίων
ἤματι, παννύχιος δὲ θοῶς ἐν κύματι ναύτης
ὄψεται ἐκ κορυφῆς πῦρ μέγα καιόμενον,
καί κεν ἐπ' αὐτὸ δράμοι Ταύρου Κέρας, οὐδ' ἂν ἁμάρτοι
Σωτῆρος, Πρωτεῦ, Ζηνὸς ὁ τῆιδε πλέων.

_____ ἄλλο

μέσσον ἐγὼ Φαρίης ἀκτῆς στόματός τε Κανώπου
ἐν περιφαινομένωι κύματι χῶρον ἔχω,
τήνδε πολυρρήνου Λιβύης ἀνεμώδεα χηλήν,
τὴν ἀνατεινομένην εἰς Ἰταλὸν Ζέφυρον,
ἔνθα με Καλλικράτης ἱδρύσατο καὶ βασιλίσσης
ἱερὸν Ἀρσινόης Κύπριδος ὠνόμασεν.
ἀλλ' ἐπὶ τὴν Ζεφυρῖτιν ἀκουσομένην Ἀφροδίτην,
Ἑλλήνων ἁγναί, Βαίετε, θυγατέρες,
οἵ θ' ἁλὸς ἐργάται ἄνδρες· ὁ γὰρ ναύαρχος ἔτευξεν
τοῦθ' ἱερὸν παντὸς κύματος εὐλίμενον.

....

with Ptolemaic copying practice. The new edition by AB (followed here) corrects simple ortho-graphical errors, but wisely eliminates the emendations (most of them unnecessary) by early editors which appear in the editions of Page (*GLP*) and Gow and Page and returns to a text closer to that given by the copyist. For example, in AB 115.5 previous editors have consistently emended τέμνειν to the participle τέμνων, whereas AB sustain the infinitive of the papyrus.
[8] I give below the text as laid-out on the papyrus. See further the discussion below.

(i) As a savior of the Greeks, this watchman of Pharos, O lord Proteus,
   was set up by Sostratus, son of Dexiphanes, from Cnidos.
For in Egypt there are no look-out posts on a mountain, as in the
   islands,
   but low lies the breakwater where ships take harbor.
Therefore this tower, in a straight and upright line,
   appears to cleave the sky from countless furlongs away
during the day, but throughout the night quickly a sailor on the waves
   will see a great fire blazing from its summit.
And he may even run to the Bull's Horn, and not miss
   Zeus the Savior, O Proteus, whoever sails this way.

(ii) Midway between the shore of Pharos and the mouth of Canopus,
   in the waves visible all around I have my place,
this wind-swept breakwater of Libya rich in sheep,
   facing the Italian Zephyr.
Here Callicrates set me up and called me the shrine
   of Queen Arsinoe-Aphrodite.
So then, to her who shall be named Zephyritis-Aphrodite,
   come, ye pure daughters of the Greeks,
and ye too, toilers on the sea. For the captain built
   this shrine to be a safe harbor from all the waves.[9]

The first epigram (AB 115) addresses Proteus, tutelary Greek divinity of
Pharos Island in the harbor at Alexandria, and tells of a dedication there by
Sostratus of Cnidos, one of the King's wealthy φίλοι. It contrasts Egypt, with its
flat plains, and the mountain peaks that serve as watch towers for sailors in the
Greek islands like Cnidos, praising Sostratus for installing in the harbor at
Alexandria such a look-out as would be a guiding Savior to sailors approaching the
harbor from a distance at sea. The second epigram (AB 116) describes the construction and dedication of a temple of Aphrodite (soon to be identified with Arsinoe)
by the Ptolemaic admiral Callicrates of Samos at Cape Zephyrium and invites
young Greek women to choral performances at her festival there.

Both epigrams interestingly showcase Ptolemaic Egypt (Alexandria, Cape
Zephyrium), its famous building projects (the lighthouse in the harbor in

---

[9] Translated after AB.

Alexandria, the temple of Aphrodite), and its famous personalities (Sostratus, Arsinoe, Callicrates). In the first, the capital of Ptolemy's realm is advertised as visible from afar, by a beacon of light that shines throughout the Greek world, as visibly as the mountain-peaks of the Greek isles. The second connects the northern shore of Egypt with the rest of the Greek world as an equally enviable place: Libya rich in sheep, Italy. In both the gaze of sailors converges from without upon a land that is as safe as it is Greek. The focus is on safety (lighthouse, harbor, breakwater), on cult (sea-god Proteus on Pharos island and Aphrodite's temple at Cape Zeuphyrium), on Ptolemaic celebrity (Sostratus, Queen Arsinoe, Callicrates), and finally and most importantly on Greekness: Egypt is not a barbarian land, nor is it a mere Macedonian possession; it is a civilized, cultured, and celebrated place, peopled by Ptolemaic Greeks.

In this respect the pair of epigrams AB 115–116 forms a piece with the new epigrams by Posidippus of the Milan roll. Egypt attracts celebrities from the entire Greek world (Cnidos, Samos). Greeks are mentioned twice: prominently in AB 115.1 and again in 116.8 nearer the end of the poem, thus forming a ring. Thus I argue that the epigrams are paired, both here on the papyrus in a manner of a mini-anthology, and in composition, as evidenced by the framing references to (i) Greekness and Sostratus at the beginning of AB 115 and (ii) to Greekness and Callicrates at the end of AB 116. However in this case the physical separation of the two monuments precludes that they were ever actually paired in an inscribed monumental context, for the two monuments in question were hundreds of miles apart. Rather, they must have originally been paired in a book.

But were the epigrams known individually, as inscribed in monumental contexts? The answer is that they very probably were. The existence of the first is recorded by Strabo XVII 791, while the second has a close partner in AB 119 on the dedication of the same temple by Callicrates and which is quoted by Athen. VII 318d (ἔγραψε δὲ καὶ Ποσείδιππος).[10] Thus there arises the possibility that the writer in fact knew them from their monumental, inscribed contexts. Did he perhaps write them down after reading them or hearing them recited? The papyrus roll that contains them consists of a privately arranged and written anthology, containing the writer's personal selection of literary passages, including those by Posidippus, Euripides, and other unidentified authors. The rest of the papers in the archive belong to two brothers, Ptolemy and Apollonius, left orphaned by their father, a Macedonian mercenary. The brothers have taken refuge as *katochoi* at the Serapaeum, but move freely in the Helleno-Memphite community at Saqqara.

---

[10] The new AB 110. 1 εἴαρος ἡ Ζεφ[υρ- may derive from such a context, and the dedications in AB 77–78 may refer to this same temple: cf. 37. 8 ναοπόλο[υ.

Their story is vividly recounted in a study by D. J. Thompson.[11] The principle of selection in the anthology is unknown, but a number of scholars have suggested that ties to Macedon may have recommended the choice of passages from both Posidippus and Euripides for copying. The documents produced by each of the two brothers are easily identified and distinguished, for the reason that the younger, Apollonius, is far more advanced and proficient, and may have been acting as tutor to the older, slower brother.

The lighthouse on Pharos island in the harbor at Alexandria was one of the most famous and celebrated monuments in the ancient world. It is illustrated in a Mosaic from Gasr el Libia.[12] Strabo, who visited Alexandria in 24 BCE, describes not only the monument but also the inscription that it bore, presumably on its base (XVII 791):

ἔστι δὲ καὶ αὐτὸ τὸ τῆς νησῖδος ἄκρον πέτρα περίκλυστος
ἔχουσα πύργον θαυμαστῶς κατεσκευασμένον λευκοῦ λίθου
πολυώροφον ὁμώνυμον τῇ νήσῳ. τοῦτον δ᾽ ἀνέθηκε
Σώστρατος Κνίδιος, φίλος τῶν βασιλέων, τῆς τῶν
πλωιζομένων σωτηρίας χάριν, ὡς φησιν ἡ ἐπιγραφή.

Lucian says that Sostratus was the builder of the monument and that he put up the inscription (cf. variation), but plastered over his own name and cut the king's in plaster, knowing that in time the plaster would fall off[13], an evident fiction sufficiently exposed by the appearance of Posidippus' epigram on papyrus. Pliny says that the monument cost 800 talents and adds that it was very generous of the Ptolemaic king to allow Sostratus' rather than his own name to go onto the monument. This discrepancy—and many more (e.g. the referent of Σωτήρ in lines 1 and 11)—was neatly solved in an ariticle by Bing, who argues that Sostratos dedicated not the monument itself, but the statue of Zeus Soter that stood astride the top of the tower.[14] The epigram, Bing suggests, may have been inscribed on the tower, rather than right beneath the statue of Zeus, where it would have been hard to see.

Ptolemaus,[15] who wrote the anthology of literary passages containing the pair of epigrams by Posidippus, happened to have recorded in another papyrus found

[11] Cited above.
[12] Chamoux 1975:214–222 with pl. III 1.
[13] *Hist. Conscr.* 62 records the wording of the inscription: Σώστρατος Δεξιφάνους Κνίδιος θεοῖς σωτῆρσιν ὑπὲρ τῶν πλωιζομένων.
[14] Bing 1998:21–43.
[15] It is his hand that is visible in the papyrus, see Turner and Parsons 1987:82–83, no.45 with addenda p. 151.

among his papers a dream (used as divination in the Serapaeum) as follows (*UPZ* 78.28–39):

ᾤμην με ἐν ᾿Αλεξαν|δρήᾳ με εἶναι ἐπάνω πύργου μεγάλου.
εἶχον | πρόσοπον καλὸν ⟨εἶχον⟩ καὶ οὐκ ἤθελον οὐθενεὶ | δῖξαί
μου τὸ πόρσοπον διὰ τὸ καλὸν αὐτὸν | εἶν[α]ι καὶ γραῦ⟨σ⟩ μοι
παρεκάθητο καὶ ὄχλος ἀπὸ βορρᾶ μου | καὶ ἀπὸ ᾿πηλιότης . . .

I thought I was in Alexandria, on top of a great tower. I had a beautiful
face, and did not want to show my face to anyone because of its beauty.
And an old woman sat down next to me, and [there was] a crowd of
people to the north and east of me . . .

When U. Wilcken read this in 1920, he could hardly believe his eyes! He
concluded that Ptolemaus could have visited Alexandria in his youth. D. J
Thompson proposed that the 'great tower' was 'perhaps indeed the Pharos.' Bing
carries his argument one step further to propose that the dreamer identifies with the
statue, and that the beautiful face is that of Zeus Soter on top of the Pharos. He
suggests further that Ptolemaus, because of his 'particular interest in the statue'
transcribed the poem. In fact the statue on top of the lighthouse on Pharos island
in the harbor at Alexandria seems to have been fairly well known as a famous monu
ment. It is, for example, apostrophized by Callimachus in a fragmentary poem (fr
400 Pfeiffer):

ἁ ναῦς, ἁ τὸ μόνον φέγγος ἐμὶν τὸ γλυκὺ τᾶς ζόας
ἅρπαξας, ποτί τε Ζανὸς ἱκνεῦμαι λιμενοσκόπῳ.

Ship, that snatched away the only sweet light of my life,
I entreat you by Zeus the watchman of the harbor.

Bing leaves open the question of whether the Ptolemaus knew the epigram
from the inscription on the monument, but allows he might have, and assumes tha
Strabo knew it from sailing in and out of the harbor. While it is tempting to thin
that Ptolemaus in fact knew the epigram from the inscription on the monument
we can be confident that he did not. Rather, he copied it, along with the epigram
on Callicrates dedication on the temple of Arsinoe-Aphrodite at Cape Zephyrium
from a Hellenistic poetry book where he found them paired. This is clear from the
graphic features which it exhibits. Among these may be counted the scribal errors
which are those of a beginner or bilingual writer copying from a book: dittographie
and hyperiotacisms abound as well as numerous errors of a visual sort caused by th
slip of the eye from one sequence to a subsequent identical sequence of letters, a

well as seeming phonetic errors caused by misremembering what a copyist has read.[16] But the tell-tale sign that Ptolemaus is copying from a professionally produced book is that, although he is copying only a pair of epigrams, he manages to replicate the significant features of the form of the Hellenistic poetry book. Note first that in the layout of the epigrams as represented by the copyist, the pentameters are not inset from the starting point of the hexameters as they conventionally are in modern printed editions. This is standard practice for Greek poetry books.[17] (The only exceptions are the Gallus papyrus, a Roman manuscript of Latin epigrams by Cornelius Gallus dating from the early Augustan period, and *SH* 982, a Greek epigram in elegiacs celebrating Augustus' victory at Actium with which its writing is virtually contemporaneous.) In addition, Ptolemaus in copying his model has squeezed in an initial title after the fact, indicating that the pair of poems are epigrams[18] by Posidippus.[19] He does this for none of the other literary passages (from Euripides, Menander, etc.) that he copied into his personal anthology. It must be regarded as a feature drawn from the exemplar from which he copied. Presumably he found this title in the colophon of the book from which he was copying at the end of the roll where titles would be expected in an ancient Greek book; he then decided to import it into the top margin before the column in which he had written AB 115 on the lighthouse and 116 on the temple.

---

[16] This is only partly due to the limited competence of the writer, young Ptolemy as he is learning to write: as noted above (in Stephens-Obbink, 'The Manuscript', in this volume) papyri of the Ptolemaic date appear to be far more tolerant than their Roman period counterparts of the sort of errors that a trained reader might have been expected to correct, and this is true of the errors of the Milan roll of epigrams of Posidippus as well.

[17] See Anderson, Parsons, and Nisbet 1979:130. For exceptional εἰσθέσις of the pentameter in Greek epigram on papyrus that prove the rule see P.Lit.Lond. 62 = *SH* 982, with Barbantani 1998:259–60 and tav. II who discusses the other evidence (e.g. the Gallus fragment) and implications (or not) for dating. Another way of viewing this feature is as the setting-out into the margin in ἔκθεσις of the hexameter (the origin of the practice?). Such ἔκθεσις is the normal graphic convention for marking inception (in this case of the elegiac couplet) in quotations, lemmata in commentaries, etc., whereas *eisthesis* in the modern sense of 'indentation' is exceptional in ancient manuscripts.

[18] Ptolemaus' initial title ἐπιγράμματα might also be considered parallel to the subtitles in the Milan roll (though might we not have expected a more specific designation, like Περὶ Ἑλλήνων?). I have wondered whether Posidippus fr. AB 147 Περὶ Κνίδου might reflect the subtitle of a section of epigrams by Posidippus (or others) in a lost edition. Cf. Posidippus' interest in AB 115.2 of the Cnidian origin of Sostratus. Mention of the place here, as in other epigrams of Posidippus, draws it into the ambit of the Ptolemaic empire.

[19] Ptolemaus' annotation Ποσιδίππου is the only testimony we have that the pair of epigrams is by Posidippus. Given that it is an addition after the fact, we might be tempted to doubt its authority, as P. van Minnen suggested to me. However, given the Ptolemaic focus of the new epigrams by Posidippus, as the lexical parallels they provide, lend new support to Ptolemaus' claim for Posidippus' authorship: e.g. with AB 115.4 ἐκτέταται cf. now AB 8.4 and 76.1.

Second, Ptolemaus began copying the pair of epigrams by writing on the firs
line of the column the first half of the first hexameter up to the caesura, the firs
four words: ʿΕλλήνων σωτῆρα Φάρου σκοπόν. Then he began the secon
line by completing the hexameter (ὦ ἄνα Πρωτεῦ). In order to do so he had t
squeeze in the entire pentameter into the remaining space, creating an inordinatel
long line that required wrapping part of Sostratus' ethnic Κνίδιος underneath. I
doing this he exhibits another feature of the Hellenistic poetry book (and o
Alexandrian bibliographic practice in copying and indexing of books): the literar
incipit. Callimachus in his *Pinakes* (an index of books in the Alexandrian Library
recorded the ἀρχή of each book, together with the author, title (if one was known)
genre, and number of lines. The practice of identifying works by their openin
words derives from Peripatetic practice among the pupils of Aristotle. Th
hypotheses of Attic dramatic works attributed to Dichaearchus, the earliest exam
ples, identify each play by incipit. Originally the intention must have been to indi
viduate the works in question, lest there be any question which play was bein
hypothesized, or which exact version of a book was being acquired for the library
By the time that Ptolemaus copied the pair of epigrams by Posidippus, the practic
of composing 'wish-lists' of poems (particularly epigrams) for transcription into a
anthology or edition was becoming common practice.[20]

Side by side with this goes the attention paid to the number of lines containe
in a given poem. Not only did a stichometric count figure in the entries i
Callimachus' *Pinakes*, but we also find them in the totals of many literary books o
papyrus. They are also of interest to the scribe of the Milan roll of Posidippus
epigrams, who gives marginal totals for the poems he copies. Ptolemaus did not giv
a count for the number of lines in the pair of epigrams of Posidippus that he copied
but he does give a stichometric total for all the passages he has copied into hi
anthology at the end of the roll.

Finally, and also as an afterthought, Ptolemaus returned to the pair of epigram
after copying them, divided the two at the margin by the short horizontal line o
punctuation known as the παραγραφός, and penned the word ἄλλο in th
center of the column between the line ending AB 115 and the one beginning AI
116. The uniquely early thematic subheadings of dividing the sections in the Mila
roll immediately come to mind as a graphic comparison. But in fact this use o
ἄλλο is familiar to us from the later anthologies of Greek epigrams, where it desig
nates a succession of epigrams on the same theme or by the same author or both
We are thus entitled to assume Posidippus' authorship of AB 116 as well as that o

---

[20] Compare the lists of epigram incipits discussed by Stephens and Obbink, 'The Manuscript' (in thi
volume).

AB 115, and that the epigrams were meant to stand as a pair. What is more, they are made to look by the writer as though they had the same graphic arrangement as a professionally produced book of poems, by a single author.

Such pairs of epigrams or 'Konkurrenzgedichte' survive both on papyri and inscribed on monuments.[21] For examples on papyrus, we may turn to the two funerary epigrams of unknown authorship sent in the form of a letter (very likely by the poet himself) to Zeno, the Fayum estate-manager of Apollonius, and Diorcetes of Ptolemy Philadelphus, memorializing Zeno's hunting-dog Tauron who was mortally wounded during the (supposed) pursuit and attack of a wild boar (*SH* 977). One is in elegiacs, the other in iambics. Both refer to the physical burial (v. 1 ὅδε . . . τύμβος, 14 τύβωι τῶιδ', 24 τᾶιδ' . . . κόνει), and were doubtless destined to be inscribed as a pair, a practice exemplified in funerary epigram elsewhere. But as Bing has noted, the letter suggests distance (plausibly sent from Alexandria), and there is no evidence that they were ever actually set up. Yet we cannot assume such practice was a purely literary exercise. Inscribed epitaphs for people's pets are not unknown. There is a new example from Termessos:[22]

- - - - -|- - - 'Ροδόπ[ης? - - - - - - - - - -
κ . . τ . ον εὐχάριτον Στέ|φανον παίζοντες ἐφώνουν, |
ἐξαπίνης θανάτῳ μεμαρμμένον ἐνθάδε κεύθ[ει, |
ἔστι κυνὸς τόδε σῆμα καταφθιμέ|νου Στεφάνοιο, |
τὸν 'Ροδόπη δά|κρυσε καὶ ὡς ἄνθρωπον ἔθαψεν. |
εἰμὶ κύων Στέφανος, 'Ροδόπη δέ [μοι] | ἔκτισε τύμβον.

The phenomenon of composing an epigram for a pet and erecting it in a monumental context is well attested elsewhere.[23]

We are thus entitled to bring the epigrams of Posidippus on papyri previously known before the discovery of the Milan roll into conjunction with the new epigrams of Posidippus from that book. The pair of epigrams informally copied by Ptolemaus can be seen to derive from a professionally produced collection like the Milan roll. As such, it comprises a subset, and can be seen in itself as a kind of mini-anthology of Posidippus. The two epigrams of Ptolemaus' collection appear neither in the Milan roll (where we might have expected them among the other poems

---

[21] See Fraser 1972: I 611 with nn. 426–30 (ii 863f).

[22] I.Termessos I. 22 (Iplikçioglu 1991:39–43 = Merkelbach and Stauber 2002:104, limestone dog-sarcophagus inscribed with 7 hexameters near the inscribed sarcophagus (*TAM* III,1 no.746) of Αὐρ(ηλία) 'Ροδόπη.

[23] Cf. comm. *ad loc.* with further inscribed examples. Literary examples: *AP* VII 211 (Tymnes), 304 (Peisandros of Kameiros on Rhodes); Herrlinger, 1930; Zlotogorska 1997.

given under the heading *Anathematika*), nor in the *Palatine Anthology* or related later anthologies, though the existence of at least one of them is noted by a perihegetical writer, and the second has a close parallel in the Milan roll with AB 119 which purports to be inscribed on the same monument. They were copied by standard scribal techniques from a collection that was either more exhaustive of the poet's œuvre than either of these, or at any rate contained additional material (and the lack of overlap between the three can hardly be said to point to the existence of a single authoritative edition on which all three are drawing). This together with the circumstances of copying might point in a sub-literary direction, or at least lead to doubts about authorial composition of any one of these particular collections. They were copied as a pair, as indicated by the connecting subtitle ἄλλο—thus constituting a mini-Posidippus anthology incorporated in a larger personal anthology. They came equipped in their source with titles (the latest book-technology of the day), including the use of the incipit as a title, as employed in Callimachus' *Pinakes*. Thus they show signs of derivation not from monument or memory but from state of the art book production. At the same time their selection for this particular anthology, as in the case of many poems in the Milan roll, seems to have been guided by geographical and political considerations.

3

Posidippus Old and New

David Sider

New York University

A review of *Posidippo premilanese* is clearly in order if we are ever to see him whole. This presents an interesting challenge, because old and new Posidippi are not the easiest of fits. I have, moreover, taken it as my task to point out, if not exaggerate, these differences. We begin with a brief review of what we knew of the poet and his work before the publication of the papyrus.[1]

There are not many facts external to the epigrams themselves known about Posidippus,[2] but oddly enough one of them is that he wrote epigrams. *IG* IX.1².17, v.24, from Thermium, grants proxeny status in Delphi to "Posidippus the epigrammatist from Pella," Ποσειδίππωι τῶι ἐπιγραμματοποιῶι Πελλαίωι,[3] and a scholion to Apollonius of Rhodes tells us that Posidippus the epigrammatist (ἐπιγραμματογράφος) followed Antimachus on the matter of Heracles' great weight (Schol. *ad* A.R. I.1289, p.116 Wendel = *SH* 703). For a while I wondered whether ἐπιγραμματοποιός, the word used in the public declaration, was the more formal of the two words for epigrammatist,[4] and whether ἐπιγραμματογράφος perhaps harbored some of the pejorative sense that λογογράφος had in contrast with λογοποιός,[5] but there are far too few instances to substan-

---

[1] Texts with commentaries on Posidippus are Schott 1905; Gow and Page 1965; Fernández-Galiano 1987; and Albrecht 1996.

[2] For the testimony see Fernández-Galiano 1987:9–17.

[3] First published by Weinreich 1918.437; see further Lloyd-Jones 1963, repr. with corrections and a postscript in Lloyd-Jones 1990; Fraser 1972:II 796n44 is good on its historical context.

[4] A third word, ἐπιγραμματιστής, lies latent behind Latin *epigrammatista* in Apollinaris Sidonius *Epist.* IV 1.

[5] Cf. Plat. *Phdr.* 257c διὰ πάσης τῆς λοιδορίας ἐκάλει λογογράφον, with schol. *ad loc.* λογογράφους γὰρ ἐκάλουν οἱ παλαιοὶ τοὺς ἐπὶ μισθῷ λόγους γράφοντας καὶ πιπράσκοντας αὐτοὺς εἰς δικαστήρια, ῥήτορας δὲ τοὺς δι᾽ ἑαυτῶν λέγοντας, Demosth. XIX 246 λογογράφους τοίνυν καὶ σοφιστὰς καλῶν τοὺς ἄλλους καὶ ὑβρίζειν πειρώμενος.

tiate this distinction. Posidippus, then, is simply an epigrammatist, although h« may have written in other forms.[6]

A survey of what was previously known is in order, sorted by source. The reason for giving lengths of individual poems [in square brackets] will appea presently.

From the *Greek Anthology* (i.e., the union of the Palatine and Planudear anthologies)[7] we have thirteen undisputed epigrams: *AP* V 134 (1 GP), 183 (1(GP), 186 (2 GP), 211 (3 GP), 213 (9 GP); VII 267 (15 GP); XII 45 (5 GP), 98 (6 GP), 120 (7 GP), 131 (8 GP), 168 (9 GP); *APl* 119 (18 GP)[8], 275 (19 GP) [average length of undisputed epigram, ca. 5 vv.]

Unfortunately, nine epigrams in the *Greek Anthology* are doubly ascribed tc Posidippus and another:[9]

Asclepiades: *AP* V 194 (Asclepiades 34 GP = *EG* 23), *AP* V 202 (Asclepiades 35 GP = *EG* 24), *AP* V 209 (Asclepiades 36 GP = *EG* 25); *AP* XII 17 (Asclepiades 37 GP = *EG* 26), *AP* XII 77 (Asclepiades 38 GP = *EG* 27); *APl* 68 (Asclepiades 39 GP = *EG* 28)[10]

Callimachus: *AP* VII 170 (Posidippus 21 GP; Καλλιμάχου C[11])

Plato Comicus: *AP* IX 359 (Posidippus 22 GP; οἱ δὲ Πλάτωνος τοῦ κωμικοῦ[12] C)

Meleager: AP V 215 (Posidippus 23 GP; ἢ Μελεάγρου PC)

Athenaeus is our source for four epigrams: VII 318c (13 GP); X 412d (14), 414d (16); XIII 596c (17). This last poem is intriguingly introduced as follows: εἰς

---

[6] Περὶ Κνίδου (*SH* 706), credited to Posidippus, could for all we know be in prose, just as Sophocles, Ion of Chios, and Callimachus wrote in both prose and verse. It is also possible that *SH* 706 was written by another Posidippus.

[7] Austin and Bastianini publish these as AB 65, 123, 124, 125, 129, 130, 132, 135, 137, 138, 139, 140, and 142. For the details on the two anthologies, see Sider 1997:45.

[8] This epigram is one of two previously known poems of Posidippus which also appear in the Milan papyrus and which thus alerted the editors to the likelihood that Posidippus was the author of all the epigrams in the papyrus.

[9] These are published in AB as nos. 126, 127, 128, 131, 133, 134, 136, and 141; for the problem of doubly ascribed epigrams in general, see Gow 1958.

[10] It will thus be observed that Gow, the GP editor primarily responsible for Asclepiades and Posidippus, and Page, the editor of the *OCT Epigrammata Graeca* (*EG* above), disagreed on these particular doubly ascribed epigrams. For the double ascriptions to Posidippus and Asclepiades in particular, see GP:II 117.

[11] C is the *siglum* for the Corrector in the *Palatine Anthology*, who, with access to mss. no longer extant and with an intelligence of his own, often alone records a correct reading or ascription; cf. GP:I, xxxv–xxxviii; Cameron 1993:103–105, 108–120.

[12] Since elsewhere there is confusion between Posidippus the epigrammatist and Posidippus *Comicus* (see below, n. 24), it is possible that this was the original confusion here.

δὲ τὴν Δωρίχαν (sc. the mistress of Sappho's brother Charaxus, who, like Δoricha, is mentioned in the poem) τόδ' ἐποίησε τοὐπίγραμμα Ποσείδιππος, καίτοι καὶ ἐν τῇ Αἰθιοπίᾳ πολλάκις αὐτὸς μνημονεύσας. [ὅτι δὲ τόδε ["17 GP"] ("Posidippus wrote this <following> epigram on Doricha, indeed mentioning her many times *also* in his *Aithiopia*. It is as follows:" [17 GP]).[13] *Aithiopia* looks very much like the title of a book. Why was *Ep.* 17 excluded from it, as καὶ before ἐν indicates? Two reasonable answers: (i) *Aithiopia* is a book containing poems in a different genre or genres from epigrams (elegies would be most likely), where the slight genre of epigram would be thought out of place;[14] or (ii) *Aithiopia* was a book of epigrams, but Posidippus wrote one or more epigrams mentioning Doricha in either an earlier or a later book of epigrams. If the latter (ii) is the case, we may know the title of that book too, for at 491c Athenaeus quotes one line from a work of Posidippus entitled Ἀσωπία· οὐδέ τοι ἀκρόνυχοι ψυχραὶ δύνουσι Πέλειαι (*SH* 698).[15] Scholars noting the similarity between *Asopia* and *Aithiopia* have suggested that one is a mistake for the other,[16] but if our inference from 596c is correct that Posidippus published more than one book of epigrams and that one of them had a title, then it is reasonable to imagine that the second book also had a title. And if our testimony provides us with a second name, why get rid of it? A quick look at any onomasticon shows how many more Greek names begin with alpha than with any other letter. It remains possible that *Asopia* was, as Lloyd-Jones suggests, one long poem, possibly an epyllion.[17]

AB 15 (Tzetzes *Chiliades* VII 660 = 20 GP), which Page 1965:121 thought was ascribed to Posidippus erroneously, also appears in P.Mil.Vogl. VIII 309, each reinforcing the other to support Posidippus as author.

---

[13] *SH* 699, designed solely to highlight the title, omits the actual text of the epigram. Although καίτοι καί occasionally serves as a strong continuative (cf. Denniston 1954:560), here the two participles seem to work independently, as here translated. Cf. Angiò 1999:157, who argues that in the *Aithiopia* Posidippus imitated Mimnermus, Antimachus, Philetas, and Hermesianax in composing a long elegy containing (*inter alia*) amorous tales in a historical setting, and that the name of the poem alludes to Aithiops, an early and poetic name for Lesbos.

[14] Catullus had not been born yet.

[15] The meaning of this line shifts, depending on which of the two adjectives is attributive and which predicate. Since the acronychal (evening) setting of the Pleiades is in the spring, either (as spelled out by Parsons and Lloyd-Jones 1983:338) "the acronychal Pleiades set but are not cold [as they would be in their autumnal setting]," or "the cold Pleiades set but are not acronychal [as they would be in the spring]." The former is the thought more likely to be expressed.

[16] Schott 1905:100 read Αἰσωπεία for both, since Herodotus II 135 says that Doricha was a fellow slave of Aesop the fabulist; "ingenious, . . . but it is in fact extremely hazardous" (Lloyd-Jones 1990:176). In his Teubner edition of Athenaeus, Kaibel suggested reading Αἰθιοπίδι for Αἰθιοπίᾳ.

[17] Lloyd-Jones 1963:176; but since Athenaeus labels AB 122 (17 GP) an epigram, Lloyd-Jones is wrong to suggest that *Aithiopia* is also an epyllion.

David Sider

AB 115–116 (*P.Firmin-Didot*) are two 10-line epigrams, 11 and 12 GP = 104a–b in Page 1942. [av. length of Ath., Tz., and *P.Firmin-Didot*, 7.7 vv.]. AB 117 (P.Tebtunis. I 3 21–25 , first century BCE, = 24 GP) contains traces of four poems in elegiac couplets. The first is anonymous and since it is 12 lines long Gow-Page wonder whether it should be thought of as an elegy, but as will be made clear below (in part by the 12-line epigrams in P.Mil.Vogl.), there is no hindrance to our considering it an epigram, just like the three that follow it in P.Tebtunis: Alcaeus of Messene 17 GP (8 vv., no heading but previously known from the *Anthology*); Posidippus 24 (4 vv.), headed Ποσειδί]ππου; and Asclepiades 47 (at least 6 vv.), headed Ἀσκληπ]ιάδου.

Stephanus of Byzantium 295.3 (AB 148 = *SH* 700), without naming the source, quotes three verses by Posidippus to illustrate that he spelled Ζέλεια as Ζελίη and that Πάνδαρος παρὰ τῷ Σιμοῦντι τέθαπται:

ὁ δὲ Λυκαονίη δέξατό σε Ζελίη
ἀλλὰ ⟨παρὰ⟩ προχοῇσι Σιμουντίσι τοῦτό σοι ῞Εκτωρ
σῆμα καὶ ἀγχέμαχοι θέντο Λυκαονίδαι.

Nor did Lycaonian Zelia receive you, but Hector and the close-fighting Lycaonians set up this tombstone for you at the mouth of the river Simois.

This could easily be from a sepulchral epigram. Only three sepulchral epigrams by Posidippus were previously known, two from the *Anthology* (AB 131–132 = 21 and 15 GP) and one from Athenaeus (AB 122 = 17 GP),[18] but P.Mil.Vogl. contains twenty. Other Hellenistic sepulchral epigrams for Homeric characters are *AP* VII 136 (Antipater on Priam), 140 (Archias on Hector), 141 (Antiphilus on Protesilaus), 145–147 (Asclepiades, Antipater, and Archias on Ajax), but none of the twenty in P.Mil.Vogl. is of this sort. Stephanus, interested only in geographical and onomastic niceties, may well have excerpted *SH* 700 from a longer poem.

AB 118 (P. Berol. 14283 = *SH* 705) is a poem now of 25 lines but originally, if the posited lacunae are correct, of at least 28 lines. As Lloyd-Jones and Gutzwiller have shown, this poem spoken in the voice of the author, who laments his old age and asks for proper honors, reads very much like a *sphragis*, whether to introduce the book as its "seal" or as an *envoi* to the readers of the book.[19] In *SH* it is headed "epigramma vel elegia: poematum σφραγίς," but as a *sphragis* it should rather be

---

[18] This is not counting the puzzling, or rather joking, epigram on the non-existent Homeric hero "Berisus" (*SH* 701); cf. Cameron 1993:372, 376.

[19] Lloyd-Jones 1963:190; Barigazzi 1968:201. Gutzwiller 1998: 154 argues that it belonged to a book called simply *Epigrammata*, but, as we are beginning see, determining the number and names of possible Posidippan epigram books is not easy.

compared to the long introductory poems to Meleager's and Philip's anthologies, neither of which is considered an elegy, although it must also be noted that most people hesitate to call them epigrams either.

In addition to the poems noted above, there are several *dubia*, most of which are conveniently printed and commented on by Fernández-Galiano (as xxx–xxxvi [epigrams] and xxxviii [elegy]), although with little critical analysis of authorship. All are anonymous, and in each case Posidippan authorship is merely a guess (and often other names have been proposed as well). AB 134 (*AP* V 168), anonymous in the two mss. of the *Greek Anthology* (= Anon. 3 GP) was held to be by Posidippus by Stadtmüller (the editor of the Teubner edition of the *Greek Anthology*), and then by Wallace and Wallace 1939 and Albrecht (1996:147–152), largely on the basis of some similarities with Posidippus AB 137 = 6 GP, but this poem in turn shares features with Asclepiades 11. In other words, these three poems (and Asclepiades 14) show the usual signs of overt debt (read "allusion") of one epigram to another, whether or not by the same poet.[20] If this anonymous poem is by Posidippus, we will need another papyrus like P.Mil.Vogl. to prove it. Fernández-Galiano (1987:30) does not even print it among his *dubia*.

This, then, however briefly, is what we had of Posidippus before the publication of P. Mil.Vogl. How do the previously known epigrams differ from those in the Milan papyrus? One not uncommon reaction among early readers, who had then only Bastianini and Gallazzi by which to judge,[21] was that the new epigrams were distinctly inferior. The notion of how epigrams are judged will be questioned below—but before questioning it I want to point out one way Old Posidippus is more in line with what we usually think of when we picture a Hellenistic epigrammatist.

Old Posidippus frequently fashioned the speaker of the poem in the persona of poet, no example of which can be found in the new material. This is most straightforward in AB 118 (*SH* 705), the so-called *Seal* of Posidippus, in which he (i.e. the speaker in the name of Posidippus) addresses the Muses as his fellow citizens (1 Μοῦσαι πολιήτιδες), who are asked now to sing along with him in chorus what they had written of his grievous old age (5–6 νῦν δὲ Ποσειδίππῳ στυγερὸν συναείσατε γῆρας . . . γραψάμεναι δέλτων ἐν χρυσέαις σελίσιν).[22] Note the Hellenistic nicety of the Muses, of all people, reciting from an already written text. The text to be sung is of course this very poem, the *Seal* of Posidippus itself,

---

[20] For this particular train of allusions, see Tarán 1979:53–65.

[21] BG 1993a and 1993b.

[22] Cf. Bing 1988:15, Acosta-Hughes and Stephens 2002:214–216n24. Does συναείσατε include Posidippus? Cf. Page's 1942:473 translation, "now join Poseidippus in his song."

the imperative συναείσατε, as usual, actually referring to the present performance; cf. μῆνιν ἄειδε θεά. The poem had been composed in the short-term memory of wax tablets; now finished it is transferred to the longer-lasting format of the book roll, and it is just such a roll that Posidippus wants to be seen reading when he is (he hopes) honored with a public statue: 16 ἔοιμι δὲ βύβλον ἑλίσσων. This last verb should be translated as "reading," not simply and literally as "unwinding" (Page), an action whose only purpose in this context is to expose columns for reading;[23] and this word may also call for further elaboration. Since Posidippus had earlier alluded to himself, along with the Muses, reading from the *Seal*, we are thus presented with a very elaborate bit of ecphrasis, where the performance—Posidippus reading/reciting—is exactly what is before the audience's eyes when he describes his desired statue. A tableau vivant in which performer, performance,[24] and content all become one.[25]

Next consider AB 137 (6 GP = *AP* XII 98):

> τὸν Μουσῶν τέττιγα Πόθος δήσας ἐπ᾽ ἀκάνθαις
> κοιμάζειν ἐθέλει πῦρ ὑπὸ πλευρὰ βαλών·
> ἡ δὲ πρὶν ἐν βύβλοις πεπονημένη ἄλλα θερίζει
> ψυχή, ἀνιηρῷ δαίμονι μεμφομένη.

> Desire holding the Muses' cicada on a bed of thorns wants to keep
> it silent by applying heat to its ribs; but the (cricket's = poet's) soul has
> done its homework and gathers other things, blaming the wretched god.

As Gutzwiller (1998:160–161) neatly demonstrates, Pothos would like to have an ἀκάνθιος τέττιξ, "mute or unmusical," but cicadas thrive in heat and chirp

---

[23] Cf. (with Lloyd-Jones) Callimachus fr. 468 Pf. γράμματα δ᾽ οὐχ εἵλισσεν ἀπόκρυφα where a literal "unrolled treatises" makes no sense (Ammonius, who cites this fragment, tells us that γράμματα here equals συγγράμματα); *AP* IX 540 (anon., but conceivably from Philip's *Garland*) μὴ ταχὺς Ἡρακλείτου ἐπ᾽ ὀμφαλὸν εἴλεε βίβλον, "don't read Heraclitus hastily." See further Acosta-Hughes and Stephens 2001:214, who demonstrate the difficulty of restoring ἐλίσσω at Callimachus *Aetia* I 5.

[24] I remain convinced that many Hellenistic epigrams were written for performance by the poet, who would thus be free to refer directly to himself. This is not the place to argue this, but cf. Sider 1997:27 for a brief account.

[25] The ghost of Posidippus must be frustrated first by the fact that this poem has been preserved only on two wax tablets rather than the book roll he describes, and second by the extant statue of a seated Posidippus merely *holding* an unopened scroll in his right hand rather than reading from it, although a stone statue in the Abbey of Grottaferrata of a boy reading shows how easily Posidippus' wish could have been fulfilled; cf. the frontispiece of Pinner 1958 for an illustration. For a convincing argument that the statue labeled "Posidippus" is the epigrammatist and not the homonymous comic poet, see Dickie 1994, who also reproduces a photograph of the statue; see also Richter 1965:II fig. 1647. The statue is now on the cover of Austin and Bastianini 2002.

even louder than before. Moreover, since cicadas (certainly those said to be "of the Muses") often stand in for poets,[26] this particular learned poet[27] makes his literary harvest[28] from all that he has pored over in the book; he is now ready for a counterattack against the god, which consists, at least in part, of this very poem.[29] This poem contrasts (perhaps intentionally) with AB 140 (Anon. 9 GP = *AP* XII 99, from Meleager's *Garland*), where the speaker, struck by Eros, gives up his devotion to the Muses, finding it useless if not an actual impediment at such a moment (5 τηκέσθω Μουσέων ὁ πολὺς πόνος)[30] Posidippus, on the other hand, not only does not give up on his art, he characterizes it as one that depends upon deep immersion in earlier literature—and himself, it would seem, as a *poeta doctus*, ready to take on the god of Desire.

Which books has Posidippus studied so carefully? We could try to compose a list, but he in fact provides his own: AB 140 (9 GP = *AP* XII 168).

Ναννοῦς καὶ Λύδης ἐπίχει δύο, καὶ φιλεράστου
Μιμνέρμου, καὶ τοῦ σώφρονος Ἀντιμάχου·
συγκέρασον τὸν πέμπτον ἐμοῦ· τὸν δ' ἕκτον ἑκάστου,
'Ηλιόδωρ', εἴπας, ὅστις ἐρῶν ἔτυχεν·
ἕβδομον Ἡσιόδου, τόν δ' ὄγδοον εἶπον Ὁμήρου,
τὸν δ' ἔνατον Μουσῶν, Μνημοσύνης δέκατον.
μεστὸν ὑπὲρ χείλους πίομαι, Κύπρι· τἄλλα δ', Ἔρωτες,
νήφοντ' οἰνωθέντ' οὐχὶ λίην ἄχαρι.[31]

Pour in two measures for Nanno and Lyde, and one for the lover's friend[32] Mimnermus and another for prudent Antimachus. For the fifth

---

[26] Cf. in particular Callimachus *Aetia* fr. 1 29–30 τῷ πιθόμη]ν· ἐνὶ τοῖς γὰρ ἀείδομεν οἳ λιγὺν ἦχον | τέττιγος, θ]όρυβον δ' οὐκ ἐφίλησαν ὄνων; Albrecht 1996:160f.

[27] As Gow 1965:II 234 ad Theocritus XIII 14 notes, this use of πονέω is largely prosaic; note in particular Aristotle *Nicomachean Ethics* 1101b35 τοῖς περὶ τὰ ἐγκώμια πεπονημένοις. With this use of the perfect, cf. Aristotle's frequent term for the educated man, ὁ πεπαιδευμένος.

[28] Cf. Philip's description of his literary culling: σελίδος νεαρᾶς θερίσας στάχυν (Philip 1.3 GP *Garland* = *AP* IV 2.3).

[29] Cf. Gutzwiller 1998:161: "The poem thus becomes the proof of its own premise, that despite Desire's attempt to silence the poet, the learned Posidippus has the means to resist by voicing condemnation of his torment."

[30] Somewhat similar is Meleager 19 GP (*AP* XII 117), which of course Posidippus could not have known; for a comparison of the three poems, cf. Albrecht 1996:166.

[31] ἄχαρι Jacobs ἄχαριν P. The entire last clause is daggered by Gow-Page and Albrecht and emended in quite inventive ways by others (see Fernández-Galiano's or Albrecht's apparatus).

[32] The ms. has φερεκάστου, but although φέρε is an appropriate word in this context I print Jacobs' emendation, even though I am tempted by Bousquet's φέρε καὶ τοῦ, which is printed and defended

measure mix in myself. Then, Heliodorus, add the sixth measure with a toast to each person who ever happened to be in love. Say the seventh is Hesiod's, the eighth Homer's, the ninth the Muses', and the tenth Mnemosyne's. I drink a cup slopping over the brim, Cypris. And then,[33] Cupids, to be sober while drunk on wine is not to be too graceless.

His literary cup runneth over. And this cup may not have been his first, to judge from the lack of tidiness in his categories. Are Lyde and Nanno women or literary works? One often toasts or dedicates a drink to a woman; cf. Meleager 42 GP (*AP* V 136) ἔγχει καὶ πάλιν εἰπέ, πάλιν πάλιν, Ἡλιοδώρας, so the poem begins with a certain erotic charge; i.e., they are women. Continuing, however, with toasts to Mimnermus and Antimachus, the respective authors of *Nanno* and *Lyde*, the poem makes the reader rethink (in good reader-response critical fashion) the preceding two toasts; i.e., they are literary creations.[34] But isn't Posidippus confusing his two poets by toasting first a work by each and then toasting them as authors? At least the choice of these two authors makes a kind of sense; both wrote erotic poetry, as does Posidippus. The fifth in the list is himself, but ἐμοῦ with συγκέρασον reads more like a partitive genitive: put some of me in the fifth measure. If this is so, however, we have to go back to the beginning once again and recognize that ἐπιχέω may also take a partitive genitive.[35] All of this seems to be turning this poem into a kind of (pardon the expression) potted literary

....

by Albrecht. Its stylistic awkwardness (played down by Albrecht in order to make his case) could be intentional, designed to make manifest the speaker's drunken state (see below). And for what it is worth, it is paleographically the easiest of the various emendations. I borrow the translation "lover's friend" from Paton; for a defense of such a literal rendering (rather than, say, "charming"), cf. Sider 1997:88.

[33] An explicit temporal reading of τἄλλα fits my reading of the poem (see below) better than vaguer renderings like "for the rest" (Paton), "der Rest" (Beckby), "por lo demás (Fernández-Galiano), or "what's more" (Gutzwiller). Buffière 1977:107 specifies that his "pour la suite" is temporal, but his understanding of what follows differs from mine.

[34] For another example of intentional confusion between Lyde and *Lyde*, cf. Asclepiades 32 GP (*AP* IX 63)

Λύδη καὶ γένος εἰμὶ καὶ οὔνομα, τῶν δ' ἀπὸ Κόδρου
σεμνοτέρη πασῶν εἰμι δι' Ἀντίμαχον·
τίς γὰρ ἔμ' οὐκ ἤεισε; τίς οὐκ ἀνελέξατο Λύδην,
τὸ ξυνὸν Μουσῶν γράμμα καὶ Ἀντιμάχου;

For further play on women = poems (including Callimachus' μεγάλη γυνή), cf. Cameron 1995:303–338. For Latin (some of which is discussed by Cameron), note Ovid *Amores* 3.1, which describes Elegeia and Tragoedia as women; e.g., v.7 *venit odoratos Elegeia nexa capillos*; id. *Remedia Amoris* 379–380 *blandas pharetras Elegia cantet Amores*; and Williams 2002:150–171, who analyzes the ways Martial (among others) personifies his epigrams in erotic terms.

[35] Cf. Theocritus II 151 ἀκράτω ἐπεχεῖτο, "he poured some unmixed wine."

history of the poet Posidippus. And even if item number six were only a toast, it still seems odd. Who offers a toast to oneself? The sixth toast is to everybody who has chanced to be in love. This, like "Lyde" and "Nanno" refers to content, which, as before, makes one back up a toast and ask whether "me" alludes to Posidippus as author or as subject. Let's keep it open, an intentional amphiboly. Homer is every poet's model, but Hesiod seems out of place. He was, though, known for his lists, the most important of which for a poet is the roster of nine Muses, the daughters of Mnemosyne. Hesiod thus may be taken as the model for the list we are currently reading, which puts the (nine) Muses in ninth place.[36] In any case, Muses and Mnemosyne form yet another category. All together, the list includes content (Lyde, Nanno, "me"), book (*Lyde* and *Nanno*), poet as author (Mimnermus, Antimachus, Posidippus), poet as persona ("me" taken together with "everyman" in love), and poetic inspiration (Muses and Mnemosyne). Since, moreover, Muses and Memory are typically appealed to in proems, their mention suddenly converts lines 1–6 into a proem, after which (τἆλλα) the poet begins the poem proper. Our poem, however, like many shorter Homeric hymns, is all prologue. Its form, though, is meant to mirror its content, which describes what a poet must do (read, think, absorb, imitate, allude to) before composition.

The confusion of categories, in other words, is an artful mess, covering the ground like a drunk who cannot walk straight, but who eventually makes his way. Here the ground is erotic poetry, as indicated by the addresses to Cypris and Erotes. The drunkenness, however, is only an act. Thus, in the last line, not only does "sober" mean as befits one ἐν βύβλοις πεπονημένος (cf. νήφω *LSJ* II a, "soberness of thought," as adapted to a poet-scholar), but νήφοντ' οἰνωθέντ' refers to the two facets of the poet's psyche at work at the same time, νήφοντα for the poet now (note present tense) crafting his poem, οἰνωθέντα for his persona within the poem.[37]

We are now in a position to recognize that Posidippus AB 139 = 5 GP (*AP* XII 45) belongs to this group of poems where the persona of the speaker represents Posidippus as poet.

---

[36] Elsewhere I hope to suggest yet another reason for naming Hesiod.

[37] The participles, that is, modify the speaker (so Skiadas 1966:188), not the (understood) *kyathos* vel sim. (so, e.g., Giangrande 1963:262f. and again, rearguing his case after Skiadas, 1969:440–448). My reading of the last clause is as follows: "And then, Erotes, it is not too graceless to be (sc. εἶναι) sober while drunk." For asyndetic coordination of contrasting participles, cf. K-G II 103. The particular turn of phrase at the end is in direct response to Theognis 467–496, a rather tedious bit about drinking in moderation in order not to lose one's wits during a symposium. Note in particular 478–480 οὔτε τι γὰρ **νήφω** οὔτε λίην **μεθύω**. | ὃς δ᾿ ἂν ὑπερβάλλη πόσιος μέτρον, οὐκέτι κεῖνος | τῆς αὑτοῦ γλώσσης καρτερὸς οὐδὲ νόου, 496 χοὕτως συμπόσιον γίνεται οὐκ **ἄχαρι**.

ναὶ ναὶ βάλλετ᾽, Ἔρωτες· ἐγὼ σκοπὸς εἷς ἅμα πολλοῖς
κεῖμαι. μὴ φείσησθ᾽, ἄφρονες· ἢν γὰρ ἐμέ
νικήσητ᾽, ὀνομαστοὶ ἐν ἀθανάτοισιν ἔσεσθε
τοξόται ὡς μεγάλης δεσπόται ἰοδόκης.

Come on, Cupids, take your best shot! I'm right here, one target
for many. Don't hold back, you ninnies, because if you conquer me,
you'll be famous among the gods as archers who are masters of a great
quiver.

This poem presents a twofold response: on the surface a challenge to the
Erotes, but just as clearly to Posidippus' readers both ancient and modern a
response to Asclepiades 17 GP (*AP* XII 166), a plaintive appeal to the Erotes by
someone wasted by love to be put out of his miseries altogether,[38] line 5 of which
begins ναὶ ναὶ βάλλετ᾽, Ἔρωτες. As such, Asclepiades' poem is part of a long
history, beginning with Sappho, of the lover passively bewailing his or her wasted
state. To which Posidippus' poem is more than that of a more bold lover telling a
more down-cast one to face up to his adversaries; rather, although this has not been
generally recognized, it is the poet Posidippus telling a fellow poet how to react
when in love; poets, after all, possess resources denied to ordinary men. They can
lend fame and glory even to immortals.

Posidippus' conditional, "if you conquer me, you will have a name," has an
unspoken negative, "if you do *not* conquer me, you will *not* be named."[39] To be
named is to be famous, but not to be named is to be abominable; cf.
Od. XIX 260 = 597 Κακοΐλιον οὐκ ὀνομαστήν, Hes. *Th.* 148 (the Cyclopes)
οὐκ ὀνομαστοί, Κόττος τε Βριάρεως τε Γύγης θ᾽, ὑπερήφανα τέκνα.
Compare Lat. *nefandus* (West *ad loc.*) and Eng. "infamous." Posidippus thus takes
the *topos* of a poem granting immortal fame (usually understood as a form of
immortality) and transfers it to the Erotes, who as much as any mortal will welcome
having their tale told forever.[40] This poem, in other words, gains its point only
when it is understood as the words of a poet *qua* poet, and quite a bold one at that.

---

[38] This at any rate is how I read the poem, which has two textually vexed passages; Gow and Page
1965:II 128 think that "the poet asks the Loves either to cease tormenting him or to kill him
outright" (intro. *ad poem.*). Asclepiades' precise meaning is not essential for my interpretation of
Posidippus.

[39] This is ordinary thinking but not logical: ~[(P→Q)→(~P→~Q)]. Or, for an example in ordinary
English, the statement "Since I live in Manhattan, I live in New York City" does not entail "Since I
do not live in Manhattan, I do not live in New York City." (Manhattanites, take note.)

[40] Pindar *Pythian* 1.35–38 applies the word to the town of Aetna. Theognis applies the word to
himself: Θεύγνιδός ἐστιν ἔπη | τοῦ Μεγαρέως· πάντας δὲ κατ᾽ ἀνθρώπους
ὀνομαστός. For our purposes, however, the most relevant passage is Posidippus AB 122.5–7 (17

We have now seen how Old Posidippus differs, in a way we have come to think of as typically Hellenistic (a poet who plays with the persona of the speaker as an "I," who in this case is a cocksure poet unafraid to take on the god of love himself), from New Posidippus, who thus starts his literary life at a disadvantage. Such a difference, however, was predictable, as we see when we consider another difference between the two, which will also help to explain the first difference and allow us to make a proper comparison between Old and New Posidippi.

It will have been noted that the epigrams found in the *Greek Anthology* are shorter than the new ones, which break down as follows: 108 poems in 630 vv. = 5.83 vv./poem (4 vv. × 54 poems, 6 × 38, 8 × 11, 10 × 2, 14 × 3). But this disparity in length does not apply to those epigrams of Posidippus previously known from papyri: The Firmin-Didot and the Tebtunis papyri contain epigrams significantly longer than the 5+ line average of the *Anthology*. The relative shortness of the epigrams from the *Anthology* can be credited to one person, Meleager, who compiled a *Garland* of poems by the first generation of Hellenistic epigrammatists, including himself and Posidippus. Thanks to the convenient gathering of these poems in Gow and Page's *Hellenistic Epigrams*, it is relatively easy to get a sense of the epigrams Meleager liked: "sharp and devastating [in] their sudden changes of register, subject, or speaker, [with] sudden revelations and surprises in their move-ment."[41] I quote Hutchinson (on Hellenistic epigrams in general and Callimachus' in particular, not specifically on Meleager's taste) not only because it is to the point, but also because he credits brevity alone with allowing all this. Asclepiades and Callimachus provided early examples of the witty and brief epigram, and they were followed very much by later practitioners. By the time Meleager came to compile his *Garland*, longer epigrams, especially if they did not have a sting in their last line, must have seemed somewhat stodgy. Meleager's published anthology would have spread the gospel of brevity even further, for an overall comparison between the average length of an epigram in his collection with that in Philip of Thessalonica's shows that poets took brevity as a challenge if not a criterion. I can't provide aver-ages here, but note that in Gow and Page's *Hellenistic Epigrams*, there are twenty-one epigrams longer than ten lines (six longer than fourteen lines); in their *Garland of Philip*, on the other hand, the only poem longer than ten lines is Philip's intro-duction of fourteen lines (far shorter than Meleager's 58-line introduction).[42]

⋯⋯⋯⋯

GP) Cαπφῷαι δὲμένουcι φίληc ἔτι καὶ μενέουcιν | ᾡδῆc αἱ λευκαὶ φθεγγόμεναι cελίδεc | οὔνομα cὸν μακαριcτὸν κτλ cf. Angiò 1999:153f.

[41] Hutchinson 1988:75.

[42] My figures are not compromised by the fact that Gow and Page added epigrams belonging to Meleager's and Philip's poets known from elsewhere (such as, in the case of Posidippus, AB 115), and even added (their readers are grateful) Theocritus, who seems not to have been anthologized by

Brevity now becomes explicit as a criterion of the epigram: Philip mentions ὀλιγοστιχίη in his introduction (Philip 1 = *AP* IV 2.6), and one of his authors actually says φημὶ πολιστιχίην ἐπιγράμματος οὐ κατὰ Μούσας εἶναι (Parmenion 11 = *AP* IX 342.1 f.). Between Meleager and Philip's two collections and the two Byzantine manuscript collections that make up the *Greek Anthology*, there was further selection, but probably not in a way that disturbs the decreasing size of epigrams between the first generation of epigrammatists (Meleager's collection) and Philip (who must be one of the very latest in his own collection).

This has not been an exercise in statistics. The inference to be drawn is that the best artists (say, Asclepiades and Callimachus), if they are recognized as such at the time, alter the development of their genre. That Meleager was both poet and anthologist almost guaranteed that what he thought good would affect literary taste for some time to come,[43] indeed until the present day. The *American Heritage Dictionary* (ed. William Morris, 1969) defines epigram as "a short poem expressing a single thought or observation with terseness and wit." This is essentially the Hellenistic definition. Any poem that deviates from this definition cannot be, or fails in its attempt to be, an epigram. This explains the initial reaction of many (myself included) to think little of the Milan epigrams. Just as audiences' expectation of music could never be the same after Mozart (ask Salieri), the essence of the epigram was forever altered after Callimachus, Asclepiades, and their contemporaries.

Among their contemporaries, of course, was Posidippus. He therefore could not, it has been argued,[44] be the author of the Milan epigrams, which seem sorely deficient in Hellenistic wit. This argument, it should now be clear, cannot be maintained. Even if "good" and "bad" were entirely objective and measurable qualities (and if one granted for the sake of the argument that the Milan epigrams were bad), the selection process that began with Meleager and ended with Maximus Planudes would guarantee that Posidippus' epigrams in the *Greek Anthology* would be better than those in any epigram book edited by Posidippus himself (if that is what the Milan papyrus is). This in fact can be "proved mathematically" by the one purely

....

Meleager. (Also added are Crates, Duris, Moschus, Phalaecus, and Zenodotus; cf. GP:II 718f.) The important point here is the increased use of brevity as a criterion for inclusion. It is further interesting to note that Martial's longer epigrams were criticized for not observing this by-then well established criterion: cf. Szelest 1980.

[43] Cf. Cameron 1993:15, "It was Meleager's *selection* [my emphasis] from this material that has shaped our perception of the character and limitations of the classical epigram. It was Meleager's selection that influenced the practice of later epigrammatists; Meleager's *Garland* that determined the character of later anthologies."

[44] Orally, by Hugh Lloyd-Jones. See also Lloyd-Jones 2003 (forthcoming).

quantifiable criterion used by epigrammatists themselves: length. The situation becomes more complex when we leave science and recognize not only that art is not quantifiable but that, as we have seen, tastes change, even within the lifetime of one artist, who may change with the times or who, like Mozart, may himself be responsible for the change in other artists. *Tempora mutantur*. . . .

New Posidippus thus challenges us to read him as he would have been read before the Hellenistic epigram took on (in no small part thanks to Old Posidippus, who may in fact have postdated his Newer form) its characteristic qualities, and to appreciate him for what he is rather than to depreciate him for being what he is not.

4

Alexandrian Posidippus: On Rereading the GP Epigrams in Light of P.Mil.Vogl. VIII 309

Benjamin Acosta-Hughes
University of Michigan

A Poem Commemorates

Δωρίχα, ὀστέα μὲν σὰ παλαὶ κόνις ἡδ᾽ ἀναδεσμός[1]
χαίτης ἥ τε μύρων ἔκπνοος ἀμπεχόνη,
ᾗ ποτε τὸν χαρίεντα περιστέλλουσα Χάραξον
σύγχρους ὀρθρινῶν ἥψαο κισσυβίων·
Σαπφῷαι δὲ μένουσι φίλης ἔτι καὶ μενέουσιν
ᾠδῆς αἱ λευκαὶ φθεγγόμεναι σελίδες.
οὔνομα σὸν μακαριστόν, ὃ Ναύκρατις ὧδε φυλάξει
ἔστ᾽ ἂν ἴῃ Νείλου ναῦς ἐφ᾽ ἁλὸς πελάγη.

Doricha, your bones are long dust, and the band
of your hair and your perfume-breathing robe,
with which you once wrapped lovely Charaxus,
and, one body, you reached the morning wine bowls.
But Sappho's white voice-giving columns of lovely song
remain and will still remain.
Blessed is your name, which Naucratis so will guard
so long as a sea-faring ship goes over the Nile's water.[2]

---

[1] I follow Albrecht 1996:73–74 in accepting Wilamowitz's (1913:20) reading for line 1. GP obelize th
problematic text of Athenaeus here, the source of this poem: Δωρίχα, ὀστέα μὲν †σ᾽ ἁπαλ•
κοιμήσατο δεσμῶν†. Cf. GP: 2.497, Fernandez-Galiano ap. crit. Austin (AB 122) conjectures ἥ•
ὅ τε δεσμός.

[2] There are many evocative translations of this poem, testifying to the changes in reception of Posidip•

42

Among the poems of pre-Milan Posidippus that at once contextualize him in a third-century BCE Alexandrian setting, and highlight some of the more revealing features of the epigrammatist's verse, this commemorative epigram is one of the more remarkable. The poem's eight lines are a series of striking juxtapositions that entwine temporal and physical distance, contrasting images of the passage of time, and a series of changing focal points, as each distich envisions a different figure: Doricha, Charaxus, Sappho, the evoked commemoration. Among the poem's more revealing features are the following:

1. Contrast of monuments: The first quatrain appears to evoke a funeral monument: yet from line 1 to line 2 there is a transition from imagery of death to imagery of life.[3] The robe of line 2, lightly personified by the phrase **μύρων ἔκπνοος**, 'perfume-breathing', evolves into the image of living embrace in the following distich. The final imagery of morning, and of *agrypnia*, provide a poignant contrast with the imagery of sleep inherently present in the imagery of death of the opening line.[4] The second quatrain evokes a different commemoration, Sappho's verse, with a transition from the imagery of life, in the singing of Sappho's 'white voice-giving columns of lovely song', to that of death in the return, in the final distich, to the figure of the dead Doricha and her commemoration. Particularly the term **μακαριστόν**, 'blessed', mainly used of the dead, captures Doricha both as dead figure and as subject of song.[5] The poem can also be read as

....

pus over time: among the most poignant is the sonnet of E. A. Robinson in his 1902 collection *Captain Craig*:

> So now the very bones of you are gone
> Where they were dust and ashes long ago;
> And there was the last ribbon you tied on
> To bind your hair, and that is dust also;
> And somewhere there is dust that was of old
> A soft and scented garment that you wore—
> The same that once till dawn did closely fold
> You in with fair Charaxus, fair no more.
> But Sappho, and the white leaves of her song
> Will make your name a word for all to learn,
> And all to love thereafter, even while
> It's but a name; and this will be as long
> As there are distant ships that will return
> Again to Naucratis and to the Nile.

[3] On the self-conscious play with form of the funerary epigram of this period, see esp. Bing 1995, Walsh 1991.

[4] Although I have adopted Wilamowitz's reading for line 1, κοιμήσατο, 'was put to sleep, laid to rest', of Athenaeus' text that preserves this epigram (Athenaeus XIII 596c) is a vivid contrast with the sleeplessness of line 4.

[5] Cf. Theocritus *Idyll* 7.83: ὦ μακαριστὲ Κομᾶτα, τύ θην τάδε τερπνὰ πεπόνθας, "O blessed Comatus, indeed you had experience of these sweet things", and Hunter 1999:177 on this line.

a kind of eclectic ecphrasis, envisioning a real or imagined funerary monument, that moves in its second half to an evocation of Sappho's songs that in turn records, in its final distich, an appropriate inscription for Doricha's tomb. And so the poem captures two commemorative media in one harmonic whole.[6]

2. Personification of objects: The perfume-breathing robe of the first quatrain and the 'white, voice-giving columns' of the second, not only juxtapose two living images, they also both evoke the imagery of enfolding. Doricha's robe enfolds the embracing couple, Sappho's columns encompass (and hence enfold) their erotic subject—and one might think further here of the imagery of the papyrus roll in turn enfolding its song.[7] There is then a transition, or transformation, of the enfolding robes into the enfolding papyrus, i.e. song. And the contents of the song are of course, in turn, the enfolding of the robe, so that the song retrospectively creates (or has created) the second distich of the epigram. Further, recall of the physical is then answered by the recall of sound. For Sappho's songs, while eternal, also recall a past voice, that of the poet.

3. Play with sound and word position: This works in the epigram on several levels. Χάραξον, μακαριστόν, Ναύκρατις transfers the poem's focus temporally from the Archaic setting of embrace to the speaker's contemporary setting of reflection on memorial. The sound repetition in line 3 χαρίεντα περιστέλλουσα Χάραξον places emphasis on Charaxus' winning qualities:[8] there is also the lovely touch that Doricha's robe actually enfolds him in the line. The repetition at line 5 μένουσι, μενέουσιν, both enacts the enduring quality of Sappho's song first and effects a marked juxtaposition of the figures of Sappho and her poetry, Sappho now become a characterization, her song personified. Further, Σαπφῷαι . . . σελίδες enclose the distich, which is marked by the repetition not only of μένουσι/μενέουσιν, but also by the repetition of ω in the initial words Σαπφῷαι and ᾠδῆς, and the predominance of the sounds μ, λ and φ.[9]

This epigram is itself emblematic of the transference of the world of Archaic poetry to an Alexandrian setting. The preservation of Doricha's memorial, and the enduring character of Sappho's poetry, (wonderfully captured in line 6: ᾠδῆς αἱ λευκαὶ φθεγγόμεναι σελίδες, 'white voice-giving columns of song', as both song

---

[6] I thank M. Baumbach for helpful discussion of this point.

[7] On the personification of Sappho's columns here as an example of personified text(s), see Bing 1988:33, and also Prins 1999:23–24.

[8] The erotic sense of χαρίεις when used of men is nicely brought out at Theocritus *Idyll* 2.115: πρᾶν ποκα τὸν χαρίεντα τράχων ἔφθασα Φιλῖνον, 'as surely yesterday I outran lovely Philinus'.

[9] There is a clear contrast of sound effects in the two quatrains: a predominance of palatals in the first is replaced by a predominance of liquids and nasals in the second. On the euphonic appreciation of *lambda* see Janko 2000:176–78.

nd text), are of the poet's contemporary world, and its relationship to its cultural
nd poetic past. At the same time the poem encapsulates an earlier Greek presence
n Egypt;[10] it also perceives the preservation of archaic Greek culture in Alexandrian
erms—the Nile's enduring course will ensure Doricha's eternal fame.

In the pages that follow I consider the pre-Milan author, under three categories
particularly evoked in the new collection. These are:

1. representation of Alexandrian monuments and ecphrastic technique;
2. resonances of other authors, especially here Sappho;
3. evocation of pathos in the representation of death (or near death).

In each case the new collection casts remarkable light on the old, and features
hat seemed perhaps less remarkable before turn out to be far more representative
of the poet's artistry than we might have thought.

On Reconsidering Posidippus

Modern knowledge and reception of Hellenistic poetry is, in large part, dependent
on the chance survival of texts: we, a much later audience, imagine a whole from
he shards that remain. Inevitably this leads to a hierarchy of authors that, rightly
or wrongly, prefers the survivors. In some cases, e.g. Euphorion, the modern audience knows, at least at one level, that it sees "through a glass, darkly," that poets of
great artistic significance for their own and later eras are now all but entirely lost.[11]
Often only the occasional reference of a scholiast is the sole hint of the artistic value
of lost work. The discovery of a lost text can lead to an enhanced appreciation of
an already valued author, as was the case with the publication of the Lille papyrus.[12]
In the case of a less valued author, the discovery of lost text can lead to a more
radical re-evaluation of the poet in terms of his place in his contemporary setting,
the scope of his work, and his role as a model. This is very much the case with
Posidippus: the publication of P.Mil.Vogl. VIII 309 has already led to a wide-
ranging reassessment of his poetry as both intertextual matrix of his own period and
influence on Latin literature.[13] But the discovery of a new text often has another
function as well—it necessitates re-evaluation of earlier known text now part of a

---

[10] On Alexandrian reconfiguration of the Archaic past, two recent and very thought-provoking studies
are Selden 1998 and Stephens 2000.

[11] As Magnelli's recent illuminating study of this poet, and of his enduring influence, makes clear.

[12] Parsons 1997. Discovery of a lost text can also lead to a negative re-evaluation, as was the case with
the Gallus fragment, and also in some sense with the Archilochus Cologne epode. Scholars who find
the pre-Milan Posidippus artistically superior to the new epigrams are faced with a similar situation.

[13] The role of the new poems, as individual works and as an artistic composite, for Latin literature is
only beginning to be appreciated: Hutchinson's 2002 study is a crucial beginning of what will be a
large area of scholarship to come.

larger, different corpus. The new epigrams, whether all, or some, are correctl
attributed to the third-century BCE Macedonian poet Posidippus, do compel us t
look again, and from a new perspective, at the author we had before and our earlie
reception of him.[14]

Prior to the publication of the Milan papyrus one might rightly have said, t
someone inquiring about this epigrammatist, that Posidippus was of particula
interest for three reasons:

First his name appears in the company of several others in the *Florentin*
Scholia to Callimachus' *Aetia* Prologue (fr. 1 Pf.). *PSI* 1219, fr. 1.1–10 appears t
equate a number of contemporary literary figures with the Telchines of the openin
line of Callimachus' poem. The text of the scholion is fragmentary, and the subjec
of considerable scholarly debate.

πολλάκ]ι[15] μοι Τελχῖνες ἐπιτρύιζουσιν ἀοιδῇ
        ]τει. δ[. . .]. . .
    ]. Διονυσίοις δυ[σ]ί, τῷ ελ
    ]νι κ(αὶ) τῷ ἵλειονι κ(αὶ)’Ασκλη-
πιάδῃ τῷ Σικε]λίδῃ κ(αὶ) Ποσειδίππῳ τῷ ονο
    ]. υρίππῳ τῷ ῥήτορι κ(αὶ) Αγα
    ]βῳ κ(αὶ) Πραξιφάνῃ τῶ Μιτυ-
ληναίῳ, τοῖς με]μφομ(έν)ο[ι]ς αὐτοῦ τὸ κάτισ-
χνον τῶν ποιη]μάτ(ων) κ(αὶ) ὅτι οὐχὶ μῆκος ηρα
. . . . . .]. . [. . . . .]ουμ(εν)ο. [.]οι. [. .].

Often the Telchines croak at my song (. . .) two Dionysus' (. . .) and
Asclepiades son of Sicelidas[16] and Posidippus (. . .) the rhetorician and
(. . .) and Praxiphanes of Miletus, those faulting the slender quality of
his poems and that not length (. . .)

While there is still much room for debate as to what is exactly going on in thi
fragmentary passage, two things are especially revealing.[17] a) The scholion list
Posidippus with a number of other literary figures in some way associated witl

[14] While the attribution of some, or all, of the new epigrams to Posidippus is still a point of vivid discus
sion, the passage of time is seeing the weight of scholarly judgment come down in favor o
Posidippus. The absence of any other known epigrammatist in the collection, and the consistency o
metrical practice both argue strongly for one author, and that this author is Posidippus. On th
metrical consistency of the collection, see now Fantuzzi 2003.
[15] This is almost certainly the correct reading for *Aetia* fr. 1.1, as confirmed by Pontani 1999:57–59.
[16] Or Sicelus. See GP 2:115.
[17] See Massimilla 1996:199–201.

allimachus: whether some or all polemically, and whether these are in fact the elchines of the *Aetia*'s opening line is of less interest than the association. There are me very intriguing points of correspondence between the two poets not only in e new epigrams, on which several contributors to this volume comment in detail, at also in the old ones.[18] b) Significantly here, as in several other contexts, cluding the opening poem of Meleager's *Garland*, Posidippus is paired with, *and llows*, Asclepiades. Although the fragment may have contained many other names, urs is a reading here at once associative and hierarchical—we have the epigramatists together, and in this order.

Secondly, when read with Asclepiades, his poems provide a revealing contrast some aspects of the former's epigrams. A. Sens has recently written a nuanced udy of ecphrastic epigrams that develops just such a contrasting reading.[19] The sociation of the two poets, and of their poetry, is not only a historical one, attested the association of their names and doubtful attribution of some poems to either the *Greek Anthology*, but one predicated on marked artistic resonance in both ets' work. Their compositions appear to reflect one another.

Thirdly, Posidippus' epigrams include one on the description of the construcon of the Pharos lighthouse AB 115 (= 11 GP) and two on the cult of Arsinoe ephyritis, AB 116 and 119 (= 12 and 13 GP). He is a witness to early Ptolemaic ltural monuments and trajectories in a way that sets him somewhat apart from her epigram authors.[20]

Looking again, in a new context, at the pre-Milan author, we encounter some roblematics' in approaching the collection, and these are worth detailing briefly.

1. Gow and Page in their 1965 edition of *Hellenistic Epigrams* give us some poems: Page in his 1975 *Epigrammata Graeca* ascribes 29 to Posidippus.[21] There e then the fragments in the *Supplementum Hellenisticum* (frr. 698–708) of which e *Seal* (*SH* 705) is of particular interest for its autobiographical voice, for its parals with the themes and imagery of Callimachus' *Aetia* Prologue, and for its rtrayal of memorial of poetry and of poet.[22] Particularly the metaphorical refer-

---

[18] See Sider this volume on AB 140 (= 9 GP).

[19] Sens 2002.

[20] The new epigram on the Colossus of Rhodes, then still standing, is another example, as D. Sider has pointed me out to me. On Posidippus and Alexandrian monuments, see esp. Bing 1998.

[21] Page ascribes to Posidippus six epigrams (23–28) that Gow ascribed to Asclepiades. He also ascribes one epigram to Meleager (54) that Gow ascribed to Posidippus (23). The final epigram in Page's edition (29) is given the wrong GP number (this should be 24, not 34). For a more detailed discussion of the pre-Milan collection, see Sider in this volume. See further Albrecht 1996:20–21, Fernandez-Galiano 1987:24–26.

[22] AB 114 (= *SH* 961), perhaps an *epithalamium* of Arsinoe, is attributed by some to Posidippus: see further Albrect 1996:10, Fernandez-Galiano 1987:38–39. The preponderance of poems on Ptolemaic queens, and on Arsinoe II in the new collection, makes this attribution the more

ences to the physicality of the text are revealing both for their resonances elsewhere in Posidippus' poetry and their correspondences in Callimachus.[23] Fernande Galiano in his 1987 edition of Posidippus includes additionally a number inscriptional epigrams, which he, following several earlier scholars, tentativel attributes to Posidippus.[24] These last I leave aside here, but in considering the re of the texts would draw attention to what might be termed a 'contested' characte of the pre-Milan collection, a corpus marked in the scholarship by query and doub The main contributing factors to this are a rather contested poetic voice, and poetry in its scholarly interpretation of contested attribution, contested quality, an a problematic dual role of the epigram poet Asclepiades. Let us consider each these for a few moments.

2. Neither in the pre-Milan epigrams in GP, nor in the new material, do Posidippus name himself, as does Asclepiades at 16 GP, or Callimachus, albe obliquely, in his two funerary epigrams 29 GP and 30. The important exceptio here is the *Seal*, a poem specifically about poetic composition, and one that astute plays on the conventions of dedicatory epigram—the statue is of the poet himsel Nor is it easy from the first-person references that might be associated with a poet voice to really derive a sense of "Posidippus": again the situation is very differe with Asclepiades. The *Seal of Posidippus* (*SH* 705, AB 118), whether understood an epigram or as a longer elegiac work, is of course a markedly first-person utte ance, and the fragment does include two self-references (lines 5 and 9).[25] In th remaining epigrams, however, it is not easy to gage the first person voice.

3. Confusion of attribution, assignation to Asclepiades or Posidippus, already at issue with six epigrams from the *Greek Anthology*: these are assigned b Gow to Asclepiades (GP Asclepiades 34–39), but subsequently by Page in his *OC* edition to Posidippus (Posidippus 23–28).[26] But the association with Asclepiades rather more complicated than one of contested attribution alone. Gow-Page remarks on a number of Posidippus' epigrams take the stance that, essentiall "Asclepiades did it better."[27] Their remarks on other epigrams of Posidippus us

....

intriguing. See Fantuzzi and Stephens in this volume. On the correspondences of the *Seal* ar Callimachus' *Aetia* fr. 1, see Sider (this volume), Acosta-Hughes and Stephens 2002:244n2 Fernandez-Galiano 1987:16–17, and in his commentary *ad loc*.

[23] On the physicality of the text, see Bing 1988:15, Goldhill 1991:224.

[24] Fernandez-Galiano 1987:27–31.

[25] The longest poems in the Milan collection are 14 verses (AB 19, AB 74, AB 78). These are not long as the *Seal* (perhaps 28 lines—see Lloyd-Jones and Parsons *ad loc*.), but attest to the variabili in size of Posidippus' epigrams. The longest of the epigrams in the pre-Milan collection is 12 lines

[26] This attribution must then have been Page's, as my colleague David Sider has pointed out to me: Pa does not, in the introduction to his *OCT* text, address this.

[27] E.g. 10 GP (= AB 124).

Asclepiades as a point of comparison and reference.[28] Clearly the association is a legitimate one, and one that can contribute much to interpretation. On the other hand, this reading of one epigrammatist in the light of another has the effect of trivializing the one compared. Posidippus becomes the Tibullus to Asclepiades' Propertius, or (to borrow a parallel from my co-contributor D. Sider), the Salieri to Asclepiades' Mozart, the secondary figure, the subject of variation rather than its object. One wonders how the new poems, if indeed by Posidippus, will affect this rapport. Surely one of the contributing factors to the older hierarchy is that there were more epigrams of Asclepiades than Posidippus, and that these formed a more comprehensive group. The new epigrams, even if there remain, in the end, doubts on the attribution of the entire collection to Posidippus, alter this ratio.[29]

4. There remain several instances in the pre-Milan corpus of poems contested on grounds of other problematic attribution or perceived quality. These include the "satiric" AB 133 (= GP 22) on the miseries of human life,[30] and the *Seal* itself, thought by some to be the composition of a later Posidippus, author of elegiac poetry. AB 65, 142, and 15 (= 18–20 GP), all poems preserved in sources other than the *Palatine Anthology*, have also been held as suspect: these of course include two of the poems found among the new epigrams in the Milan roll.

What this brief survey does, I think, suggest is that our pre-Milan collection is in some respects a rather unstable one, and may, in the context of a larger corpus, come to be perceived quite differently. And then there is the odd experience of reading this collection of epigrams in light of the new ones. For the epigrams of Posidippus from the *Palatine Anthology* are not, of course, contiguous: the associations made between them, now contiguous on the modern page, are partly ours, the modern readers, as, in some cases, their separation in the new *editio minor* makes clear. The Milan epigrams are, on the other hand, contiguous, and the experience of reading them necessarily very different, one that experiences their order, their position, and their respective quality to Posidippus.

Posidippus and the Monuments

The pre-Milan epigram collection encompasses a number of categories, a rather large number given the relatively small number of epigrams: these include symposistic epigrams (among them drinking and erotic epigrams), ecphrastic, funereal, and satiric epigrams. The ecphrastic epigrams are remarkable for the juxtaposition (in category, not in text) of very large and very small objects, the Pharos lighthouse

---

[28] E.g. 2, 4, 5, 15, 18 GP (= AB 125, 130, 135, 132, 65).
[29] See Fantuzzi 2003.
[30] *AP* 9.359, assigned either to Posidippus or Plato *Comicus*.

and the snakestone of AB 15 (= 20 GP). There is the further revealing character tha the epigram on the Pharos lighthouse, AB 115 (= 11 GP), and those on the cult o Arsinoe Zephyritis, AB 116 and 119 (= 12 and 13 GP), themselves in turn provide a small ecphrasis of Alexandria. Alexandria is far less present in e.g. the surviving epigrams of Callimachus. The reader of Posidippus reads the city through hi poetry.[31]

A remarkable characteristic of these three epigrams is the variety of perspective While all three play on the traditional conventions of inscribed epigram, the rela tionship of speaker and audience is differently configured in each one. AB 11' (= 11 GP), on the Pharos lighthouse, addresses the figure surmounted on the struc ture's summit.[32] AB 116 (= 12 GP), on the shrine of Arsinoe-Aphrodite a Zephyrium, assumes the first person voice typical of dedicatory epigram: here the monumental object, the shrine, is the speaker. AB 119 (= 13 GP) has neither apos trophe of the monument nor first person self-reference: it addresses an otherwise unidentified second person plural audience. The variation in the three epigram extends to their evocation of topographical setting, beneficiary of the monument and imagery of the sea. Their points of similarity and difference are necessarily highlighted in part by their adjacent position in GP, and are thus emblematic of the real challenges that positioning of epigrams renders for the reader.[33] At the same time all three also illustrate both variety of technique in ecphrastic composition and in the encompassing of large monuments in small poems, an artistic inclination Posidippus shares with other Hellenistic poets.[34]

AB 116 and 119 (= 11 and 12 GP), the two 10-line poems preserved by the Firmin-Didot papyrus, share particularly an extended play of image and monu ment, and sense of geographical place.[35] As P. Bing has evocatively shown, the image (of Zeus Soter) in the first and last distichs encloses the *aition* of the monumen (lines 3–4), and its daytime (lines 5–6) and nighttime aspects (lines 7–8, with the pointed juxtaposition at the opening of 7 ἤματι, παννύχιος δέ).[36] The image o

---

[31] *P.Firmin-Didot* comes from a collection of papers belonging to two brothers, Macedonians, associ ated with the temple of Sarapis at Memphis. See Bing 1998:21n2, Thompson 1988:259–261. Th brother(s) are already reading the city through epigrams on its monuments: see Bing, 1998:30–31.

[32] Bing 1998:22–27.

[33] The editors of the *editio minor* have, in their structure of the corpus, restored something of the asso ciation of these two poems in the Firmin-Didot papyrus by separating them from the *AP* epigrams

[34] Two of the many signal features of Hellenistic ecphrasis are small objects delineated in great deta and large objects captured *in Kleinem*, both exemplified by the new Posidippus epigrams.

[35] On the possibility that these epigrams are emblematic of a guide to monuments, see Bin 1998:30–31, Thompson 1987:109. Callimachus in his *Aetia* and *Iambi* similarly provides panorama of celebrated statuary. See Acosta-Hughes 2002:287–288.

[36] Wonderful moments of recall in lines 9–10 reflect lines 1–2: Φάρου σκοπόν, Ταύρου κερας

the tower shining forth at great distance in lines 5–6 is answered in lines 7–8 with the light of the tower's summit perceived by the distant sailor—distance perceived at each end of the spectrum. The eye of the reader/viewer moves first up, then outward, then back. There is similar play in direction in several poems of the new collection: cf. AB 90 (from the *Nauagika*) γῆν ἔνθεν τε καὶ ἔνθεν ὁρώμενον, where the verse captures the swimmer's wandering gaze. AB 116 (= 12 GP) displays similar touches of prefigure and recall. The opening distich configures monument and place, the monument, in a nice touch in the first hemieps, is set indeed 'between' μέσσον ἐγὼ Φαρίης. These two lines, encompassing place and monument, are followed by two juxtaposed distichs, one on place (lines 3–4), one on monument (5–6).[37] The monument evolves into the divinity at lines 7–8, and then back into the monument in the final line.

Several sections of the new epigrams markedly feature viewing, the gaze, audience evoked. In particular the *Anathematika*, the *Nauagika*, and the *Iamatika* appear to 'read' physical settings: the shrine of Arsinoe-Zephyritis, funeral votaries, perhaps a shrine of Asclepius.[38] The *Oiônoskopika* also center on viewing; the gaze of both figures in the poems and the external audience is constantly drawn to new birds, their movements, and the direction of their flight. In a similar way the epigrams of the Firmin-Didot papyrus appear to 'read' the Alexandrian shoreline, both from land and from sea, and to preserve its light, wide spaces, and sea-faring activity in the compass of the small poem.

Posidippus and Sappho

The epigram on Doricha's tomb (AB 122 = 17 GP), discussed above, is remarkable both for the characterization of Sappho's verse as physical text, and particularly as a collective cultural metaphor. The appearance of Sappho's verse in a similar guise in one of the new epigrams (AB 55.2) and its conjecture in another (51.6) encourages us to re-consider Posidippus' use of Sappho, and also Posidippus' place in a long tradition of reception of Sappho in Hellenistic and Latin poetry. Both passages in the new epigrams occur in the contexts of funerary lament, and so share with the epigram on Doricha's tomb the association of Sappho and death:

....

(remarkable geographic features, same position in the line); σωτῆρα, σωτῆρος; Πρωτεῦ, Πρωτεῦ. Further close reading might garner many more.

[37] The phrase ἐν περιφαινομένῳ (line 2) occurs also at AB 93.5 (from the *Nauagika*) ἐν περιφαινομένωι Κύμης, καὶ τὸν νέκυν, ὡς χρή. The setting is quite different (albeit both are poems, in a sense, about sea-faring); the further sound parallel in κύματι/Κύμης is worth noting.

[38] See respectively Stephens, Thomas, Bing, this volume.

πάντα τὰ Νικομάχης καὶ ἀθύρματα καὶ πρὸς ἐώιαν
κερκίδα Cαπφώιουc ἐξ ὁάρων ὁάρουc
ὤιχετο Μοῖρα φέρουcα προώρια· τὴν δὲ τάλαιναν
παρθένον 'Αργείων ἀμφεβόηcε πόλιc.
"Ηρηc τὸ τραφὲν ἔρνοc ὑπ' ὠλένοc· ἃ τότε γαμβρῶν
τῶν μνηcτευομένων ψύχρ' ἔμεινεν λέχεα.

All of Nicomache's possessions, her playthings and Sapphic songs
upon songs, lasting until the morning shuttle, all these
has Fate, untimely, come and borne away. The wretched
maid does Argos' city cry aloud,
a young shoot raised under Hera's care. Alas then, for those
suitors who would be bridegrooms—cold remain their beds.[39]

'δακρυόεccα[ι ἔπεcθε, θε]οῖc ἀνατείνατε πήχειc',
τοῦτ' ἐπὶ πα[ιδὸc ἐρεῖτ' αὐ]τόμαται Καρύαι,
Τηελφίηc, ἧc [κεῖcθε πρὸ]c ἠρίον· ἀλλὰ φέρουcαι
εἴαρι πορφυρέ[ου κλῶν' ἐc ἀ]γῶνα νέμουc
θῆλυ ποδήν[εμον ἔρνοc] ἀείδετε, δάκρυcι δ' ὑμέων
κολλάcθω Cα[πφῶι' ἄιcμ]ατα, θεῖα μέλη.

In tears [follow], your arms stretch to the gods!
Say this freely [for the girl], Carian women,
she, Telephia at whose tomb [you lie]. But bearing
in spring a [spray] from purple meadow to this gathering,
sing of the maiden, with wind-swift feet, and to your tears
be joined Sa[ppho's] odes, divine songs.[40]

In their comments on AB 55.2, the editors of the *editio princeps*, comparing this use of the adjective Cαπφώιουc with that of 17.5 GP, doubt that the phrase Cαπφώιουc ἐξ ὁάρων ὁάρουc referred to Sappho's poetry. "Qui Cα⟨φ⟩ώιουc dovrebbe invece genericamente significare 'femminili' (cfr. παρθενίουc τ' ὁάρουc in Hes. *Theog.* 205) come induce a credere anche il confronto con altre inconsuete formazioni aggettivali presenti nel rotolo: per es., δελφὶc . . . 'Αριόνο[c di VI 19, dove all'aggettivo pare essere attribuito il generico

---

[39] Translation by B. Acosta-Hughes and E. Kosmetatou.
[40] Translation by B. Acosta-Hughes and E. Kosmetatou.

scopo di designare un delfino 'qual era quello di Arione' . . ." In their translations of this epigram both the Italian and English renditions reflect this: "conversari femminili", "conversations à la Sappho". Concerning the sense of AB 51.6 their interpretation is similar.[41] Yet we might choose to look at this evocation of Sappho from another perspective, that of Archaic poet now become poetic motif—Sappho as metaphor, as it were. Sappho is by no means the only figure who is present, through evocation or as intertext, in the epigrams of Posidippus; in particular the poets Theocritus and Callimachus have a marked presence in the epigrams, as several recent studies have well shown.[42] But the simple recurrence of the epithet. Ϲαπφῷοϲ in the collection might suggest looking again, from a different perspective, at other epigrams that appear to recall Sappho.

One example would be AB 139 (= GP 8), the prayer of Callistion:

ἃ Κύπρον ἅ τε Κύθηρα καὶ ἃ Μίλητον ἐποιχνεῖϲ
    καὶ καλὸν Ϲυρίης ἱππκρότου δάπεδον,
ἔλθοιϲ ἵλαοϲ Καλλιϲτίῳ, ἣ τὸν ἐραϲτήν
    οὐδέποτ᾽ οἰκείων ὦϲεν ἀπὸ προθύρων.

> You who frequent Cyprus and Cythera and Miletus
>   and the lovely plain of horse-beaten Syria,
> may you come favorably to Callistion, who a lover
>   never thrust away from her own door.

Commentators have been troubled by the inconsistency of dialect forms in the poem, particularly the jarring contrast of Doric ἅ in the anaphora of line 1 and Ionic ἥ of line 2.[43] A. Sens in this volume has a nuanced study of the light the new epigrams cast on Posidippus' use of Doric dialect in his verse: he argues for a specific Doric/Ionic demarcation in Hellenistic poetics. In this case, though, I think one might also wonder whether the dialect evoked in the first line is not Aeolic, and the image evoked not Sappho, specifically the voice of Sappho fr. 1.[44] The structure of the epigram is clearly one of rather striking contrast: the apparent solemnity of the

---

[41] See their comments to AB 51.6: "Riguardo al senso, dovremmo forse pensare che le fanciulle dolenti cantino veramente carmi di Saffo? Ciò non sembra probabile, e saremmo propensi a ritenere che l'aggettivo Ϲαπφῷοϲ, ammessa la giustezza dell'integrazione, sia usato in senso analogico . . ."

[42] On Theocritus and the new epigrams, see Petrain 2003; on Callimachus and the new epigrams, Fantuzzi and Sider in this volume.

[43] GP: 2.487, Albrecht 1996:167–68. Artistically the anaphora is clearly meant to draw attention to the dialect form.

[44] Albrecht 1996:172–73 has some very good observations on this poem and thematic parallels in Sappho: I would just take it a step further and say that Posidippus is indeed evoking Sappho here.

first distich contrapoised with the far more mundane, yet piquant second one.⁴ The association of Sappho fr. 1 as opening poem of the Alexandrian edition c Sappho is clearly important for later authors (e.g. Horace 4.1):⁴⁶ the question her would be whether this is already true for Posidippus. While there are some tanta lizing specific parallels among the fragments of Sappho, at issue here is a rathe broader type of evocation, one again that reflects Sappho as cultural metaphor.⁴ Callistion's prayer for the goddess' attendance is, in it first distich, in its setting imagery, and relative pronoun, set in part in Sappho's realm, in the second ver much in Callistion's own.⁴⁸

The use of Sappho's name as epithet in the new epigrams raises a number c intriguing questions about Posidippus' reading of Sappho, and of the reception c Sappho in this period, particularly, again, as cultural metaphor. Once again the nev epigrams cast light back on the old, and vividly make clear for us the significance which we may not have perceived, of the verses we already had. The final line c BA 123 (= 1 GP) μέλοι δ' ἡμῖν ὁ γλυκύπικρος "Ερως has always been undei stand as a resonance of Sappho's image (fr. 130 V: "Ερος δηὖτέ μ' ὁ λυσιμέλη δόνει, | γλυκύπικρον ἀμάχανον ὄρπετον. The degree, and variety, c Sappho's resonance in Posidippus is only now becoming clear.

Posidippus and Pathos

A surprising number of the epigrams preserved by P.Mil.Vogl. VIII 309 have deat as their focus: these include the categories on grave offerings (*Epitymbia*), shipwrec (*Nauagika*), sickness and cure (*Iamatika*) and the somewhat enigmatic *Tropo* Poems in other categories, particularly the *Oiônoskopika*, also include poems tha have death as a central image. The poems exhibit a great innovation in the conven tions of funerary epigram, and as well a wide range of treatment of pathos. It i particularly with this variation in pathos in mind that I would like, in the fina portion of this paper, to look again at a pre-Milan epigram of Posidippus that play in revealing ways with conventions of pathos, and with the audience's expectation: AB 131 (= 21 GP) appears twice in the *Palatine Anthology*, the second time ascribe to Callimachus: in the *Planudean Anthology* it is ascribed to Posidippus. Gow remark on the epigram, "its tenderness or sentimentality does not accord very we with what we know of Pos.", would need re-thinking in light of the new collectior

---

⁴⁵ As Sens, this volume, well captures.

⁴⁶ See Barchiesi 2000:172–73.

⁴⁷ A nice parallel here is Theocritus *Idyll* 2, with the 're-writing' of Sappho fr. 31 in Simaetha's descriptio of her experience of the ἐρωτική νόσος at lines 88–90 and 106–110. See Dover 1971 to line 108.

⁴⁸ A contemporary poem that has Aeolic coloring, similarly for associative reasons, is Callimachu *Iambus* 7. See D'Alessio 1996:627.

Τὸν τριετῆ παίζοντα περὶ φρέαρ ᾿Αρχιάνακτα
εἴδωλον μορφᾶς κωφὸν ἐπεστάσατο,
ἐκ δ᾽ ὕδατος τὸν παῖδα διάβροχον ἥρπασε μάτηρ
σκεπτομένα ζωᾶς εἴ τινα μοῖραν ἔχει.
5   Νύμφας δ᾽ οὐκ ἐμίηνεν ὁ νήπιος ἀλλ᾽ ἐπὶ γούνοις
ματρὸς κοιμαθεὶς τὸν βαθὺν ὕπνον ἔχει.

The silent image of his form drew
the three-year old Archianax playing at the well.
And from the water his mother snatched the boy all wet
wondering what part of life he yet retained.
The infant did not pollute the nymphs, but upon the knees
of his mother lulled fell into a deep sleep.

The sequence of action in the distichs is remarkable (cf. e.g. AB 74) as is the
change of viewer and viewed in each distich: each depicts an image and suggests a
reaction. Revealing also are some of the vivid adjectives. The εἴδωλον κωφόν of
line 2 at once draws the boy's gaze and prefigures his subsequent state (cf. Euripides
Medea 1162: ἄψυχον εἰκὼ προσγελῶσα σώματος). τὸν παῖδα
διάβροχον of the following line at once captures the child seized by the mother
and recalls the image perceived through the water of the previous distich. The
apparent recollection at line 5 of Theocritus 13.53–54: Νύμφαι μὲν σφετέροις
ἐπὶ γούνασι κοῦρον ἔχοισαι | δακρυόεντ᾽ ἀγανοῖσι παρεψύχοντ᾽
ἔπεσιν, is truly very striking: [49] the boy, apparently represented in death here (and
hence perhaps the sense of the final ἔχει) is at the same time in a sense captured, as
is Hylas in *Idyll* 13, as though alive. The 'viewer' of poem (and monument) is left,
at the epigram's end, with the same question given the boy's mother at line 4—
whether indeed the boy is still alive. Is the juxtaposition of *thanatos* and *hypnos* here
contrast or confluence of imagery?

Conclusion

As the present volume was on the eve of going to press, C. Austin's and
G. Bastianini's *editio minor* of Posidippus appeared, the first volume to include all
of extant Posidippus between two covers. Their positioning of the poems was of
course crucial for their reception—for while the edition follows a logic at once

---

[49] Well articulated by Piacenza 1998:348–50. Cf. also [Theocritus] 23.56 εἵματα πάντ᾽ ἐμίανεν
ἐφαβικά. I thank M. Fantuzzi for this reference.

material and chronological, it also effectively incorporates the pre-Milan epigram together with the new, both through continuous numeration and placement o categories. A continuous reading of the volume results in an appreciation of the ol epigrams informed by the new—the reader perceives the old epigrams anew, wit new association and meaning.

5

Homeric Echoes in Posidippus

Gregory Nagy
Harvard University

The word 'echoes' in the title is meant as a substitute for 'allusions', which is inadequate for conveying the awareness of Homeric poetry in the poetics of Posidippus. The subtle ways in which Posidippus demonstrates this awareness reveal an understanding of Homeric poetry that transcends conventional views in later eras, as typified by Aristarchus of Alexandria in the middle of the second century BCE. In the earlier era of Posidippus, in the third century BCE, Homeric poetry was viewed more broadly. In this earlier era, as most prominently typified by Callimachus, the Homeric text was understood differently from the later era of Aristarchus, whose more narrow understanding of Homer has set the standards of Homeric textual criticism to this day.

In the era of Posidippus, Homeric poetry was thought to include a periphery of meanings and forms that later generations of Homeric scholars excluded as non-Homeric. The poetry of Posidippus, following a poetic vogue best exemplified by Callimachus, cultivated this Homeric periphery. Even if Posidippus may be considered a rival of Callimachus, we can still think of these two poets as parallel forces in the cultivation of this vogue. A strong interest in what I am calling here the Homeric periphery was typical of Hellenistic poetry in general.

It was not a question of simply alluding to Homer. It was more, much more, than that. Poets like Posidippus—especially Callimachus—alluded to a special kind of Homer, distancing themselves from the core of Homeric poetry while privileging its periphery. Their self-distancing from the Homeric core helps explain my description of their allusiveness in the title of my presentation. This allusiveness was a kind of distant echoing.

What was being echoed by these Hellenistic poets was indeed Homer, but this Homer was destined to become something other than Homer in the post-Callimachean era of Aristarchus and beyond.

Aristarchus' rigorous system of excluding various meanings and forms as non Homeric elements in the Homeric tradition had actually been anticipated by contemporary of Callimachus and Posidippus. This was Zenodotus, generall acknowledged as the first editor of Homer at the Library of Alexandria. Althougl the approach of Zenodotus in the third century may have been less systematic that that of Aristarchus in the second, what stands out is the overall similarity betwee the methods of these two editors of Homer. The overall criteria used by Zenodotu for excluding various meanings and forms as non-Homeric turn out to be remark ably convergent with those of Aristarchus. Such convergence raises a question tha is essential for my presentation: why did Callimachus and other Hellenistic poets including Posidippus, cultivate precisely those Homeric meanings and forms tha were deemed to be non-Homeric by the leading contemporary editor of Homer?

The answer has to do with the poetic sensibilities that characterized the age o Callimachus. As scholar poets of the Hellenistic era, the likes of Callimachus an Posidippus preferred the peripheral to the central, the exotic to the conventiona They were interested in variation for the sake of variation, treating variants not a distractions from the core of Homeric poetry but instead as sources of fascinatioi about exotica deemed peripheral to this poetry. By contrast, Aristarchus and sucl predecessors as Zenodotus stayed focused on what th͜ey considered to be the essen tial core of Homeric poetry—whatever they thought belonged to the real Home Everything non-Homeric was for them post-Homeric and 'newer'.

The rigorous methodology of Aristarchus in excluding 'newer' elements in th Homeric text is reflected in his rigorous usage of the word *neôteroi* as a designatioi of 'newer' poets and *neôterikos* as an adjective describing features that distinguis! the 'neoterics' from the genuine Homer. As the exhaustive study of Severyns ha made clear, this rigorous usage of Aristarchus is reflected even indirectly in the usag of these same words by the excerpters and epitomators of Aristarchus, as reflecte in the Homeric scholia.[1]

What Aristarchus was doing, and what his predecessor Zenodotus had bee doing beforehand, though perhaps not as systematically, represented a radica departure from earlier ways of thinking about Homer. The Classical idea of Home as reflected in the conventional usage of most authors in what we know as th Classical period, pictured the poet of the *Iliad* and *Odyssey* as a figure more recen

---

[1] Severyns 1928. A particularly noteworthy follower of Aristarchus in applying the criterion of *neôter* was Apollodorus of Athens. (On Apollodorus as a student of Aristarchus, see Apollodorus *FGrHi* 244 T 1; cf. Pfeiffer 1968:261; Rusten 1982:32n10.) A striking example is P. Col. inv. 5604, whei Apollodorus comments on a manuscript of the *Meropis* (*SH* 903A) that he found (on which see espe cially Henrichs 1993:188–189; cf. Rusten1982:32). Apollodorus describes the anonymous author a *neôteros tis* 'someone newer'; he explains his interest in the manuscript in terms of the *idiôma* of it content (ἐδόκει δέ μοι τὰ ποήμα|[τα] νεωτέρου τινὸς εἶναι . . . τὸ ἰδίωμα τῆς ἰστορίας)

than such primeval and superannuated figures as Orpheus and his 'scribe' Musaeus.[2] The idea of Homer as the oldest of all standard poets became a standard idea in its own right only in the era of Alexandrian scholarship. A moving force that led to this shift was Aristotle, who thought of Orpheus as a mythical figment post-dating Homer.[3] It needs to be emphasized that fifth-century authors like Herodotus were far ahead of their times in thinking of Homer as the oldest poet—older even than Orpheus and Musaeus.[4]

This rethinking of Homer in the Hellenistic era affected radically the editing of Homer. For example, Aristarchus made it his editorial practice to athetize or even omit Homeric verses that could be characterized as 'Orphic', treating them as interpolations; also, within individual verses, he preferred variant wordings that seemed to him Homeric as opposed to other variants that seemed by comparison 'Orphic'.[5]

Zenodotus anticipated the editorial practice of Aristarchus, in treating Homer as the oldest poet and in treating all other poets as *neôteroi* 'newer'. This predecessor's approach to the Homeric text was in many ways even more radical than that of Aristarchus. For example, Zenodotus athetized the Shield of Achilles passage in *Iliad* XVIII (483–608), condemning it as a non-Homeric interpolation. Nevertheless, even within the athetized text of the Shield, Zenodotus went on make judgments about individual words within given verses, evidently on the grounds that some variant words were more Homeric than others (as at XVIII 485).

Such exercising of editorial judgment in making distinctions between what was Homeric and what was non-Homeric—or even between what was relatively more likely and less likely to be Homeric—amounted to a scholarly skill in the procedures of *diorthôsis*—that is, in the ongoing process of 'correcting' the Homeric text in order to recover, ultimately, the true or 'correct' Homer.[6] The Hellenistic scholar-poets of Alexandria, such as Callimachus as well as rivals like Posidippus, transformed this scholarly skill into a poetic skill. In the 'Seal of Posidippus' (AB 118 = *SH* 705), the poet alludes to his mastery of *diorthôsis* by referring to himself as *orthoepês* (verse 24).

The Hellenistic poets of Alexandria were exponents of the kind of poetry that concentrates on displaying—artistically—the learning it took to distinguish the newer from the older kind of poetry. What was being echoed in their poetry was

---

[2] In the traditions of fifth- and fourth-century Athens, the figure of Orpheus—along with Musaeus—are conventionally pictured as if they were earlier than Hesiod and Homer; the *locus classicus* is Aristophanes *Frogs* 1032–1035. Other important testimonia include Hippias 86 B 6 DK; Plato *Apology* 41a; *Republic* 363a, 377d, 612b; Ephorus *FGrHist* 70 F 101.

[3] Cicero *De Natura Deorum* I 38.

[4] Herodotus II 53.3.

[5] Nagy 2001.

[6] More on *diorthôsis* in Nagy 1996:115–116, 118–122, 125–127, 186, 191, 198–200, 203–204.

not so much the idea that something happens to be not Homeric but rather that it must not be Homeric. What they cultivated was the poetics of the anti-Homeric, not just the non-Homeric. To do this successfully, they had to know, and know well, what was considered to be genuinely Homeric and what was post-Homeric.

In actively applying to their own poetry their notion of whatever was 'newer' than Homer, the Hellenistic poets of Alexandria cultivated usages of post-Homeric poetry that seemed overtly distinct from Homeric usage, as they understood it. This way, their own poetic usage became an implicit demonstration of their ability to discriminate post-Homeric from Homeric usage. Because their discrimination favored, at least on the surface, the 'newer' usage, the poetics of these Hellenistic poets may be characterized as 'neoteric'.

For my part, I prefer to use this term 'neoteric' instead of 'non-Homeric' or 'post-Homeric' or 'anti-Homeric' in describing the stance of these Hellenistic poets, since their own criteria for determining what is or is not truly Homeric need to be treated objectively—and since I do not agree with these criteria.

Despite whatever disagreement we may have with whatever criteria developed by these Hellenistic poets, we need to treat objectively the actual application of these criteria to their own poetry, resulting in conscious choices of what they judged to be non-Homeric forms in preference to what they judged to be Homeric forms. We may disagree with their judgments, but these judgments still add up to a genuine poetics of discrimination, which can serve as a body of evidence for studying the history of variations in the Homeric tradition.

As we are about to see, Aristarchus already understood the evidentiary value of this poetics of discrimination. He and his followers treated the poetic usage of Hellenistic poets as a litmus test for isolating post-Homeric variants in the Homeric textual tradition. Before I turn to a specific example, however, I need to repeat that I prefer to call these variants 'neoteric'—merely describing an ancient value-judgment and without accepting the implicit idea that any 'neoteric' variant found in the Homeric textual tradition must *ergo* post-Homeric and *ergo* non-Homeric or even anti-Homeric.

In a pioneering study, F. Montanari has shown that Aristarchus in his Homer commentaries evidently took great interest in Callimachean usage.[7] Building on Montanari's work, Rengakos went on to show that Aristarchus studied the usage of Hellenistic poets in general—including Posidippus—in an ongoing search for forms and themes that he deemed post-Homeric.[8] What evidently made the study of these poets most valuable for Aristarchus and the Aristarcheans is that the Hellenistic poets cultivated poetry that was deemed in their own time to be post-

---

[7] Montanari 1995.
[8] Rengakos 2000.

Homeric. Invoking again the concept used by the Aristarcheans, I stress that these Hellenistic poets gravitated toward the 'neoteric' aspect of Homer, turning this aspect into a 'neoteric' poetics of its own.[9] By contrast, the usage of earlier poets studied by the Aristarcheans was 'neoteric' only in the sense that it was post-Homeric. To put it another way, the Hellenistic poets were actively 'neoteric' in their outlook, whereas earlier 'post-Homeric' poets were only passively 'neoteric'— only insofar as they were supposedly preceded by Homer.

My specific example of the 'neoterism' that characterized the Hellenistic poets is an attestation, in the poetry of Posidippus, of the name 'Berisos' (*SH* 701). The witness to this attestation is Aristarchus himself, as reported by his Aristarchean successor, Didymus (whose life overlapped the first centuries BCE and CE). The reportage of Didymus survives in this compressed account, as transmitted by the A scholia to *Iliad* XI 101:

αὐτὰρ ὁ βῆ ῥ' ˣἶσον τε. Ζηνόδοτος ἔξω τοῦ **ρ** "**βῆ** ˣἶσον". μὴ ἐμφέρεσθαι δέ φησιν ὁ 'Αρίσταρχος νῦν ἐν τοῖς Ποσειδίππου ἐπιγράμμασι τὸν "**Βήρισον**", ἀλλ' ἐν τῷ λεγομένῳ Σωρῷ εὑρεῖν. εὔλογον δέ φησιν ἐξελεγχόμενον αὐτὸν ἀπαλεῖψαι.

(The lemma is) "αὐτὰρ ὁ βῆ ῥ' ˣἶσον." Zenodotus has it without the ρ, "βῆ ˣἶσον". Aristarchus says that "Βήρισον" is not attested now in the epigrams of Posidippus, but that he [= Aristarchus] had found it in the so-called *Soros*. He [= Aristarchus] says that it was reasonable that he [Posidippus] deleted it [= the word Βήρισον] upon being challenged [concerning it].

We may infer that Aristarchus thought of the *Soros* as a publication that predated the publication of the epigrams of Posidippus.[10] In the version of the epigrams of Posidippus that were in circulation 'now' (νῦν)—that is, in the time of Aristarchus—the name of the hero Berisos was no longer attested (μὴ ἐμφέρεσθαι δέ φησιν ὁ 'Αρίσταρχος), whereas it was indeed attested in the *Soros*. To put it another way, this particular attestation involved an epigram by Posidippus that Aristarchus had 'found' (εὑρεῖν) in the *Soros* but not in the epigrams that were 'now' (νῦν) in circulation.

Aristarchus may have thought that the *Soros* was an earlier publication on the grounds that the epigram he found there about Berisos was in his opinion an earlier epigram. This supposedly earlier poem seems to have been part of a series of epigrams for Trojan heroes who were mentioned in the *Iliad*, arranged in acrostic

---

[9] This formulation is meant as an alternative to the views of Cameron 1980, especially pp. 135–137.
[10] See Rengakos 2000:329, with bibliography on the problem of identifying the *Soros*.

order from alpha to omega.[11] The Trojan hero Berisos filled a gap by supplying a name starting with beta, since otherwise there is no attested Trojan hero whose name starts with beta.[12] According to Didymus, as we infer from the reportage of the A scholia, Aristarchus thought that Posidippus must have changed his mind about using a form like Βήρισον. That is why, Aristarchus reasoned, a Berisos epigram was no longer attested in the publication of Posidippean epigrams circulating 'now' in the time of Aristarchus, about a century after the era when Posidippus flourished. But why would Posidippus change his mind? According to Aristarchus, it was because Posidippus was being 'challenged' (ἐξελεγχόμενον) concerning his use of the form Βήρισον. For Aristarchus, the most obvious source of such a challenge would have been the Homer edition of that eminent precursor of his, Zenodotus himself, who flourished in the era of Posidippus and Callimachus. Aristarchus must have thought of Zenodotus as his forerunner in the task of guarding against 'neoteric' forms that threatened to infiltrate the Homeric text as he saw it. As we learn from the same reportage of Didymus, Aristarchus here invokes a variant reading adduced by Zenodotus, βῆ ᾽ Ἰσόν instead of βῆ ῥ᾽ ᾽Ἰσόν. Now BHPICON could be read as either Βήρισον or βῆ ῥ᾽ ᾽Ἰσόν, but the reading adduced by Zenodotus, BHICON, necessarily ruled out Βήρισον and left no choice: now the reading must be βῆ ᾽Ἰσόν, and the unique name Berisos becomes a phantom, to be replaced by another name unique to the *Iliad*, Isos.

Following the lead of Zenodotus, who was in turn followed in this case by Aristarchus, we would have to read the relevant passage of the *Iliad* (XI 101–102) in the form that we find in the *editio maior* of T. W. Allen:

αὐτὰρ ὃ βῆ ᾽Ἰσόν τε[13] καὶ ῎Αντιφον ἐξεναρίξων
υἷε δύω Πριάμοιο νόθον καὶ γνήσιον ἄμφω

What Posidippus must have read, on the other hand, was something like this:

αὐτὰρ ὃ Βήρισόν τε καὶ ῎Αντιφον ἐξενάριξεν
υἷε δύω Πριάμοιο νόθον καὶ γνήσιον ἄμφω

---

[11] See the comments of Lloyd-Jones and Parsons p. 339 on AB 148 (*SH* 700), which is an epigram by Posidippus for Pandaros, a hero who fights on the Trojan side in the *Iliad* (II 827, IV 88, V 168, 171, 246, 795); cf. also Lloyd-Jones 1963:95–96 = 1990:190–191.

[12] Merkelbach 1956:123–124 = 1996:152–153.

[13] Aristarchus read ᾽Ἰσόν τε, not ᾽Ἰσόν τε, according to a scholion in the margin of Vindobonensis 39 (= Vi² Allen): ᾿Αρίσταρχος δὲ ᾽Ἰσόν τε. From what we read in the T scholia to XI 101, it seems as if Zenodotus too may have read ᾽Ἰσόν τε· Ζηνόδοτος δὲ χωρὶς τοῦ ῥ᾽, "βῆ ᾽Ἰσον τε" (*pace* Erbse III p. 144, who deletes the τε).

Both versions, in fact, are justifiable on the basis of the internal evidence provided by Homeric diction.

On the one hand, to start with the 'Posidippean' version, it is essential to note that the form ἐξενάριξεν is actually attested in one *Iliad* manuscript, Vat. gr. 26 (= V¹ Allen, V West). Moreover, as George Huxley has shown, '[i]n taking the letters BHPICON in [*Iliad* 11] 101 as one word [Posidippus] understood them to be the name of the eponymous hero of the *polis* of the Βηρύσιοι in the Troad'.[14] The syntax of XI 101 is made straightforward by ἐξενάριξεν, whereas the ἐξεναρίξων necessitated by the αὐτὰρ ὅ βῆ of the 'Zenodotean/Aristarchean' version produces a syntax that seems strained by comparison. The closest parallels I can find to the αὐτὰρ ὅ βῆ . . . ἐξεναρίξων at *Iliad* XI 101are βῆ δ' ἴμεν ἀνστήσων at *Iliad* X 32 and βῆ δ' ἴμεν αἰτήσων at *Odyssey* xvii 365.

On the other hand, the reading of verse-initial αὐτὰρ ὅ βῆ for XI 101 in the 'Zenodotean/Aristarchean' version is closely paralleled by verse-initial αὐτὰρ ὅ βῆ ῥ' at *Iliad* V 849, X 73, XX 484, and XXI 205. Moreover, the omission of the ῥ' in some medieval manuscripts (at XX 484 and at XXI 205) provides evidence for the authenticity of the wording αὐτὰρ ὅ βῆ ⁺Ισόν, without ῥ', as adduced by Zenodotus. Finally, the name Isos, unique to the *Iliad* just like Berisos, is attested in a fragment of a hexameter poem 'The Kathodos of the Atreidai', quoted by Athenaeus IX 399a (*Nostoi* F 9 Davies = *Nostoi* F 11 Bernabé).

On the whole, then, both the 'Posidippean' and the 'Zenodotean/Aristarchean' versions of *Iliad* XI 101 can be justified on the basis of the internal evidence provided by the textual attestations and by formulaic analysis (ἐξενάριξεν argues for the 'Posidippean' version, while the attestations of αὐτὰρ ὅ βῆ without ῥ' at XX 484 and at XXI 205 argue for the 'Zenodotean/Aristarchean'). Both versions can also be justified on the basis of existing external evidence for names like Berisos and Isos.

Still, the fact remains that the 'Posidippean' Berisos variant is exotic, whereas the 'Zenodotean/Aristarchean' variant Isos seems by comparison generic. Aristarchus and his followers made it their practice to purge as 'neoteric' the exotic forms and meanings cultivated by the Hellenistic poets in their echoings of Homer.[15]

In this light, even the primary genre of Posidippus as poet, the epigram, can be viewed as an echo of a 'neoteric' Homer. The non-Aristarchean and non-Zenodotean 'Homer' was himself an epigrammatist: according to the Lives of Homer traditions, Homer himself was commissioned to compose the epigram for

---

[14] Huxley 1992:153.

[15] See Rengakos 2000:331–334.

the tomb of Midas.[16] Such a 'neoteric' Homer became the non-Homer of later Alexandrian scholarship, but echoes of this alternative Homer can be heard in the epigrams of earlier Alexandrian scholar-poets like Callimachus—and like Posidippus as epigrammatist par excellence.

---

[16] *Vita Herodotea* 131–140 pp. 198–199 Allen; *Certamen* 260–274 pp. 235–236 Allen. The epigram, VII 143 in the *Palatine Anthology*, is alternatively attributed to Kleoboulos of Lindos. The sources for the alternative attributions are summarized in the apparatus of Allen 1912:198–199.

6

Doricisms in the New and Old Posidippus[1]

Alexander Sens
Georgetown University

Introduction

Posidippus AB 139 (8 GP = *AP* XII 131) is a prayer for Aphrodite to favor a woman named Callistium:

ἃ Κύπρον ἅ τε Κύθηρα καὶ ἃ Μίλητον ἐποιχνεῖς
καὶ καλὸν Συρίης ἱπποκρότου δάπεδον,
ἔλθοις ἵλαος Καλλιστίῳ, ἣ τὸν ἐραστὴν
οὐδέποτ᾽ οἰκείων ὦσεν ἀπὸ προθύρων.

You who visit Cyprus and Cythera and Miletus
and the beautiful ground of Syria resounding with horses,
come propitious to Callistium, who never
pushed her lover out of the doors of her own house.

As it survives in the single manuscript witness, the dialect coloring of the poem is inconsistent. In the opening verse the feminine nominative singular of the relative pronoun appears three times in the Doric form ἅ[2] but in the third verse the manuscript transmits ἥ. The text of the rest of the poem is consonant with the latter rather than the former: thus the second verse has epic/Ionic Συρίης rather

---

[1] I am deeply grateful to Marco Fantuzzi, Richard Hunter, David Lightfoot, Enrico Magnelli, Charles McNelis, Gregory Nagy, S. Douglas Olson, and Calvert Watkins for advice on drafts of this paper and for helpful discussion of the dialectal practices of Hellenistic poets generally. Although I cite poems by their enumeration in AB, I give the text of the *editio princeps*.

[2] I use "Doric" and "West Greek" interchangeably. The retention of *alpha* for inherited /a:/ is a feature of Aeolic dialects as well, but as Redondo (forthcoming) has recently pointed out, Callimachus fr. 203.18 suggests that the basic distinction envisioned at least by that poet (and in great likelihood by his contemporaries) was between Ionic (in which he implicitly includes Attic) and Doric.

65

than Doric (and Attic) Συρίας; and the third, ἐραστήν rather than ἐραστάν.[3] Gow and Page, who make the sensibly conservative decision to print the paradosis, nonetheless note that they find it "difficult to believe" that the poet could have written both ἅ and ἥ in the same epigram, and incline toward replacing the Doric pronouns on the ground that Posidippus "does not favour Doric." Such uncertainties about dialect are common in our texts of Hellenistic poetry, and the difficulty of resolving them in any satisfactory way is compounded by a number of considerations. The category "Doric" is not monolithic but includes a variety of widely dispersed local dialects, each with its own phonological peculiarities. By the end of the fourth century, moreover, spoken and literary forms of the dialect regularly combined traditional characteristics of Doric phonology and morphology with elements drawn from other dialects, including the Attic *koine* (especially in the case of the spoken language)[4] and (in the case of poetry, at least) the complex, predominantly Ionic literary language of the early epic hexameter poems. Hellenistic poets, moreover, often overlaid Doric phonology on epic vocabulary and morphology. As a result of all this, the Doric found in Hellenistic poetry is highly variable. In fact, the evidence that was available even before the publication of P.Mil.Vogl. VIII 309 shows that the earliest texts of some Hellenistic poems had both Doric and epic/Ionic forms side by side,[5] and indeed Callimachus in *Iambus* 13 seems to justify his own use of precisely such a combination of dialects (fr. 203.17–18 Pf. τοῦτ' ἐμπ[έ]πλεκται καὶ λαλευσ|[. .] . . [| Ἰαστὶ καὶ Δωριστὶ καὶ τὸ σύμμικ|τον[.).[6]

As studies of the textual tradition for the Theocritean corpus show, this artificial and variable language was easily altered in the process of transmission,[7] so that the manuscript evidence for dialect coloring must be considered highly suspect. Modern readers of Hellenistic poems preserved in medieval manuscripts thus cannot have confidence either that the appearance of dialectal regularity in a given poem does not mask a more complex original picture, or that what at first appears

---

[3] In verse 4 οὐδέποτ(ε) is of indeterminate dialectal coloring, since literary Doric allows ποτε (e.g. Pindar *Pythian* 4.4) as well as ποκα (cf. e.g. Theocritus 13.10 οὐδέποκ(α)). Cf. Molinos Tejada 1990:344–347. Despite Theocritus 15.126 (cf. Theocritus 1.1 GP, for which the Palatine ms. has Μίλατον) Μίλητον is the expected form; cf. Timotheus *PMG* 791 234 (Μίλητος δὲ πόλις νιν ἁ θρέψασ(α)).

[4] For the development of a Doric *koine* by the end of the fourth century, cf. Buck 1955:176–178; Horrocks 1997:40–41.

[5] Cf., e.g., Wilamowitz-Moellendorff 1886:25–28; Molinos Tejada 1990:38; Hunter 1996:31–45, esp. 36.

[6] Cf. above note 2.

[7] Cf. Molinos Tejada 1990 *passim*; Hunter 1996. For the problems raised by dialect in the medieval manuscript tradition of ancient authors, cf. Colvin 1999.

to be a chaotic and unlikely jumble of different dialect forms was not what the poet wrote. The new Posidippus papyrus offers a rare opportunity for exploring the use of dialect in an extensive, mostly continuous and complete Hellenistic text produced not long after the poems it contains were composed and assembled.[8] Given that P.Mil.Vogl. VIII 309 (like any manuscript) naturally contains slips and errors of various sorts,[9] it cannot be taken as providing a wholly accurate image of what its author wrote, but its early date and the care with which it was produced make it likely to give a far better picture of the poet's practices than the medieval manuscript tradition does for the "old" Posidippus.

Dialectal Characteristics of the Corpus of Posidippus

For most of the epigrams of Posidippus known prior to the publication of the papyrus, the basic dialectal coloring preserved in the witnesses is Ionic with a heavy admixture of features characteristic of the Attic *koine*. Thus, for example, the endings of first-declension nouns and adjectives consistently have Ionic η rather than Attic (and Doric) long α even after ρ, ι, and ε (e.g. AB 116.1 [12.1 GP]; AB 117.2 [24.2 GP]; AB 118.17 [*SH* 705.17]); AB 129.2 [3.2 GP]; AB 148.1 [*SH* 700.1], but (as in much other early Hellenistic poetry) the endings of nouns and verbs often contract in the Attic manner. The Attic-Ionic modal particle ἄν (AB 15.6 [20.6 GP]; AB 116.4–5 [12.4–5 GP]; AB 120.2 [14.2 GP]; AB 122.8 [17.8 GP]; AB 125.4 [2.4 GP]; AB 135.2 [5.2 GP]) predominates over κε(ν) (AB 115.9 [11.9 GP]), the form characteristic of most other dialects and preferred in early epic. Moreover, the obvious influence of the Attic *koine* suggests that features characteristic of that dialect but alien to Ionic should be understood as Atticisms, even when the form in question would be equally appropriate in other dialects. A case in point is the use of -αις as the ending of the first-declension dative plural at AB 137.1 (6.1 GP),[10] a passage that conforms to the usual Hellenistic practice of placing these forms only at verse end.[11]

The situation is much the same for the poems contained in the new papyrus. In most of these epigrams η rather than α follows ρ, ι, and ε in the endings of the first-declension (e.g. AB 10.3; AB 12.5; AB 16.5; AB 23.4; AB 24.6; AB 28.4; AB 32.6; AB 37.1; AB 38.3; AB 40.3, AB 42.3, 4; AB 45.5; AB 48.3, 4; AB 51.3; AB 53.2; AB 55.5; AB 60.2; AB 63.4; AB 63.6), although AB 55.1 has the Attic

---

[8] For a preliminary study of dialect, on the basis of the specimen poems published in Bastianini and Gallazzi 1993 and 1993a:34–39, cf. Palumba Stracca 1993–1994:405–412.

[9] That the papyrus contains a number of itacizing errors (cf. BG:19–20) is particularly problematic, the distinction between η and ει in certain linguistic contexts has important dialectal implications.

[10] Contrast epic/Ionic προχοῆσι at *SH* 700.2.

[11] Cf. Sens 1997:88 on Theocritus 22.16.

form ἑώιαν[12] and at AB 89.3 the genitive Ἀκαδημείας is used (appropriately) of the Athenian philosophical school. The contraction of verbs and nouns is common (e.g. AB 15.5). The genitive of the second declension is almost always -ου; epic -οιο seems not to occur. Dative -αις is possible at AB 58.5 and secure at AB 74.4 and AB 83.2, all at verse end. The modal particle is consistently ἄν; κε(ν) appears nowhere on the papyrus, although it has been introduced by the editors at AB 20.3. Once again, certain forms that are common to Attic and to other dialects, including Doric, should probably be taken as Atticisms, given that some overtly Attic forms occur in poems otherwise of epic/Ionic coloring but identifiably Doric features (other than proper names; see below) do not. Thus, for example, at AB 37.8 ναοπόλο[υ is equally appropriate to the Attic *koine* (cf. J. *AJ* 14.73) as it is to Doric (cf. Pindar fr. 51d), and is best taken as a natural feature of the prevailing Attic-Ionic dialectal coloring.

Despite the predominance of Attic-Ionic, however, both the previously known and the new, expanded corpus of Posidippus contain poems in which at least some "Doric" coloring is in evidence. The paradosis of AB 141 (*APl*[A] 68), a short ecphrastic poem in which the speaker claims not to be able to tell whether a portrait he is viewing depicts Aphrodite or Berenice, uses forms with Doric *alpha* (ἄδ(ε), Βερενίκας and ὁμοιοτέραν), but the epigram may be by Asclepiades, to whom it is alternatively ascribed by the lemma, rather than Posidippus.[13] Two other instances in which the witnesses preserve α rather than Attic-Ionic η for inherited /a:/ in the "old" Posidippus involve references to the Muse. At Posidippus AB 123 (1.3–4 GP), the Doric form of the article in the phrase ἅ τε Κλεάνθους | μοῦσα, occurs in close conjunction with the markedly Attic contraction of ε+ο to ου (Κλεάνθουc)[14] and with the Attic-Ionic pronoun ἡμῖν, while at 23.2 GP, a poem also ascribed to Meleager,[15] the speaker refers to Μοῦσαν ἐμὰν ἱκέτιν in the context of complaining of his desire for a woman whose name has the apparently Attic form Ἡλιοδώρας (genitive).[16] The function of the Doric coloring in these epigrams is not immediately clear—Cleanthes' surviving fragments do not show any trace of Doric coloring—but the passages illustrate an important feature of the majority of the Doricisms in the entire corpus of Posidippus. Whereas the use of α as a reflex of inherited /a:/ is a common feature of the entire Doric group, the

---

[12] The short initial syllable produced by quantitative metathesis in Attic (Ionic ἠοῖος, Doric ἀοῖος) is here metrically convenient.

[13] On this epigram, cf. Sens 2002:249–262.

[14] Cf. Buck 1955:40.

[15] Cf. GP 2.636–637.

[16] The dialect of μιαιφονίαν at the end of the poem is ambiguous. For φωνεῦντ' in the fifth verse as an acceptable Doricism, and for the dialect coloring of proper names, see below.

various local dialects treat the products of contraction and compensatory lengthening of /e/ and /o/ in different ways. In some dialects, which constitute a group Ahrens called "Doris mitior," secondary long /e/ and /o/ are represented as ει and ου respectively, but in a handful of others (which Ahrens calls "Doris severior"), they converge with the inherited long vowels and are written as η and ω.[17] The vast majority of instances of secondary long /e/ and /o/ in the corpus of Posidippus are written ει and ου, as in the case of Μοῦσα (rather than Μῶσα [e.g. Alcman *PMG* 8; 14; 28; 30; 31; 46; 59 Page; scholium to Theocritus 1.9, p. 34 Wendel]) in 1.4 GP and 23.2 GP.

Other than these passages, the only instance of Doric coloring in the "old" Posidippus occurs in a poem also found on the new papyrus. AB 65 contains the text of an epigram ascribed to Posidippus at *APl*[A] 119 (= 18 GP):

Λύσιππε,ι πλάςτα Cικυώινιε, θαρςιαλέα χείρ,
　　δάϊε τεχνίιτα, πῦρ τοι ὁ χαιλκὸς ὁριῆι,
ὃν κατ' Ἀλεξάινδρου μορφᾶς ἔθευ· οὔ τι γε μεμπτοὶ
　　Πέρςαι· cυγγνώιμα βουςὶ λέοντα φυγεῖν.

1 θαρςαλέη Pl : δαιδαλέη Himerius *Or.* 48.14　3 χέες Pl　4 cυγγνώμη Pl

Lysippus, Sicyonian sculptor, bold hand,
　　cunning[18] craftsman, the bronze, which Lysippus put down over
the form of Alexander, has a look of fire in its eyes.
　　The Persians are to be forgiven: it's excusable for cattle to flee a lion.

The poem offers important evidence for the loss of Doric forms in the process of transmission. Alongside forms consonant with Doric (including not only μορφᾶς but also ὁρῆ, which shows the standard Doric contraction of α and ει to η rather than to ᾳ),[19] the later witnesses have Ionic θαρςαλέη/δαιδαλέη and cυγγνώμη where the papyrus shows evidence of Doric θαρςαλέα and cυγγνώμα instead. Furthermore, whereas *Pl* has the unaugmented form χέες in the second hexameter, the papyrus seems to contain ἔθευ. The form raises an interesting point. The contraction of ε and ο to ευ was widespread in Ionic, but it was not a universal feature of Doric, although it occurred in some local dialects,

---

[17] Ahrens 1839–1843: II 153–72, 201–207, 403–422. Bartoněk 1972 recognizes a "Doris media" in which the compensatory lengthening of /e/ produces either η or ει.

[18] I have elsewhere argued that the adjective, which is traditionally associated with fire, links Lysippus to his subject matter (cf. πῦρ ... ὁρῆ and thus implies a more common sense "fierce" as well as "cunning." See Sens in Gutzwiller 2004 (forthcoming).

[19] Cf. Buck 1955:37.

including Rhodian and Cretan. In Hellenistic poetry, however, it seems to have been treated as a generalized Doric characteristic, occurring in the Doric poems of Theocritus[20] and Callimachus (cf. *Hymn* 6.127) as well as in Posidippus 23.5 GP φωνεῦντ(α), an epigram in which (as we have seen) the presence of ἐμάν suggests a Doric coloring. Nonetheless, the contraction was also a feature of Corinthian, which is closely related to the dialect spoken at Sicyon, and, in an epigram in which Lysippus' Sicyonian background is explicitly asserted, it may therefore be thought specially appropriate.[21]

In addition to this epigram, a number of other poems on the papyrus show aspects of Doric coloring. As is to be expected, the most obvious and consistent marker of Doric in the epigrams is the presence of *alpha* rather than *eta* as the reflex of inherited /a:/. Because this feature was the most recognizable feature of all forms of Doric, literary Doric from an early period sometimes generalized it even to cases where Attic-Ionic *eta* represents not /a:/ but /e:/, for which Doric properly uses η. Although it is often difficult to tell whether analogically generated forms of this sort are original or the product of transmission, papyrological evidence shows that many such forms were represented in the tradition at a very early stage and may thus be original. The phenomenon, however, seems largely foreign to the new Posidippus. The only plausible example occurs at AB 87.3, where the original copyist seems to have written the *alpha* of [πο]λυθρύλατον over the *eta* he produced initially. Adjectives in -τος from verbs in -έω properly terminate in -ητος in Doric (e.g., Pindar *Olympian* 1.21 ἀκίνητον; 7.25 ἀναρίθμητοι; Theocritus 14.6 ἀνυπόδητος, 48 ἀρίθμητοι), although hyperdoric -ατος is occasionally attested for adjectives of this sort in the manuscript tradition of both choral lyric (e.g. Pindar *Isthmian* 5.6 ὠκυδίνατος) and Hellenistic bucolic (e.g. Bion fr. 2.15; *Adonis* 58 τριπόθατος)[22], and some at least are probably authentic.[23] Posidippus seems to have used a "proper" Doric form of a comparable adjective at AB 64.4, where the editors' [ἀδό]νητος is highly likely (despite their unnecessary puzzlement about why Posidippus has not written -ατος; cf. above). Although it is impossible to exclude the possibility that Posidippus wrote πολυθρύλατον at AB 87.3, the most economical explanation is that the form is a hyperdoric miscorrection by the copyist after he wrote the proper form πολυθρύλητον. If this is the case, then despite the small size of the sample, it seems reasonable to conclude that

[20] Cf. Molinos Tejada 1990:88–96.

[21] Cf. Buck 1955:164. In this regard, it is worth noting that although βωσί would be expected in some Doric areas (Buck 34), βουσί is the normal form in many West Greek dialects, including that spoken at Sicyon.

[22] Cf. Reed 1997:35.

[23] For hyperdoricisms in the bucolic corpus, cf. Molinos Tejada 1990:38–46; for Callimachus, cf. Cassio 1993:903–1010.

osidippus understood and was attentive to the difference between Doric α = /a:/
nd η = /e:/.

Besides those cases in which Doric *alpha* is used in place of Attic-Ionic *eta*, the
ew papyrus contains only a few traces of other distinctly Doric features. The first-
erson pronoun ἁμές and the first-person plural verbal ending -μες occur several
mes each, but only in the ἱππικά (AB 87.1 and AB 88.1 ἁμές; [cf. AB 75.1];
B 88.2 νικῶμες; AB 87.2 ἀγάγομ[ε]ς).[24] With two notable exceptions, the
econdary long /e/ and /o/ sounds are represented as ει and ου, as in Attic-Ionic and
ne "mild" Doric dialects, even in forms that show other features of Doric.[25] At AB
4.2, however, the aorist ἠργάσατο appears in an ecphrastic epigram on a statue
f the Cretan hero Idomeneus by the Cretan sculptor Kresilas. Although the
ugmented first syllable of this verb is at least sometimes treated as ἠ- rather than
ι- in Attic and the *koine*,[26] the form—if it is in fact what Posidippus wrote[27]—
rould also be appropriate to the overall Doric coloring of the epigram, which seems
ο have γαρύει, Μηριόνα, and δάν.[28] Other than in this poem, the only
istances in which η and ω represent secondary long /e/ and /o/ occur in an
pitaph in which Menoitios, the dead man who is the purported speaker, explicitly
laims to be from Crete. The augmented aorist ἤασατε (= Attic-Ionic εἰάσατε)
t the end of the first verse shows the "severe" Doric treatment of the first syllable
nd is in fact attested in an inscribed epitaph of Doric coloring from the first
entury CE (*GVI* 969.2).[29] Similarly, Φιλάρχω is the only example in the papyrus
f -ω instead of ου, and—despite the tendency of proper names to retain special
ialectal characteristics—must be considered a particularly marked Doricism.

The restriction of η for secondary long /e/ and υ for secondary long /o/ to
ontexts involving Cretans is highly suggestive. Bastianini and Gallazzi (21–2; 189)
lausibly suggest that the use of Doric in these poems may be generally mimetic of

---

[4] As BG note *ad* XII 8 (= AB 75.1), the scribe's alteration of ειλομες to ειλομεν is most easily understood as a banalization.

[5] E.g., from contraction of ε + ε and ο + ε, cf. AB 75.1 εἵλομε⟨ς⟩; AB 87.4 ἀφειλόμεθα; AB 68.6
ἐχαλκούργει. With one exception (discussed below), the gen. sg is -ου; cf. AB 65.3
Ἀλεφά↓νδρου; AB 75.2 ἀνιόχου, AB 75.4 Λακεδαιμονίου.

[6] E.g. Aeschylus *Eumenides* 213; Euripides *Iphigeneia at Aulis* 326; Aristophanes *Wasps* 787, 1350;
Birds 323; *Women of the Thesmophoria* 743; *Assembly Women* 134; Lysias VII 4; XIII 76; Plato
Phaedrus 244b; *Laws* 885b; Septuagint *Job* XXIV 6, XXXIV 32.

[7] The text of the first line appears to contain the itacising error ιδομενεια for Ἰδομεν⟨ῆ⟩α.

[8] The editors' Κρησίλ⟨α⟩ is a natural and highly likely correction of κρησιλε in the second verse,
though it is at least theoretically possible that Posidippus wrote Ionic Κρησίλεω or Κρησίλω, or
even Attic -ου; cf. also πλασται (dative?) in the final verse.

[9] The total number of possible examples of augmented indicatives of verbs beginning in epsilon is
small. Of those expected to produce ει-, the papyrus has III 1 εἶχε (= AB 15.2) and XII 1
ἐφειλκύσα[το (= AB 74.8) in Ionic contexts, XII 8 εἵλομε⟨ς⟩ (= AB 75.1) and XIII 34
ἀφειλόμεθα (= AB 87.4) in Doric poems.

71

the Doric color of Cretan speech, but the point may be pushed even farthe Although the use of -ω as the genitive singular of second-declension nouns cam to be treated as a generalized feature of literary Doric, it occurs regularly only i Cretan, Heraclean, and Laconian.[30] Cretan also ranks among a handful of Dori dialects in which η rather than ει regularly represents secondary long /e/. The pre ence of "severe" Doric phonology independently and exclusively in poems involvin Cretan subject matter may suggest an attempt to capture the particular, region: characteristics of the language spoken on the island.[31] That both poems contai direct speech placed in the mouth of Cretans supports this view,[32] even if in th Cresilas poem ἠργάcατο forms part of the narrative rather than the speec ascribed to Idomeneus' statue.

It is important to note, however, that even if the severe Doricisms in these tw epigrams are intended to suggest actual features of Cretan speech, any mimet effect they produce remains somewhat stylized inasmuch as the poet makes n attempt to capture all the peculiarities of Cretan speech. Moreover, the poems als contain forms apparently alien not only to Cretan but to Doric as a whole. Thu the first verse of the Idomeneus-statue poem has, in addition to the appropriatel epic form of the adjective χάλκειον, the Attic demonstrative ἐκεῖνον, a wor found also in an otherwise Doric context at AB 68.5, rather than κῆνοc, the forr used in Crete and elsewhere, or τῆνοc.[33] Together with severe Doric Φιλάρχϲ and ἠάcατε, the Menoetius-epigram contains εἰμι rather than ἠμι, as well ε several forms in which η rather than Doric α appears. Indeed, the "Doric" used b Posidippus throughout the papyrus may be understood as an artificial creatio influenced by a number of literary traditions. Thus, if (as seems likely) the edito are correct to supplement [εἰν] at AB 85.4, the preposition is best explained as a epicising admixture in a purely literary language rather than as a reflection of th way actual people spoke. Like Pindar and other lyric poets, Posidippus us πρῶτοc (AB 68.5; AB 88.1) rather than Doric πρᾶτος; Theocritus, by contras appears to favor the latter in his Doric poems.[34] Characteristic of both Pindar an Theocritus, on the other hand, is the use of the cardinal numbers τρεῖc at AB 88. and τέccαρεc at AB 75.1 (as opposed to τρῖc / τρῆc and τέτορεc) alongsi such forms as Doric εἴλομε⟨c⟩ and ἀμέc. These cases are more complicated tha

---

[30] Cf. Buck 1955:28–29; Hopkinson 1984:45.

[31] For Hellenistic poets' sensitivity to local variations in "Doric," cf. Theocritus 15.80–95, with Hunt 1996:120–123 and 1996a:152.

[32] AB 99, a cure poem concerning a Cretan apparently named Asclas, shows no trace of Doric.

[33] Cf. Buck 1955:101. ἐκεῖνος recurs beside Doric forms in other Hellenistic epigram at e.g. Theocrit 5.1 GP (= *AP* VI 336.1); Erycius 12.5 GP (= *AP* VII 230.5); cf. Theocritus 11.3 GP (= *AP* VII 663. ἀντὶ τήνων (ἀντεκείνων P).

[34] Molinos Tejada 1990:259–260.

that of εἰν, however, since Attic-Ionic elements seem also to have been character-istic of the Doric *koine* that had developed by the end of the fourth century.[35]

Thus the presence of these forms in Doric contexts could be due to the influ-ence of other literary traditions, but the words are also consistent with the way in which some people actually spoke.[36] This fact has important implications for the way in which we evaluate the "dialect mixing" we find in the epigrams of Posidippus, since the influence of the *koine* means that even forms like ἐκεῖνος need not be seen as strikingly out of place in a Doric context, though the use of Attic-Ionic η for inherited /a:/ (especially in the endings of first-declension nouns) alongside other clearly Doric features would presumably still have been felt as highly marked, since the distinction between α and η was upheld even in the Doric *koine*.[37]

Reading Doricisms in the New Posidippus

The epigrams in which Doric forms occur are not uniformly distributed throughout the papyrus but are instead restricted to the section containing epigrams on statues (ἀνδριαντοποιικά); to the section containing poems on the equestrian victories (ἱππικά); and to the last extant section, labeled τρόποι; else-where the only forms with identifiably Doric coloring occur at AB 47.1, where the speaking tomb calls its occupant Ὀνασαγορᾶτι⟨ν⟩, despite using ἥ(τις) as the relative pronoun to refer to her throughout the epigram, and at 94.4 AB, where μίκκος may also be a proper name.[38] The vast majority of these Doric-colored poems occur in the ἱππικά, and these appear to conform to an interesting pattern. Bastianini and Gallazzi may be correct to suggest that the relatively high number of poems in Doric in this section has something to do with the prominence of the Peloponnese and of the projection of the power of the Lagid dynasty at the Peloponnesian athletic competitions, but the association of Doric with epinician lyric also makes it appropriate for poems celebrating equestrian victories.[39] It is crucial to note, however, that only poems for Olympic victories appear in Doric, whereas the dialect of the epigrams on the outcome of Pythian, Isthmian, and

---

[35] Cf. Buck 1955:176–178. Inscriptional evidence suggests that the Cyrenean dialect, which Ruijgh 1984:56–88 thought may have been a prominent feature of the linguistic landscape at Alexandria, contained a number of elements of the *koine*; cf. Dobias-Lalou 1987:29–50.

[36] Indeed, features of the Doric *koine* and of Attic seem to have been widespread in certain parts of Crete (Buck 1955:171; Brixhe 1993:37–71) and the presence of strictly non-Doric forms in the Idomeneus-statue epigram and in the epitaph for Menoetius may thus not be wholly unrealistic.

[37] Buck 1955:177.

[38] Personal names, like place names, show a high degree of linguistic continuity even in "foreign" dialectal contexts; cf. Threatte 1980:136; Morpurgo Davies 2000:15–39.

[39] Cf. Fantuzzi in Gutzwiller 2004 (forthcoming).

Nemean contests is consistently epic/Ionic. The only example of a Doric form among the latter group of poems occurs at AB 86.4, where the narrator refers to himself as Εὐβώταν, but given the use of Ὀνασαγορᾶτι⟨ν⟩ at AB 47.1, this sort of dialect coloring in a proper name may have been felt as a special case and thus not strongly marked.[40] Conversely, with two clear exceptions, the poems on Olympic victories for which there are unambiguous markers of dialect have Doric coloring.

The dialectal distinction between poems on Olympic victories and those on all others becomes particularly striking when one considers AB 81.1–2, where the marked reference to the "Dorian" parsley (Δ]ωρικὰ φύλλα cελίνων) awarded for a Nemean victory stands in striking juxtaposition to the Attic-Ionic form κεφαλήν. Why the equestrian poems should for the most part divide neatly by dialect is unclear. The only exceptions occur at AB 83 and AB 78. The only clear dialectal marker in the first of these is μνῆμ(α) at AB 83.2.[41] The epigram, in which the supposed speaker is a victorious Thessalian horse, introduces a series of three poems involving Thessalians. The next epigram (AB 85), celebrating an Olympic victory by a Thessalian named Phylopidas, contains no certain dialectal marking, but the following poem, on an Olympic victory by Amyntas of Thessaly, contains a number of Doric forms. More can be said about AB 78, a long epigram that celebrates the Olympic achievements of Lagid royalty, culminating in the Olympic chariot victory of Berenike II.[42] This poem belongs to a sequence of five epigrams, all with Ionic coloring, for victories by the queen at various athletic contests. The victory celebrated in AB 78 seems to have taken place in 248 BCE, and the epigram must thus have been composed relatively late in Posidippus' life, perhaps at a chronological distance from the other Olympic victory poems, and almost certainly from those celebrating the Olympic victories by other members of the Lagid dynasty.

As far as it goes, the very limited evidence from other poems unambiguously or dubiously attributed to Posidippus may suggest a regular (and natural, given the supposed Dorian ancestry of the Macedonian ruling class)[43] connection between

---

[40] See above, n. 38.

[41] The almost universal use of ἱερός rather than ἱαρός in choral lyric and Theocritus (e.g. Pindar *Olympian* 2.9 and often; Theocritus 1.69; cf. Molinos Tejada 1990:109–110) means that ἱερόν is not marked for dialect; for ἱερός as a feature of spoken Doric by the fourth century, cf. Buck 1955:177.

[42] Thompson in Gutzwiller 2004 (forthcoming) rather identifies this Berenice with the Syrian queen, sister of Ptolemy III Euergetes.

[43] Although the Macedonian elite adopted a form of the Attic *koine* in the fourth century (cf. Horrocks 1997:32–33; Brixhe1999:66–69), the alleged Argive origins of the Macedonian royal house and the connection between the Ptolemies and the Doric hero Heracles (cf. Theocritus 17.26–27 would have lent Doric a particular ideological importance for the Alexandrian court; cf. Hunter 2003 (forth-

Doric and epigrams on early Macedonian royalty. Thus an epigram attributed either to Asclepiades or Posidippus, *APl* [A] 68, seems to have had a Doric coloring, while the Doricism of the epigram on Lysippus' statue of Alexander (like Asclepiades' poem on a statue of the king by the same sculptor) is appropriate both to the artist's Sicyonian origins and to Alexander's background. The connection between Doric and the Ptolemaic court was not universal in early epigram (e.g. Asclepiades 64 GP), however, and in any case by the time of Berenike II it may have seemed less important to underscore the alleged Argive ancestry of the Macedonian royal house.[44]

All three Doric epigrams in the ἀνδριαντοποιικά describe statues by sculptors who would themselves have spoken a West Greek dialect. In these poems the narrator is thus represented as a member of the linguistic community of the artist he praises,[45] as is suggested by the narrator's use of the severe Doric form ἠργάσατο in a poem praising a statue by a Cretan.[46] In two of the three poems, the narrator also shares a common dialect with the artist's subject, since both the Macedonian king Alexander in the case of AB 65 and the Cretan hero Idomeneus in the case of AB 64 could be thought to have spoken a form of Doric "in real life."[47] The placement of Doric in the mouth of Idomeneus is particularly interesting, and has important implications for our understanding of Posidippus' project in the epigram in which it occurs. I give the full text of AB 64:

αἴ]νεέ γ'{ε} Ἰδομεν⟨ῆ⟩α θέλων χάλκειον ἐκεῖν[ον
Κρησίλ⟨α⟩· ὡς ἄκρως ἠργάσατ' εἴδομεν εὖ·
γ]αρύ[ει] Ἰδομενεύς· ἀλ[λ'] ὦ 'γαθὲ Μηριόνα, θεῖ
......] πλάσται δὰν [ἀδό]νητος ἐών.'

ιδομενεια pap.

....

coming). Ruijgh 1984 argues that the Doric dialect of Cyrene was much spoken in Alexandria and influential on the poetry of Theocritus; for criticism, cf. Molinos Tejada 1990; Abbenes 1996:1–19. For evidence for "Macedonian" from a *defixio* found at Pella, cf. Dubois 1995:190–197; Voutiras 1998:20–34; Brixhe 1999:41–69.

[44] Such a view is at any rate consistent with the tradition that Ptolemy I placed special emphasis on his Macedonian ethnicity; cf. Bearzot 1992:39–53.

[45] Although the ἀνδριαντοποιικά may be read as a highly unified section (cf. Gutzwiller, this volume; Sens in Gutzwiller 2004 (forthcoming) a); the use of Doric in three poems means that the section cannot be taken to have a single consistent narrative voice.

[46] Cf. Asclepiades 43 GP (Asclepiades or Archelaus *APl* [A] 120), where Doric forms are used both by the narrator and by the statue of Alexander.

[47] For such dialect marking, cf. Asclepiades 26.4 GP (*AP* V 185.4), where the Doric form τέτορας occurs in the instructions given to a slave to buy specific provisions from a certain Amyntas, whose name suggests that he was of Macedonian origin (for Macedonian nomenclature, cf. Hatzopoulos 2000:99–117). I am grateful to M. Fantuzzi for calling my attention to the relevance of this passage.

> Willingly praise that bronze Idomeneus
> Of Cresilas. How precisely he made it, we know well.
> Idomeneus cries: "Good Meriones, run!
> ... having long been immobile (?)."

Like a number of passage of early Hellenistic poetry, the epigram depends for its point on the ecphrastic topos in which the viewer of a work of art asserts that it would be wholly realistic but for its lack of a voice,[48] so that the attribution of direct speech to the statue of Idomeneus suggests that Cresilas' piece has transcended even this limitation.[49] In this context, as we have seen, the Doric coloring of the words placed in the mouth of the Cretan hero Idomeneus underscores the realism of the statue. By attributing such language to Idomeneus, Posidippus "brings to life" a character whose existence was established for the poet only through his presence in the Homeric poems.[50] Read in this light, the epigram may be seen as engaging in a project of hyper-realism that departs from and implicitly rejects the epic manner of representing individuals, who in the Homeric poems all speak a relatively undifferentiated and elevated epic-Ionic *Kunstsprache*.[51] This departure from Homeric practice is typically Hellenistic, but may come as a surprise after the first verse, which contains no Doric elements and leaves the initial impression that—as might be expected in a poem about a Homeric hero—the epigram will have an Ionic or (given ἐκεῖνον) at least Attic-Ionic coloring. In any case, the poem's "realistic" treatment of Idomeneus' speech makes the epigram a fitting complement to the immediately preceding epigram, in which Hecataeus is praised for producing a realistic sculpture of Philitas in which he mixed in nothing from the form of heroes (AB 63.4 ἀφ' ἡρώων δ' οὐδὲν ἔμειξ'{ε} ἰδέης): read against that verse, the Idomeneus-statue epigram may be taken as an example of a treatment of "epic" subject matter in which the stylized language is replaced by a more realistic (if naturally still stylized) representation of Idomeneus' native dialect.

The final Doric poem in the ἀνδριαντοποιικά (AB 68), on the colossal statue of Helios at Rhodes, also seems to use dialect as a marker of realistic speech, although in this case the speech is indirect and implicit rather than direct:

---

[48] Cf. A. fr. 78a.6–7; Erinna 3.3–4 GP (*AP* VI 352.3–4); Herodas IV 32–34 with Headlam *ad* 33.

[49] For the technique, cf. Asclepiades GP 43.4 (*AP* 1 120); Dioscorides GP 15.5-6 (*AP* VI 126.4–6); later, Agathias *AP* IX 619.4–5.

[50] Note also the colloquial (and unepic) character of the address ὦ 'γαθέ at AB 64.3 (cf., e.g., Aristophanes *Clouds* 675, 726; *Wasps* 286, 920, 1145, 1149, 1152; Pherecrates fr. 43.3; Metagenes fr. 2.1; for ἀγαθέ as a term of address, cf. the passages assembled by Dickey 1996:277–278).

[51] As the first editors note, Idomeneus' shout in the second couplet finds an analogue at *Il.* XIII 477–86, where he calls on a number of his companions, including Meriones, to come to his aid (cf. 477–481 αὖε ... Μηριόνην ... 'δεῦτε, φίλοι, καί μ' οἴῳ ἀμύνετε).

ἤθελον Ἥλιον Ῥόδιοι π[εριμάκε]α θεῖναι
δὶς τόσον, ἀλλὰ Χάρης Λίνδιο[ς] ὡρίσατο
μηθένα τεχνίταν ἔ⟨τ⟩ι μείζονα [τ]οῦδε κ[ο]λοσσόν
θήσειν· εἰ δὲ Μύρων εἰς τετράπ[ηχ]υν ὅ[ρον
σεμνὸς ἐκεῖνος ἀνῆκε, Χάρης πρῶ[τος μ]ετὰ τέχνα[ς
ζῷ⟨ι⟩ον ἐχαλχούργει γᾶς μεγ[......].[..]ν

v. 1 π[εριμάκε]α edd. pr., sed π[εριμήκε]α supplere possis   v. 4 θησεῖν ?

The Rhodians wanted to make the enormous (?) Sun
Twice this size, but Chares of Lindus set it down that
No craftsman would make a statue even bigger than this one.
If that venerable Myron reached a limit
Of four cubits, Chares was the first with his art
To forge in bronze a figure . . . [the size?] of the earth . . .

The dialect is notable for several reasons. Although the poem has Doric α rather than Attic-Ionic η after the first verse (τεχνίταν, τέχνα[ς]; γᾶς), the second word, Ἥλιον, may naturally lead readers to assume at first that the coloring of the epigram will be epic/Ionic. This use of an apparently "out-of-place" Ionic form early in the poem finds a close parallel in the equestrian poem at AB 73, where the opening words, εὐθὺς ἀπὸ γραμμῆς, stand at odds with ἁδύ in the third verse.[52] That epigram, the first in the ἱππικά to celebrate an Olympic victory, is thus also the first poem in the section to contain Doric forms. The initial, isolated Ionicism could easily be the product of a slip by a scribe who was not expecting Doric coloring but who later correctly wrote Doric forms without amending his earlier mistake. A similar explanation could also account for the presence of ἠέλιον rather than ἀέλιον at AB 68.1 (contrast GP adesp. 58A.1–3 [AP VI 171.1–3]), but the numerous examples of mixed dialect in both contemporary inscribed epigram and in other early Hellenistic poetry, as well as the care with which the papyrus has been produced in general, make it reasonable to explore other, less pedestrian solutions.

In the case of AB 68.1, one possibility is that the poet did not wish to use the form ἀέλιον, a common "artificial" Doric form created by analogy with epic ἠέλιος,[53] but this hypothesis, despite the absence of ἀέλιος from the Doric poems

---

[52] ἁδύ also suggests that the dative Ὀλυμπίαι in the opening hexameter should be interpreted as a Doricism rather than an Atticism; that AB 73.3 should be supplemented ταχυ[τᾶτι rather than ταχυ[τῆτι seems likely.

[53] Cf. Forsmann 1966:6–8.

of Theocritus (who uses only ἅλιος), requires the improbable assumption that Posidippus placed a greater premium on the "purity" of Doric forms—even in the face of the well established use of ἀέλιος in literary Doric (e.g. Pindar *Olympian* 1.5; 2.32; *Pythian* 4.214; Bacchylides 5.161; Theocritus 16.76; Callimachus *Hymn* 5.89; 6.91)—than on uniformity of dialect in a single epigram. The issue is further complicated by the gaps in the poem, especially that at the end of the first verse. The first editors adopt Austin's suggestion π[εριμάκε]α, a word well fitted to both the available space and context, but even if this is the adjective Posidippus used, we have no basis for knowing whether he wrote it with the Doric -μακ- or with Attic-Ionic -μηκ-, and the point at which identifiable Doricisms rather than epic/Ionic equivalents first appear in the poem must remain uncertain.[54]

As the first editors suggest, the Doricisms in the epigram seem appropriate to the content of the poem, since the dialect spoken at Rhodes belonged to the Doric family, but the nature of the "ossequio . . . alla doricità dell' isola" needs to be explored further[55] The narrator seems initially to be a speaker of Ionic, but he soon adopts the Doricisms of his putative location, since he presents himself as standing in the presence of the statue (cf. τόcοc, τοῦδε). Given the incomplete state of the end of the first verse, we cannot know whether he switches to Doric already in that line. If he did not, the first unambiguously Doric forms appear at the head of the second hexameter in the indirect statement introduced by ὡρίcατο, "ordained" (*LSJ* s.v. III). The subject of that verb is Chares, a Rhodian from the city of Lindus, and the Doric coloring of the dependent clause vividly reflects the dialect Chares would have used in establishing a limit to the size of the Colossus.

In this regard, μηθένα in v. 3 is particularly interesting. The forms οὐθείς / μηθείς appear in Attic inscriptions as early as 378/7 BCE and are widespread in inscriptions and papyri throughout the Greek-speaking world by the end of the fourth century.[56] The form with a *theta* is thus not in itself unusual or necessarily marked, though it is unique in the papyrus, which elsewhere has οὐδείς (AB 62.6; AB 63.4; ambiguous at AB 77.4 οὐ[δ]έν). Heraclides of Miletus (fr. 25 Cohn *ap.* Eust. 452.20–1), however, reports that Doric speakers pronounced *delta* as *theta* and gives the examples of ἔθω for ἔδω, μαcθόν for μαδόν, and ψύθος for ψεῦδος, and Archestratos of Gela (if the transmitted text is correct) seems to have used ἔθοντεc (= ἔδοντεc) to parody speakers of Sicilian Doric (fr. 60.11

---

[54] θεῖναι is properly foreign to Doric, in which athematic infinitives terminate in -μεν rather than -ναι cf. Buck 1955:122; for the evidence for athematic infinitival endings in the bucolic corpus, cf. Molinos Tejada 1990:317–319.

[55] BG:195.

[56] Mayser 1906 (i.1):180–182; Threatte 1980 (i):472–476.

Olson–Sens).[57] Moreover, the use of ζ to represent original δ (τόζ[´ = τόδε) in a sixth-century Rhodian inscription (*IG* XII 1.737; *GDI* 4140) suggests that in that local dialect inherited /d/ had come to be pronounced as a spirant.[58] All of this makes it possible, despite the widespread use of μηθείς and οὐθείς in the third century BCE, that the aspirated form of the adjective in its context serves, in conjunction with its referent τεχνίταν, as a marker of a stylized version of Rhodian Doric.[59] Our ignorance about the end of the first verse complicates the picture, but if the phrase μηθένα τεχνίταν is the first recognizably Doric language in the poem, the effect would be especially striking and pointed. If that was the case, the narrator, having begun in epic/Ionic, switched to Doric in order vividly to represent the actual words of the Rhodian sculptor. The influence of that "quotation" then continues throughout the remainder of the poem (τέχνα[ϲ]; ᾶϲ), as if the narrator's description of Chares' accomplishments were expressed by the artist himself.

Perhaps the most intriguing juxtaposition of Doric and epic-Ionic forms within a single poem in P.Mil.Vogl. VIII 309 occurs at AB 102, the first epigram in the section of the papyrus labeled τρόποι:

> τί πρὸς ἔμ᾽ ὧδ᾽ ἔϲτητε; τί μ᾽ οὐκ ἠάϲατ᾽ ἰαύειν,
> εἰρόμενοι τίϲ ἐγὼ καὶ πόθεν ἢ ποδαπόϲ;
> ϲτείχε⟨τέ⟩ μου παρὰ ϲῆμα· Μενοίτιόϲ εἰμι Φιλάρχω
> Κρήϲ, ὀλιγορρήμων ὡϲ ἂν ἐπὶ ξενίηϲ.

> Why did you stop near me like that? Why didn't you let me sleep,
> asking who I am and whence and where born?
> Go past my tomb. I am Menoetius, son of Philarchus,
> Cretan, a man of few words inasmuch as being in a foreign land.

As in AB 64, Doric forms in the speech of a Cretan speaker may be intended as a realistic feature, "come riflesso della parlata dorica del defunto."[60] We have already observed that the two "severe" Doric forms (ἠάϲατε and Φιλάρχω) that are preserved in the poem may, like ἠργάϲατο in the epigram on Cresilas' statue of Idomeneus epigram, be introduced to suggest specific features of actual Cretan speech. Despite the presence of such specially marked Doricisms, however, the

---

[57] Cf. Olson and Sens 2000:232.
[58] Cf. Buck 1955:58–59.
[59] Given the Doric character of the indirect discourse, one could conceivably write the contracted Doric future infinitive θηϲεῖν rather than θήϲειν at the head of the second pentameter.
[60] BG:229.

dialectal coloring of the epigram is not consistent, since the poem also contain cῆμα (AB 64.3) and ξενίης (AB 64.4), for which the poet could easily have written cᾶμα and ξενίαc had he wished. As Palumbo Stracca has pointed out,[61] the existence of similar variations in inscribed epigram from an early period cautions against emending away the inconsistency of the transmitted text. If this i preserved, however, the combination of strongly Doric forms with others that are foreign to Doric would seem at odds with any attempt to capture, even in a styl ized manner, the speech of the Cretan narrator.

For Hellenistic readers attuned to nuances of dialect, however, the mixture of Doric and non-Doric forms may have formed part of the point. The poem, of which a text was made available in the preliminary publication of select epigram from the papyrus, has already received a relatively large degree of critical attention most of it directed to unpacking the significance of the speaker's explanation for hi taciturnity in the final verse.[62] Whatever the precise connection between the speaker's Cretan background and his reticence, however, the speaker represents hi unwillingness to speak at length as a natural consequence of his actual location in a foreign land,[63] and the simplest conclusion is that the speaker, having been buried away from Crete, explains his reticence by reference to the expected behavior of living foreigners.[64] The precise significance of the generic label τρόποι given to the section to which this poem belongs is uncertain, but the epigram and those tha follow may well be intended to illustrate certain types of character through first person speech. In this case, the poem turns on its head the epitaphic convention in which the deceased person or his tomb calls for passersby to stop and pay attention and in so doing the epigram paints a humorous and vivid picture of a certain type of speaker, the taciturn foreigner.

When viewed in this context, the juxtaposition of Doric and non-Doric form may be seen as part of a subtle characterization of the speaker, Cretan by birth bu resident, in life and death, in an alien land. For people like him, speech serves as a fundamental marker of foreign origin. Implicit in the poem's suggestion tha foreigners are naturally taciturn may be the idea that they are so not only because

---

[61] Palumbo Stracca 1993:408.

[62] Gronewald 1993:28–29; Voutiras 1994:27–31; Dickie 1995:5–12; Celentano 1995:67–79; Cairn 1996:77–88.

[63] *Pace* D'Alessio 1996:227n22, who claims that the final phrase means "as one *would be* in a foreign land" rather than "inasmuch as being in a foreign land" (cf. Gronewald 1993:28–29); cf. AB 94. and Asclepiades 28 GP (*AP* VII 11), where the small quantity of Erinna's work is explained by th clause ὡς ἂν παρθενικᾶς ἐννεακαιδεκέτευς, "as (is natural given that) she was a nineteen-year old maiden." On the Asclepiadean poem, see Sens 2003 (forthcoming).

[64] Thus Gronewald 1993:28-29, adducing an Athenian proverb about the restricted *parrhesia* of metics That the speaker is also ἐπὶ ξενίης in the sense that he has come to reside in the place of the dea may also contribute to the point.

ticence is expected of them, but also because by speaking they expose their status.
a the mouth of an alien like Menoetius, the mixture of Doric and non-Doric
rms represents a stylized version of the way in which foreigners actually speak,
mbining features of their native tongue with elements of the language indigenous
» the place in which they find themselves. If the dialectal variation of the poem is
nderstood in this way, the Ionic coloring of the final words, ἐπὶ ξενίης, takes on
ecial significance, since that phrase both announces the speaker's foreign status
nd serves as an icon of his position as social and linguistic outsider: the very word
hich means foreign is itself uttered in a dialect "alien" to the speaker's own.[65]

Conclusion

he use to which dialect seems to be put in this poem—and elsewhere in the
apyrus—provides a helpful backdrop for thinking about the juxtaposition of
oric and Ionic forms of the relative pronoun in the text of the poem with which
is essay began, Posidippus AB 139 (8 GP = *AP* XII 131). On the one hand, the
apyrus offers some justification for regularizing the forms in that epigram, since a
mparison of the text of the Alexander-statue epigram contained in the single
anuscript witness and that preserved on the papyrus suggests that some but not
l of the original Doricisms were displaced in the course of transmission. Given the
latively scarcity of Doric forms in the poems of Posidippus that are preserved in
ae *Anthology*—and the predominance of Attic-Ionic in the *Anthology* in general—
ae Doricisms in the paradosis of *AP* XII 131 seem more likely to have been subject
» alteration, and if one were to regularize, it would (*pace* Gow-Page) therefore
aake best sense to replace transmitted East Greek forms with Doricisms. On the
ther hand, the juxtaposition of Doric and Ionic forms of the relative pronouns in
P XII 131 is not inherently less likely than the use of markedly non-Doric forms
ke γραμμῆς or ξενίης in close conjunction with Doric elements in individual
oems of the new papyrus. Let us therefore briefly explore the consequences of
suming that Posidippus did in fact write ἅ three times in the first verse of
P XII 131 but Συρίης and ἥ elsewhere.
    To understand what function this variation might have served, we must
nsider the poem as a whole more closely. The epigram, cast as a prayer to
phrodite, opens in the elevated manner of hymn,[66] and the language and style of

---

[5] It is tempting to suggest that the other word of markedly non-Doric coloring, σῆμα, is equally
significant: taken together, σῆμα and ξενίης serve precisely as the σήματα of the speaker's foreign
status.
[6] For the relative clause as a typical hymnic feature, cf. Janko 1981:9–10; Norden 1913:168–172. For
the invocation of the goddess by reference to her habitual haunts, cf. Sappho frr. 1.7; 127; Alcaeus
fr. 34.1; Aristophanes *Lysistrata* 1296; Theocritus 1.125. For ἔλθοις ἵλαος, cf. Pindar *Pythian* 12.4;

the first couplet are evocative of "high" lyric poetry in general. The verb shared b
the opening relative clauses, ἐποιχνεῖς, is an interesting marker in this regard. Th
word is rare, occurring in literature apparently only in two contextually simila
passages: at Bacchylides 10.1–2, where it is a likely supplement in an address t
personified Fame (Φή]μα, σὺ γ[ὰ]ρ ἀ[ἐπ]οιχνεῖς | [φῦ]λα),[67] and in th
Delphic paean by Aristonous, where it appears as part of an address to Apoll
(verses 11–12, p. 163 Powell μαντοσύναν ἐποιχνεῖς, ἰὴ ἰὲ Παιάν).[
Posidippus' use of the word, whether or not it has a specific model in anteceder
poetry, thus helps to evoke the tradition of choral lyric. That the other passages i
which ἐποιχνέω occurs have a Doric coloring is telling, and the historical assoc
ation of Doric with lyric poetry in general makes the use of the Doric forms of th
pronoun in the invocation of Aphrodite in the first verse of Posidippus' epigram
particularly appropriate.[69]

At first glance, therefore, the generic background of the poem's opening migh
offer some justification for regularizing all of the Ionic forms to their Doric equiv
alents. A closer reading, however, suggests that the dialectal variation might itself b
significant. Some of the wit of the epigram, indeed, depends on the disjunctio
between the elevated manner of the invocation of the goddess in the first coupl
and the coarse content of the final description of the human Callistium. Th
speaker, whether the woman herself or someone else, uses "special" Doric form
with their marked association to choral lyric, to refer to the goddess in the first lin
but reverts to "ordinary" Ionic forms elsewhere. The effect is to create an oppos
tion between the goddess, addressed at the opening of the epigram via Doric form
of the relative pronoun, and the sexually willing Callistium, who is described wit
the "unmarked" language of Ionic in the final relative clause, ἣ τὸν ἐραστὴν
οὐδέποτ' οἰκείων ὦσεν ἀπὸ προθύρων.

Given our ignorance about the text, such a reading of the dialect forms in th
epigram must be provisional, and the fact that the paradosis has Συρίης rathe
than Συρίας complicates the opposition that I have suggested. Taken cumulativel
however, the evidence offered by the new papyrus cautions against dismissing th
and other passages in which the dialect seems to be inconsistent as merely the resu
of errors in transmission or as products of authorial carelessness. To the contrary
the new papyrus shows that Posidippus was interested in the nuances of dialec

....

Aeschylus *Eumenides* 1040; Aristophanes *Women of the Thesmophoria* 1148; anonymous *PM*
934.19; Herodas IV 11; Furley and Bremer 2001: I 54–55.

[67] Maehler 1982:180–181.
[68] Elsewhere, cf. Hesychius ε 5483 ἐποιχνεῖ· ἐπιφοιτᾷ.
[69] For the Hellenistic association of Doric and lyric, cf. Fantuzzi 1993:932; Hunter 1996:31.5.

which he uses as a powerful if often subtle tool not only for affiliating his compositions with the various literary traditions on which he draws, but also for creating other, more complex, forms of meaning. In this respect, as in many others, P.Mil.Vogl. VIII 309 offers unparalleled access into the practices of an important figure in the literary history of the third century BCE, and by implication into those of other learned Hellenistic epigrammatists as well.

7

A New Hellenistic Poetry Book: P.Mil.Vogl. VIII 309[1]

Kathryn Gutzwiller
University of Cincinnati

The earliest Greek poetry books come from the third century BCE, and surviving examples include Callimachus' *Iambi* and *Aetia* and Herodas' *Mimiambi*, known from papyrus, and a few manuscript possibilities, such as Callimachus' *Hymns* and portions of Theocritus. Collections of epigrams were also among the earliest poetry books, and Meleager apparently used these single-authored collections in compiling his *Garland*, which became the primary source for Hellenistic epigrams preserved in the later Byzantine anthologies. Up to this point, however, direct evidence for epigram collections has been slight, consisting of a few papyrus scraps containing contiguous epigrams, ancient references to the *Epigrammata* of various poets, and a small *sylloge* of epigrams attributed to Theocritus that descends in bucolic manuscripts.[2] The new Posidippus papyrus now provides us with an epigram collection securely dated to the third century BCE. The editors point out, on the basis of the care given to the script and outlay of the text, that this papyrus was the product of a scriptorium, not a personal copy. They also recognize that the arrangement of the poems was not just formal or convenient, but refined, aesthetically designed to appeal to a reading public.[3]

One of the most surprising aspects of the papyrus is its division into sections, each with its own title, placed within a column and centered. Nine such sections are clearly visible on the papyrus, and the editors believe that a tenth may be lurking in the scraps at the end of the surviving text.[4] The Byzantine anthologies are

---

[1] This is a slightly expanded version of a paper that was given at the annual meeting of the American Philological Association in January of 2001. The paper was then published on the APA website at http://www.apaclassics.org/publications.

[2] For discussion, see Cameron 1993:3–18; Gutzwiller 1998:15–46; Argentieri 1998:12–17.

[3] BG:24–26; Bastianini 2001:114–118.

[4] BG:18–19.

rranged in categories of larger scope, and Planudes subdivides his major sections nto smaller ones with specific headings somewhat reminiscent of Posidippus. It has een argued that Meleager's *Garland* consisted of at least four such sections— *pitymbia, anathematica, erotica*, and one other of less certain content.[5] In addition, he collection of Theocritean epigrams in the bucolic manuscripts, of uncertain late, is easily divided into three sections, but without transmitted titles.[6] The 'osidippus papyrus shows that this type of division goes back to the third century, hough some of the headings are unexpected. They are nevertheless, I suggest, hematically connected to poetic arrangement in a way that the Byzantine headings re not. The editors point out that the distribution and arrangement of epigrams vithin sections is arbitrary:[7] certain poems would fit in more than one category, specially dedicatory and sepulchral epigrams, and some epigrams are only margin- lly related to the heading of their section. This is not, however, because the head- ngs are formally inadequate or because the ancient editor was careless in his rrangement. It is rather because the sections are ordered to create a certain poetic xperience and themes take precedence over formal categories.

Most of the epigrams in this collection belong to inscriptional types, connected vith dedications, grave monuments, or art objects. Erotic and sympotic epigrams y Posidippus are known from the *Anthology*, but no example of this more personal, ubjective type appears in the surviving portion of the papyrus. As a result, the voice eard most commonly in the collection is that of the objective epigrammatic arrator, who only occasionally addresses an internal auditor or ventriloquates other oices. Artistic arrangement for a collection of the more objective type requires that ohesion be achieved within the natural variety of epigrams dealing with a wide ange of subjects and individuals;[8] the Posidippus collection displays a number of ophisticated techniques for creating such cohesion. Thematic and structural simi- rities are easily emphasized by the grouping of poems within sections, and the 1ost similar poems are often given contiguous placement. In at least two instances 1e collection contains a pair of epigrams on the same topic, placed side by side AB 6–7 and 11–12), creating a knot of density within the flow of the collections'

[5] Cameron 1993:24–33; Gutzwiller 1998:278–321.

[6] For the sectioning within the Theocritean collection, see Tarditi 1988:47–52, Gutzwiller 1998: 42–45, and Rossi 2001:367–371. Since Meleager seems not to have known a *sylloge* of the Theocritean epigrams, it was likely not formed until after his *Garland*. In Gutzwiller 1996 and 1998:41–42 I have argued that Vergil's imitations of key Theocritean epigrams in programmatic passages in the *Eclogues* indicate that an epigram collection similar to the one in the bucolic manu- scripts existed by ca. 40 BCE. Rossi 2001:363–371 posits a more stratified collection, with pre- Vergilian sections supplemented with material from the imperial period.

[7] BG:25 and Bastianini 2001:115.

[8] For this type of arrangement in an epigram collection and the likely reaction of readers to it, see Gutzwiller 1998:11–12.

variety.[9] There is also a remarkable amount of verbal linkage between poems, mostly contiguous epigrams, but strong verbal parallels occur over larger spaces as well.[10] This technique also appears in the longer *Anthology* sequences deriving from Meleager's *Garland*, particularly the erotic section, where the poet-editor links his own epigrams both to earlier epigrams he anthologizes and to other epigrams of his own, through similarity of vocabulary and phrasing.[11] In Posidippus the phenomenon seems, in part, a result of natural verbal repetitions in poems on similar topics, but over the course of the collection the links are numerous enough, and often repeated in key or identical positions within poems, so as to suggest that they function to foster continuity within the ever changing subject matter endemic to epigram books.[12]

Another important element for giving the collection cohesion is the rhythm of the arrangement within sections. Certain sections, like the short one on shipwrecks, are ordered for the purpose of variation on a given theme, as the problem of commemorating the drowned is differently focalized by the empty tomb, the grieving family, the deceased buried by a stranger, or even the possible survivor of

[9] Other sets of "companion pieces" are known, such as Callimachus *AP* VII 525 and VII 41 (29–30 GP), Leonidas *AP* VII 648 and VII 440 (10–11 GP), Theocritus (?) *AP* VII 658 and VII 65 (7–8 GP), and Meleager *AP* VII 195 and VII 196 (12–13 GP), *AP* V 172 and V 173 (27–28 GP), *AP* V 151 and V 152 (33–34 GP); see Kirstein 2002:113–135. It appears that Meleager V 151–152 and V 172–173 have descended to us in their original *Garland* sequence, and the Posidippus collection now provides evidence that juxtaposition of such paired epigrams began in an earlier period.

[10] For instance, the phrase καλὸc ἠέλιοc or καλὸν ἠέλιον occurs in three noncontiguous poems always at the end of an epigram (AB 13.4, 16.6, 52.6). This sort of verbal repetition argues strongly for a single author for the collection.

[11] The principal studies are Radinger 1895:100–107, Wifstrand 1926:8–22, and, more comprehensively, Gutzwiller 1998:277–321.

[12] A few examples will illustrate the technique. The first two poems (AB 1 and 2), fragmentary as they are, seem linked in their first and last words ('Ινδὸc 'Υδάcπηc, 'Ινδ[); for this technique of linkage, cf. Meleager *AP* XII 52 and XII 53 (81 and 66 GP) with the discussion of Gutzwiller 1998:286–287. The last two poems in the first section on stones are also linked verbally (κύμα[τc νῆcον, AB 19.1, 19.14; κύματι, νήcων, AB 20.1, 20.5), while in the omens section the last line of AB 22 (κῦμα, ἠερίων) echoes in the first line of AB 23 (ἠερίην, κῦμα). The first two dedicatory poems, AB 36 and 37, are linked by the same beginning phrase ('Αρcινόη, coί), as in the equestrian section Βερενίκηc . . . cτέφανον at the end of one poem, AB 78.13–14, echoes in Βερενίκη . . . cτεφάνουc at the beginning of the next, AB 79.1–2. Likewise, the last two poems in the epitaphic section share language as well as theme (βαρύγηρωc, AB 60.5, κοῦφοc 60.4 εὔγηρω, 61.1, κοῦφον, 61.4). Epigrams in other sections are linked by vocabulary that reinforces the theme of that section: note, for instance, the words πλάccω/πλάcτας (AB 63.2, 64.4, 65.1, ἄκρος/ἄκρον/ἀκριβής/ἀκρομέριμνοc (AB 63.2, 63.5, 67.4), τέχνη/τεχνίτας (AB 63.5, 65.2, 68.3, 68.5), and χείρ (AB 62.3, 65.1, 66.3, 67.2, 67.4, 70.3) in the bronze statue section; ἵπποc (71.4, 75.2, 76.2 78.4, 79.3, 79.5, 82.2, 83.1, 84.1, 85.1, 85.4, 86.2, 87.1, ἄεθλοc/ἀεθλοφορέω/ἀεθλοφόροc (71.3, 76.2, 78.8, 78.12, 79.2, 82.6, 85.1), and cτέφανος/cτεφανόω (AB 73.3, 74.6, 74.11, 75.3, 76.4, 78.14, 79.2, 80.2, 84.3, 86.4, 87.2) in the equestrian section.

wreck. But in some sections unique or special poems are placed first or last, or even at transitional points between sequences within one section. And importantly, several sections also display a movement from the specific to the general, the private to the political, or the small to the large. These movements work to identify the political world encompassing the various subjects of Posidippus' collection, from its historical background in the Argead dynasty and Alexander's conquests to the three generations of Ptolemaic rulers who apparently supported Posidippus' poetic endeavors. More speculatively, I will argue that arrangement combined with interconnection between poems offers a key to the aesthetic principles underlying Posidippus' epigrammatic collection.

A quick overview of the nine sections will highlight major themes and the flow of the arrangement. I warn that this discussion is based on only a preliminary reading of the text and reflects my initial impressions, which will surely be subject to change. The gaps in the papyrus certainly hinder a holistic reading, and it is unfortunate that the first few poems have almost completely disappeared. We lack as well a knowledge of the full scope of the collection, whether the papyrus breaks off near the original conclusion or continued with additional sections.

The first section concerns stones, and the title λιθικά suggested by the editors fits well the gap in the papyrus. It begins with a long sequence of (probably) sixteen epigrams on engraved gemstones, several of which mention the stone's origin in India or Arabia, or a Persian context for the object. Most of these stones, then, became available through Alexander's eastern conquests, and at least two of them were carved by Cronius (AB 2.2, 7.3), who was mentioned by Pliny as a successor to Pyrgoteles, Alexanders' favorite engraver (Pliny *Natural History* XXXVII 8). One piece of carnelian appears to be an old Persian stone that perhaps belonged to Darius (AB 8), and another poem concerns the famous ring of Polycrates, here engraved with a lyre belonging to a court poet, apparently Anacreon (AB 9).[13] This combining of contemporary subjects with famous predecessors of another era will appear in other sections as well.

The editors note that the first seven epigrams, as best they can tell, concern gemstones belonging to women,[14] but they fail to notice that the transition from this group is marked at the beginning of the eighth poem concerning an enormous carnelian engraved with Darius and a chariot. That epigrams begins, "No neck or finger of any woman wore this carnelian, but the lovely stone . . . was attached to a gold chain" (AB 8.1–3). Next is the Polycrates epigram, which opens with the

---

[13] On interest in collecting antique gems on the part of the Romans and late Hellenistic monarchs, see Plantzos 1999:108. Posidippus' collection now shows that the phenomenon goes back to the early Ptolemaic period.

[14] BG:25.

narrator addressing the tyrant, who is a suitable archaic predecessor for the Hellenistic owners of gemstones, because, as Herodotus (III 40–41) tells the story he loved his ring better than any other possession. The sequence then advances to stones that were engraved with special craft, so that they change their visual properties, show contrast between surface and background, or display very miniature images (AB 11–15). The gemstone sequence is followed by a shorter section of natural or extraordinary stones (AB 16–18), culminating in a fourteen-line poem about a huge boulder cast up onto Euboea by Poseidon (AB 19). The final epigram not about stones at all though verbally and thematically connected to the preceding poem, is a prayer to Poseidon not to harm Ptolemaic lands with earthquake (AB 20). This poem brings closure to the section by its expansive reference to the Ptolemaic kingdom, which may be perceived as the setting from which the poet has made his comments on various stones – from the small and artistically worked, to the natural and the unusual, to the enormous and threatening.

The next section, entitled οἰωνοσκοπικά, consists of fifteen epigrams pertaining to omens. It begins with a sequence concerning bird signs, particularly as relevant for sailors, farmers, and fishermen. This initial group may suggest to the reader that the title is to be understood in its narrow sense, as bird augury, but the section then proceeds to omens applicable to other situations, some of which do not concern birds.[15] The tenth through thirteenth poems involve military omens (AB 30–33). One warns that a sweating god signals an attack on a city, and another delineates omens that helped the Argeads—an eagle, lightning, and a statue of Athena that moved its foot, the latter appearing to Alexander before he attacked the Persians. The final two epigrams concern specific seers, one an unknown Carian and the other a certain Strymon who aided Alexander's campaign against the Persians with bird augury (AB 34–35). The movement in this section is, then, from omens for ordinary people to specific military omens, with special references to Alexander's conquests.

The third section, given the title ἀναθεματικά, known from later anthologies, consists of only six poems. The initial four concern dedications to Arsinoe II Philadelphus. In the first of these (AB 36), a girl of Macedonian ancestry offers Arsinoe a linen handkerchief (or perhaps a headband?) from Naucratis, which the goddess requested during a dream in which she appeared sweating from her labor and holding spear and shield.[16] The poem links back to the war omens in the previous section, which included a sweating deity, and so fosters a theme of

---

[15] For a somewhat different structure for this section, see the essay of M. Baumbach and K. Trampedach in this volume.

[16] The object dedicated is specified by two rare nouns, βρέγμα and κανόνισμα, the known meaning for which do not work here. BG:151–152 think of a handkerchief, Lapini 2002:47 of a headband.

Ptolemaic inheritance of the Argead hegemony. But Arsinoe, who in her epiphany has ceased her labors, may here signal a *pax Ptolemaica* in contrast to the military expansiveness emphasized in the omen section. In the next poem Arsinoe's temple attendant offers her a lyre brought from the sea by Arion's dolphin (AB 37), in the third a freedwoman offers a phiale (AB 38), and the fourth concerns Arsinoe's role as protectress of sailors commemorated in the temple built by Callicrates at Zephyrium (AB 39). The final two poems are puzzling and fragmentary, but the section as a whole is dominated by the great queen Arsinoe in her various capacities as warrior, patron of sailors and poets, and protectress of the humble.

The fourth section, whose title is lost, consists of twenty sepulchral poems. The great majority of these are about women, and the section seems to begin with epitaphs for initiates in the mysteries. Particularly interesting is a poem concerning a girl from Pella who was initiated in Dionysiac mysteries (AB 44). As we know from a poem by Posidippus found on a wax tablet, his so-called *sphragis* or elegy on old age (AB 118.24–28 [*SH* 705.21–25]), the poet himself was a Dionysiac initiate, and a gold lamella from a Macedonian grave bearing the name Posidippus has been taken as evidence that one of his ancestors participated in the mysteries.[17] This section is organized, as is the sepulchral section from Meleager, by type of individual—old women (AB 45–47), maidens (49–51, 53–55)[18], women who died in childbirth (56–57). The last two epitaphs are for men, both of whom died in their prime with loving descendants; both poems contain the theme of "no need for tears" (μὴ κλαύσητέ με, AB 60.3; τὸν ἀδάκρυτον βλέψον λίθον, 61.3), which appears as well in Posidippus' elegy (μηδέ τις οὖν χεύαι δάκρυον, AB 118.24 [*SH* 705.21]), where it is connected with the happy life of the initiate. Since this theme is very rare, the coincidence is remarkable.[19] If the request for "no tears" were characteristic of initiates, then the last two epigrams in this section would link back to the first set about female initiates. But at the very least, the parallels with Posidippus' elegy support his authorship for these two poems, in addition to the two ascribed to him elsewhere (AB 15 [20 GP], AB 65 [18 GP]).

---

[17] Dickie 1995 and 1998:65–76, Rossi 1996.

[18] AB 52, which occurs in the midst of the epitaphs for maidens, concerns Timon, whose sundial, erected by his tomb, will be guarded by a female figure, whom the editors think is his daughter. It is a good example of how thematic focus, here on the girl, is more important to the arranger than strict typology.

[19] See the note of BG:184, although "Simonides" *AP* X 105.2 seems to me not a good parallel because the theme there is malicious happiness at another's death. The editors cite as a close parallel οὐδὲν ἔχω θρήνων ἄξιον οὐδὲ θανών, Carp(h)yllides *AP* VII 260.2 (1.2 GP), where the deceased just may be an initiate of the mysteries. Not only does he "not die" but his descendants send him to sleep "the sweet sleep" in the "land of the blessed" (ἐπ' εὐσεβέων); cf. Posid. AB 43.1 where the initiate Nicostrate has gone ἐπ' εὐcεβέων.

The fifth section, entitled ἀνδριαντοποιικά, concerns bronze statues and links with the first section, dealing largely with carved stones. The connection involves both similarity and difference, since sculpting in bronze and carving in stone were conceived as antithetical forms of artistic creativity (Aristotle *Nichomachean Ethics* 1041a). The first of the nine poems in this section begins with a direct address to sculptors: "Mimic these works, sculptors, and leave aside ancient rules for larger-than-life-size statues" (μιμήσασθε τάδ' ἔργα, πολυχρονίους δὲ κολοσσῶν, ὦ ζῳοπλάσται, ναί, παραθεῖτε νόμους, AB 62.1–2); it then proceeds to praise the new art of Lysippus in comparison with the old style of earlier sculptors. Serving an obviously introductory function, the poem was perhaps composed for this position in the collection,[20] and here the poet himself speaks, alluding to the subjects of the remaining poems in the section with the phrase τάδ' ἔργα. The first of these works is a statue of Philetas, commissioned by Ptolemy and remarkable for the realistic manner in which the poet-scholar's old age and intelligence are represented (AB 63). The sculptor Hecataeus is also praised because he constructed the Philetas statue in human rather than heroic proportions and so realistically that he is "like one about to speak" (AB 63.7), if the editors' supplement here is correct. The following poem addresses the reader, or viewer, who is asked to praise the bronze Idomeneus sculpted by Cresilas, and the words that Idomeneus seems to speak to his companion Meriones are then quoted (AB 64). The point seems to be that, even if the Idomeneus statue is heroic in subject matter in the older fashion, it is nevertheless so lifelike that the viewer may perceive the very words the figure wishes to speak.

The following poems emphasize the realism, polish, or limited size of the bronzes (AB 65–70); their subjects are an Alexander statue by Lysippus (a poem known from the *Greek Anthology*, XVI 119), the famous cow by Myron (the subject of a long series of later epigrams), a self-representation by the sixth-century sculptor Theodorus in which he holds a miniature chariot in one hand and a file in the other, the colossus of Rhodes by Chares who made it only half the size the Rhodians wished, another statue by Myron, of Tydeus, and, lastly, another Lysippan statue of Alexander. This section obviously has something to say about the aesthetic principles of the age, as it reaches back to the late archaic and classical periods to find predecessors for the new realism, here associated particularly with Lysippus, the favorite sculptor of Alexander.[21] In particular, I call attention to the symbolism of

---

[20] Many of the epigrams on the papyrus were likely occasional in nature, later gathered for collection. But this first poem in the statue section does not fit with known types of epigrams and seems particularly well suited to its literary context.

[21] For a more detailed analysis of the structure and significance of the section, see Gutzwiller 2002. There I argue that the section is a carefully arranged sequence, which "constitutes nothing less than

he Theodorus statue, with its clear allusion to miniaturism and polish;[22] it seems
ignificant as well that this Theodorus was the engraver of Polycrates' famous ring
Herodotus III 41), so that the epigram about his self-representation creates another
though unexpressed) link back to the section on stones.

The sixth section, entitled ἱππικά and concerning equestrian victories,
:ontains eighteen poems which appear, according to the editors, in two series.[23] The
'irst series begins with seven poems (AB 71–77) that celebrate victories in single
1orse racing or chariot racing all apparently by men, including Callicrates of Samos
AB 74), the Ptolemaic nauarch lauded in previously known epigrams by
Posidippus (AB 116, 119 = 12–13 GP). Some of these mention commemorative
statues of horses or victors, and yet others seem suitable for inscription in such
:ontexts. The next five poems may all concern victories by Berenice II (AB 78–82),
including one or two Nemean victories datable to 249 or 247 BCE, which may
:orrespond to the one celebrated by Callimachus at the opening of the third book
of the *Aetia* (AB 79-80).[24] In the first of the five poems (AB 78), fourteen lines in
length, the speaker appears to be Berenice herself,[25] who calls on all Macedonian
poets to tell of her κλέος – the victories of her grandfather Ptolemy I Soter, her
grandmother Berenice I, her father Ptolemy II Philadelphus, and Arsinoe II, as well
as now her own triumph in chariot racing. The next four poems, possibly all about
her other victories, may be taken as Posidippus' answer to that request, and this
reading is supported by the last poem in the series where the poet directly addresses
the queen as internal auditor: "Only you, queen, brought it about that your house
was so many times heralded as victorious at the Isthmus" (AB 82.5–6). The second
section of six ἱππικά has a similar structure (AB 83–88). The first four poems
concern victories apparently by individual men and the fifth an Olympian chariot
victory by Berenice I, spoken by the victorious horses, who boast that their owner
has taken away from the Spartan Cynisca the claim to be the only woman victor at
Olympia (AB 87); the last is spoken by her son Ptolemy II, who celebrates the
κλέος gained by himself and his parents in Olympian victories (AB 88). The two
sequences in this section, the first ending with a victory in the early 240s and the
second with a victory in 284, may define, at least generally, the chronological

....

a brief history of Greek bronze statuary, one in which Lysippus is the culmination of the development toward true naturalism and precision in detail and Myron his principal predecessor."

[22] Pliny *Natural History* XXXIV 83 stresses that the self-portrait was famous because of its realism
(*similitudo*) and fineness (*subtilitas*); for discussion of Theodorus, see Stewart 1990.1:244–46.

[23] BG:197. For a revisionary assessment of the structure, see the essay by Fantuzzi in this volume.

[24] See BG:206, 208.

[25] It is just possible that the speaker is Ptolemy III Euergetes, but I agree with BG:206 that the queen
is the better possibility.

boundaries for the composition of Posidippus' collection, as they praise the various Ptolemies who have supported his work.

The seventh section, entitled ναυαγικά, concerns men who died at sea (AB 89–94). While in the Byzantine anthologies epigrams on the shipwrecked appear in the sepulchral books, here they are given a separate section.[26] The arrangement has the advantage of highlighting the difficulty of maintaining the conventions of sepulchral inscription in the case of death by shipwreck, since any tomb erected by the family will lack a body and any epitaph for a body found will lack name and homeland. This short section, neatly conveying the pathos of those lost at sea, works changes on this theme. The first poem (AB 89) performs its work as introduction by commenting on the "empty tomb" of Lysicles, a friend and patron of Polemo who was head of the Academy (Diogenes Laertius 4.22). Though his philosophy would teach rational calm in the face of a friend's loss at sea, here the cenotaph is asked, perhaps ironically, to weep and blame the gods for Lysicles' fate. In another epigram the cenotaph, one may suppose, warns the viewer against sailing lest, like the deceased, he lie unburied far from home (AB 91). In another a kinsman, as it seems, asks Poseidon to send home the body of the lost one (AB 93), and in the last poem the deceased expresses thanks to a passerby for performing the last rites of lamentation and burial (AB 94).[27] We move, then, through the various possibilities, from "empty tomb" to a body in need of a tomb, so that the organization of the section conveys the pathos inherent in the separation of the shipwrecked from his proper mourners.

The eighth section consists of seven ἰαματικά, or poems on cures. In the introductory poem a physician, who has discovered a cure for the bite of the asp, dedicates to Apollo a bronze statue of an emaciated man (AB 95). The next five celebrate cures obtained by individuals (AB 96–100), in several instances from Asclepius, while in the last poem (AB 101), on a more general theme, a man asks Asclepius for moderate wealth and health, "two cures", the "high acropolis" for men's characters (ἠθέων). Once again, we find that key poems are placed in the positions of introduction and conclusion for the section.

The ninth section, apparently consisting of eight poems (AB 102–109), is somewhat mysteriously called τρόποι, and the editors debate the meaning of the title. The poems in this section that are still readable are spoken by deceased persons to those who pass by their tombs. Taking note of the phrase ἤθη τε καὶ τρόπους

---

[26] It does appear, though, that deaths at sea were grouped together in Meleager's sepulchral section, as they are in Planudes' anthology: see Gutzwiller 1998:312–314.

[27] The fact that the person who buries the shipwrecked's body, Leophantus, is named and the deceased who speaks remains unnamed suggests that we are to imagine Leophantus as the one responsible for the inscription. Callimachus *AP* VII 277 (50 GP) contains a similar play with voicing.

in Plato's *Laws* (924d), we may understand that here ἠθέων in the last line of the eighth section looks forward to the title τρόποι and that the ninth section concerns various character types, at least the first of which are revealed through their speech from the grave. So, for instance, in the first poem the deceased complains that passersby pester him with questions about his identity (AB 102), while in the second a deceased of the opposite persuasion complains that a passerby hurries on without making the customary inquiries (AB 103). If this interpretation is the correct one, then the τρόποι section displays the poet's skill at distinguishing and delineating particular or idiosyncratic character traits, just as Hecataeus' statue of Philetas is said to be lifelike because it was "made distinct with so much character" (ὄσωι ποικίλλεται ἤθει, AB 63.7). Apparently at the beginning of a tenth section, for which no title can be discerned, the text of the papyrus breaks off.

The new Posidippus collection is clearly a remarkable poetry book that deserves a much more detailed and careful reading than I have been able to give it in this paper. The force of many scholarly minds now being brought to bear on the papyrus will do much to illuminate the meaning of individual poems and to help us understand the fragmentary passages. But I suspect that in the end the most exciting discovery will be the way in which the collection as a whole creates meaning from the interrelationship of its epigrams. The strategic placement of references to monarchs, the Argeads and Ptolemies, defines the chronological and spatial limits of the multifarious individuals named in the collection. The grouping of contemporary subjects with key predecessors from the late archaic and classical ages suggests those portions of Greek heritage that shape Posidippus' artistic vision. The two sections on works of art, emphasizing miniature carvings on gemstones and accurate, realistic portraits in bronze, may reveal the aesthetic principles that underlie Posidippan poetics. As in the instance of Polycrates' ring, carved by Theodorus who polishes with a file, containing a representation of Anacreon's lyre, and specifically named a *sphragis* (AB 9.1), the works of art described in Posidippus' collection are carefully designed emblems of his own epigrammatic art.

8

Notes on the *Lithika* of Posidippus[*]

Richard Hunter
University of Cambridge

The first group of epigrams is one of many surprises on the Milan papyrus, though perhaps it should not have been so. *Lithika* is indeed a genre not previously well attested at so early a date,[1] although the considerable interest in precious stones in, say, the *Periegesis* of Dionysius, to whom a *Lithika* or *Lithiaka* is also ascribed, should have led us to expect a rich background in Hellenistic literature; it may indeed be that Posidippus was an innovator in this type of ecphrastic epigram.[2] As for the title, Λιθικά is not of course preserved on the papyrus, but *lithika* is indeed what these poems are; I shall continue to use the title, but shall return presently to the generic sense of the collection. As we cannot be sure how the roll originally began and ended, we must be very cautious about the structure of the whole, but we know from the preserved stichometric marks[3] that we certainly have the complete *Lithika* section (though, of course, some individual poems are more complete than others), and the likelihood that the whole epigram collection began

---

[*] Earlier versions of this paper were presented at colloquia on Posidippus at the Center for Hellenic Studies in Washington (April 2002) and in Florence (June 2002) and at seminars in Cambridge and Oxford. I am grateful to all these audiences and to the editors of this volume for helpful criticism. A (rather earlier) version has appeared in the papers of the Florence colloquium (*Il Papiro di Posidippo un anno dopo* (Florence 2002) 109–19). I have tried as far as possible to maintain the exploratory tone of the oral presentation and have not at every step cited and/or argued with the outpouring of scholarship on these poems which has appeared or become known to me since I drafted this essay. I would, however, in particular draw attention to Bernsdorff (2002), Lapini (2002), and Petrain (2002) as three important contributions, all written quite independently of each other and of my essay; unsurprisingly, the observations and conclusions of all four of us overlap in important respects.

[1] Cf. Gutzwiller 1995.

[2] The *Lithika* certainly do not weaken, and may be thought to add some color to, the case for Posidippan authorship of AB 113 (*SH* 978), an ecphrasis of a bathing-house, if chronology allows this; cf. now Lehnus 2002:12–13. The description of gemstones, including the ecphrasis of an amethyst engraved with an elaborate pastoral scene, at Heliodorus *Aithiopika* V 13–14 also suggests a rich tradition that we have now lost.

[3] Cf. BG:15–16.

with this section seems overwhelming: P. Bing[4] has called attention to how these poems would give a 'brilliant' and programmatic opening to the collection through the obvious analogy between the small-scale and detailed craftsmanship of gem-working and the art of the epigrammatist. I turn first to the general shape of the *Lithika* section.

The tattered remains of the opening poem offer (probably) Ζην[, perhaps—as the editors suggest—the start of the name of a lady who received the gem as a gift. The possibility that at least the collection of *lithika*, if not the whole collection, 'commences from Zeus' (cf. Aratus, *Phaenomena* 1, Theocritus 17.1 etc), as the lady's name may have done, may be at least given a certain color by 'Kronios' in what looks like the second poem, presumably a reference to the jeweler named also in AB 7.3 (and cf. AB 6.2); that this name also suggests Zeus' paternity, memorialized in the standard appellation Κρονίων or Κρόνιος (παῖς), is of course a speculation, but I think an attractive one. If there is anything in this, we cannot of course say whether there was a corresponding close to the collection as a whole, but we do at least have the close of the *lithika*, AB 20.5 a prayer to Poseidon which might remind us of the prayers which close hymns (e.g. the end of Callimachus *Hymn to Demeter*)[6] and poetry books; G. Hutchinson[7] has noted that the final *iamatikon* (AB 101) might be considered an adaptation of the hymnic close on ἀρετή and ὄλβος. Be that as it may, the *Aetia* of Callimachus closes (fr. 112.8) with a prayer to Zeus to save the 'house of the rulers' (i.e. Ptolemy III and Berenice II), as the last *lithikon* seeks to keep 'the land of Ptolemy' and the islands free from earthquakes and other natural disturbance.[8] Whether we should connect this with the tradition, discussed by A. Barchiesi in connection with Callimachus and Virgil,[9] that Delos, Apollo's island, was ἀκίνητον ('not subject to earthquakes')[10] is not clear, but both Callimachus and Theocritus make much of Apollo's relationship to Delos as parallel to that of Ptolemy II to Cos, and a gesture here towards Ptolemy's divinity would reinforce the weight of the reminder of divine pleading in the second couplet.

---

[4] Bing 2002; cf. also Hutchinson 2002:2–3.

[5] C. Austin prefers to make all of AB 19 and 20 one poem, but I follow the indications of the papyrus and the arguments of Bastianini and Gallazzi.

[6] See Hopkinson's note on verses 134–137, Richardson on *Homeric Hymn to Demeter* 490–495.

[7] Hutchinson 2002:1. On the *Iamatika*, cf. Bing (this volume).

[8] For 'the islands' as a designation in the poetry of Posidippus cf. AB 115.3 and perhaps *SH* 705.15. For the closing prayer, cf. also Callimachus *Hymn* 5.142 Δαναῶν κλᾶρον ἅπαντα σάω.

[9] Barchiesi 1994.

[10] Cf. Herodotus VI 98, Pindar fr. 33c.4, Schol. Callimachus *Hymn* 4.11. Areas of Ptolemaic power and influence in the Aegean and Asia Minor were, of course, prone to earthquakes, cf. *RE* Suppl. 4.351–358.

The actual form of the prayer to Poseidon is a particularly interesting version of traditional modes: the god is first reminded of his power to destroy (Helike), but then of his past willingness to listen to intercession (the *da quia dedisti* form);[11] the central couplet lends the weight of Demeter's physical supplication (more possible for her than for a mortal)[12] to the current prayer, for the goddess too has been in this position of dependence (the assonance in ἐκύνησε and ἀκίνητην reinforces the parallelism). Her kissing of Poseidon's hand, an unusual gesture in poetic descriptions of supplication, perhaps recalls the only such Homeric gesture, *Iliad* XXIV 478–479 where Priam kisses 'the terrible man-slaying hands of Achilles, which had slain many of his sons' (cf. also XXIV 506); the rôle of Poseidon's 'hand' in the 'natural' destruction he causes has already been made clear in the previous, closely related epigram (AB 19.9-13).[13] Unfortunately, we have no idea to what this couplet refers, but the poetic technique is noteworthy: although the sparing of any 'Eleusis' might reasonably be assigned to an intercession by Demeter,[14] the god's previous granting of a prayer is here, as for example in Sappho fr. 1, a poetic fantasy of the poet (for who else would know of the relations between Demeter and Poseidon?), and this creates that intimate link between mortal and god which is so crucial for the granting of prayers.[15] As for Poseidon, a god with whom anyone named 'Poseidippos' might have felt a special relationship, there is (as far as I know) not much evidence for his cult in Alexandria,[16] but his famous connection with Euboean Geraistos (AB 20.5) appears also in the *Argonautica* of Apollonius (III 1244) and in Callimachus' account of the birth-myth of Apollo (*Hymn* 4.199), and Ptolemaic interest in Euboea (and dedications at Geraistos?) in the middle of the century would certainly not surprise.[17]

---

[11] Cf., e.g., Pulleyn 1997:17, 65–66.

[12] On mortal 'supplication' of the divine see, however, Pulleyn 1997:56–57.

[13] It is probably at least worth noting that the Theocritean Cyclops who appears in the previous poem (cf. below) fantasizes about kissing Galatea's hand (11.55). A. Sens (priv. comm.) suggests that the motif of Poseidon's hand varies the emphasis of earlier *lithika* on the skill of the sculptor's hands.

[14] The editors and Lehnus 2002:13 produce arguments for believing that this is the Eleusis near Alexandria; for Demeter's important cult status in Alexandria cf. Fraser 1972: I 198–201. The matter seems to me, however, to remain at least open. If the Attic Eleusis were meant, the closing *lithikon* would gracefully plot a shift of power (and divine protection) from the mainland Greece of the classical period to the new Ptolemaic realm of Egypt and the Aegean islands.

[15] M. Fantuzzi (priv. comm.) points out that Demeter is a very suitable 'representative' for the initiate Posidippus.

[16] Cf. Visser 1938:30.

[17] Cf., e.g., Walbank 1984:246–248; the presence of Euboea in Callimachus' catalogue of islands led by Delos, the center of the pro-Ptolemaic Island League, at *Hymn* 4.20 is noteworthy in this regard. For different approaches to the 'Ptolemaic' dimension of the *Lithika*, cf. Bing 2002 and Petrain 2002. There is another prayer to Poseidon on the new papyrus at AB 93.3.

Although the prayer to Poseidon is tied into the *Lithika* through various links with the preceding poem, it clearly also stands apart as a poem that is not about a single stone or rock, and this too strengthens its force as a closural prayer. Nevertheless, it closes something of a ring around the *Lithika*, in which both the opening and closing pairs are linked together:[18] we begin, as I have suggested, with Zeus and close with Poseidon, and—in a complementary structure—we begin with Alexander (the Hydaspes, famous in the mid third century only as the site of Alexander's victory over Poros)[19] and close with Ptolemy, Zeus' representative and manifestation here on earth and Alexander's true successor, as (e.g.) Theocritus' *Encomium of Ptolemy* makes clear.

The internal arrangement of the *Lithika* has been briefly sketched out by the editors:[20] first, incised gems (AB 1–15), perhaps themselves divided into gems given as gifts (AB 1–7) and those not (AB 8–15); then, poems about 'remarkable' stones or rocks (AB 16–19), and then the prayer to Poseidon of AB 20. A new text such as this naturally tests our interpretative resolve (and our methodology) in finding patterns and meaning in juxtaposition, and the new text of Posidippus is no exception; K. Gutzwiller has already opened certain lines of enquiry.[21] The *Lithika* offer juxtaposed poems on mother-of-pearl (AB 11 and AB 12) and, very probably, juxtaposed poems about a precious necklace (AB 6 and AB 7). More interestingly, perhaps, we can now see how AB 15 (= Posidippus 20 GP) begins with a rejection of the 'river topos' of, say, AB 1.1 and AB 7.1–2,[22] as AB 8.1–2, οὔτ' αὐχὴν ἐφόρησε τὸ σάρδιον οὔτε γυναικῶν | δάκτυλος, 'no throat or woman's finger wore this carnelian', 'rejects' the subject-matter of the immediately preceding pair of poems.[23] The general impression is that the collection becomes more miscellaneous, and the stones get bigger, as we proceed, but nothing, I think, in either Theophrastus' *On Stones* or in Books 36 and 37 of Pliny's *Natural History* would have prepared us for the poem on the Euboean rock (AB 19) or for the final poem (AB 20). The first of this final pair is linked to what precedes by the opening notion of 'calculation', for the central conceit of AB 18 seems to be exact measurement (cf. Callimachus *Iambus* 6 on the exact dimensions of the statue of Zeus at Olympia);[24] in the current state of the text, a number or measure appears in every verse of this poem except the third, and who is to say that one should not be found there also.

---

[18] Cf. further below.

[19] It is not obvious to me that Virgil *Georgics* IV 211 *Medus Hydaspes* is 'an evident use' of Posidippus, *pace* Hutchinson 2002:3.

[20] BG:25.

[21] Gutzwiller 2002; cf. also Hutchinson 2002:1.

[22] Cf. BG on AB 10.3.

[23] Cf. Gutzwiller 2002:4.

[24] On this poem cf. Luppe 2002.

As for the final pair of poems themselves, they are both prayers to Poseidon in connection with his brutal natural power (with ἐνὶ κύματι in AB 20.1 perhaps picking up AB 19.4) and both identify famous Euboean landmarks that were also very close together, the Capharean rocks and the temple of Poseidon at Geraistos both prayers feature Poseidon's 'hand' (AB 19.11, AB 20.4).[25] The penultimate *lithikon* is apparently imagined as delivered at the site of the rock (perhaps indeed inscribed upon the rock as a talismanic protection for the island at its border with Poseidon's realm),[26] and I do not see any reason why the final poem could not be imagined as delivered at Geraistos itself.

The surprise of the final two poems is not lessened by the fact that one of them is indeed about a *lithos*, though of a rather different kind than all which have preceded. In interpreting this variety we are hampered by our ignorance of the generic expectations which titles such as λιθικά, οἰωνοσκοπικά, and τρόπο would raise in readers of an early collection such as this: how familiar, and how settled in meaning, were such titles? What kind of unity of subject do such titles lead us to expect? Ought we to see the final two poems, or at least the penultimate poem, as a kind of 'generic joke', which relies upon a familiar, but unexamined sense of distinction between types of epigram, or rather as a sign that category boundaries were still far from rigid? The latter explanation is perhaps more likely but a few brief observations about the rest of the collection will, I hope, indicate that the matter may not be straightforward.

The *Oiônoskopika* collect both poems about ominous 'birds' (οἰωνοί) and about omens (οἰωνοί) drawn from other spheres, but it is birds that predominate and open the section (the first four poems), and which therefore establish a 'generic sense' from which the other poems can be seen to deviate. The final two poems, as with the *Lithika*, are on related subjects and also differ from what has gone before being about οἰωνοσκοποί rather than about omens. As the *Lithika* closed with Ptolemy, the *Oiônoskopika* close with Alexander's defeat of the Persians, which was of course, for the Ptolemies a very ideologically charged piece of history. As for the dedicatory *Anathematika*, one might have thought that this type of epigram was so common that it would have been easy enough to fill a section with 'straightforward' poems, but again this proves not so: the first three poems (to Arsinoe) are indeed dedicatory poems of a very common kind, thereby suggesting that we are indeed in familiar territory, but the fourth, though linked to them through the figure of

---

[25] With AB 19.11 cf. *Iliad* XV 694–695 τὸν δὲ (sc. Ἕκτωρα) ὦρσεν (ὧσεν Aristarchus, cf. AB 19.5) ὄπισθεν | χειρὶ μάλα μεγάληι. It may be worth noting that the first *oiônoskopikon*, which follows immediately after the final *lithikon*, is about dangers to shipping, for which this coast of Euboea was notorious, and the second and third also have waves in them.

[26] Cf. Lapini 2002 and Livrea 2003.

Arsinoe, is in fact quite different, being on the subject of the temple and cult of Arsinoe as Aphrodite Euploia. The final two, apparently on a carved wolf and a tortoise shell, both appear to have been indeed dedicatory, but are again quite different from what has preceded. As a whole, the section again forces us to wonder what kind of unity is imposed by the collective title.

Like the *Anathematika*, the *Epitymbia*, if that is the correct title, collect epigrams of a very familiar, indeed perhaps the original 'epigrammatic', type; they are mixed in mode and voice, and a few are barely *Epitymbia* at all (cf. AB 52 on Timon's sundial). The final two poems are again linked: they are the only two that concern men, and both use the theme of a happy death after a fulfilled life which requires no weeping. More striking perhaps is the fact that, although a passerby is addressed at AB 52.3 earlier in the section, only in the final poem do we have the classic 'stop, passerby and look at the tomb of . . .'; this is particularly notable as what is left of the *Tropoi* section suggests that these poems were standardly epitaphic and address to a passerby was there a regular feature. Perhaps, then, the arrangement of the *Epitymbia* suggests an attempt to impose, rather than disrupt, a generic identity at the conclusion; at the very least, it would seem again that category-boundaries were very fluid or that the arranger of our new collection placed a high premium on generic surprise and uncertainty. About the remaining sections there is less to say. The ἀνδριαντοποιϊκά and the ἱππικά have been admirably discussed elsewhere;[27] both sections end with 'Ptolemaic' subjects (Alexander, AB 70, and Ptolemaic chariot-victories, AB 88), but it is noteworthy that the final two ἱππικά are again closely linked in subject and theme. In view of the patterns I have been tracing, it is perhaps important that the final ναυαγικόν clearly signals its affiliation in the opening word, ναυηγόν με κτλ, and that this is the only occurrence of the word in the section; we have already noted how the final *iamatikon* functions closurally,[28] and it is distinguished from the other poems in that section in being a request to Asclepius for 'moderate wealth and health'.

In sum, there is clearly enough variety in the arrangement of the sections to enjoin caution; nevertheless, there are also suggestive indications of play with ideas of 'unity' and 'sameness', and generic wit of this kind fits easily with the early date of the papyrus: some categories are more obvious and more settled than others, but others are being fashioned for the first time, perhaps never to return. The primary position of the *Lithika*, with its remarkable closing poems, alerts us to this aspect of readerly pleasure.

[27] Cf. Gutzwiller 2003, and the essays of Fantuzzi in this collection and in Gutzwiller 2004 (forthcoming).
[28] Cf. above p. 95.

Let me now turn to the penultimate poem itself, the longest *lithikon* for the largest rock, and one of the three fourteen-verse poems on the papyrus.²⁹

μὴ] λόγιcαι με⟨γ⟩άλ⟨η⟩ν τ[αύτη]ν πόcα κύμα[τα λᾶαν
τη]λοῦ μαινομένηc ἐξ[εφόρηc]εν ἁλόc·
τή]νδε Ποcειδάων βρια[ρῶc ἐδ]όνει καὶ ἀπ[οκλάc
ῥίμφ']ί{α} ἐφ' ἑνὸc cκληροῦ κ[ύματο]ς ἐξέβαλεν
ἡμι]πλεθραίην ὥcαc προ[τὶ τ]ἄ[c]τεα πέτρην,
τοῦ Πολυφημείου cκαιοτέρ⟨η⟩ν θυρεοῦ·
οὐκ ἄ⟨ν⟩ μιν Πολύφημοc ἐβάcταcε, cὺν Γαλατείαι
πυκνὰ κολυμβήcαc αἰπολικὸc δύcερωc·
οὐδ' 'Ανταί⟨ου⟩ ὁ γυρὸc ὁλοίτρ⟨ο⟩χοc, ἀλλὰ τριαίνηc
τοῦτο Καφηρείηc τε⟨ι⟩ρα⟨τ⟩οεργὸν ἁλόc·
ἴcχε, Ποcειδᾶον, μεγάλην χέρα καὶ βαρὺ κῦμα
ἐκ πόντου ψιλὴν μὴ φέρ' ἐπ' ἠϊόνα·
τετρακαιεικοcίπηχυν ὅτ' ἐ⟨κ⟩ βυθοῦ ἦραο λᾶαν,
ῥεῖα καταμήcειc εἰν ἁλὶ νῆcον ὅλην.

Do not calculate how many waves carried [this rock] far from the raging sea. Poseidon shook it fiercely and [having broken it off] with one powerful [wave] cast out this rock, [?]-plethra in size, shoving it towards . . ., this rock more wild than the door-stone of Polyphemus. Polyphemus could not have lifted it, the lovesick goatherd who often dived with Galatea; nor does this round boulder (?) belong to Antaeus (??), but this marvel of the sea of Caphareus is the work of the trident. Poseidon, stay your great hand and do not bring a mighty wave from the sea against the defenseless coast; having raised a rock of twenty-four cubits from the deep, easily would you lay waste in the sea a whole island.³⁰

The god's power, in the face of which all we can do is pray, is marked by the difference between the opening of the poem, where we are all but certainly advised not to engage in the proverbially fruitless activity of counting waves,³¹ and its close, where we are told that, with typical divine ease, Poseidon can 'harvest the sea',

---

²⁹ Cf. AB 74, AB 78, BG 2001:130.
³⁰ All translations are by the author.
³¹ Cf. Gow on Theocritus 16.60.

Notes on the Lithika of Posidippus

another proverbial waste of time (at least for mortals).[32] Καταμήσεις, 'you will reap', a verb of complex semantics,[33] suggests that the wave knocks over, and thus covers, everything in its path (cf., e.g., *Homeric Hymn to Apollo* 70–78, Plato *Timaeus* 25d); it is to be seen in counterpoint to ἦραο 'you lifted up'. The huge rock, which stands as testimony to the god's powerful effort (marked by the heavy spondaic opening of AB 19.5), and which twice fills the first half of a hexameter with a single measurement (AB 19.5 and 19.13), is larger than the most famous rock of the *Odyssey*, the Cyclops' door-stone.[34] In AB 19.6 σκαιοτέρην (s.v.l)[35] picks up Nestor's description of the dangerous Cretan coast:[36]

ἀλλ' ὅτε δὴ καὶ κεῖνος ἰὼν ἐπὶ οἴνοπα πόντον
ἐν νηυσὶ γλαφυρῆσι Μαλειάων ὄρος αἰπὺ
ἷξε θέων, τότε δὴ στυγερὴν ὁδὸν εὐρύοπα Ζεὺς
ἐφράσατο, λιγέων δ' ἀνέμων ἐπ' αὐτμένα χεῦε
κύματά τε τροφόεντα πελώρια, ἶσα ὄρεσσιν.
ἔνθα διατμήξας τὰς μὲν Κρήτῃ ἐπέλασσεν,
ἧχι Κύδωνες ἔναιον Ἰαρδάνου ἀμφὶ ῥέεθρα.
ἔστι δέ τις λισσὴ αἰπεῖά τε εἰς ἅλα πέτρη
ἐσχατιῇ Γόρτυνος ἐν ἠεροειδέϊ πόντῳ·
ἔνθα νότος μέγα κῦμα ποτὶ σκαιὸν ῥίον ὠθεῖ,
ἐς Φαιστόν, μικρὸς δὲ λίθος μέγα κῦμ' ἀποέργει.

(*Odyssey* III 285–296)

But when he in turn had launched his ships again on the wine-dark sea
and came in his rapid course to the sheer headland of Maleia, then
thundering Zeus devised a distressing voyage for him, loosing upon him
the violent breath of whistling winds and rearing huge heavy waves that
were mountains high. Then, dividing his company, he brought some
ships to that part of Crete where the Cydonians lived by the waters of

---

[32] Cf. Theognis 105–107 (with van Groningen's note) and certain ancient explanations of ἀτρύγετος, cf. *LfgrE* s.v.

[33] Cf. Jebb and Griffith on Sophocles *Antigone* 601, Petrain 2002. I have considered the possibility that ἀμησάμενος at *Odyssey* IX 247 has been influential here (cf. below).

[34] I remain sceptical that the corrupt opening of AB 19.9 really contained the name of Antaios, another monstrous son of Poseidon, though I have nothing better than the editors' reconstruction to suggest; at the Washington conference D. Obbink attractively suggested οὐδ' Αἰτναῖος ὁ γυρὸς κτλ.

[35] Lapini 2002 proposes σκαιότερον θυρεόν. Petrain 2002 suggests that the unusual word is chosen to allow Polyphemus' uncultured 'gaucheness' to resonate.

[36] Cf. now Bernsdorff 2002:12.

Iardanus. There is a smooth cliff in the misty deep at the verge of the territory of Gortyn; it stands sheer above the sea where the southwest wind drives a great surge towards the western headland, and the narrow rock-face checks the great surge on its way to Phaestus.

Here a 'small rock' offers protection from a 'great wave', and verse 295, ἔνθα Νότος μέγα κῦμα ποτὶ σκαιὸν ῥίον ὠθεῖ, has been broken up by Posidippus and distributed over his poem;[37] σκαιός occurs only here in the *Odyssey*, and the scholia note that opinion was divided as to whether it meant 'western' or 'δεινὸν καὶ ἄγριον', as it plainly does in Posidippus. The echo links two coastlines that brought terrible danger to ships (cf. *Odyssey* III 298–299).

Posidippus appears to have used, perhaps indeed conflated, two distinct elements of Homer's portrayal of the Cyclops. First, of course, there is the massive (ἠλίβατος IX 243, μέγας IX 313, 340) 'door-stone' to which the Euboean rock is directly compared. The Cyclops can 'lift it up high' (ὑψόσ᾽ ἀείρας IX 240, 340 cf. AB 19.13 ἦραο), though 'twenty-two four-wheeled wagons could not have raised it from the ground' (IX 241–242), a description that echoes in τετρακαιεικοσίπηχυν at AB 19.13; Odysseus tells us that he and his men would not have been able ἀπώσασθαι λίθον ὄβριμον (IX 305, cf. AB 19.5]πλεθραίην ὤσας . . . πέτρην), whereas we have seen the Cyclops do this 'easily' (IX 313). The second part of *Odyssey* IX that is relevant here is verses 480ff. in which the blind and enraged monster attacks the departing Greeks: he 'breaks off' (ἀπορρήξας IX 481, cf. ? AB 19.3 ἀπ[. . .) a mountain peak and hurls it (κὰδ δ᾽ ἔβαλε IX 482) *into* the sea (contrast cf. AB 19.4 ἐξέβαλεν); as the rock sinks it causes a great wave (πλημμυρίς IX 486, a standard later term for 'natural' floods and 'tidal waves' such as Poseidon is here asked not to cause) which drives the Greek boat towards the land. In the epigram, one great wave drove the huge boulder *onto* the shore, rather than into the sea. After Odysseus has taunted him and he has learned the truth as to what has happened, Polyphemus *prays to his father Poseidon* (who hears the prayer), and then he 'lifted up a far larger rock' (πολὺ μείζονα λᾶαν ἀείρας IX 537, cf. AB 19.13) and the pattern is repeated, except that this time the wave carries the Greeks to safety. It is clear, then, that there is a complex and sophisticated intertextual relationship between the epigram and *Odyssey* IX. Where Homer shows us the terrible power of Poseidon's son, in Posidippus it is the divine father, now made to resemble his Homeric son, whose 'great hand' is to be feared.[38]

---

[37] For another discussion of a Homeric reworking in the *Lithika*, cf. Bing 2002:4–6.

[38] Cf. Virgil *Aeneid* III 624, *magna manu* of the Cyclops; note too how the Virgilian Cyclops is given terrible earth-shaking powers which resemble those of his father (*Aeneid* III 673–674). For the great

Nothing, however, is as surprising in this poem as the apparent echo[39] of Theocritus' lovesick Cyclops, and specifically of Theocritus *Idyll* 6, βάλλει τοι, Πολύφαμε, τὸ ποίμνιον ἁ Γαλάτεια | μάλοισιν, δυσέρωτα καὶ [Meineke: τὸν codd.] αἰπόλον ἄνδρα καλεῦσα, 'Galatea pelts your flock with apples, Polyphemus, calling you ill-starred in love and a goatherd'; we must ask how the Theocritean Cyclops and the Theocritean text are superimposed upon the Homeric pattern, for we clearly have here a very interesting example of so-called 'window allusion' in which a model text is traced back in turn to its own model.[40] Both *Idylls* 6 and 11 locate the young Cyclops on or near the seashore, and *Idyll* 11 places him 'on a high rock' looking out to sea (11.17–18, cf. Ovid *Metamorphoses* XIII 778–780), a detail which perhaps turned Posidippus' mind to the Cyclops. Be that as it may, though Homer's monster might have been able to lift the Euboean rock, Theocritus' unhappy young Cyclops, 'growing thinner [and hence weaker] day by day' (11.69), could not have done so: the Theocritean rewriting of Homer allows Posidippus both to use the great door-stone of the *Odyssey* and to surpass it, not merely in size, but by identifying a version of the Cyclops who would have found the task beyond him. Unlike Theocritus' Cyclops, however, who could not swim and seemed to regard the sea as a nasty, inhospitable place, Posidippus' Polyphemus 'often went diving with Galatea'. Although the Homeric character is thus brought nearer (in one respect) to his father Poseidon, the reversal of the Theocritean situation is at least very remarkable. The editors note that δύσερως most naturally suggests that Posidippus does not want us to think that Polyphemus and Galatea are a 'happy couple', as they are in a rare, but probably Hellenistic, version of the story.[41] Rather, according to the editors, this Polyphemus appears to have had the courage to go swimming, and Polyphemus is indeed depicted in the water near Galatea in Roman art.[42] Σὺν Γαλατείαι does not, of course, necessitate that Galatea welcomes his presence, but the editors' translation 'dietro a Galatea' reveals the awkwardness they feel. It may be, as R. Thomas has suggested, that we should understand κολυμβήσας conditionally, 'the lovesick Cyclops could not have lifted it from the sea-floor, *even if* he dived frequently with Galatea,' or perhaps the swimming should be seen as taking place

....

hands of marine deities cf. Ap. Rhod. *Arg.* I 1313 στιβαρῆι . . . χειρί (Glaukos) and D. Petrain (priv. comm.) adds *manu magna* at *Aeneid* V 241 of another sea god, Portunus, propelling a ship through the water.

[39] The onus of proof seems to me clearly upon those who would deny allusion to Theocritus here.

[40] Cf., e.g., McKeown 1987:37–45.

[41] Cf. Hunter 1999:242, 244. A number of scholars have observed that the combination of a lovesick Cyclops and the hurling of great rocks might make one think of Ovid's story of Acis and Galatea.

[42] Cf. BG on AB 19.7–8.

solely in the Cyclops' erotic fantasy (cf. Theocr. 11.54–62), but it is clear that αἰπολικὸc δύcερωc identifies this Cyclops as 'Theocritean'; the words are, as it were, in inverted commas to mark citation. By viewing Homer through Theocritus' rewriting, Posidippus can demonstrate that, though he may ransack the text of *Odyssey* IX for ways in which to describe this massive boulder, the events and characters of that book offer no real parallel to the marvel he is describing; what Theocritus has done to the Homeric monster has disarmed his threat. Whatever terrors the Homeric Cyclops held, he has now been 'humanized', reduced (by poetry) to a 'lovesick goatherd'. All that remains is the power of Poseidon: the gap which is thus opened between the text and its model is precisely where meaning lies.

Finally, let me return to the generic question. It may, or may not, be relevant that Homer too marks the distinction between past and present by the ability of the figures of the past to hurl massive rocks which would be way beyond the powers of men 'of the present day' (*Iliad* V 302–304, XII 380–383, 445–9, XX 285–287), but like all Hellenistic poets, Posidippus knew that all things flow from the Homeric source. Just as Homer certainly wrote about bird omens, shipwrecks, and victories in chariot races, so—Posidippus assures us—he also wrote *Lithika*: you just have to know where to look.

9

Elusive Stones: Reading Posidippus' *Lithika* through Technical Writing on Stones

Martyn Smith
Emory University

Posidippus[1] writes with an acute sense of the exceptional. In several places within the *Lithika* section of the new papyrus he highlights the "marvel" or "wonder" resulting from a stone.[2] The stones selected by Posidippus include *sapeiron* (AB 5.1), *beryllion* (AB 6.3), *xanthe* (AB 7.1), *sard* (AB 8.1), *anthrax* (AB 8.5), *margaritis* (AB 11.3), *smaragdos* (AB 12.3), *iaspis* (AB 14.1), *kyanus* (AB 14.4), the snakestone (AB 15.2), *krustallon* (AB 16.1), the touchstone (AB 16.4) and the magnet (AB 17.4). If we had the complete text for the fragmentary sections from the Posidippus papyrus, no doubt this list would grow.[3] The names for these stones are not used ornamentally by Posidippus; rather it is often the case that the nature of the stone, some exceptional quality, is tied directly to the meaning of the epigram.

K. Gutzwiller has pointed out this close tie between the nature of the stone and the epigram in her discussion of the Pegasus epigram (AB 14).[4] Posidippus notes that the craftsman has done well to carve on blue chalcedony the riderless horse disappearing into the blue sky. Posidippus is not simply applying a fanciful adjective to the *iaspis* when he calls it ἠερόεσσαν, 'airy'. Rather, he is making reference to an actual variety of the gem which was recognized by technical writers on stones (cf. Pliny XXXVII 115). When Posidippus praises the craftsman for carving well according to hand and mind he is pointing out the skill of the craftsman not only

---

[1] Throughout this chapter I refer to Posidippus as the author for the sake of convenience. Also for convenience I use AB numeration, while retaining the BG text.

[2] Cf. AB 8.7; AB 13.2; AB 15.7; AB 17.5; AB 19.10.

[3] Four fragmentary sections seem especially to demand the name of a stone: AB 1; AB 2; AB 4; AB 10.

[4] Gutzwiller 1995:383–398.

in depicting the horse, but also in selecting a singularly fitting stone for his subject, one that mimics the air into which the real Pegasus flew.

This careful use of stones and their qualities connects Posidippus to technical writers on stones, who were drawn to the same unique characteristics. Theophrastus was one of the earliest of these technical writers, and certainly the earliest writer whose work on this topic has survived largely intact.[5] In his *On Stones*, he is concerned with stones that are rare or have some special quality:

εἰσὶ δὲ πλείους καὶ ἄλλαι κατὰ ταύτας ⟨διαφοραί⟩. αἱ μὲν οὖν κατὰ τὰ χρώματα καὶ τὰς σκληρότητας καὶ μαλακότητας καὶ λειότητας καὶ τἆλλα τὰ τοιαῦτα, δι' ὧν τὸ περιττόν.

Numerous stones, then, posess characteristic differences in respect of colour, hardness, softness, smoothness, and other such qualities which cause them to be exceptional (δι' ὧν τὸ περιττόν).[6]

Nearly all of the stones mentioned by Posidippus are also treated by Theophrastus, the exceptions being the snakestone (AB 15), the conjectural reading of *Beryllion* (AB 6.3), and of course the great boulder used at the end to praise the power of Poseidon (AB 19).

This coincidence of material leads me to question the nature of the relationship between the epigrams found in the *Lithika* and the technical writing of authors such as Theophrastus and Pliny. We have already seen how Posidippus could use a technical name for a variety of stone, but there are other more subtle uses of technical writings hidden in the *Lithika*. At AB 8.5 Posidippus implies that the gem *anthrax* has an especially brilliant glow. When Theophrastus turns to this gem he mentions this same characteristic:

ἐρυθρὸν μὲν τῷ χρώματι, πρὸς δὲ τὸν ἥλιον τιθέμενον ἄνθρακος καιομένου ποιεῖ χρόαν.

It is of a red hue and when placed towards the sun produces the color of live charcoal.

(III 18)

From parallels such as this it is clear that Posidippus is relying to some degree on technical writing. One or two instances of such technical correctness could be explained by personal experience or hearsay, but for the whole we need to posit the presence of technical sources from which Posidippus could mine his details about stones and their exceptional properties.

---

[5] For an overview of ancient studies in mineralogy, see Halleaux and Schamp 1985:XIII–XXXIV.

[6] Theophrastus *On Stones* I 6; text and translation by Eichholz 1965:6.

There are two works which are by far the best witnesses to ancient technical writing on stones. First is the *On Stones* by Theophrastus, already mentioned above. The second is book XXXVII of the *Natural History* by Pliny. These books stand as bookends for a long history of technical writing on stones.[7] Theophrastus stands toward the beginning of technical writing on stones, and Pliny is the later inheritor of the knowledge collected by many writers (he lists 40 sources in his introduction to the *Natural History*, including Theophrastus). *On Stones* is important because its probable date of composition around 314–15 BCE[8] means that Posidippus could reasonably be expected to have known this work, and thus any parallels with it have an assured value. Pliny's work, although much later than Posidippus, is also essential to our reading of Posidippus because of his frequent use of older sources. Pliny often preserves information not present in Theophrastus, but which could well have an early source or reflect much earlier knowledge.

The *On Stones* is also important since it gives a realistic view of the range and scope of works on stones available in the time of Posidippus. Pliny's work by its very encyclopedism obscures the humbler size of the *On Stones*. Pliny mentions upward of two hundred stones, and when Posidippus is approached from this vantage point he appears to have chosen merely a random sprinkling of possible stones. Theophrastus' *On Stones*, on the other hand, mentions perhaps two dozen stones.[9] When considered alongside this smaller work on stones the *Lithika* section takes on a more programmatic appearance, as if Posidippus were attempting to cover most of the important stones by mentioning them at least once.

In order to clarify the relationship between Posidippus and technical writings such as we possess by Theophrastus and Pliny, I will examine four of the epigrams in the *Lithika* section, noting the intersections between the epigrams and technical writing. The goal of the readings will be not only to find these references, but further to note how this technical information allows us to update or deepen our interpretation of the epigram. We begin with the first epigram in the collection that is reasonably complete (AB 5):

Τιμάνθης ἔγλυψε τὸν ἀστερόεντα σάπειρον
τόνδε χρυσίτην Περσικὸν ἡμίλιθον
Δημύλωι· ἀνθ᾽ ἁπαλοῦ δὲ φιλήματος ἡ κυανόθριξ
δῶρον Ν̣[ι]καίη Κῶια ἔδ̣[εκτ᾽ ἐρατόν.

---

[7] Compare Wellmann 1935.

[8] The date is based on the argument worked out by Eichholz 1965:8–11.

[9] An exact count depends on whether sub-classes are counted or not, i.e. whether one counts the "male" and "female" varieties of *kyanus* as separate stones.

> Timanthes carved the starry sapeiros,
> This gold-dusted Persian semi-stone,
> For Demulos. In return for a gentle kiss, the dark-haired
> Coan Nikaie received it as a lovely gift.

Theophrastus gives a slightly different spelling for this stone (which we know as lapis lazuli), but any doubt as to whether he refers to the same stone is allayed by the brief description: '[it] is speckled with gold' (αὕτη δ᾽ ἐστιν ὥσπερ χρυσόσπαστος) (IV 23). In a later mention of the stone Theophrastus adds that the stone is 'dark' (μέλαινα (VI 37). It is also (IV 23) classed among 'stones, on which signets are carved' (ἐξ ὧν καὶ τὰ σφραγίδια γλύφουσιν).

Theophrastus has not provided a lot of information, but it is striking that Posidippus has encapsulated all the information contained in Theophrastus within this brief epigram. The *sapeiros* is correctly portrayed as a stone that is carved. His adjective ἀϲτερόεντα, 'starred', incorporates the sprinkled look of the stone, as well as implying the stone's relative darkness by calling to mind the nighttime ground of the stars. The second line gives us the adjective χρυϲίτην, 'gold-containing', which completes our picture of the stone since we now understand that the stone is not simply starred, perhaps with white stars like the nighttime sky, but is golden-speckled. The adjective Περϲικὸν adds a further touch of the exotic to the stone, going along with the evocation of nighttime and gold. This is not a piece of information present in Theophrastus, but lest we imagine that Posidippus has arbitrarily decided that Persia suits his poetic interests, Pliny assures us that Persia is indeed the best site for *sapeiros*: "The best are in Persia" (XXXVII 120).[10]

We encounter in the epigram about the *sapeiros* a re-fashioning of scientific description into an evocation of a beautiful object. Its equation of the gift of a stone with a tender kiss imbues the stone with all the emotional warmth of that exchanged kiss. The stone is on its way to becoming what Pliny, at the beginning of his book on stones, professes that some people find in stones: ". . . for many people a single gemstone is sufficient for a high and perfect contemplation of the things of nature" (XXXVII 1).[11] That is, the stone is no longer a point of scientific interest, but rather a matter of aesthetic, even passionate, experience.

In highlighting the process of exchange, this short epigram becomes a useful entrance to the poetic project of Posidippus. In the *Lithika*, but also notably in the *Oiônoskopika* section, Posidippus is taking over knowledge whose natural domain might be thought to rest in didactic poetry or scientific treatises. But the manifest

---

[10] *Caeruleae perlucidae et sappiri, rarumque ut cum purpura. optimae apud Medos, nusquam tamen perlucida.* My text for Pliny throughout this chapter is drawn from Eichholz 1971.

[11] *ut plerisque ad summam absolutamque naturae rerum contemplationem satis sit una aliqua gemma.*

lack of scientific system, and the presence of the long epigram on a great boulder (AB 19), betray the fact that Posidippus did not intend to write a poetic textbook on gems in a way parallel to Aratus' poetic translation of a textbook on constellations and weather signs. Rather, in the same way that the stone is worked by a craftsman and transformed into an object exchanged for a kiss, the technical writing of a scientific philosopher such as Theophrastus is skillfully re-worked until it becomes a work that gives aesthetic pleasure.

Because the *Lithika* often relies on technical sources, the more knowledge a reader has of those sources, the more pleasure can be derived from the short epigrams. In trying to demonstrate this I will now consider two epigrams in which the meaning may be dependent on a correct understanding of the stone at hand, as it is represented in technical writing on stones. The first is an epigram that has already drawn some attention (AB 7).[12]

ἐξ Ἀράβων τὰ ξάνθ᾽{α} ὀ[ρέων κατέρ]υτα κυλίων,
εἰς ἅλα χειμάρρους ὣκ᾽ [ἐφόρει ποτα]μός
τὸν μέλιτι χροιὴν λίθ[ον εἴκελον, ὅ]ν̣ Κρονίο[υ] χείρ
ἔγλυψε· χρυσῶι σφι⟨γ⟩κτ̣[ὸς ὅδε γλυκερ]ῇι
Νικονόηι᾽ κάθεμα τρη[τὸν φλέγει, ἥ]ς ἐπὶ μαστῶι
συ⟨λ⟩λάμπει λευκῶι χρωτὶ μελιχρὰ φάη.

Out of the Arabian mountains rolling the fallen yellow stones,
    the storm-rushing river brought swiftly to the sea
the stone, honey-like, which the hand of Cronius
    carved. This stone, bound with gold for delicate Niconoe,
flames as an inlaid necklace, as on her breast
    its honey-sweet light shines along with her white skin.

Again we find in this epigram a noteworthy technical correctness. To begin with, *xanthe* (ξανθή) is a precious stone mentioned by Theophrastus (VI 37).[13] I argue that the use of the neuter plural adjective in this epigram, *ta xantha* (τὰ ξάνθα), results from his evocation of the unvariegated yellow detritus, the end result of which will be the precious stone *xanthe*. Posidippus has gotten the general source of this stone correct. In Theophrastus, *xanthe* is mentioned among a group of precious stones which are 'rare and come from only a few places' (οἱ περιττοὶ σπάνιοι καὶ ἐξ ὀλίγων τόπων). No locale is connected to *xanthe* by

---

[12] Cf. Bing 2002a.
[13] Eichholz 1965:114, tentatively identifies this as yellow jasper or brown hematite.

Theophrastus, but an exotic and foreign place, such as Arabia, would be expected. Perhaps contemporary accounts of the Ptolemaic exploitation of gem resources in Arabia[14] provided the means by which Posidippus learned of this specific source. Finally, Cronius is no fictional craftsman, but an historical figure whom Pliny mentions as one of the great engravers of the Hellenistic period (XXXVII 8). The use of a well-known gem carver such as Cronius here and elsewhere in the *Lithika* (cf. AB 2.2 and possibly AB 6.2) adds a link to the real world that increases the expectation of technical accuracy in the epigram, and this also looks forward to the multiple references to important sculptors in the section *Andriantopoiika*.

Posidippus goes further than mere correctness in this epigram, he may also be interested in critiquing an earlier opinion on the stone *xanthe*. In a short note Theophrastus takes issue with the color of *xanthe*, writing that it is 'not so much yellow in color as whitish' [or 'off white'] (οὐ ξανθὴ μὲν τὴν χρόαν, ἔκλευκος μᾶλλον) (VI 37). He buttresses this with an explanation that the word *xanthos* means 'whitish' for speakers of Doric Greek, not yellow.

When we turn back to the epigram we notice that color gets emphasized to an unusual degree. Both the third and sixth lines describe the stone as 'honey-colored', as if he could not quite trust the word *xantha* to stand by itself for the color. Then perhaps to prove his point, he sets the stone on the truly white skin of Niconoe's breast. Given this beautifully white background, the yellowness of the stone stands out vividly in the reader's imagination, and the doubts of the scholar who might remember the description of Theophrastus are banished.

The next epigram is unique among its neighbors in that it obstinately refuses to name its described stone (AB 13).[15]

κ̣[ερδα]λ̣έη λίθος ἥδε· λιπα[ινομένη]ς̣ γε μὲν α̣ὐτῆς,
   [φέγγο]ς̣ ὅλους ὄγκους θαῦ[μ᾽ ἀπάτη]ς̣ περιθεῖ·
ὄ̣[γκων] δ᾽ ἀ̣ς̣κελέων, ὠκὺ γ[λυπτὸς λ]ὶ̣ς ὁ Πέρςης
   [τε]ί̣νων ἀςτράπτει πρὸς καλόν ἡέλιον.

This is a crafty stone. First, when it is rubbed with oil,
   a light runs around the entire mass, marvel of illusion.
Then, when the mass is dry, a carved Persian lion
   flashes sharply, stretching to the beautiful sun.

---

[14] Nenna 1998:156–61.

[15] Line 3 of this epigram has a significant gap, and the reading supplied by the editors is highly conjectural. What is missing is the noun that accompanies the adjective 'Persian'. One might want to supply the word *smaragdos* here, which would be attractive since 'Persian' is a variety of the *smaragdos* that is

Although the number of conjectures in this epigram is quite large, it is clear that Posidippus is contrasting two states, first oiled or wet, then dry, and two different ways that light responds to this stone.

The terse opening to this epigram, "This is a crafty stone", calls attention to the fact that this is a specific kind of stone, and further, it highlights the author's crafty silence as to its identity. This riddling quality in the epigram provides an example of what Bing has called *Ergänzungsspiel*, referring to the kind of play and literary association required from the reader in order to arrive at an understanding of a poem.[16] In this case the epigram pointedly does not provide all the necessary information, but rather the reader must supplement the information from other sources if any answer to this riddle is to be located.

I would like to suggest that the stone *smaragdos*, a name for a class of green precious stones, is a possible solution to this riddle epigram. Theophrastus twice singles out a remarkable power: its ability to lend its color to a body of water that surrounds it.

The *smaragdos*, on the other hand, possesses also certain powers (δυνάμεις τινάς). For, as we have mentioned, it imparts its color to water (τοῦ τε γὰρ ὕδατος . . . ἐξομοιοῦται τὴν χρόαν ἑαυτῇ).

(IV 23)

This optical power is remarkable enough to Theophrastus that he mentions the stone in company with both the magnet and the touchstone,[17] i.e. it is a stone with an actual power, not just an optical quality.

When Pliny writes about the stone he also lingers over the unique optical power of the *smaragdos*, though applying the effect to the air rather than to water:

praeterea longinquo amplificantur visu inficientes circa se repercussum aëra.

Besides this, being viewed from a distance [the *smaragdi*] appear larger because they color the air which has rebounded around them.

(XXXVII 63)

The mechanism may be suspect, but his meaning is quite clear: the air that bounces up against the stone is colored, and thus when viewed from a distance the stone naturally looks larger.

---

mentioned by Pliny (cf. XXXVII 69). But the trace of a "Γ" at the beginning of the gap precludes that option, and makes something like what the editors arrived at the most likely reading.

[16] Bing 1995:115–131.

[17] *On Stones* I 4.

The second quality that Pliny describes is its power of blazing. He tells an odd story about the statue of a lion, set up next to a tunny-fishery, which had eyes fitted with *smaragdos* from Cyprus.[18] The eyes of this lion flashed so brightly into the depths of the sea that the tunny-fish fled the vicinity, to the obvious consternation of the fishermen (XXXVII 66).[19] One could add this to Pliny's discussion of the Persian variety of the *smaragdos*. He writes, citing Democritus as his source (likely a work falsely attributed to him):

> . . . felium pantherarumque oculis similes, namque et illos radiare nec perspici, eosdem in sole hebetari, in umbra refulgere et longius quam ceteros nitere.

He compares them to the eyes of cats and leopards, which likewise shine without being transparent, and mentions, moreover, that the stones are dimmed in sunlight, glisten in shadow and shine farther than other stones.

(XXXVII 69)

Oddly, the eyes of cats, real or statue, figure in both of these examples from Pliny, and it is interesting that in the editorial restoration of line 31 we find a lion.

It thus seems plausible to understand this short epigram as a reference to the stone *smaragdos*. The optical quality of light literally 'running around' (περιθεῖ) the mass, as described by Posidippus, seems closely connected to the optical effect of the stone in both Theophrastus and Pliny. And the second quality of blazing solves nicely the last two lines of the epigram. And these dual optical effects seem sufficient to earn for a stone the title 'crafty' (κερδαλέη).

Perhaps in order to give the reader another hint to the answer of this riddle, Posidippus, or whoever compiled our poems, sandwiched this epigram between two suggestive epigrams. In the previous epigram we can make out the word *smaragdos* and the first line of the following epigram mentions the stone *iaspis*, which Theophrastus tells us is closely related to the *smaragdos*.[20] This may seem a quite bookish hint, but if it is correct to see Posidippus as working with and commenting on technical writings, then these are the kinds of hints to which we must become sensitive.

In conclusion we will look at the epigram on the snakestone, one of the two previously known epigrams attributed to Posidippus that turned up in the new papyrus. In his commentary on this epigram Gow called it "undistinguished" and

---

[18] Cyprus happens to also be the place that Theophrastus knows as the origin of the stone (VI 36).

[19] *oculos et smaragdis ita radiantibus etiam in gurgitem ut territi thynni refugerent . . .*

[20] "It is stated that in Cyprus a stone was once found one half of which was *smaragdus* and the other half an *iaspis*, as though the transformation of the stone from water were not yet complete" (IV 27).

ɔubted its authenticity.[21] By considering once again the possibility that Posidippus working from technical sources, we may be able to set this epigram in a more ɔsitive light.

Unlike the other stones mentioned above, the snakestone does not correspond ɔ an actual stone. Pliny starts off with a general account of the supposed origin of .is stone:

> Draconitis . . . e cerebro fit draconum, sed nisi viventibus absciso capite non gemmescit invidia animalis mori se sentientis, igitur dormientibus amputant.

> The "draconitis" (snakestone) . . . is obtained from the brains of snakes, but unless the head is cut off from a live snake, the substance fails to turn into a gem, owing to the spite of the creature as it perceives that it is doomed. Consequently the beast's head is lopped off while it is asleep.

> (XXXVII 158)

As Gow dryly noted, "Stones in the heads of snakes however are like jewels in e heads of toads; they do not exist."[22] The question for us is what to make of this ɔn-existence: is this an actual class of stones recognized at the time but to which false origin had been ascribed, or did the snakestone never exist except in the ɔrld of technical writing on stones?[23]

Having described briefly the origin of the snakestone, Pliny defers to an earlier urce in order to give us more details about the stone. By so doing he preserves the count of Sotacus, one of the earliest writers on stones, and one whose work could ɪve been known by Posidippus.[24]

> Sotacus, quo visam eam gemmam sibi apud regem scripsit, bigis vehi quaerentes tradit et viso dracone spargere somni medicamenta atque ita sopiti praecidere. esse candore tralucido, nec postea poliri aut artem admittere.

Gow 1954:197.

* Gow 1954:198.

ɔ An example of this separate book existence can be glimpsed in the case of the *lyngurium*, literally: "lynx-urine." Theophrastus, on the authority of a Diocles, maintains that this stone has its origin as the buried urine of a lynx (V 28). Later Pliny, having quoted Theophrastus, was ready to dismiss this stone as simply a legend: "I for my part am of the opinion that the whole story is false and that no gemstone bearing this name has been seen in our time" (XXXVII 53). The stone lived only in texts, and Pliny recognized this and was ready to banish it.

* Sotacus was a Greek writer whom Pliny calls one of the very oldest of his sources (XXXVI 146). His date may be as early as the beginning of the third century BCE (as estimated by Eichholz 1965:7). See also Kind 1927:1211.

Sotacus, who writes that he saw such a gem in the possession of a king, states that those who go in search of it ride in two-horsed chariots, and that when they see the snake they scatter sleeping-drugs and so put it to sleep before they cut off its head. According to him, the stone is glossily-white and transparent, and cannot be polished or submitted to any other skilful process.

(XXXVI 158)

This account of the snakestone, the earliest we know about, we can no[compare with the epigram by Posidippus (AB 15):

οὐ ποταμϳὸς κελάδων ἐπι χείλεϲιν, αλλὰ δράκοντος
εἶχέ ποτ᾽ εὐπώγων τόνδε λίθον κεφαλῇ
πυκνὰ φαληριόωντα· τὸ δὲ γλυφὲν ἅρμα κατ᾽ αὐτ[ο]ῦ
τοῦθ᾽ ὑπὸ Λυγκείου ⟨βλέ⟩μματος ἐγλύφετο
ψεύδεϊ χ⟨ειρ⟩ὸς ὅμοιον· ἀποπλασθὲν γὰρ ὁρᾶται
ἅρμα, κατὰ πλάτεος δ᾽ οὐκ ἄν ἴδοις προβόλους·
ἧι καὶ θαῦμα πέλει μόχθου μέγα, πῶϲ ὁ λιθουργός
τὰϲ] ἀτενιζούϲαϲ οὐκ ἐμόγηϲε κόραϲ.

No river rolled this stone onto its banks, but at one time
the well-bearded head of a snake held it,
streaked with white. The chariot engraved upon it,
resembling a white mark on a nail,[25] was carved
by Lynceian eyes. For after an imprint is taken
the chariot is seen, but on the surface you do not see any projections.
In which fact resides a great marvel of labor,
how the craftsman while straining did not damage his eyes.

We should imagine a stone smaller than the head of a snake, streaked wi[white, and with one streak containing an engraved chariot which is impossible [see with the naked eye but which shows up clearly when an imprint is taken.

It is immediately apparent that there are a couple of similarities between t[poetic account given by Posidippus and Sotacus. Most notable is the presence o[

---

[25] These three words (ψεύδεϊ χ⟨ειρ⟩ὸς ὅμοιον) have been variously translated. Gow argues stron[for the reading that I have adopted, which makes these three words refer to blemishes on fingern[(Gow 1954:198, and GP:500–501). This reading has been accepted by recent commentat[(Fernandez-Galiano 1987:128).

chariot in both accounts. Noting this similarity, K. Gutzwiller writes: "In all likelihood, then, the tiny chariot carved on the gem provided a reference to the difficult process by which the gem had been ostensibly obtained."[26] A second similarity is in the color, or colorlessness, that is attributed to the snakestone. Posidippus writes, using a couple of rare and poetic words, that the snakestone has white streaks and that it resembles to some extent the nail of a hand. This description is comparable to Pliny's note that Sotacus described the stone as *candore tralucido*, 'transparent glistening-white'. The idea of whiteness is present in both, and by the allusion to a fingernail, a degree of transparency is also introduced by Posidippus. Pliny gives us no hint that Sotacus mentioned any streaks or marks on the stone, but these do not contradict the brief description by Sotacus, and can be read as an elaboration of that description by Posidippus. As we saw with the epigram on the *sapeiros*, Posidippus often uses technical sources and re-states their flat descriptions in a more poetic manner. The epigram on the snakestone appears to be another case of this re-statement, as Posidippus has taken the same basic elements and made them more vivid.

One major difference stands out between these two earliest accounts of the snakestone: its ability or inability to be carved. Sotacus is quite clear on the matter, writing that the stone "cannot be polished or submitted to any other skilful process." This directly contradicts the insistence by Posidippus that the stone is carved. Gow explains this by assuming that since this is not a real stone, but simply a name ascribed to some group of stones that have a similar size and color, Posidippus must know of a variety that was "evidently not too hard to work."[27] But this explanation assumes that Posidippus was working from an actual precious gem, instead of relying, in a more bookish fashion, on a technical source.

Since we have already had cause to note the accuracy of Posidippus when it comes to his descriptions of stones, we should be cautious in asserting a contradiction between Posidippus and his sources. The Byzantine writer Tzetzes read this epigram differently and calls snakestones αὐτόγλυφοι ('self-carved') and then supposed that on this particular snakestone a chariot had been engraved on its own, or naturally (ὧν ἐν ἑνὶ καὶ ἅρμα ἐγγεγλυμμένον κατιδεῖν αὐτοφυῶς . . . .).[28] The idea of an elaborate design such as a chariot being self-carved or naturally appearing may seem fantastic to the modern reader, but this is simply another exceptional feature that a stone may have. Toward the beginning of his book on stones, Pliny mentions an agate upon which could be seen the nine Muses with Apollo holding the lyre. He goes on to explain the origin of this complex design:

---

[26] Gutzwiller 1995:388.

[27] Gow 1954:198. Fernandez-Galiano 1987:127 writes similarly "Segun Sotaco en Plinio . . . la piedra no podia ser tallada, pero evidentemente Posidipo pensaba lo contrario . . ."

[28] GP:2.500.

"This was due not to any artistic intention, but to nature un-aided [*non arte, sed naturae sponte*]; and the markings spread [*discurrentibus maculis*] in such a way that even the individual Muses had their appropriate emblems allotted them" (XXXVII 5). This famous stone was reported by Pliny to be a possession of Pyrrhus who lived only slightly before Posidippus (319–272 BCE). A stone that contains a natural carving would fit nicely into this category of wonder, a category which we know existed during the time of Posidippus.

The internal references to the eyesight of a stoneworker are compatible with this reading. There are two references to the eyesight necessary for this kind of carving: line 4 with the reference to the incredible vision of the Argonaut Lynceus, and lines 6–7 with the note that it is a 'wonder' (θαῦμα) that the stoneworker did not damage his eyes by such minute attention. The reader encounters the stone through the eyes of the narrator, and follows the narrator's reasoning about the necessity of superhuman eyesight and miraculous craft in order to make such a carving. But the reader may well begin to wonder about the conclusions drawn by the narrator, since the conclusions seem to point to a level of skill that is impossible for a human being. One begins to question the reliability of the narrator since this stoneworker is too skilled, the vision required is too great, for an actual stoneworker to have carved the invisible chariot upon the streak of white. Then if the reader recalls the note by Sotacus that this is a stone which cannot be carved, the true nature of this stone appears: it is a natural wonder, a self-carved stone. The hidden riddle mirrors the hidden carving present on the snakestone.

It is also possible to read this in a different way. One could argue that this is another case of Posidippus subtly correcting his source, either by the use of information gained from some other technical source, or by personal knowledge of some stone that was purported to be a snakestone. Posidippus, on this reading, affirms the basic facts about the origin and color of the snakestone as presented by Sotacus but then differs by presenting a case where the snakestone has been successfully carved. As with the *Xanthe* discussed earlier, the point is to be aware of Posidippus' subtle correcting of his sources.

By my reading, which Tzetzes also stumbled upon, the poem becomes another case of a riddle within the *Lithika*. The challenge for the reader is to perceive rightly the actual nature of this marvel. In this light an "undistinguished" epigram may become elusive and brilliant. This makes the snakestone epigram similar to the epigram on *smaragdos*, in that they both demand playful work on the part of the reader if they are to be understood. And this demand for work on the part of the reader is a trait of Hellenistic poetry. Bing notes: ". . . the authors of the age ask their readers to supply a great deal. They are expected to recognize, and bring to the text an understanding, not just of literary allusions . . . but of those to history, geography, medicine, religion, etc."[29]

The snakestone contains a design invisible to the eye glancing upon it, a design that appears only after an imprint is taken. It is a picture of the process that a reader must go through in understanding these epigrams: there is a brilliance invisible at first, but which becomes visible as soon as one is willing to delve into its more elusive aspects.

[29] Bing 1995:131.

10

A Garland of Stones: Hellenistic *Lithika* as Reflections on Poetic Transformation

David Schur
Miami University, Ohio

Drawing inspiration from the importance of floral metaphors for poetry in the Western literary tradition and in our conception of the Hellenistic epigram tradition particularly, I think it would be worthwhile to consider the relationship between stones and poetry; more specifically, the conceit that likens stones or gemstones to poems.[1] What I wish to suggest is that the lithic poems collected in the Milan papyrus (AB 1–20) illuminate the self-presentation of literary epigram. Since we are here dealing with a form of poetry that presumably began as, and continued to emulate, epigraphy, stone is not a neutral topic when addressed in the epigram form.[2]

The poems, possibly by Posidippus,[3] tend to describe stones that have been transformed. These stones are not so much inherently precious as artistically or geographically distanced from their sources. As K. Gutzwiller has remarked: "The epigram placed in a book, whatever its intended purpose at the time of composition, gives meaning to its referents through exemplification: its subjects become types, presented, *gemlike*, through brief but specific details" (my emphasis).[4]

---

[1] On lapidary lore in antiquity, see Gutzwiller 1995:383, especially n1.

[2] Hence the valence in, e.g., funerary epigrams of "this stone". Cf. Bing 1995; Bing 1998:21–43; Gutzwiller 1998:47–114; Rossi 2001:3–13; Bing (this volume).

[3] The fact that no authorship is indicated in the surviving portions of the papyrus led a few scholars to initially dispute the attribution of the entire collection to Posidippus. The most notable objections were voiced by H. Lloyd-Jones in 2002 at the APA annual meeting in Philadelphia. Significantly, in his first publication on the Milan papyrus Lloyd-Jones seems to avoid reference to Posidippus. See Lloyd-Jones 2001. However, he appears to have changed his mind. See Lloyd-Jones 2002. Scholarly consensus seems to move decidedly towards the attribution of all epigrams to Posidippus. Cf. the proceedings of the Florence conference in 2002, in particular Fantuzzi's stichometric analysis (pp. 79–97). See also Sider (this volume).

[4] Gutzwiller 1998:8.

Gemlike in this sense of particularity, the stones themselves are travelers, and the distance traveled may remind us that just as a stone can be made into a gem through human artifice, so too can a lithic inscription become a literary epigram. It is a journey of transformation, which P. Bing has called "the journey from physical source to cultural application," that takes inert material far from its presumed source.[5] Since this is largely a question of context and reception, let us pause for a sweeping consideration of the *topoi* or conventional conceits involved. An anthology is understood etymologically as a collection of flowers, along the lines of Meleager's *Garland* and through association with garlands worn during *symposia*.[6] Though by no means the first to associate poetry with flowers, Meleager even refers to "newly-written shoots" (ἔρνεα . . . νεόγραφα, 1.55 GP), thus giving the conceit a sense rather close to that of the German word *Blatt*, meaning both leaf and page. In such a phrase, plant material and written form become inextricable; whereas a typical simile might make an explicit association between two separate images, and a metaphor might substitute one for the other, here the vehicle (plant) and tenor (writing) are combined in a hybrid form. Meleager's written shoots exemplify a poetics of transformation. Interestingly this concept is already found in another epigram by Posidippus (6.3 GP = *AP* XII 98) in which he describes his intellectual labors with books in these terms (ἐν βύβλοις πεπονημένη, which was incidentally translated into the title of this volume).[7]

Historically, the weaving of poetic garlands or wreaths has been reinforced by an etymological connection between texts and textiles. And the commonplace of poetic vegetation has persisted in famous examples such as Sa'adi's *Gülistan*, or *Rose Garden* (1258), the German selection of poetry entitled *Venusgärtlein* (1656), Frances Lincoln's *A Garden of Greek Verse*, Baudelaire's *Flowers of Evil*, *A Child's Garden of Verses* by Robert Louis Stevenson, and Whitman's *Leaves of Grass*. The string of poetic stones has been a somewhat less popular convention, though it hardly seems unfamiliar. Perhaps the early ancient anthology that is attributed to Posidippus by ancient and modern authors, called the "heap" (Σωρός), was conceived as a pile of quarried poems.[8] More recent parallels include the

---

[5] Bing 2002a:4. Cf. discussion *infra* of epigram AB 7 which describes the journey of a gem from the Arabian mountains to the sea, finally resting on the neck of a woman.
[6] Gutzwiller 1998:227–322.
[7] Gutzwiller 1998:160–161. Philip also equates the making of an anthology to harvesting the grain of a new page. Cf. *AP* IV 2.3 = L3 GP *Garland*.
[8] Gutzwiller 1998:18–19, 155–157, 169–170. Reitzenstein (1893) assumed the *Soros* to be an anthology of epigrams by Asclepiades, Posidippus, and possibly Hedylus as well. Gutzwiller is probably right to attribute it to a single author, namely Posidippus.

Renaissance crown of (jewel-like?) sonnets, the Romantic association of stone ruins with literary fragments, and the Symbolist poets' search for crystalline perfection in their writings.[9] Just as telling are cases where stones and flowers are conflated. Thus a 1913 translation of the *Greek Anthology* is entitled *Ancient Gems in Modern Settings*. And on a lighter (or heavier) note, we have the Rolling Stones' song "Ruby Tuesday" appearing first on the album called *Flowers*, and later anthologized in a collection of hits called *Hot Rocks*. These examples may simply serve to show how aptly the title *Lithika*—a title standing, if it is there at all, at the head of the entire Milan papyrus as we have it—fits a gathering of poems when the *topos* is seen through a modern lens largely forged in ancient times.[10]

Now to the poems themselves. If stone is indeed conceived as *the* fundamental material for epigram, then it is extraordinarily suited to represent the epigram form. The *Lithika* are essentially presented as inscriptions about inscriptions, when inscription is understood broadly in terms of carving, engraving, and marking. This is one crucial significance of verbs that characterize the stoneworker's craft. "As art contemplating art," writes P. Bing, "they invite a self-reflexive interpretation."[11] The conceit of stones as poems, carried into new contexts, literalizes the linguistic parallel between the word "metaphor" itself and its Latin counterparts "translation" and "transformation". I am not suggesting that this view is consciously adopted in the *Lithika*; instead, I would argue that very early in the history of epigram composition, conceptual connections had already begun fueling certain underlying rhetorical conventions or generic self-representations.

In general, the attribution of specific carvings to named artisans raises questions of creation and authorship. We might envisage a series of transformations, compositions moving from improvised speech to carvings in monuments, then to engraving in smaller stones, then perhaps to written tags anchored to stones, and finally to poems on papyrus.[12] Each step takes us further away from the presumed source or original context, leaving us in possession of literary texts that are less seemingly anonymous and less strictly referential than would previously have been

---

[9] This romantic notion of the quest for perfection in a miniature literary world is further found in Jane Austen who described her novels as "the little bit (two inches wide) of ivory on which [she works] with so fine a brush, as produces little effect after much labour" (*Letter to James Edward Austen*, 16–17 December 1816). Related to this assessment of her work is her other reference to her *Pride and Prejudice* as "too light, and bright, and sparkling" (*Letter to Cassandra Austen*, 4 February 1813).

[10] On the important observation that *Lithika* may have been the possible title of the entire collection preserved on the Milan papyrus, see also Bing 2002a and Hunter (this volume).

[11] Bing 2002a:2.

[12] Evidence for the actual association of tags with small objects that served as votives is provided by inventory lists from the Classical and Hellenistic periods associated with the Athenian Acropolis and Asclepion, as well as with various Delian temples. Cf. Tod 1954:1–8; Harris 1995:23–24.

erceived. The deliberate creation of such distance in epigram allows for what
Bing has called *Ergänzungsspiel*.[13]
We may identify several types of transformational distance in the new
pigrams. One is geographical, as in the poem that traces a stone's journey from
rabian mountains to a woman's breast (AB 7). A more personal change of location
s seen in the theme of exchange, exemplified by stones changing hands as gifts
AB 4, AB 5). The poem about a stone with unusual, dual magnetic qualities
AB 17) touches on the theme of attraction and repulsion, another kind of give and
ake that echoes throughout the *Lithika* section in verbs such as ἕλκω ('to drag'),
ορέω ('to carry'), κυλίω ('to roll'). We can understand this as a tension between
istancing and attraction. Stones are repelled—dragged, carried, and rolled
bout—yet they can be attractive and valuable. In fact, distance makes them more
aluable (compare AB 16.6). And in the case of gemstones, carving itself is a kind
f *translatio*. We should not ignore the overt associations between carving,
iscribing, and writing that unfold in the poetic glyptic and graphic handling of
:ones.

With these observations in mind, I shall conclude by reading the following
pigram (AB 5):

Τιμάνθης ἔγλυψε τὸν ἀστερόεντα σάπειρον
τόνδε χρυσίτην Περσικὸν ἡμίλιθον
Δημύλωι· ἀνθ᾽ ἁπαλοῦ δὲ φιλήματος ἡ κυανόθριξ
δῶρον Νικαίη Κῶια ἔδεκτ᾽ ἐρατόν.

Timanthes carved this starry lapis lazuli,
a gold-speckled Persian half-stone,
for Demylus; in exchange for a soft kiss, dark-haired
Nicaea of Cos accepted the erotic gift.

The poem celebrates the achievement of a skilled stone-worker. The sequence
f events forms a small narrative that follows the stone through two stages,
xpressed in two main clauses. First the Persian stone is carved by Timanthes and
ansferred to Demylus. The initial position of the name Demylus in line 3,
illowing the hapax ἡμίλιθον, marks the halfway point of transition to a second
:age, as the stone is given by him to Nicaea. While the word ἡμίλιθον may have
imething to do with the stone's softness,[14] it also literally stands as a go-between.

---

³ Bing 1995; cf. Hunter 1992:114.
⁴ BG:114.

And the sequence of sounds heard in the words ἡμίλιθον | Δημύλωι· ἀνθ' trace
an elegant, almost palindromic route of exchange. When composed, the narrative may certainly have been referential. In it
current context, however, the poem's emphasis is twofold, focusing on the carve
stone's starry, golden brilliance and on its value in an amorous exchange. The lapi
apparently presents the dark blue of a night sky against which "gold pyrite inclu
sions" shine like stars.[15] It may recall the rare word ἀντιϲέληνον, which occurs i
the collection's preceding, fragmentary epigram (AB 4.3). Since, as Bastianini an
Gallazzi note, ἀντιϲέληνον has been translated elsewhere as "shining like th
moon",[16] our stone exchanged for (ἀνθ') a kiss has comparable celestial brillianc
The stone's brilliance and hardness seemingly melt into the woman's contrastiv
dark hair and soft kiss.

In this interpretation, the artist/artisan is ultimately responsible for the *translat*
or exchange that takes place. It is therefore fitting that the major theme of exchange
expressed by the preposition ἀνθ' (ἀντί), echoes the second element in the artist
name Τιμ-άνθηϲ. The name, which at first may have looked like a "preciou
flower", upon further reading becomes a *nomen loquens* personifying "exchange
value" itself.

[15] Spier 1992:6. Cf. Schumann 1995:172.
[16] BG:113.

11

'Winged Words': Poetry and Divination in Posidippus' *Oiônoskopika*[*]

Manuel Baumbach

University of Heidelberg

Kai Trampedach

University of Konstanz

ὄρνιθες δέ τε πολλοὶ ὑπ' αὐγὰς ἠελίοιο
φοιτῶσ', οὐδέ τε πάντες ἐναίσιμοι[1] . . .

Homer, *Odyssey* II 181–182

Bird-augury is one of the oldest mantic practices found in Greek literature. In Homer it is an important means of getting and deciphering divine messages, and Hesiod regards bird-augury as the most striking form of mantic practice.[2] Birds appear as potential 'messengers of the gods' as they not only live among the dwellings of gods and men[3] but also move in a seemingly arbitrary and voluntary way. This behavior cannot be influenced by human beings but is regarded as a proof of their divine inspiration.[4] However, the unpredictability of flying birds and their everyday occurrence make bird-augury one of the most difficult mantic forms, and it seems that in Greek culture no overall accepted doctrine (τέχνη) had been estab-

---

[*] We are grateful to Markus Asper, Helga Köhler, Ivana and Andrej Petrovic for their suggestions and helpful criticism.

[1] "Many birds there are that pass to and fro under the rays of the sun, and not all are fateful." Murray 1995: I 59.

[2] Hesiod *Works and Days* 826–828. Also see below V: 'Poetry and Didactics in the *Oiônoskopika*.'

[3] Cf. for instance Homer *Iliad* XXIV 315–16, Xenophon *Memorabilia* I 3 and Porphyrius *De Abstinentia* III 5.3. For further discussion and reference see Pollard 1977:116–129; for bird-augury in general cf. Bouché-Leclerq 1879–1882: I 127–145, Dillon 1996, Pritchett 1979:101–108, and Stengel 1920:57–59.

[4] Cf. Stengel 1920:57–58.

lished.[5] From this perspective the quoted verses from the *Odyssey* can be read as an early literary reflection upon the uncertainties of bird-augury and its mantic interpretation, even if in this case the speaker Eurymachus is proved wrong by events, which show that his opponent, the specialist[6] Halitherses, came forward with the correct interpretation of the omen.

The aim of this article is to explore the literary account of bird-augury in the recently published epigram collection transmitted on P.Mil.Vogl. VIII 309. The group of 15 epigrams (AB 21–35) entitled *Oiônoskopika* is of particular interest, as bird-augury was a common narratological motive in genres such as epic, historiography, tragedy and didactic poetry. Until the publication of the Milan papyrus no series of epigrams on bird-augury had come down to us, and only sporadic poems dealing with this topic are transmitted in the *Greek Anthology*.[7] From a literary point of view this poses questions regarding: a) the literary tradition in which these epigrams are to be placed; b) their generic models; and c) an explanation of their limited occurrence within the genre of epigram. The aspect of *Sitz im Leben*[8] and the relation of the epigrams with the actual mantic practice shall be addressed from the historian's perspective. We will discuss the possibility of reading the *Oiônoskopika* as a poetic translation of mantic knowledge into a series of epigrams, by which the poet transmits divine messages in the form of 'winged words' (ἔπεα πτερόεντα). Furthermore, a possible relation between the *Oiônoskopika* and didactic poetry will be considered, against which we will evaluate the collection as a generic experiment in epigrammatical didactic poetry.

We will first examine the structure and sequence of the *Oiônoskopika*, which, regardless of whether the Milan papyrus represents the work of one author or of an anthologist,[9] not only reveal a systematic internal composition by which the reader

---

[5] Cf. Bouché-Leclerq 1879–1882: I 129 and Pollard 1977:121–126.
[6] Homer *Odyssey* II 158–159: . . . ὁ γὰρ οἶος ὁμηλικίην ἐκέκαστο | ὄρνιθας γνῶναι καὶ ἐναίσιμα μυθήσασθαι· (". . . for he [Halitherses] surpassed all men of his day in knowledge of birds and uttering words of fate.") Murray 1995: I 57–59. The seer interprets the flight of two birds, which were spotted fighting against each other during an assembly of the Ithacians, as a negative omen for Penelope's suitors. For his expertise in prediction also cf. *Odyssey* XXIV 452: ὁ ['Αλιθέρσης] γὰρ οἶος ὅρα πρόσσω καὶ ὀπίσσω ("For he alone saw before and after") Murray 1995: II 445.
[7] The only comparable example is epigram XI 186, in which the song of a night-raven is taken as a prediction of death and destruction: Νυκτικόραξ ᾄδει θανατηφόρον· ἀλλ' ὅταν ᾄσῃ | Δημόφιλος, θνῄσκει καὐτὸς ὁ νυκτικόραξ ("The night-raven's song bodes death, but when Demophilus sings the night-raven itself dies") Paton 1999: IV 161. Other epigrams, in which birds appear, are mostly grave-epigrams like VII 191 (magpie), VII 199 (unknown bird), VII 202 (cock), 203–206 (partridge), 210 (swallow). The oracle-epigrams of book XIV in the *Greek Anthology* do not deal with bird-*omina*/-oracles.
[8] Cf. Käppel's analysis of the *Paian* (1992:17–21).
[9] Up to this point the question of authenticity cannot be finally solved. However, the lack of distinguished linguistic and stylistic differences amongst the epigrams as well as the careful composition of

is invited to perceive the section as an organic whole, but also fit harmoniously into the composition of the whole epigram book—an aspect which can be seen as the attempt to establish the *Oiônoskopika* among the more 'traditional' sections of epigrams like *Anathematika* or *Epitymbia*.

I. Title and Topic

Within the thematically arranged Milan papyrus the *Oiônoskopika* (AB 21–35) form the second section, framed by the *Lithika* and the *Anathematika*.[10] The title is taken from the fourteenth epigram (AB 34), which does not contain an omen itself but describes the praxis of augury, especially of bird-augury:

ἐκ τού⟨του⟩ τοῦ πάντα περισκέπτοιο κολωνοῦ
Δάμων Τελμ⟨η⟩ccεὺc ἐκ πατέρων ἀγαθόc
οἰωνοcκοπίαc τεκμαίρεται· ἀλλ' ἴτε φήμην
καὶ Διὸc οἰωνοὺc ὧδ' ἀναπευcόμε[νοι.

From this very hill that is seen from all sides
Damon from Telmessos, good in bird-augury
from his forefathers proclaims; but come here
and ask for Zeus' prophetic utterance and signs.[11]

The transference of the term οἰωνοcκοπία to the title of the whole section (οἰωνοcκοπικά) may, however, not lead to the assumption that all epigrams of the *Oiônoskopika* deal with bird-augury. The predominance of bird-augury in early Greek literature has influenced the linguistic usage and from Homer onwards the words for 'bird of prey' or 'bird', οἰωνός and ὄρνιc, bear the semantic meaning of 'bird of omen' or 'omen' in general.[12] Aristophanes is exploiting this metonymical

....

the whole epigram-book and its single sections, in which the epigrams are thoroughly interrelated not only in regard to their contents but also linguistically (see below section II), strongly suggests one poet as author and probably also as anthologist of the epigram book. Thus we follow BG:22–24 in associating the papyrus with Posidippus of Pella.

[10] The different sections of the book are: [λιθ]ικά, οἰωνοcκοπικά, ἀναθηματικά, [ἐπιτύμβια], ἀνδριαντοποιϊκά, ἱππικά, ναυαγικά, ἰαματικά, τρόποι followed by two fragments of epigrams from an unspecified tenth section. For the composition of the epigram book, see BG:24–27 and Gutzwiller (this volume).

[11] Translated by B. Acosta-Hughes and E. Kosmetatou.

[12] See *LSJ* s.v. οἰωνός and ὄρνιc. Also cf. Stengel 1920:59 and Pollard 1977:120 for the *termini technici* of bird-augury. The common terms for (bird-)augury are οἰωνοcκοπική, οἰωνοcκοπία and ὀρνιθομαντεία (Proclus *ad* Hes. *Op.* 824). The verbs οἰωνίζομαι and (the more seldom used) ὀρνιθεύομαι bare exclusively the mantic meaning 'to foretell from birds' or 'to prophesy' in general;

transference in an ironic remark in his *Birds*, who take the term ὄρνις literally in order to stress man's constant unconscious worship of the birds:

> ὄρνιν τε νομίζετε πάνθ' ὅσαπερ περὶ μαντείας διακρίνει·
> φήμη γ' ὑμῖν ὄρνις ἐστί, πταρμόν τ' ὄρνιθα καλεῖτε,
> ξύμβολον ὄρνιν, φωνὴν ὄρνιν, θεράποντ' ὄρνιν, ὄνον ὄρνιν.

Whatever's decisive in prophecy you deem a bird: to you, an ominous utterance is a bird, a sneeze you call a bird, a chance meeting's a bird, a sound's a bird, a good luck servant's a bird, a braying donkey's a bird.[13]

Due to the transference of the specific meaning 'bird' to 'omen' the term οἰωνοσκοπικά can also be interpreted as reference to epigrams on bird-*omina* as well as on other kinds of *omina*, so that this is an appropriate title for Posidippus' second preserved section, in which the author plays with the double meaning of the word: of the 15 epigrams clustered together in this section, ten deal with bird-augury whereas five present different but similarly constructed signs.[14] There is, however, a close link between both groups as eight epigrams (1–5, 8, 9, 12 = AB 21–25, 28, 29, 32) belong to the common category of ἐνόδιοι σύμβουλοι, which can be expressed by birds as well as other signs. Such 'wayfaring signs' mostly refer to a single individual recipient and mirror the dangers and uncertainties, which were associated in antiquity especially with traveling. In connection with warfare ἐνόδιοι σύμβουλοι could also get public significance.[15] Nevertheless the quantitative dominance of bird-*omina* over other signs as well as the observation that all three epigrams allude to mantic practice as a τέχνη by mentioning male or female seers (6, 14, 15 = AB 26, 34, 35), while they explicitly refer to bird-*omina* and not to other signs, strongly argues for a narrow meaning of *Oiônoskopika*, which is dominated by epigrams on bird-augury.[16]

....

the specialists for bird-augury in Homer are οἰωνισταί or οἰωνοπόλοι, later attested terms are ὀρνιθόμαντις and οἰωνόμαντις. Pausanias (IX 16,1) calls the place of bird-augury οἰωνοσκοπεῖον.

[13] Aristophanes *Birds* 719–722. Translation by Henderson 2000:121. Also cf. Dunbar 1995:456f.

[14] Epigrams 5, 8, 10, 12, 13 (AB 25, 28, 30, 32, 33). For the interpretation of πρέσβυς in epigram 8 (AB 28) see below II.4.

[15] The term is used by Aeschylus *Prom.* 487; σύμβουλοι of this kind are also mentioned by Pindar *Olympian* 12.8 (with scholia), Aristophanes *Birds* 721 (with scholia) and Xenophon *Memorabilia* I 1.3; cf. McCartney 1935:97–112.

[16] One could even say that the structure of the *Oiônoskopika* mirrors the linguistic development, as we find 'pure' bird-*omina* in the first couple of epigrams, which give way to other signs the more the section proceeds. See below II.4. Hunter (this volume) derives a 'generic sense' from the fact that the first four epigrams depict bird-*omina*.

II. Internal *Ergänzungsspiel*

At first glance the structure of the *Oiônoskopika* appears to be typical of an anthology, as the epigrams thematically belong to the topic of augury, yet do not show any systematic order or interrelation among each other.[17] For a reader this could be taken as an invitation to enjoy the variety and diversity of these epigrams, to approach them individually, and to use his imagination to contextualize the single epigrams with a fictional or real object or even associate it with another literary work. Such an *Ergänzungsspiel*[18] is a common characteristic of Hellenistic epigram, and it becomes especially stimulating in the case of collections of loose epigrams, which do not help the reader to interpret the texts by offering a literary contextualization in the form of a dialogue between neighboring epigrams.[19] On these grounds the editors' difficulty in detecting a clearly distinguishable structure in the *Oiônoskopika*[20] is no surprise, because this apparent lack of internal structure might be part of the game. However, the careful arrangement of the epigrams in sections framing the *Oiônoskopika*, such as the *Lithika* and *Anathematika*,[21] raises the question of whether the *Oiônoskopika*, too, have an inner structure on the basis of which the epigrams are deliberately arranged. This question focuses on the literary contextualization of epigrams with other poems of the same section. In this context the reader is asked to participate in an internal *Ergänzungsspiel*, i.e. to look specifically for links among the 15 epigrams of the *Oiônoskopika*.[22] As a result, the section can be approached as a *Gesamtkunstwerk* to which each epigram contributes. Such a focused *Ergänzungsspiel*, intended by the text, however, by no means limits the reader's imagination in exploring the different and multiple contexts that can be found outside the *Oiônoskopika*. Quite to the contrary, it constitutes a sign of the auctorial art that preserves the individuality of the epigrams, which thus become the starting point for an open process of supplementation. On the other hand, these poems are carefully arranged as a group, so that they also participate in the specific internal *Ergänzungsspiel* within the *Oiônoskopika*. And it is this aspect that we will examine further here. For an

---

[17] For the order of epigrams in anthologies cf. Cameron 1993:19–48 and Gutzwiller 1998:277–321 with a discussion of verbal linkage between epigrams.

[18] Cf. Bing 1995:116 and Ludwig 1968 for the intertextuality of epigrams by different authors.

[19] Cf. Gutzwiller (this volume).

[20] BG:25: "Nella sezione οἰωνοσκοπικά (IV 7–VI 8) la disposizione interna dei testi non è altrettanto evidente ed articolata come nella serie dei λιθικά."

[21] Cf. Hunter and Stephens in this volume. Also the *Hippika* and *Iamatika* are artfully arranged as Fantuzzi and Bing (both this volume) can show.

[22] Cf. also Bing 1998:38. Such a literary contextualization of course reflects the increasing transition of epigram from stone to book in the Hellenistic period.

overview of the epigrams and their topics our reader is invited to refer to the scheme at the end of this paper (section VII).

Let us begin with the question of how the epigrams are arranged and put in dialogue with each other; this will provide us with a starting point for reading the *Oiônoskopika* as a whole. So far, three suggestions have been made. First, the editors of the *editio princeps*, Bastianini and Gallazzi, propose a rather rough and unspecific three-part structure:

> i primi quattro riguardano l'apparire di uccelli che costituiscono un
> buon auspicio per la navigazione o per la pesca (IV 8–29); poi vi sono
> nove testi in cui il presagio descritto è fornito da incontri casuali o da
> uccelli o da eventi di varia natura, portentosi oppure no (IV 30–V 39);
> e in conclusione sono posti due conponimenti che non parlano di
> presagi, ma di indovini (VI 1–8).[23]

The first group of four epigrams (1–4 = AB 21–24) seems perfectly reasonable as all the poems deal with bird-augury; thematically they form a nice pair of two epigrams on sea-travel followed by two epigrams on fishing. However, the second group of nine epigrams (5–13 = AB 25–33), which contains "eventi di varia natura," falls completely apart. Given that epigrams 14 and 15 (AB 34–35) form the last group, the suggested arrangement provides us with a frame of two distinguishable sets flanking an unsorted main bunch of *Oiônoskopika*. Such lack of order supports an anthological reading of the section, whose second and most numerous group is no more than a loose collection of various *omina* containing different motives and mantic qualities.

K. Gutzwiller tries to further clarify this arrangement by grouping epigrams 10–13 (AB 30–33) according to the military *omina* they describe.[24] Like Bastianini and Gallazzi her approach only offers a partial structure of the *Oiônoskopika* and confines itself to the general observation that there is a "movement . . . from omens for ordinary people to specific military omens, with special reference to Alexander's conquests"[25]—an interpretation which, in our opinion, becomes problematic.

Finally D. Petrain has suggested a subdivision of the *Oiônoskopika* into five sections,[26] which he develops in connection with his possible but not entirely convincing interpretation of epigram 8 (AB 28).[27] Petrain tries to show that the

---

[23] BG:25.

[24] Cf. Gutzwiller 2002b:5: "The tenth through thirteenth poems involve military omens."

[25] Gutzwiller 2002b:5. Cf. also Gutzwiller (this volume).

[26] Petrain 2002:10–11: "IV. 8–29: bird omens pertaining to maritime occupations; IV. 30–35: advice on finding a husband; IV.36 – V.15: omens pertaining to domestic affairs and land travel; V. 16–39: other types of omens (not birds); VI. 1–8: noteworthy interpreters of omens."

[27] Petrain takes πρέσβυς as referring to a 'wren' and integrates the epigram amongst the bird-*omina*; for

"poems tend to fall in groups of four," but the definition of the three groups that fulfill this criterion is not always clear, especially in the case of epigrams 9–13 (= AB 29–33) which contain "other types of omens (not birds)."[28] A further inconsistency can be found in the relation between the single groups. Whereas according to Petrain's structure two of the groups of four epigrams are linked by a transitory epigram (5 = AB 25), there is no such bridge between the second and the third groups, which thus constitutes a "decisive break"[29] not only between the two sections but also within Petrain's structure of the *Oiônoskopika*.

We would like to propose a different structure by taking into account linguistic evidence such as quotations and verbal allusions, which can be used to create links between certain epigrams, as well as by looking at four possible structural elements deriving from the content: 1) the persons by whom *omina* are experienced or to whom they are addressed; 2) the situations in which the *omina* occur; 3) the mantic significance and quality of the *omina*; 4) the kinds of *omina* involved.

II.1 Persons

Two thirds of the epigrams involve persons of different professions and backgrounds: sailors (Timon, 1 = AB 21), fishermen (Archytas, 4 = AB 24), private citizens (Hieron, 6 = AB 26; Euelthon, 9 = AB 29), soldiers (Timoleon, 8 = AB 28; Antimachos, 12 = AB 32; Aristoxenos, 13 = AB 33), seers (Asterie, 6 = AB 26; Damon, 14 = AB 34; Strymon, 15 = AB 35) as well as the Argead kings, and Alexander the Great who is mentioned twice (11, 15 = AB 31, 35). The variety of persons as well as the selective usage of names throughout the section thus makes a grouping of the epigrams according to addressee difficult and even Gutzwiller's general observation that *omina* about ordinary people are followed by military *omina* in the second part of the *Oiônoskopika* cannot stand up to scrutiny.[30] Some military *omina* also refer to ordinary people and the sequence of explicit military *omina* seems to be interrupted by epigram 9 (AB 29), which is dealing with an unspecified omen for a traveling man. Furthermore, Gutzwiller does not take into account the epigrams which do not refer to specific persons but rather indicate that *omina* in Greek mantic are not limited to a specific group of recipients; with the exception of the Alexander-*omina*, all signs can principally happen to anybody in a given situation. Thus the variety of names rather seems to stress the idea that the *Oiônoskopika*, especially those collected in this section, could affect and refer to

....

further discussion of Petrain's suggestion and the interpretation of the epigram, cf. below II.4.

[28] Petrain 2002:11.

[29] Petrain 2002:11.

[30] Gutzwiller 2002b:5 and Gutzwiller (this volume).

anybody regardless of profession or social position. The author attempts to attract the attention of a wide readership as the persons displayed in the *Oiônoskopika* function as a kind of '*Platzhalter*' for the reader.[31]

At the same time, the frequent connection of names with marks of origin and short references to historical circumstances[32] might suggest that the poet also alludes to 'historical' persons and events that were familiar to a Hellenistic—or more specifically, an Alexandrian—audience.[33] There are, however, two objections against this assumption. On the one hand it is striking that especially the omina and oracles connected with Alexander—in epigram 11 (AB 31) the statue of Athena moves her right foot indicating his victory over the Persians and in epigram 15 (AB 35) the raven of the seer Strymon foretells Alexander three victories over the Persians—are not known from other sources. With regard to the extensive use of *omina* and the variety of mantic events in the historiography on Alexander,[34] we would expect to know about Posidippus' *omina* from a second source, if they were indeed 'historical'. Thus the fact that Posidippus' examples are not transmitted elsewhere either indicates his deliberate usage of less famous *omina* or can be taken as part of his poetic invention and creativity in adding something new to a well-known corpus of Alexander (hi)stories.[35]

On the other hand the occurrence of 'speaking' names in some of the epigrams seems to be an argument against historical allusions in the *Oiônoskopika* as the names are used to increase the aesthetic pleasure of the single epigrams by raising (and disappointing) certain expectations of the reader. Thus for example in epigram 6 (AB 26) the 'holy' Hieron is rewarded for his trust in a sacrificial ritual and in epigram 8 (AB 28) Timoleon, who 'respects the lion', is killed, because he did not respect a bad omen on his way to war. A similar fate happens to Antimachos who is killed by the enemies he is 'fighting'. And whereas Hieron and Antimachos

---

[31] For ways of interaction between poetry and readership in the Hellenistic period, cf. Asper 2001:94–116.

[32] Marks of origin are found in epigram 8 (AB 28), where Timoleon from Phocis is mentioned, as well as in epigrams 13–15 (AB 33–35), which introduce the Arcadean Aristoxenos, Damon from Telmessus and the Thracian hero Strymon. Historical events are presented in epigrams 11 and 15 (AB 31, 35), which refer to Alexander's war against the Persians and in epigram 12 (AB 32), where the Illyrian army is mentioned.

[33] The fact that we do not know anything about the persons presented and the described events except for Alexander and the Argead kings might be caused by the loss of texts especially from the Hellenistic era.

[34] See also III below. We just want to mention the temporal coincidence of the increased occurrence of bird-augury and mantic practice in the Alexander literature and Posidippus' epigrams. From this point of view the reference to Alexander in Posidippus could be read as his homage to the very person who helped to make bird-augury popular again.

[35] We can of course not rule out the possibility that the poet alludes to events that were familiar to the Alexandrians of the third century BCE whose reports disappeared in the course of later transmission.

confirm the mantic meaning of their names in one way or the other, in the case of Euelthon, 'who is on a good or safe way', the expectation raised by his name is transferred into the contrary as he will get killed by robbers on his journey to Sidene (epigram 9 = AB 29). In all cases the use of speaking names stresses the relation between person and event, as the names become *omina* themselves and contain a prediction of the future events. However, if the person in question ignores or misinterprets the *omina*, even euphemistic names do not prevent a bad outcome and in the case of Euelthon we might even take this as tragic irony.[36]

The occurrence of 'speaking' names as well as the difficulties in associating the persons with historical figures,[37] however, should not lead to the conclusion that all names except for Alexander's are fictional. We are probably rather dealing with a typical Hellenistic mixture of both historical figures (Alexander) and fictional names by which the poet intends to attest and authorize the presented *omina*. The underlying idea seems to be the credibility of the material, which is granted by the usage of names together with marks of origin[38] and sporadic details of 'historical' circumstances. Thus the *Oiônoskopika* begin with an attested, i.e. legitimized *omen* by mentioning Timon in the first epigram (AB 21.6) and guide the reader through a number of unattested *omina* to authorized ones in the last five epigrams which all contain names (11–15 = AB 31–35). Such dynamics of legitimization allow the poet to gain authority as a credible transmitter of credible *omina*.

II.2 Situations

In approaching the *Oiônoskopika* with regard to the situations in which *omina* occur we find a starting point for a parallel structure: The first six epigrams (1–6 = AB 21–26) cover the private sphere with their focus on four different areas: Sea-traveling (1–2 = AB 21–22), fishing (3–4 = AB 23–24), wedding (5 = AB 25) and buying slaves (6 = AB 26). Taking these epigrams together as a group we can add the observation that there is a movement from the outside world towards the life

---

[36] A similar ironic use of speaking names can be found in Callimachus, for instance in the cases of Callignotos (11 GP = 25 Pf.), Euaenetus (25 GP = 56 Pf.), or Conopion (63 GP = 63 Pf.).

[37] Neither a clear historical reference nor a clear functionalization as a speaking name can be detected in the case of the Arcadian Aristoxeinus (13 = AB 33). The name together with the mark of origin might however characterize him—like the Phocean Timoleon in epigram 8 (AB 28)—as a mercenary. Similarly Timon (1 = AB 21) and Archytas (4 = 24) do not show clear references. The Thracian seer Strymon (15 = AB 35), who is also characterized as a hero, has the name of a Thracian river (and river-god), which at its lower stretches forms the traditional border between Thrace and Macedon. This could perhaps be taken as a poetic attempt to align the seer with Alexander.

[38] The only explicit mark of origin can be found in epigram 9 (AB 29), where the city Sidene in Aeolia is mentioned (cf. Strabo XIII 1.11, 42). Perhaps the author intended to 'prove' the tragic irony indicated by the name by evoking an historical background.

within the οἶκος of a Greek citizen as the last line of epigram 6 (AB 26) explicitly indicates by referring to the house:

οἰκῆα κτήσαςθαι ἐρωιδιὸς ὄρν‹ις› ἄριστος
πελλός, ὃν Ἀ[c]τερίη μάντις ἐφ' ἱρὰ καλεῖ·
ὧι πειςθεὶς Ἱέρων ἐκτ[ή]ςατο τὸν μὲν ἐπ' ἀγροῦ
τὸν δ' οἴκων ἀγαθῶι εὐ‹ν› ποδὶ κηδεμόνα.

To aquire a (house-)slave the dusky heron is an excellent sign,
   whom Asterie the seer summons to her holy rites;
heeding this omen, Hieron obtained one slave for the fields
   and one for the house with lucky foot.[39]

As we shall see this movement towards the οἶκος comes to an end in epigram 7, which deals with the topic of childbirth. Thus we can define the first group as a cluster of epigrams dealing the domestic affairs of private persons, and the unity of this group is further characterized by a peaceful atmosphere, common in all six epigrams.

In contrast to this first cluster, a second group of six epigrams deals with war and crime (8–13 = AB 28–33). It starts with AB 28, in which a soldier sets out for war and meets an old man crying at a crossroads,[40] and ends with the narration of Aristoxeinus' dream and subsequent death in battle in AB 33. All epigrams in this group depict *omina* which bear a dangerous, mostly life-threatening prediction, and compared with the first group these epigrams move away from the *oikos* of the living towards the realm of the dead, or, as the last words of AB 33 make clear, εἰς Ἀΐδεω.

The suggested distinction of these two pairs of six epigrams is underlined in epigram 7 (AB 27) which functions as transitory epigram. It describes the importance of a special bird-omen for childbirth and explains the function of the vulture for the child's success within society as well as in war:

τέκνων εἰρ[ο]μένω‹ι› γενεὴν οἰωνὸς ἄριστος
φήνη·[41] μαρτυρίην οὐδὲ θεοῦ δέχεται
οὐδὲ συνεδρεῦcαι μέγαν ἀετόν, ἀλλὰ τελείη{ι}
φαίνεται· οἰωνῶν χρῆμα τελειότατον,

---

[39] Translation by B. Acosta-Hughes and E. Kosmetatou.
[40] For further discussion of this omen, cf. below II.4.
[41] The punctuation (colon) should be behind φήνη and not at the end of the first verse (cf. BG:51 and AB:48).

φήνη παῖδ᾽ ἀγαγοῦςα καὶ ἐν θώκοιϲ ἀγορητήν
ἡδυεπῆ θήϲει καὶ θοὸν ἐν πολέμωι.

> For someone who is seeking the birth of children, the vulture is the best sign:
> it neither receives a message from god nor appears together with
> the mighty eagle, but is alone meaningful—the most effective omen of all.
> The vulture makes a child a well-versed speaker in public and agile in war.[42]

The internal movement of the epigram from the peaceful, almost idyllic sphere of the *oikos* to war (ἐν πολέμωι, AB 27.6) reflects the topics and movements of the two groups mentioned above. Thus the epigram constitutes a harmonic transition between the two groups, and it is also nicely mirrored linguistically. The opening hexameter of epigram 7 (AB 27) quotes in variation the opening line of the previous epigram (6 = AB 26, as the ὄρν⟨ιϲ⟩ ἄριϲτοϲ of the one is echoed by the οἰωνὸϲ ἄριϲτοϲ in the other. This allusion is further underlined by the parallel structure of the two opening verses:

οἰκῆα κτήϲαϲθαι ἐρωιδιὸϲ ὄρν⟨ιϲ⟩ ἄριϲτοϲ (epigram 6)

τέκνων εἰρ[ο]μένω⟨ι⟩ γενεὴν οἰωνὸϲ ἄριϲτοϲ (epigram 7)

The epigram perfectly integrates itself into the first group by stressing the most important aspect of an *oikos*: childbirth, which, as in this case, secures not only the continuity of the family but ideally also grants prosperity as well as success and glory in society.

At the same time we find a second verbal linkage as epigram 7 (AB 27) closes with the word ἐν πολέμωι (AB 27.6), which points to the following epigram (8 = AB 28), where the word is taken up twice: εἰϲ ἕτερον πόλεμον (AB 28.4) and ἐκ πολέμου (AB 28.6).[43] Epigram 7 (AB 27) is therefore a perfect starting point for the second group and can be regarded as a deliberately chosen transitional bridge by which the poets links the two groups, i.e. the private and the public life of a citizen. The perfect harmony of the transition creates the illusion of an ongoing story so that the reader accompanies the child (7 = AB 27) going to war (8 = AB 28) and getting killed.

Thus the following structure emerges:

---

[42] Translation by the authors.

[43] Epigram 8 (AB 28): ἢν ἀνδρὸϲ μέλλοντοϲ ἐπ᾽ Ἄρεα δήϊον ἕρπειν | ἀντήϲη⟨ι⟩ κλαίων πρέϲβυϲ ἐπὶ τριόδου, | οὐκέτι νοϲτήϲει κεῖνοϲ βροτόϲ· ἀλλ᾽ ἀναθέϲθω | τὴν τόθ᾽ ὁδοιπορίην **εἰϲ ἕτερον πόλεμον**· | καὶ γὰρ Τιμολέων κεκλαυμένοϲ ἦλθεν ὁ Φωκεύϲ | **ἐκ πολέμου** τούτωι ϲήματι μεμψάμενοϲ.

First group: 1–6 (AB 21–26)	domestic affairs; movement towards the οἶκος and the prospect of life (children)
Transition: 7 (AB 27)	childbirth as goal of private and beginning of public life
Second group: 8–13 (AB 28–33)	public sphere and military movement away from the οἶκος to war and death

However straightforward this arrangement of the first 13 epigrams of the *Oiônoskopika* might appear, one epigram of the second group (9 = AB 29) seems to fall out of this scheme as it deals with an unspecific omen rather than a military one:

ἐχθρό⟨ν⟩, ἀνὴρ κορυδοὺς καὶ ἀκανθί⟨δ⟩ας ἦν ἐνὶ χώρωι
ἀθρήςη⟨ι⟩· χαλεποὶ ςύνδυο φαινόμενοι·
ὡς Εὐέλθων εἶδε· κακοὶ δέ μιν αὐτὸν ὁδίτ⟨η⟩ν
κλῶπες Cιδήνη⟨ι⟩ κτεῖναν ἐν Αἰολίδι.

It is a hostile sign, when a man sees larks and finches in the same spot:
they are dangerous when they both appear together.
This is how Euelthon saw them and evil thieves murdered him
as he was walking on the road at Sidene in Aiolia.[44]

Two observations can be made: On the one hand the epigram is closely connected with the preceding one (7 = AB 27) as both deal with 'wayfaring signs'. On the other hand, the verbal linkage between the epigrams reminds us of the internal *Ergänzungsspiel* within the *Oiônoskopika* and we could ask whether the context of epigram 9 (AB 29) provides us with a further hint that it might indeed fit into the group of military epigrams. The epigram itself does not contain any information about the identity of Euelthon or his motives for traveling, so that we can either accept the general meaning of the omen as principally referring to any traveler, or try to fill in the open space with our imagination. If we ask for instance why Euelthon was traveling, we could find a possible answer in the neighboring epigrams. As both epigrams explicitly deal with military omens and situations it is tempting to expect a military context also in epigram 9 (AB 29). Thus a possible supplementation could be that Euelthon, like Timoleon in epigram 8 (AB 28), is on his way to war, so that the overall theme of the second group would be also (indirectly) present in epigram 9 (AB 29).[45] In any case, by not providing the reader

[44] Translation by C. Austin and G. Bastianini, AB:51.
[45] The term ὁδίτης is not restricted to a 'peaceful' traveler, but can be used with a negative and even

134

with any information whatsoever about Euelthon and by linking the epigram to the preceding one, which contains exactly such information, the poet is deliberately appealing to the readers' desire and ability to supplement the missing information in epigram 9 (AB 29) from its context.

A further reason for the placement of epigram 9 (AB 29) in the second group can be found with regard to the quality of the *omina* involved.

II.3 Mantic Significance and Quality of the *Omina*

In all epigrams the quality of the *omina* is defined by authorial statements. It is clear from the beginning that we are dealing with a kind of "black and white" scheme as the described constellations of signs and situations indicate either a good or a bad outcome. Epigrams which give examples of both, like the first one (AB 21), where we learn that a falcon is a good omen for shipping in contrast to a shearwater,[46] clearly focus on one of the possibilities, which is then further illustrated by a concrete example. As a result, every epigram stresses one specific quality of an omen.

The category of mantic quality provides us with further evidence for the suggested arrangement: Whereas the first group consists of six epigrams (AB 21–26) with positive *omina*, the epigrams of the second group mostly depict negative ones.[47] Looking at the position of AB 29 from this point of view, its placement amongst the military *omina* is justified by the negative omen, which leads to the same outcome as the purely military *omina*. Thus our suggested structure of the *Oiônoskopika* is can be further established:

First group: 1–6 (AB 21–26)	positive *omina* and peaceful atmosphere
Second group: 8–13 (AB 28–33)	negative omina in connection with war and crime

....

hostile connotation (cf. Sophocles *Philoctetes* 147: δεινὸς ὁδίτης).

[46] AB 21: νηῒ καθελκομένηι πάντα πλέο⟨c⟩ ἰνὶ φανήτω ἴρηξ, αἰθυίης οὐ καθαροπτέρυγος. ('At the launching of a ship may a hawk appear all full of strength | as the shearwater's wings are not of good omen.') Translation by C. Austin and G. Bastianini, AB:43. The ἴρηξ which can be a hawk or a falcon (cf. Pollard 1977:144), was frequently regarded as a bird of omen and is linked to Apollo in Aristophanes' *Birds* 516 (cf. Dunbar 1995:354–355). As such, the occurrence of a falcon/hawk in the first epigram can be seen as programmatic as the bird evokes the god and the mantic art traditionally associated with Apollo, which is also the topic of the *Oiônoskopika*. For the different types of falcons/hawks and their characteristic features, cf. Thompson 1966:114–118.

[47] A possible exception is epigram 11 (AB 31), which contains a positive omen for Alexander that is, however, negative for his enemies, the Persian army, as it indicates fire and destruction for them (AB 31.6).

II.4 Kinds of *Omina*

As a final criterion for structuring the *Oiônoskopika* we will look at the kinds of *omina*. Although the diversity of *omina* (ten epigrams present bird-omina whereas five deal with human beings, statues, or dreams) does not seem to be very helpful in arranging the epigrams at first glance, an interesting constellation can be detected. Whereas in the first group (1–6 = AB 21–26) all epigrams except the fifth (AB 25) deal with bird-*omina*, birds in the second group (8–13 = AB 28–33) either play no role at all[48] or are subordinate to a different, more decisive sign,[49] but again with one exception: epigram 9 (AB 29) is a pure bird-omen. We thus find a parallelism in regard to the absolute number of *omina*, six of which are bird-*omina* and six depict *omina* of a different kind.

However, in composing the two groups according to the depicted situations and the quality of the *omina*,[50] the poet has avoided the creation of a strict symmetry in the kinds of *omina* involved. Instead he has integrated a bird-*omen* in the otherwise bird-free second group and the omen of an encounter with certain human beings (5 = AB 25) with the five bird-*omina* depicted in the first group. This surprising inconsistency[51] in the otherwise strictly parallel arrangement, however, is not only subordinated to the two structuring criteria of situations and quality— which both epigram 5 (AB 25) and epigram 9 (AB 29) share with the other epigrams of their groups[52]—but also serves an important function with regard to the overall topic of the *Oiônoskopika*. The unpredictable surprise in the otherwise parallel arrangement of the epigrams is a symbolic reminder by which the poet shows his audience that the material he is dealing with, i.e. *omina*, is itself unpredictable, even if a well-ordered and 'secure' way of interpretation seems to have been established. Form and content thus comment on each other and the τέχνη of arranging the *Oiônoskopika* mirrors the search for, as well as the difficulty in, finding a reliable τέχνη in dealing with mantic *omina*.

---

[48] From this angle Petrain's (2002) interpretation of πρέcβυc as a bird in epigram 8 (AB 28) seems unlikely as it would spoil the proposed arrangement of the epigrams, which revealed itself with regard to the quality of *omina* and situations in which they occur. Thus it seems more plausible to assume that also the criterion of the kind of *omina* follows this grouping, which it does if we take πρέcβυc (like in epigram 5, AB 25) as referring to an 'old man'. We might, however, accept Petrain's notion that the name contains a deliberate ambiguity by which the author could underline the point that different *omina* could have similar meanings, such as a crying wren and a crying old man.

[49] As in epigram 11 (AB 31), where the focus is not on the eagle as a sign but on the statue of Athena.

[50] Cf. II.2 and II.3 above.

[51] Which itself shows a parallel structure as epigrams 5 and 9 'circle' around the transitional epigram 7, of which they both are separated by only one other epigram.

[52] Epigram 5 (AB 25) deals with marriage and has a positive outcome, whereas epigram 9 has a negative outcome and integrates itself among the military *omina* (cf. II.2 above).

It is exactly this search that leads the reader to the seers in the last two epigrams
f the *Oiônoskopika*, which form a third and final group (14–15 = AB 34–35).
Iaving read thirteen examples of different *omina*, the reader is not only reminded
f the importance of consulting a seer. To a certain degree the reader has now been
evated to the position of a seer himself, insofar as he has read and learned about
ertain omina, of which some are important for everyday-life occurences, and for
ιe ways of approaching them. The structure of the *Oiônoskopika* can therefore be
ɔnsidered as didactic, as the reader is led from simple *omina* in the first couple of
ɔigrams, i.e. *omina* which can be easily interpreted and are partly expressed in the
ιrm of country sayings,[53] to more complicated and rare ones, which make it neces-
ιry to consult a seer. This didactic structure of the *Oiônoskopika* (compare texts on
ιltural development or aitiological texts) reveals itself by way of the internal
rgänzungsspiel. It could also lead the way to finding the generic models of the
)iônoskopika, which might be regarded as the transformation of a technical prose
xt on mantic art into the poetry of epigrams.[54] The question of intertextuality also
ɔens a path towards reading the *Oiônoskopika* as a kind of didactic poetry.
[owever, as such a transformation cannot be achieved by a single epigram, our
ading of the *Oiônoskopika* as a collection of epigrams that are closely connected
ith each other becomes the *conditio sine qua non* for such an assumption. On
ounds of the Hellenistic play of genres[55] it seems however possible that the
)iônoskopika as a collection translated the characteristics of other literary forms
to epigram. To take this idea a little further, we have to ask how far the
)iônoskopika reflect the actual mantic practice, and how it can be placed in the
:erary tradition of transporting mantic knowledge, be it technical literature or
dactic poetry.

II. Bird-augury and Mantic Practice

οὐ γάρ τι μικρὸν οὐδ' ἄδοκον, ἀλλὰ πολὺ καὶ παμπάλαιον
μαντικῆς μόριον οἰωνιστικὴ κέκληται· τὸ γὰρ ὀξὺ καὶ νοερὸν
αὐτῶν καὶ δι' εὐστροφίαν ὑπήκοον ἁπάσης φαντασίας ὥσπερ

---

[53] Country sayings can be found in epigram 2 (AB 22) and epigram 3 (AB 23), in which the diving
shearwater indicates successful fishing. A straightforward interpretation by analogy can be found in
the first epigram (AB 21), where a diving bird is depicted as a negative omen for launching a ship
that will most likely sink.

[54] The same can be said for the structure of the *Andriantopoiika*, which reflect prose works on art-
historical theory. See Kosmetatou (this volume).

[55] For different aspects of the Hellenistic 'genre-crossing' cf. the volume on *Genre in Hellenistic Poetry*
(for example Harder's [1998:95–113] study on 'Generic Games' in Callimachus' *Aetia*) as well as
Taran 1979 and Ludwig 1968 (with emphasize on the erotic epigram).

ὀργάνῳ τῷ θεῷ παρέχει χρῆσθαι καὶ τρέπειν ἐπί τε κίνησιν
ἐπί τε φωνὰς καὶ γηρύματα καὶ σχήματα νῦν μὲν ἐνστατικὰ
νῦν δὲ φορὰ καθάπερ πνεύματα ταῖς μὲν ἐπικό-πτοντα ταῖς
δ' ἐπευθύνοντα πράξεις καὶ ὁρμὰς εἰς τὸ τέλος. διὸ κοινῇ μὲν
ὁ Εὐριπίδης θεῶν κήρυκας ὀνομάζει τοὺς ὄρνιθας.

It is, in fact, no small or ignoble division of divination, but a great and
very ancient one, which takes its name from birds; for their quickness of
apprehension and their habit of responding to any manifestation, so
easily are they diverted, serves as an instrument for the god, who directs
their movements, their calls or cries, and their formations which are
sometimes contrary, sometimes favouring, as winds are; so that he uses
some birds to cut short, others to speed enterprises and inceptions to
the destined end. It is for that reason that Euripides calls birds in
general "heralds of the gods".[56]

Plutarch's criteria of movements, utterances and constellations, in which different
birds collaborate, are particularly prominent for an interpretation of bird-*omina* i
Greek culture. However, his text does not provide an answer to the questio
whether these criteria have ever been integrated into a semantic system of bird
augury and considering our poor sources this will probably remain uncertair
Nevertheless, there is some literary evidence that contains certain patterns c
(bird-)augury, which provide quite a detailed picture of the nature of Greek mantic
First of all, there is the coincidence of an extraordinary incident and a significar
moment, which creates the symbolic value. On this occasion, against a backdrop c
its habits, the behavior of a bird (or a number of birds) is understood as a symboli
code, which can be deciphered in regard to the situation in which it occurrec
Beyond this basic assumption, however, material concurrences within Greek manti
are by no means guaranteed. The code is not fixed but flexible, and elements c
arbitrariness not only arise from the situation in which a sign occurs but also fror
eclectic observation. Thus in bird-augury the following ways of behavior must b
especially considered: the manner of flying, the direction of flight, the place of
possible landing, the food intake, and the interaction with other birds or anima
in general.[57]

[56] Plutarch *De sollertia animalium* 975 A. (Translation by Helmbold 1957:413).
[57] Cf. Aeschylus *Prometheus* 488–492:

γαμψωνύχων τε πτῆσιν οἰωνῶν σκεθρῶς
διώρισ', οἵτινές τε δεξιοὶ φύσιν
εὐωνύμους τε, καὶ δίαιταν ἥντινα
ἔχουσ' ἕκαστοι, καὶ πρὸς ἀλλήλους τίνες

Furthermore, a bird can get into contact with a human being on its own account and thus present itself as a messenger from the gods. Although specific birds are associated with specific deities (for instance the eagle with Zeus or the falcon with Apollo), the connection between the species and other factors remains significant particularly since Greek mantic does not seem to know any explicitly 'lucky' or 'fateful' birds/birds of good or bad tidings. If we take a look at the Alexander literature for instance, we find examples of both a positive and a negative interpretation of the raven[58] and a similar ambivalence can be observed in the case of owls.[59]

When applied, even the differentiation which had remained the only distinction in Greek mantic of signs that was generally acknowledged and being used since Homer, namely the 'technical' classification into right-promising and left-unfortunate, seems to be governed by a certain randomness. Either it might simply become redundant due to the symbolic property of the sign (for instance through the metaphoric implication of the 'flying ahead' or 'flying over') or it could be taken as an accidental statement merely confirming an assessment of a sign, which had already been established by means of symbolic configuration as favorable or unfortunate. The fact that there are only a few post-Homeric and pre-Hellenistic records of bird-*omina*, in which the indication of direction becomes markedly significant for the interpretation,[60] undoubtedly links with the trends of literary representation of such signs. In a reality in which symbolic explanations were not always at hand, the simple distinction between 'right' and 'left' presumably played a more important role. An ἀετὸς αἴσιος spotted by a seer during a sacrifice would simply have been seen as an eagle flying to the right.[61] Yet there is no doubting that symbolic and metaphoric interpretations had a greater persuasiveness in Greek mantic.

....
ἔχθραι τε καὶ στέργηθρα καὶ συνεδρίαι·
"The flight of crook-taloned birds I distinguished clearly—which by nature are auspicious, which sinister—their various modes of life, their mutual feuds and loves, and their consortings." (Translation by Weir Smyth 1922:I 259).

[58] Plutarch tells us (according to the general knowledge that a raven is eating carrions, cf. Bouché-Leclerq 1879:133 and Pollard 1977:127f.) about some ravens, which appeared as symbols of death when Alexander arrived at Babylon (*Alexander* 73.1). On the other hand we hear of helpful ravens that led Alexander and his followers through the desert to the Ammoneion. Cf. Callisthenes (*FGrHist* 124) F 14 (= Strab. XVII 1.43; Plutarch *Alexander* 27.2); Arrian *Anabasis* III 3.6; Diodorus XVII 49.5; Curt. IV 7.15. For the motive of birds leading the way also cf. Plutarch *Theseus* 36.1 and Pausanias IX 38.3–4. See Dillon 1996:115n56 with further bibliography.

[59] The owl was regarded as a bird of death (cf. Wellmann 1909:1065f. and 1069f. with sources), but was also associated with Athena and thus regarded as a bearer of positive messages (especially for the people of Athens), cf. Plutarch *Themistocles* 12.1 and Diodorus XX 11.3.

[60] An exception is Xenophon *Anabasis* VI 1.23.

[61] Cf. Xenophon *Anabasis* VI 5.2; VI 5.21.

Since in most cases bird-*omina* were not especially sought for but occurred spontaneously, the simple classification of 'right' and 'left' cannot be taken as objective data but depends on the accidental standpoint of the spectator at the very moment he sees the unexpected bird. It would of course be possible to establish such an objective orientation in which 'right' and 'left' became connected to specific cardinal points, if we assume that the sky would be observed with the intention of gaining bird-*omina*. However, concrete examples of such a particular method are not recorded in Greek literature, at least not in pre-Hellenistic times.

Nonetheless, there is some evidence showing that also the Greeks enacted bird-augury as provoked mantic: in replying to the interpretation of a bird-omen by Polydamas, the Homeric Hector identifies 'right' with East and 'left' with West:

τύνη δ' οἰωνοῖσι τανυπτερύγεσσι κελεύεις
πειθέσθαι, τῶν οὔ τι μετατρέπομ' οὐδ' ἀλεγίζω,
εἴ τ' ἐπὶ δεξί' ἴωσι πρὸς ἠῶ τ' ἠέλιόν τε,
εἴ τ' ἐπ' ἀριστερὰ τοί γε ποτὶ ζόφον ἠερόεντα.

But thou biddest us be obedient to birds long of wing, that I regarded not, nor take thought thereof, whether they fare to the right, towards the dawn and the sun, or to the left towards the murky darkness.[62]

However, this identification is not universally applicable and it is valid for neither the concrete sign, which Hector reacts to, nor other bird-*omina* in the epos, which always occur spontaneously or are semi-provoked but at any rate appear uncalled-for.[63] Furthermore the reference to one side strongly depends on the present location of the receiver. To give an example, when Odysseus and Diomedes are prowling through the darkness of the night to the camp of the Trojans as spies, the following omen occurs:

τοῖσι δὲ δεξιὸν ἧκεν ἐρωδιὸν ἐγγὺς ὁδοῖο
Παλλὰς Ἀθηναίη· τοὶ δ' οὐκ ἴδον ὀφθαλμοῖσι
νύκτα δι' ὀρφναίην, ἀλλὰ κλάγξαντος ἄκουσαν.

And for them Pallas Athene sent forth on their right a heron, hard by the way and though they saw it not through the darkness of night, yet they heard its cry.[64]

[62] Homer *Iliad* XII 237–240 (Translation by Murray 1988: I 561).
[63] Cf. Stengel 1920:58 and Pollard 1977:120f. Semi-provoked signs are signs that occur during or shortly after a prayer or sacrifice and can thus be regarded as an "answer" of the gods.
[64] Homer *Iliad* X 274–276 (Translation by Murray 1988: I 457). Also cf. *Iliad* XXIV 315f. and Pollard 1977:121.

It seems very unlikely that the two heroes would determine a cardinal point for bird-watching in the darkness. Furthermore, since they were on their way from the Greek to the Trojan camp they were moving south and thus they must have heard the heron coming from the west. But how is Hector's remark to be taken? He probably hints at a mantic habit, in which the observer of birds faces north and gathers bird-signs by observing and interpreting the movements of the heavenly messenger.[65]

The literary texts do not provide any further first-hand reports of such a 'technical' mantic; at best speculations can be made. The warning transmitted by the only bird-sign in Hesiod's *Works and Days*, which cautions to beware of the cawing crow on the roof, does not exclude technical means. Furthermore, Hesiod's lost *Ornithomanteia* might have contained some rules for a stationary observation of birds.[66] In tragedy, traces of mantic technique can be found in Aeschylus' *Seven Against Thebes* when Eteocles, on ordering the Thebans to occupy and watchfully guard the walls, towers, and gates of the city, refers to the prophecy of a seer in order to justify his command:

νῦν δ᾽ ὡς ὁ μάντις φησίν, οἰωνῶν βοτήρ,
ἐν ὡσὶ νωμῶν καὶ φρεσίν, πυρὸς δίχα,
χρηστηρίους ὄρνιθας ἀψευδεῖ τέχνῃ·
οὗτος τοιῶνδε δεσπότης μαντευμάτων
λέγει μεγίστην προσβολὴν Ἀχαιίδα
νυκτηγορεῖσθαι κἀπιβούλευσιν πόλει.

But now, as the seer, the shepherd of birds, informs us, pondering in ears and mind, with no help from fire, the omens of prophecy with unerring skill—he, master that he is of such means of divination, declares that the fiercest assault of the Achaeans is proclaimed in nightly council, and that they will devise plans for the capture of our city.[67]

The seer, who enjoys Eteocles' trust, infers precise information from the bird-flight, which can hardly be gained from symbolic interpretation alone. Likewise characterizations such as 'master of prophecies' (δεσπότης μαντευμάτων) and 'shepherd of birds' (οἰωνῶν βοτήρ) imply an active part of the seer without however learning more about his 'unerring art' than the mere fact. The question

---

[65] In this case, the east is of course always on the right hand side.
[66] For a possible influence of this work on texts like Posidippus' *Oiônoskopika*, cf. V below.
[67] Aeschylus *Seven against Thebes* 24–29. (Translation by Weir Smyth 1922:I 325).

remains whether Aeschylus and his contemporaries actually still knew anything a all about the methods and contents of such a mantic art (τέχνη).[68]

Concerning the possible location of mantic art, the outcome is comparably meager. One of the few hints can be found in Sophocles' *Antigone*, when Teiresia talks to Creon:

> Γνώσῃ, τέχνης σημεῖα τῆς ἐμῆς κλύων.
> Εἰς γὰρ παλαιὸν θᾶκον ὀρνιθοσκόπον
> ἷζων, ἵν᾽ ἦν μοι παντὸς οἰωνοῦ λιμήν,
> ἀγνῶτ᾽ ἀκούω φθόγγον ὀρνίθων, κακῷ
> κλάζοντας οἴστρῳ καὶ βεβαρβαρωμένῳ·
> καὶ σπῶντας ἐν χηλαῖσιν ἀλλήλους φοναῖς
> ἔγνων· πτερῶν γὰρ ῥοῖβδος οὐκ ἄσημος ἦν.

You shall learn, when you hear the indications of my art! As I took my place on my ancient seat for observing birds, where I can mark every bird of omen, I heard a strange sound among them, since they were screeching with dire, incoherent frenzy; and I knew that they were tearing each other with bloody claws, for there was a whirring of wings that made it clear.[69]

In the *Bacchae* of Euripides the seat of the old bird-watcher is also referred to.[70] In view of such patterns it is not surprising that in the second century CE the Thebans wanted to show their tourists this legendary place, which Pausanias mentions as the οἰωνοσκοπεῖον of Teiresias and locates between the sanctuaries of Ammon and Tyche.[71]

Considering this exceedingly poor evidence one might indeed wonder whether the mantic 'science' in Greece is not just a fiction proposed by the literary sources, which has been re-projected into an idealized past. There is, however, one fragment of an inscription found in Ephesos and dated to the second half of the sixth or the beginning fifth century BCE, that strongly confirms the hypothesis of an elabo-

---

[68] Cf. Bouché-Leclerq 1879–1882: I 142: "La science augurale des Tirésias et de Calchas était déjà une science morte pour les anciens historiens eux-mêmes."

[69] Sophocles *Antigone* 998–1004. (Translation by Lloyd-Jones 1994: II 95). The interpretation of the blind seer, who is told the events by a young boy, is by no means a "technical" one but again symbolic: Teiresias learns about the situation of Thebes by the unusual behavior of the birds, as the croaking noise of the birds, which are tearing each other apart, tells him that something is wrong.

[70] Euripides *Bacchae* 346–351: Pentheus demands to destroy the seat from which Teiresias watched the birds.

[71] Pausanias IX 16.1.

ated mantic τέχνη in Greece. The inscription pins down in detail the significance
f bird movement:

[- - - - - ἐγ μὲν δεξι-]
[ῆς ἐς τὴν · ἀριστερὴν · πετ-]
[όμεν]ος · ἦμ μὲν · ἀποκρύψε-]
[ι, δε]ξιός · ἦν δὲ · ἐπάρει · τὴ[ν]
[ε]ὐώνυμον · πτέρυγα · κἂν
[ἀπά]ρει · κἂν ἀποκρύψει · ε
[ὐώ]νυμος · ἐγ δὲ · τῆς ἀριστ-
[ερῆ]ς · ἐς τὴν δεξιὴν · πετό-
[μ]ενος · ἦμ μὲν · ἰθὺς · ἀποκρ-
[ύ]ψει · εὐώνυμος · ἦν δὲ · τὴν
[δεξ]ιὴν πτέρυγα · ἐπάρας
[κἂν · ἀπάρας · ἀποκρύψει]
[δεξιός - - - - - - - - - - - - -]⁷²

If [a bird] which is flying from right to left disappears [from sight], [the
sign] is good; if it lifts his left wing, flies up and disappears, [the sign] is
bad; if it disappears flying from left to right however, [the sign] is bad.
But if it disappears after lifting the right wing, [the sign] is good.

In manner and content, the inscription is unique since here the criteria, which
erve to analyze and evaluate bird-flight, are indeed technical and not symbolic. The
ommon distinction of 'right' and 'left' exists and is connoted in the common
manner, but it only becomes the crucial factor if the bird does not settle within the
iewer's field of vision. If it does, the movement of its wings becomes decisive. This
elevance of wing movements lacks any parallel in the Greek mantic of birds, at least
s far as we know from the descriptions in literary texts. In view of the fragmentary
haracter of the inscription it remains uncertain whether the Ephesian rules also
ake into account the species of birds or might even refer to a very specific type. In
ny case, the regulations presuppose that the movements of birds were observed
rom a very particular viewpoint with a specific direction (probably northwards).⁷³
Thus the inscription seems to confirm the poor literary evidence suggesting a tradi-
ion of active bird-augury in Greece.

The uniqueness of the inscription has raised doubts about its origin, and
Wilamowitz for example regarded the rules of the inscription as hardly being

---

⁷² The most important editions are: *LSAM* 30 A; *CIG* II 2953; Syll.³ 1167; *SGDI* 5600; *DGE* 708;
   IvEphesos V 1678 A.
⁷³ Cf. Dillon 1996:107.

Greek.[74] For all we know, bird-augury indeed had so great a tradition in Old Anatolia[75] that the present regulations might have been transmitted from there to Ephesos. But this, of course, remains speculation and even if this was the case, th question remains whether and how such influences had any effect within a Greek context. A partial answer to this question might be given by the epigraphic context The block of marble, which carries the inscription, probably belongs to an exten sive collection of texts, which were apparently fastened to a wall in the Artemision Of these texts a second block has been preserved showing a different inscription. I records an oath-offering, which a witness had to accomplish before the judges in trial.[76] This connection suggests that it is unlikely that the augury inscription ca be taken as a consecration of an οἰωνοσκόπος as proposed by Jacoby.[77] One coul rather say that the Ephesian people apparently used to publish binding rules o sacral character at a wall of their main sanctuaries. Pritchett thus deduced a connec tion between the two preserved matters of law:

> The auspices were taken for some official purpose. Since one fragment
> has to do with the taking of an oath before *dikastai* by the use of a boar
> (οἰμύντα κάπρωι τὸν Ζῆνα ἐγμαρτυρεῖν), the augury text must
> presumably relate to the ritual of taking omens for some official body.[78]

Such a connection is conceivable but by no means definite for numerou examples show that the spatial proximity of archaic inscriptions on a wall does no yet indicate a textual relation.[79] Furthermore, following Pritchett's hypothesis on might conclude that in Ephesus there existed an augury-tradition, which corre sponded to the Roman pattern at least from a formal point of view. But as far as w know the Greek community did not know of any of this. The same, of course applies to the more far-reaching finesse of Roman augury-tradition such as th differentiation of celestial areas or the fixation of a *templum*.[80] Hence, a standard ized connection between the rules of assessing the bird-flight and political execu tions and institutions seems rather doubtful. But what does it mean if the rules which apply to the gathering of bird-*omina*, are displayed in public? On the on hand this guarantees that at least theoretically every Ephesian can learn and prac tice the art of augury if only in its outline. However, since possibly not all Ephesian

---

[74] Wilamowitz 1931:148: "wohl schwerlich griechisch."
[75] Haas 1994:27, 691; cf. Cicero *De Div.* I 25–26.
[76] *LSAM* 30 B; Koerner 1993: nr. 82.
[77] *FGrHist* 3b (Suppl.) 2, 261 Anm. 6.
[78] Pritchett 1979:103.
[79] Cf. Hölkeskamp 1999:114 and Dillon 1996:106.
[80] Cf. Wissowa 1896:2313–2344 and Rübke 2001:77, 180–82.

ad a cause, the time, or the desire for this, at least the inscription enabled them to ontrol the specialists, whom they could consult in private or public matters qually, and check their interpretations. On the other hand, due to the fixation on he rules of interpretation contradictory explanations, at least if founded on the ame observation, were ruled out. As a consequence we can say that the Ephesian nscription complies with the Greek trend to prevent exclusive specialization and ecret knowledge in religious issues. Despite the existence of specialists in augury, n principle everyone can interpret bird-*omina* provided he has the social status that llows him to take part in public discourse.

The setting up and publication of the inscription is a concomitant of the ontemporary trend of depersonalizing and objectivizing norms that is clearly vident in archaic legislation. Although Greek signs owe their persuasiveness rather o situative and metaphorical interpretation than to abstract rules, the trace of an ctually existent *techne* of bird augury within Greek civilization has thus been stabiized and solidified. Against this backdrop it seems perfectly justified to render ?osidippus' *Oiônoskopika* not only in the context of the literary tradition of augury ut to look for traces of potential scholarly and technical references, which in the nanner of the inscription mentioned above reflect poetically on the "technical" or ather the regulated dealing with mantic.

IV. Posidippus' *Oiônoskopika* and Mantic Practice

Although bird-augury seems to have played only a minor role as a public mantic)ractice in the fifth and fourth centuries BCE, it remained—and not only in poetic exts—the most respected and heroic branch of Greek mantic. Especially the historical' signs (i.e. signs that are embedded in a historical context) reveal the :normously striking continuity of the Homeric patterns. Thus it is no wonder that o vast an amount of bird-*omina* transmitted in connection with Alexander's varfare fit in perfectly with the Homeric self-image of the Macedonian king and he heroic stylization of his deeds by the historians, especially Callisthenes.[81] By nentioning Alexander twice and presenting a collection of bird-*omina*, Posidippus' *Oiônoskopika* probably reflect this historical restoration of bird-augury in particular ind augury in general.

Reading the *Oiônoskopika* in the light of the literary and technical sources on bird-)augury, we see a basic characteristic of Greek mantic, namely the predomiiance of symbolic interpretation. The following pattern emerges. The first three :pigrams contain analogies, as can be seen for example in the first epigram (AB 21).

---

[81] Cf. Pearson 1960:9, 48.

If a ship is pulled into the sea and a falcon shows up flying high above, the ship wil sail safely. If, on the other hand, a shearwater appears (a bird which being incapabl of flying high dives into the sea), a shipwreck could be expected. Thus the fate of ship is determined by the flight patterns of birds appearing at the moment of it departure. Similarly, in the second epigram (AB 22) a flying bird, a crane, stand for a successful sea voyage, whereas in the third epigram (AB 23) the diving shear water augurs successful fishing.[82] In the last two instances the signs (which are remi niscent of country sayings) also have an empiric dimension. The contradictor outcome that the shearwater portends in epigrams 1 and 3 (AB 21, 23) clearly indi cates that the interpretation of a sign depends more on the situation in which i occurs than on the type of bird involved.

This "situative" character of *omina* is further developed in epigrams 4 to ? (AB 24–27) which display different coincidences that lead to the mantic signifi cance of signs. Although the exact semantics of the *omina* in epigrams 4 and 5 (AI 24, 25) remain dubious owing to the lack of parallels,[83] in epigram 6 (AB 26) a bir appears at a sacrifice—a traditional constellation well exemplified in Greek litera ture.[84] However, it is atypical that the seer Asterie demonstrates magical powers by calling a bird for help. We should take this unusual act as the poet's attempt t underscore an exceptional event—the judgment of the seer who prays and sacrifice in order to achieve a client's goal of buying a good slave is confirmed by a bird However, it remains unclear what the link is between the πελλὸς ὄρνις and the buying of slaves. That the vulture is helpful with regard to offspring, as stated ir epigram 7 (AB 27) can be concluded from his εὐτεκνία, as the editors have shown.[85] With the notion that a vulture enables a child to become a good speake and an agile soldier we find the variation of a Homeric and Hesiodic *topos*.[86]

---

[82] AB 23:

> ἠερίην αἴθυιαν ἰδὼ[ν ὑπ]ὸ κῦμ[α] θαλάc[cηc]
> δυομένην, ἁλιεῦ, cῆ[μα φ]ύλα[c]c' ἀγαθ[όν·]
> καὶ πολυάγκιcτρον κ[αθίει] καὶ βάλλε cαγ[ήνην]
> κ]αὶ κύρτουc ἄγρηc οὔ[ποτ' ἄ]πε[ι] κενεόc.

> When you see the shearwater diving from high in the air
>   under the wave of the sea, consider it, fisherman, a good sign.
> [Send down] your line with its many hooks and throw the drag [net]
>   and traps: you'll never come home without a good catch.

>   (Translation C. Austin)

[83] For the interpretation of epigram 5 (AB 25) cf. Lapini 2002.

[84] Cf. For instance Xenophon *Anabasis* VI 5.2 and 21; *SEG* 36, 1986, nr. 351. Callisthenes (*FGrHis.* 124) F 22a (= Cicero *De Div.* I 74).

[85] BG:141. Also cf. Pollard 1977:79.

[86] Cf. below V.

Epigrams 8 and 9 (AB 28, 29) contain typical ἐνόδιοι σύμβουλοι which are constructed as analogies. In epigram 8 (AB 28) a soldier who sets out to war sees an old man crying at a crossroads.[87] This omen reflects the death of the soldier symbolically as the old man resembles the father of the soldier who laments his dead son. The crossroads can also be interpreted symbolically because it offers a soldier the alternative of dying at war or cowardly retreating from it. Epigram 9 (AB 29) is subtle as the interpretation of the behavior of the birds is based on the knowledge and observation of their ways of life. Larks and goldfinches normally do not gather at the same place. However, if they do so, they warn the spectator that something terrible will happen. As a matter of fact, in Greek mantic irregular natural phenomena inherently have negative connotations: the addressee, whose identification may be disputed, has to face disaster.[88]

Epigrams 10 and 11 (AB 30, 31) contain signs associated with the religious sphere, which is also a familiar motif in Greek literature, as the gods often deliver their messages in form of *omina* at the place of religious communication, i.e. the sanctuaries.[89] In this regard sweating statues were especially prominent and it is not astonishing that we find such an omen in Posidippus (10 = AB 30), although he presents the omen in an unusual way:

ξέcματοc ἰδρώcαντοc ὅcοc πόνοc ἀνδρὶ πολίτηι
καὶ δοράτων ὅcc⟨οc⟩ προcφέρεται νιφετόc·
ἀλλὰ τὸν ἰδρ[ώcα]ντα κάλει θεὸν ὅcτιc, ἀπώcε[ι
πῦρ ἐπὶ δυ[cμε]νέων αὔλια καὶ καλάμα[c.

If a *xoanon* sweats what great trouble it spells for a citizen
and what a blizzard of spears it signifies!
But he who invokes a perspiring god, he will deflect
fire to the folds and crops of his unfortunate enemies.[90]

---

[87] For a discussion of Petrain's reading of πρέcβυc as a bird, cf. II.4 above.

[88] As a consequence, in times of conflict such occurrences have positive significance for the addressee's enemies. Cf. Chaniotis 1998.

[89] Special attention in this context was not only given to catastrophes like fire, lightning strikes, or flooding but also accidents of visitors and the unusual behavior of priests and animals living in the sanctuary (cf. Herodotus VIII 41.2–3, Xenophon *Hell.* I 3.1; I 6.1;V 4.58; Pausanias III 9.2; Diodorus XV 48.1, 49.4; Plutarch *Alexander* 3.4). Furthermore, miraculous signs (*terata*) happened very often in sanctuaries, such as the sweating of a cult statue or other *peculiari* on statues, the disappear-ance of sacred weapons and their reappearance at different places in the sanctuary, and the 'auto-matic' opening of doors (cf. Herodotus VI 82; VIII 37.1–2; Xenophon *Hell.* VI 4.7 and Plutarch *Timoleon* 12.9).

[90] Translation by B. Acosta-Hughes and E. Kosmetatou.

The sweating of the cult statue is a conventional sign that always indicates destruction or devastation in war.[91] In Greek (and Roman) literature such an omen is symptomatic: it happens *before* the actual catastrophe and is verified *ex eventu*. The frequent use of this omen in literature can be explained by the narratological effect of symptomatic *omina* in guiding the expectations of a reader and explaining the causality of an event. Coming back to Posidippus, however, it seems odd that he does not present the omen retrospectively (as he does in most of the other epigrams) but takes the view of the addressee whom he gives surprising advice on how to avert the predicted devastation. If we compare this treatment of the omen with an episode taken from the Alexander literature, an interesting observation can be made. The Alexander episode runs as follows. Before Alexander's march against the Persians, a statue of Orpheus in a Prierian sanctuary was seen sweating. Whereas the other seers who were consulted gave the expected negative prediction, the Telmessian Aristandros gave a different answer. He not only took into account the sweating of a statue but related it to the person depicted in the statue (i.e. Orpheus). Aristandros, transferring the metaphorical meaning of Orpheus as a poet to the actual situation, explained the sweating by saying that the poets of his time would have a lot to do (i.e. to sweat) in order to praise Alexander and his future deeds.[92]

The pattern of this story is a typical one in Greek mantic. In dealing with negative *omina* the seers often tried to avert the most obvious reference of the divine message by way of creative reinterpretation.[93] If we compare this pattern with Posidippus, we find that he achieves this, not by reinterpretation, but by ritual. The transference of the negative semantics to the enemy is achieved by the evocation of the sweating god. Such ritual methods in reaction to negative *omina*, however, are found only sporadically in Greek literature and mantic. Posidippus' epigram probably reflects an actual practice and we can assume that also in Greece people 'answered' to such negative *omina* with prayers and sacrifices. The reliability of such averting means, however, was not valued as highly as it was, for example, in Rome.[94]

---

[91] Cf. the evidence collected by BG:143. Also cf. *AP* IX 534 (anonymous), which regards a sweating Artemis statue as messenger of a devastating war: Ἄρτεμις ἰδρώουσα προάγγελός ἐστι κυδοιμοῦ. Similarly *AP* XIV 92 gives an example of a sweating statue as harbinger of destruction in war.

[92] Plutarch *Alexander* 14.5 and Arrian *Anabasis* I 11.2. Also cf. BG:143–144.

[93] Cf. Herodotus VII 37.2–3; Plutarch *Nik.* 23.5 = Philochorus (*FGrHist* 328) F 135b; Xenophon *Hell.* IV 7.4; Plutarch *Dion* 24.1–3 and with regard to the Alexander history: Arrian *Anabasis* I 18.6–9; III 7.6; Plutarch *Alexander* 26.5–6 and Curt. IV 8.6; IV 10.1–7. Also cf. Bearzot 1993:102–110. The pattern is frequently used in reaction to oracles too.

[94] The Romans reacted to *prodigia* with *procurationes*, which (if performed correctly) could avert the negative prediction and reestablish the *pax deorum*. In Greece no comparable way of communication

Whereas Posidippus in the other epigrams reflects the fixation of Greek mantic on questions of interpretation, epigram 10 (AB 30) introduced into literature a mantic practice which, hitherto, had been mostly sub-literary.

In epigram 11 (AB 31) we find a statue of Athena in front of her temple (which is unfortunately not further located by the poet) that moves her right foot, which is made of lead.[95] This sign proves to be an auspicious τέρας for Alexander who is planning his war against the Persians. Compared with the conventional signs the previous Macedonian kings received, Alexander's τέρας is superior and more specific. The movement of the right foot of the Athena-statue is a positive sign which becomes clear for three reasons: a) because it is the right, i.e. the better foot. b) The incident occurs while Alexander is planning his war. We thus have a clear situation to which the sign must refer. In this specific context the movement of the foot can only mean that Athena indicates she will march alongside Alexander against the Persians. c) The heaviness of the foot symbolizes that the undertaking will be difficult but nonetheless possible.

Epigrams 12 and 13 (AB 32, 33) concentrate on the reactions of the figures involved. In epigram 12 (AB 32), a servant, who is carrying the weapons of his master Antimachos, falls down. The incident anticipates Antimachos' fate—that his weapons will be of no avail. Although Antimachos reacts to the sign with dismay and is puzzled, he takes part in the war and returns reduced to ashes. The protagonist of epigram 13 (AB 33), by point of contrast, reacts in exactly the opposite way. Aristoxeinos misinterprets his symbolic dream as being auspicious for his participation in the battle. But he ends up being killed. In both cases the result is the same but the cause of events is different. Antimachos interprets the sign correctly but does not draw the necessary consequences while Aristoxeinos, led by hubris or stupidity, interprets the sign wrongly but reacts consistently. In the two epigrams the poet suggests that the gods, whose will is indicated in omens and dreams, are always right and always achieve their goals.

The concluding epigrams 14 and 15 (AB 34, 35) celebrate the competence of two seers in interpretating the birds' flight (14 = AB 34) as well as in understanding the birds' language (15 = AB 35).[96] Thus these epigrams 'correct' the wrong interpretation of the preceding one and pave the way for the overall and final success of

....

with the gods is known. Even in Posidippus the ritual does not aim to undo the message. As always in Greek mantic, the prediction of an omen will fulfill itself (in this case only upon a different addressee).

[95] For a somewhat different reading of the epigram, cf. Schröder 2002:28–29.

[96] A seer (Asterie) is also mentioned in epigram 6 (AB 26), which, however, does not put the focus on mantic practice or the competence of the seer, but on the πελλὸς ὄρνις as a specific omen.

bird-augury in the collection. In the latter epigram the raven functions as a carrier of divine messages which are associated with Alexander (apparently early in his war against the Persians) and which hint at the three battles of Granikos, Issos and Gaugamela. The seer who is able to translate the language of the raven[97] is characterized as a hero: ἥρως Θρηίξ ὀρνίθων ἀκρότατος ταμίης (AB 35.2). His competence is based on a τέχνη, which has been described as a family tradition in epigram 14 (AB 34.2): Δάμων Τελμηςςεὺς ἐκ πατέρων ἀγαθὸς οἰωνοςκοπίας. The Carian Telmessos is already praised by Herodotus for its mantic specialists[98] and Alexander's most important seer was born in Telmessos.[99] Although the Telmessians are represented in Greek sources mostly through symbolic interpretation, they seem to have regularly practiced certain mantic techniques, such as extispicy, dream divination, and bird augury.[100] In this regard epigram 14 (AB 34) confirms the use of a specific technique in Greek mantic as the seer operates from a specific location, a hill, where he meets his clients.[101]

Summarizing these observations on mantic in the *Oiônoskopika* we get a twofold picture. On the one hand, most epigrams display the patterns familiar from the literary sources (which we can describe as situative or figurative mantic). On the other hand, the epigrams contain traces of a technical mantic known to us especially from the Ephesian inscription mentioned above. Thus the *Oiônoskopika* seem to reflect both literary and technical approaches towards Greek mantic. This observation recommends that we should not search for one generic model alone.

V. Poetry and Didactics in the *Oiônoskopika*— the Literary Tradition

As stated in the beginning, bird-augury is an integral facet of epic poetry in which it often serves as a narratological device to motivate action, to connect episodes, and as a justification of specific events. Whereas bird-augury in epic as well as in other literary genres (such as historiography or tragedy) remains an isolated, episodic phenomenon, it is also—if only very schematically—a topic of whole works, a fact which reflects the profound interest in augury and its great significance in Greek civilization. First to be mentioned is the lost ὀρνιθομαντεία ascribed to Hesiod.

---

[97] Schröder's (2002:27–28) observation that the epigram starts with the description of a gravestone that depicts a raven (AB 35.1) does not alter the mantic significance of the raven and the use of him as a means of prediction by Strymon and Alexander: τῶι τούτου χρηςάμενος κόρακι (AB 35.4).

[98] According to Herodotus I 78.84 the Lydian king Croesus consulted the Telmessians.

[99] Cf. Berve 1926:I, nr. 117 (s.v. Ἀρίστανδρος).

[100] Cf. Cicero *De Div.* I 91 and the commentary of Pease 1920–1923:256f.

[101] A similar place to that of Posidippus is mentioned by a Pergamene inscription of the Imperial period (cf. Habicht 1969, no.115).

This work, which was athetized by Apollonius Rhodius,[102] might indeed have contained a complete bird-mantic. It probably followed the *Works and Days* as the following lines suggest (826–828):

> τάων εὐδαίμων τε καὶ ὄλβιος, ὃς τάδε πάντα
> εἰδὼς ἐργάζηται ἀναίτιος ἀθανάτοισιν,
> ὄρνιθας κρίνων καὶ ὑπερβασίας ἀλεείνων.

That man is happy and lucky in them who knows all these things and does his work without offending the deathless gods, who discerns the omens of birds and avoids transgressions.[103]

One can only speculate on the structure and the mantic implication of this ὀρνιθομαντεία. Above all it seems possible that it might have been a kind of didactic poetry composed in the manner of the daily calendar of the *Works and Days* (which also alludes to bird-signs)[104] and could have included an anthology of the most important or the most frequent signs and their significance. At the same time one cannot rule out a treatment limited to the function of bird-*omina* as—for example—weather indicators. In such a way bird-*omina* are presented in the *Phaenomena* of Aratus, who has imitated Hesiod's didactic poetry[105] and who has incorporated or transferred a prose text 'On Signs'—be it Theophrastus' *De Signis* or a more extended one[106]—into his own didactic poem. Similarly Posidippus could have "translated" a (lost) technical prose text on (bird-)augury or a didactic poem— be it Hesiod's ὀρνιθομαντεία, a lost poem or parts of Aratus' *Phaenomena*—into his epigrammatic poetry. In any case, the example of Hesiod and Aratus show that bird-augury appears to have had its place also in didactic poetry as a potential topic of an individual work, which could have functioned as a model for the *Oiônoskopika*.

Our assumption seems further justified in view of the Hellenistic renaissance, not only of didactic poetry in general, but also, as the example of Aratus indicates, of the poetical reception of bird-augury as a special topic of this genre. Even without being able to illustrate a direct reception of Aratus (let alone Hesiod) by Posidippus, comparison clarifies the following. Unlike Aratus, Posidippus tries to present the whole range of mantic augury in an exemplary study. In his epigrams we find both weather indicators and signs referring to everyday-life as well as polit-

---

[102] Cf. Pausanias IX 31, 4f. Also see Schwartz 1960:29–31.

[103] Translation by Evelyn-White 1982:65

[104] Verses 747 and 801. Also cf. West 1978:364f.

[105] Cf. Kidd 1997:8–10 and Hutchinson 1988:216.

[106] Cf. Hutchinson 1988:214f. and Kidd: 1997:21–23.

ical and 'historical' *omina*. This reflects the poet's claim to present (with the brevity of the epigrammatic form) as complete a picture of (bird-)augury as possible. From this point of view we might say that Posidippus' epigrams outgrow the limits of a didactic poem that is restricted in theme such as Aratus's *Phaenomena*. Thus a potential double intention of the *Oiônoskopika* emerges, namely to integrate a new topic into the genre of the epigram and at the same time to establish and introduce the new epigrams as a rival to other genres that had previously dealt with this topic.

Such a breaking of genre-boundaries is particularly characteristic of the Hellenistic epigram,[107] and in the case of the *Oiônoskopika* a dialogue with at least four different genres takes place. Whereas the inner *Ergänzungsspiel* of the *Oiônoskopika* reveals the didactic structure of the section, single epigrams of the collection allude to and play with themes and motifs taken from didactic poetry, epic, historiography, and technical writings on augury. Thus we are familiar with the type of weather-indicator and country-saying (2–3 = AB 22–23) from didactic poetry (Hesiod, Aratus) and from the Homeric Epos; political and military *omina* have their traditional place in historiography and epic; and the technical details concerning seers and their art which are presented in epigrams 14 and 15 (AB 34, 35) mirror the presentation of bird-augury in technical writings. With his *Oiônoskopika*, Posidippus thus combines a scientific approach of (bird-)augury with a poetical combat of genre.

The intended appeal to different genres can be supported by three further observations. At the beginning of the *Oiônoskopika* a striking allusion to Homer suggests itself in the language of epigram 1 (AB 21):

νηὶ καθελκομένηι πάντα πλέο⟨c⟩ ἰνὶ φανήτω
ἴρηξ, αἰθυίης οὐ καθαροπτέρυγος·
δύνων εἰς βυθὸν ὄρνις ἀνάρcιος, ἀλλὰ πετέcθω
ὑψο..[.....]..[....].[..].φ' ὅλωc·
οἷοc ἀπὸ δρυὸc ὦρτ' Ἰακῆc ὠκύπτεροc ἴρηξ
ἰρῆι, Τίμων, cῆ⟨ι⟩ νηὶ καθελκομένηι⟨ι⟩.[108]

---

[107] Compare for example the erotic and sympotic epigrams, which take over topics from love-elegy and sympotic literature and transform them—although in a highly selective way—to the genre of epigram. Cf. Giangrande 1968. For the sympotic and erotic epigram in Hellenistic period also cf. Gutzwiller 1998:117 and—with regard to Asclepiades 25 GP—Bettenworth 2002.

[108] AB:43:
> At the launching of a ship may a hawk appear all full of strength,
> as the shearwater's wings are not of good omen.
> A bird that dives to the deep is unpropitious, but let it fly
> on high . . . completely.

In AB 21.3 and especially 21.5, Posidippus, at a prominent spot of his introductory epigram, quotes a Homeric description of a hawk or falcon,[109] which appears, after Poseidon had transformed into the bird-interpreter Calchas (*Iliad* XIII 45) and delivered his warnings to the two Aias (*Iliad* XIII 62–70):

αὐτὸς δ', ὡς ἴρηξ ὠκύπτερος ὦρτο πέτεσθαι,
ὅς ῥά τ' ἀπ' αἰγίλιπος πέτρης περιμήκεος ἀρθεὶς
ὁρμήσῃ πεδίοιο διώκειν ὄρνεον ἄλλο,
ὡς ἀπὸ τῶν ἤιξε Ποσειδάων ἐνοσίχθων.
τοῖιν δ' ἔγνω πρόσθεν Ὀιλῆος ταχὺς Αἴας,
αἶψα δ' ἄρ' Αἴαντα προσέφη Τελαμώνιον υἱόν·
Αἶαν, ἐπεί τις νῶι θεῶν, οἳ Ὄλυμπον ἔχουσι,
μάντεϊ εἰδόμενος κέλεται παρὰ νηυσὶ μάχεσθαι,
οὐδ' ὅ γε Κάλχας ἐστί, θεοπρόπος οἰωνιστής·

And he himself, just like a hawk, swift of flight, rises to fly, and posing himself aloft above a high sheer rock, darts over the plain to chase some other bird; so from them sped Poseidon, the shaker of earth. And of the two swift Aias, son of Oïleus, was first to recognize the god, and immediately spoke to Aias, son of Telemon: "Aias, since it is one of the gods who hold Olympus who in the likeness of the seer tells the two of us to flight beside the ships—he is not Calchas, the prophet and reader of omens."[110]

The following aspects can be observed. Posidippus not only alludes to the Homeric passage by language, quoting from him almost word for word in line 62, but also establishes a connection to the context of the cited passage, thus inaugurating a dialogue between the two texts on different levels. First of all, as in Posidippus, the Homeric sign appears in connection with the topic 'ship'. In contrast to Homer, where Poseidon joins the Greeks in order to prevent the impending destruction of their fleet, Posidippus refers to the far more general and peaceful situation of launching a ship.[111] But in both cases it is nonetheless the falcon/hawk that is associated with the ship. Posidippus thus uses his quotation of

So from an Ionian oak soared a swift-winged hawk
At the launching, Timon, of your sacred ship.

[109] For the term and meaning of ἴρηξ, cf. below n. 46.

[110] Translation by Murray 1999: II 7.

[111] The contrast between the situation of war in Homer and Posidippus' peaceful launching of a ship may be taken as a poetic game Posidippus is playing with his model.

153

a Homeric verse to transfer the Homeric context, i.e. the link of the falcon/hawk with Poseidon into his epigram, and thus lays the foundation of the mantic significance of this particular bird for navigation. Furthermore, from the viewpoint of the observer, the god and falcon/hawk become so closely bound up to each other in the Homeric omen that one could almost think of metamorphosis.[112] This image impressively evokes the fundamental mantic theme of the *Oiônoskopika*, which claims that in every observed (bird-)omen there is a divine message to be discovered.

A further important link between Posidippus' epigram and the Homeric passage is that in Homer the previous appearance of Poseidon in the shape of the seer Calchas is closely connected to the topic of bird-augury since Calchas is characterised by Aias explicitly as θεοπρόπος οἰωνιστής, as an 'interpreter of bird-flight' (verse 70). In evoking this context Posidippus not only legitimizes his topic as Homeric but also raises the reader's expectation that in the course of the epigrams an expert on bird augury such as Calchas will show up. This is indeed the case in the last two epigrams which thus end the dialogue with Homer. As a result Posidippus deliberately links his *Oiônoskopika* via the linguistic bonds (verse 62 of *Iliad* XIII is cited in AB 21.5), the resemblance of motives (ship, hawk/falcon), and thematic allusions (bird-augury) to the *Iliad* XIII 167–177, which thus can be seen as a classical, textual model for the οἰωνοσκοπικά (col. IV 7). This supplementary game with epic poetry is an important key for reading the *Oiônoskopika* and the discussion of its generic models.

A second intertextual dialogue can be found in epigram 7 (AB 27), where the *topos* of inspiration, which a muse or a god bestows on poets and singers as well as their gift of eloquence,[113] is taken up from the tradition of Homer and Hesiod (AB 27.5–6):

φήνη παῖδ' ἀγαγοῦϲα καὶ ἐν θώκοιϲ ἀγορητήν
ἡδυεπῆ θήϲει καὶ θοὸν ἐν πολέμωι.

The vulture makes a child a well-versed speaker
in public and agile in war.[114]

---

[112] Cf. Pollard 1977:158: "Poseidon did take bird form or rather the two Ajaxes imagined that he had done so when, as they were listening to Calchas, they suddenly spied a falcon taking wing." Against the assumption of an actual metamorphosis cf. Janko 1992:50: "Poseidon leaves with the speed of a hawk, not in the shape of one. . . ."

[113] The *loci classici* for this motive are Homer *Odyssey* VIII 167–177 and Hesiod *Theogony* 91–97. Also cf. Solmsen 1954:1–15.

[114] Translation by the authors.

One could say that Posidippus' intention in evoking this *topos* in such an untraditional way was simply to show his poetic creativity by way of variation. However, a metapoetical aspect cannot be ruled out. With the *topos* of granting eloquence Posidippus is deliberately evoking the two *loci classici* in Homer and Hesiod, but only in order to distance himself from both texts. By replacing the Homeric god and the Hesiodic muses with the vulture as the bestower of eloquence, Posidippus not only gives the *topos* a new shape and a different context but also establishes his epigram(s) in an ironic way as a new and more appropriate medium than Homeric or Hesiodic epic. We might even say that Posidippus is correcting his predecessors by naming the real (i.e. mantically approved) bestower of eloquence, a bird, in the appropriate form, an epigram on bird-augury. And as the vulture needs no other bird or even god to express his message and to become a proper omen, Posidippus and his readers need no other text to understand the gift of eloquence correctly. As the Posidippan vulture competes with the Homeric god and the Hesiodic muses, so Posidippus competes with Homer and Hesiod in his presentation of it. Thus epigram 7 (AB 27) (which anyhow has an important function in the structure of the *Oiônoskopika* and has a central position) can be seen as a poetological dialogue between epigram and epic, between the established, somehow *topos*-forming poetry of Homer and Hesiod and the innovative poems of Posidippus. Furthermore the link to Hesiod could be taken as a further indication of the suggested reading of the *Oiônoskopika* as a translation of didactic poetry (which Hesiod's works represented) into the form of epigram.[115]

Finally, the naming of Alexander the Great might raise a third point. As we have seen, two epigrams (11 and 15 = AB 31, 35) mention Alexander, the only name that is historically secure.[116] In view of the new mantic revival both in literature and in actual practice, the naming of Alexander could be seen as a direct reflection of this renaissance and of the literary genre that transmitted this knowledge (i.e. historiography). The number of 'historical' *omina* within the *Oiônoskopika* supports such a connection to the genre of historiography.

These observations of possible literary relations of the *Oiônoskopika* and other genres such as epos, didactic poetry, historiography, as well as technical writings on mantic support the impression that the collection of epigrams as a whole can and wants to be read poetologically. We are dealing with a careful and thorough composition of epigrams, or rather their transmittance into a new work of art; it is based on a didactic structure through which mantic knowledge is transmitted in a poet-

---

[115] It might be also noted that the *topos* of inspiration in Hesiod is part of the proem of the *Theogony*, so that Posidippus' epigram is alluding to a text which deliberately establishes and discusses the didactics of the specific poem and poetry in general, i.e. of how knowledge is perceived and transmitted.

[116] Cf. above II.1.

ical form.[117] The appeal to different genres springs from the strife of authorization and combat with previous texts of mantic content. We may even say that Posidippus combined his didactic presentation of Greek mantic with a history of its literary sources which chronologically runs from Homer, who is alluded to in the first epigram (AB 21), to Alexander in the last epigram (AB 35).

VI. The Invention of *Oiônoskopika* as an Epigrammatic Subgenre

Posidippus' *Oiônoskopika* do not deal with concrete (fictional or real) objects but with *omina*, which completely lack the kind of referentiality traditionally linked to the form of epigram as a (stone)-inscription. Thus they are in accord with the Hellenistic tendency of systematic delapidarization of epigram which of course progressed with the ongoing transformation of epigram from stone to book.[118] Poets such as Posidippus tried to explore new topics and integrated them into the epigrammatic genre, no matter where they emerged from or how established they were in terms of generic sense. The erotic and sympotic epigrams are typical examples of this development which translated the topics of love-elegy and sympotic literature into the form of an epigram. With the publication of the Milan papyrus further transformations have emerged. Among them are the *Oiônoskopika*. They could well be an innovation by Posidippus, if he is indeed the author.

Transforming a genre into epigram is one thing, establishing the transformation another. As we have seen, Posidippus' *Oiônoskopika* open up a poetological dialogue with a series of different genres in which (bird-)augury was at home, such as epic, didactic poetry, historiography, and technical writings. By way of inner *Ergänzungsspiel* a carefully worked out structure emerged which serves a didactic purpose and although we do not possess a didactic poem on which Posidippus could have modeled his epigram-collection, didactic poetry seems to be a possible generic model for the *Oiônoskopika*. One way to establish such an invention as a subgenre of epigram would be to integrate it among already established subgenres (and if we take a look at the structure of the whole epigram book this is what the poet might have intended). For the book seems to have an equally elaborate struc-

---

[117] The transformation of technical texts into poetry of epigrams might also be connected with the intention of presenting the material in a more memorable form. This aspect can be found in some epigrams which have been used in schools. Cf. Wißmann 2002.

[118] An early example (fifth century BCE) of an epigram playing with the conventions of inscription by asking the passerby to start the process of delapidarization and to transfer it from its inscribed place into different (con)texts can be found in Simonides' famous epigram ὦ ξεῖν' ἀγγέλλειν. . . . Cf. Baumbach 2000.

ture as the single sections and at least the *Oiônoskopika* is harmonically embedded between the preceding *Lithika* and the *Anathematika*. The following observations can be made. On the one hand both *Lithika* and *Oiônoskopika* seem to be new epigrammatic subgenres, possibly invented by Posidippus.[119] Placed at the beginning of a book, the *Lithika* not only have a surprising effect on the reader but can be also taken programmatically as a title for the whole epigram book because of the analogy between the art of gem-working and of writing epigrams.[120] And whereas this art is obviously revealed already in the first section, the following *Oiônoskopika* have a share of this programmatic meaning. They become the first example of the art of the epigrammatist established in the *Lithika*. Thus Posidippus introduces himself with two innovative subgenres, which also establish a generic sense of the art of the Posidippan epigram. We are to expect innovations as well as a creative treatment of established epigrammatic themes and subgenres. They can be as surprising as the opening sections of this Hellenistic epigram book.

Furthermore the close link between *Lithika* and *Oiônoskopika* is underscored by the harmonic, almost natural transition of the two sections; this is achieved linguistically as well as with regard to the content. At the end of the *Lithika* the attention of the reader is more and more shifted away from stones towards the element of water, which is introduced in its superior powers over stone in the form of a prayer to Poseidon (AB 19.11–14, col. III 38–41):[121]

ἴϲχε, Ποϲειδᾶον, μεγάλην χέρα καὶ βαρὺ κῦμα
ἐκ πόντου ψιλὴν μὴ φέρ' ἐπ' ἠϊόνα·
τετρακαιεικοϲίπηχυν ὅτ' ἐ⟨κ⟩ βυθοῦ ἤραο λᾶαν,
ῥεῖα καταμήϲειϲ εἰν ἁλὶ νῆϲον ὅλην.

Check, Poseidon, your mighty hand, and the heavy wave
Do not drive from the sea to the unprotected shore.
Since you lifted from the depth a twenty-four cubit rock,
You will easily mow down a whole island in the sea.[122]

The reader who has been looking at stones in the preceeding eighteen epigrams and has learned of their value, size, and origin is forced to change perspective. His glance shifts from the rock to the sea, the great power of which now gets into the

---

[119] For the *Lithika*, cf. Bing 2002 and Hunter (this volume).

[120] Cf. Bing 2002:1f.

[121] For a detailed interpretation of the epigram as a whole, cf. Hunter (this volume) and Bernsdorff 2002.

[122] Translation by C. Austin and G. Bastianini, AB:41.

focus of attention. Thus the reader is prepared to leave the *Lithika* behind and turn to a new section, which again starts with the motif of water and sea: the first two epigrams (AB 21–22) of the *Oiônoskopika* deal with shipping.[123] Similarly the *Oiônoskopika* are linked with the following *Anathematika*, as we can see from two final examples.[124] Not only is the motif of shipping, which was the topic of the first two *Oiônoskopika* (AB 21–22), taken up in the second epigram of the *Anathematika*, but we also find that the sign (a bird), which was the decisive criterion for shipping in the *Oiônoskopika*, has been replaced in the *Anathematika* by the prayer to Arsinoe (AB 37, AB 39). This shift in focus on the one hand underscores the intended praising of Arsinoe, who is likewise elevated into the position of the gods as she gains the power of a protecting goddess for shipping.[125] On the other hand the invoking of Arsinoe to protect shipping can be seen as a consequence of the lessons of the *Oiônoskopika*: omina are not always forthcoming when needed; and given that they admit various interpretations, ideally a seer should be consulted. A prayer to Arsinoe seems to be the more reliable and faster alternative.

A further link between both sections is established by the first epigram of the *Anathematika*, which is connected with two epigrams of the *Oiônoskopika*. First of all we find a link with AB 33 as in both epigrams a dream is reported. But whereas Hêgêsô interprets her vision of Arsinoe correctly, Aristoxeinos in the *Oiônoskopika* misinterprets his dream and gets killed. Thus Arsinoe is again praised for her much greater credibility compared with an omen, which is more likely to be misleading. Secondly epigram 1 of the *Anathematika* echoes epigram 10 (AB 30) of the *Oiônoskopika* in referring to the motive of a sweating cult statue. And in this case, too, the negative connotation of the omen in the *Oiônoskopika* is converted into the 'sweet sweat' (γλυκὺν ἱδρῶ, AB 36.3) of Arsinoe whose positive appearance is further stressed. Thus the *Anathematika* are in an ongoing dialogue with the preceding *Oiônoskopika* and both sections comment on each other in a playful manner. At the moment of leaving the *Oiônoskopika* and entering the 'classical' section of *Anathematika*, the reader recognizes familiar themes and motifs taken from the *Oiônoskopika* and picked up in the *Anathematika*. Thus the *Oiônoskopika* prove to be an important key for reading the *Anathematika*, which themselves become the starting point of re-reading and re-estimating the mantic messages of the *Oiônoskopika*.

[123] In regard to the underlying topics of the two sections, the transition is visualized in AB 19; the epigrams move away from hard and in the case of the rock also static objects of stones to the flying (birds) and changing omens of the *Oiônoskopika*. Furthermore the reader is asked to raise his glance from the stones on the ground to the birds in the sky.

[124] Also cf. Stephens (this volume), who discusses further evidence for the intertextuality between the *Oiônoskopika* and the *Anathematika*.

[125] Cf. Stephens (this volume).

To summarize these observations we can say that the *Oiônoskopika* are not only artfully structured as a section but also harmonically fit into the sequence of the epigram book. The first three sections build upon each other, so that the *Lithika* introduce the *Oiônoskopika*, which pave the way for the praise of Arsinoe in the Anathematika. Posidippus has introduced his 'new' *Oiônoskopika* into an epigram book and established it amidst the classical epigrammatic subgroups. Thus Posidippus has tried to establish his 'new' *Oiônoskopika* by way of *Ergänzungsspiel* with other and—in the case of the *Anathematika*—'classical' epigrammatical subgroups.

The fact that later anthologies did not include *Oiônoskopika* neither separately nor as a whole section reflects a certain conservatism towards the genre of epigram. Posidippus' fascinating innovation thus remained an unchallenged poetic experiment.

VII. Topics and Structure of the *Oiônoskopika* (οἰωνοσκοπικά)*

epigram	kind of omen	situation	person	quality
1 (AB 21)	ἴρηξ (αἴθυια)	sea travel	Timon	positive
2 (AB 22)	γέρανος (ὄρνις βουκαῖος)	sea travel	—	positive
3 (AB 23)	αἴθυια	fishing	—	positive
4 (AB 24)	ὁ Θηβαῖος ὄρνις (αἴθυια)	fishing	Archytas	positive
5 (AB 25)	(old man) priest/relatives	(traveling) marriage	—	positive
6 (AB 26)	πελλὸς ὄρνις	buying slaves	Hieron/ Asteria	positive
7 (AB 27)	φήνη	childbirth	—	positive
8 (AB 28)	crying old man at a crossroads	warfare	Timoleon	negative
9 (AB 29)	κορυδός/ἀκανθίς	(traveling)	Euelthon	negative
10 (AB 30)	sweating statue	warfare	—	negative
11 (AB 31)	(ἀετός/στεροπή) moving bronze-statue of Athena	warfare	Alexander	(negative) positive
12 (AB 32)	servant falling down with armor	warfare	Antimachos	negative
13 (AB 33)	dream of being a suitor of Athena	warfare	Aristoxeinos	negative
14 (AB 34)	seer	mantic art	Damon	open
15 (AB 35)	seer/κόραξ	mantic art	Strymon/ Alexander	positive

* The brackets indicate a subordinate situation, kind, or quality of omen.

12

For You, Arsinoe . . .

Susan Stephens

Stanford University

The recent publication of P.Mil.Vogl. VIII 309 not only provides us with a substantial portion of an epigram collection from the early Hellenistic period, it allows us important new insights into the ways in which the images of the Ptolemaic monarchs were being integrated into contemporary poetry. At critical points throughout the collection we find discrete epigrams that implicate the Ptolemies. Further, the epigrams are set out in sections, each of which is headed with a title in such a way that the interplay of title, section size, and subject matter of the epigrams within each section courts an immediate reader response. Two of these sections—the third and the sixth—are in large part devoted to the celebration of Ptolemaic queens. The nature of any such collection of poems, but especially one organized like the Milan roll, will be to have many focal points and many converging lines of interpretation. What follows is a discussion weighted to expose the nature and significance of the role of the Ptolemies, and in particular Arsinoe II, the sister-wife of Ptolemy II, both as it is set out in the third section and within the new epigram collection as a whole. My argument rests upon two critical assumptions: the poetic collection was intentionally organized (whether by author or editor) and that reading an epigram within a sequence of poems produces a reader response that differs from reading the same epigram in isolation.

The third surviving section of the roll is titled *Anathematika*, or 'Dedications' (AB 36–41).[1] It consists of six epigrams arranged in an order of 8–8–4–8–4–6 lines, and its total of 38 lines provides a marked contrast to the first two sections. These

---

[1] The word seems to be post-classical in its use, the earliest occurrence from the second century BCE. Polybius (XXVII 18.2) refers to statues of a living ruler—Eumenes II of Pergamon—as ἀναθη-ματικὰς τιμάς in contrast to inscriptions (ἐγγράπτους τιμάς). The term (whether spelled ἀναθεμ- or ἀναθημ-) may also refer to dedications in a more general sense. The sixth book of the *Palatine Anthology* is devoted to *Anathematika*.

contain respectively 21 epigrams in 126 lines (on stones)[2] and 15 epigrams in 80 lines (*Oiônoskopika*). The section immediately following *Anathematika*, consisting of tomb inscriptions, is also large—20 epigrams in 116 lines. The relative proportions of these four sections, 126–80–38–116 lines,[3] or three large with one considerably smaller, would seem to be reversed in the next four sections. In these, labeled *Andriantopoiika*, *Hippika*, *Nauagika*, and *Iamatika*, we find respectively 50, 98, 26, and 32 lines.[4] If the *Anathematika* is set apart because of its brevity, in these next four it is the large unit (98 lines) that differs.[5] Both of these sections, differentiated by relative size, showcase Ptolemaic queens. Within the sequence of six poems of the *Anathematika* the first four are dedications to Arsinoe, the fifth is to Leto, the dedication of the final poem is now missing.

Because these texts are very fragmentary, I have set out the parameters for interpretation:

1. The first epigram (AB 36) is complete, though there are a number of problems with understanding the text. It is a dedication of a linen object[6] from Naucratis made to Arsinoe Philadelphus by Hêgêsô, a Macedonian girl. She makes the dedication in response to a request made by the queen, who appeared to her in a dream. Hêgêsô's correct interpretation of the dream forges an immediate connection with the previous *Oiônoskopika* on the proper understanding of omens and provides a foil for AB 33 in which the subject misinterprets a dream about Athena.

2. The second epigram (AB 37) has a number of lacunae that impede understanding.[7] A lyre of unknown date and origin was brought "to Arsinoe" by a dolphin. The dolphin bears the epithet *Arionios*, a word that should mean "like Arion's" or "worthy of Arion." It is not clear if we are to imagine that the lyre was washed up on the shore near the temple or arrived in Arsinoe's kingdom by other means. Nor is it clear whether we are to imagine that the dedication is the lyre or a

---

[2] The title is now missing, as is that for the fourth section. For this reason I use English descriptions rather than the Greek titles suggested in the *editio princeps*. Where titles exist I transliterate the Greek.

[3] The ratio is roughly 3:2:1:3.

[4] The ratio is roughly 2:3:1:1, though the basis for the ratio is smaller (ca. 25 lines) than in the previous grouping, where the basis is ca. 40 lines.

[5] Nine sections have survived in considerable part, and intercolumnar numbering (XVI 17–19, between AB 109 and 110) makes clear that there must have been a tenth. But it is not possible to determine the original size of the collection.

[6] The object is called *bregma*, which normally refers to bones at the front of the head. Possibly, as the editors conjecture (BG:151n11), the word is used here in a sense closer to its cognate verb, βρέχω, and would therefore mean something moistened. The fact that it is of linen and later referred to as λευχέανον κανόνισμα and that its purpose is to wipe away sweat, requires it to be a cloth of some sort, perhaps to wipe the forehead (*bregma*). See also my discussion in "Battle of the Books", Gutzwiller 2004 (forthcoming).

[7] See BG:152–153nn23–25.

poem written by Arion or both.[8] The dedication itself was made by a temple guardian (ναοπόλος), most likely at the Cape Zephyrium temple celebrated in the fourth epigram of this series.[9]

3. Next is a dedication made to Arsinoe (AB 38) by a manumitted slave woman after she drinks or pours her first free libation.[10] This epigram also serves as a link to the following section of tomb inscriptions, since one of these (AB 48) purports to be an inscription from a slave woman who finds good masters and the fine tomb "better than freedom" (κρέccον' ἐλευθερίης). The slavewoman's name, Epicratis (=Mistress), may be a speaking name. Often the names in these poems express the inverse of actual circumstances, for example, Euelthôn (= Mr. Good Journey) is killed on a journey (AB 29).

4. The fourth epigram (AB 39) commemorates the dedication of Arsinoe's temple at Cape Zephyrium by Callicrates. In presentation it closely resembles a poem of Posidippus on this subject preserved in Athenaeus (VII 318d = 13 GP = AB 119). The scale of Callicrates' dedication makes a decided contrast to that of the freed slavewoman or the Macedonian girl.

5. The fifth epigram (AB 40) breaks the pattern of the first four: it is a dedication to Leto. Brief and witty, it seems to depend on a pun for its point—a man named Wolf (Λύκος) leaves a dedication in the mouth of a statue of a wolf. The circumstances suit a context now known only from Delphi. If so, the epigram possibly points forward to the *Hippika*, all of which are located in the Panhellenic sanctuaries of the Greek games—Olympia, Nemea, Delphi, and Isthmia.

6. Only a few phrases survive from the final epigram (AB 41). It would appear to be the dedication of a tortoise shell probably by the man upon whose head the live animal was dropped. The name of the dedicatee is now missing. The opening of the epigram has verbal reminiscences of an anecdote on the death of Aeschylus.[11]

I. Arsinoe as warrior

The centrality of Arsinoe to the *Anathematika* in combination with the sixth section on victories in chariot and horse racing (*Hippika*), where Ptolemaic queens are again foregrounded, gives the epigrammatic collection as a whole a decidedly imperial focus. But the fact that their queens seem to eclipse the male members of

---

[8] For example, see C. Austin's restorations and translation in AB 37.

[9] BG:152n19.

[10] The context for the slavewoman's libation could have been the *Arsinoeia* or a private dedication. Note that Arsinoe had cult titles of *Eleêmôn* and *Sôzousa* (Fraser 1972:1.237).

[11] The anecdote survives in various sources: see *Vita Aeschyli* 9; Suda s.n.; Sotades *apud* Stobaeum, *Flor.* 98.9; Pliny *NH* X 3.7; Valerius Maximus IX 12; Aelian *On Animals* VII 16. And see discussion in BG:156–157.

the family will not necessarily be poetic hyperbole, so much as the reflection of a calculated policy. Two queens—Arsinoe II and Berenice II—were deliberately promoted in cult by their male kin, and both were linked after death with the cult of Alexander.[12] In contrast, the male members of the family did not include themselves in the cult as individuals, but always coupled with their spouses—as *Theoi Adelphoi* (Ptolemy II and Arsinoe II) or *Theoi Euergetai* (Ptolemy III and Berenice II).[13] We find an analogous process at work within the opening sections of the collection, as the reader is encouraged to associate Arsinoe with Alexander via several strategically placed poems that move us from the great Persian king Darius to Alexander, who defeated the Persians, to the Ptolemies. This trajectory culminates in the image of Arsinoe II holding the accoutrements of battle in the opening poem of the *Anathematika*.

Because historical figures are rare in these poems, the context of each occurrence becomes commensurately more important for the patterning of the whole text. Darius seems to be the first named historical figure (AB 4.1–2), introduced probably as a patron of the stone cutter's art.[14] He reappears in the eighth poem of the opening section, now as the artistic subject:

οὔτ᾽ αὐχὴν ἐφόρηcε τὸ cάρδιον οὔτε γυναικῶν
δάκτυλοc, ἠρτήθη δ᾽ εἰc χρυcέην ἄλυcιν
Δαρεῖον φορέων ὁ καλὸ[c] λίθοc—ἅρμα δ᾽ ὑπ᾽ αὐτὸν
γλυφθὲν ἐπὶ cπιθαμὴν μήκεοc ἐκτέταται—
φ]λέγγοc ἔνερθεν ἄγων·

No woman's neck or finger has ever worn this carnelian. The beautiful stone, readied for a golden chain, depicts Darius and glows from within—the chariot carved under him extends a span in length.

(AB 8.1–5)

The fact that Darius is said to be on his chariot implies a specific context.[15] In the famous "Alexander mosaic" from Pompeii, which reflects a late classical painting,[16] Darius is depicted on his chariot facing Alexander on his horse, either at Issos or Gaugamela.[17] The pathos of the encounter is enhanced as the eyes of the two monarchs meet across opposing battle lines. Plutarch, in his *Life of Alexander*

---

[12] Quaegebeur 1988:41–42.
[13] Fraser 1972:1.214–215.
[14] So BG:112n15.
[15] See Kosmetatou 2003a.
[16] See the extensive discussion of Stewart 1993:130–150 and Cohen 1997, a book devoted to the subject.
[17] Stewart 1993:134 argues for Issos; cf. Cohen 1997:84 who favors Gaugamela.

(XXXIII 3–4) similarly emphasizes the encounter of the two kings as one of tragedy and nobility as the Persian king faces his enemy and defeat:

[’Αλέξανδρος] πόρρωθεν γὰρ αὐτὸν [Δαρεῖον] κατεῖδε, διὰ
τῶν προτεταγμένων ἐν βάθει τῆς βασιλικῆς ἴλης ἐκφανέντα,
καλὸν ἄνδρα καὶ μέγαν ἐφ’ ἅρματος ὑψηλοῦ βεβῶτα,
πολλοῖς ἱππεῦσι καὶ λαμπροῖς καταπεφραγμένον . . . ἀλλὰ
δεινὸς ὀφθεὶς ἐγγύθεν ’Αλέξανδρος . . . ἐξέπληξε καὶ
διεσκέδασε τὸ πλεῖστον.

[Alexander at Gaugamela] saw him at a distance as he appeared deep within the drawn up ranks of the royal cohort, a fine-looking man, and stately upon his high chariot, surrounded by a distinguished and numerous cavalry . . . but when Alexander was seen near by, with his terrifying looks he struck fear into their hearts and put them to flight.

In isolation an epigram on Darius' chariot might simply be read as an elegant example of poetic ecphrasis. Its status is altered, however, when its implicit message of Persian defeat returns in *Oiônoskopika*.

In contrast to the Persian monarch portrayed at a moment that recalls his defeat, the Ptolemies first occur at the end of the opening section as monarchs over a broad domain. In the last poem of the section, Poseidon is invoked to "preserve the land of Ptolemy undisturbed with its islands and coastline" (AB 20.5–6). The Ptolemies next appear at the end of the *Oiônoskopika* as Macedonian kings, where they are coupled with Alexander:

ἀετὸc ἐκ νε[φέω]ν καὶ ἅμα cτεροπὴ καταβᾶ[cα
νίκηc οἰων[οὶ δε]ξιοὶ ἐc πόλεμον
’Αργεάδαιc βα[cιλε]ῦcιν, ’Αθηναίη δὲ πρὸ ναο[ῦ
ἴχνοc κίνη[cαc’ ἐ]ξιὸν ἐκ μολύβου
οἷον ’Αλεξά[νδρ]ωι ἐφάνη τέραc, ἡνίκα Περc[ῶν
ταῖc ἀναρ[ιθμ]ήτοιc πῦρ ἐκύει cτρατιαῖ[c.

An eagle coming from the clouds and, simultaneously, flashes of light-ning are auspicious omens of victory in war for the Argead kings. But Athena in front of her temple moving her foot out from the lead[18] appeared as such a sign to Alexander, when he bred fire for the innu-merable armies of Persians.

(AB 31)

---

[18] I have in part adapted the supplements and punctuation of Schröder 2002:28–29.

According to the epigrammatist, both the Argead kings and Alexander enjoy propitious omens, but in different ways. The symbols of Zeus, the eagle and the lightning bolt, signal the success of the one, while the other receives a sign from Athena. For Alexander, the omen is specifically linked to his defeat of the Persians. This epigram relies on the familiar iconography of Ptolemaic coinage to reinforce its meaning. An eagle perched on a thunderbolt appeared on Ptolemaic coins for generations,[19] while coins of Alexander often featured Athena brandishing spear and shield on the obverse. On one important series of silver tetradrachs, minted by Soter in Alexandria, a head of Alexander appears on one side, on the other, Athena with spear and shield is shown protecting the eagle on a thunderbolt.[20] This brief epigram, therefore, not only links the Ptolemies with Alexander, it does so in a way that indicates orderly succession. The coinage that stands behind the epigram was deliberately adopted by Soter and his successors to legitimate themselves as the heirs of Alexander, in image if not in fact.

At this point we reach the first poem of the *Anathematika*, where Arsinoe II Philadelphus[21] is introduced as the first named Ptolemy.

> Ἀρσινόη, σοὶ τοῦτο διὰ στολίδων ἀνεμοῦϲθαι
> βύϲϲινον ἄγκειται βρέγμ' ἀπὸ Ναυκράτιοϲ,
> ὧι ϲύ, φίλη, κατ' ὄνειρον ὁμόρξαϲθαι γλυκὺν ἱδρῶ
> ἤθελεϲ, ὀτρηρῶν παυϲαμένη καμάτων·
> ὡϲ ἐφάνηϲ, Φιλάδελφε, καὶ ἐν χερὶ δούρατοϲ αἰχμήν,
> πότνα, καὶ ἐν πήχει κοῖλον ἔχουϲα ϲάκοϲ·
> ἡ δὲ ϲοὶ αἰτηθεῖϲα τὸ λευχέανον κανόνιϲμα
> παρθένοϲ Ἡγηϲὼ θῆκε γένοϲ Μακέ[τη.

Arsinoe, to you is dedicated this *bregma* of linen from Naucratis with folds to be caught by the wind, with which you, dear lady, in a dream wished to wipe your sweet sweat,[22] after ceasing from your sharp toils. You appeared, Philadelphus, holding a spear in your hand, Lady, and with a hollow shield on your arm. The girl, Hêgêsô, a Macedonian in lineage, at your request, dedicated this white strip.

(AB 36)

---

[19] See Svoronos 1908:pls.A, nos.22–38 and B throughout. Theocritus *Idyll* 17.71–75 notes the appearance of an eagle at Ptolemy II's birth; see notes *ad loc.* in Gow 1950:2.337–338.

[20] See Stewart 1993:231–243, especially 239–241 and pls.8c, 78, and 79.

[21] On the introduction and use of "Philadelphus" for Arsinoe, see Fraser 1972:1.217 and 2.367n228 and Quaegebeur 1998:83–84,107.

[22] "Sweet sweat" may mark nothing more than Arsinoe's divine status, but in light of the subsequent

Arsinoe is portrayed as a warrior, with spear and shield, and sweating. Arsinoe's status as a goddess is implied by the fact that she has appeared in a dream to Hêgêsô. The atypical nature of the dedication—a *parthenos* who is not making the usual request for marriage, but rather complying with a dream omen—immediately links this epigram to those on the interpretation omens that precede. It simultaneously positions Arsinoe as a type of divinity, because at the end of the previous section the reader has learned that a sweating divinity would be propitious if properly summoned:

ξέϲματοϲ ἱδρώϲαντοϲ ὅϲοϲ πόνοϲ ἀνδρὶ πολίτηι
καὶ δοράτων ὅϲϲοϲ προϲφέρεται νιφετόϲ·
ἀλλὰ τὸν ἱδρ[ώϲα]ντα κάλει θεόν, ὅϲτιϲ ἀπώϲε̣[ι
πῦρ ἐπὶ δυ[ϲμε]νέων αὔλια καὶ καλάμα[ϲ.

When a statue sweats, what great trouble presents itself for the male citizen and what a great snow storm of spears. But summon[23] the sweating god, who will divert fire upon the folds and reed huts of his enemies.

(AB 30)

This epigram becomes the more relevant to the first of the *Anathematika* because its immediate predecessor in the sequence gave us the example of Athena's propitious omen to Alexander (AB 31).[24] Athena as a warrior goddess who regularly carries a shield and spear, by virtue of her poetic proximity, becomes the obvious association for an armed Arsinoe. And this is particularly reinforced in the context of coin iconography. Further the epigram quoted immediately above blurs the distinction between sweating statue and sweating god, just as the Hêgêsô dedication does. In the fourth of the *Anathematika* we learn that Arsinoe—like the sweating deity of the earlier epigram—acts favorably towards those who call upon her for aid.[25]

There is some historical evidence to reinforce an identification of Arsinoe with Athena. For example, Alexandrian street names that employ cult titles of Arsinoe include two that suggest association with Athena—Arsinoe *Nikê* and Arsinoe

....

argument linking her with Alexander, it may be relevant that Plutarch finds the εὐωδία of Alexander's skin and breath noteworthy (*Life of Alexander* 4.4–5). I am endebted to B. Acosta-Hughes for this observation.

[23] Accepting κάλει, the reading of Gronewald 2002:2; so also Lloyd-Jones 2002:6.

[24] Alexander regularly sacrificed to Athena *Nikê* before battle, see Curt. III 12.27, IV 13.15 (before Gaugamela); VIII 2.32 and 11.24. For the omen of Athena's statue sweating see Plutarch's *Life of Lucullus* 10 (cited in BG).

[25] Sweating statues of divinities are quite commonly attested. See BG:143–144nV16–19 and151nVI12–13.

167

Susan Stephens

Chalkioikos.[26] Athena *Nikê* is often portrayed on Alexander's coinage,[27] while *Chalkioikos* was a cult title of Athena, known elsewhere only from Sparta.[28] The assumption of the epithet *Chalkioikos* by or its attachment to Arsinoe may have commemorated the particularly close association with Sparta at the time of the Chremonidean War.[29] Other frequent Olympian associations for Arsinoe include Aphrodite, of course, with whom she was identified in her temple at Cape Zephyrium.[30] She also appears as a Demeter-Isis-Tyche figure in *oinochoae* with a double cornucopia and phiale.[31] However, there is no unimpeachable evidence to indicate that the epigram commemorates any real military activity on Arsinoe's part, though much has been made of her power and influence upon Ptolemy II's overall foreign policy.[32] The principal piece of evidence for this is *SIG*[3] 434/5, a decree proposed by Chremonides, the Athenian who most aggressively opposed the Macedonian policies of Antigonus, in 268/7. The decree states in part: "King Ptolemy in accordance with the policy of his ancestors and his sister is visibly concerned for the common freedom of Greece."[33] It is possible that this Milan epigram is intended to recall these or similar historical circumstances. It is also possible that the epigram alludes to a specific cult statue of an armed Arsinoe. We do not know, for example, how she was represented in the Alexandrian Arsinoeion, though according to Pliny the statue itself was of topaz.[34] But even if Arsinoe was never represented as a warrior queen, the sequence of images that runs from Darius to his conqueror, Alexander, and from him to his successors, the Argead kings, by

---

[26] Fraser 1972:1.35.

[27] See Stewart 1993:159–160.

[28] Fraser 1972:1.238 and see Pausanias III 17.2–7 on her temple in Sparta, "the Bronze House".

[29] See Cartledge and Spawforth 1989:35–37 for the relations of Sparta and the Ptolemies at the time of the Chremonidean War of 267/262. For a recent discussion of the Chremonidean war, see Huss 2001:271–281.

[30] Aphrodite also may be represented as an armed goddess, though not as consistently as Athena. See Pausanias II 5.1; III 15.10; III 23.1. See Bing 2003, who would identify this armed Arsinoe with Aphrodite rather than Athena.

[31] See Fraser 1972:1.242–243 and Thompson 1973:31–33. For other links to Demeter, see Minas 1998:44–49.

[32] See Burstein 1985 for a skeptical view. The whole controversy is reprised in Hazzard 2000: 93–100.

[33] ὅ τε βασιλεὺς Πτολεμαῖος ἀκολούθως τῶι τῶν προγόνων καὶ τῶι τῆς ἀδελφῆς προ[α]ιρέσει φανερός ἐστιν σπουδάζων ὑπὲρ τῆς κοινῆς τ[ῶν] Ἑλλήνων ἐλευθερίας. Other evidence includes the Pithom stele, according to which she accompanied her husband as he inspected the irrigation repairs and oversaw the return of the gods from Persia. For the relevant text, see Roeder 1955:121–122, 124–125. On Arsinoe in the Pithom stele see Hauben 1993:155–162.

[34] Pliny *NH* XXXVII 108. In an earlier book (XXXIV 148) Pliny mentions that the roof of the temple was magnetic so that an iron statue of the queen could float above it. These cult statues of the dead queen provide a useful reminder of the extravagance of imperial display and the context in which these Milan epigrams would have been composed.

virtue of her shield and spear, locates Arsinoe as the culmination of a process of conquest.

The connection that the reader is encouraged to make between Alexander and Arsinoe is not arbitrary. It accords well with the historical fact of her association with Alexander in ancestor cult and with her promotion to divinity by her male kin. For example, on gold and silver tetradrachmas apparently issued at the time of her death to mark her inclusion in the Alexander cult, Arsinoe is shown with a diadem and veil, from which a ram's horn protrudes below her ear. The ram's horn identified Alexander with his "father" the ram-headed god, Zeus Ammon, and was employed in Ptolemaic coin portraiture to connect individual Ptolemies with the divinized founder of the dynasty. The use of this iconography for Arsinoe on commemorative coins was certainly meant to associate her with Alexander.[35] Moreover, a statue of Alexander probably created for his Alexandrian cult shows him wearing a short cloak covered with the aegis. Alexander as "Aegiochos" links him, of course, with Zeus Aegiochos, but it must also to Athena, whom Alexander favored elsewhere, particularly on coinage.[36] Thus a sequence of images that locates Arsinoe in a context of both Alexander and Athena plays out or plays with, perhaps, standard elements in the iconographic repertory of the early Ptolemies.

In contrast to this portrait of Arsinoe, in the rest of the epigram sequence we find no male Ptolemies mentioned in the context of war, and when they are introduced in the *Hippika*, their accomplishments are overshadowed by the victories of their queens. Arsinoe, therefore, as a sweating warrior queen in the first half of the collection finds her closest parallel in the *kudos*-acquiring Berenice of the second half, who competes with men in her chariot victories. M. Fantuzzi, in his discussion of the *Hippika*, argues that the gaining of *kudos* by this queen, or more precisely her appropriating or surpassing the *kudos* of Cynisca of Sparta (AB 87), was as close as it was possible for a Greek to approach heroization.[37] Arsinoe, though clearly located in Egypt in the *Anathematika*, is via the associations of the epigrams identified with Greek divinities and Greek cult, just as the Ptolemaic queens in this later section are constantly identified as Macedonian in lineage and associated with Greek queens and heroes. The 'divine' status of the one queen as opposed to the mere athletic prowess of the others might simply reflect the fact that Arsinoe was dead and at least one Berenice[38] was still alive at the time of the compo-

---

[35] See Kyrieleis 1975:79 and plates 70, 1 and 2.

[36] Stewart 1993:248–250 and fig. 83. I am endebted to Ann Kuttner for pointing out this connection.

[37] "Posidippus at Court", in Gutzwiller 2004 (forthcoming).

[38] BG and others have assumed that the younger Berenice of the *Hippika* was Berenice II, the wife of Ptolemy III. D. Thompson, in Gutzwiller 2004 (forthcoming), has suggested that the terms *pais* and *parthenos* would be more appropriate for Berenice, the daughter of Ptolemy II and Arsinoe I.

sition of the collection. More likely, the divinization of Arsinoe was a phenomenon that could only be comfortably elaborated within the Egyptian context, while in the rest of the Greek world different symbols were required to publicize the excellence and superiority of the Ptolemies. Athletic victories were clearly one such symbol, the importance of which the poet emphasizes by identifying them as acts of gaining *kudos*. And it is significant that in the *Hippika* several generations of Ptolemies are linked as *athlophoroi*.[39] Indeed, the athletic victories of Berenice II (again a queen, not a king) came to be regarded as commensurate with the cultic elevation of Arsinoe. Well after her death, Ptolemy IV in 211/210 BCE introduced Berenice II into the Alexander cult to join Arsinoe and his other divine ancestors. The eponymous priestess of Berenice II's cult was designated "*athlophoros*" in contrast to the priestess of Arsinoe's cult, who was a "*kanêphoros*".[40]

II. Geopoetics

The first poem of the *Anathematika* plays out another theme found in these opening poems—geographic movement. The Macedonian girl, Hêgêsô, who is now in Egypt, dedicates a markedly Egyptian object made of linen and from Naucratis to Arsinoe. This dynamic of objects in motion is similar to that found in Callimachus' epigram on the nautilus (Athenaeus VII 318b–c = *Ep.* 6 Pf. = 14 GP). The shell of a nautilus, a creature that wanders the sea, is beached at Iulus in Ceos, where it is presumably acquired by Selenaea, the daughter of Smyrnean Cleinias, then finally comes to rest as a dedication in Arsinoe's temple at Cape Zephyrium. In both poems, there is a sense of the flow of people and objects from around the Mediterranean to end up in Egypt.[41] This "geopoetics" is played out from the beginning of the whole collection. The roll opens with epigrams on gemstones that have been finely carved to epigrams on larger, uncarved stones and ostraca to a vast boulder hurled up on the beach. The stones seem to migrate from their original locations on periphery of empire—India, Persia, the Caucasus—to their position as jewel, signet, or ostracon moving ever closer to Ptolemaic Egypt. The first section concludes with a prayer for the well-being of the Ptolemies, while the second epigram in the *Oiônoskopika* features a ship's journey embarking upon "the Egyptian sea", and tracing the flight of cranes as a guide for their journey. The cranes migrate annually between Thrace and Egypt.[42] Within the section mention

---

[39] AB 78.12: παίδων παίδας ἀεθλοφόρο[υ]ς.

[40] *Kanêphoroi* were found in many cults throughout the Greek world, though one of the most prominent was the Athenian Panathenaia, held in honor of Athena. On Arsinoe's *kanêphoros*, see Minas 1998.

[41] Selden 1998:309–313.

[42] Cranes figure prominently in the opening of Callimachus' *Aetia* (fr. 1.13–14Pf.). There they are banished from Egypt.

of Alexander and the Argead kings replicates the movement of the cranes—from Thrace to Egypt, while dedications in Egypt dominate the third section. In contrast, the tomb inscriptions begin with girls in Thrace or Macedon, and the *Hippika* focus on mainland Greece and the Ptolemies as a Macedonian line. In the fifth section (*Andriantopoiika*) the second poem commemorates a statue of Philitas of Cos, Ptolemy II's tutor (quoted below) and the final poem mentions Alexander in the context of victory over the Persians.[43] In at least six sections of the collection, therefore, the exchange between Egypt and Macedon delimits the axes of Ptolemaic power and projects an empire that appears to absorb—at least imaginatively—whatever lies around and between.

If Hêgêsô as a Macedonian girl living in Egypt is a human instantiation of the ship that moves between Thrace and Egypt in the *Oiônoskopika*, the fourth of the *Anathematika* evokes seafaring in general. The poem begins by recommending that those who are about to embark upon a sea-journey "offer a greeting to Arsinoe, summoning the Lady goddess from her temple" (AB 39.1–2). It further announces that Callicrates dedicated the temple especially for the seafarer, and that those who call out to her on land and sea "will find her receptive" (AB 39.7–8). At the end of the first section, Poseidon, the divinity with power over the sea, was invoked to protect the Ptolemies and their lands. Now Arsinoe Euploia is positioned as a protecting goddess for the individual who travels these same seas, but with an important difference—Poseidon was associated with violence, geological instability, and earthquakes. Arsinoe, first as Athena[44] and now as Euploia, is portrayed as entirely beneficent. This accords well with actual practice in Egypt where devotions to Arsinoe II were extremely popular, not only in the organized dynastic cults, but also within Egyptian temples, where she was co-templed (made "*sunnaos*") with members of the Egyptian pantheon.[45] Even private devotions to Arsinoe seem to have been encouraged, if they did not develop spontaneously.[46]

This fourth poem is in many ways a doublet of a poem preserved in Athenaeus as one of Posidippus displaying similarities of phrasing as well as overall structure.

καὶ μέλλων ἅλα νηὶ περᾶν καὶ πεῖϲμα καθάπτειν
χερϲόθεν, Εὐπλοίαι 'χαῖρε' δὸϲ 'Αρϲινόηι,

---

[43] The last three extant sections do not have the same geographic movement, though all feature individuals from many locations in the Mediterranean in motion. We find a Coan dedication to Aesclepius, for example, or the Cretan misanthrope of the *Tropoi*.

[44] The contest of Poseidon and Athena for Attica figures in Callimachus' sixth *Iambus*. It is possible that the shift of Poseidon to an Athena-like Arsinoe is an allusion to this mythological struggle.

[45] Quaegebeur 1988.

[46] Satyrus, *On the Demes of Alexandria* (P.Oxy. 2465 fr.2, col.1.7–23) provides the evidence for this claim. See also Thompson 1973:117–122.

πό]τνιαν ἐκ νηοῦ καλέων θεόν, ἣν ὁ Βοΐϲκου
ναυαρχῶν Ϲάμιοϲ θήκατο Καλλικράτηϲ
ναυτίλε, coì τὰ μάλιϲτα· κατ' εὔπλοιαν δὲ διώκει
τῆϲδε θεοῦ χρήιζων πολλὰ καὶ ἄλλοϲ ἀνήρ·
εἵνεκα καὶ χερϲαῖα καὶ εἰϲ ἅλα δῖαν ἀφιεὶϲ
εὐχὰϲ εὑρήϲειϲ τὴν ἐπακουϲομένην.

When you are about to cross the sea in a ship and fasten a cable from
dry land, give a greeting to Arsinoe Euploia, summoning the lady
goddess from her temple, which Samian Callicrates, the son of Boiscus,
dedicated especially for you, sailor, when he was nauarch. Even another
man in pursuit of a safe passage often addresses this goddess, because
whether on land or setting out upon the dread sea you will find her
receptive to your prayers.

(AB 39)

τοῦτο καὶ ἐν πόντωι καὶ ἐπὶ χθονὶ τῆϲ Φιλαδέλφου
Κύπριδοϲ ἱλάϲκεϲθ' ἱερὸν 'Αρϲινόηϲ
ἣν ἀνακοιρανέουϲαν ἐπὶ Ζεφυρίτιδοϲ ἀκτῆϲ
πρῶτοϲ ὁ ναύαρχοϲ θήκατο Καλλικράτηϲ·
ἡ δὲ καὶ εὐπλοίην δώϲει καὶ χείματι μέϲϲωι
τὸ πλατὺ λιϲϲομένοιϲ ἐκλιπανεῖ πέλαγοϲ.

Both on the sea and on land venerate this temple of Arsinoe
Philadelphus Cypris, to whom, commanding Cape Zephyrium, the
admiral Callicrates first dedicated. She will grant safe passage and in
the midst of a storm smooth the vast sea for those who implore her.

(AB 119 = 13 GP = Athenaeus VII 318d)

Note that both poems begin with generalized exhortations to pray to the
goddess in her temple, then in the fourth line, in very similar language, both identify Callicrates as nauarch and dedicator of the temple.[47] In both she is identified as
a goddess (τῆϲδε θεοῦ, Κύπριδοϲ). Both conclude with the sentiment that
Arsinoe when implored (λιϲϲομένοιϲ, εὐχὰϲ . . . ἐπακουϲομένην) will respond
favorably. In each, Arsinoe's domain encompasses the traveler on land as well as the
sea. In contrast to the anxiety of omen interpretation found in the *Oiônoskopika*,

---

[47] On Callicrates, see Bing 2003.

now we find that a prayer to Arsinoe brings both predictable and favorable results.[48] Coming as it does as the fourth and probably the last of the dedications to Arsinoe, it is by far the grandest since it commemorates the whole temple, not merely a small object.[49] On a reduced scale these four dedications to Arsinoe replicate the dynamic of the opening section where the epigrammatic sequence describes ever larger objects and includes the commonplace as well as objects valued for rarity or artistry.

III. Patroness of the Arts

The second epigram of this set, on the lyre and the dolphin, not only involves geographic movement—the lyre like the earlier stones wanders the Mediterranean only to arrive on Egyptian shores—it introduces the idea of artistry and artistic patronage as well. The reader of this collection first encounters a lyre in the epigram on the ring of Polycrates (AB 9), and the language of that dedication: ἀνδρὸϲ ἀοιδοῦ | [τοῦ φο]ρμίζ[οντοϲ coῖϲ] παρὰ π[occ]ὶ λύρην (AB 9.1–2) is echoed here: λύρην ὑπὸ χειρ[. . . . . .]. | φθεγξαμ[ένην] (AB 37.1–2). Polycrates was a tyrant of Samos and well known as a patron of the arts. Ibycus and Anacreon and even Pythagoras were connected with his court in ancient anecdotes, if not in fact.[50] The poetic subject of the earlier epigram, the ring of Polycrates, was famous because it was a highly valued object thrown into the sea, swallowed by a fish, and returned accidentally to Polycrates when a fisherman brought him the extraordinary catch.[51] Arsinoe's lyre seems to have experienced an equally fortuitous sea journey—it was conveyed to Arsinoe's realm by a dolphin. Moreover, the dolphin is characterized as *Arionios*, thus evoking the tale of Arion, the quasi-mythical poet attached to the court of Periander of Corinth.[52] Periander was not only a renowned patron of the arts like Polycrates, he was said to have written poetry and was occasionally counted as one of the Seven Sages.[53] The story goes that while sailing from Italy to Corinth, Arion was attacked with murderous intent by the ship's crew, but was saved from drowning by a passing dolphin. Allusively, *Arionios* creates a link between those famous tyrants of old who subvented the arts and the

---

[48] I am endebted to M. Baumbach for this observation.

[49] Callicrates' munificence is seen again in the fourth epigram of the *Hippika*, which celebrates his dedication of a bronze group consisting of the victorious chariot and charioteer to the *Theoi Adelphoi* (Ptolemy II and Arsinoe II).

[50] Ibycus' "Hymn to Polycrates" has survived in a fragmentary state (P.Oxy. 1790); for Anacreon, see Herodotus III 121; and for Pythagoras, see Diogenes Laertius VIII 3.

[51] Herodotus III 39–43. The fact that it was Amasis, a king of Egypt, who encouraged Polycrates to throw away the ring in order to avert the envy of the gods, may not be entirely irrelevant for these poems.

[52] Herodotus I 23–24 and Plutarch *Septem Sapientium Convivium* 18 (160F–162B).

[53] See the *Diegeseis* VI 13 Pf. for Callimachus' first *Iambus*.

Ptolemies, as well as a link between archaic poets and their successors in this new imperial court. Just as Arsinoe is a warrior queen with whom the action of conquest culminates, so too she is imaginatively positioned as the successor of earlier artistic patrons,[54] as now a lyre—an emblem of the poet's art—has found its way to her temple. Like the gemstones and other objects that are attracted to the Ptolemaic court as an almost inevitable response to the new empire, poets and poetry similarly gravitate to this new milieu.

The last poem in this section on the tortoise shell surely plays out this idea from a slightly different perspective. Though very fragmentary, the following may be said. The event described is reminiscent of the anecdote on the death of Aeschylus, another peripatetic artist enjoying support of an imperial patron. In this sixth dedication, an eagle clutching a tortoise in its talons apparently dropped it onto the head of an unknown person.[55] Although Aeschylus is killed, this man apparently survives to dedicate the tortoise shell. In proximity to the earlier poem on the lyre and the dolphin, it may be relevant that it is the tortoise that gave up his shell involuntarily so that Hermes could invent the lyre.[56] The lyre as both subject and source of poetry and the tortoise shell as a common element that can become a musical instrument seem obviously programmatic for these poems. This is stated quite explicitly in the first epigram of the *Andriantopoiika* where the human and the non-heroic are praised as the proper canons of art:

τόνδε Φιλίται χ[αλ]κὸν [ἴ]ϲον κατὰ πάνθ' Ἐκ[α]ταῖοϲ
    ἀ]κ[ρ]ιβὴϲ ἄκρουϲ [ἔπλ]αϲεν εἰϲ ὄνυχαϲ,
καὶ με]γέθει κα[ὶ ϲα]ρκὶ τὸν ἀνθρωπιϲτὶ διώξαϲ
    γνώμο]ν', ἀφ' ἡρώων δ' οὐδὲν ἔμειξ' ἰδέηϲ,
ἀλλὰ τὸν ἀκρομέριμνον ὅλ[ηι κ]ατεμάξατο τέχνηι
    πρ]έϲβυν, ἀληθείηϲ ὀρθὸν [ἔχων] κανόνα·
αὐδήϲ]οντι δ' ἔοικεν, ὅϲωι ποικίλλεται ἤθει,

---

[54] Even the Persian Darius might belong to this sequence of patrons of the arts if the original editors are correct in that he is introduced in AB 4.2 as the stone cutter's patron (see above and n. 14).

[55] The opening words of the epigram: ἀετοῦ ἐ[ξ and]χ[ελ]ώνη seem to echo the Aeschylean anecdote. K. Gutzwiller observes that ἀετόϲ also occurs as the opening word of the epigram on omens for the Ptolemies and Alexander discussed above, pp. 165–166. It is possible, therefore, that the *Anathematika* section may have been bounded by the parameters of this earlier poem, moving from Alexander's Athena to Ptolemy's eagle.

[56] See, e.g, *Homeric Hymn to Hermes* 25–55. An anecdote from the fragmentary novel of "Metiochus and Parthenope" now found only in a very late Persian version suggests a possible connection. In that novel, Parthenope is the daughter of Polycrates of Samos and while visiting her father's court Metiochus relates an account of how the lyre was invented from a tortoise shell. See Stephens and Winkler 1995:74–75.

ἔμψυχ]ος, καίπερ χάλκεος ἐὼν ὁ γέρων·
ἐκ Πτολε]μαίου δ᾽ ὧδε θεοῦ θ᾽ ἅμα καὶ βασιλῆος
ἄγκειτ]αι Μουσέων εἵνεκα Κῷος ἀνήρ.

Hecataeus has formed this bronze likeness of Philitas accurate in every
respect to the tips of the fingers. Following a measure proper to man in
size and form, *he has incorporated no aspect of the heroic, but fashioned
the old man accurately with all his skill, adhering to the proper canon of
the truth* (emphasis mine). He (Philitas) is represented as a man about
to speak with such realism that he seems alive, just like an old man,
although he is bronze. In this way by order of Ptolemy, both god and
king, was the Coan man dedicated for the sake of his talent (?) [for the
sake of the Muses].

(AB 63)

As we see in the lyre dedication of the *Anathematika*, in this epigram the proximate
cause of an art that allows the celebration of such an *anthrôpisti gnômôn* is a
Ptolemy.

The fifth epigram seems to move away from royal patrons at least momentarily
since it is a dedication to Leto. Though Leto herself enjoyed a connection with
Alexandria. Satyrus in his treatise *On the Demes of Alexandria* records a shrine dedicated to her, and she may also have been commemorated in a deme name.[57] While
the subject matter of the epigram is presumptively about an ordinary man, like the
poems on the lyre or the tortoise shell it is allusively rich. According to Aelian, Leto
became a she-wolf to avoid Hera's wrath when she became pregnant with Apollo,
and for this reason a statue of a wolf was set up in Delphi.[58] (The anecdote also
provides an *aition* for Apollo's cult title of Λύκιος.) Leto's presence must inevitably
suggest her son, who is the divine patron of poets. It may not be fortuitous in this
context that Apollo *Lukios* is slyly evoked by Callimachus at the opening of the
Aetia—it is the Wolf-god Apollo who instructs Callimachus to raise fat sheep
(fr.1.21–24Pf.). We saw an earlier confluence with the opening of the *Aetia* in the
mention of Thracian cranes in the *Oiônskopika* (AB 22.3–6). If we consider that
the third and fourth books of the *Aetia* are framed with poems for Berenice II,[59] and
that the dedication of Berenice's lock in the final poem of the *Aetia* is made in
Arsinoe's temple at Cape Zephyrium, the Milan epigrammatist's treatment of these

---

[57] P.Oxy. 2465 fr.11, and see Fraser 1972:1.44 and 196.

[58] *On Animals* X 26 and Aristotle *HA* 580a16–19.

[59] Assuming that Berenice II is the queen of the *Hippika*, then both epigrammatic sequences include
poems on Berenice's Nemean victory, which gives them the same poetic *terminus post quem*.

same two queens may well have been structured as an intertextual dialogue with Callimachus.[60] In any case, Leto, lyres, poets, and tortoise shells adumbrate a poetic universe of royal patrons and fellow poets with Arsinoe at its center.

The *Anathematika*, like every other section in this fascinating text, has an internal coherence as well as extensive links with many of the poems that precede or follow. Internally, the epigrams celebrate Arsinoe as an embodiment of Ptolemaic Egypt. They reflect the historical reality of her cults and shrines, and the breadth of her popularity—ranging from the extravagant gesture of the imperial admiral Callicrates, to the humble devotion of a freed slave. They portray Arsinoe as queen, goddess, and patron of the arts, as the successor of Alexander on the one hand and as an instrument of succor and mercy on the other. The dedications of Hêgêsô, the Macedonian girl, the manumitted slave woman, and the prayers of the unnamed seafarers suggest the mundane context in which denizens of Ptolemaic Egypt would have turned to the deified queen. Even the epigram on Leto reinforces this—as a goddess of the second rank, not quite Olympian, with good Alexandrian credentials as well as associations with Delos and Delphi, she makes a fit companion for Arsinoe. These six poems also play out a theme that pervades the whole collection—the juxtaposition of ruler and subject, rich and poor, the exalted and the absurd, in fact, human nature in all its variety. Throughout the collection we find a concomitant emphasis on the transformation of the mundane or ordinary into a fit subject for poetry, and this, of course, is enabled by the Ptolemies.

[60] See Fantuzzi's remarks in this volume.

13

Posidippus and the Mysteries: *Epitymbia* Read by the Ancient Historian

Beate Dignas
University of Michigan

Grave Inscriptions—Grave Epigrams

Ancient historians and epigraphists rarely consider Hellenistic poetry in their research. Although literally transmitted funerary epigrams have been absorbed frequently in epigraphic corpora, skepticism prevails even with regard to this category. But neither Posidippus nor other Hellenistic poets, nor their impact on historical insights can be ignored altogether. P. Bing calls the distinction between 'inscribed' and 'quasi inscriptional' texts "a hermeneutical crux"—looking at Hellenistic epigrams from the philologist's angle he observes that "the possibility of inscription bedevils scholars who deal with funerary epigram."[1] In analogy, the historian should complain to be bedeviled by the possibility of literary fiction. But is this so? Does it matter whether Posidippus composed an epigram for it to be inscribed, or composed it and then it happened to be inscribed, or composed it knowing that it would never be inscribed, or was inspired by a monument that he thought should be inscribed, or used an inscribed epitaph as a model, or thought of an epitaph for a person he knew? The possible scenarios are many. On both 'sides', scholars have denied that it matters, because the generic conventions of both types—meter, structure, formulae, and themes—are the same; the history of the term 'epigramma' and its meaning confirm that one cannot really be understood without the other.[2]

Epitaphs both in meter and prose began to appear in the mid-seventh century BCE: the dead person's name, sometimes accompanied by patronymic or ethnic,

---

[1] Bing 1998:29.
[2] For references to works regarding the relationship between Greek epigram and epigraphy see Rossi 2001:3n2; Rossi calls epigram the "literary *alter ego*" of epigraphs; see also Gutzwiller 1998:47–49.

was incorporated into a short formula. Soon this was expanded, with the main intention to commemorate the deceased as an ideal type. From early onwards the reader was envisaged as moving along, encouraged to stop, to praise the deceased as well as the poem and the monument. This dialogue between monument and passerby can take many forms: the stone can speak for itself; the dead person, the dedicator who composed or commissioned the inscription, or the passing reader's voice can be heard. The texts inform the reader not only about the deceased's name and homeland but also about how he died, who performed funeral rites, and about the feelings of survivors. Moreover, inscribed epitaph was an integral part of grave monuments. A three-dimensional character, the fact that the text was an essential part of a monument that often showed secondary decoration reinforcing the praise and characterization of the dead person, is thus crucial for its interpretation. However, this monumental aspect of grave inscriptions was often imitated in literary epigrams that appear to describe the relief or sculpture of a grave monument.[4] As R. Thomas puts it, "the fiction of functionality is part of the essence of the developing epigrammatic genre."[5] Hellenistic epigram books, which were preceded by a growing interest in authorship in the fourth century BCE, and which can be traced to the first half of the third century, were thus not an antidote to inscriptions but a form of literary expression that imitated and further developed what poets found on stone and composed for epigraphic purposes. Not surprisingly, some historians have included the literary epigram in their analysis of particular themes in grave inscriptions[6] and, vice versa, philologists have observed epitaphic rhetoric as inspiration and boundary for the Hellenistic poet.[7]

---

[3] It is remarkable that the correspondence between epigram and sculptural ornamentation, which does apply in most cases in the Archaic and Classical periods, often does not exist in the Hellenistic period. Although at this time epigram was very concerned with private matters and with grief and emotion, reliefs on public grave *stelai* tend not to be. These differing messages might be a result of "mass production" with only the epitaph having been specifically commissioned for a given situation/individual; for a detailed analysis on second century grave reliefs from Smyrna, see Zanker 1993:212–230; Rossi 2001:20 and n24 denies altogether that funerary inscriptions had any explanatory function with regard to the iconographic aspect of the monument. She explains this observation by pointing out that each had its own tradition of formulaic conventions.

[4] Lefkowitz 2001 explains epigram AB 56, "The epigram may describe a representation of the dead woman and her son on a grave stele," although in this case no monument is mentioned.

[5] Thomas 1998:205.

[6] In his dissertation on women's praise in Greek funerary epigram, Pircher 1979:11, explains the selection of texts, "Die in der *Anthologia Palatina* literarisch überlieferten Epigramme konnten nicht ausgeschlossen werden, da sie, wenngleich oft fingiert, in Formular und Thematik durchaus in die Nähe der echten Grabgedichte zu stellen sind."

[7] Walsh 1991:77–105, observes the influence of epitaph rhetoric outside the graveyard and sees the Hellenistic poet as the reader of inscriptions, as an interpreter of signs who uses the constraints and possibilities of real epitaphs for his art; it is also possible, of course, that vice versa certain formula

There are, however, epigrams that can most likely be identified as literary and in which the conventional features of epitaphs are absent or even reversed; even texts that carry the bedeviling possibility of inscription may be more different from epitaphs than assumed. P. Bing argues that there is indeed a basic difference between the two types of texts and labels this difference as one of reader response: the reader of epigram deals with the lack of context that a monument would provide by way of engaging his imagination.[8] This response is of concern to the ancient historian, as he or she scrutinizes any context provided at least for its plausibility, if not authenticity. If the text had been inscribed, he or she would still hesitate to take it at face value[9] but the information would at least gain a concrete setting: names and places, institutions and activities.

In what follows, I shall not offer any solution to the 'hermeneutical crux'. Reading the section of the Milan papyrus that features 'epitymbia', one theme in particular catches the interest of the historian of Greek religion: epitaphs for initiates in the mysteries. Trying to avoid the 'imaginative play'[10] of a casual reader but nevertheless contextualizing the texts, we can find out more about the author of the epigrams as well as his subject.

Posidippus' *Epitymbia*

The heading of the section '*epitymbia*' has been completely restored by the editors of the text.[11] In comparison with some of the other sections of the papyrus this one is long, as it comprises 20 epigrams, covering the columns VII.9–X.6 (AB 42–61). It is remarkable that the epitaphs almost exclusively regard women; only the last two poems (AB 60–61) were written for men. The section starts with three epitaphs for women who had been initiated in mystery cults. These poems are followed by four epitaphs for older women, seven epitaphs for young girls, two epitaphs for women who died in childbirth, two more epitaphs for old women, and the final two for men. On the whole, the themes of the texts are very familiar both from 'inscribed' and 'quasi inscriptional' funerary epigrams: the praise of longevity, the lament for young girls who died before marriage and before having given birth to

....

originated in literature and then passed to epigraphy.

[8] Bing 1998:35; Rossi 2001:5, however, insists that even manifestly fictitious epigrams always featured at least a single epigraphic marker.

[9] A good example is the statement by Garland 1985:xi, "Epitaphs are in fact of limited value to this study since, with some signal exceptions, the majority record little more than the achievements and virtues of the deceased and the sense of loss which he has bequeathed to his relatives."

[10] Bing 1998:35.

[11] For arguments in favor of this restoration see the commentary in BG:157. As the adjectives were synonymous, we could also restore *epitaphia*.

children, the sorrow for death in childbirth, etc.[12] In contrast to the anthologies, which also include these groups, the focus on women takes priority over epitaphs for famous men, noble men, philosophers, warriors, and sons. The majority of the *epitymbia* show a third person narrative, dialogues with frequent changing voices but no puns or jokes, as were common among epitaphs. The poems rather describe and express compassion for the typical lives and activities of women.

Let us turn to the first three epigrams. Scholars are surprised about this group as few epitaphs concerning initiates in mystery cults exist from the Hellenistic and Roman periods.[13] The largest group among the grave inscriptions that refer to Dionysus, Dionysiac activities, or Bacchic activities represents epitaphs for members of Bacchic organizations who are promised continued participation in the *thiasos* of Dionysus.[14] This is followed by epitaphs for children initiated by their parents, whose grief even Dionysus cannot take away. What is even more remarkable than the scarce number of relevant texts is the difficulty in identifying such texts. Most obviously, pictorial representations suggesting a Dionysiac context (ivy leaves, grape clusters, *cantharoi* etc.) may be misleading as sole indicators.[15] In other cases particular terms in the texts can be associated with initiation but do not provide a clear indicator. They may touch on ideas about the lands of the blessed, the Elysian Fields, or the special sphere of the pious, but do not explicitly mention mysteries.[16] Throughout, a clear eschatological message does not appear in grave inscriptions on stone, nor does the myth of Dionysus feature.[17] When the texts themselves mention initiation explicitly it may not be possible to distinguish between Dionysiac initiates and those of other mystery cults. When specified, reference is mostly made to the Eleusinian mysteries.

---

[12] Rossi 2001:13 claims that the interest in categories of the dead rather than the defunct as an individual marks the difference between funerary epigram and epigraphic model—this shift in interest might, however, occur after composition.

[13] The great majority of the texts date from the imperial period; see BG:158; the editors refer to *GV* 1344 (= Merkelbach-Stauber 1998:01/20/21), Merkelbach-Stauber 1998:01/20/45; *GV* 1916; *GV* 509 (= Merkelbach-Stauber 1998:03/02/74), *GV* 974; *GV* 2012; *GV* 694; *GV* 879, Merkelbach-Stauber 1998:04/19/02. See also *GV* 1179 (= Merkelbach-Stauber 1998:05/01/50), Merkelbach-Stauber 2001a:10/03/02; Merkelbach-Stauber 2001b:14/07/06; Merkelbach-Stauber 2002:17/09/04, 18/01/22, 21/12/02, 01/19/29; Betz 1998:400n7 with a list of epitaphs that allude to the initiation of the deceased.

[14] Cf. Cole 1993:280–292; Cole counts a total of 75 sepulchral inscriptions, 25 of which fall under this category. She observes that only four texts relate to women; cf. Cole 1993:283.

[15] See, e.g., Merkelbach-Stauber 2001b:16/34/24; the editors entitle the epitaph for a certain Daphne from Dorylaion (imperial period) "Daphne, eine Dionysosmystin?" because a grape cluster is depicted above the inscription.

[16] For a survey of themes, see also Chaniotis 2000:166.

[17] Cole 1993 observes a marked contrast in this respect between the early gold tablets (see below) and later public inscriptions on stone.

These "ambiguities" apply also to the three epigrams discussed here. The first text in the section (AB 42) is actually too fragmentary for restoration.

ἡ Ἑκατ[±26   ].ων
κεῖτα̣[ι   ±18   ].[.....].[
c ὣc ἔτι κ̣[±11   ]η̣cιη ἐ⟨κ⟩ δ.[...]ων
γνήcιον ἀμφοτέρω̣ν̣ αἷμ', ἀγαθὴ γ̣ε̣ν̣ε̣ή.[18]

The [servant] of Hecate . . . lies . . . still safe . . . of . . . genuine blood of both . . . good descent.

Given the content of the following two epigrams it seems plausible that this first one, too, was an epitaph for a female initiate. This is possibly confirmed by the letters εκατ[in the first line. Although a restoration ἑκατὸν or ἑκατονταέτις (cf. AB 47, l.5) would also be possible, Hecate's connection with the mysteries comes to mind. In the Homeric *Hymn to Demeter* (438–40) her actual cult title is *propolos* of Demeter or Persephone, so that she has her role and prerogatives at Eleusis. On an Attic red-figure bell-krater of ca. 440 BCE she is shown leading Persephone up from Hades, thus acting as a mediator between the worlds.[19] The editors of the Milan papyrus therefore suggest the genitive dependent of a noun such as as θεράπνη or πρόπολος, which would characterize the deceased.[20] The expression ἀγαθὴ γενεή (line 4) might refer to the offspring of the deceased woman, who was then supposedly married and of fairly old age. As the second epigram is also for an old woman, this would match the composition of the whole section, which has epitaphs for older women precede those of young girls.

The second epigram in the section (AB 43) is an epitaph for Nicostrate, who had been initiated in the Eleusinian mysteries.[21]

ἦλθεν ἐπ' εὐcεβέων Νικοcτράτη ἱερὰ μυcτῶν
ὄργια καὶ καθαρὸν πῦρ ἐπὶ Τριπτολέ[μου.
ἦν ἄψ ἡ φ..[.....]... Ῥαδαμάνθυος [
Αἰακὸc ε[......]. δῶ̣μα πύλας τ' {ε̣} Ἀΐδεω

---

[18] Although I cite the epigrams with their AB numeration, I give the text of the *editio princeps*. All translations by the author except where otherwise stated.

[19] See Foley 1994:61, figure 4.

[20] BG 158 (with parallels); in Merkelbach-Stauber 2001b:14/07/06 the Κόρης τε θεᾶς πρόπολοι καὶ Διονύσου (l.14f) join the parents of the deceased in mourning.

[21] The editors do not necessarily see her as an Attic woman but point out that mysteries of Kore, Demeter, and Triptolemus existed also in other places. The Eleusinia in Alexandria were not necessarily a festival that included mysteries, therefore I would argue for an initiation at Eleusis; this does not, however, mean that Nicostrate was an Attic woman.

τέκνων [πλῆθος] ἰδοῦϲαν· ἀεὶ δ᾽ ἀπα[λώτερο]ϲ οὕτω
ἀνθρώπ[οιϲ λυγρ]οῦ γήραός ἐϲτι λιμή[ν

Nicostrate came to the dwellings of the blessed, to the sacred rites of the
initiates and the pure fire before the house of Triptolemus. Again the
. . . of Rhadamanthys . . . Aeacus . . . her to the house and gates of
Hades, she who had seen the [crowd] of her children; in this way the
harbor of sad old age is always softer for mankind.

The fact that Nicostrate is transferred into a world that she had glimpsed already
during her lifetime (indicated by ἄψ) is important in order to make the case that she
was indeed an initiate. Described is not just the transition to the underworld, which
may be part of any epitaph. The final sentence, "the harbor of sad old age is softer
this way," has a double meaning in that her comfort could either lie in having seen
her children grow up or in the initiation with the promised blessed afterlife.

The third epitaph (AB 44) is for a young girl named Niko from Posidippus'
birthplace Pella. She was a servant of Dionysus, a young Bacchant.

ἐκ τέκνω[ν νεάτ]ην δυοκαίδεκα καὶ .[.....]ϲα.
παρθένο[ν ἔκλαιο]ν Πέλλ[α] καὶ Εὐιάδ[εϲ
αἳ τρίϲ, ἐπ[ειδὴ Μοῖ]ρα Διωνύϲοιο θερά[πνην
Νικὼ βαϲ[ϲαρικῶν] ἤγαγεν ἐξ ὀρέων.

Pella and the Bacchants were lamenting the [youngest] of twelve children, a . . . young girl, "Alas", three times, since Fate led the servant of
Dionysus, Niko, down from the Bassaric mountains.

The Εὐιάδ[εϲ in this case are not the mythological Maenads but the local
women initiated in the Dionysiac mysteries. Their exclamation αἳ τρίϲ refers to
the threefold invocation of the deceased that we encounter already in Homer (e.g.
Odyssey IX 65), which also makes the restoration of the imperfect ἔκλαιον more
plausible than the rather too long aorist ἔκλαυϲαν. The ἐξ ὀρέων contrasts with
and at the same time reminds of the famous cry of the Bacchants in Euripides'
Bacchae (163ff.), εἰς ὄρος, εἰς ὄρος. A famous inscription from Miletus illustrates
nicely that walking to the mountains was a central feature in Bacchic rites:[22]

"τὴν ὁσίην χαίρειμ" πολιήτιδες εἴπατε βάκχαι
"ἱρείην" χρηστῇ τοῦτο γυναικὶ θέμις,
ὑμᾶς κεὶς ὄρος ἦγε καὶ ὄργια πάντα καὶ ἱρὰ

---

[22] Herrmann 1998, no.457.

ἤνεικεμ πάσης ἐρχομένη πρὸ πόλεως
τοὔνομα δ᾽ εἴ τις ξεῖνος ἀνείρεται· ᾽Αλκμειωνίς
ἡ ῾Ροδίου, καλῶμ μοῖραν ἐπισταμένη.

You Bacchants in the city say, "Be greeted, pure priestess"; this is proper for a good woman.

She led you to the mountain and carried all the sacred symbols, walking before the whole city.

But if a stranger asks about her name: she was Alkmeionis, daughter of Rhodios, and she had the destined understanding of the good things.

The final ἐπειδή-clause at the end of Niko's epitaph is rather enigmatic. Does he comment "fate led her down from the mountains" merely symbolize her death as such, or could it be that she actually died during the orgiastic rites on the mountains? Plutarch's famous fourth-century story about the maenads of Delphi comes to mind: during a winter night the exhausted maenads fell asleep in the marketplace of war-shaken Amphissa and were only rescued by local women, who made sure that they returned safely to Delphi.[23] In spite of such allusions, however, we see Bacchic rites and a priestess of Dionysus well integrated into the world of *polis* religion—which was not exceptional at all. Dionysiac sacrifice, which is documented well in sacred calendars and cult regulations, took place side by side with sacrifices to other civic divinities.[24] In contrast, evidence of Bacchic initiation ritual is virtually absent.

In particular the third epigram makes us wonder about the concrete context and even the authenticity of what we are told. Posidippus' birthplace Pella is concerned, and from other written and material evidence we know that Dionysiac rites and orphic mysteries existed in Macedonia, and indeed in Macedonian Pella.[25] Numerous tombs painted with Dionysiac scenes have been found. In the literary accounts the royal family features prominently as followers of Dionysus: Argaeus, the first king supposedly installed the cult of Dionysus with virgin maenads.[26] Plutarch describes Alexander the Great's mother Olympias vividly as a maenad.[27] Alexander himself started to identify with the god and promoted the worship of the god tremendously. Not least, there is the Derveni papyrus which contains an

---

[23] Cf. Plutarch *Mulierum Virtutes* 13.

[24] Note in particular the expression πρὸ πόλεως, which alludes to the fact that the Bacchic rites were performed outside the city—the term occurs frequently in that context and meaning—but which in this case shows the priestess's important role within civic life. See Henrichs 1990.

[25] For Bacchic evidence from Macedonia, see Gioure 1978; for evidence from Pella, see also below.

[26] Polyaenus IV 1; cf. also Herodotus VIII 137f.

[27] Plutarch *Alexander* 2f.

account of rites and eschatological beliefs, together with a prose allegorical-philosophical interpretation of a theogonic Orphic poem.[28]

Given that other texts, such as Posidippus' elegy *On Old Age*[29] and proxeny decrees for him by the Aetolian League at Thermum[30] and from Delphi,[31] show the poet's close contacts with his birthplace Pella, it is not too far-fetched to assume that Posidippus might have known Niko or other initiates in Pella. In fact, already before the new papyrus collection was known, M. Dickie and L. Rossi argued that Posidippus was deeply involved in religious life and was himself an initiate. Both scholars have referred to pieces of evidence that might not have been conclusive on their own but certainly deserve to be reconsidered in light of the new papyrus.[32] A few years ago several gold leaves were discovered in tombs in Pella, one of which dates to the late fourth century and bears the following inscription:

ΠΕΡΣΕΦΟΝΗΙ
ΠΟΣΕΙΔΙΠΠΟΣ ΜΥΣΤΗΣ
ΕΥΣΕΒΗΣ[33]

This and comparable leaves or tablets found not only in Macedonia originated among groups of worshippers who were initiates of Dionysus and shared beliefs about the afterlife.[34] Unlike this particular text others actually describe the landscape of the underworld and give instructions to the dead person. A gold leaf from Southern Italy helps our understanding of the dative on the Pella leaf: it is not a dedicatory dative but an abbreviated form of the phrase "tell Persephone/bring to the attention of Persephone." The text leaves no doubt that Bacchic mysteries are concerned and that Persephone played a key role in the initiate's admittance to the underworld.[35]

νῦν ἔθανες καὶ νῦν ἐγένου, τρισόλβιε, ἄματι τῶιδε.
εἰπεῖν Φερσεφόναι σ' ὅτι Βάχ⟨χ⟩ιος αὐτὸς ἔλυσε.[36]

And now you have died and now you have been born, three times blessed, on this day.
Tell Persephone that Dionysus himself has freed you.

---

[28] Cf. Laks and Most 1997 where previous bibliography is cited.
[29] *SH* 705.
[30] *G* IX 1² 17. 24 (263/2 BCE).
[31] *FdD* III 192. 9f (273/2 BCE).
[32] Cf. Dickie 1995; Dickie 1998; Rossi 1996.
[33] Dickie 1995:81; Lilimbake-Akamate 1992:91–101.
[34] For texts and commentary, see Riedweg 1998.
[35] See Graf 1993.
[36] Riedweg 1998:P(elinna) 1–2, ll 1f (= IIB 3–4 Pugliese Caratelli; end of fourth century BCE).

Although the "pious initiate" in the fourth century leaf from Pella cannot be
ur poet and although the name Posidippus is reasonably common in Macedonia,
. family connection seems plausible.[37] If one takes hints from these gold leaves and
.llows for a connection with the epigrammatist, several passages in the so-called
eal of Posidippus or *Poem on Old Age*[38] take on far more concrete meanings than
hey would otherwise. At least two passages in the poem feature the language of
ysteries and initiation.

εἴ τι καλόν, Μοῦσαι πολιήτιδες, ἢ παρὰ Φοίβου
    χρυσολύρεο καθαροῖς οὔασιν ἐκλύετε
Παρνησοῦ νιφόεντος ἀνὰ πτύχας ἢ παρ' Ὀλύμπου
    Βάκχῳ τὰς τριετεῖς ἀρχόμεναι θυμέλας,
νῦν δὲ Ποσειδίππῳ στυγερὸν συναείσατε γῆρας
    γραψάμεναι δέλτων ἐν χρυσέαις σελίσιν.[39]

If, Muses of my city, you have heard anything beautiful
    in your pure ears from Phoebus of the golden lyre
in the glens of snowy Parnassus or when celebrating
    in Olympus the triennial festivals for Bacchus,
now help Posidippus to sing of his hateful old age,
    inscribing the golden leaves of his tablet.

μηδέ τις οὖν χεύαι δάκρυν. αὐτὰρ ἐγὼ
γήρᾳ μυστικὸν οἶμον ἐπὶ Ῥαδάμανθυν ἱκοίμην
    δήμῳ καὶ λαῷ παντὶ ποθεινὸς ἐών.[40]

So may no one shed a tear. But in old age
may I travel the mystic path to Rhadamanthys,
    adored by the city and all its people.[41]

It is possible that the lines have a metaphorical meaning and merely describe
he initiation of the poet in his craft by the muses.[42] One may also argue, however,

---

³⁷ AB 2002 include the leaf in their list of testimonia and take up Dickie's suggestion that the initiate
    might have been Posidippus' grandfather.
³⁸ We cannot be entirely sure that this poem should be attributed to Posidippus but most scholars do
    see it as an autobiographical statement of our poet.
³⁹ *SH* 705.1–6.
⁴⁰ *SH* 705.21–23.
⁴¹ Translated by Gutzwiller 1998:153–154.
⁴² Lloyd-Jones 1963.

that they truly reflect the language and confidence of an initiate of Dionysus.[43] To tip the scales, the new epigrams for female initiates would appear to be strong support for this second, more concrete interpretation. Given how scarce their epigraphic counterparts were, they show an exceptional interest, familiarity, and even involvement in the language and rites of Dionysiac worshippers. The fact that the epigrams are the first three 'epitymbia' and that they form a section of their own within this group gives them a special quality. If Posidippus' epigrams functioned as a "model book," they would have attracted an interesting 'clientele' and would have promoted Dionysiac worship. As such, or if used for inscription on stone, they would have been widely read.[44]

Posidippus' epigrams hence grow on the ancient historian. As reflections of contemporary reality they are potentially significant.[45] As expressions coming "from within," they are undoubtedly significant for our knowledge of ancient mystery cults and their worshippers.

---

[43] See the publications by Dickie 1995 and Rossi 1996 for—in my view convincing—arguments.

[44] Bing 2002c argues that inscribed epitaphs up through the early Hellenistic period were read only by exceptional persons and that wide reading of inscriptions did not develop until epigram became a genre composed or collected for the book. I do not agree with Bing's emphasis on a radical indifference towards inscribed texts, but would argue that it was precisely the deep familiarity with epitaph that made the development of the genre possible.

[45] Cf. Rossi 2001:21.

14

Vision and Visibility: Art Historical Theory Paints a Portrait of New Leadership in Posidippus' *Andriantopoiika*[1]

Elizabeth Kosmetatou

Katholieke Universiteit Leuven

μιμ[ή]cαcθε τάδ' ἔργα, πολυχρονίους δὲ κολοccῶν,
ὦ ζ[ωι]οπλάcται, ν[αί,] παραθεῖτε νόμους·
εἴ γε μὲν ἀρχαῖαι .[..].πα χέρεc, ἢ Ἀγελάιδηc
ὁ πρὸ Πολυκ⟨λ⟩είτο[υ πά]γχυ παλαιοτέχνηc,
ἢ οἱ Διδυμίδου cκληρ[οὶ τύ]ποι εἰc πέδον ἐλθεῖν
Λυcίππου νεάρ' ἦν οὐδ[ε]μία πρόφαcιc
δεῦρο παρεκτεῖναι βαcάνου χάριν· εἶ[τα] δ' ἐὰ⟨ν⟩ χρῆι
καὶ πίπτηι ⟨ὦ⟩θλο⟨c⟩ καινοτεχνέων, πέραc ἦν.[2]

Imitate these works, and surpass,
    sculptors, statuary's ancient norms.
For if the ancient hands of [. . .]pas or of Hagelaides
    who before Polyclitus was a craftsman of the ancient style
or if Didymides' rigid forms were to enter the field,
    no reason whatsoever would there be for Lysippus' new forms

[1] I owe a great debt to the generosity of Professor Guido Schepens of the Katholieke Universiteit Leuven, director of the *Fragmente der griechischen Historiker* project, who put Felix Jacoby's *Nachlaß*, in particular his notes on ancient *Kunstgeschichte*, at my disposal. Ruth Scodel graciously provided me with a copy of the forthcoming publication of her brilliant restoration of AB 63. Benjamin Acosta-Hughes, Manuel Baumbach, Jan Bollansée, Gloria Ferrari-Pinney, Hans Hauben, and Nassos Papalexandrou should be gratefully acknowledged for offering comments on this paper. As ever, I assume responsibility for all errors and flaws. All translations of the *Andriantopoiika* are by B. Acosta-Hughes and E. Kosmetatou.
[2] Agreeing with Austin's attractive restoration; cf. AB 62.8. The papyrus has πετεcηι.

187

to lie out here and be put to the test; were it then necessary
and a contest of new craftsmen took place, he would be the limit.

Posidippus opens his fascinating *Andriantopoiika* section with this dynamic manifesto (AB 62), which was most likely specifically composed to head the cluster that follows.[3] Prevalent scholarly views on the structure and purpose of the *Andriantopoiika* notwithstanding, this author would rather view the group primarily as a study in a nutshell of sculptors (ἀνδριαντοποιοί), set in the context of a latter-day mini competition of technical invention in sculpture (τορευτική), and of the age-long debate on style, rather than as a gallery of statues that may even have been put together incidentally. In this context, the term *kolossos* is used to indicate a lifelike rather than a larger-than-life statue.[4] Indeed, in characteristically ambiguous fashion, the poet seems to have thematically presented individual sculptural works elsewhere.[5] The *Andriantopoiika* section seems to serve a multitude of purposes: first, it praises Lysippus, official sculptor by appointment to the Macedonian court, who held exclusive rights in producing portrait statues of Alexander the Great.[6] He was probably Posidippus' own favorite sculptor, very likely also of the latter's employers.[7] Next, this constellation of epigrams recasts the

---

[3] Cf. Gutzwiller (this volume). The programmatic nature of the opening epigram in the *Andriantopoiika* is similar to the first of the *Hippika*, which evokes the vivid image of a crowned victor, followed by an *in medias res* of sorts in the epigrams that follow relating races in detail. Cf. Kosmetatou on *Hippika* (this volume).

[4] See Kosmetatou-Papalexandrou 2003 (forthcoming) where previous bibliography is cited. On various proposals on the structure of the *Andriantopoiika*, see Gutzwiller (this volume); Gutzwiller 2002c. Without rejecting the possibility that the epigrams comprising the *Andriantopoiika* may have been composed for this collection, Sens 2002:9 also considers A. Cameron's view, expressed during a panel discussion at the *APA* meeting in Phiadelphia (2002) that each epigram be viewed as a potential independent entity, as well as part of the group. In the opinion of this author, the epigrams included in the *Andriantopoiika* belong to a different category than most ecphrastic poems that praise objects by simply describing them. In such cases emphasis is placed on the work of art itself, rather than its sculptor, whose name is not supplied most of the time. Their internal links suggest, again according to this author, that they were exclusively composed for this, or perhaps a longer, section on ancient *andriantopoioi* reflecting specific art-historical theories of the time. Cf. Gutzwiller 2002:88 on Erinna 3 GP, its antecedents and successors.

[5] Several of the *Hippika* can also be interpreted as references to statues and statuary groups that recall harnessed victories. They certainly reflect monuments that may have constituted a source of inspiration for Posidippus, additional to his actual attendance in athletic events. See articles by Kosmetatouon on *Hippika*, Papalexandrou, and Hoffman (this volume). Lefkowitz 2002 also makes a case for the reflection of funerary statuary in AB 56 of the *Epitymbia*. Contrast Dignas (this volume). AB 95, the first of the *Iamatika* certainly refers to the dedication of a statue. Cf. Bing (this volume); Bing 2002b.

[6] Plutarch *Moralia* 335A–B. On Lysippus, see Edwards 1996.

[7] Cf. Kosmetatou (this volume). Posidippus composed several epigrams in praise of Lysippus: AB 62, 65, 70, 142 (=19 GP, not part of the Milan papyrus).

old debate on art historical theory, reflecting contemporary trends, as well as earlier, mainly prose, works on style and art history. This is why every vivid description of sculptures is carefully associated with specific artisans, an element which is not generally found in ordinary ecphrastic poems.[8] Last, but not least, as a poet by appointment to the Ptolemaic court, Posidippus takes part in the political and philosophical discourse of his time, in which style played a role carrying additional important implicit meanings, associated in this case with the new regime in Egypt.[9] At the end of the section, the poet has presented his case to the reader, and from his programmatic scrutiny Lysippus emerges victorious, his predecessors' ideas lie gasping for relevance, and the work of his successors is forever doomed to play second fiddle to his own unsurpassed achievement.

All theories that dominated art-historical debate until Lysippus are therefore seemingly pronounced as defunct and destined for the dustbin of discourse. This view appears to have been prevalent and is echoed later in Pliny, who states that bronze art was dormant from about 290 to 155 BCE.[10] Yet, even though one may assume that Posidippus speaks the word of doom for old, and several new, sculptors in his retrospective, all does not seem to be lost for their survival in the good opinion of posterity. The poet's repeated references to μίμησις, best interpreted as 'creative adaptation', rather than 'imitation' (μιμήσασθε),[11] 'truth' (ἀλήθεια), and 'the measure thereof' (κανών), associated with his review of past and contemporary achievement, culminates in a proto-Darwinian view of sorts: theories and ideas, just like species, evolve from a primordial swamp, adapt to their environment, and thrive. This article will argue that despite Posidippus', and Ptolemaic, taste for Lysippus and his successors, the *Andriantopoiika* do not represent a polemic, even though they are structured as a *plaidoyer*. The rhetoric used by the poet is old; the seemingly differing visions of sculptors, here outlined, are in tune with the cornerstone of Greek aesthetics: the search for truth and realism that had been in the mind of all artists since the artistic explosion occurred.

This exploration is going on today even though truth is not defined in the same way.[12] Modern science may offer a physiological explanation for the transformations of art and aesthetics as a result of the co-evolution between mind and

[8] Most ecphrastic epigrams contain elaborate descriptions of sculptures, but very few in conjunction to the specific style associated with certain sculptors. Cf. Posidippus, AB 142 (on Lysippus); *APl.* 54 (on Myron); 60 (Simonides on Scopas); 81 (Philip on Phidias); 84 (on Cimon), 120 (Asclepiades or Archelaus on Lysippus), 275 (Posidippus on Lysippus), etc.
[9] Cf. Edelman 1995:24.
[10] Pliny XXXIV 52. Cf. Preisshofen 1979; Isager 1991:97–98.
[11] Following the thoughtful interpretation of Connor 1987:50. Cf. Gray 1987:467–486; Childs 1994:38.
[12] For the most important deconstructionist view on the truth in art, see Derrida 1987. Cf. also Stewart (forthcoming).

brain, which particularly witnessed the development of the prefrontal cortex, driven by the adaptive advantages of superior cognitive functions.[13] However, in attempting to define the sublime, creativity and invention are still in part associated with the incomprehensible of the act of beholding. Indeed, the feeling of the sublime seems to have remained as impenetrable to reason, yet comprehensible in the imagination, as it ever was in the days of Kant.[14] Whether physiology has still to work out the details in capturing and dissecting it, or whether the sublime will remain as elusive as ever, one cannot say. However, the mystery of creativity notwithstanding, a work of art may function as catalyst in the interaction between artist and spectator, and ensuing debate, driven by language, be that pedantic scholarly prose or poetry, may contribute in the end to the development of collective cognitive functions which form future artistic trends.[15] Even though brain physiology was a complete unknown in Posidippus' time, the contribution of artistic discourse both in the development of art and in personal improvement was acknowledged and appreciated.[16]

The unfortunate loss of the greater part of Greek literature has left us with pitiful fragments and echoes of this important debate, especially its earlier stages, in the remaining sources. The historian's task is to bring together this information and place it in its appropriate context by examining its position within a certain historical, political, philosophical, aesthetic, theoretical, and cultural framework. Even though it is unclear when the debate was first formulated and to which literary genre committed, its earliest appearance is associated with ecphrastic passages in Homer's *Shield of Achilles* and the pseudo-Hesiodic *Shield of Heracles*, both of which reflect their contemporary artistic developments.[17] Later works from the Classical and Roman periods describe the achievement of the legendary sculptor Daedalus, who is credited with such innovations in technique that his reportedly lifelike works were supposed to move almost by magic.[18] All reports reflect myth, rather than

---

[13] Ramachandran-Hirstein 1999:15–51; Harth 1999:105, 113–114.

[14] Kant 1960/1764. Cf. Gadamer 19892:42–60.

[15] Cf. Brown 1999:158–160.

[16] A group of articles on art and its perception by humans was instigated by the essay by Ramachandran and Hirstein 1999, and was published in three consecutive issues of the *Journal of Consciousness Studies*. The achievement of this critically acclaimed interdisciplinary dialogue is of paramount importance as it brought together scholars from seemingly distant and even unusual disciplines, including neuroscientists, neurologists, neurobiologists, neuropsychologists, physiologists, psychologists, physicists, philosophers, art historians, computer scientists, and artists. Cf. Goguen 1999, Goguen 2000, Ramachandran and Freeman 2001. On ancient ideas on the role of art in society, see Andronikos 1986:23-108; Childs 1994:39–40.

[17] Janko 1986:37–42; Becker 1995; Snodgrass 1998:especially 40–66.

[18] Philipp 1968; Donohue 1988:179–194 where testimonia are cited; Morris 1995:2. Information on the ancient perception of Daedalus is furnished by a wealth of sources including: Aristophanes,

reality, and no work could be attributed with certainty to Daedalus in antiquity. As a result, ancient perception of the origins of Greek statuary was set as fact through the centuries, influencing antiquarian and Christian authors, as well as modern scholars who did not take the existing material remains into account in their initial reconstruction of artistic developments.[19] The literary tradition on Daedalus' achievement surely predates the authors who lived through the enlightenment that was the fifth century BCE and witnessed important strides in rational discourse and the development of method in historical studies. However, one may assume that the issue of accurate imitation of life preoccupied artists and spectators as much in the Archaic as in later periods, including Posidippus'. Indeed, Posidippus' select bronzes are described as looking almost alive through the skill of both their sculptor and the great poet whose poetry brings them to life (AB 63 [ἔμψυχ]ος, καῖπερ χάλκεος ἐὼν ὁ γέρων; AB 64 [γ]αρύ[ει] 'Ιδομενεύς). Nevertheless, the reader is continuously reminded that these are works of art, lifelike, but not actually alive. In this respect, by stressing the lifeless material of which they are made (AB 65: πῦρ τοι ὁ χα[λκὸς ὁρ]ῆι,), the poet does not allow us to forget reality. The reader therefore keeps his cool and his mind ready for rational discourse. Earlier accounts on Daedalus' statuary are more fanciful: Aristophanes says that the legendary sculptor's works were reputed to be chained to prevent them from actually walking away.[20] In this respect, these daedalic sculptures were not far removed from the Homeric tripods-*automata* that served Hephaestus, and whose soon to be added highly decorated handles are interestingly described as δαιδάλεα.[21]

Although art historians in Posidippus' time mainly wrote in prose, the poet felt at home in his chosen medium. Indeed the origins of ecphrasis in the context of rational discourse are found in the ancient dramatists as an integral part of the spectacle that is theater. Scholars have drawn attention to an important fragment of Aeschylus' satyr play entitled *Theoroi* or *Isthmiastai* (*Spectators at the Isthmian Games*)[22] that probably belonged to its *parodos*.[23] The satyrs are carrying masks in the form of images of themselves destined to be hung as votive offerings on the

....

fr. 194 Kock = Hesychius, s.v. *Daidaleia*; Plato *Euthyphro* 11b–e; Aristotle *De Anima* I 3.406b; Diodorus IX 76.1–3; *Lexeis Rhetorikai* X; Philostratus *VA* VI 4.

[19] Donohue 1988:177–194.

[20] Aristophanes, fr 194 Kock = Hesychius, s.v. *Daidaleia*.

[21] Homer *Iliad* XVIII 373–379; Becker 1995. Papalexandrou 2003 argues that Homer does not insinuate that the unfinished state of the tripods does not allow them to move, but that he would rather refrain on purpose from presenting his audience with an ecphrasis of visual elements in order to promote the ideology of the visual decoration on Achilles' shield.

[22] For the various meanings of the term *theoros*, see Rutherford 2000.

[23] P.Oxy. 2162; fr. 78a Radt.

façade of the temple of Poseidon Isthmius. They take the opportunity to comment on their portraits whose unnamed artist captured his subjects so remarkably well that they look alive (Fr. 1, col. I, lines 5-7, 11–17). An allusion to Daedalus' life-like works is made:

ἄθρησον εἰπ [. .] . . [
εἴδωλον εἶναι τοῦτ' ἐμῆι μορφῆι πλέον
τὸ Δαιδάλου μ{ε }[ί]μημα φωνῆς δεῖ μόνον.
. . .
εὐκταῖα κόσμον ταῦτ[α τ]ῶι θεῶι φέρω,
καλλίγραπτον εὐχάν.
τῆι μητρὶ τἠιμῆι πράγματ' ἂν παρασχέθοι·
ἰδοῦσα γὰρ νιν ἂν σαφῶς
τρέποιτ' ἂν αἴζοιτό θ' ὡς[24]
δοκοῦσ' ἐμ' εἶναι τὸν ἐξ-
έθρεψεν· οὕτως ἐμφερὴς ὅδ' ἐστίν.

Pray look and tell [me
this image if it could be more like me,
this likeness made by Daedalus, it only lacks a voice.
. . .
These votive offerings I bring to the god
a beautifully painted payment of vow.
If these were shown to my own mother
she would turn and cry for she would think
that it is I, the one she raised; so like me is this effigy.

Skinner and Gutzwiller have already taken note of the striking similarities between this passage in Aeschylus and an epigram by Erinna on the portrait of the maiden Agatharchis (3 GP):

Ἐξ ἀταλῶν χειρῶν τάδε γράμματα, λῶιστε Προμαθεῦ,
ἐντὶ καὶ ἄνθρωποι τὶν ὁμαλοὶ σοφίαν.
ταύταν γοῦν ἐτύμως τὰν παρθένον ὅστις ἔγραψεν,
αἰ καὐδὰν ποτέθηκ', ἧς κ' Ἀγαθαρχὶς ὅλα.

---

[24] The text is corrupt here. Cf. Lobel, Roberts, Wegener 1941:21.

Delicate hands produced this painting, most excellent Prometheus,
indeed humans can have as much wisdom as you.

Had he but given her a voice, whoe'er it was that painted the maiden
so accurately, this would have been Agatharchis in everything.

Other parallels have also been drawn, and the theme of mimesis seems to have
been particularly popular in Hellenistic poetry.[25] Callimachus used extensively
ecphrasis in his *Aetia* and in *Iambi* 6, 7, and 9, focusing on the innovative form of
individual statues.[26] The new Posidippus furnishes more examples of ecphrastic
epigrams, belonging to the same tradition and describing statues so lifelike that
seem about to speak, this an additional allusion to their inscribed base
(AB 63–64).[27] In his introductory AB 62 his appeal in favor for the new Lysippean
sculpture may reflect his own, new, poetry, short and delicate, just like Lysippean
art. In this respect, Posidippus' praise for Lysippean art is sung in its appropriate
form, from the poet's perspective—the epigram—which he praises through his
praise of his favorite sculptor.[28] Realism in sculpture is a recurring theme in the
Hippika and *Andriantopoiika*, the two sections that are dedicated to the artful
crafts.[29] However, an effective description in the tradition that may have begun with
Homer, from which Aeschylus may have been influenced, is not all that the
Andriantopoiika epigrams have to offer.

Let us dwell on Aeschylus for a little longer: Zeitlin has brilliantly interpreted
the satyrs and their masks in *Theoroi* as the scene of a paradigmatic encounter
between the two representational modes of theater and its contemporary arts.[30] In
this context, theater with its conventions as a framed space, defined by spatial and
mental horizons, made use of figurative arts, mainly architecture and painting
(*skenographia*), therefore becoming the ideal forum where artistic advances could be
presented to their best advantage. Indeed, it was at the time that Aeschylus staged
his *Theoroi* that important developments took place in perspective, coloration, and
the pictorial space. These were applied in contemporary scene-painting, an invention of the painter Agatharchus especially for Aeschylus' plays. Agatharchus is also
credited with authorship of a treatise on perspective, and his interest in optical
phenomena was shared by his contemporary philosophers Anaxagoras and
Democritus in their respective works.[31] Euripides, himself reputed to have also been

---

[25] Skinner 2001:207–208; Gutzwiller 2002:88–91.

[26] Acosta-Hughes 2002:265–303.

[27] Cf. important new reading on AB 63 by Scodel 2003.

[28] On Hellenistic epigram as a miniature perfection, see Schur (this volume).

[29] See articles by Kosmetatou, Papalexandrou, and Hoffman (this volume).

[30] Zeitlin 1994.

[31] Zeitlin 1994:139–140. Cf. Vitruvius *De architectura* VII pref. 11; Demosthenes *Ad Meidiam* 147;

a remarkable painter, went further than his predecessors in using ecphrasis, both symbolically and, most importantly, in his exploration of vision and the interplay between illusion and reality.[32] As the Athenians viewed it, theater was a place of education in the democratic polity functioning as bridge between the élite and popular culture. Its importance in forming spectators' minds and challenging them to take part in the political debate of the day has been discussed, of course, at great length.[33] At the same time, it also acquainted the same public with the current art-historical debate going on in the highest circles of the élite and drew spectators in to experience visual art by provoking impassioned responses to it. True enough, spectators were not expected to feel as tourists, focusing on the poet's display of art, as images were subordinate to the action and functioned as symbols, rather than having their own life.[34] However, by drawing attention to the achievement of the dramatist's artist-collaborators, playwrights also aimed at bringing the world that had been there all along to the attention of that same public: to ambush them with the passions and dreams of the artist and invite them to look at that same world through the eyes of another.

By opting for ecphrastic epigram, epigrammatists from the middle of the fourth century BCE onwards entered a territory that had been previously occupied by art historical treatises written by the artists themselves and by tragic poets. Indeed, the tragic stage constituted an ideal forum, as it was partly defined by the dialectical relationship between the visible and invisible which transcended to the epistemological discourse of the time on insight, knowledge, revelation, and truth. The reciprocal influence between the visual and dramatic arts with regard to the debate on the sources of knowledge and double perspective was a frequent theme in plays, and it found its best expression in tragic irony.[35] Hellenistic epigram took ecphrasis one step further: although this genre is set in a purely mental framework, the poet's vision invites the reader to experience art and what is no longer visible with the eyes of his/her imagination. The epigram form was an ideal host to this interaction; by challenging the reader's erudition, it invited audiences at the same time to participate in what Bing described as *Ergänzungsspiel,* or process of supple-

....

schol. *ad loc.*; Pseudo-Andocides *Ad Alcibiadem* 17; Plutarch *Alcibiades* 16; Diogenes Laertius *Vit. Dem.* IX 46, IX 48; Simon 1988. Democritus wrote two treatises that touched on art entitled *On Colors* and *On Painting.*

[32] On reports on Euripides' parallel career as a painter, see Satyrus *Lives* in P.Oxy. 1176 (= Pack 14560 = P.Lit.Lond. 2070); Arrighetti 1964. Cf. Zeitlin 142–147.

[33] Cf. Euben 1990.

[34] The same can be said about Euripides' famous passage from *Ion* 184–231, offering a tour of the sanctuary of Delphi. See also Zeitlin 1994:147–156; Childs 1994:36.

[35] Seale 1982:20–21; Zeitlin 1994:140–142. Cf. Sophocles *Oedipus Rex* 300–305, 380–428.

mentation.[36] Hellenistic poets exploited the transition of epigram from stone to book by further severing it from its context: they offered part of the wider picture, which the reader was intrigued to reconstruct based on the few clues, hints, and allusions that were provided. As is obvious from the new Milan epigrams, Posidippus became a master in this art, and his *Andriantopoiika* provide significant information to allow audiences to construct multiple contexts.[37]

The *Andriantopoiika* certainly provide a valuable account on art history in the Hellenistic age, echoing the earlier debate as well. However, as I will argue, Posidippus' musings on sculptors are not incidental but rather programmatic, and they also fit in with this poet's service in the court of the Ptolemies, where he promoted their own vision of a different kind of world, successor to Alexander's.[38] Art certainly played an important role in Ptolemaic self-definition, but the contribution of the Alexandrian scholars in contemporary art-historical debate also aimed at rationalizing Ptolemaic royal positions and further influencing their audiences by settling meanings. Art has always formed an integral part in the process of arguing the merits of a political leader because it conceptualizes and reflects on the outcome of policies. In such a context art does not only use visual but also political language in order to construct, reconstruct, and rationalize the courses of action of leadership.[39] It is naturally difficult for artists, especially those that are employed in the service of the powers that be, to override these barriers, and reactionaries are a very rare phenomenon. However, exceptional talent and powerful arguments in support of political decisions and against constructed enemies can produce classics of enduring influence. Indeed, classic works of art have the ability to maneuver audiences into particular ways of seeing and understanding realities that can be reconstructed by future generations of leaders into acquiring new meanings appropriate for the times.

In his retrospective on ancient and modern sculptors Posidippus sketches then a brave new world ruled by the Ptolemies, the presumed lawful successors of Alexander. At the same time, by contributing to the process of legitimization of the Ptolemies, the poet promotes his own art as well by seeking his own share in the advertised novelty. It is no coincidence that Lysippus, the Macedonian conqueror's favorite sculptor, happens to be the honoree of the section. His juxtaposition to earlier and contemporary sculptors and the emphasis that the poet places on his novelties (παλαιοτέχνης vs. νεάρ') shapes the readers' beliefs in a constructed

---

[36] Bing 1995.

[37] This brilliant use of *Ergänzungsspiel* is also found in his 'old' epigrams. Cf. AB 131 (21 GP).

[38] For more on the role of Alexander the Great in Ptolemaic dynastic propaganda, see Kosmetatou on *Hippika* (this volume).

[39] Edelman 1995:38.

whole new world, which is a fundamental element in every new regime seeking legitimacy. Indeed, even though Lysippus is pronounced to be the greatest of all sculptors, AB 63 praises Hecataeus' portrait of Philadelphus' mentor, Philitas, sponsored by the king for his newly constructed Mouseion.[40] The poet was a popular subject in Hellenistic poetry, and Posidippus' text is reproduced below and includes Scodel's excellent reading:[41]

τόνδε Φιλίται χ[αλ]κὸν [ἴ]ϲον κατὰ πάν⟨θ⟩'{α} Ἑκ[α]ταῖος
ἀ]κ[ρ]ιβὴϲ ἄκρουϲ [ἔπλ]αϲεν εἰϲ ὄνυχαϲ,
καὶ με]γέθει κα[ὶ ϲα]ρκὶ τὸν ἀνθρωπιϲτὶ διώξαϲ
γνώμο]ν', ἀφ' ἡρώων δ' οὐδὲν ἔμειξ'{ε} ἰδέηϲ,
ἀλλὰ τὸν ἀκρομέριμνον ὅλ[ηι κ]ατεμάξατο τέχνηι
πρ]έϲβυν, ἀληθείηϲ ὀρθὸν [ἔχων] κανόνα·
αὐδήϲ]οντι δ' ἔοικεν, ὅϲωι ποικίλλεται ἤθει,
ἔμψυχ]οϲ, καίπερ χάλκεοϲ ἐὼν ὁ γέρων·
ἐκ Πτολε]μαίου δ' ὧδε θεοῦ θ' ἅμα καὶ βασιλ⟨ῆ⟩οϲ
ἄγκειμ]αι Μουϲέ{ι}ων εἵνεκα Κῶιοϲ ἀνήρ.

This bronze, like Philitas, Hecataeus in all respects
    moulded, accurately, even down to the finger tips,
both in size and form aiming for human standard,
    he added in no heroic element;
but with all his skill fashioned the old man,
    realistically, with the right measure of truth.
Like one about to speak, with such nature embellished,
    the old man is as though alive, yet made of bronze.
"By order of Ptole]my, at once god and king,
    am I vowed] for the Muses, a Coan man."

---

[40] Cf. a fragment by Hermesianax of Colophon (Powell fr. 7.75–78) mentioning a statue of Philitas on Cos, represented much in the same manner as the commemorative statue that Posidippus wished his native Pella to set up in his own honor after his death. Cf. Posidippus AB 118.15–18 (= *SH* 705); Angiò 2002. Hardie 1997:56–62 suggested that Philitas received heroic honors at his death, and his statue mentioned by Hermesianax was set up at a sacred plane grove dedicated to the Muses.

[41] Scodel 2003. An anonymous funerary epigram for Philitas was preserved by Athenaeus IX 401e. Cf. also Theocritus *Idyll* 7.39–41. Philitas was also the subject of other Hellenistic poets. Cf. Callimachus fr. 1.9–10 Pf.

Scodel's restoration of [ἄγκειμ]αι on line 10, works perfectly with the convincing [αὐδήϲ]οντι that the original editors proposed for line 7. The last two lines of the epigram function then as a virtual quote of an epigram within an epigram. Placed second in the *Andriantopoiika*, AB 63 forms a link with the section's manifesto that precedes it, as it looks like Hecataeus, a sculptor who is otherwise known as a famous metal-worker,[42] borrowed heavily from the characteristics of Lysippean art that are spelled-out in AB 62. We may conclude then that in Posidippus' view, it was Lysippus' work that exercised a great influence over Hecataeus to the extent that the younger sculptor created a particularly compelling statue of the philosopher. An analysis of the specifics in Hecataeus' bronze, read under the light of surviving ancient sources on Lysippus' art and craft, suggests that by reading both epigrams together, we do not only understand Philitas' portrait as the consummate study of human nature because it reflects the philosopher's character and doctrines.[43] We are also able to complete the list of characteristics and innovations associated with Lysippus' workshop, to whose tradition then Hecataeus, at least according to Posidippus, clearly belonged.[44]

While on the subject of lifelike bronzes, Posidippus presents one more example of a successful bronze in retrospect, thereby defining a long trajectory of sculptors leading to Lysippus. In this case the reader is presented with a statue of the Homeric hero Idomeneus made by the late-fifth-century BCE sculptor Cresilas (AB 64):

αἴ]νεέ γ᾽ {ε} ᾽Ιδομεν⟨ῆ⟩α θέλων χάλκειον ἐκεῖν[ον
Κ̣ρηϲίλ⟨α⟩· ὡϲ ἄκρωϲ ἠργάϲατ᾽ εἴδομεν εὖ
γ]α̣ρύ[ει] ᾽Ιδομενεύϲ· ᾽ἀλ[λ᾽] ὦ ᾽γαθὲ Μηριόνα, θεῖ,
] πλάϲται δ̣ὰ̣ν [ἀδό]ν̣ητοϲ ἐών᾽.

Praise willingly that bronze Idomeneus
by Cresilas. How perfectly he worked, we see.
Idomeneus cries: "good Meriones, run
. . . . . .] molded being immobile for too long.

The scene evoked by this epigram is probably from the *Iliad* (XIII 240–294) featuring a hurried dialogue between the Cretan heroes Idomeneus and Meriones

---

[42] Pliny *NH* XXXIII 156, XXXIV 85; cf. Overbeck 1868:417–418. Assuming that Posidippus' Hecataeus is the one meant in the text, this sculptor is considered by Pliny as second-rate at best. Of course, this opinion may only reflect Pliny's personal taste and the aesthetics of his time regarding ancient art. At any rate, in the current state of the evidence, we cannot draw conclusions on the reception of Hecataeus' art in antiquity.
[43] This epigram has been the object of two important studies: Sens 2002; Angiò 2002.
[44] Cf. Sens 2002:3–4.

before they rush together to battle. Interestingly, Meriones is described there as πόδας ταχύς.[45] Although Idomeneus' imagined voice constitutes a remote allusion to the Homeric text, the epigram is nevertheless linked with AB 63 that precedes it, which also features an imaginary short speech of the subject portrayed. In both cases, the texts evoke actual epigrams that can be traced back to inscribed bases of Archaic statues, deemed to look "alive," like the famous Phrasicleia, who seemingly "speaks" to the passer-by:[46]

cε̃μα Φραcικλείαc· κόρε κεκλέcομαι αἰεί,
ἀντὶ γάμο παρ' θεō̃ν τοῦτο λαχō̃c' ὄνομα.

This is the grave of Phrasicleia. "I will always be called a maiden,
having received this fateful name from the gods instead of marriage."

In AB 64 the poet urges his readers to applaud Cresilas' achievement with the same vigorous expressions he uses in his manifesto: continuous usage of imperatives (AB 62: μιμ[ή]cacθε, παραθεῖτε, AB 63: αἴ]ϝεέ γ'), superlatives, and antithesis between the stillness of an object and its inherent movement that its lifelike appearance renders (γ]αρύ[ει], θεῖ vs. [ἀδό]ϝητοc). Cresilas of AB 64 is portrayed then as a worthy predecessor of Hecataeus and by extension of Lysippus as well. His work is as lifelike as Hecataeus' which is due in both cases to the perfection of the two artists' workmanship (AB 63: ἀ]κ[ρ]ιβὴc ἄκρουc, ἀκρομέριμνον; AB 64: ἄκρωc). As in AB 63, the hero looks so lifelike that the poet puts actual words in his mouth.

Furthermore, Posidippus' reference to Cresilas enhances the idea of contest among sculptors that he introduced in AB 62. Along with Pheidias, Polyclitus, and Phradmon, Cresilas famously took part in a competition that was organized by the Ephesians for the commission of the statue of an amazon.[47] Given Posidippus' clear preference of Lysippus over Polyclitus in AB 62 (ὁ πρὸ Πολυκ⟨λ⟩είτο[υ πά]γχυ παλαιοτέχνηc), and his classification of Cresilas among the former's worthy predecessors, one may easily conclude which of the four fifth-century BCE masters won his personal vote. Pliny mentions several works of this sculptor, but his other-

---

[45] For Homeric echoes in Posidippus, cf. Nagy (this volume).

[46] *IG* 1³, 1261; cf. Svenbro 1988; Childs 1994:35.

[47] Pliny *NH* XXXIV 53. The text is corrupt, mentioning a fifth sculptor by the name of Cydon, which probably derives from Cydonia, the locality from where Cresilas came. Whether Pliny's passage reflects reports on an ancient competition is disputed, but Posidippus' text may indicate that there may have been a competition along the lines of similar, earlier ones between Alcamenes and Agoracritus and other sculptors. Cf. Pliny *NH* XXXVI 17; Ridgway 1974:2. On the Amazons of Ephesus and Cresilas, see Ridgway 1974; Ridgway 1976; Weber 1976; Ridgway 1981:181, 191; Cohen 1994:74, 78–79.

wise unattested Idomeneus mentioned by Posidippus is a Cretan subject fitting for a Cretan sculptor.[48]

The energy and vigor oozing from this first cluster of four epigrams culminate in AB 65 in praise of Lysippus' portrait of Alexander:

[Λύϲιππε,] πλάϲτα Ϲικυώ[νιε, θαρϲ]α̣λέα χείρ,
δάϊε τεχνί]τα, πῦρ τοι ὁ χα[λκὸϲ ὁρ]ῆ̣ι,
ὅν κατ' Ἀλεξά]ν̣δρου μορφᾶϲ ἔθε̣υ· οὔ τί γε μεμπτοί
Πέρϲαι· ϲυγγνώ]μα βουϲὶ λέοντα φυγεῖν.

Lysippus, sculptor of Sicyon, daring hand,
cunning craftsman, the bronze has a look of fire
in which you set Alexander's form; in no way at fault
are the Persians; cattle are forgiven for fleeing a lion.

As this author has argued elsewhere, Lysippus' statue oozes valor in battle that even affects the sculptor's hand that flashes momentarily through the reader's mind, described as θαρϲαλέα, sure and firm. This adjective, which is directly related to the sculpture described, immediately conveys to the reader the image of an artist, who, in the fervor of his creativity, almost single-mindedly brings his work to life as he separates it from the lifeless-material (ὁ χαλκὸϲ ὁρῆι). The poet alludes to the fever of battle throughout by using the words θαρϲαλέα, πῦρ and by comparing the opponents to cattle (the Persians) and a lion (Alexander).[49] Both animals functioned as symbols of valor and were used in ancient divination, especially in comparisons of Alexander the Great with worthy opponents and predecessors.[50]

At the same time, the theme of the concentration of all life in the eyes of a sculpture is present in AB 95 from the *Iamatika*[51] and perhaps in AB 64, the

[48] Pliny *NH* XXXIV 53, 74–75. On testimonia on Cresilas, see Overbeck 1868:157–158, nos. 870–876; Orlandini 1961:405–408.

[49] This poem by Posidippus significantly departs from the usual reports on Lysippus' representations of Alexander the Great. The sculptor's innovating mark in them was a melting glance of his eyes (ὑγρότηϲ τῶν ὀμμάτων) which contrasts sharply with Posidippus' reference to a fiery glance (πῦρ τοι ὁ χαλκὸϲ ὁρῆι). Cf. Plutarch *Alexander* 4.1–2. Plutarch reports that it was the painter Apelles who was famous for his depiction of Alexander κεραυνοφόροϲ, warrior-like, dark, and formidable (φαιότερον καὶ πεπινωμένον). On further analysis of AB 65, cf. Kosmetatou 2003b.

[50] Philip II of Macedon reportedly dreamt of sealing pregnant Olympias' womb with a signet ring bearing an incised representation of a lion, which led Aristander of Telmessos to interpret this as a sign of Alexander's future bravery. Plutarch *Alexander* 2.2–3. Cf. Lycophron's *Alexandra*, where Roman valor is compared to lion's strength; Kosmetatou 2000:33 (where previous bibliography is cited).

[51] Cf. Papalexandrou (this volume); Bing 2002b; Bing (this volume).

Elizabeth Kosmetatou

Cresilas epigram as well. Indeed, in his praise for Cresilas' statue of a man succumbing to his wounds, Pliny, undoubtedly drawing upon an earlier author, comments on how the viewer could barely discern whatever life was left in the figure's expression.[52] This may have been then a remarkable characteristic of Cresilas' art that particularly spoke to Posidippus' heart, and his allusion to it in connection with various sculptors may reflect another passage from Aeschylus. In his *Agamemnon* (v. 415–419) the tragic poet mentions statues (κολοσσοὶ εὔμορφοι) that stood in the palace of Menelaeus. Following Helen's seduction by Paris and upon his return to Sparta, Menelaeus gazed at these statues which he thought had an "empty look" (ὀμμάτων δ᾽ ἐν ἀχηνίαις | ἔρρει πᾶσ᾽ Ἀφροδίτα), being deprived of magic and lifelike appearance as his wife was no longer there.[53] AB 62 advises sculptors to prefer lifelike bronzes (πολυχρονίους δὲ κολοσσῶν, | ὦ ζ[ωι]οπλάσται, γ[αί,] παραθεῖτε νόμους), and in AB 63 he praises Hecataeus' preference for the human over heroic standard, even in the depiction of heroized mortals like Philitas. The qualities of heroes are then visible in humans as long as sculptors can convey all their fervor and passion in their eyes, as happens in the presumably lifelike statue of Alexander in AB 65.

Sens has taken note of the remarkable similarities in form, subject, and vocabulary between AB 65 and *AP* XVI 120, which is doubly ascribed to Archelaus and Asclepiades but may actually have been composed by the latter:[54]

Τόλμαν Ἀλεξάνδρου καὶ ὅλαν ἀπεμάξατο μορφὰν
Λύσιππος· τίν' ὁδὶ χαλκὸς ἔχει δύναμιν.
αὐδήσοντι δ᾽ ἔοικεν χάλκεος ἐς Δία λεύσσων
"Γᾶν ὑπ᾽ ἐμοὶ τίθεμαι, Ζεῦ, σὺ δ᾽ Ὄλυμπον ἔχε."

Both Alexander's boldness and his entire form has Lysippus
molded; what great power does this bronze have.
For this bronze figure looks as if it almost says, looking at Zeus:
"I am the master of the Earth, o Zeus, you keep Olympus."

The second and final group of epigrams within the *Andriantopoiika* is unfortunately fragmentary, but it is possible to reconstruct its contents to some extent. It began with another retrospect, this one further into the past, of works of great realism made by Lysippus' worthier predecessors who had all tried their hand in sculptures of varying sizes. AB 66 praises the famous sculpture of a cow by the

[52] Pliny *NH* XXXIV 75.
[53] Childs 1994:35–36. Cf. Vernant 1990:25–34; Denniston and Page 1957:106–107.
[54] Sens 2002:5–7.

culptor of the so-called "Severe" style Myron (ca. 480–440 BCE) that is well-
ttested in ancient authors[55] and seems to have been a favorite subject for the
pigrammatists of the Hellenistic and Roman periods:

±13   ].ηϲε τὸ βοίδιον ἄξιον ὁλκῆς
±14   ] καὶ τριϲεπαργύριον
±13   ] χεῖρα, ϲοφὸν χρέος εἶδ᾽ ἐπ᾽ ἀδόξου
±11   ἀλλὰ Μύρων ἐπόει.

.........] the cow worthy of the plough

.........] and most valuable

.........] the hand, he unexpectedly beheld a clever thing:

.........] but Myron made it.

The ninth book of the *Greek Anthology* includes no fewer than thirty-six
pigrams dedicated to this apparently formidable sculpture that was reportedly set
p on the Athenian Acropolis (IX 713–742, 793–798).[56] They are attributed to
amous epigrammatists like Anacreon (IX 715–716), Leonidas of Tarentum
[X 719), and Dioscorides (IX 734), and the sculpture's lifelike, deceiving appear-
nce is a common theme in most of these. Clustered together they also give the
npression of a series of comments, commonly expressed by passers-by. Praises of
Myron's cow can be divided into two groups: the first one comprises epigrams that
eemingly deceitfully invite the reader to believe that the animal is real or was once
live, having been later turned miraculously into bronze (IX 713–714, 716,
19–720, 721a, 722–723, 725, 732). The second group, with which we can asso-
iate Posidippus' AB 66, includes poems that draw the readers' attention to the
eceiving, lifelike appearance of the sculpture, at the same time stressing the fact
1at it is lifeless (IX 715, 717–718, 721, 724, 726–731, 733–742). Among these is
n interesting sub-group alluding to parallels between Myron's extraordinary skills
nd the legendary abilities of Prometheus to mold real human beings by breathing
fe into them (IX 717, 724, 726–727, 729, 736–737). Interestingly, some of these
pigrams represent the "voice" of the cow (IX 713, 719–720, 723, 729, 731–732,
42), a technique that Posidippus also used in AB 63 and 64 in order to underline
1e realism with which his favorite artists worked.

⁵ Ovid *Ex Ponto* IV 1.34; Pliny XXXIV 57; Cicero *In Verr.* IV 60.135; Lucil. Iun. *Aetna* V 592; Aelian
De Natura Animalium epilog.; Ausonius *Ep.* 58–68; Tzetzes *Chil.* VIII 370; Procopius *De Bello
Gothico* IV 21. Cf. Overbeck 1868:98–109.

⁶ For a discussion of the "Cow-epigrams" and their arrangement within the anthology, see Gutzwiller
1998:245–250.

Ancient literary sources hint at a significant debate that was instigated b
Myron's presumed formidable production. This sculptor worked on different medi
and produced life-size and under-life-size statues.[57] True to his initial manifesto i
AB 62, Posidippus only deals with this sculptor's smaller works which he, as other
before him, praises for their realism.

Indeed, Myron is credited with having revolu
tionized the human posture, especially in his statues of athletes, the most famous o
which was the *Discobolus*. He was, like Lysippus, prolific, but Pliny voices som
criticism that his works received, perhaps after his death, for their lack of emotiona
expression and some imperfections with regard to the naturalized rendering o
hair.[58] However, the influence that this sculptor exercised on sculptors and art
historians was enormous. Quintilian and Pliny, surely echoing the same source
that Posidippus used for his *Andriantopoiika*, discuss its impact: the Archaic *kouro*
now looked like a thing of the past in all their stiffness, an opinion that is share
by Posidippus in AB 62 where he discusses the elusive [. . .]pas, Hageladas, an
the otherwise unattested Didymides who were probably all sculptors belonging t
the Archaic tradition.[59] Pliny, like Posidippus in AB 62, considers Myron to be
greater sculptor than Polyclitus, having a greater sense of rhythm than the Argiv
artisan.[60]

Myron was probably highly esteemed by Posidippus for both his artistic an
technical achievements, especially in smaller-sized works because he figures i
AB 68 and 69. AB 68 constitutes an anecdotal account and serves as compariso
between Myron and Posidippus' contemporary Chares of Lindus, a student c
Lysippus, the creator of the Rhodian Colossus:

ἤθελον Ἥλιον Ῥόδιοι π[εριμάκε]α θεῖναι
δὶς τόσον, ἀλλὰ Χάρης Λίνδιο[ς] ὡρίσατο
μηθένα τεχνίταν ἔ⟨τ⟩ι μείζονα {τ}οῦδε κ[ο]λοσσόν
θήσειν· εἰ δὲ Μύρων εἰς τετράπ[ηχ]υν ὄ[ρον

---

[57] On the *colossi* of Myron, see Strabo XIV 1.14; Lucian *Gall.* XXIV 30; Kosmetatou-Papalexandro
2003:53–58. On Myron in general, see Ridgway 1970:84–86; Stewart 1990:148–149, 237–23
255–257; Mattusch 1996:195.

[58] Pliny *NH* XXXIV 58. Cf. Isager 1991:99–100.

[59] Quintilian II 13.8. Cf. Stewart 1990:148. BG:186 think that the unattested Didymides represents
corruption in the text, being rather a reference to Deinomenes, a student of Polyclitus. In the opinio
of this author, these three sculptors are grouped together on the basis of their stylistic affinities, the
rigid forms, as the poet puts it. Hence they should be considered as chronologically close. Polyclitu
a later sculptor, even though dismissed in favor of Lysippus, is not really accused of sharing their cha
acteristics, even though he may be considered by Posidippus as belonging to the same tradition
they did, probably for the strict formalism of his work. In this case, formalism would be seen
successor to rigidity.

[60] Pliny *NH* XXXIV 57–58. Cf. Stewart 1990:255–256.

cεμνὸc ἐκεῖνοc ἀνῆκε, Χάρηc πρῷ[τοc μ]ε̣τὰ τέχνα[c
ζῶ⟨ι⟩ο̣ν ἐχαλκούργε̣ι γᾶc μεγ[......].[..]ν̣.

The Rhodians wanted to set up a Helios so very tall
    twice as much, but the Lindian Chares made sure
    that no artisan would ever create a larger colossus
    than this; if that venerable Myron reached
    the limit of four cubits, Chares was the first with his craft
    to make a statue in bronze [comparable in size ?] with the earth.

The Rhodian Colossus was a very controversial sculpture in its time, a marvel
of engineering, rather than art, a view that may be reflected in AB 68 especially
since the poet discusses its size rather than craftsmanship and beauty and compares
it to Myron, one of his favorites.[61] His neutrality in judging Chares as a sculptor
may be due to the fact that the Lindian had been a disciple of Lysippus, the greatest
master of all. At the same time, his praise of the smaller-sized works of Myron indicates that Posidippus distances himself from Chares' flair for the colossal.

AB 69 is unhappily too fragmentary for us to reconstruct, but it seems to have
been dedicated to Myron and may have again dwelled on the theme of realism that
deceives the viewer (ε̣ἰ δ' ἐπιθιξ̣ει):[62]

εἶμαι χάλκειᾳ προτ̣...[±10   ].του μου̣
    Τ̣υδεὺc μηπ[±20   ]νο̣c
εἰ δ' ἐπιθιξει[±20   ]. Μύρων εὖ
    θῆκ' ἐπ' ἔμ' ἱμ[άτιον   ±15   ]c.

I'm plated in bronze . . . me
    Tydeus . . .
    for if you touch . . . Myron well
    placed on me a . . .

Although it is impossible to reconstruct the content of this fragmentary
epigram, this author will venture to make a case for the association of AB 69 with
representations of a dying Tydeus before the Gates of Thebes. The *Andriantopoiika*
deal with single representations of heroes, common mortals, and animals, and a
study of the iconography of Tydeus suggests that images of the hero succumbing to

[61] Pliny *NH* XXXIV 41; Sextus Empiricus *Adv. Mathem.* VII 107; Philo Byzant. *De Sept. Mirac. Mundi*
14.
[62] Pausanias X 10.3 mentions a statue of Tydeus set up in Delphi but offers no further description of it.

his wounds were especially popular.[63] If indeed Posidippus described such a statue, AB 69 would then be nicely linked with AB 64, the Cresilas epigram, alluding to a similar representation of an otherwise unidentified wounded hero by the Cydonian sculptor.[64]

As is obvious from AB 62, innovation in technique was also a subject that interested Posidippus, a subject that is brought back in his retrospective of the sculptor Theodorus in AB 67. Dealing with a favorite subject of Posidippus statuary commemorating victories in the chariot-races, on which more is said in the *Hippika*, the poet praises the sculptor's superior abilities in the workmanship of detail:

±14   ]..[..]. ἄντυγος ἐ‹γ›γύθεν ἄθρει

τῆς Θεοδωρείης χειρὸς ὅσος κάματος·

ὄψει γὰρ ζυγόδεϲμα καὶ ἡνία καὶ τροχὸν ἵππων

ἄξονά ‹θ›’ [{ε} ἡνιό]χου τ’ ὄμμα καὶ ἄκρα χερῶν·

ὄψει δ’ εὖ [±12   ]...εος, ἀλλ’ ἐπὶ τῷιδε

ἑζομέν[ην   ±15   ] μυῖαν ἴδοις.

. . . .] of the rail, observe from close

with what great care the hand of Theodorus;

for you will see the yoke, and reins, and ring of the horses' bit,

and axle, and the charioteer's eye, and fingertips;

and you will see well [. . . . .] , but upon it

sitti[ng . . . .] you could see a fly.

Pliny discusses Theodorus of Samos, after Boutades and Rhoecus, just before reporting on Duris' discussion of Lysippus. Theodorus had been a great metal-worker, sculptor, and engineer of the Archaic period. Following the tradition of Boutades and Rhoecus he was a great innovator in the clay-modeling that was necessary for the production of bronze statues. Posidippus' interest in him is multi-fold: Theodorus (second half of sixth century BCE) stands behind Lysippus in the evolution chain leading to the splendors that were the Sicyonian's works. The Samian sculptor is credited with inventions that eventually led to Lysippus' technical experiments and innovations in the casting of bronze alluded to in AB 62.[65] Like Myron he had been an artisan with multiple interests, being credited with the construction of enormous metal vessels,[66] a marvelous gold vine which he made for

---

[63] Simon and Lorenz 1997:142–143.
[64] Pliny XXXIV 75.
[65] Cf. Pausanias X 38.6–7; Pliny *NH* XXXV 153; Mattusch 1996:71–72.
[66] Herodotus I 51.

the Persian king Darius I,[67] and of the so-called Labyrinth, as the temple of Hera of Samos was known.[68] At the same time, his attention to detail and his work in miniature, another favorite of Posidippus judging from his *Lithika*, was legendary. He was supposed to have carved Polycrates' legendary ring[69] which Posidippus praises in another tantalizingly fragmentary epigram from the Milan papyrus (AB 9). AB 67 focuses on Theodorus' miniature workmanship related to the self-portrait that he set up at the Labyrinth of Samos. It concentrates on the chariot and charioteer that, according to Pliny (XXXIV 83) stood on the three fingers of the sculptor's left hand, and could be covered by the wings of a fly that may have stood on one of his remaining fingers, functioning perhaps as a measure for comparison.[70]

Sadly, AB 70, which wraps up the *Andriantopoiika*, is hopelessly fragmentary, but it probably featured a final comparison of Polyclitus and Lysippus, from which the Sicyonian emerged victorious even though the achievement of the former sculptor could not be denied:

κοὶ τὰ Πολυκ[λείτου   ±12   ] πάντων
      cάρκινα καὶ θ.[±18   ]αι
πάντ' ἐπ' Ἀλεξά[νδρου   ±14   χ]ειρῶν
      τῶν Λυcιππε[ίων   ±19   ]ς.

Also Polyc[litus' [. . . . . .] of all
      fleshy and [. . . . .
all on Alexa[nder's . . . .] of the hands
of Lysippus . . . [. . . . .

The above inquiry does not only concern the structure of the *Andriantopoiika* section of the Milan papyrus; it rather defines the framework for an art-historical model that Posidippus drew from one of his contemporary art-historians. Consequently, we readers are not only invited to "view" what the poet makes "visible" to our imagination through his vivid descriptions. We are also led to discover the principles on which Posidippus' unnamed sources established the *Canon*, in this case the rule and trajectory, of perfection in sculpture. This *Canon* comprises then the artists Theodorus, Myron, Cresilas, Lysippus, Chares, and Hecataeus, whose achievements have been examined in the section against their contemporaries and predecessors, some of whom were rejected. The first four

---

[67] Herodotus VII 27; Athenaeus XII 514f. A mysterious golden vine is also mentioned in several Delian inventory lists, a new study of which is in progress by this author. Cf. ID 101, line 26 (367 BC).
[68] Pliny *NH* XXXIV 83.
[69] Herodotus III 41.
[70] Pliny *NH* XXXIV 83. Pliny's text is not clear about the position of the fly.

masters were renowned for their technical achievement and their realism, which appealed to the emotions of the viewer. Of course, it is unclear whether these four constituted a *Canon* to which Posidippus added his two contemporary sculptors, Chares and Hecataeus, in accordance with the tastes of the new leadership in Egypt that set the style. At any rate, even though the attribution of the ideas behind the *Andriantopoiika* must be conjectural, an overview of Posidippus' contemporary trends is in order.

Many of the ideas expressed in *Andriantopoiika* are also reflected in Pliny's treatise on bronze sculpture, and scholarly research has focused on three main sources for the Roman author's work: Duris of Samos for anecdotes, Xenocrates of Athens for technique, and the Pergamene scholar of the mid-third century BCE Antigonus of Carystus for schools. For several reasons that mostly have to do with chronology Antigonus is probably not the author that influenced Posidippus. Additionally, Antigonus was probably the one who defined, or contributed to the definition, of the so-called Pergamene *Canon*, which is different from Posidippus'.[71]

The next candidate is Xenocrates of Athens, a sculptor who lived in the first half of the third century BCE and also wrote treatises on sculpture and painting.[72] He was reportedly a disciple of the sculptor Tesicrates or Euthycrates and seems to have had connections with the Pergamene court, judging from the discovery of a base bearing his signature on the citadel.[73] This is hardly surprising given the fact that the Attalid rulers were especially fond of Athens and Atticism and had associated themselves mainly with the Academy and, less so, with the Peripatos.[74] Xenocrates' ideas can be partially reconstructed on the basis of fragments and testimonia that have survived in the ancient sources. He may have defined his own tradition of sculptors as characterized by rhythm and symmetry, tracing its roots to the philosopher Pythagoras who was reputed by legend to have also been a sculptor. His association with the Pergamene court might also be deduced by the fact that Pliny discusses Pergamene art immediately after a passage that is most likely based on the Athenian sculptor and art historian.[75] Xenocrates' work was largely a chronological exploration of Greek sculpture whose *Canon* featured an artistic evolution towards naturalism as defined by Pythagoras, Myron, Pheidias, Polyclitus, and

[71] Cf. Dorandi 1999a:ciii. The Pergamene *Canon* comprised the following sculptors: Callon, Hegias, Calamis, Myron, Polyclitus, Phidias, Alcamenes, Praxiteles, Lysippus. On the scholarly circle around the Pergamene library, see Nagy 1998.

[72] On Xenocrates, see Pliny *NH* XXXV 83; Diogenes Laertius VIII 46; Pernice 1939:320, 326–327; Sprigath 2001.

[73] IvP 138. Rumpf 1967 mentions a second base as well.

[74] Habicht 1990, Kosmetatou 1993:178–180, Nagy 1998, Dorandi 1999a:103, Kosmetatou 2003a.

[75] Cf. Isager 1991:102.

ysippus.[76] In the opinion of this author, Xenocrates then cannot be the master-mind behind the *Andriantopoiika*: his proposed *Canon* differs significantly from Posidippus' who, moreover, beyond his apparent disregard for Atticism, appears to e critical of Polyclitus (AB 62 and AB 70). This critical view may also be reflected n Pliny XXIV 58, according to which Myron was "more prolific in his art and nore careful in his proportions," despite Polyclitus' celebrated care for symmetry which was widely publicized, in part thanks to his own treaty entitled *Canon*. Last, ut not least, scholars in Hellenistic courts promoted the propaganda of their mployers, and it would be surprising if a Pergamene scholar set the style in Ptolemaic Egypt.[77]

To which author does Posidippus then nod in his display of the splendor of ysippus' work? There is little doubt that the Pellaean poet had read the famous writings of his contemporary popular historian and philosopher Duris of Samos ca. 340–260 BCE) who belonged to the Peripatetic school, and who also wrote on rt history. Duris was about one generation older than Posidippus, his ideas had een widely established, and he was much admired by the epigrammatist's contem-poraries. He came from a very prominent family: both his father and himself were yrants of Samos before it passed under Macedonian, Thracian, possibly Seleucid, nd eventually Ptolemaic domination (by 279 BCE).[78] He claimed descent from he notorious and fascinating Alcibiades, owing his existence to one of the Athenian olitician's numerous flings on the island in ca. 411 BCE.[79] Duris reportedly had a air for high drama, loved to trigger the emotional response of his readers, and was ne the representatives of "tragic historiography," aiming at emotional responses on he part of his readers, a trend that was criticized in antiquity, especially by Polybius.[80] A highly educated scholar, unusually versatile in many fields, he had written a *History of Macedonia* (which covered Alexander's conquests) and had also hown Egyptian interests, having written on the pyramids.[81] Interestingly, Duris lso shared Posidippus' fascination with Panhellenic festivals and is credited with everal works on ancient games and their victors.[82] Last, but not least, being a eripatetic he fitted perfectly with the traditions of the Museum.[83]

---

[76] Pollitt 1974:20–21, 74–77; Dorandi 1999a:103; Sprigath 2001. On Polyclitus, see also Donohue 1995.

[77] Atticism had been strongly promoted by Philetaerus and Eumenes I of Pergamon. Cf. Nagy 1998:185–194; Kosmetatou 2003a.

[78] Cf. Hauben 1970:33–34.

[79] Pausanias VI 13.5. For a collection of the testimonia and an analysis of Duris' work, see Jacoby, *FGrHist* 76; Okin 1974; Kebric 1977.

[80] On tragic historiography, see Haegemans and Kosmetatou 2003 and Schepens 2003 where previous bibliography is cited.

[81] Jacoby, *FGrHist* 76 T 12.

[82] Cf. Okin 1974:128–130.

[83] Nagy 1998:190; Dorandi 1999b:35–37.

Duris' reputation as a superb historian notwithstanding, Posidippus probabl felt special ties to his work. Ptolemaic domination over Samos certainly played role, especially if the Milan book, or parts of it, were commissioned by Callicrate of Samos.[84] Callicrates was a Ptolemaic protegé with connections to Ptolemai queens, founder of the cult of Arsinoe II at Cape Zephyrium, eponymous priest o the cult of Alexander and the *Theoi Adelphoi*, and he figures prominently amon, the Milan epigrams.[85] If Posidippus' *Canon* may be identified as Duris' own, th presence of the Samian sculptor Theodorus (AB 67), alone rather than alongsid the equally resourceful Boutades, may account for the Samian historian's persona interests and sensibilities. Posidippus' attachment to Duris' ideas may also hav stemmed from the historian's interest in Macedonian history and his hostil account of the Antigonids, the rivals of the Ptolemies who ruled Macedonia. Th Ptolemaic court also promoted Peripatetic ideas as is evident from ancient report on the fate of the Aristotelian corpus, as well as on the activities of Peripateti philosophers, starting from Demetrius of Phalerum and Strato of Lampsacus another mentor of Philadelphus, in Egypt.[86]

Duris' art-historical oeuvre comprised two treatises entitled *On Painting* an *Toreutike* (*On Sculpture in Metal*)[87], the latter having probably served as a source o inspiration for Posidippus' Andriantopoiika. We hear that he loved anecdotes, som of which may be reflected in epigrams AB 66 and, especially, AB 68.[88] Second-han reports on his art-historical work, especially his discussion of Lysippus, hav survived in Pliny. Jacoby and Mattusch's reconstruction of Duris' *On Paintin* shows significant affinities in structure and content with Posidippus Andriantopoiika to the extent that this new text can now serve as a *testimonium* fo the specific work, further updating Jacoby's entry 76.[89] Pliny's account of Duris treatment of Lysippus begins as follows:

> Lysippum Sicyonium Duris negat ullius fuisse discipulum, sed primo
> aerarium fabrum audendi rationem cepisse pictoris Eupompi responso.

---

[84] Bing discussed Callicrates of Samos as one of Posidippus' potential employers at a recent conferenc at Columbia University. Cf. Bing 2002d.

[85] Hauben 1970; Hauben 1989.

[86] Nagy 1998:189–192 (especially on the differences between Ptolemaic and Attalid scholarship) Barnes 1999; Rowe 2000:392–395. The Peripatetic Strato of Lampsacus wrote the treatise *On th Philosopher King* for Ptolemy II Philadelphus.

[87] Jacoby *FGrHist* 76 T 12d, F 31–32. Pliny uses the term *toreutike* to refer to sculpture, but in Gree authors it signifies works in metal or relief. Cf. Jacoby *FGrHist* 76 F 85; Clemens Alexandrinus I 4.26; Eustathius, *Schol. ad Od.* II 190.

[88] Dorandi 1999a:civ.

[89] Pliny *NH* XXXIV 61.

Eum enim interrogatum, quem sequeretur antecedentium, dixisse monstrata hominum multitudine, naturam ipsam imitandam essem non artificem.

Duris denies that Lysippus of Sicyon was a disciple of anyone but says that he was originally a bronze-worker and conceived the idea of venturing to sculpture from a response by the painter Eupompus. For when someone asked him (Eupompus) which of his predecessors he would follow, pointing at a crowd, he said that it was Nature herself that one should use for a model, rather than an artist.

Despite the anecdotal character of the above quoted passage a study of the amian's oeuvre makes it obvious that we cannot associate Duris' art-historical work nainly with anecdotes, preferring to link discussions in Pliny on technique exclu-ively with Xenocrates.

The similarities between Duris and Posidippus' first two *Andriantopoiika* are triking. The opening epigram denounces the rigid works of Archaic sculptors in avor of, presumably, more natural forms, forming a valid deductive argument onsisting of a series of true premises and a logical conclusion: a) rigidity is to be voided in favor of natural representation; b) colossal statues are undesirable; c) in his respect Lysippus is the sculptor whom all young artisans are urged to take for model, d) the καινοτέχνης Hecataeus followed the rules of truth (AB 63: κληθείης ὀρθὸν [ἔχων] κανόνα) and used the human standard (καὶ με]γέθει α[ὶ ca]ρκὶ τὸν ἀνθρωπιcτὶ διώξαc γνώμο]ν', ἀφ' ἡρώων δ' οὐδὲν μειξ'{ε} ἰδέηc,) in molding Philitas' portrait. It follows then that Hecataeus is a vorthy successor of Lysippus, and the two artists shared common characteristics. The Sicyonian's realism is further alluded to in a description of the work of 'hiladelphus' sculptor. AB 62 also mentions Lysippus' innovations (νεάρ'), which probably echo other parts of Duris' discussion of the Sicyonian sculptor. Born to a amily that owned a foundry, and following in the footsteps of his founder brother ysistratus, Lysippus is credited with important technical innovations in the field of portraiture that formed the pathway to achieving realism more directly than before. Mattusch has plausibly argued that Lysippus' experiments led him to develop a way o substitute for the artist's original model one that could be taken directly from an ndividual's face, thus molding "from nature." This idea may very well have come ollowing a conversation with his compatriot Eupompus and led to higher quality nd quantity of portraits.[90]

[90] Ancient authors state that Lysippus was prolific, and about 1500 bronzes were attributed to him. Cf. Pliny *NH* XXXIV 37; Mattusch 1996:68–76.

Pliny offers an even more intriguing account on Lysippus' innovations possibly drawing from Duris:[91]

> Hominis autem imaginem gypso e facie ipsa primus omnium expressit ceraque in eam formam gypsi infusa emendare instituit Lysistratus Sicyonius, frater Lysippi, de quo diximus. Hic et similitudines reddere instituit; ante eum quam pulcherrimas facere studebant. Idem et de signis effigies exprimere invenit, crevitque res in tantum, ut nulla signa statuaeve sine argilla fierent.

> The first to form an image in plaster from the face itself and who devised a method of pouring wax into this plaster mold and then making corrections on it, was Lysistratus of Sicyon, the brother of Lysippus, whom we are discussing. He also established a method for reproducing images; before him they had tried to make them as beautiful as possible. The same person also devised a method of making casts of images, and it became popular to such an extent that no longer were figures or statues made without clay.

Mattusch interprets Lysistratus and Lysippus' technique as a pure form of indirect lost-wax casting. Casts were made of real human beings from which master molds were taken. These were lined with wax, and artists thus obtained wax working models which they may have touched up, and then passed on to their technicians for further processing: master-mold taking, wax-making, coring, investing and casting. The rate of successful casting was increased, and the whole process of casting bronzes saved time, effort, and money. Exact copies could be made, an innovation that opened the road for the mass-reproduction of popular sculptures in the centuries to come. Lysippus' ingenuity certainly won him the reputation of an artist that worked directly from nature.[92]

The above-discussed passage from Pliny may be drawing upon Duris and belongs to a longer discussion on modeling that is organized chronologically. Since it forms an integral part with it and seems to be comparing Lysippus' innovation with those of his predecessors, one may plausibly attribute the whole to Duris' lost work on sculpture. Lysippus and his brother were then pioneers in casting, but before them, came the three innovators in clay modeling: Boutades, Rhoecus, and Theodorus, the last of whom is the subject of Posidippus' AB 67. We may therefore

---

[91] Pliny *NH* XXXV 153. Pollitt 1990:104n53, argues that casts were possibly made of the entire body as well as the face. At any rate, real body casts were used in heat therapy for the treatment of pain.

[92] Mattusch 1996:71–72. Cf. Lucian *Zeus Tragoidos* 33.

conclude that the *Andriantopoiika* is probably a free adaptation of Duris presenting to readers his *Canon,* complete with commentary in a nutshell.

Even though Duris' art historical work is hard to reconstruct from Pliny alone, substantial fragments of his *History of Macedonia* allow us to reconstruct his ideas. His preference for "tragic historiography" that induced strong emotional responses in his readers fits with the passion found in Lysippus' sculptures in the *Andriantopoiika,* which comes a long way in the evolution chain that starts with his illustrious predecessors. It also ties well with Posidippus' impassioned advice to sculptors to follow Lysippus' lead, which may reflect in part the Samian historian's own comments. We know that the issue of *mimesis* occupied Duris in his historical works where he muses about historical reality in a *plaidoyer* against his predecessor historians Ephorus and Theopompus.[93] In his opinion truth in historiography can be understood as *mimesis* that is as close to reality as possible, even though it must remain *mimesis* rather than be transformed into reality itself. Interestingly, in his search for truth in historiography, Duris compared his concept of *mimesis* with "lifelike painting," an idea that is also found in his discussion of Lysippus and his encounter with Eupompus, which led to an interesting definition of how an artist can copy nature.[94] Finally, Duris' criticism of Ephorus and Theopompus fascination with the beauty of writing style, rather than truth, echoes Pliny's juxtaposition of Lysistratus and Lysippus' works on the one hand and of their predecessors on the other who were mostly interested in beauty in sculpture.[95]

Posidippus' *Andriantopoiika,* like all Hellenistic ecphrastic poetry should be viewed in its specific context, against its specific cultural and intellectual background.[96] This fascinating section can only be understood against its contemporary intellectual discourse, and suggests to the reader a certain approach to viewing that is associated with the historical setting and its philosophy. As a work produced in order to support Ptolemaic self-definition, it should be expected to define seeing, as works of art, contemporary and past, are assigned new meanings that trigger expected responses of viewers and are reconstructed in such a way as to occupy their proper place in the illusion created by Ptolemaic politics in the first half of the third century BCE.

---

[93] Jacoby, *FGrHist* 76 F 1; cf. Schepens 1998.

[94] On general reflections about the concept of *mimesis* in Greek sculpture, see Stewart 1990:73–75. On naturalism and the peripatetics, see Miller 2000.

[95] Cf. above discussion of Pliny XXXIV 37. For a study of Duris' historical and art-historical oeuvre, see Schepens 1998:106–107.

[96] Goldhill 1994:223.

15

The Structure of the *Hippika* in P.Mil.Vogl. VIII 309

Marco Fantuzzi

University of Macerata
and Graduate School of Greek and Latin Philology
of the University of Florence

In their introduction to the *editio princeps*, Bastianini and Gallazzi already noted the complexity of artistic structuring in the *Hippika* section of the new Milan papyrus (AB 71–88). Their discussion is part of their valuable analysis of the poetry book's "artistic intentions," the establishment of criteria on which epigrams were grouped together within different sections.[1] In the *Hippika*, the editors discern a bipartite structure; in their view, individual epigrams are arranged in two distinct groups comprising twelve and six poems respectively (AB 71–82 and AB 83–88).[2] They perceive the poems dedicated to Ptolemaic queens as marking the conclusions of each group.[3] Their observations on the contents of each group led them to take a skeptical stance on the presence of underlying reasons and aims for the organization of the *Hippika*, and to doubt even whether there was an intentional organic/artistic arrangement of the whole. Specifically, they conclude:

> Le ragioni per cui i testi sono così suddivisi non sono evidenti, tanto più che i due raggruppamenti mostrano una struttura analoga. Gli epigrammi furono forse attinti da due raccolte differenti e non furono coordinati insieme?[4]

The main problem involved in Bastianini and Gallazzi's hypothesis is the lack in unity of the epigrams on the royal victories. Seven of the *Hippika* celebrate

---

[1] BG: 24–27.
[2] This bipartite structure of the *Hippika* is also accepted by Bernardini-Bravi 2002:154.
[3] BG: 197.
[4] BG: 26.

Ptolemaic victories: five of them name (often together with other Ptolemies) a queen Berenice who may be identified with Berenice II or, as D. J. Thompson has convincingly argued, with Berenice the Syrian (AB 78–82), while the last two epigrams mainly focus on Berenice I (AB 87–88).[5] Royal victors are the common denominator here, and above all, as we shall see, the epigrams in question are in many ways different from the rest whose laudandi are non-royals. This is also very different from the *Anathematika*, where the four epigrams involving Arsinoe (AB 36–39) are set at the beginning of the section. One wonders then why the royal epigrams are not gathered together, but rather are divided into two clusters, one placed at about the middle of the *Hippika*, the other at its end. Are we to follow Bastianini and Gallazzi's suggestion that the arrangement of the *Hippika* in two mixed groups, each one including epigrams for non-royal and for royal victors, derives from the existence of two separate, earlier collections? My article aims at proposing a different solution for the structure of this section, and at suggesting a specific principle for this arrangement which, if correct, would serve highly artistic purposes.

Let us first consider the possibility that the distinction between non-royal and royal victors is the main criterion for the arrangement of the *Hippika*. If this is the case, we may distinguish four groups of texts: AB 71–77, AB 78–82, AB 83–86, and AB 87–88.

According to my hypothesis, the *Hippika* would be headed by a first group comprising seven epigrams. The first six honor victors in the κέλης event ('steed-races'; 1–3, 6) and in the chariot-races (4–5), but all place a strong emphasis on horses at least as much as on their owners. Indeed, in most cases the horses are κέλητες, which were traditionally accorded a protagonistic role in equestrian victories.[6] But also in the case of the two victories in four-horse chariots (AB 74 and 75) the main focus is on the horses: they are the real protagonists of the first three out of four lines in AB 75, and the real victor/protagonist in the competition commemorated by the epigram AB 74 is the right horse that shows extraordinary intelligence. The special attention on horses in the first six epigrams of the *Hippika* may also have led the anthologist (perhaps Posidippus himself, if all the texts of the P.Mil.Vogl. VIII 309 are by Posidippus), to place epigram AB 71 strategically first

---

[5] Bastianini and Gallazzi identified Berenice quoted at AB 78.13, AB 79.1, and 82.1 with Berenice II, the daughter of Magas of Cyrene and wife of Ptolemy III, whose Nemean victory in a chariot race was celebrated by Callimachus (*SH* 254–69). Thompson (forthcoming) argues, persuasively in my opinion, that this Berenice should be identified with Berenice the Syrian, daughter of Ptolemy II and Arsinoe I, and sister of Ptolemy III. Married to Antiochus II after the Second Syrian War, she was killed along with her son by Antiochus immediately after her husband's death in 246 BCE by Laodice, Antiochus' former wife.

[6] Some evidence is collected by Bernardini-Bravi 2002:155.

because of its strong parallelism between the victory of the owner and the "personal" victory of his horse. Emphasis in this perspective is placed on both distichs by the use of rather heavy pleonasm through repetition:

οὗτος ὁ μουνοκέλης Αἴθων ἐμὸς ἵ[ππος ἐνίκα
κἀγὼ τὴν αὐτὴν Πυθιάδα ςτ[άδιον·
δὶς δ᾽ ἀνεκηρύχθην Ἱππόςτρ[ατος] ἀ̣θλοφ[όρος τ᾽] ἦν
ἵππος ὁμοῦ κἀγώ, πότνια Θεςςαλία.

This, my single horse, Aithon, [won victory]
  and I was crowned at the same Pythian Games;
twice was I, Hippostratos, heralded victor,
  my horse, as well as I, Lady Thessaly.[7]

Both the emphasis on the victorious horse in the κέλης-race and the position of a κέλης-epinician in the beginning of a section on equestrian victories are also well paralleled in the collection of Pindar's *Epinicians*. Indeed, according to the schol. Pind. I, p. 7.14f. Drachmann, the first *Olympian Ode*, composed in commemoration of the Syracusan tyrant Hieron's victory in single-horse racing (476 BCE), occupies the first position in the *Epinicians* tout court, at least from the time when Pindar's corpus was edited by Aristophanes of Byzantium (since Aristophanes lived between 265/257 and 190/180, the chronology of his *akme* fits the age the anthology of P.Mil.Vogl. was presumably compiled: see below n. 28). Interestingly, it also constitutes the only epinician for a victory with the κέλης to be found in Pindar and is followed by five Olympian odes for winners with the horse- or mule-chariot, and so violates the criterion of importance of the agonistic specialty, which appears to have orientated Aristophanes' arrangement of Pindar's epinician poems (chariot-races are elsewhere more important), in order to feature the presence in *O.* I of the paradigm of Pelops, who had been the first Olympian winner (cf. schol. Pind. I, p.7.16f. Drachmann). Furthermore, Pindar's ode places the horse Pherenicus as protagonist in a manner that prefigures the first of the *Hippika* of P.Mil.Vogl. VIII 309: the courser is said by Pindar to have 'joined' his owner Hieron of Syracuse in his triumph (lines 20–22):

. . . παρ᾽ Ἀλφεῷ σύτο δέμας
ἀκέντητον ἐν δρόμοισι παρέχων,
κράτει δὲ προσέμειξε δεσπόταν.

---

[7] Translation by B. Acosta-Hughes and E. Kosmetatou.

. . . he sped beside the Alpheos,
giving his limbs ungoaded in the race,
and joined to victorious power his master.[8]

In commemorating the same Olympic victory by the same horse and owner,
Bacchylides also highlighted the achievement of Hieron's κέλης (5.183–186):

πο]σσὶ νικάσας δρόμῳ
ἦλθ]εν Φερένικος ⟨ἐς⟩ εὐπύργους Συρακόσ-
σας Ἱέρωνι φέρων
εὐδ]αιμονίας πέταλον.

Pherenicus sped to victory in the race
and so returned to well-towered
Syracuse bringing Hieron
the leaves of good fortune.[9]

Also the very few inscriptions that have survived, or are quoted by ancient
authors, commemorating victories with a κέλης, strongly suggest that this
emphasis was traditional at least as early as the Archaic period. This protagonistic
role of the animal in the victory was possibly motivated by the fact that actual
commemorative monuments often displayed the horse itself. An epigram from the
Greek Anthology, attributed to Anacreon, presumably refers to the dedication of the
sculpture of such a κέλης which won victory for the Corinthian Phidolas in the late
sixth century BCE (*AP* VI 135, *FGE* 502 f.):[10]

οὗτος Φειδόλα ἵππος ἀπ᾽ εὐρυχόροιο Κορίνθου
ἄγκειται Κρονίδᾳ μνᾶμα ποδῶν ἀρετᾶς.

The horse of Phidolas from spacious Corinth
is dedicated to Zeus in memory of the might of its legs.[11]

Pausanias describes this monument's dedication in detail, offering additional
information on victories in the same event scored by the horse belonging to
Phidolas' sons. He also quotes an epigram that was associated with their own votive
and focused all the same on the horse as protagonist.[12]

---

[8] Translation by W. H. Race.
[9] Translation by D. A. Campbell.
[10] Cf. Ebert 1972:46–48, no.6.
[11] Translation by W. R. Paton.
[12] Pausanias VI 13.9–10; Ebert 1972:48–49, no.7. On Pausanias' interests in epigraphy and his relia-

ὠκυδρόμας Λύκος "Ἰσθμι' ἄπαξ, δύο ἐνθάδε νίκαις
Φειδόλα παίδων ἐστεφάνωσε δόμους.

The swift Lycus by one victory at the Isthmus and two here
crowned the house of the sons of Pheidolas.[13]

The victorious owner of a four-horse chariot dominates only the seventh of the
Hippika (AB 77), where his personal οὐκ ὀλίγα δαπάνα is stressed, as well as his
concern about his own δόξα:

ἄρμ[ατι ±11   ]. τελέωι τρὶς 'Ọ[λύμ]πια νικῶ
  Εὐ.[±13   ο]ὐ̣κ ὀλίγαι δαπ[άνα]ι.
[±15   ] κομιδᾶς .[.....].[
  εἴ γ' ἀ[ρ]κ̣εῖ δόξαι, λείπεται οὐ[δ]ὲν ἐμοί.

With the full chariot I won three times in the Olympic games
. . . not inconsiderable cost (?)
. . . supplies (?) . . .
though suffices for fame, I am left with nothing.[14]

I suggest that this last epigram in the first section of the *Hippika* (AB 83),
which is dedicated to non-royal winners, may owe its final position to its separate
emphasis on the figure of the chariot's owner, rather than the horse's. This feature
may have led the (author?-)anthologist of the epigrams of the P.Mil.Vogl. to isolate
the poem at the end of this first cluster of the *Hippika*.[15] We observe the same editorial stratagem in the case of two epigrams for deceased men (AB 60–61) at the end
of the section of the ἐπιτύμβια, a section that primarily features dead women.

....

bility in transmitting inscribed texts, especially in Books Five and Six, cf. Tzifopoulos 1991:1–23. A
victory in chariot-racing was further commemorated by a similar inscription carved on a monument
at Delphi which dates to the mid-fourth century BCE (Moretti 1953:65–66, no.27; Ebert
1972:136–137, no.42):

εἰκόνες αἵδ' ἵππ[ων], αἳ Πύθια [ποσσὶν ἐνίκων]
'Ἰσθμοῖ τε στεφ[άνοις] Κ̣αλλιά[δην πύκασαν]
σκηπτροφόρ[ō τε Διὸς π]ατρὸς [ἄροντ' ἄεθλον].

These are the images of the horses that won the Pythia by their feet
and covered Calliades at the Isthmus thick with crowns
carrying off the prize of the sceptre-bearing Father Zeus.
(Translated by E. Kosmetatou)

[13] Translation by W. H. S. Jones.
[14] Translation by M. Fantuzzi.
[15] As acknowledged by BG:26.

After all the epigram AB 77 of the *Hippika*, with its stress on the specifics of he δόξα that is garnered by victory in chariot-racing, marks perfectly the transiion from the first to the second cluster, consisting of five epigrams which are dedi-ated to queen Berenice II (or Berenice of Syria), and to her ancestors, and are haracterized by a strong emphasis on the royal owners of the victorious chariots.[16] t seems that there was some kind of historically attested hierarchy of relevance etween victories in the κέλης events on the one hand and in chariot-racing on the ther. Apart from Aristophanes' opinion, cited above, Pindar had already declared hat among the equestrian victories success with the chariot is 'sweeter' γλυκυτέρα) than with the κέλης.[17] The anthologist (or the author at the noment he was the anthologist of his own work) may have liked to pave the way or epigrams celebrating royal δόξα gained in chariot victories by accurately lefining the implications of this glory in his last epigrams dealing with non-royal vinners (AB 77). Indeed, if the reading provided by the editors for the problematic ast line of this epigram is correct (AB 77.4: ε̣ἴ γ' ἀ̣[ρ]κ̣ε̣ῖ δόξαι, λείπεται ο̣ὐ[δ]ὲν ἐμοί), it follows then that the poet adheres to the idea that δόξα—this vord at least is sure—is gained through chariot victories as a consequence of the ieavy (οὐκ ὀλίγαι) expenditures for the κομιδά (AB 77.3, = ἱπποτροφία), roved by the fact that the winner "is left with no revenue."[18] Assuming that also

---

[16] It is of course impossible to restore AB 81 with certainty, but it is logical to assume that it, too, dealt with the queen, since it is placed in her section, so to speak: cf. BG:210. As for AB 80, the final ἐπὶ παιδὶ μόνη, when compared to παῖδα (AB 82.4) and μόνη βασιλίς (82.6) as references to Berenice I (or the Syrian), lead us to deduce that the epigram deals with the same queen. Cf. Thompson (forthcoming).

[17] At the end of the first Olympian ode, which was dedicated to the third victory of Hieron with the κέλης at the Olympic Games of 476 BCE, Pindar anticipates the victory with the chariot which indeed took place in 468 with the words (1.106–111):

> θεὸς ἐπίτροπος ἐὼν τεαῖσι μήδεται
> ἔχων τοῦτο κᾶδος, Ἱέρων,
> μερίμναισιν· εἰ δὲ μὴ ταχὺ λίποι.
> ἔτι γλυκυτέραν κεν ἔλπομαι
> σὺν ἅρματι θοῷ κλεΐ-
> ξειν ἐπίκουρον εὑρὼν ὁδὸν λόγων, κτλ.

> a god acting as guardian makes this his concern: to devise means, Hieron, for your aspirations, and unless he should suddenly depart, *I hope to celebrate an even sweeter success with a speeding chariot* (my emphasis), having found a helpful road of words . . .
> (Translation by W. H. Race)

Beyond this undoubted surface meaning, the reference to the chariot may also have been used metaphorically to imply the chariot of the Muses: "if Hieron wins with his chariot, Pindar hopes to be able to celebrate the victory with the aid of the Muses' chariot" (so Gerber 1982:165).

[18] I agree with Gärtner 2002:32 that this is the correct interpretation of the second hemistich of AB 77.4.

the reading ϼόξ[α at the end of what we can read of AB 78.2 in the first roya
epigram is correct, the explicit statement of the non-royal winner of AB 77 on th
relevance of glory coming from success in chariot-racing would anticipate the ide
that could be taken for granted for the monarchs without further remarks i
AB 78.2 (μοι ϼόξ[α παλαιόγονος], 'my renown is of ancient origin').

This idea would have found full support in contemporary mentality, as exem
plified in a famous speech of Thucydides' Alcibiades. In the spring of 415 BCE
during a discussion on the Sicilian expedition at the Athenian Assembly, th
Athenian general Nicias stood firmly against it, and Alcibiades spoke in favor of th
proposed campaign. In attempting to strengthen his position in favor of wa
Alcibiades made the following statement on his authority based on his spectacula
performance in the chariot-racing during the 416 BCE Olympic games:

> καὶ προσήκει μοι μᾶλλον ἑτέρων, ὦ ᾿Αθηναῖοι, ἄρχειν . . .
> οἱ γὰρ ῞Ελληνες καὶ ὑπὲρ δύναμιν μείζω ἡμῶν τὴν πόλιν
> ἐνόμισαν τῷ ἐμῷ διαπρεπεῖ τῆς ᾿Ολυμπίαζε θεωρίας,
> πρότερον ἐλπίζοντες αὐτὴν καταπεπολεμῆσθαι, διότι
> ἅρματα μὲν ἑπτὰ καθῆκα, ὅσα οὐδείς πω ἰδιώτης πρότερον,
> ἐνίκησα δὲ καὶ δεύτερος καὶ τέταρτος ἐγενόμην καὶ τἆλλα
> ἀξίως τῆς νίκης παρεσκευασάμην. νόμῳ μὲν γὰρ τιμὴ τὰ
> τοιαῦτα, ἐκ δὲ τοῦ δρωμένου καὶ δύναμις ἅμα ὑπονοεῖται.

It belongs to me more than to others, Athenians, to have command . . .
For the Hellenes, who had previously hoped that our state had been
exhausted by the war, conceived an idea of its greatness that even transcended its actual power, by reason of the magnificence of my display as
sacred deputy at Olympia with which I represented it at the Olympic
games, because I entered seven chariots, a number that no private
citizen had ever entered before, and won the first prize, and the second
and the fourth, and provided everything else in a style worthy of my
victory. For by general custom such things do indeed mean honor
(νόμῳ μὲν γὰρ τιμὴ τὰ τοιαῦτα) and from what is done men also
infer power.[19]

(Thucydides VI 16.1–2)

Further, in his introduction to this speech, Thucydides reveals that in this
passion for horse-breeding, among many others, Alcibiades had been wasting
almost all his property, more or less in the same way as the winner of P.Mil.Vogl.
AB 77, at least according to Gärtner's interpretation:

---

[19] Translation by C. F. Smith.

ὧν γὰρ ἐν ἀξιώματι ὑπὸ τῶν ἀστων, ταῖς ἐπιθυμίαις
μείζοσιν ἢ κατὰ τὴν ὑπάρχουσαν οὐσίαν ἐχρῆτο ἔς τε τὰς
ἱπποτροφίας καὶ τὰς ἄλλα δαπάνας.

he indulged desires beyond his actual means, in keeping horses as well
as in other expenses.[20]

(Thucydides VI 15.3)

If the first seven epigrams of the *Hippika* correspond, as is suggested here, to a first cluster of texts, we may then observe an internal symmetrical structure in it as well. The section begins with three epigrams comprising four lines each. These are followed by one long central epigram of fourteen lines (AB 74) narrating the tale of an unusual, indeed paradoxographical, final judgment, with unusual descriptive quality, and consequently of unusual narrative length—an anomalous dimension which may also point out the great political relevance of the victor, Callicrates of Samos, the famous nauarch of the Ptolemies and first eponymous priest of the cult of the *Theoi adelphoi*, who also were the dedicatees of the bronze chariot erected by Callicrates to celebrate his victory (AB 74.12–14).[21] The first cluster is rounded-up by three further epigrams each four lines long. The symmetry here described is of course artistically refined and self-explanatory in itself, but it also finds another parallel within the Milan papyrus. Indeed it seems to be mirroring the structure of the ἐπιτύμβια, where, in a series of seven epigrams for deceased maidens (AB 49–55), the fourth (AB 52) stands out from the beginning and the last ones because of its peculiar content: the girl on whom the epigram concentrates is not dead, but the deceased is her father, whose tomb beside his sundial she guards faithfully.

---

[20] This parallelism between 77.4 and the passage of Thucydides has already been noted by Gärtner 2002:31. Euripides is credited by Plutarch (*PMG* 755) with the composition of an *epinician* in honor of Alcibiades' Olympic victory of 416. It, too, stresses the unprecedented nature of the Athenian general's participation and achievement in the games.

[21] See Bing 2003: the author has been so kind as to allow me to see the text before publication; Bing points out well the anomaly of the fact that "it is not Callicrates who is the *honorand* of the dedication (though it doubtless does him honor, too), nor even the god of Delphi—though he *is* the poem's addressee with Φοῖβ' ε v. 4—but rather the *Theoi adelphoi.*" This dedication may actually have stood for another form of indirect celebration of the equestrian glory the Ptolemies appear to have established and advertised not only for themselves, but also for the members of their 'court' (*lato sensu*), like the court member of Ptolemy III and Ptolemy IV Sosibios (see Call. fr. 384) or the mistress of Ptolemy II Bilistiche (see *FGrHist* 257aF6). The intentionality of the gesture of Callicrates as an 'image-maker' would not surprise, if we consider the couple of statues erected by him to Ptolemy II and Arsinoe at Olympia in between the temple of Zeus and of Hera, most probably to parallel them with the couple of the supreme gods (and brother-sister): cf. Hintzen-Bohlen 1992.

According to my interpretation of the structure of the *Hippika*, a second cluster of five epigrams follows the first one, and this is dominated by the chariot-victor Berenice, to be identified (see above n5) either with Berenice II Euergetis or Berenice the Syrian (AB 78–82). The third cluster consists of four epigrams honoring non-royal winners in the κέλης event (AB 83–86). Once again, as in the first group of epigrams, the epigrams of the third group place the main emphasis on racing horses, mirroring in size the first three and the last three of the seven epigrams in total of the first cluster: each epigram is four lines long. The third cluster of epigrams would separate the previous five epigrams in honor of Berenice (Euergetis or the Syrian) and other Ptolemies from the two epigrams which conclude the *Hippika* and make up the last (fourth) small group of texts: of these the first one (AB 87) as a whole honors Berenice I, while the second one at least ends by commemorating her victory (AB 88).

Of course, the structure that I have suggested above presupposes the awareness by the author of the epigrams of a distinction between the courtly voice of the epinician/encomistic poet celebrating Ptolemaic queens and kings on the one hand, and the purely epinician voice of the singer of the victories of all other, non-royal, victors on the other. If poet and anthologist are not the same,[22] the latter managed to catch the courtly tone of the epigrams commemorating victories of kings and queens remarkably well, distinguishing it from the voice of the celebrator of other equestrian victors.

I suggest that this distinction, which mainly deals with the orientation in the advertisement of *kydos*, is especially obvious in the first and last of the royal *Hippika* (AB 78 and AB 88). In the *Hippika* epigrams which praise non-royal victors, the protagonists, namely the human victors themselves and their horses, are celebrated for *their own* single, or iterated, exploits. In this context, the text of each epigram fulfills the task of *establishing* and recording their own *kydos*. On the other hand, AB 78, in which queen Berenice (Euergetis or the Syrian) seems to speak in her own voice,[23] the glory (κλέος) the poets are invited to sing is deemed as already well-known (γνωστά: AB 78.2). Additionally, the name of the victor in this, as well as in the last of the *Hippika* (AB 88), comes only in the penultimate line. This choice of emphasis by the poet is probably due to the fact that the victories of individual kings and queens appear to have become a point of departure for the celebration of the super-individual equestrian glory encompassing the entire dynasty—a glory which had to be seen as proof for the continuous presence of divine favor and of

---

[22] See below n. 28.

[23] Alternatively, the persona loquens may have been Ptolemy III (according to BG *ad loc.*) or Ptolemy II, the father of Berenice the Syrian, if Thompson's proposed identification is correct. Cf. Thompson (forthcoming).

dynastic "identity" which the Ptolemies liked to show perpetuated in their lives.[24] This practice precisely mirrors the presentation of Berenice II in the *Victoria Berenices* by Callimachus (*SH* 254), where the queen does not appear to have been explicitly mentioned by name, but is just introduced with the patronymic designation κασιγνήτων ἱερὸν αἷμα θεῶν, which on one side certainly pays a reverent homage to the official title of the reigning Ptolemaic couple[25], but on the other stresses the belonging of the un-named Berenice (here not individualized) to the dynasty in which every reigning couple usually had the title. However a special and individual emphasis was accorded at least to the victory of Berenice I, since it was she who started the long-lasting line of *female* victors, which functioned as another special family-record testifying to Ptolemaic gift in equestrian victories.[26]

My idea of the arrangement of the *Hippika* involves an interpretative key that explains the inclusion of a cluster of epigrams (the third) in honor of non-royal victors between the epigrams mainly centered on Berenice (Euergetis or the Syrian), located in the middle of the section, and the epigrams focused on Berenice I at the end. In arranging this collection, its anthologist may have broadly adopted as template a structure also found in Callimachus' *Aetia*, another collection of apparently unrelated pieces on different *aetia* within a very thin narrative frame of the dialogue with the Muses (in the first two books), or no frame at all (as it appears to be the case in the last two), where the coherence of the encomiastic voice of the author celebrating Ptolemaic *queens* at the middle and at the end of the work could be especially characterized and identifiable inside the work.[27] Of course, I am not referring to a numerically or qualitatively precise attempt at miniaturization. I simply suggest that the author of the epigrams when editing them, or their anthologist, may have tried to mimic the alternation of poetic voices found in the *Aetia*, namely Callimachus' mixing of courtly and non-courtly voices, through the same kind of alternation: the *Aetia* would actually have instantiated the idea that to celebrate the glory of the kings at the middle and at the end is a better and more effective homage than to concentrate the celebration in a single point of the work. In the *Hippika* this alternation results not only in juxtaposing unrelated non-royal protagonists—the owners of the κέλητες together with their horses—versus the well-known, coherent, and dominating figures of two queens and of other royal

---

[24] I have recently stressed and expanded this point in a paper entitled "Posidippus in Court." Cf. Fantuzzi (forthcoming).

[25] Cf. Fuhrer 1992:88–90.

[26] In general on the significance of Berenice I in Ptolemaic dynastic propaganda, see Gutzwiller 1992:364–366. Cf. also Kosmetatou on Ptolemaic *Familiengruppe* in this volume.

[27] Or, to express the issue in a more drastic way, with Parsons 1977:50: "*Aetia* I–II, and *Aetia* III–IV, form two distinct wholes, one united by the Muses, the other by Berenice."

members of the Ptolemaic dynasty, but also in refraining from gathering in the same position all the epigrams to honor victories of kings and queens.

If the supposition proposed above is correct, the beginning, fairly long series of *Hippika* discussing disparate non-royal winners would 'correspond' to the first two books of the *Aetia*. In both sections neither the epigrammist's nor Callimachus' voices as courtly encomiasts are heard or anticipated. However, at about the middle of the *Hippika* occurs a cluster of coherent epigrams commemorating victories by Ptolemaic queens and kings: this 'corresponds' to Callimachus' long poem on the equestrian victory of Berenice II, the *Victoria Berenices*, which Callimachus placed at the beginning of his third book, namely in the middle of the *Aetia*. Turning back to P.Mil.Vogl. VIII 309, the sequence of four more epigrams commemorating further non-royal winners in the κέλης event would aim at re-establishing the alternative kind of emphasis on the κέλητες, which can be found in the first epigrams of the *Hippika*: this third section would then 'correspond' to the non-courtly aetiological tales of the third and fourth books of the *Aetia*, that separated the "Victory" of Berenice II from the "Lock" of Berenice II. Only at the end of the series of the *Hippika* would the anthologist of the epigrams (or maybe the author-anthologist of his own work) have reproposed again the courtly voice and focused on royal victors. This 'second installment' of the courtly voice would find its parallel in the divinization of the *plokamos* of Berenice II sung by Callimachus at the end of the fourth book of his *Aetia*.[28]

Especially the penultimate epigram of the *Hippika* (AB 80), namely the first of the couple of texts which mainly aim at the commemoration of the greatness of the equestrian success of Berenice I, may have been proposed by the (author?-)anthol-

---

[28] According to BG:17 the roll of P.Mil.Vogl. VIII 309 more probably dates to the end of the third century than to the half of the same century or to the beginning of the second. The dedication of the *plokamos* by Berenike II and its disappearance, followed by Conon's interpretation of this event as a *katasterismos*, most probably took place at the end of 245 BCE, and Callimachus' poem could nothave been composed a long time later. We do not know when Posidippus died, and cannot rule out that a poet who was most probably commissioned for the epigram on the Pharos of Alexandria and therefore must have been an established man of letters by 282-280 BCE (cf. Fernández Galiano 1987:13) was still alive (and anthologized his own work) forty or fifty years later. Anyway my interpretation of the structure of the *Hippika* is neither bound by the identification of the author of the *Hippika* as Posidippus, nor by the chronology of the author(s) of the epigrams in case he/they were not Posidippus. The only relevant issue for me is the chronology of the anthologist who arranged the collection of P.Mil.Vogl., and may have been both the author of the epigrams or a bright reader of his poetry: if the papyrus is of the last tenth of the third century, the anthologist may well have arranged the collection a few years before that date, under the impression of the structure which Callimachus had conceived for his own collection of *aetia* (+ the encomiastic pieces he had decided to include in the *Aetia*). Not very differently, as noted above in this paper, he may have placed the epigrams on victories in steed-racing at the beginning of the collection under the influence of Aristophanes' arrangement of Pindar's *Olympian* odes.

ogist as a parallel to the *Plokamos* of Berenice II. It is possible that after a first reading of the entire *Hippika* a learned reader would hear in this collection of epigrams the echo of alternating voices and topics which had featured in the *Aetia* (Ptolemaic queens versus non-royal, disparate characters/disparate aetia not connected to the Ptolemaic family)[29]: if the memory of this template was activated in the readers' minds, it is very tempting to suggest that the form of presentation of AB 87—the epigram adopts the *persona loquens* of the statuary group of the horses who won the victory for Berenice I and takes the form of a flashback recollection—might sound like (though not necessarily conceived by the author to be) a distant echo of the *persona loquens* of the Callimachean πλόκαμος. More specifically, the wishful thinking of the πλόκαμος remembering its past life on the head of the queen might be read underlying the beginning ἵπ[ποι] ἔθ' ἁμὲς ἐοῦσαι of AB 87. In the same way that the πλόκαμος wished to provide the queen with a memorial equivalent to Ariadne's *corona* in heaven (cf. Cat. 66.59–62), the statuary horses would remember the precise moment when they won the στέφανος for Berenice (AB 87.2), and the fact that they are "speaking" again and again through the voices of the readers of their inscription (or anyway of their epigram), re-enacts that moment eternally, thereby "crowns" Berenice for ever.[30] Last but not least, in the same way that the protagonists of the epigram on the victory of Berenice are horses, the πλόκαμος was said to have been carried to the sky by the wind Zephyros, and in an expression that is unclear and has provoked much scholarly debate, this wind is once metaphorically described as "the horse of Arsinoe" (Callim. fr. 110.53–5; cf. Cat. 66.52–54.).[31]

After all, the possibility of paralleling in some way the *Lock of Berenice* with an equestrian courtly epinician may not have occurred only to Callimachus alone as editor, when he sought a model for his new edition of the *Aetia*, or to the anthologist of the *Hippika* of the P.Mil.Vogl. It likely took place elsewhere at least once: in P.Oxy. 2258, which apparently preserves an annotated anthology of Callimachus' poems, the *Coma Berenices*, here not in the role of epilogue that it plays in the *Aetia*, is immediately followed by an equestrian epinician in honor of Sosibios.[32] Furthermore, Callimachus' placement of an encomiastic piece for Berenice II both in the middle of the *Aetia*, at the beginning of the third book, and at the end of another eulogy, most probably attracted the attention of another author, Virgil, who in his *Georgics* appears to have placed two passages in honor of the military

---

[29] With the partial exception of the Callicrates of AB 74, on which see above n. 21.

[30] Cf. Kurke 1993:141–149.

[31] On this problematic identification of Zephyros, cf. Gutzwiller 1992:380f.; Koenen 1993:103–105, and the *status quaestionis* in Marinone 1997:151–157.

[32] Cf. Parsons 1977:48; Gutzwiller 1992:382; Marinone 1997:41f.

successes of Octavian at exactly the same position, namely at the beginning of the third of a four-books work, and shortly at the end (III 1–48 and IV 559–566).[33] In contrast to the first Ptolemies, Octavian could be proud of a properly military *kydos*, which of course was a more traditional and impressive path to glory than equestrian success.

[33] The beginning apostrophe to Octavian (I 24–42) does not include any mention of his victories. A detailed analysis of the structure of *Aetia* III and IV as possible template for the arrangement of the eulogies of Octavian in *Georgics* III and IV is offered by Thomas 1983:92–113 (= Thomas 1999:68–100) and Thomas 1988:41 and 239.

16

Constructing Legitimacy: The Ptolemaic *Familiengruppe* as a Means of Self-Definition in Posidippus' *Hippika*[1]

Elizabeth Kosmetatou

Katholieke Universiteit Leuven

Scholarly interest in the Hellenistic epigram has recently soared, and important studies have been published on its specific characteristics, context, models, and development.[2] Of particular relevance is the ongoing vivid discussion of the process by which these short, almost incidental, poems acquired new life in their transition from stone to book. The lucky survival of the new Milan papyrus, plausibly associated with Posidippus, has been a most welcome addition to this significant body of texts, as it sheds light on a variety of old questions, raises new problems, and opens paths for renewed debate. Indeed, one cannot stress enough its importance for our understanding of ancient poetry collections, the early book roll, and the aesthetics of organizing texts. However, interesting though this new cultural monument may be a variety of disciplines, art historical, archaeological, historical, philosophical, or literary, its context remains primarily associated with the early Ptolemaic political spectacle.[3]

---

[1] It is a pleasure to thank the following scholars for discussing with me previous versions of this article: Benjamin Acosta-Hughes, Manuel Baumbach, Peter Bing, Marco Fantuzzi, Nassos Papalexandrou, Dorothy Thompson, and Stephen V. Tracy.

The term "Familiengruppe" was first introduced by Borbein. See Borbein 1973:88–90. See also relevant discussion in Smith 1988:16–17; Hintzen-Bohlen 1990:129; Schmidt-Dounas 2000:102–119. Rose introduced the English term "dynastic group monument"; cf. Rose 1987 and Rose 1998. Since this article will be dealing with echoes of a specific type of dynastic group monument, i.e. the genealogical statuary group, which is not exclusively associated with royalty, this author has preferred to use the German term "Familiengruppe."

[2] Cf. Bing 1988; Bing 1998; Gutzwiller 1998:229–230; Rossi 2001; Fantuzzi and Hunter 2002:389–448; Gutzwiller 2002.

[3] On the consequences of the public's access to information for ideology, action, and quiescence and the need to view political news as spectacle, see Edelman 1988:1–11.

It is a *topos* among students of the Hellenistic period that much of its contemporary literature resulted from royal initiative to take positions opportunistically and to devise means for misleading public presentations of self.[4] It is a universal law of politics that in order for a leader to climb up the greasy pole and establish a regime, winning the support of disparate and often conflicting groups is crucial. These entities include the referential hinterland consisting of a ruler's "immediate mirrors", or his immediate entourage, the governed mass, the wider international community, as well as posterity.[5]

In such a context, legitimacy can first be viewed as a term of international law. Any state or organization is deemed to be legitimate after having been recognized and accepted by the international community, in other words by its peers with whom it expects to interact in the future. Even though the third century BCE was by no means a peaceful period, and conflicts among the Hellenistic kingdoms remained unresolved, the *status quo* established at Ipsus in 301 BCE was pretty much secure.[6] Alexander's empire, whose initial survival rested on the personality and image of the Macedonian conqueror, had been a "great patient" since its birth, its size and diversity requiring the setting up of a specific state structure and institutional functions that never came to be. A few short years after Alexander's premature death, it was therefore definitively parceled out among his generals, a new model of state developed, and it soon became obvious that reviving the dead in all its unstable glory would prove a futile endeavor. However, the official policy of self-promotion and misinformation ensured a continuous recognition of the newly emerged Hellenistic kingdoms as legal entities and powers to be reckoned with. After all, states were still being formed and could still disappear as the example of Lysimachus' kingdom of Thrace instructed everyone in 281 BCE.[7] Every forged alliance counted.

Egypt, like Syria, was faced with additional concerns, as it was ruled by a Greek minority, an elite that had to be accepted by the wide population. As the kingdom gradually took shape, and new populations blended in living side by side with the native Egyptians, there arose the usual problems that any government deals with in its attempt to survive.[8] The manipulation of public opinion into winning the confidence of the ruled could only be achieved through the construction and reconstruction of a public persona in the form of illusions that aimed to discourage

---

[4] The bibliography on literature as a product of royal patronage is substantial. Cf. Stephens 1998; Kosmetatou 2000:35–39; Stephens 2003, all of which cite earlier bibliography.

[5] Muller and Jobert 1987; Edelman 1988:57; Barker 2002:30–35; Geuss 2002:31.

[6] Green 1990:21–35; Billows 1990.

[7] Lund 1992; Kosmetatou 2003.

[8] Cf. Quaegebeur 1983; Thompson 1987; Thompson 1988; Clarysse 1992; Thompson 1992a; Thompson 1992b; Thompson 1992c; Thompson 1993; Clarysse 1998; Stephens 1998.

critical evaluation of policy, to maintain the social peace, and to define the ruler as a binding power that the ruled ought to take into account.[9] Additionally, it was equally important for the Ptolemies to retain a close relationship with their roots in Greece proper, especially its culture as formed by the old aristocracy and royalty over the centuries. The success of the early Ptolemies as image-makers lay on their linking themselves closely to their subjects and peers and on integrating themselves in their community on the basis of a shared set of expectations, values, and patterns. The use of social and religious structures, including processions and festivals was of paramount importance in this policy.[10]

Several of the new Milan epigrams highlight these recurring themes in Ptolemaic dynastic propaganda as it was formulated in the first decades of Lagid rule over Egypt.[11] This paper will examine the use of dynastic imagery as reflected in Posidippus' *Hippika*, a section that attempts to mould the reader's perception of the Ptolemies, in part by alluding to their use of statuary groups. Ptolemaic dynastic group monuments, featuring the reigning monarch and members of his immediate family, sometimes alongside his illustrious predecessors, were set up in areas under Ptolemaic influence and in major sanctuaries and cities. This form of representation, an extension of the usual gift of statue to an influential patron, was not new: it had already developed as a phenomenon among the Greek aristocracy in the mid-sixth century BCE, had declined with the rise of democracy in the Classical period, and had been revived in late 4th century BCE, among others, by Philip II of Macedonia. It was thereafter widely used by monarchs throughout the Hellenistic period as a means of legitimating their power, as well as for their self-glorification. Portraits of the honorees that were usually set up in public places, also functioned as monuments of royal euergetism toward cities, sanctuaries, and individuals who thus rewarded their patrons and invited future benefactions. At the same time, these sponsors advertized their own high connections at the Hellenistic courts.[12]

Very few surviving statues can be associated with confidence to Ptolemaic dynastic statuary groups. Most of our evidence about them comes from a wealth of inscriptions that have been discovered in sanctuaries and cities of Greece, Egypt, and Asia Minor. Their texts provide partial information about donors, statue mate-

[9] Cf. Stephens 1998:167–171; Geuss 2002:35–36.

[10] Connor 1987:40–50.

[11] Fantuzzi (this volume); Hunter (this volume); Kosmetatou on "Vision and Visibility: Art Historical Theory Paints a Portrait of Ideal Leadership in Posidippus' *Andriantopoiika*" (this volume); Stephens (this volume); Fantuzzi in Gutzwiller 2004 (forthcoming); Thompson in Gutzwiller 2004 (forthcoming).

[12] On royal euergetism and the city-states see: Gauthier 1985:39; Welsh 1904–1905:32–43; Poland 1909:425–445; Henry 1983:294–310; Smith 1988:15; Hintzen-Bohlen 1990:129; Hintzen-Bohlen 1992; Rose 1998:3–4; Savalli-Lestrade 1998; Bringman 2000.

rials, and, sometimes, the occasion for the dedications.[13] Of these undoubtedly the most interesting are the inscribed bases that once supported bronze or marble life, or larger-than-life, honorific or cult statues. Although none of the sculptures that were associated with the existing dedicatory inscriptions have survived to the best of our knowledge, we get an idea of how they may have looked from the few surviving portraits in stone and on portrait-coins.[14] Moreover, echoes of them can now be found in the new epigrams of the Milan papyrus.

Posidippus' *Hippika* section comprises some of the most fascinating and spectacular epigrams on victories in the κέλης and chariot-racing events. A tremendous speed and energy stemming from the euphoria of victory comes across from the opening epigram, as the reader's attention and the eyes of his/her imagination are repeatedly directed from the victorious horse to its owner and back, as they are both being crowned at the Pythia (AB 71):

> οὗτος ὁ μουνοκέλης Αἴθων ἐμὸς ἤ[ρατο νίκην]
> κἀγὼ τὴν αὐτὴν Πυθιάδα στ[εφόμην]
> δὶς δ' ἀνεκηρύχθην Ἱππόστρ[ατος] ἀθλοφ[όρος τ'] ἦν
> ἵππος ὁμοῦ κἀγώ, πότνια Θεσσαλία.

> This, my single horse, Aithon [won victory]
> and I was crowned at the same Pythian games;
> twice was I, Hippostratus, heralded victor
> my horse, as well as I, lady Thessaly.[15]

The epigram in question stresses the dazzle of victory, as it gives way *in medias res* to the following epigrams featuring the successful races themselves. This sense of energy is further accentuated in the two epigrams that follow (AB 72–73), evoking at the same time vivid visual images:[16]

> τοῦ πώλου θηεῖσθε τὸ λιπαρές, ὡς πνόον ἕλκει
> παντὶ τύπωι καὶ πᾶς ἐ⟨κ⟩ λαγόνων τέταται
> ὡς νεμεοδρομέων· Μολύκωι δ' ἤνεγκε σέλινα
> νικήσας ἄκρωι νεύματι καὶ κεφαλῆι.

---

[13] See Smith 1988:15.

[14] Kyrieleis 1975; Stambolidis 1982:297–310, figs. 1–3; Smith 1988:86–98, cat. nos. 46–82. On the types and styles of Egyptian royal portraits, see Stanwick 1999.

[15] Translated by B. Acosta-Hughes and E. Kosmetatou. I have chosen to retain the Greek text of the *ed. princ.*

[16] Cf. articles by Papalexandrou and Hoffman (this volume).

Behold the colt's splendor, how it draws in breath
with every stroke and from its flanks is all taut
as though running the Nemean race; for Molycus it brought the
celery crown
on winning with the furthest motion of its head.[17]

εὐθὺς ἀπὸ γραμμῆς ἐν Ὀλυμπίαι ἔτρεχον οὕτω
κέντρα καὶ ἐξώ[ϲειϲ οὐδ᾽ ἐπιδεξά]μενοϲ,
ἁδὺ βάροϲ ταχυ[τᾶτι.......ἐϲτ]εφάνωϲαν
θαλλῶι Τρυγαῖ[ον.......]..[.].[ο]υ

Straight from Olympia's starting line so I ran
not awaiting the whip's bidding
a sweet weight for spe[ed (?) . . . . . .] they crowned
Trygaeus with a branch[. . . . .[18]

Indeed, this enormous energy is found in the characters and in the action within this cluster of epigrams, as it transcends from animal to human. While all the epigrams reflect the actual games that took place in major Panhellenic sanctuaries, the reader's interest is captured throughout by the complexity and variety of events. People and animals are dashing about in thrilling races, achieving unparalleled glory and renown. Anecdotal stories are reconstructed featuring Ptolemaic protegés (AB 74):[19]

ἐν Δελφοῖϲ ἡ πῶλοϲ ὅτ᾽ ἀντιθέουϲα τεθρίπποιϲ
ἄξον‹ι› Θεϲϲαλικῶι κοῦφα ϲυνεξέπεϲε
νεύματι νικήϲαϲα, πολὺϲ τότε θροῦϲ ἐλατήρων
ἦν ἀμφικτύοϲιν, Φοῖβ᾽{ε}, ἐν ἀγωνοθέταιϲ
ῥάβδουϲ δὲ βραχέεϲ χαμάδιϲ βάλον, ὡϲ διὰ κλήρου
νίκηϲ ἡνιόχων οἰϲομένων ϲτέφανον·
ἥδε δὲ δεξιόϲειρα χαμαὶ νεύϲα[ϲ᾽ ἁ]κεραίων
ἐ[κ ϲ]τηθέ̣ων αὐτὴ ῥάβδον ἐφειλκύϲα[το,
ἡ δεινὴ θήλεια μετ᾽ ἄρϲεϲιν· αἱ δ᾽ ἐβόηϲ[αν
φθέγματ[ι] πανδήμωι ϲύμμιγα μυριάδ[εϲ

---

[17] Translated by B. Acosta-Hughes and E. Kosmetatou.
[18] Translated by B. Acosta-Hughes and E. Kosmetatou.
[19] On Callicrates from Samos, see Hauben 1970; Bing 2003 (forthcoming).

κε[ίν]ηι κηρῦξαι ϲτέφανον μέγαν· ἐν θορ[ύβωι δέ
Καλ[λικ]ράτης δάφνη⟨ν⟩ ἦρατ' ἀνὴρ Cάμι̣ο̣[ϲ,
Θε̣ο̣ῖϲι̣ δ' 'Αδ̣[ε]λφε{ι}οῖϲ εἰκὼ ἐναργέα τῶν τότ' [ἀγώνω]ν̣
ἅρ̣[μα καὶ ἡνί̣]ο̣χον χάλκεον ὧδ' ἔθετο.

In Delphi when this filly competed in the four-horse race
  swiftly it arrived at the finish, racing against a Thessalian chariot,
  winning by a nod. Then there was great uproar among the charioteers
  before the Amphictyonic judges, Phoebus.
They cast their short staffs to the ground, for by lot
  the charioteers ought to have won victory's crown.
But then the horse on the right side inclined to the ground and
      without guile
  at heart (?) herself she drew up a staff,
an excellent female among males; whereupon roared
  in one commingled voice all those myriads
to proclaim a great wreath for her. In the up[roar
  Callicrates, a man from Samos, won the laurel crown.
And to the Brother-Loving gods the life-like image of that contest then
  he set up here—the chariot and the charioteer in bronze.[20]

These first epigrams in the *Hippika* are of particular interest because they
feature certain structuring devices that link them with each other and the rest,
thereby bringing some order to the moving figures. As a concluding epigram of this
first cluster, AB 74, already from its opening, resumes on the topics mentioned by
the first two: The foal of AB 74 that won by a nod (νεύματι νικήϲαϲα) therefore
echoes Molycus' horse in AB 72 whose victory was also close (νικήϲαϲ ἄκρωι
νεύματι καὶ κεφαλῆι). Likewise, the double victory in AB 71 is remembered in
the last line of AB 74 (εἰκὼ ἐναργέα τῶν τότ' [ἀγώνω]ν̣ ἡ ἅρ[μα καὶ
ἡνί̣]ο̣χον χάλκεον ὧδ' ἔθετο), also alluding to a long tradition of victory monuments to which the surviving Charioteer of Delphi (5th c. BCE) belongs (Figure 1).
In this respect, AB 74 also repeats in some detail the story of the three previous
epigrams so to speak (AB 71–73).

As is the case with the *Anathematika* and the *Andriantopoiika*, the structure of
the *Hippika* serves certain programmatic purposes related to the glorification of two

---

[20] Translated by B. Acosta-Hughes and E. Kosmetatou.

Ptolemaic royal women (Berenice I and Berenice of Syria) and by extension of the entire dynasty, present in the epigrams that follow.[21] These poems serve then as ideological texts, through which the political leaders of Egypt figure as signs of competence and promise; the energy vibrating in the *Hippika* section, reflects their own strength, and their virtues introduce meaning to a confusing political world.[22]

Among the diverse eulogies with which Posidippus' employers are showered, two stand out, AB 78 and AB 88 in honor of the royal sister and brother: the Syrian Berenice and the future Ptolemy III Euergetes.[23] The first and longest one places emphasis on three generations of victorious Ptolemaic women:

ε]ἴπατε, πάντες ἀοιδοί, ἐμὸν [κ]λέος, ε[ἴ] π[οτ' ἀρέσκει
γνωστὰ λέγειν, ὅτι μοι δόξ[α παλαιόγονος·
ἅρματι μὲ⟨ν⟩ γάρ μοι προπάτω[ρ Πτολεμ]αῖος ἐν[ίκα
Πισαίων ἐλάσας ἵππον ἐπὶ στα[δίων,
καὶ μήτηρ Βερενίκη ἐμοῦ πατ[ρός· ἄ]ρ[μ]ατι δ' αὖτ[ις
νίκην εἷλε πατὴρ ἐ⟨κ⟩ βασιλέω[ς] βας[ι]λεύς
πατρὸς ἔχων ὄνομα· ζευκτ[ὰς δ'] ἐξήρατο πάσας
'Αρσινόη νίκας τρεῖς ἑνὸς ἐξ ἀέ[θλου·
π.[±13   ] γένος ἱερὸν [... γυ]ναικῶν
κε[±12   ] παρθένιος [......]ς
τα[ῦ]τ[α] μὲ[ν εὔχε' ἐ]πεῖδεν 'Ολυ[μπ]ία [ἐξ ἑ]νὸς οἴκου
ἅρμασι καὶ παίδων παῖδας ἀεθλοφόρο[υ]ς·
τεθρίππου δὲ τελείο⟨υ⟩ ἀείδετε τὸν Βερ[ε]νίκη[ς
τῆς βασιλευούσης, ὦ Μακέτα[ι], στέφανον

Recount, all poets, my glory, if ever it pleases you

to tell of what is known, as my renown is ancient;

for with the chariot my forefather Ptolemy won

driving his horses through Pisa's [stadium,

---

[21] Bastianini and Gallazzi identified the queen quoted at AB 78, 79, and 82 with Berenice II, daughter of Magas of Cyrene and wife of Ptolemy III Euergetes, whose Nemean victory in a chariot race was celebrated by Callimachus (*SH* 254–69). Thompson (forthcoming) has convincingly argued, in the opinion of this author, that Posidippus' Berenice in this case is the daughter of Ptolemy II and Arsinoe I, and sister of Ptolemy III. She married Antiochus II in 252 BCE and was murdered along with her son by Antiochus immediately after her husband's death in 246 by his former wife Laodice. Cf. Fantuzzi (this volume).

[22] Cf. Edelman 1988:37–38.

[23] See Thompson (forthcoming) on queen Berenice of Syria. BG:206 and AB:102 identify the queen as Berenice II who was retroactively adopted into the family of her husband.

and Berenice, my father's mother. With the chariot again
my father scored victory, a king descended from a king,
named after his father. And in a single competition
Arsinoe[24] scored all three victories for harnessed races;
. . . .] the holy race . . . of] women
[. . . . .] virginal [. . . . .]
These victories from a single house Olympia beheld
children's children victors with their chariots.

Her crown for the victorious four-horse chariot,
Sing, Macedonians, for your queen Berenice.[25]

Verse 12 of the above epigram with its emphasis on the repeated victories by the younger generation (αἰ παίδων παῖδας ἀεθλοφόρο[υ]ς), in a manner that echoes the repetitive references to the victory of horse and owner in AB 71, also links AB 78 with AB 88 relating a victory by the later Ptolemy III Euergetes, perhaps during the same Olympic Games (before 252 BCE):

πρῶτο[ι] τρεῖς βασιλῆες 'Ολύμπια καὶ μόνοι ἀμέc
ἅρμαcι νικῶμεc κᾳὶ γονέεc καὶ ἐγώ·
 εἷc μὲν ἐγὼ [Π]τολεμαίου ὁμώνυμος, ἐ⟨κ⟩ Βερενίκαc
υἱ[ος], 'Εορδαία γέννα, δύω δὲ γονεῖc·
πρὸ⟨c⟩ μέγα πατρὸc ἐμὸ⟨ν⟩ τίθεμαι κλέος, ἀλλ' ὅτι μάτηρ
εἷλε γυνὰ νίκαν ἅρματ⟨ι⟩, τοῦτο μέγα.

We alone were the first three kings to win at Olympia
in chariot-racing, my parents and I.
I am one, of the same name, Ptolemy, and Berenice's son
of Eordean descent—my parents (the other) two.
I have added to my father's great glory, but my mother,
a woman, won a victory in the chariot races—a great feat.[26]

---

[24] This author agrees with Gallazzi, Bastianini, and Austin in identifying the Arsinoe of AB 74 with Arsinoe II. Contrast Thompson (*apud* AB 74) who identifies her with Arsinoe I, the biological mother of Ptolemy III and the Syrian Berenice. It is noteworthy that Arsinoe I was divorced and disgraced, after which Ptolemy II married his sister Arsinoe II. The latter adopted his children. Cf. Gutzwiller 1992. It is therefore unlikely that Posidippus would recall Arsinoe I in such a late context, dated to the 250's BCE.

[25] Translated by B. Acosta-Hughes and E. Kosmetatou.

[26] Translated by B. Acosta-Hughes and E. Kosmetatou.

The above two epigrams certainly belong to the epinician tradition in poetry that had been developed by Simonides, Pindar, and Bacchylides, but move even further. Placed among epigrams on equestrian triumphs, many of which clearly evoke victory monuments with their visual language and their use of demostratives,[27] these two epinicians for the two royal children also allude to a different kind of monument, the extensive *Familiengruppe* that was in vogue during the fourth and third centuries BCE. The presence of epigrams describing sculptures in the *Hippika*, rather than the *Andriantopoiika*, is not surprising. Indeed, the poet often displays in it, as in previously known work, his love for ambiguity, a tool that served him well in challenging his reader's erudition and forcing him to become an active participant in the process of supplementation, Bing's so-called *Ergänzungsspiel*.[28] The epinician epigrams in honor of the early Ptolemies do not only serve as flashbacks of their victories; they also allude to single or group monuments in their honor for athletic and political achievement. Last, but not least, they argue that Ptolemaic glory was further embedded in the Greek past.

Indeed, family renown seems to have been a standard element in the commemoration of members of Greek aristocracy as early as the seventh century BCE, before they found their visual expression in *Familiengruppen*. Interestingly, the earliest known epigram that praised a prominent family is associated with a daedalic votive-offering to Artemis, set up by a woman, Nicandre, on Delos.[29] It is dated to ca. 650 BCE, and the *boustrophedon* text inscribed on its base boasts:

Νικάνδρη μ' ἀνέθεκεν h⟨ε⟩κηβόλοι ἰοχεαίρηι, ϙόρη Δεινο-
δίκηō τō Ναhσίō, ἔhσοχος ἀ(λ)λήōν, Δεινομένεος δὲ κασιγνέτη,
Φhράhσō δ' ἄλοχος ν⟨ῦν⟩.

Nicandre dedicated me to the goddess who shoots from afar, the
pourer of arrows,
daughter of the Naxian Deinodices, the greatest of all, and sister of
Deinomenes,
now wife of Phraxus.[30]

27 Cf. AB 72; AB 74, v. 14 (ὧδε).

28 Bing 1995. Significantly, the *Andriantopoiika* is not dedicated to sculpture, but rather to style, representing a fascinating analysis of art theory debate during the Classical and early Hellenistic periods.

29 Levin 1970:157–165; Lejeune 1971:209–215; Marcadé 1987:369–375; Ridgway 1993:147–149. The statue, most likely of Artemis as πότνια θηρῶν, may have held the reins of lions. On Archaic lions, see Kokkorou-Alewras 1993.

30 Translated by E. Kosmetatou.

As was stated above, the origins of dynastic group monuments can be traced back to the middle of the sixth century BCE, the date of the so-called Geneleos group that was set up at the Heraion of Samos in honor of the queen of the gods (560–550 BCE). This *Familiengruppe* was set up prominently in the sanctuary and featured the reclining figure of the patriarch [- - -]arches, probably an aristocrat, and his wife Phileia on either end of a long base, flanking their four children.[31] Two hundred years separate it from the next surviving *Familiengruppe*, the so-called monument of Pandaetes and Pasicles that was set up on the Athenian Acropolis in the second half of the fourth century BCE.[32]

However, Ptolemaic dynastic group monuments were conceived on the basis of two parallel traditions. Modelling themselves after Alexander the Great's Argead dynasty, they were probably influenced by the Philippeion, built by Philip II after 338 BCE as a circular Ionic structure that was set up at Olympia, the site of the Olympic Games. It reportedly contained chryselephantine statues of three generations of the royal family: Philip II and his chief wife Olympias, his parents Amyntas and Eurydice, and his son and successor, Alexander. The Philippeion was significant in another way as well: it interacted with the major temples in the sanctuary, a practice that would be adopted by Ptolemy II Philadelphus as well.[33] Additionally, the use of gold and ivory in the statues of the Macedonian royal family drew an unmistaken parallel with the chryselephantine cult statue of Zeus and established a link between the Olympian god and the Macedonian kings.[34]

The Philippeion at Olympia was perhaps modelled after the lavish Mausoleion, the tomb of queen Artemisia's husband Mausolus at Halicarnassus. The tomb was envisaged as a massive dynastic group monument featuring free-standing portraits of some thirty-six members of the royal family that were placed in the intercolumniations of its superstructure. The same program was later adopted by other Hellenistic dynasties, most notably the Attalids of Pergamon.[35]

The monument which comes closest to the ones echoed in Posidippus' AB 78 and 88 is the so-called Daochus *Progonoi* monument—a variation of the *Familiengruppe*, which was set up in Delphi by the homonymous Thessalian dynast

---

[31] Freyer-Schauenberg 1974:104–130; Walter–Karydi 1985:91–104; Hintzen-Bohlen 1990:149; Hintzen-Bohlen 1992:15–17; Ridgway 1993: 135–136, 190–193, 209–210.

[32] *IG* II/III² 3829; Loewy 1885:63–65, no.83; Borbein 1973:88, no.226.

[33] Ptolemy II set up colossal statues of himself and his sister–wife Arsinoe II on columns in front of the Stoa of Echo which faced the temples of Zeus and Hera, thereby creating a visual representation of his own consanguinous marriage and underlying his newly assumed divine status. Cf. Theocritus 17.131–134; Hoepfner 1971:11–54; Hintzen-Bohlen 1992:77–81, 210, no.8; Rose 1998:5–6.

[34] Miller–Collett 1973; Ridgway 1981:161–163, 168–170; Hintzen–Bohlen 1990:131–134; Rose 1998:4–5. On chryselephantine statuary, see Lapatin 2001.

[35] Cf. Hoepfner 1989; Hoepfner 1996; Ridgway 2000:19–102; Stewart 2000:32–57.

between 336 and 333 BCE. The group in question consisted of nine statues portraying the donor and his ancestors, real or fictitious, if indeed Apollo had also been featured in it. What is significant in this case is that two of these ancestors, Agias and Telemachus, had been Olympic victors between 490 and 480 BCE, while they had also scored victories at the Pythia together with their brother Agelaus, facts that were stressed by their portrayal in heroic/athletic nudity.³⁶ Each sculpture is identified by an epigram, and the athletes of the family boast their victories in a manner that is echoed in Posidippus:³⁷

> Ἀκνόνιος Ἀπάρου τέτραρχος Θεσσαλῶν
> Acnonius, son of Aparus, Tetrarch of the Thessalians

> πρῶτος Ὀλύμπια παγκράτιον, Φαρσάλιε, νικᾶις,
> Ἀγία Ἀκνονίου, γῆς ἀπὸ Θεσσαλίας,
> πεντάκις ἐν Νεμέαι, τρὶς Πύθια, πεντάκις Ἰσθμοῖ·
> καὶ σῶν οὐδείς πω στῆσε τροπαῖα χερῶν.

> First victory at the Olympian pankration you scored,
> Pharsalian Agias, son of Acnonius, from the Thessalian land,
> five victories at the Nemea, three at the Pythia, five at the Isthmus;
> and no one has yet taken this record from your hands.

> κἀγὼ τοῦ{ο}δε ὁμάδελ[φος ἔ]φυν, ἀριθμὸν δὲ τὸν αὐτὸν
> ἤμασι τοῖς αὐτοῖς [ἐχφέρ]ομαι στεφάνων,
> νικῶν μουνοπά[λης], Τ[··]σηνῶν δὲ ἄνδρα κράτιστον
> κτεῖνα, ἔθελον τό[γε δ' οὔ]· Τηλέμαχος δ' ὄνομα.

> And I was born his full-brother; and on the selfsame day
> I carried off the same number of crowns
> having scored victory in wrestling. I killed a mighty man from T[- -],
> but not on purpose. My name is Telemachus.

> οἵδε μὲν ἀθλοφόρου ῥώμης ἴσον ἔσχον, ἐγὼ δὲ
> σύγγονος ἀμφοτέρων τῶνδε Ἀγέλαος ἔφυν·

---

³⁶ Smith 1910:168–174; Pouilloux 1960:67–80; Dohrn 1968:33–53; Borbein 1973:79–84, 88–90; Ridgway 1989:46–50; Hintzen-Bohlen 1990:134–137; Hintzen-Bohlen 1992:205, no.4; Ridgway 1997:289; Rose 1998:5; Jacquemin-Laroche 2001:305–332.
³⁷ Ebert 1972:137–145, nos.43–45. Translated by E. Kosmetatou.

νικῶ δὲ στάδιον τούτοις ἅμα Πύθια παῖδας·
μοῦνοι δὲ θνητῶν τούσδ' ἔχομεν στεφάνους.

And these have shared an equal strength for victory, while I,
Agelaus, was born a kinsman of both;
I won the stadion for youths at Pythia, just like they did;
we alone of all mortals have carried off these crowns.

The similarities between Posidippus' *Hippika* and the three epigrams associated with the victors featured in the Daochus monument are striking. First, there is emphasis on the considerable number of victories scored by the *periodonikai* Agias and Telemachus which are especially recounted in the Agias epigram in a clear attempt to overwhelm the reader.[38] The same technique is used by Posidippus, especially as he relates the story of the owner of a horse with obvious ambitions to win eventually a periodos in AB 76:[39]

ἐκτέτα[τ]αι π[ρ]οτ[ρ]έχων ἀκρώνυχος, ὡς 'Ετεάρχωι
οὗ]τος κ[λεινὸς "Α]ραψ ἵππος ἀεθλοφορεῖ
[ν]ικήσ[α]ς Πτολεμαῖα καὶ "Ισθμια καὶ Νεμέαι δίς,
[τ]οὺς Δελφοὺς πα[ριδ]εῖν οὐκ ἐθέλει στεφάνους.

At full stretch running on the tips of its hooves, so for Etearchus
this famed Arabian horse was victorious.
Having won in the Ptolemaea, and Isthmia, and Nemea twice,
he does not wish to shun the crowns of Delphi.

It is undoubtedly by design that Posidippus mentions the Ptolemaea, a Panhellenic festival instituted by his employer Ptolemy II in memory of his father Ptolemy I Soter, which occupies here the first place, carrying off the glory that is a victory in the Olympic Games.

The same theme of multiple victories at the Olympic, Nemean, and Isthmian games is featured in the series of epigrams in honor of princess Berenice (AB 78, 79, and 82). Rather than present these achievements in a nutshell, Posidippus spread them out by dedicating a poem for each event. However, this sense of energy and concentrated victory is still conveyed by the poet's reference to the later Syrian queen's multiple scores in chariot-racing. This device may have been first used by

---

[38] On the *periodonikai*, who scored victories in all four, later more, Panhellenic games, see *IG* III 809; *IG* V(1) 669; Philo II 438; P.Oxy. 1643, v. 2; Dio LXIII 8.

[39] Multiple victories are also recounted in AB 77 and 86.

he tragic poet Euripides in 416 BCE in his epinician for the Athenian general
\lcibiades, the first Greek to enter seven chariots for one event and to score three
 victories:⁴⁰

Σὲ δ' ἀείσομαι, ὦ Κλεινίου παῖ
καλὸν ἁ νίκα· κάλλιστον δ', ὃ μηδεὶς ἄλλος Ἑλλάνων,
ἅρματι πρῶτα καὶ δραμεῖν καὶ δεύτερα καὶ τρίτα,
βῆναί τ' ἀπονητί, Διὸς στεφθέντα τ' ἐλαίᾳ
κάρυκι βοᾶν παραδοῦναι.

Your praises I'll sing, child of Cleinias.

To win is beautiful; yet this is the fairest of all that no other Greek
has achieved:
to score first and second and third victory in the race of the chariots
and effortlessly to succeed and be crowned with the olive of Zeus
and the object to be of the herald's proclamation.⁴¹

Although this intriguing text is fragmentary, the few verses from its opening
nclude a fascinating reference to the ease with which victory was achieved
ἀπονητί), the same that is also found in Posidippus' AB 79 in praise of princesss
3erenice's effortless en bloc victories at the Nemea:

παρθένος ἡ βασίλισσα σὺν ἄντυ[γ]ι, ναί, Βερενίκη
πάντας ἅμα ζευκτοὺς ἀθλοφορεῖ στεφάνους,
Ζεῦ παρὰ σοὶ Νεμέατα· τάχει δ' ἀπελί‹μ›πανεν ἵππων
δίφρος ἐπεὶ [κάμψη]ι τὸν πολὺν ἡνίοχον,
δαλ[οῖς δ' εἴκελοι ἵ]πποι ὑπὸ ῥ[υτ]ῆρι θέοντες
πρῶ[τοι ἐς 'Α]ργολικοὺς ἦλθον [ἀγω]νοθέτας.

A virgin the queen with her chariot, yes, Berenice,
carries off all victory crowns for chariot-racing
from you, Nemean Zeus. By the speed of her horses, her chariot
left many charioteers far behind, whenever she turned;
her horses running under the rein [like meteors]
came first before the Argive judges.⁴²

⁴⁰ Plutarch *Alcibiades* 12.2. Cf. Thucydides VI 16.1–3; also Fantuzzi (this volume).
⁴¹ Translated by E. Kosmetatou.
⁴² Translated by B. Acosta-Hughes and E. Kosmetatou.

A second common theme occurring both in the epigrams from the Daochu monument and Posidippus' AB 78 and 88 in praise of princess Berenice and th« later Ptolemy III Euergetes is the emphasis on the collective achievement of th« Ptolemaic clan. Agias, placed first for his seniority, lists his extraordinary victories which may have been surpassed by his brother's accidental, yet nevertheless impres sive, killing of a mighty opponent (Τ[··]σηνῶν δὲ ἄνδρα κράτιστον | κτεῖνα ἔθελον τό[γε δ᾽ οὔ]·). However, Telemachus' achievement is presented through : link to his brother's, the blood relationship of the two being declared first as furthe praise of the honoree (κἀγὼ τοῦ{ο}δε ὁμάδελ[φος ἔ]φυν). Kinshiμ (σύγγονος ἀμφοτέρων τῶνδε) is also stressed in the epigram in honor o« Agelaus which also incorporates the youngest brother's Pythian victories in th« family tradition begun by the elder brothers, a piece of information that become available only in the third poem, in addition to the Olympic achievement of th« two. The unprecedented athletic glory of the family of Daochus (μοῦνοι δι θνητῶν τούσδ᾽ ἔχομεν στεφάνους) may echo Euripides' boasting fo Alcibiades (ὃ μηδεὶς ἄλλος Ἑλλάνων).

Euripides' *Epinician for Alcibiades* and commemorative monuments in th« tradition of the Naxian Nicandre probably influenced Cynisca's epigram that wa inscribed on a victory monument that this daughter of king Archidamus II an« sister of kings Agesilaus II and of Agis II of Sparta set up at Olympia. She was th« first woman to score victory in chariot-racing at the Olympic Games of 396 o: 392 BCE.[43] Her epigram was preserved on stone and was also transmitted by th« *Greek Anthology* (XIII 16):

> Σπάρτης μὲν βασιλῆες ἐμοὶ πατέρες καὶ ἀδελφοί·
> ἅρματι δ᾽ ὠκυπόδων ἵππων νικῶσα Κυνίσκα
> εἰκόνα τάνδ᾽ ἔστασα, μόναν δ᾽ ἐμέ φαμι γυναικῶν
> Ἑλλάδος ἐκ πάσας τόνδε λαβεῖν στέφανον.

My ancestors and brothers were kings of Sparta;
and having won with a chariot drawn by swift-footed horses
I set up this image, and I boast that I'm the only woman
of all in Greece to have carried off this crown.[44]

Posidippus obviously nods to this monument in AB 87 which focuses or Berenice I, challenging Cynisca's *kydos*. Fantuzzi has brilliantly discussed the context of these two mini-epinicians and has drawn parallels between Ptolemaic

---

[43] Pausanias III 8.1; III 15.1; V 12.5; Ebert 1972:33.
[44] Translated by E. Kosmetatou.

reoccupation with ancestral glory and several odes by Pindar in honor of promi-
ent aristocratic victors.[45] This theme of challenge is important in the *Hippika*, and
he glove is thrown, so to speak, explicitly to such glorious figures of the past as
Cynisca, but the element of competition is also present in the continuous allusion
o the long tradition to which the Ptolemies aspired. In this respect, the Lagid kings
merge victorious from their implicit juxtaposition with Alcibiades and aristocratic
amilies of the remote past and, especially the illustrious quasi-royal family of
Daochus, to whose victory monument may allude continuous references to his
ative Thessaly.[46]

Ptolemaic dynastic group monuments that focused on athletic victories of the
ulers and their extended family may have existed, although the literary sources and
he archaeological record have yet to furnish information on them. Remains of
nore mundane statuary groups standing on inscribed bases without epigrams have
een associated with the early Ptolemies. These monuments are closer in concept
o the Geneleos rather than the Daochus groups. A Ptolemaic statuary group was
et up by the Aetolian League, an important Ptolemaic ally, at the sanctuary of
Apollo in Thermos perhaps around 239 or 238 BCE.[47] Fragments of the base have
urvived and suggest that the group featured Euergetes, Berenice, and their six chil-
ren from left to right: the heir to the throne, the later Ptolemy IV Philopator,
Arsinoe III, the deified princess Berenice, a son whose name has not survived, but
vho may have been called Lysimachus, Alexander, and Magas. The group was
ompleted by at least one more figure whose name has also not survived. Scholars
ave suggested Apollo for the last figure of this dynastic group, the honored god of
he sanctuary, but Ptolemy I or Alexander the Great are likely candidates as well.[48]

A second dynastic group monument in honor of Ptolemy III was dedicated by
he Aetolians in the venerable Panhellenic sanctuary of Apollo at Delphi which they
ontrolled during the third and second centuries BCE. A few fragments of its base
ave survived, but its reconstruction suggests that it was very similar to the one
rom Thermos and represented again Euergetes and his immediate family. Both
Ptolemaic groups meant more to the Aetolians than a mere expression of gratitude
nd displayed at the same time the League's high connections. The prominent posi-
ion of prince Ptolemy, the heir to the Egyptian throne, in the group was an expres-

---

[45] Fantuzzi (forthcoming). On the importance the Ptolemies placed on their Macedonian heritage see
   also Thompson (forthcoming).

[46] Cf. AB 71, 74, 82–86. This is particularly interesting in AB 74, where the intelligent horse owned
   by the Ptolemaic protegé Callicrates of Samos wins against a Thessalian chariot.

[47] Cf. Bennett 2002.

[48] *IG* IX.1.1256 = Moretti 1978:II, no.86; Huss 1975:312–320; Hintzen-Bohlen 1990:144–145; Hintzen-
   Bohlen 1992:134; Scholten 2000:138n31; Kotsidu 2000:168–170, no.104; Bennett 2002:141–145.

sion of the Aetolians' hope for the continuation of Ptolemaic military support int
the reigns of Euergetes's successors.[49]

At the same time, both monuments advertised the excellent relationshi
between king and queen, as well as the importance of children in the state propa
ganda under Euergetes, who thus functioned as symbols for dynastic succession.[⁵
Indeed, this latter theme was mostly promoted by Euergetes, and later by his so
Philopator, in an era before the murderous habits of his successors turned agains
members of their family, real or constructed challengers. Ptolemy III and Berenic
II's young children are mentioned in inscriptions; they escorted their parents o
official visits, and the death of the infant Berenice initiated a cult in her honor o
an unprecedented nature.[51] It was during that time that miniature intaglio portrai
of Ptolemaic children became especially in vogue and circulated widely, like th
oionochoai in fayence that were massively produced featuring Arsinoe II and othe
queens in relief.[52] This line of propaganda, later adopted by Augustus at a tim
when he constructed his own portrait of leadership,[53] had always been an effectiv
means of creating ideal types. An image of a strong, perpetually united ruling famil
appealed to the common man who could thus relate to his ideal leader by identi
fying with his conservative habits. Moreover, the ubiquity of the royal childre
during the reign of Euergetes constitutes a subtle visual expression of an importan
term of political rhetoric that presented the public with the powerful ideas of secu
rity and austerity that one usually associates with a father figure.[54]

Whether Posidippus' *Progonoi* epigrams in the *Hippika* are an ecphrasis of rea
or imaginary dynastic groups, he may have derived inspiration for their composi
tion from monuments like the Daochus group. At any rate, he had probabl
noticed the specific group, set prominently at Delphi, given his attested relation
ship with the sanctuary where he himself had been honored.[55] This theory become
even more attractive if we take into account that Lysippus, Posidippus' apparentl
favorite sculptor (cf. AB 65), had made at least one bronze statue of Agias that wa
set up at Pharsalus. Although the Lysippan associations of the surviving Delphi

---

[49] Colin 1930: 275–278, nos.232–234; Hintzen-Bohlen 1990: 145–146.

[50] On the role of the passionate relationship between Euergetes and Berenice II in state propaganda, se
Gutzwiller 1992.

[51] Bennett 2002:142–143 (where previous bibliography is cited). Cf. Canopus decree on the honors fo
the dead princess Berenice: *OGIS* 56. On Philopator's dynastic group monument that was set up i
the royal yacht see Athenaeus V 205f; Borbein 1973:88n225; Grimm 1998; Pfrommer 1999.

[52] Cf. Vollenweider 1984; On the Ptolemaic *oinochoai*: Burr-Thompson 1973.

[53] Rose 1990; Rose 1998:11–21.

[54] Kosmetatou 2002:406; Kosmetatou 2003.

[55] Cf. *IG* IX.12.17, verse 24, from Thermium, granting proxeny status to Posidippus at Delphi. O
inscribed epigrams and their readers in antiquity, see Bing 2002.

marbles are possible, yet fiercely debated among scholars, the likelihood of a connection between the group monument and the Sikyonian sculptor makes the question of Posidippus' models even more intriguing.[56] Posidippus attempted to display continuity in the rule of Egypt from Alexander the Great to the Ptolemies. Indeed, the Macedonian conqueror is mentioned by several epigrams, directly or indirectly, or is alluded to by the mere mention of the Persians, as well as of the boundaries of his kingdom.[57] Even though his allusion to Ptolemaic dynastic group monuments is limited, the literary evidence suggests that Alexander the Great featured in some of these. It is not surprising that state propaganda in the first years of the Ptolemaic rule focused on underlining the ruler's legitimacy as heir to Alexander's empire and legacy. In this context, Ptolemy I, former general in the Macedonian army, had successfully manipulated the politically confusing situation which ensued after the conqueror's death, occupied Egypt and areas around it, and eventually seceded from the rest of the empire. His grip over his territory was secure, but Ptolemy also sought to gain the respect and obedience of his subjects, as well as prestige among the Greeks as a legitimate king. In a mastertroke, he seized Alexander's body in ca. 321 BCE, while it was being transferred to the Ammoneion at modern-day Siwa desert or Macedonia and buried it in Memphis, in accordance with both Macedonian and Egyptian practices, which dictated that the ascension of the new king to the throne was marked by his burying of his predecessor. It was in Alexandria that Alexander's earthly remains eventually found their resting place, however, under his son and successor, Ptolemy II.[58]

Throughout his reign, Ptolemy sought to emphasize his closeness to the Macedonian conqueror. The publication of his own history of Alexander's wars exercised influence over the way posterity remembered the Persian campaign. The former general undoubtedly made sure that he figured prominently in the narrative, while he surely exaggerated the importance of his actions and contribution to its success.[59] But the close relationship between the two great men was further

---

[56] Cf. Preuner 1900; Ridgway 1989:47, 68n33; Edwards 1996:135–137.

[57] AB 1, 2, 4, 5, 8, 31, 35, 65, 70. Cf. Bing (forthcoming).

[58] The principal ancient accounts on Alexander's resting place and his cult are: Strabo XVII 1.8, 794; Diodorus XVIII 26.3–28.2–4; Arrian in *FGrHist* 156 F 9, no.25; Mar. Par. in *FGrHist* 239 F B 11; Pausanias 1.6.3; 1.7.1; Curt. Ruf. 10.10.20; Pseudo-Callisthenes III 34; Aelian *VH* XII 64; Zenobius III 94; Suetonius *Augustus* 18; Dio LI 16.3–5; Herodian IV 8.9. For recent modern discussion on the subject see: Fraser 1972:15–17n79, 225–226; Pollitt 1986:19; Hammond and Walbank 1988:120; Green 1990:13–14; Stewart 1993:209–225. Rose 1998:4–5 erroneously states that Ptolemy I, rather than his successor Philadelphus, buried Alexander in Alexandria.

[59] Ptolemy's history is mainly known from Arrian. See: *FGrHist* 138–139; Errington 1976:154–156; Pearson 1983:150–211; Roisman 1984:373–385; Stewart 1993:11–12.

emphasized, particularly towards Ptolemy's subjects, when a blood relation between Alexander and Ptolemy was invented. According to rumours that were spread by the king's entourage and which are reflected in the texts of various authors, Arsinoe Ptolemy's mother, married his father, Lagus, while she had already been impreg nated by Philip II of Macedonia and therefore carried the future general and king of Egypt. By claiming Alexander as his half-brother, Ptolemy also sought member ship to the Macedonian Argead House and thus genealogical continuity for his dynasty.[60]

Ptolemy's retroactive adoption into Alexander's family was emphasized when ever possible. Posidippus' AB 31 suggests that the dynasty that the Ptolemaic o Lagid dynasty was also known as "Argead":

ἀετὸς ἐ⟨κ⟩ νε[φέω]ν καὶ ἅμα στεροπὴ καταβᾶ[σα
νίκης οἰων[οὶ δε]ξιοὶ ἐς πόλεμον.
Ἀργ⟨ε⟩άδα⟨ι⟩ς βα[σιλε]ῦσιν, Ἀθηναίη δὲ πρὸ ναο[ῦ
ἴχνος κινή[σας' ἐ]ξιὸν ἐ⟨κ⟩ μολύβου·[61]
οἷον Ἀλεξά[νδρ]ωι ἐφάνη τέρας, ἡνίκα Περς[ῶν
ταῖς ἀναρ[ιθμ]ήτοις πῦρ ἐκύει στρατιαῖ[ς.

An eagle coming down from the clouds and lightning together
were favorable omens for victory in war,
for the Argead kings, and Athena, in front of her temple
brought forth her foot from the lead.
A similar sign appeared to Alexander when he upon the Persians'
innumerable armies brought forth fire.[62]

Evidence from the Delian inventory lists mentioning Ptolemaic gifts to the sanctuary make it obvious that, like Alexander the Great had done before him Ptolemy I evoked two different fathers, according to the occasion. We know that he dedicated an elaborate gold thericleian kylix, weighing about one modern kilo which bore the inscription "ἀνάθημα Πτολεμαῖος Λάγου Μακεδὼν Ἀφροδίτηι."[63] At the same time, Theocritus in his seventeenth *Idyll* (17.13–33)

---

[60] See Satyrus in *FGrHist* 631 F 1; P.Oxy. 2465; Curt. IX 8.22; Pausanias 16.2. Cf. also *OGIS* 54, l.5
For modern discussion on the subject see: Bosworth 1976:28; Errington 1976:154 ff.; Stewar 1993:229.

[61] Accepting Schröder's restoration. Cf. Schröder 2002.

[62] Translated by B. Acosta-Hughes and E. Kosmetatou.

[63] It appears on inventory lists dated from 279 to after 166 BCE. Cf. *IG* XI (2) 161, B, lines 26–27
On the importance of Aphrodite in Ptolemy's propaganda, especially with regard to his last wife Berenice I, the mother of his heirs, see Gutzwiller 1992.

mentions Ptolemy I as son of Lagus but at the same time groups the king together with Alexander and with his own son, Ptolemy II in a continuing father-son structure. Such an apparent discrepancy should not surprise: the close association of rulers with divinities and heroes was a regular feature of civic ceremonial and political manipulation that dated from at least Pisistratus' time, and audiences were not as gullible as scholars had initially assumed; they rather understood and appreciated the symbolism that was embedded in the theatricality of public life as controlled by the powers that be.[64]

Visual advertisement of the fictional brotherly relationship between Alexander the Great and Ptolemy I found its expression in several dynastic group monuments, according to the sources. In the grand procession for the Alexandrian Ptolemaea statues of Ptolemy I and Alexander were carried together, flanked by personifications of Greek regions.[65] Nicolaus Rhetor (ca. 400 CE) also mentions a similar elaborate group in his description of the now lost circular Tychaion of Alexandria. This building was commissioned by one of the first two Ptolemies, was located in the center of Alexandria, and probably constituted a shrine adjoining or incorporated to Ptolemy II's Mouseion. On the side leading to the latter stood bronze statues of prominent kings, unspecified by Nicolaus, while on the opposite wall was a marble laurel crown flanked by the statues of two philosophers. Bronze stelae stood in the center on which the laws of the city of Alexandria were inscribed. The two adjoining sides each contained seven niches which were separated from each other by engaged columns. The central niche on the left side of the room, contained a larger-than-life-size statue of Ptolemy I holding a cornucopia which was flanked by six Olympian gods represented on a smaller scale. Facing the king across stood Charis (Grace) flanked by the remaining six Olympians. In the center of the room stood a sculptural group representing Alexander being crowned by the personification of Gaia. The latter was in turn crowned by Tyche, flanked by statues of Victory.[66]

Although Alexander's statue occupied the center of the sanctuary and his extraordinary conquests were clearly emphasized, the primary focus of the

---

[64] Connor 1987. Cf. Herodotus I 60.2–5 and his incredulity on Pisistratus' staged return to Athens on a chariot escorted by an actress dressed as Athena.

[65] Rice 1983; Thompson 2000:365–368.

[66] The principal ancient account of the Alexandrian Tychaion is in Pseudo-Libanius (Nicholaus Rhetor) *Progymnasmata* XXV 1–9. Several post-4th century CE authors mention this monument in passim. Theoph. Simoc. VIII 13; Theoph. Chron. PG 108 col. 616A; Georg. Mon. II pp. 663–664; Nic. Call. *Hist. Eccl.* XVIII 41; Ps.-Call. I 41.4. According to Palladas in the *Greek Anthology* IX 180, the Tychaion was converted into a wine–shop or a restaurant after CE 391. For modern discussion on the building see: Schweitzer 1931:218–220; Fraser 1972:I, 241–242; II, 392n417; Hebert 1983:10–25; Stewart 1993:243–246, 383–384.

Tychaion's sculptures was Ptolemy I, his presumed half-brother and legitimate heir by the grace of the gods. According to Nicolaus, the entire ensemble culminated in the group which was set against the back wall and which included the laurel crown, the philosophers and the bronze stelae rather than Alexander. In his own clever and subtle way, Soter thus discreetly projected an idea whose debate was to occupy ancient philosophers: Alexander's successes were mostly due to the benevolence of Fortune. The heavy duty of governing his spear-won territories weighed upon Ptolemy, his next of kin, who ruled by divine right. His absolute power would never become a tyranny, however, as his subjects were ingenuously informed: Soter was an enlightened ruler and patron of the arts and sciences who abided by the laws that he instituted and consulted the best and wisest advisors.

Until recently, scholars who attempted to reconstruct the Alexandrian Tychaion, incorporated the building in the Roman Imperial architectural tradition of Asia Minor.[67] Stewart has convincingly argued for a higher date for the Alexandrian Tychaion, however, by plausibly dating its intellectual roots to the mid-320's BCE.[68] Alexander's military successes had been considered as a gift of Fortune as early as 327 BCE, when the philosopher Theophrastus, Aristotle's disciple and head of the Peripatos, wrote a treatise entitled *Callisthenes or On Grief.*[69] The significance of Fortune's benevolence toward the Macedonians was further treated by Demetrius of Phalerum in a long treatise which may have been commissioned by Ptolemy I after 307 BCE when the exiled Athenian philosopher-"tyrant" fled to Soter's court.[70] Their attractive ideas certainly influenced contemporary religious practice and triggered the foundation of various cults of Tyche. In this context most notably, Seleucus I of Syria commissioned a famous statue of Tyche for Antioch, his kingdom's capital. The goddess was represented seated on Mount Silphion and holding a sheaf of wheat with the personification of the river Orontes at her feet.[71]

The theme of the triumph of divine and enlightened monarchy which influenced the commission of the Alexandrian Tychaion was further amplified by other philosophers who worked at the court. Indeed the philosopher Euhemerus is credited with the introduction of the theory on "divine monarchy," according to which the traditional gods had once been great rulers who were eventually deified. In order to illustrate his point, Euhemerus compared Ptolemy's kingdom to the legendary court of Osiris and Isis. A passage from Diodorus attempting to trace the position of intellectuals and their influence over the Hellenistic courts back to the

---

[67] The architectural parallels are listed by Hebert 1983:24–25. Cf. Fraser 1972:II, 392n417.
[68] Stewart 1993:244–245.
[69] *Tusc.* III 21; 5.25; Diogenes Laertius V 44. Cf. Plutarch *Alexander* 4.1–7; Athenaeus *Deipn.* X 435a.
[70] Polybius XXIX 21.3–6.
[71] Pollitt 1986:277–279; Stewart 1990:201–202.

physicians, who took part in the Trojan War and served Agamemnon, may reflect the ideas of Euhemerus and his followers. Several intellectuals of the period lived under the illusion that they exercised positive influence on their patrons' policies.[72] The representation of royal statuary groups reflects the ideology of the period: Rulers are crowned by personifications underlining their virtue already in the early third century BCE. In particular, Pausanias describes two groups from Olympia which bear similarities to the Alexander group of the Tychaion. In one, the region of Elis crowns Demetrius Poliorcetes and Ptolemy I, while in a later group, the personification of Hellas crowns Antigonus Doson and his son and successor Philip V.[73]

The presence of Olympian gods in the dynastic group monument of the Alexandrian Tychaion, may owe to late fourth-century BCE antecedents. In particular, Philip II of Macedon reportedly introduced this practice. The Macedonian ruler celebrated the wedding of his daughter Cleopatra at Aegai in 336 BCE and concluded the festivities with games which took place in the theater. An elaborate procession opened the events featuring a float which carried the statues of the Olympian gods and of Philip II as one of them.[74] Philip's divine aspirations reportedly came as a shock to the Greeks who explained his ensuing assassination as the punishment of Nemesis for his hybris. By the time Ptolemy I commissioned the Tychaion, however, the Greek world had become used to royal claims to divine status. Soter went one step further than Philip II by placing his statue as second only to Alexander's, but certainly more prominently than the once revered and feared Greek Pantheon.

The identity of the kings who were represented against the Tychaion's wall which led to the Mouseion, necessarily remains a mystery, but we may plausibly assume that this, too, was an elaborate Ptolemaic dynastic group monument. That

---

[72] Several scholars sought advancement in the employ of kings, and some of them even had the illusion that they exercised significant influence over these rulers' deeds. As early as the sixth century BCE the Milesian Thales lived under the protection of the tyrant Thrasyboulus of Miletus, while Solon enjoyed the patronage of king Croesus of Lydia (Diogenes Laertius I 22.27; Herodotus I 30–33). Thucydides, Euripides, and Agathon lived for a while in the court of king Archelaus of Macedonia during the late fifth century BCE. Plato and Aristotle also served as advisors and protégés of Dionysus of Syracuse and Philip II of Macedonia respectively (Diogenes Laertius III 9.18–23; 5.5–6.11; Plutarch *Alexander* 8.53–55.77; Aristotle, Fr. 666 [Rose]). On Euhemerus, see: Diodorus I 15.4; IV 71.4; Diogenes Laertius V 46.2–7; VI 63, 69; Pollitt 1986:10 ff.; Green 1990:57. On the debate in political philosophy during the Hellenistic period see Harnsey 2000:404–414; Moles 2000:415–434; Schofield 2000:435–456; Hahm 2000:457–476.

[73] Pausanias VI 16.3; Stewart 1993:244.

[74] Plutarch *Alexander* 10.1–4. Philip II's daring inclusion of his statue among the images of the twelve Olympian gods was mirrored in the parade that opened the Ptolemaia penteteric festival. Cf. Rice 1983.

these statues may have been expanded in the three hundred years that followed by the addition of prominent Ptolemies who wished to associate their policies to that of Alexander and Ptolemy I, is an attractive theory, which cannot be stated with certainty, however. If this be the case, the Tychaion may therefore have been an ever-growing dynastic group monument extending over the centuries of Ptolemaic rule over Egypt and linking the later Ptolemies to their illustrious past. Such seems to have been the intention of most of these kings, starting from Ptolemy II Philadelphus, who chose to be buried near the tomb of Alexander thereby creating a large funerary complex which at the same time served as a royal group monument and functioned as visual expression of dynastic continuity.

Even though there is little evidence for the planning and setting up of elaborate Ptolemaic *Familiengruppen* during the second and first centuries BCE, the ideas that were first formulated and implemented under the early Ptolemies were always present in the language that these kings used in their appeal to their world for support. All political terms in the later period of the Ptolemaic dynasty evoked the importance of dynastic continuity that had been served well in the past by visual propaganda and could be traced back to that era when the young kingdom was still taking its form and link it with the Greek remote past. Posidippus' retrospect of present and past victories in the *Hippika* recalls the viewer's gaze upon monuments stemming from a long tradition that was shaped by the Greek elite from the seventh century BCE onwards. Initially it consisted of an elaborate praise of the *Progonoi* on inscriptions that were especially associated with great deeds: elaborate dedications to the gods, many of them in commemoration of prestigious athletic victories. The popularity of such stone epigrams made their transition from stone to book especially smooth, and longer epinicians often employed the theme of ancestral glory which found its visual expression in the *Familiengruppe*. The Ptolemies embraced this form of self-definition throughout the history of their dynasty and remained especially proud of their ancestry. Indeed, the reported eulogy over the dead body of Cleopatra VII, the most famous of the Ptolemies, pronounced by her dying maid Charmion seems to echo the words of Posidippus more than two hundred years before: she died as was becoming a queen, descendant of so many kings.[75]

---

[75] Plutarch *Marcus Antonius* 85.5–6.

17

Reading as *Seeing*: P.Mil.Vogl. VIII 309 and Greek Art

Nassos Papalexandrou

University of Texas at Austin

O Queen of Egypt with the lovely brow—
To you—thou smilest and to me it seems
The earth has owned but one such smile; 'twas thou
Visitedst Lionardo in his dreams.

(Kenyon Cox 1888)

This essay is motivated by a fascinating collection of ancient poetry, but it opens with a poem dating only to the nineteenth century. Kenyon Cox, who conceived the lyric reverie of these lines, was certainly stirred by an intense emotional impulse. His poetic words channel his energy to the object of his desire and admiration, an unspecified Queen of Egypt. Brief and evocative as they are, they entice us to visualize the Queen as someone combining the simple perfection of Nefertiti's facial lines with the sunny warmth of an Archaic Greek *kore*. As we decipher this poetry and its messages, we are made to engage in several concurrent dialogues: first, the poem is a fragment of an encounter between the poet and the Queen of Egypt. Following this, we, the readers, meet with the author and his imagination but also with his interlocutor as we try, in the inner folds of our minds, to delineate the "lovely brow" and the near uniqueness of the celebrated smile. The reference to Leonardo da Vinci expands the field of dialogic confrontations to include fine conduits between the poet and Leonardo, between Leonardo and the Egyptian Queen, and perhaps between us and Leonardo. And if the universal uniqueness of the Queen's smile and the reference to Leonardo are meant to evoke the most celebrated smile in Western culture, the possibilities of uncovering more nuanced layers in the simple lines of Cox's poem seem to multiply indefinitely. Herein, then, lies the power of poetry: it evokes what is not present; it spawns a vision out of the unseen; it guides our fantasy to the very roots of the sparks that generated it. In other words, it makes us *wonder* about many things and, in this particular case, about the Queen of Egypt: who is she? How did she manage to visit Leonardo's dreams? What is the relationship between her and the poet? Does the poet imply that we, the readers, will be subject to the lures of this mysterious Queen by means of the transformational quality of his poetry? What is the essence of the Queen's irresistible smile?

Our hermeneutic effort will be pleasantly surprised—but also drastically reoriented—if we consider the function of Kenyon Cox's lines not merely as a poem but as an *epigram*. They are, in fact, part of a larger painted vision that recreates the sculpted head of an unknown Egyptian Queen (Figure 4).[1] The painting captures the appearance of a particular plaster cast that was exhibited at the Metropolitan Museum of Art in New York from the mid-eighties of the nineteenth century onward.[2] With simple means such as a reduced palette, clear and elegant lines, and a subtly balanced gradation of light and shadow, Cox has rendered the ambivalent nature of this object. The apparent coldness of the material of the cast is mitigated on the painting by the animated smile of the figure. In this way the spectral emptiness of the cast is transformed into an intimation of character, even idiosyncrasy. Certainly this figure is someone we can converse with. Indeed, we easily surrender ourselves to the charm of the gaze and the smile of the Queen of Egypt.

But Kenyon Cox has accomplished much more than just the successful reproduction of an alluring, if derivative, likeness. His vision of the *Head of the Queen of Egypt* is not a faithful recording of the cast as this would have been seen in its actual setting at the gallery of casts in the Metropolitan.[3] It is, in fact, not difficult to reconstruct his actual experience of viewing. The cast would have been placed on a pedestal, and in the best of circumstances it would have been accompanied by a simple label intended to communicate something about the representation. The

---

[1] Kenyon Cox, *Head of the Queen of Egypt*, 1888: oil on canvas, 18 1/8 x 15 in. (46.1 x 38.2 cm.) National Museum of American Art, Smithsonian Institution, Washington D.C. Bequest of Allyn Cox. I am indebted to and thankfully acknowledge the valuable assistance of Drs. Jennifer Hardin (Museum of Fine Arts, St. Petersburg, Florida), and Richard Murray (Smithsonian American Art Museum) in my research on this painting.

[2] Hardin 1996:12. For the cast, see the MMA 1908, no.32. The original is the head of a limestone statue from Karnak (18th Dynasty) in the National Museum at Cairo. I am grateful to my colleague Professor Susan Rather, for this reference. The MET's collection of sculptural casts was not put together until 1886 (see MMA 1908:vii).

[3] The setting is hinted at by a streak of light that illuminates the head and the surface on which it rests. We are meant to understand a pedestal, on the vertical front of which Cox has painted the label with his poem.

one of such a label still resonates in the brief entry for this cast in the *Catalogue of the Collection of Casts*, published in 1908: "No. 32. Head of a Queen of the XVIII dynasty. There is no evidence as to its identification. Of limestone. Found at Karnak and now in the Cairo Museum."[4]

In place of the factual coldness of a label, Cox's painterly vision substituted a piece of paper bearing a hand-written epigram that transcribed his spontaneous, poetic response into a format no less informal than the work of art it accompanies. It is certainly not by accident that we can see the creases of the unfolded paper. We can also easily detect its careless mounting on the pedestal below the head. The improvisational character of these elements jibes with the unpolished diction of the poem and the secondary nature of the cast. This extemporaneousness is motivated by Cox's *normative* vision, one which privileges the essence of things over their appearance. There is little doubt that Cox intended label and poem to be of an importance commensurate with the rest of the painting. He carefully signed his name on the label immediately below the epigram, thereby underlining the unequivocal integration of poetry and painting within the image. Although placed in a position visually subservient to that of the sculpted head, Cox's poem—the epigram of the sculpted head—is a semantic gesture that makes manifest his artistic impulse. Not only does it indicate the focus of seeing (Cox's and the beholders') as a playful and necessary interplay between word and painted likeness; it also establishes the artist's poetic dialogue with the painted object as an essential component of *every* subsequent beholder's encounter with the image. In doing so, it directs in explicit terms the focus of our gaze and our visual decoding of the painted head.

The fruitful coexistence of sculpture and poetry in Cox's painting parallels the perceptual background of the epigrams on P.Mil.Vogl. VIII 309. It matters little why they were compiled together in this now fragmentary papyrus; in many cases the reader's appreciation of them was originally—and still should be—inextricable from their intended function in their original contexts.[5] For their nature and various levels of referentiality often point to the world of ideas and experience embedded in the materiality of human life. As is the case with Cox's painting, their motivation stemmed from the need to articulate formalized discourse about objects present or absent.[6] A very brief overview of the compiler's categorization of this poetry points to the material or pragmatic basis for its inspiration: the *Lithika* are

---

[4] MMA 1908, no.32.

[5] Some epigrams were certainly composed as purely literary artifacts. Even in this case their consumption must have been conditioned by the original experiential determinatives of the genre.

[6] A detailed and rigorous archaeological commentary on these epigrams is urgently needed. As Hoffman points out in this volume, the hermeneutic analysis of the P.Mil.Vogl. VIII 309 as a whole should be based on interdisciplinarity.

motivated by the need to articulate, or even dictate, a taste for exotic, intricately carved gemstones. Likewise, the *Oionoskopika* presuppose observation of natural phenomena and the *Andriantopoiika* focus on statuary and its ecphrasis. The *Epitymbia* and *Nauagika* evoke the actualities of funereal commemoration whereas the *Anathematika* and *Iamatika* have to do with material objects. It is therefore worthwhile to probe the material basis that inspired this poetry. In particular, I will argue that the elucidation of the meaning of certain epigrams (*Hippika, Iamatika*) should rest upon the consideration of the material culture that framed their original function as objects of perception.[7] Inversely, these epigrams can be shown to preserve insights or commentaries valuable for understanding the aesthetic motivation that informs certain works of Hellenistic figurative art. Their value for reconstructing the experience of *seeing* as an essential component of Hellenistic visuality cannot be emphasized enough.[8]

Hippika

There is no doubt that the epigrams grouped under the title *Hippika* evoke the actuality of the major panhellenic sanctuaries at Olympia, Delphi, Nemea, and the Isthmus.[9] They all celebrate the *kleos* of either a victorious horse or a victor, or both, in one or more of these prestigious athletic arenas.[10] But the poetry of *kleos* is a poetry of physical and mental action, that is, its purposes are fulfilled upon recurrent readings or performances of their content in specific contexts.[11] It is, therefore, useful to search for internal clues in the poems regarding the material referentiality of their content. In this respect, demonstrative adjectives such as οὗτος (AB 71.1, AB 76.2, AB 77.2), τοῦτον (AB 84.2, AB 85.2), ὅδ' (AB 86.2) always refer to the objects of celebration, πῶλος or ἵππος, thus suggesting a strong and deliberate deictic function. This is easily explainable if we consider that the epigrams were originally meant to be read or performed in the presence of actual likenesses, which I understand as sculptural visualizations of the epigrams' objects of reference.[12] This is indicated, for example, in the concluding lines of the epigram AB 74:

---

[7] For a similar approach, see the contributions by Kosmetatou in this volume.

[8] On ancient visuality, understood as the culturally conditioned practice of seeing and being seen as meaningful action, see Nelson 2000.

[9] See BG 2001:197–216. For the structure of the *Hippika* see Fantuzzi's contribution in this volume. The function of certain epigrams in the context of Ptolemaic dynastic commemoration is addressed in Kosmetatou's analysis of *Familiengruppen* in this volume.

[10] See col. AB 78.1 for a specific identification of the poetry of the epigram as a poetry of *kleos*.

[11] This was precisely Pausanias' experience of Olympian victory monuments. See Pausanias VI 1.3–VI 18.7 and recent discussion in Elsner 2001:14–16.

[12] BG 2001:198 on AB 72.1, talk about "un forte valore deittico."

Θεοῖϲι δ' Ἀδ[ε]λφε{ι}οῖϲ εἰκὼ ἐναργέα τῶν τότ' [ἀγώνω]ν
ἅρ[μα καὶ ἡνί]οχον χάλκεον ὧδ' ἔθετο.

[Callicrates] dedicated this bronze chariot and the charioteer to the
Fraternal Gods, as a vivid image of the past races.[13]

Callicrates of Samos monumentalized his victory in an equestrian event at the
Pythian games by setting up a bronze quadriga and its charioteer. The demonstrative ὧδε in AB 74.14 clearly points to the monument, and in this way it signals
the implied conceptual and physical space of the epigram. Interestingly enough, in
the same epigram the monument is termed εἰκὼ ἐναργέα, a vivid likeness, a
representation redolent with the splendor, the vitality, and the emotional charge of
the reality it represents.[14] Thus, the beholders are made to understand that they
witness a glorious moment of the past in its perpetual reenactment and, in this way,
they are immediately transformed into idealized spectators of a unique athletic
event. Unfortunately the concerted tenor of these words and their figurative object
of reference is now lost. Something of their cooperative efficacy, nonetheless, can be
appreciated in monuments such as a gravestone from Athens for a Phoenician
visitor who died there.[15] Inscribed in both Phoenician and Greek, this μνῆμα
combines a suggestive image with an epigram that verbalizes the subtly dense mood
of the former. This extraordinary monument cannot be discussed here in detail, but
I would like to emphasize the directive force of the demonstrative in the first line
of the epigram <εἰκόνα τήνδε>, which functions like the demonstratives in the
Hippika: one is immediately made to understand that the poetry has to do with the
relief but also that the relief cannot stand alone without the poetry. Inherent in this
explicit gesture of verbal *deixis* is the latent message that the communicative efficacy of the monument depends on the simultaneous viewing of image and poetry,
of the visual and the aural.

A great number of Hellenistic works of art were accompanied by epigrams,
that is, verbal enablers intended to function as essential components of ensembles
which were programmatically conceived in terms of both poetically articulated
words and images. Unfortunately, the intended effect of these ensembles has been
lost or largely ignored as a result of the systematic or accidental dislocation of

---

[13] Although I use AB numeration, I cite the text(s) of the *editio princeps* throughout. All translations by
the author.

[14] Inherent in these words and the specific viewing attitude they recommend is the resonance of the
philosophical theory of *phantasia*. See discussion in Goldhill 1994:208–209.

[15] First published in *AM* 13 (1888) 310–316. For the text see Peek 1955, no.1601. For a detailed
discussion see Clairmont 1970:114–117, no.38, pl.19.

epigrammatic poetry from its actual experiential contexts.[16] The compilation, for example, of epigrams on P.Mil.Vogl. VIII 309 is perhaps one of the earliest testimonies of their transformation into purely literary or textual artifacts. It stands at the beginning of a long tradition of publications which includes the *Greek Anthology* as well as more recent collections such as those by Kaibel or Peek.[17] This process has resulted in the scholarly neglect of the original format of epigrams as a determinative component of visual experiences much more complex and nuanced than the consumption of poetry available in book form.[18] Equally problematic is the often fragmentary and dispersed nature of monuments that originally combined sculptural or painted images with inscribed epigrams. Pausanias' account of Olympia, for example, reveals how much of the communicational multivalence of the original monuments he experienced is now lost. Their figurative components have all perished, whereas the few surviving epigrams are often treated as isolated textual data only partially capable of evoking the determinative ambience of their original context.[19] Further, the traditional disciplinary focuses within classical archaeology have privileged the study of the figural components of artworks (e.g. sculptures in the round, reliefs) at the expense of their verbal paraphernalia and vice versa. This is true even when the latter have survived together with the former and their mutual relationship is archaeologically verifiable.[20]

The sheer abundance of originally "functional" poetry in P.Mil.Vogl. VIII 309 provides yet another testimony of the incompleteness or distortion of the surviving record of Hellenistic visual arts. Against this unfortunate situation, certain epigrams enable a fresh understanding of "canonical" works of Hellenistic art that survived detached from their original contexts. For example, it is tempting to juxtapose the enigmatic horse of Artemision (Figure 2), the well-known and celebrated masterpiece, with epigrams such as AB 72 or AB 76. The horse and its jockey, now on

---

[16] By "context" I mean ". . . the totality of its relevant environment, where 'relevant' refers to a significant relationship to the object—that is, a relationship necessary for discerning the object's meaning" (Hodder 1991:143).

[17] Kaibel 1878; Peek 1955.

[18] On the hermeneutical difficulties created by the textual objectification of the inscribed word in collections and corpora, see the observations in Papalexandrou 2001:259–260; see also Stears 2000:206.

[19] See, for example, the epigram celebrating the monument of Xenombrotos in Dittenberger and Purgold 1897:293–296, no.170 (mentioned in Pausanias VI 14.12). For an example from Delphi, see Bourguet 1929:41–43, no.510.

[20] A good case is the well-known stele of Hediste from Demetrias-Pagasai: the connotations of the tragic theme of the painted image are inconceivable without the accompanying epigram, the efficacy of which (as an indispensable component of the image) is never addressed. See, for example, Pollitt 1986 where this monument is discussed in two different contexts (Pollitt 1986:4 and 194). See also Fowler 1989:92–93, who ignores the epigram altogether.

display at the National Archaeological Museum in Athens, were recovered in 1926 just off the northwest coast of the island of Euboia.[21] This group has been praised for the accuracy of realistic modeling it displays both in the rendering of its overall movement and for its graphic details. M. Robertson, for example, has stated that the jockey is "a more direct and detailed transcript of observed nature, and a more vivid impression of life in action, than in any other work of major art that has come down to us from ancient Greece."[22] The same author, however, is perplexed by what exactly the dynamic pose of this horse aims to convey. He is disturbed by its "extremely spread movement (*not, I fancy, a good racing style*)" which he explains in terms of the artist's need to accommodate the far superior jockey.[23] Robertson is perhaps right in criticizing the racing style of this horse. The flying gallop with outstretched legs is naturally impossible, but it has had a tenacious career as a conventional schema for representing the impressively fast running of horses.[24] How are we then to account for this paradoxical departure from reality in a composition motivated by the aspiration to be an *eikon enarges*, a photographic evocation of reality? B. Ridgway is close to the truth when she understands the bronze group to represent the moment "close to the goal."[25] The horse and its jockey are striving to attain victory and glory; they are conceived at the pinnacle of their performance.

This interpretation is now convincingly corroborated by the *Hippika* AB 72 and AB 76 on the newly published papyrus. Both epigrams are informed by the same realities as those we see crystallized in the animated bronze. Not unlike the epigram in Cox's painting, both of them "guided" the beholders toward a meaningful dialogue with the subtleties of the formal vocabulary of their objects of viewing (AB 72):[26]

τοῦ πώλου θηεῖϲθε τὸ λιπαρέϲ, ὡϲ πνόον ἕλκει
παντὶ τύπωι καὶ πᾶϲ ἐ⟨κ⟩ λαγόνων τέταται
ὡϲ νεμεοδρομέων· Μολύκωι δ' ἤνεγκε ϲέλινα
νικήϲαϲ ἄκρωι νεύματι καὶ κεφαλῆι.

---

[21] Athens, NM Br 15177. The group has recently been the subject of a series of excellent studies by Hemingway, of which the most recent is Hemingway 2000.

[22] Robertson 1975:559.

[23] Ibid., emphasis my own.

[24] Gombrich 1984:10–11. He based his analysis on Eadweard Muybridge's series of photographic frames that capture all successive stages of a horse's gallop.

[25] Ridgway 2000:311.

[26] See Goldhill 1994 on this type of dialogue as a deeply embedded strategy in epigrammatic poetry of the Hellenistic period.

Look how persistent is this foal, as he stirs up a wind throughout the image,[27] and how his whole body is tensed from the ribs, as he races in the Nemean games. He brought glory to Molycos, having won with a nod of the tip of his head.

The epigram is replete with admiration for a remarkable animal captured at the peak of its potential and beauty through the art of the sculptor. The epigrammatist's voice dictates the perceptual terms that guide our gaze throughout the image. His directives are explicit: we are confronted with a virtual replication of a Nemean competition (AB 72.3). We are meant to understand that, both in reality and in its re-presentation, an abstract quality of the horse (τὸ λιπαρές) has been transformed into palpable signs: the horse's blasting gallop is faster than the wind.[28] His formidable motion is manifest in the tension of his ribs, which is a visual trope that orchestrates the forward movement of the animal. The epigrammatist also wants us to pay particular attention to the head of this animal, a meaningful and well-timed nod of which won him the victory. In this way, the symbiotic coexistence of epigram and image chronicle the unique performance of an outstanding animal.

Likewise, in AB 76 a memorable stallion is celebrated thus:

ἐκτέτα[τ]αι π[ρ]οτ[ρ]έχων ἀκρώνυχος, ὡς Ἐτεάρχωι
οὗ]τος κ[λεινὸς "Α]ραψ ἵππος ἀεθλοφορεῖ
[ν]ικής[α]ς Πτολεμαῖα καὶ "Ισθμια καὶ Νεμέαι δίς,
[τ]οὺς Δελφοὺς πα[ριδ]εῖν οὐκ ἐθέλει στεφάνους.

He races ahead fully stretched and hardly touching the ground
    with the tip of his hooves
  as this glorious Arabian horse wins prizes for Etearchos;
having won at the Ptolemaia, the Isthmia and twice at the Nemea,
  he does not want to miss a Delphic victory.

In both epigrams the imagery evokes a representation akin to the Artemision horse, the conception of which points to a victory context and to the same gamut of values that have subtly been translated into the tension and dashing energy of Molycos' and Etearchos' racers. That the Artemision horse was intended to monu-

---

[27] Although *tupos* is most likely to refer to a figural work in relief, it is not impossible that it is used here to denote a three dimensional work like the Artemision bronze. See discussion in Pollitt 1994:272–293, esp. 291 where he concludes that this term might also have been used to refer to ". . . any sort of statue that resembled a mold-made image."

[28] See BG:199, commentary on AB 72.1–2 for an interpretation of πνόον ἕλκει as 'breathing' or 'panting'.

mentalize a victory is corroborated by the brand on the horse's right hind thigh: it is a flying Nike holding out a wreath.[29] Both bronze original and the epigrams celebrate an admirable exertion of heroic proportions. We need only look at the garment flying behind the bronze jockey to realize the import of AB 72.1–2: ὡc πνόον ἕλκει παντὶ τύπωι. Likewise, the bronze horse's outstretched legs in full flight convey the struggle of the noble animal towards victory as in AB 72.2 (καὶ πᾶc ἐ⟨κ⟩ λαγόνων τέταται) and AB 76.1 (ἐκτέτα[τ]αι π[ρ]οτ[ρ]έχων ἀκρώνυχος). His ears, turned completely back to his rider, no less than the pulsating nervousness of his muscles, denote his eagerness for victory (λιπαρέc)— the celebrated quality of Molycos'and Etearchos' chargers.[30]

As it stands now, the bronze monument lacks epigrams such as AB 72 or AB 76. That is, it lacks its *kleos*. Conversely, the *Hippika* lack their visual associations. As a result, their communicational efficacy remains no less unfulfilled than that, for example, of lyrics that are devoid of their musical notation. Neither horse nor epigrams make sense when perceived detached from each other. Nevertheless, the *Hippika* can trigger new evaluations of many decontextualized monuments, for they embody the same values and sentiments as the figural works they were meant to complement or amplify. They were products of an age accustomed to reading the poetry in representational arts and, inversely, to "hearing" the visual in verses like the *Hippika*.

Iamatika

It is not always easy to recover the original context of the *Iamatika* in P.Mil.Vogl. VIII 309. To this end, an explicit testimony is offered by AB 97, which is essentially a dedicatory epigram labeling a silver *phiale* dedicated to Asclepius at Cos as payment and thanksgiving for a successful and miraculous cure. The epigram was probably inscribed either directly on the *phiale* or, more likely, on a perishable medium appended to it.

Perhaps the most intriguing epigram in terms of its function as verbal qualifier of a figurative work of art is the epigram AB 95:

οἶος ὁ χάλκεος οὖτος ἐπ' ὀcτέα λεπτὸν ἀνέλκων
πνεῦμα μόγι[c] ζωὴν ὄμματι cυλλέγεται,

---

[29] This was originally inlaid with silver or gold. See Hemingway 2000:234 and accompanying drawing on 229, fig.3.

[30] In the specialized language of horsemanship, the Artemision horse and the victorious stallions of the *Hippika* are by all means "sharp racers," that is, competitive athletes keen on winning. On this see Ainslie and Ledbetter 1980:164–167.

ἐ⟨κ⟩ νούϲων̣ ἐϲάου το⟨ί⟩ουϲ ὁ τὰ δεινὰ Λιβύϲϲηϲ
δήγματα φα̣ρ̣μά⟨c⟩cειν ἀcπίδοc εὑρόμενοc
Μήδειοc Λάμπωνοc ᾽Ολύνθιοc, ὧι πανάκειαν
τὴν ᾽Ασκληπιαδῶν πᾶσαν ἔδωκε πατήρ·
coὶ δ᾽, ὦ Πύθι᾽ ῎Απολλον, ἑῆc γνωρίcματα τέχνηc
λείψανον ἀνθρώπου τόνδ᾽ ἔθετο cκελε̣τόν.

Like this brazen one, who takes a thin breath on his bones and hardly
draws together some life in his eyes, such were those Medeios, son of
Lampon, from Olynthos saved from illness, as he discovered the cure
from the awful bites of the Libyan asp. To him his father bestowed the
all-healing power of the Asclepiads. To you, o Pythian Apollo, as tokens
of his skill, he dedicated this skeleton, the relic of a man.

The demonstrative *houtos* in AB 95.1 emphatically points to something made
of bronze, but it is not until the final line that the object of the epigram
is specified as a skeleton, a relic of a man (λείψανον ἀνθρώπου τόνδ᾽ ἔθετο
cκελε̣τόν). What type of figurative work of art was meant to supplement
this epigram?

I am tempted to juxtapose this epigram with a small Hellenistic bronze in the
Byzantine Collection of Dumbarton Oaks representing an emaciated man of indeterminate age seated on a stool (Figure 3).[31] In its opening lines the epigram
conjures up the image of a represented—but as yet unspecified—somebody
(*houtos*) whose bones are animated by an insubstantial, flickering sparkle of spirit
(*pneuma*). If there is some life left in this figure, it is concentrated in his eyes.
Interestingly enough, the Dumbarton Oaks bronze features the same pathetic life-
lessness in his emaciated torso which is kept together by a transparent layer of thin
flesh. Likewise, his arms are inorganically appended. If there is some life remaining
in them, it is slowly dripping out of his numb fingers. The figure is at the threshold
of death, an awful and unappealing spectacle, an image of helplessness and suffering
that inspires sentiments of pity, curiosity, and fear in the past and in the present. It

---

[31] Dumbarton Oaks, no.47.22 (H. 11.5 cm). The cultural biography of this bronze after its discovery
near Soissons, France in the nineteenth century is no less exciting than the formal appearance of the
object: see Richter 1956:32–35; True in Kozloff and Mitten 1988:151–3; Garland 1995:118. At this
point, I should note that I attempt this juxtaposition for heuristic purposes only. The bronze has been
dated to the late Hellenistic period and it features a series of individualizing details, such as two
inscriptions in punctured letters (one of which is the name of a certain Eudamidas) and the deformity of the right foot, which point to a conception different from that of Medeios' dedication.
However, as Richter and True point out, the Dumbarton Oaks bronze may well be a replica of a
larger original that may have also provided a model or inspiration for Medeios' bronze.

is the spectral appearance of an uncanny state of existence. As is the case in the opening lines of the epigram, the represented is withering away and the only sign of life is that which is traceable in his sparkling eyes. Coming from nowhere, his gaze is directed to a vacuum. AB 95.12 affords us an epigrammatic statement of the unhappy object of ecphrasis in this poem. We are not supposed to look at a human but rather at a skeleton, a *leipsanon anthropou*.

This bronze has always been viewed as an enigma, as yet another specimen of the well-documented penchant in Hellenistic art for the graphically realistic or even the grotesque. In sharp contrast to Classical art, Hellenistic art often portrays liminal situations of human existence, the reversion of normality or the non-stereotypical. This figure, viewed in very generic terms, could fit nicely into this category. The lack, however, of a specific context regarding its experience as a work of art has hindered its interpretation and its appreciation in terms of the sentiments and the experience of contemporary viewers. Contrary to this state of knowledge, AB 95 provides insightful information for a type of situation that could have motivated the commissioning as well as the viewing of this bronze figure. The effect of both figure and bronze is actualized by *inversion*. As we learn from the epigram, the figure in front of us exemplifies a gruesome past of malady and affliction. It typifies a physical and, perhaps, mental state which was successfully cured by the healing art of Medeios, the son of Lampon from Olynthos (AB 95.3: ἐ⟨κ⟩ νούϲων ἐϲάου το⟨ί⟩ουϲ ὦ Μήδειοϲ). His *kleos* as a healer, as an inventor of medicines, and as a successful heir (or rival?) to the tradition of the Asclepiads is celebrated by image and epigram alike. The image induces the beholder to think of the diametrically opposite situation, of the multitude of healed persons who owe their happiness to Medeios and Apollo, his divine patron. The motivation for the image is formulated in the *apostrophe* to Apollo (AB 95.11–12): it was dedicated as a token of Medeios' healing art, as a sign of his power to effect miraculous transformations. As a dedicatory object or *agalma*, the value of the image is paradoxically invested in *what it is not*, that is, the representation of a fully recovered and healthy individual.

The juxtaposition of the Dumbarton Oaks bronze and the *Iamatikon* AB 95 shows the potential of considering their efficacy in concert. Moreover, it shows how much of the affective power of this poetry is lost because of its reification as literary artifact. Where then should we recontextualize the original coexistence of image and epigram? How were they meant to be viewed together? The invocation of Apollo Pythios, considered together with the mention of the Asclepiads, point to the sanctuary of Apollo at Delphi.[32] The kind of statuary represented by the Dumbarton Oaks bronze was seen at Delphi by Pausanias, who reports: "Among

---

[32] Jouanna 1999:33–35.

the votive offerings of Apollo was an image in bronze of a man in an advanced stage of decay, whose flesh has already fallen off so that he has nothing left except for the bones. The Delphians said that it was "a dedication of Hippocrates the physician" (Pausanias X 2.6). In view of this precedent, Delphi turns out to be an appropriate context for the expression of Medeios' piety and his thankfulness to Apollo. It is also an appropriate, panhellenic context for the advertisement of his successful practice and his expertise. The reference to the revered, healing clan of the Asclepiads (AB 95.6), the clan to which Hippocrates of Cos belonged, may be motivated by his rivalry with them. He is not an Asklepiad himself, but he has inherited his father's all-healing power, a power commensurate to that of the Asklepiads.[33]

It is possible that the bronze skeleton and an epigram like AB 95 were somehow displayed together, thus mutually reinforcing their communicative power in a manner clearly illustrated by Cox's *Head of the Queen of Egypt*. Unfortunately, the archaeological record has not preserved any traces of this co-existence. Should we reconstruct the placement of the statuette (or of a large-scale prototype, of which the statuette is but a replica) on top of a stone pedestal? In this case AB 95 was inscribed in stone. Or is it possible that the epigram was written on a perishable medium to be reconstructed as an appendage to the figurative component of the dedication? Given the present state of the available evidence we cannot even attempt to answer these questions. We can, however, enjoy the art of the statuette in light of the poetry treasured in the Milan papyrus and vice-versa. In this way we enrich our sensibilities, and we come somewhat closer to the bizarre and exotic life-world of the Hellenistic Mediterranean.[34]

---

[33] Ibid. See Bing's contribution in this volume regarding a possible identification of Medeios with a physician active in the Ptolemaic court during the time of Posidippus. Also cf. Bing 2002c.

[34] In May 2002 I was able to examine the Dumbarton Oaks bronze in person due to the valuable assistance of Drs. Susan Boyd and Stephen Zwirn, curators of the collection, both of whom I thank wholeheartedly. I also express my thanks to Elizabeth Kosmetatou, Manuel Baumbach, Amy Papalexandrou, and Glenn Peers, for insightful comments and criticism.

18

"Drownded in the Tide": The *Nauagika* and Some "Problems" in Augustan Poetry[*]

Richard F. Thomas

Harvard University

Phlebas the Phoenician, a fortnight dead,
Forgot the cry of gulls, and the deep sea swell
And the profit and loss.
      A current under sea
Picked his bones in whispers. As he rose and fell
He passed the stages of his age and youth
Entering the whirlpool.
      Gentile or Jew
O you who turn the wheel and look to windward,
Consider Phlebas, who once was handsome and tall as you.

             T.S. Eliot, *The Waste Land* 312–321

In "The New Posidippus and Latin Poetry," G. Hutchinson began the task of considering "how this big accession of new material enlarges our appreciation of the Hellenistic background to Latin literature, and our understanding of Latin elegy in particular."[1] The Milan papyrus contains one six-line and five four-line epigrams of the type ναυαγικόν, a title here attested (XIV 2) for the first time. Hutchinson notes a parallel between XIV 12 (AB 91.2) and Ovid's *Tristia* IV 4.55–58 (dangers of the Euxine), and otherwise on this group of 26 lines notes:[2]

---

[*] I am grateful to David Petrain for helpful comments and suggestions.
[1] Hutchinson 2002:1–10.
[2] Hutchinson 2002:6.

xiv.4 θεοῖς μέμφεται οἵ ἔπαθεν (the empty tomb laments the death of Lysicles at sea); xiv.23-4 τὸν νέκυν, ὡς χρή, πατρώηι, πόντου δέσποτα, γῆ ἀπｏδｏς. Both passages give relevant context for the speech of the drowning Paetus, Prop. 3.7.57–64; the whole poem is like a huge expansion of an epigram in the class ναυαγικά. The speech begins with the complaint to *di maris Aegaei*, mentions Neptune (*caeruleo . . . deo*) in 62, and ends asking the gods (cf. *mandata* 55) *at saltem Italiae regionibus evehat aestus; | hoc de me sat erit, si modo matris erit.*

Again, Hutchinson makes no claims to comprehensiveness, and is to be applauded for initiating this important inquiry into the reception and intertexts of the papyrus. We could, of course, already see the role played by Hellenistic ναυαγικά in Propertius III 7, since we already had two runs of the sub-genre in the *Palatine Anthology* (*AP* VII 263–279, 282–294), though most of the second group are post-Augustan.[3] Incidentally, as noted by Bastianini and Gallazzi, one of these poems (*AP* VII 267) is by Posidippus, but is absent from the ναυαγικά of the papyrus—one of the reasons for skepticism about Posidippan authorship of *all* the new poems.[4] As for these pre-existing ναυαγικά, *AP* VII 263, ascribed to Anacreon, and certainly Hellenistic or earlier,[5] would seem to have a connection to Propertius, with each conflating erotic and sepulchral: *AP* VII 263.3–4 (narrator) ὑγρὰ δὲ τὴν σὴν | κύματ᾽ ἀφ᾽ ἱμερτὴν ἔκλυσεν ἡλικίην = Prop. III 7.57–9 (Paetus) "*di maris Aegaei quos sunt penes aequora, venti, | et quaecumque meum degravat unda caput, | quo rapitis miseros primae lanuginis annos?*"

Nevertheless, the six new poems preserved by the papyrus permit us to see just how intensely a poem like Propertius III 7 may indeed seem to represent a "huge expansion" of epigram in the process of creating a genre, Roman elegy, that is rooted in Hellenistic epigram. In this respect, the elegist may be seen to be working in the tradition of expansion observable in Catullus 68, which takes sepulchral

---

[3] See Gutzwiller 1998:313 for the proposition that the shipwreck poems in the Cephalan section at VII 263-73 were in last section of the Meleagrian book with VII 494–506, 650–654, 738–739.

[4] Cf. BG 216. In other words the absence of a Posidippan ναυαγικόν from the ναυαγικά of the papyrus may argue as much for a multi-authored anthology as the presence of two possibly Posidippan poems argues for a single-authored book. (Gow-Page say of one [*APl.* 199 = Pos 18 GP = AB 65] there are "reasons for questioning [with Schott] the ascription to Pos.," of the other [*ap.* Tzetz. *Chil.* 7.660 = Pos 20 GP = AB 15] "its authenticity seems open to considerable doubt"). This is especially true given the variation in quality of the new poems, the oddity of the collection (whose lemmata seem to be the organizing principle), and the absence of more familiar Hellenistic subgenres (straightforward sympotic, and erotic, in particular). I would be prepared to accept Posidippan authorship; the case, however, given the slightness of the evidence, has yet to be made.

[5] Cf. GP I xxii.

epigram (already "translated" in Catullus 101) as a starting-point and expands that genre into a complex proto-elegy.[6] These new poems may be usefully viewed in relation to two other Roman poets, who are similarly involved in generic appropriation and renovation. In all three cases we will see that readers and critics have found something odd or strange about the lines in question. I believe that the Milan papyrus allows and encourages us to see this oddness as part of the compositional condition of these epigrams, and also allows us to reconstruct the peculiar essence of that corpus of Roman poetry that most looked to Alexandria for much of its inspiration and innovation.

The Archytas Ode (Horace, *Odes* I 28)

The new papyrus does not at first sight seem to provide a transformative lens through which to view *Odes* I 28, the Archytas ode. As Nisbet-Hubbard already noted in their introduction, "the poem includes many traditional elements from Greek sepulchral epigram."[7] We can however, see certain important elements of Horace's poem coming into sharper focus through the appearance of the new ναυαγικά, when we consider them as a group. It may be worth noting at the outset that the first of the Milan epitaphs (AB 89) records the grief of Polemon at the loss by drowning of his friend Lysicles. That Polemon, like Archytas, was a philosopher may not be irrelevant, since the epigram and the ode may both be seen as being rooted in the tradition of literary epitaphs for philosophers, to be found at *AP* VII 94–132 (VII 103 is for Crates and Polemon).

As for shared themes and actual intertexts, the new epigrams offer one detail that, although already available to Horace in part from Meleager's anthology and elsewhere, is closer than examples we already had. Horace's poem ends with the injunction that the traveling merchant pause to give burial to the unburied speaker (35–6 *quamquam festinas, non est mora longa: licebit | iniecto ter pulvere curras*). Nisbet-Hubbard (*ad* I 28.35) refer to various texts, including Asclepiades 33 GP (= *AP* XIII 23), dealing with the necessity to interrupt one's business in order to mourn the dead. Their examples, however, are not specifically from shipwreck poems, the context of the plea of Horace's ναυαγός. But now we have a model in the final poem of our series in the Milan papyrus (AB 94):

ναυηγόν με θανόντα καὶ ἔκλαυcεν καὶ ἔθαψεν
Λεώφαντοc cπουδῆι, καὐτὸc ἐπειγόμενοc

---

6 On this see Thomas 1998:214–216.
7 Nisbet and Hubbard 1970:318.

ὡς ἂν ἐπὶ ξείνης καὶ ὁδοιπόρος· ἀλλ' ἀποδοῦναι
Λεωφάντι μεγάλην μικκὸς ἐγὼ χάριτα.

"I died in a shipwreck and was mourned and buried
hurriedly by Leophantus, as too he was hastening
like a traveler in a foreign land. But I am too small
to give great thanks in return to Leophantus."[8]

Although the ending is either obscure or lame,[9] the poem gives us a closer situation to that of the ending of *Odes* I 28 than we hitherto had. Both texts represent the voice of the shipwrecked in the first person, each either gives thanks for or requests burial by a trader, and both refer to the haste of the trader. The differences are merely ones of aspect and temporal progression: while the Latin poem urges burial, the Greek one records burial that has been granted.[10]

Perhaps more important than this intertext is the fact that we now have the Milan epigrams in their original, Hellenistic context, not just as six poems preserved in a later redaction, but as a run of 26 lines of related and varied poems, so placed by Posidippus or the third-century BCE anthologist. Nisbet-Hubbard have rightly defended Horace's 36-line poem against those who would see it as a "chaotic youthful experiment." Whatever the oddities, as they note, "anybody who likes this poem has discovered something about poetry."[11] Nisbet-Hubbard have also designated it "undeniably bizarre in conception."[12] The basis for finding *Odes* I 28 "chaotic," "bizarre" or otherwise odd, has purely to do with voice and identity. Who speaks the opening lines (1–4 *Te . . . cohibent, Archyta,* | *pulveris exigui . . .* | *munera*)? The corpse of a drowned man? The passing *nauta* of line 23? Horace himself? And what is the relationship of the *te* of line 2 to the *me* of line 21? Is the poem a monologue or a dialogue—or neither? These are the questions that have vexed all critics of this poem ever since it has been read. Frischer has a good survey

---

[8] Translation C. Austin in Austin and Bastianini 2002:119.

[9] See BG:221 for discussion, and for the possibility (ultimately rejected) that there is a play on the name Μίκκος. Without some such play, the poem is rather feeble.

[10] BG: 220–221 give no reference to Horace, but they do point to the parallel with Callimachus, *Ep.* 58 Pf. = *AP* VII 277 (the model for Eliot's lines at the beginning of this article), which records Leontichus' (cf. Leophantus) burial of an unnamed ναυαγός. A far superior poem to that of the Milan papyrus, Callimachus' epigram is however distinct from it and from *Odes* I 28 in that it addresses the deceased and narrates the burial, while they are addresses by the deceased. David Petrain points out that the opening of Callimachus' poem (τίς ξένος . . .) raises questions of voice that bring it closer to *Odes* I 28 but not to the Milan poem.

[11] Nisbet and Hubbard 1970:320.

[12] Nisbet and Hubbard 1970:319.

of recent work on the question, citing the "standard interpretation" of Nisbet-
Hubbard:[13]

> the poem is spoken by a corpse of a drowned man. First the dead man
> apostrophizes the great fourth-century BCE Pythagorean Archytas of
> Tarentum, as he lies buried in his grave. Then at 23 he turns to a
> passing *nauta* and asks for burial himself. The structure of the poem
> causes perplexity because we do not know till 21 the speaker is not
> Horace but a corpse.

Frischer's own view is that the opening speaker is Horace, who sarcastically
addresses the dead Archytas (1–20):[14]

> Horace's purpose in attacking Archytas and his beliefs is to create a situ-
> ation in which Archytas would not fail to reply, if he could, to Horace's
> abuse. In 21–36, the epitaph on Archytas' tomb is quoted as the only
> response that Archytas can make after Horace's address. The wit of the
> poem consists in the fact that Archytas' epitaph in no sense responds to
> the issues Horace raises. All the text of the epitaph can do is endlessly
> repeat the same empty threats and promises, the irrelevance of which
> reinforces the point of Horace's attacks on Archytas' beliefs in the
> survival of consciousness in the afterlife and in the possibility of
> communication between the living and the dead at the tomb.

There are attractions to such a reading, but it too calls for an act of faith, since
the dramatic setting and the movement from the first part to the second is by no
means explicit or even implicit in the text. Frischer's reading is possible, but it
hardly resolves the issue of identity and voice in any compelling or final way. Other
possibilities remain, as does the question of coherence.

Let us return briefly to the Milan poems, and to the issue of voice. They are
quite varied in this respect:

AB 89	**B**	Third-person narration by text on stone or reader
AB 90	**A¹**	Third-person narration, no text/stone; focalization of swimmer (ὀρώμενον)
AB 91	**C¹**	Address to reader/passerby by text/stone; deceased in third person[15]

---

[3] Frischer 1984:71–102; cf. also Nisbet-Hubbard 1970–1978: 317–20.

[4] Frischer 1984:73.

[5] Following AB. The edition of BG (14 καὶ ⟨μ'⟩ αἱ θῖνες ἔχουςιν ἁλός) would have the deceased
addressing the reader (C).

AB 92	A	Third-person narration, no text/stone
AB 93	D	Address to earth/sea to cover lightly/return to shore
AB 94	E	First-person narration by deceased

Horace's poem, on the other hand, falls into the following categories:

1-20	F	Address to deceased (Frischer)
	E¹	Apostrophe by deceased (Nisbet-Hubbard)
21–22	E	First-person narration by deceased
23–36	C	Address to passerby by deceased

In other words, Horace's poem demonstrates a combination of voices, such a one finds in the epigrams—only there across poem-boundaries. Nisbet-Hubbard noted of I 28.21ff.: "Horace now weaves in themes from the other type of Greek epitaph, where the dead man does the speaking himself."[16] Horace cannot give us an epigram in the *Odes* (though IV 10 will come close), but, particularly with the impulse from a string of thematically connected but varied epigrams such as we find on the Milan papyrus, he can combine and conflate, and in the process produce lyric poem of some mystery, a poem that looks like two or three epigrams, and yet still somehow works as a poem, if only we listen to, and *appreciate*, its disparate voices.

Propertius III 7: Epigrams or Elegy?

At a number of points the third book of Propertius' elegies seems to respond to the recently published collection of *Odes* 1–3.[17] It may therefore be worth considering Propertius III 7, in connection with *Odes* I 28, but also in the light of the new epigrams. Again the words of Hutchinson on this poem: "the whole poem is like huge expansion of an epigram in the class ναυαγικά." There is some truth to that particularly if we accept the multiple transpositions, and claims for interpolation that have been made by editors in a frantic attempt to create a coherent poem of 3.7. Housman is representative, as he reads the poem thus: 1–10/43–66/17–18/11–16/67–70/25–32/37–38/35–36/19–20/33–34/21–24/39–42/71–72.[18]

---

[16] Nisbet and Hubbard 1970:319.

[17] For the connections between the two poets see Solmsen 1948:105–109; Flach 1967:*passim*.

[18] Butler and Barber 1933:275 record the interventions of four critics: Scaliger, Housman, Postgate, and Richmond. Fedeli's 1984 Teubner and Goold's 1990 Loeb (rev. 1999) have slightly different arrangements.

But as Butler and Barber note, "While few are likely to regard any of these suggestions as wholly acceptable, and fewer still will venture to explain how such disloca-
tions could have been brought about, all four schemes are fundamentally inspired
by the desire to eliminate three genuine difficulties."[19] All three difficulties have to
do either with confusion of adressees (as in the case of *Odes* I 28) or with logical
problems in the narrative unity of the poem.

Butler and Barber record the attempt of Vahlen to explain the poem without
these transpositions.[20] His argument is one "which may be summarized as a plea
that Propertius' method is not to exhaust any one motive once introduced, but to
recur to it and add new touches; and that consequently all wholesale transpositions
are based on a misconception." Butler and Barber concede some ground, but while
they preserve the order of the MSS, as does Barber's *OCT*, they ultimately resist
Vahlen's suggestion: "Such a defense . . . is an assertion that a rambling style and a
love of parenthesis is characteristic of the Propertian elegy. And while there is some
truth in such an assertion, the present elegy provides an extreme example of the
poet's particular art or lack of it. . . [T]he most cursory analysis at once reveals the
eccentricity of the structure and arouses strong suspicions of the soundness of the
tradition."[21]

The experimental and innovative aspects of Propertius' third book are well
acknowledged. What if, with the help of the Milan papyrus, we were to revive
Vahlen's hypothesis that the "rambling" style is intended, and is indeed part of the
art? When we accept and consider the poem as it is preserved in the MSS, we are
left, not in the words of Hutchinson with a "huge expansion of an epigram," which
might describe the text produced by Housman and others, but rather with a reduc-
tion of elegy to its constituent component string of epigrams, all of them
αυαγικά for Paetus (some naming him, others not). This is what leads to an
appearance of "rambling style and a love of parenthesis." When the parenthesis
becomes a poem in its own right it is no longer a parenthesis, rather an epigram.

Such a hypothesis could have been proffered before the appearance of the
Milan papyrus, on the basis of the pre-existing runs at *AP* VII 263–79, 282–94.
But what we can now for the first time do is make two further, notable observations: 1) since scholars have already begun to see the thematic groupings of the
papyrus as having some unitary status within the group,[22] the Greek poems give us
direct or indirect model, precisely for a poem such as III 7, read as Vahlen

[19] Butler and Barber 1933:275.
[20] Vahlen 1883:36–90.
[21] Butler and Barber 1933:276.
[22] Notably, in this volume, Fantuzzi for the ἱππικά, Baumbach and Trampedach for the
οἰωνοσκοπικά.

proposed to read it; 2) the once popular question of the origin of Roman elegy comes back into play, since the papyrus gives us a book of at least ten "poetic units" ranging in length from 26 to 126 verses (excluding col. XVI.18ff., the last grouping, of 8 lines). Propertius III 7 looks very much like one of those "poetic units", but it is unique among the poems of Book 3 in doing so. To this extent the Latin poem may be seen as reversing the process apparent in much elegy (but *not* in III 7), wherein the genre can indeed be viewed as a "huge expansion" (both in size and poetic complexity). This expansion is heralded by the opening of the *Monobiblos* (Prop. I 1 1–4), translating and transgendering as it does the homoerotic Meleager 103 Page (= *AP* XII 101), which serves only as the opening intertext. Propertius' string of ναυαγικά at III 7, on the other hand, shows us where Roman elegy largely came from, precisely by giving us a poem that is to be read as epigrams, as the *disiecta membra* that are the basis for the "poem's" making sense. It is truly experimental precisely in its revisionism, which especially comes into focus and appears familiar now that we have the Milan papyrus.

Here then is Propertius III 7 (*Nauagica Paeti*), with individual "epigram titles" supplied:[23]

Perils of the marine merchant

> Ergo sollicitae tu causa, pecunia, vitae!
> > per te immaturum mortis adimus iter;
> tu vitiis hominum crudelia pabula praebes;
> > semina curarum de capite orta tuo.
> tu Paetum ad Pharios tendentem lintea portus   5
> > obruis insano terque quaterque mari.
> nam dum te sequitur, primo miser excidit aevo
> > et nova longinquis piscibus esca natat.

Cenotaph and a mother's grief

> et mater non iusta piae dare debita terrae
> > nec pote cognatos inter humare rogos,   10
> sed tua nunc volucres astant super ossa marinae,
> > nunc tibi pro tumulo Carpathium omne mare est.

---

[23] Many of these "epigrams" demonstrate the presence of antithesis or paradox that is so marked a feature of the Hellenistic genre.

Cruelty of Neptune and the North Wind

infelix Aquilo, raptae timor Orithyiae,
    quae spolia ex illo tanta fuere tibi?
aut quidnam fracta gaudes, Neptune, carina?   15
    portabat sanctos alveus ille viros.

Too late a son's plea and cry for his mother

Paete, quid aetatem numeras? quid cara natanti
    mater in ore tibi est? non habet unda deos.
nam tibi nocturnis ad saxa ligata procellis
    omnia detrito vincula fune cadunt.   20

Even Agamemnon suffered such loss, by water and on land

sunt Agamemnonias testantia litora curas,
    quae notat Argynni poena Athamantiadae.
hoc iuvene amisso classem non solvit Atrides,
    pro qua mactatast Iphigenia mora.

Bring his body to the shore, to be a sailors' warning

reddite corpus, aquae! posita est in gurgite vita;   25
    Paetum sponte tua, vilis harena, tegas;
et quotiens Paeti transibit nauta sepulcrum,
    dicat 'et audaci tu timor esse potes.'

Human skill brings human loss

ite, rates curvate et leti texite causas:
    ista per humanas mors venit acta manus.   30
terra parum fuerat fatis, adiecimus undas:
    fortunae miseras auximus arte vias.

Stay at home or suffer this fate

ancora te teneat, quem non tenuere penates?
    quid meritum dicas, cui sua terra parum est?

ventorumst, quodcumque paras: haud ulla carina   35
consenuit, fallit portus et ipse fidem.

Nature more cunning than culture hero

natura insidians pontum substravit avaris:
  ut tibi succedat, vix semel esse potest.
saxa triumphalis fregere Capherea puppes,
  naufraga cum vasto Graecia tracta salo est.   40
paulatim socium iacturam flevit Ulixes,
  in mare cui soliti non valuere doli.

Better poverty at home than wealth across the sea

quod si contentus patrio bove verteret agros,
  verbaque duxisset pondus habere mea,
viveret ante suos dulcis conviva Penates,   45
  pauper, at in terra nil nisi fleret opes.
noluit hoc Paetus, stridorem audire procellae
  et duro teneras laedere fune manus,
sed thyio thalamo aut Oricia terebintho
  effultum pluma versicolore caput.   50

The sum of his evils: wave-torn, night-blinded, drownded in the tide

huic fluctus vivo radicitus abstulit ungues:
  Paetus ut occideret, tot coiere mala.
hunc parvo ferri vidit nox improba ligno,
  et miser invisam traxit hiatus aquam.

Melodious tears, last words: "Look homeward angel"

flens tamen extremis dedit haec mandata querelis   55
  cum moribunda niger clauderet ora liquor:
'di maris Aegaei quos sunt penes aequora, venti,
  et quaecumque meum degravat unda caput,
quo rapitis miseros primae lanuginis annos?
  attulimus longas in freta vestra manus.   60

ah miser alcyonum scopulis affligar acutis!
in me caeruleo fuscina sumpta deo est.
at saltem Italiae regionibus evehat aestus:
hoc de me sat erit si modo matris erit.'
subtrahit haec fantem torta vertigine fluctus;   65
ultima quae Paeto voxque diesque fuit.

"Where were ye nymphs?"

o centum aequoreae Nereo genitore puellae,
et tu, materno tacta dolore, Theti;
vos decuit lasso supponere bracchia mento:
non poterat vestras ille gravare manus.   70

Sea of love for me!

at tu, saeve Aquilo, numquam mea vela videbis:
ante fores dominae condar oportet iners.

The antepenultimate and penultimate titles' references to Milton's *Lycidas* (formally a ναυαγικόν for Milton's friend, Edward King, like Paetus lost at sea and dead "ere his prime"), are not casual. Like Propertius III 7, that great poem has regularly been criticized for its excessive art in engaging so openly and emphatically with the intertexts in its tradition. Its fractured state may be parallel to that of Propertius III 7, precisely because the two poets are engaged on parallel confrontations with their traditions.

Rather than transposing sequences of lines in Propertian elegy, we might do better to reflect on the sort of sequences that the Milan papyrus gives us, and to see in a poem like Prop. III 7 a radical encounter with the tradition reperesented by the papyrus. The Roman elegy is still a poem—just—but it is a poem with looser narrative logic and progressions, and more propensity to disunity, than we are traditionally capable of tolerating. Perhaps the papyrus will increase our tolerance, and also give a basis for similar findings elsewhere in the corpus of Roman poetry, that of Propertius in particular.

Palinurus (Virgil, *Aeneid* V 833–71, VI 337–83)

Virgil's Palinurus is a character of some complexity in terms of literary genealogy and intertextuality. As has long been noted, his Homeric counterpoint is Elpenor, like Palinurus the first familiar character encountered by the hero in the course of his *katabasis* (*Od.* XI 51–83 ~ *Aen.* VI 337–83), just as he shared with Aeneas' navigator the fate of being the last to die in the upper world (*Od.* X 552–60 ~ *Aen.* V 833–71).[24] At the same time, Virgil draws from *Od.* III 278–85, Nestor's account of Menelaus' loss (to the arrows of Apollo) and subsequent burial of the helmsman Phrontis. And Aeneas' burial of Misenus (*Aen.* VI 149–53) further complicates things.[25] That parallel establishes the Odyssean moments as genre models for Virgil, but as so often his artistic genius is most on display and at its most subtle precisely when he departs from the details of those models. The greatest distance between the two characters lies in the manner of their death, which, however, both involve a fall, Elpenor's from the roof of Circe's house.

Throughout both Palinurus passages Virgil engages intensively with the tradition of the shipwreck epigram, embedding it into his larger narrative, and so creating an expansion and appropriation of the genre, as he blends it into the Homeric genre model. This is, again, something we could know before the discovery of the Milan epigrams, but these latter help to strengthen our appreciation of the Hellenistic overlay on the Homeric foundation.[26] Given that the narrative draws attention emphatically to Palinurus' struggles and death at sea, one could even conclude that the epigrammatic intertext assumes a greater impact in its new, epic context.

What does the papyrus give us, then, as readers of Virgil's Palinurus? First it demonstrates the fact, unsurprising perhaps, that the ναυαγικά were even more prevalent than the Meleagrian examples would suggest. The particularly powerful grief and pathos they evoke, since the deceased in such cases potentially or in fact go without burial, were available for Virgil to activate, and he indeed invokes these emotions throughout both passages. But there are also significant intertextual observations to be made. When Palinurus encounters Aeneas in the Underworld, he gives details of his fate:

> tris Notus hibernas immensa per aequora noctes
>
> vexit me violentus aqua; vix lumine quarto
>
> prospexi Italiam summa sublimis ab unda.
>
> paulatim adnabam terrae; iam tuta tenebam,
>
> ni gens crudelis madida cum veste gravatum
>
> prensantemque uncis manibus capita aspera montis

---

[24] See Knauer 1979: 135–9 for Homeric aspects, particularly the connection with Elpenor.

[25] See Knauer 1979:136–137; 137n1 for the possibility that Naevius' account of the death of Prochyta would have provided another doublet. On this see Mariotti 1955:40–47; also Horsfall 1991:101.

[26] See Norden 1970: 230–231 for reference to shipwreck epigrams in connection with Palinurus.

ferro invasisset praedamque ignara putasset.
nunc me fluctus habet versantque in litore venti.

(*Aen.* VI 355–62)

The lines convert to the first person the narrative account of Odysseus' being washed ashore on Phaeacia (*Od.* V 388–435), as Knauer and others have noted. But Palinurus' less happy ending (362 *nunc me fluctus habet versantque in litore venti*), take us in a different direction, to the language of the ναυαγικόν. The self-contained one-line sentence creates epigrammatic effect.[27] It is true that this line also has a (syntactically distinct) Homeric intertext, in the anxieties Telemachus expresses about his father's fate at *Od.* I 161–2 (ἀνέρος, οὗ δή που λεύκ' ὀστέα τύθεται ὄμβρωι | κεῖμεν' ἐπ' ἠπείρου, ἢ εἰν ἁλὶ κῦμα κυλίνδει),[28] but the actual language is more reminiscent of sepulchral epitaph. So, at Euripides *Hec.* 28–30, the ghost of Polydorus similarly refers to its fate: κεῖμαι δ' ἐπ' ἀκταῖς, ἄλλοτ' ἐν πόντου σάλῳ, | πολλοῖς διαύλοις κυμάτων φορούμενος, | ἄκλαυτος ἄταφος·.[29] And Euripides' and Virgil's language have reminiscences in two of the Milan ναυαγικά:

AB 89.5–6 τὸν δέ που ἤδη ἀκταὶ καὶ πολιὸν κῦμα [θανόντ'
ἔλαχον (Austin and Bastianini) | κῦμ' {α} [ἐπέχουcι ἁλόc
(Bastianini and Galazzi)

AB 91.13–14 κενεὸν Δώρου τάφον, ὃν Παριανῶν τῆλέ που
εἰκαῖαι θῖνες ἔχουcιν ἁλόc.

Virgil's verb *habent* (cf. ἐπέχουcι; ἔχουcιν) is particularly notable, and is paralleled by our Horatian ναυαγικόν discussed above (*Odes* I 28.9–10 *habentque Tartara Panthoiden*).[30]

Aen. VI 362 functions as a pivot from the narrative that precedes to what could almost be an actual sepulchral epigram. Except for the fact that it is addressed to Aeneas, it looks in large part like the conventional address to the passerby, requesting at least a perfunctory burial (365–366 *aut tu mihi terram inice*):

---

[27] For similar gnomic or epigrammatic effects (I exclude instances where forms of *hic*, etc. connect to what precedes, or *sic*, etc. to what follows), as a clausula, just from *Aen.* 1–2, see I 33 *tantae molis erat Romanam condere gentem*; 334 *multa tibi ante aras nostra cadet hostia dextra*; 401 *perge modo et, qua te ducit via, derige gressum*; 630 *non ignara mali miseris succurrere disco*; II 49 *quidquid id est, timeo Danaos et dona ferentis*; 354 *una salus victis nullam sperare salutem*.

[28] See Knauer 1979:*ad loc.*

[29] See Norden 1970:*ad loc.*

[30] Also *Aen.* IX 490–1 (sepulchral, of the whereabouts of Euryalus' headless corpse) *quae nunc artus avulsaque membra* | *et funus lacerum tellus habet?* Cf. *ThLL* s.v. *habeo* 2431.53–69.

271

"quod te per caeli iucundum lumen et auras,
per genitorem oro, per spes surgentis Iuli,
eripe me his, invicte, malis: aut tu mihi terram   365
inice, namque potes, portusque require Velinos;
aut tu, si qua via est, si quam tibi diva creatrix
ostendit (neque enim, credo, sine numine divum
flumina tanta paras Stygiamque innare paludem),
da dextram misero et tecum me tolle per undas,   370
sedibus ut saltem placidis in morte quiescam."

The model, of course, is *Od.* XI 66–78, Elpenor's request that Odysseus burn
him with his armor and set up a σῆμα for him, when Odysseus returns to Aeaea.
But Palinurus' speech is modified to suit the Roman sepulchral tradition, and also
to suit the new situation (death at sea). And a significant detail is added: since
Aeneas is in the Underworld and about to cross the Styx, Palinurus assumes he has
the divine aid of Venus (367–369), and that he may in fact be able to lift the
helmsman from the waves and take him to the other side for his final rest
(370–371, "*da dextram misero et tecum me tolle per undas,* | *sedibus ut saltem placidis
in morte quiescam*"). The least well-preserved of the Milan ναυαγικά is to be
found at AB 92, a poem apparently dealing with a divine rescue of a swimmer,
following the loss of his ship and crew:

νηὸς ἀπολλυμένης συναπώλετο πᾶς ἁμαεργὸς
   ναύτης, νηχομέ[νωι δ᾽ ἦν   ] ε̣υ̣τι φυγή·
τὸν γὰρ ἐπαμ[   ]α̣ δαίμων
   νηχόμενον [   ]ς.

Here is Austin's translation:

As the ship was sinking, down with it went the whole crew
   on board but [. . .]noeis escaped by swimming.
[Coming to his rescue] a god wrapped [him up as he gently] swam
   [and saved him from the ice-cold sea].[31]

---

[31] Following his exemplary supplementing of 3–4: τὸν γὰρ ἐπαμ[πίσχων cωτήριος ἠρέμ]α̣
δαίμων | νηχόμενον [ψυχρῆς ἐξεcάωcεν ἁλ]ο̣c. Unless Austin is wrong in this general
reconstruction, this poem must number among the most miserable on the papyrus. The poems
given as parallel by BG (e.g. *AP* VII 289, 290, 550; 9.269) all involve some sort of paradox, with
the even-tual death (but not by drowning,) of the shipwrecked man. Our poem would be better if,
for instance, the last two lines involved some ill fortune (?κακὸc δαίμων) coming up against him

From *Aen.* VI 362 (*nunc me fluctus habet versantque in litore venti*), we are to ꞏmagine that Palinurus is still amidst the waves of the sea when he pleads with ꞏeneas to rescue him; whether or not there is any direct relationship, what we find ꞏ Palinurus' plea for rescue from the divinely empowered Aeneas is a (non-Homeric) equivalence to the situation of the epigram, so supplemented.

There is another feature of the Virgilian treatment that warrants comment in ꞏhe light of the Milan papyrus. As occurred in the case of Prop. III 7, so Virgil's two ꞏassages on Palinurus have been convicted of inconsistency on a number of ꞏrounds.[32] Although these inconsistencies are part of the larger fabric of ambigui-ꞏes and oddities in the poem, no other instances rise to the level of the Palinurus ꞏections, which Horsfall proposes may have been the only sections that Virgil would ꞏave changed had he had those three years to polish up the poem. He well summa-ꞏizes the major inconsistencies (100–101):

Aeneid V	*Aeneid* VI
• Somnus throws P. overboard	• No divine actor present
• Calm sea	• Stormy sea
• Aeneas thinks it an accident	• Aeneas speaks of divine cause
• Event occurs between Sicily and Italy	• Virgil speaks of *Libyco cursu*
• The trip lasts just one night	• P. tells of swimming for three nights

It is as if the two sections tell different stories. And even within each of the two ꞏections there is a sense of episodicity, which may be seen as a result of the presence ꞏf sepulchral epigram throughout. Likewise there is some play with voice, some of ꞏhe confusion between narration and focalization that one finds in the tradition of ꞏuch epigram.[33] The fifth book ends with what is most immediately an address by ꞏeneas to his dead helmsman:

....

(ἐπαμβαίνει), or enfolding him (ἐπαμπίσχων), in the form, say, of a shark, as occurs in an epigram of Leonidas of Tarentum (*AP* VII 506.10 = Leon. Tar. 75 GP ἥμισυ δὲ πρίστις ἀπεκλάσατο). Or perhaps some god (δαίμων) sent a man-eating fish (κῆτος) against him while he was swimming, one of the primal fears of the swimming ναυαγός, as at *Od.* V 417–22:

εἰ δέ κ᾽ ἔτι προτέρω **παρανήξομαι**, . . .
δείδω μή μ᾽ ἐξαῦτις ἀναρπάξασα θύελλα
πόντον ἐπ᾽ ἰχθυόεντα φέρηι βαρέα στενάχοντα,   420
ἠέ τί μοι καὶ **κῆτος** ἐπισσεύηι μέγα **δαίμων**
ἐξ ἁλός, οἷά τε πολλὰ τρέφει κλυτὸς Ἀμφιτρίτη·

[32] See Horsfall 1991:Ch. 6 "Incoerenze." J. O'Hara will treat the topic in Virgil and other Latin poets in a forthcoming monograph.

[33] For this topic see the forthcoming Harvard PhD dissertation of Michael Tueller.

> ipse ratem nocturnis rexit in undis
> multa gemens casuque animum concussus amici:
> "o nimium caelo et pelago confise sereno,   870
> nudus in ignota, Palinure, iacebis harena."
>
> *Aen.* V 868–71

The words belong to Aeneas, but the absence of a verb of speaking and th gnomic nature of the final couplet, along with its sepulchral content, identify it a a cenotaph, whose voice is not just Aeneas', but also that of the narrator of *Aen.* V and of us, readers of the inscription and of the poem. Indeed the inscription ma even be seen as attaching to the story that proceeds, whose narrative ἐνάργεια beginning with *ecce* at V 854, functions almost as a narrative image, to which th closing epigram lends its epigrammatic commentary.

We have similar variety in *Aen.* VI, where the Palinurus episode again begin with the arresting marker, *ecce*:

> ecce gubernator sese Palinurus agebat,
>
> qui Libyco nuper cursu, dum sidera servat,
>
> exciderat puppi mediis effusus in undis.
>
> *Aen.* VI 337–9

The ensuing exchange between Aeneas and the shade of Palinurus (340–71) may be reduced to the following: A: "How did you die?" P: "This is how I died." Such a conversation is possible only in two situations, in *katabasis* and in sepulchra epigram (also in dreams, presumably). Ultimately the model for this exchange is to be found in the genre model, at *Od.* XI 57–80, where Odysseus asks Elpenor how he came to Hades (57 "Ἐλπῆνορ, πῶς ἦλθες ὑπὸ ζόφον ἠερόεντα;"), and is given a reply, along with the request for burial, to which Odysseus assents, after which the two converse. Significantly, in Virgil's version there is no reply by Aeneas, and no conversation, just the question and response, and to that extent the passage exhibits similarities to sepulchral epigrams with similar exchanges[34]—unimaginable in the Homeric version, where the text narrates a conversation between Odysseus and Elpenor following the exchange (*Od.* XI 81–83).

The culmination of the whole episode has no Homeric intertext. The Sibyl, and not Aeneas, replies to Palinurus, first rebuking him and denying him passage across the Styx, but then consoling him by predicting the fame that will come to Cape Palinurus, and that will be spread precisely by the presence of a cenotaph:

[34] E.g. *AP* VII 163–5; 317 (Callimachus); 470 (Meleager); 503 (Leon. Tar.)

274

"nam tua finitimi, longe lateque per urbes
prodigiis acti caelestibus, ossa piabunt
et statuent **tumulum** et **tumulo** sollemnia mittent,   380
aetern umque locus Palinuri nomen habebit."

Aen. VI 378–81

The culmination of the Palinurus story in *Aen.* V was a virtual epigram, while that of *Aen.* VI is a prediction of the cenotaph to which such a ναυαγικόν, already elaborated through the complex narrative of *Aen.* V and VI, would be affixed.

Conclusion

In Horace *Odes* I 28, Propertius III 7, and Virgil *Aen.* V 833–71, VI 337–83 we have three roughly contemporary Latin engagements with the ναυαγικόν. Whether or not any of these poets was specifically aware of any of the epigrams on the Milan papyrus, those poems nevertheless first of all add to the Hellenistic context of the Augustan texts, a context whose presence Latinists so oddly resist, but that becomes less resistible whenever a new literary papyrus adds to our store of Hellenistic poetry. More importantly, the "problems" of episodicity, of unity, of voice, of consistency, shared by all of these Latin poems, perhaps become less problematic if we see that each poet is in different ways engaging with thematically ordered epigrams. Whether Virgil, Horace and Propertius found their ναυαγικά in the *Garland* of Meleager or on a text such as P. Mil.Vogl. VIII 309, we cannot be sure. What cannot be doubted, however, is the fact that they read and integrated such texts into the eclectic genres of Augustan poetry, just as Eliot, in the epigram with which we began, integrated the same sub-genre into the larger, innovative project of *The Waste Land*.

19

Posidippus' *Iamatika**

Peter Bing
Emory University

The Milan papyrus confronts its modern readers with many surprises, among them—due to its singular subject matter—the short section entitled ἰαματικά (AB 95–101). To help us get our bearings in the terrain of this extraordinary new text, I want in this paper to pose some rudimentary questions such as the following:

1. What are the epigrams about?
2. Do they function as an ensemble?
3. Where should we seek their generic antecedents or models?

and finally,

4. What kind of reader-response do they elicit?

To begin with the most basic: What are these epigrams about? The ἰαματικά comprise only seven poems, all four verses long except the first, which is eight,[1] and all concerning cures, ἰάματα. These cures are sudden and miraculous; they appear as testimony to the beneficent power of the healer-god, Asclepius.[2] With the exception of AB 95, the poems consistently invoke Asclepius,[3] or have to do with his cult.[4] Indeed, even the doctor of poem 1, who discovered a cure for the bite of the Libyan asp, owes his success to having received "all the panacea of Asclepius' sons" (AB 95.5–6).[5]

---

* For their penetrating—and therapeutic—critique of earlier drafts I thank Profs. D. Bright, J. Lee and C. Perkell. If the paper nonetheless remains uncured of all its defects, that is due entirely to the author's pathological stubbornness.

[1] In other words, it totals 32 verses, as does the following section, τρόποι. The only section with fewer verses is that immediately preceding, the ναυαγικά with 26 (AB 89–94). B. Acosta-Hughes points out that these short sections grouped together resemble Callimachus' *Iambi* 2 and 3.

[2] For suddenness as a characteristic of miraculous cures, see Weinreich 1909:197–198.

[3] AB 96.1 Ἀσκληπιέ; AB 97.1 Ἀσκληπιέ; AB 98.3 Παιάν; AB101.1 Ἀσκληπιέ.

[4] AB 99.3 ἀπ᾽ εὐχωλέων Ἀσκληπιοῦ; AB 100.1 τὸν ἥσυχον ὕπνον ἰαύειν, incubation.

[5] His dedication is strictly speaking to Apollo. It is a statue portraying a wasted remnant of a man— the sort of patient he used to save through his discovery. Aristotle (*History of Animals* 8.607a) men-

Proceeding to our second question we ask, in light of so unified a subject matter, whether the poems comprise an artfully arranged set, i.e. a deliberately planned sequence with marked beginning and end. Let us assume as a working hypothesis that they do. Given the section-heading ἰαματικά this is an inherently plausible hypothesis. The title, like that of almost all the other sections, calls attention to the process of editing and classification, in that it consists of the substantivized neuter plural with the denominative suffix -ικά, indicating a *collection* of things classed together, in this case things having to do with cures, ἰάματα.[6] Whether the editorial hand belonged to the poet himself or to a somewhat later compiler we need not say. In any case, the hypothesis allows us to ask potentially useful questions about the ways in which the poems may work together to form a meaningful whole. What, for instance, can we say about the topics covered in the epigrams? Do they signify as a group? I believe they do. For the god is portrayed in the poems as curing an impressive range of illnesses. Taking the epigrams in order, we find—in addition to the snakebite of the first poem—cases of paralysis, epilepsy (the sacred disease), an infected wound made by a metal weapon, deafness, and blindness. It is striking that there is no overlap in these illnesses, that they are each quite different in kind. I think we may thus plausibly conclude that they were intended to be a representative assortment, to stand collectively for the entire spectrum of disease.

That exemplarity squares well with another consideration, namely the identity of the doctor who is the subject of the initial poem, Medeios of Olynthos, son of Lampon. It is highly probable that this doctor was the man of identical name and patronymic known to have held the prestigious position of eponymous priest of Alexander and the *Theoi Adelphoi* at Alexandria in the year 259/8 BCE, and attested in the following year as overseeing the proceeds of the royal tax for medical services, τὸ ἰατρικόν.[7] He was, in other words, a V.I.P., a player in the upper reaches of Philadelphus' court. The section thus opens in a distinctly Ptolemaic key. But more, considering the first poem's markedly greater length (double that of any other in the

....

tions a remedy for this snake's bite—the so-called "septic" drug—without specifying its inventor: ἐξ οὗ ὄφεως ποιοῦσι τὸ σηπτικόν (scil. φάρμακον), καὶ ἄλλως ἀνιάτως. Other authors insist that the bite of the asp is incurable and fatal, cf. Apollonius Rhodius 4.1508–1512, Aelian *On the Characteristics of Animals* 1.54; 9.15. On the identity of this doctor, Medeios of Olynthos, son of Lampon, cf. below.

[6] Cf. Kühner, Blass, and Gerth 1983:I.2,294; no.334.5. This is by far the earliest instance of the adjective ἰαματικός. The same appears to be the case for λιθικός (Diodorus 7.1.1–3), ἀναθηματικός (otherwise first in Polybius 27.18.2–3), and ναυαγικός.

[7] I present the case for identification fully in Bing 2002b. Bastianini and Gallazzi overlook the possibility.

section) and emphatic position, we may reasonably wonder whether the Ptolemaic note carries over into the remaining six poems, and whether that representative assortment reflects the medical interests of this courtier, and was perhaps even compiled in his honor.[8]

Further signs of unified design appear when we ask if the epigrams collectively evoke a particular social context? Again we can answer in the affirmative, they clearly do. The context is that of sanctuaries of Asclepius such as Epidaurus, the most famous, where pilgrims flocked from throughout the Greek world to seek the god's aid in overcoming illness. In the shrine, they offered sacrifice and prayers, and —most strikingly—underwent incubation in the hope that the god would appear to them in their sleep, either to cure outright or show them the road to health. Taken together the epigrams echo the rhythms of life at precisely such a shrine: Patients journey to the god.[9] They sacrifice and pray,[10] they experience the god's power in the night,[11] and make thank-offerings.[12] Finally they go back home again when they're done.[13]

Still other meanings emerge from these poems if we view them as an ensemble. I would suggest that the section offers readers the impression, as they turn from poem to poem, of strolling through a shrine of Asclepius. It allows them to play the part of imaginary pilgrim, or—in a more detached mode—uninvolved observer. In fact, as we shall presently learn, the official testimonials collected and inscribed by

---

[8] Cf. my discussion below of the ἄριϲτοϲ ἀνήρ who is the subject of the section's final poem (AB 101.1). One may wonder why Posidippus is silent concerning Medeios' political appointments. Though there can be no certainty, I can imagine a couple of scenarios. 1) The poem comes from late in Medeios' life, when he was thinking about how he wanted to be remembered. The imperfect tense of the verb referring to his therapeutic activity, ἐϲάου, "[the ones] he used to save" (AB 95.3), would suit a time when he looked back on his medical career as something in the past. It brings to mind the epitaph of Aeschylus (*Life of Aeschylus* 11), which makes no mention of his poetry at all, saying of his life only that "the famous grove of Marathon could tell of his prowess and the thick-haired Mede learned it well." 2) The poem comes from early in Medeios' life, i.e. it reflects his activities prior to his remarkable political rise.

[9] AB 96.1–2: "Antichares came to you, Asclepius, with two canes, dragging his step along the path." (πρὸϲ ϲὲ μὲν Ἀντιχάρηϲ, Ἀϲκληπιέ, ϲὺν δυϲὶ βάκτροιϲ | ἦλθε δι' ἀτραπιτῶν ἴχνοϲ ἐφελκόμενοϲ·).

[10] ϲοὶ δ[ὲ θυη]πολέων (AB 96.3), ἀπ' εὐχωλέων Ἀϲκληπιοῦ (AB 99.3), αἰτεῖται δ' ὑγίειαν (AB 101.3).

[11] AB 97.4: δαῖμον, ἀποξύϲαϲ ᾤχεο νυκτὶ μιῆι, "divinity, you departed having wiped away (the disease) in a single night"; AB 98.3-4: Παιάν, ϲ' εὔ[νοον εἶδεν ἀνώ]δυνοϲ, ὡϲ ἐπ' ὀνείρωι | τὸν πολὺν ἰηθεὶ[ϲ ἐξέφυγ]εν κάματον, "when painless [he beheld you gracious], Paean. So after the dream, being cured [he escaped] his great toil."; AB 100.1: ἡνίκ' ἔδει Ζήνωνα τὸν ἥϲυχον ὕπνον ἰαύειν, "When Zenon had to sleep that gentle sleep".

[12] ἰητήρια ϲοὶ νούϲων, Ἀϲκληπιέ, Κῷοϲ | δωρεῖται Ϲωϲῆ⟨ϲ⟩ ἀργυρέην φιάλην (AB 97.1–2).

[13] οἴκαδ' ἀπή⟨ι⟩ει, (AB 99.3).

the authorities at Epidaurus themselves provide the model for such a reading of the *Iamatika*: they repeatedly envision visitors to the shrine strolling about and perusing inscriptions.[14] In this guise, Posidippus' reader encounters diverse monuments—a cross-section typical of what a pilgrim might actually have seen at a healing-shrine—and pauses to read about them, as the pilgrim might have done through inscriptions: There is the statue in AB 95, the votive phiale of Coan Soses (AB 97), numerous testimonies recounting the wondrous cures of the god, like those on the countless *pinakes* that filled the shrine (AB 96, AB 98, AB 99, AB 100), or finally a worshipper's prayer (AB 101).[15]

The evocation of such a setting in these poems leads to our third question: To what genre do Posidippus' ἰαματικά belong? What is their model? There are notably few epigrams about cures in the *Greek Anthology*, and the handful we possess are mostly late in date.[16] Among inscribed epigrams there is a comparable dearth.[17] Those that we have, most datable in the fourth century BCE and after, are strikingly reticent about anything miraculous in the cures. Take for example the hexameter epigram by the orator Aeschines, which survives both in the *Greek Anthology* and as an inscription at Epidaurus (and happens to be our earliest acrostic):

[Αἰσχίνης Ἀτρο]μήτου Ἀθηναῖος | [Ἀσκληπιῶι ἀ]νέθηκεν.
θνητῶν μὲν τέχναις ἀπορούμενος ἐς δὲ τὸ θεῖον
ἐλπίδα πᾶσαν ἔχων, προλιπὼν εὔπαιδας Ἀθήνας,
ἰάθην ἐλθών, Ἀσκληπιέ, πρὸς τὸ σὸν ἄλσος,
ἕλκος ἔχων κεφαλῆς ἐνιαύσιον, ἐν τρισὶ μησίν.

Aeschines, son of Atrometus, from Athens dedicated (this) to Asclepius.

Despairing of mortal skill, and putting all hope

in the divine, I left Athens of the fair youths

and coming to your grove, Asclepius, was cured

in three months of a sore I'd had on my head for a year.

---

[14] The most explicit is *IG* IV², 1, no.121.22, but cf. also *IG* IV², 1, no.121.33.

[15] Though framed as a maxim, the epigram in fact functions as a prayer, though indirect, for good fortune and health. Cf. my discussion below.

[16] Cf. VI 203 (Philip of Thessalonica); VI 330 (Aeschines); IX 46 (Antipater of Thessalonica); IX 298 (Antiphilos); IX 511 (Anonymous).

[17] Cf. *CEG* 776, Aeschines' acrostic inscription from the first half of the fourth century, 808, 818; Kaibel 803–805; *IG* IV², 1, no.125 = T 431 Edelstein and Edelstein 1998. Except for the last, these references are from L. Rossi's discussion of Theocritus *Epigram* 8 in Rossi 2001:197.

Here there is neither a spectacular illness (a headsore), nor sudden miraculous cure. It takes three months for the sore to heal. A comparable reticence appears in other fourth-century inscriptions.[18] None of them sound like what we find in Posidippus, where the sudden, miraculous cure, which may include paradox, is the rule.

Interestingly, what the marvelous tales in Posidippus' *Iamatika* most closely recall, by contrast, are the *prose* inscriptions set up by temple authorities in the second half of the fourth century BCE at the sanctuary of Epidaurus (*IG* IV², 1, nos.121–124).[19] Four large, carefully incised stelae survive,[20] containing accounts of some 66 miraculous cures.[21] They are entitled not ἰαματικά but ['Iά]ματα τοῦ 'Απόλλωνος καὶ τοῦ 'Ασκλαπιοῦ. You could just as well call them "Asclepius' greatest hits": They were evidently culled from the great mass of votive tablets (*pinakes*), which filled the shrine, and were periodically cleared and buried by temple personnel so as to make room for more.[22]

We catch a glimpse of the transition from private votive to that official, collective text, as well as the addition of a notably miraculous element in the process, in the very first narrative on the stele, for here the private and relatively modest votive inscription is quoted within the text:[23]

---

[18] *CEG* 808: [τόν]δ' ἰατορίας 'Ασκλαπιοι Αἰγινάτας | ηυιός με ηαγίλλοι μνᾶμ' ἔθετο 'Ανδρόκριτος. "Androcritus, the son of Hagillus of Aegina, dedicated me to Asclepius for his healing skill." *CEG* 818: ἀντ' ἀγαθῶν ἔργων, 'Α[σ]κλαπιέ, τόσδ' ἀνέθηκε | αὐτο κα' παίδων δῶρα τάδ' 'Αντίφιλος. "In exchange for good works, Asclepius, Antiphilos dedicated these; they are gifts from himself and his children."

[19] In addition to the *IG*, see the treatments of these inscriptions in Herzog 1931; Edelstein and Edelstein 1998: no.423; LiDonnici 1995. For further inscriptions (not, however, including the above stelae) from Epidaurus and elsewhere, cf. Girone 1998.

[20] Pausanias evidently saw these stelae (II 27.3) since his description is a close match: "In my day there are six left of the stone tablets standing in the enclosure, though there were more in antiquity. The names of men and women healed by Asclepius are engraved on them, with the diseases and how they were healed; the inscriptions are in Doric." Cf. Tzifopoulos 1991:19–20.

[21] Though similar inscriptions also occur in the second century BCE at the sanctuary of Lebena on the S. coast of Crete, they are not found elsewhere. As L. LiDonnici has observed (1995:42), "The preserved finds from the three known major mainland Asklepieia, Epidaurus, Corinth and Athens present the appearance of a . . . regional style or preference for certain types of votives over others. Epidauros is best known for narrative inscriptions; Corinth lacks inscriptions but is rich in terra-cotta body-part votives, while Athens and Piraeus have many stone votive reliefs, without any text. Each of these types is poorly represented from the other sites. This may reflect the taste of the respective districts and the availability in each area of craftsmen and materials."

[22] LiDonnici (1995:66) suggests that "Collection may have occurred every few years as the sanctuary became overloaded with votives . . ." and that there may have been "*several* episodes of collection and arrangement of tales onto successively larger and probably less numerous stelai . . ."

[23] The included votive seems to have been metrical (two hexameters and a pentameter):

Οὐ μέγε[θο]ς πίνακος θαυμαστέον, ἀλλὰ τὸ θεῖον,
πένθ' ἔτη ὡς ἐκύησε ἐγ γαστρὶ Κλεὼ βάρος, ἔστε

[Κλ]εὼ πένθ' ἔτη ἐκύησε. αὔτα πέντ' ἐνιαυτοὺς ἤδη κυοῦσα ποὶ τὸν | [θε]ὸν ἱκέτις ἀφίκετο καὶ ἐνεκάθευδε ἐν τῶι ἀβάτωι· ὡς δὲ τάχισ | [τα] ἐξῆλθε ἐξ αὐτοῦ καὶ ἐκ τοῦ ἱαροῦ ἐγένετο, κόρον ἔτεκε, ὃς εὐ | [θ]ὺς γενόμενος αὐτὸς ἀπὸ τᾶς κράνας ἐλοῦτο καὶ ἅμα τᾶι ματρὶ | [π]εριῆρπε. τυχοῦσα δὲ τούτων ἐπὶ τὸ ἄνθεμα ἐπεγράψατο· Οὐ μέγε | [θο]ς πίνακος θαυμαστέον, ἀλλὰ τὸ θεῖον, πένθ' ἔτη ὡς ἐκύησε ἐγ γασ | τρὶ Κλεὼ βάρος, ἔστε ἐγκατεκοιμάθη καί μιν ἔθηκε ὑγιῆ.

Cleo was with child for five years. After she had been pregnant for five years she came as a suppliant to the god and slept in the Abaton. As soon as she left it and got outside the temple precincts she bore a son who, immediately after birth, washed himself at the fountain and walked about with his mother. In return for this favor she inscribed on her offering: "Admirable is not the greatness of the tablet, but the divinity, in that Cleo carried the burden in her stomach for five years, until she slept in the Temple and he made her sound."

(*IG* IV², 1, no.121, 3–6).[24]

The only miraculous element in the quoted tablet is the five-year pregnancy—and even here one may wonder whether the original votive truly concerned child-birth, as it describes what Cleo carried simply as βάρος, and makes no mention of delivery. The framing narrative embellishes this nucleus with Cleo's urgent depar-ture from the temple and immediate birth. It has her deliver, moreover, a child of incredible maturity, who washes himself in the fountain as soon as he is born, and is able to walk around—and presumably home, as well—with his mother. The modest votive is thus transformed from a personal commemoration into a wonder-tale celebrating the god's miraculous benevolence—an aretalogy, in other words.

We see here how the texts selected for preservation were exceptional and wondrous in character (or capable of being made so), able to fulfill an ongoing aretalogical function that set them apart from workaday commemorations of less spectacular illnesses. Four of Posidippus' epigrams (AB 96, AB 98, AB 99, and AB 100) share this aretalogical character, apparently not conforming to any other epigrammatic type (though see the discussion of AB 100 below).

....
ἐγκατεκοιμάθη καί μιν ἔθηκε ὑγιῆ.

The inscription does its best, however, to mask the meter and assimilate it to the surrounding prose by breaking lines in mid-verse and mid-word (μέγε | [θο]ς, γασ | τρὶ) and using *scriptio plena* (ἐκύησε ἐγ, ἔθηκε ὑγιῆ).

24 Translation by Edelstein.

I would suggest that inscriptions such as those at Epidaurus provided
Posidippus with a model for these poems, particularly with regard to his content.
In general, the maladies enumerated in those poems concerned with Asclepius find
close parallels in the Epidaurian inscriptions, as do the character of the cures.[25]
Recent scholars have explored how the early Hellenistic poets display in their
epigrams a keen awareness of their genre's inscriptional roots, and often play—as
epigrammatists of later generations do *not*—on contemporary epigraphic topics
and style.[26] Posidippus was well-positioned to indulge in such play, for in addition
to being a master of the *literary* tradition—ἐν βύβλοις πεπονημένη, as he
describes his soul in a previously known epigram (*AP* XII 98.3 = 6.3 GP)—he also
knew his way around monuments, winning acclaim at particular shrines as a poet
of inscribed verse. An inscription at Thermon from 263/2 records that the Aetolian
league granted him proxeny in his capacity as ἐπιγραμματοποιός (*IG* IX² 1
17 A = Testimonia 3 AB), and he also seems to appear in a proxeny list from the
270s at Delphi (*Fouilles de Delphes* III 3 no.192 = Testimonia 2 AB). As to the
Iamatika, we need not think exclusively of Epidaurus. I wonder whether
Posidippus' work in Egypt exposed him to the cult of Imouthes/Asclepius at
Memphis where, as D. J. Thompson (1988:210) notes, "the prayers and expectations of the Egyptian stelae with tales of miracles the god performs are indeed
similar in tone and content to contemporary Greek inscriptions from the shrine of
the god Asklepios at Epidaurus." Poems by Posidippus certainly made it to
Memphis, as we know from the Firmin-Didot papyrus, so why not the poet
himself? In the ἰαματικά Posidippus used his familiarity with such settings to draw
on an epigraphic model that scholars had not previously contemplated. Yet in principle it is a typically Hellenistic move: The poet here translates the subject matter

---

[25] The lame man who approaches the god on two canes in AB 96 resembles a paralytic in the inscrip-
tion (*IG* IV² 1 123.123ff.), εἰσελθὼν | [εἰς τὸ ἄβατ]ον μετὰ δύο βακτηριᾶν ὑγιὴς ἐξῆλθε
The epilepsy that plagued Coan Soses in AB 97 is likewise represented at Epidaurus, *IG* IV², 1
no.123.115. Numerous cases in the inscription record cures from weapons lodged and festering in
the body. Posidippus' Archytas, who "had kept the deadly bronze for six years/in his thigh . . . a
festering wound" (AB 98) recalls the Epidaurian example of Euhippos, who "had had for six years
the point of a spear in his jaw" (*IG* IV², 1, no.121.95 = T 423, 12 Edelstein and Edelstein 1998. Cf
also *IG* IV², 1, no.122.55 and 64 = T 423, 30, 32 Edelstein and Edelstein 1998). Interestingly there
don't appear to be any cases of deafness among the Epidaurian *Iamata* to compare with that of Ascla
the Cretan in AB 99. But compare the late Epidaurian inscription of Cuttius the Gaul, *IG* IV², 1
440. Finally, blindness is a common ailment in the sanctuary of Asclepius (cf. *IG* IV², 1, no.121.33
72, 120, 125; *IG* IV², 1, no.122.7, 64; *IG* IV², 1, no.123.129, cf. also *AP* IX 298). In *Iamatika* (
(AB 100) Posidippus gives it a paradoxical twist, however, by having the aged Zenon's restored sigh
last for only two days before he dies.

[26] See particularly Rossi 2001 and Fantuzzi and Hunter 2002:397–448 in the section, "L'epigramma
funerario e dedicatorio: convenzioni epigrafiche e variazioni epigrammatiche tra il IV e il II secolo
a.C." of the chapter "L' epigramma."

of a prose-genre into poetic form, and shifts it from its inscriptional medium onto the scroll.[27]

[27] Of course Aristophanes recreated in comic verse, and to hilarious effect, the workings of such a shrine in his *Plutus*. Comedy, however, does not evoke the inscribed tradition, while epigram insists on it through its generic history and retention of epigraphic conventions.

Interestingly, among the Epidaurian inscriptions we may find an epigraphic counterpart to the transferral of prose narrative into verse, *inscribed* verse in this instance. On the first of the Epidaurian stelae (*IG* IV², 1, no.121.107 = T 423, 15 Edelstein and Edelstein 1998) there is a third person account of the miraculous transformation of Hermodikos of Lampsakos from helpless paralytic into mighty muscleman, capable of superhuman feats:

Ἑρμόδικος Λαμψακηνὸς ἀκρατὴς τοῦ σώματος. τοῦτον ἐγκαθεύ | δοντα
ἰάσατο καὶ ἐκελήσατο ἐξελθόντα λίθον ἐνεγκεῖν εἰς τὸ | ἱαρὸν ὁπόσσον
δύναιτο μέγιστον· ὁ δὲ τὸμ πρὸ τοῦ ἀβάτου κεῖμε | | νον ἤνικε.

Hermodikos of Lampsakos was paralyzed in body. This one, when he slept in the Temple, the god healed and ordered him upon coming out to bring to the Temple as large a stone and he could. The man brought the stone which now lies before the Abaton.

(transl. Edelstein)

As the commentary in the *IG* notes, this stone has been found: *repertus est lapis proxime a templi latere orientali. Pondus computandum fecit Bl. C. 334 kg.* Indeed, Herzog 1931:102, estimated the weight at 375 kg, that is 845 pounds! An inscription *post-dating* this narrative, apparently from the third century BCE—*litterae saec. III a. Chr. elegantes*, as stated in the *IG*—translates it into first person poetry (*IG* IV², 1, 125 = T 431 Edelstein and Edelstein 1998=II.3 Girone 1998:53–57):

Ἑρμόδικ[ος Λαμψακ]ηνὸς
σῆς ἀρετῆς [παράδειγμ]', Ἀσκληπιέ, | τόνδε ἀνέθηκα
π]έτρον ἀειρά | μενος, πᾶσι[ν ὁρᾶν φανερόν, | |
ὄψιν σῆς τέχνης· πρὶν γὰρ | σὰς εἰς χέρας ἐλθεῖν |
σῶν τε τέκνων κεῖμαι | νούσου ὕπο στυγερᾶς |
ἔμπυος ὢν στῆθος χει | | ρῶν τε ἀκρατής· σὺ δέ, | Παιάν,
πεῖσάς με ἄρασθαι | τόνδε, ἄνοσον διάγειν.

Hermodikos of Lampsakos

As an example of your power, Asclepius, I have put up this
    stone which I had lifted up, clear for all to see,
a manifestation of your art. For before I came under the care of your hands
    and those of your children, I was stricken by a wretched illness,
an abscess in my chest, my hands paralyzed. But you, Paean,
    by ordering me to lift up this rock made me live free from disease.

(transl. after Edelstein)

It may be, of course, that the prose version was taken from an original verse-inscription, damaged or worn over time, and hence re-inscribed. Could it be, however, that the verse-inscription is the secondary phenomenon, and that literary epigrams such as Posidippus' prompted, in their turn, demand for poetic versions? It is worth noting that the epigram heightens the miraculous element by specifying paralysis of the hands and an abscess in the chest—precisely those parts of the body with which Hermodikos presumably hefted the huge boulder—while the prose inscription leaves the ailment as the more general paralysis of the body, ἀκρατὴς τοῦ σώματος.

Peter Bing

This brings us to our final question, regarding reader-response: How should a reader evaluate the miraculous cures in Posidippus' epigrams, situated as they are at a remove from both their generic model (the prose inscription, already remote from its source in private votives) and its physical setting in a shrine?[28] Do the poems endorse the cures or subvert them? In inquiring thus, we implicitly ask as well how Posidippus, an erudite and sophisticated reader, evaluated the cures he encountered on stone at shrines like Epidaurus, and how his literary reworking of such material reflects his response, as mediated for his readership. Indeed, it is well to bear in mind the multiple layers of interpretive mediation in play here, for in experiencing the *Iamatika* an audience is reading Posidippus' readings of the sanctuary authorities' readings of the personal votives. In any case, to contemplate the *Iamatika* on the scroll is to have an altogether different experience from that of the stricken pilgrim encountering engraved *Iamata* at a shrine, and the distance between these experiences may incline the poet's readers toward a more detached, perhaps even skeptical stance—an inclination no doubt even stronger for a modern scholar/reader with the added distance of time, the attendant change in mentality.

Leaving the epigrams aside for a moment, it is useful to recall that in ancient times people could be quite skeptical of what went on in healing-sanctuaries. While the archaeological record leaves no doubt that a sanctuary like Epidaurus enjoyed enormous popular esteem, particularly from the mid-fourth century onwards,[29] nevertheless the cult did not elicit universal trust. There is the story that tells how Diogenes the Cynic once saw a woman prostrate herself before the god. "Wishing to free her [and those like her] of their superstition, . . . he dedicated to Asclepius a fierce ruffian who, whenever people prostrated themselves, would run up to them and beat them up." (βουλόμενος αὐτῆς περιελεῖν τὴν δεισιδαιμονίαν . . . τῷ ᾽Ασκληπιῷ ἀνέθηκε πλήκτην, ὃς τοὺς ἐπὶ στόμα πίπτοντας ἐπιτρέχων συνέτριβεν, Diogenes Laertius VI 37–38). Now one might consider the skepticism of a Diogenes an extreme case, but we find similar sentiments voiced among the inscribed Epidaurian ᾽Ιάματα themselves. One text in particular, *IG* IV², 1, no.121.22, placed near the start of the first stele, and so perhaps intended programmatically, presents starkly conflicting assessments of the god's miraculous cures. Perhaps it can also help us set interpretive parameters, and provide a baseline for evaluating possible reader-response to Posidippus' *Iamatika*:

᾽Ανὴρ τοὺς τᾶς χηρὸς δακτύλιους ἀκρατεῖς ἔχων πλὰν | ἑνὸς
ἀφίκετο ποὶ τὸν θεὸν ἱκέτας· θεωρῶν δὲ τοὺς ἐν τῶι ἰαρῶι |

---

[28] For epigram's shift from monument to scroll, and its impact on reader-response, cf. Bing 1995:115–131; Bing 1998:21–43; Bing 2002a:39–66; Gutzwiller 1998:47–114; Fantuzzi/Hunter 2002:397–448.

[29] Cf. Tomlinson 1983:25; LiDonnici 1995:10f.

πίνακας ἀπίστει τοῖς ἰάμασιν καὶ ὑποδιέσυρε τὰ ἐπιγράμμα
│ │ [τ]α. ἐγκαθεύδων δὲ ὄψιν εἶδε· ἐδόκει ὑπὸ τῶι ναῶι
ἀστραγάλιζον │ [τ]ος αὐτοῦ καὶ μέλλοντος βάλλειν τῶι
ἀστραγάλωι, ἐπιφανέντα │ [τ]ὸν θεὸν̣ ἐφαλέσθαι ἐπὶ τὰν
χῆρα καὶ ἐκτεῖναί οὐ τοὺς δακτύ⟨λ⟩ │ λους· ὡς δ' ἀποβαίη,
δοκεῖν συγκάμψας τὰν χῆρα καθ' ἕνα ἐκτείνειν │ τῶν
δακτύλων· ἐπεὶ δὲ πάντας ἐξευθύναι, ἐπερωτῆν νιν τὸν θεόν,
│ │ εἰ ἔτι ἀπιστησοῖ τοῖς ἐπιγράμμασι τοῖς ἐπὶ τῶμ πινάκων
τῶν │ κατὰ τὸ ἱερόν, αὐτὸς δ' οὐ φάμεν. "ὅτι τοίνυν
ἔμπροσθεν ἀπίστεις │ αὐτο[ῖ]ς οὐκ ἐοῦσιν ἀπίστοις, τὸ λοιπὸν
ἔστω τοι," φάμεν, "Ἄπιστος │ ὄν̣[ομα]." ἁμέρας δὲ γενομένας
ὑγιὴς ἐξῆλθε.

A man whose fingers, with the exception of one, were paralyzed, came as
a suppliant to the god. While looking at the tablets in the Temple he
expressed incredulity regarding the cures and scoffed at the inscriptions.
But in his sleep he saw a vision. It seemed to him that, as he was playing
at dice below the temple and was about to cast the dice, the god appeared,
sprang upon his hand, and stretched out his [the patient's] fingers. When
the god had stepped aside it seemed to him [the patient] that he [the
patient] bent his hand and stretched out all his fingers one by one. When
he had straightened them all, the god asked him if he would still be
incredulous of the inscriptions on the tablets in the Temple. He answered
that he would not. "Since, then, formerly you were incredulous of the
cures, though they were not incredible, for the future," he said, "your
name shall be 'Incredulous'." When day dawned he walked out sound.[30]

I believe that we have here one potential roadmap for interpreting the *Iamatika*
of Posidippus. For this is a text about how to read accounts of miraculous cures. In
it we are presented with two models of reader-response, twin poles marking the
end-points along an axis of belief, the one skeptical, the other favoring credence. Of
course, the narrative strongly endorses the latter: readers should believe wholeheartedly in the powers of the god. That conclusion should not surprise, given the
document's setting at the god's chief shrine. On the other hand it scarcely compels
Posidippus' readers, who operate under quite different circumstances, to discard
whatever skepticism they may have had. Posidippus does not stage as a guide for his
audience any comparable encounter with divinity (nor even provide them an
authoritative voice or point of view), and so their experience must *a fortiori* remain

---

30 Translation by Edelstein.

open to both poles of interpretation set out on the Epidaurian stele, and all gradations in between.

Consider the case of Soses of Cos in AB 97:

> ἰητήρια coὶ νούcων, Ἀσκληπιέ, Κῶιος
> δορεῖται Cωcῆ‹c› ἀργυρέην φιάλην,
> οὗ cὺ τὸν ἑξαετῆ {α}κάματον ‹θ›' ἄμα καὶ νόcον ἱ{ε}ρήν,
> δαῖμον, ἀποξύcαc ὤιχεο νυκτὶ μιῆι.

> In payment to you for curing his sickness, Asclepius, Coan
> Soses dedicates a silver libation bowl,
> he whose six-year illness, together with the sacred disease,
> divinity, you came and wiped away in a single night.

Nothing in this epigram militates against our considering it a stock expression of popular piety. To be sure, a silver phiale is a particularly handsome gift, but ἰητήρια (= ἴατρα), "thank-offerings for cure", are attested in numerous inscriptions at Epidaurus (cf. *LSJ* s.v. ἴατρα). Similarly epilepsy, the sacred disease, is well known in the Epidaurian stelae (*IG* IV², 1 no. 123, 115). Six years is a conventional duration for an illness (*IG* IV², 1 no.121, 95, Hippocrates *Epidemics* 5.46, and AB 98). And the traditions of the god's healing hand, which here "wipes away" the disease, and also of his nocturnal appearance to the pilgrim, are likewise quite common, as Weinreich has shown in detail.[31]

But Soses turns up again in a starkly different light after just five poems, in the second epigram of the section entitled τρόποι (AB 103):[32]

> οὐδ'[{ε}] ἐπερωτήcαc με νόμου χάριν οὔτε πόθε‹ν› γῆc
> εἰμὶ παραcτείχειc οὔτε [τίc o]ὔτε τίνων·
> ἀλλὰ cύ μ' {ε} ἡcυχι[ωc ἴδε κείμεν]ον, εἰμὶ δ' ἐγὼ παῖc
> Ἀλκαίου Cωcῆc Κῶ[ιοc, ὁμόc, ποτ]ε, cοῦ

> You didn't even ask, for custom's sake, what land I'm from;
> no, nor who I am, nor descended from whom. You just walk by.
> Come on, [look at] me [lying] peaceably. I'm the son
> of Alcaeus, Soses of Cos, [alive once, same] as you.

[31] Weinreich 1909:1–45 and 76–79 respectively.
[32] As Bastianini and Gallazzi note, the reconstruction of the second couplet is quite speculative. I prefer their alternative supplement, ὁμόc, ποτ]ε, cοῦ rather than ὁμόc, φίλ]ε, cοῦ, for AB 103.4, since it better suits the feisty speaking voice of the first couplet.

286

Though he had appeared cured of both epilepsy and his unspecified six-year illness in the third *Iamatikon* (AB 97), poor Soses is envisioned here as having suffered a grave setback—the gravest: he is dead! Might the title τρόποι refer among other things to such sharp "turns" of fortune as we see between these two poems (*LSJ* s.v. I)? In any case, it is hard retrospectively not to find humor in the earlier poem. For, despite his pious gratitude before, Soses has become a cranky old corpse. That silver phiale, precious as it was, did not ensure happiness. Now Soses makes no allusion to prior blessings, no reference to divinity at all. He just berates the passerby for his breach of decorum in not inquiring about his identity. The four-fold repetition of negatives in metrically emphatic positions—including verse-start, bucolic diaeresis, and following the caesura of the pentameter—is a humorously over-the-top way of having Soses express his indignation. One thing is certain: Nothing about the way he lies in his tomb is "peaceable" (ἡϲυχι[ωϲ . . . κείμεν]ον)! On the contrary he makes darn sure that, willy-nilly, the passerby *will* hear his full provenance, patronymic included (which had been omitted from the first poem), especially as he had so rudely failed to ask about it. In light of this unexpected reversal in fortune, the first poem—and with it, Soses—appear tinged with comic irony.[33]

An epigram that permits a comparably double reading is the sixth *Iamatikon* (AB 100), about the elderly blind man, Zenon:

ἡνίκ' ἔδει Ζήνωνα τὸν ἥϲυχον ὕπνον ἰαύειν,
    πέμπτον ἐπ' εἰκοϲτῶι τυφλὸν ἐόντα θέρει,
ὀγδωκονταέτηϲ ὑγιὴϲ γένετ' ἠέλιον δέ
    δὶϲ μοῦ[νον βλέψαϲ τὸ]ν βαρὺν εἶδ'{ε} Ἀίδην.

When Zenon had to sleep that gentle sleep,
    in blindness for the twenty-fifth summer,
at age eighty he was cured. But glimpsing
    the sun only twice, he beheld oppressive Hades.

A pious reading (which can certainly be justified given the epigram's location in the *Iamatika*) might construe this poem as conventionally aretalogical. When Zenon, elderly though he was and blind for a quarter century already, sought divine help for his affliction through incubation ("When [he] had to sleep that gentle

---

[33] Indeed, we may even find an explicit link to the earlier poem if, instead of Bastianini and Gallazzi's νομου χάριν in v.1, we read νόϲου χάριν, i.e. "on account of [my unspecified] sickness". The passerby is squeamish about stopping at the tomb due to that disease, which proved fatal. The god, it appears, had not *definitively* cured Soses.

sleep", line 1), the god gladdened his final days by miraculously restoring his sight
If, according to the proverb, one should count no man happy till he dies, then
surely (that pious reading suggests) Zenon may be accounted such.
But the poem also allows a darker construction: on a purely formal level it
could just as well be an epitaph. One would not have been surprised to find it in
Book VII of the *Greek Anthology*.[34] Indeed, I believe one could assign it to a well
known, presumably epideictic sepulchral type, the "paradox in death". Unique
among the poems of the *Iamatika*, this one contains no mention of the healing god
That, of course, could be supplied from the context within the section. Thus it was
obvious to read the first verse as referring to incubation. In itself, however, the
phrase ὕπνον ἰαύειν in the first verse could just as well refer to death (as a
GV 455, 1874.7, *AP* XVI 375; for death as a "sleep" cf. *LSJ* s.v.). That is, when
Zenon was going to die, his sight was suddenly restored—a bitter blessing, as it
turned out. For with its pointed final words, εἶδ᾽ {ε} Ἀίδην, the epigram manifestly plays on the etymology of Hades as "invisible", ἀιδής, the place where
"nothing is seen" (cf. e.g. Plato, *Cratylus* 403a).[35] Rather than enjoy the sightless
sleep of death (ὕπνον ἰαύειν), Zenon now can see. But what does he behold?
Nothing, *for ever*—a grimly ironic, paradoxical demise.[36]
A further epigram that seems to invite double reading is that on Asclas of Crete
(AB 99):

> ὁ Κρὴς κωφὸς ἐὼν Ἀcκλ[ᾶc, μη]δ᾽ οἷος ἀκούειν
> αἰγιαλῶν οιος μηδ᾽ ἀνέμων πάταγον
> εὐθὺc ἀπ᾽ εὐχωλέων Ἀcκληπιοῦ οἴκαδ᾽ ἀπή⟨ι⟩ει
> καὶ τὰ διὰ πλίνθων ῥήματ᾽ ἀκουcόμενοc.

Asclas the Cretan, deaf and unable to hear either
the [crash] of the surf or clatter of winds,
suddenly because of his vows for Asclepius went home
a man about to hear conversations even through brick walls.

How we interpret this poem depends on a linguistic nicety—a nuance of
aspect—to which a hasty reader might turn a deaf ear. Until the final line a pious
interpretation seems perfectly appropriate. Asclas' deafness is absolute; it cuts him

---

[34] I owe this observation to Richard Thomas.
[35] Indeed, in an active sense the adjective can also mean "blind" (cf. *LSJ* s.v.).
[36] For comparable "paradox in death", cf. e.g. Dioskorides 33 GP = *AP* VII 76, where a mariner aban-
dons sea-faring for farming, only to be overtaken after death by the flooding Nile, which consigns
him to the watery grave of a shipwrecked man, ναυηγὸν τάφον verse 6.

off from even the loudest sounds of nature. Upon visiting the shrine, he makes vows to Asclepius, then heads back home. The start of verse 3, εὐθὺς, leaves us primed for a sudden, miraculous cure in the manner of the Epidaurian inscriptions, and the beginning of verse 4 appears to confirm that expectation (καὶ τὰ διὰ πλίνθων ῥήματ'). But the future participle ἀκουσόμενος, pointedly placed as the poem's last word, creates a space for irony. For it suggests that Asclas left the shrine as yet unaware of what he had acquired there: "a man *about to hear* conversations even through brick walls". That ignorance sets the pilgrim in a comic light. The verb of cognition moreover functions as a cue, inviting the reader retrospectively to hear humor in other elements of the poem. Asclas did not simply gain the ability to hear, but (as he presumably discovered not long after) the superhuman capacity to over-hear conversations "even through brick walls". No doubt διὰ πλίνθων is miraculous, but it is also very funny, suggesting a range of domestic or public contexts in which his new-found talent might be used. There is comic potential, too, in his ethnicity: Cretans famously prized reticence, so the prospect of indiscriminately hearing *everyone's* conversation might seem more torment than blessing. Bastianini and Gallazzi may have been right when they comment that the poet describes this cure "con una sfumatura di sorriso."

Of course it is important to recall that humor is not necessarily at odds with a pious reading. Greek religion embraces the comic in ways that startle modern sensibilities schooled in the Judaeo-Christian tradition. The tales in the Epidaurian inscriptions, too, are at times distinctly, and no doubt deliberately, funny.[37] Thus humor alone should not suffice to make Posidippus' readers incredulous—unless that incredulity has the semantic range it has in the narrative of the skeptical visitor in the Epidaurian stele, where the term could signify distinct things under different circumstances, and the name "Incredulous" in fact bespoke *credence*.

I want to close with a look at the last of the *Iamatika* (AB 101), an epigram once again susceptible to double reading, but which perhaps illuminates a different point along the interpretive axis traced above:

ὄλβον ἄριστος ἀν[ήρ], Ἀσκληπιέ, μέτριον αἰτεῖ
    —coὶ δ' ὀρέγειν πολλὴ βουλομένωι δύναμις—
αἰτεῖται δ' ὑγί‹ει›αν· ἄκη δύο· ταῦτα γὰρ εἶναι
    ἠθέων ὑψηλὴ φαίνεται ἀκρόπολις.

---

[37] Weinreich 1909:89–90 makes the following comment about several of the Epidaurian miracles (a cure for baldness: *IG* IV², 1, no.121.122; a cure for lice, in which the god sweeps away the vermin with a broom: *IG* IV², 1, no.122.45): "Bei diesen Wundern möge man bedenken, dass die Aretalogie nicht nur erbauen, sondern auch unterhalten will. Deshalb wird Humor und Komik nicht verschmäht."

> The noblest man, Asclepius, asks for moderate wealth
> —great is your power to bestow it when you wish—
> and he asks for health: remedies both. For these appear to be
> a towering citadel for human conduct.

Coming after the particular instances of divine cures in the previous poems, this epigram appears to confirm their value by generalizing the importance of health.[38] With its idealized subject—the indefinite ἄριϲτοϲ ἀν[ήρ—and its impersonal, metaphor-rich summation (ἄκη δύο· ταῦτα γὰρ εἶναι | ἠθέων ὑψηλὴ φαίνεται ἀκρόπολιϲ lines 3–4), the poem functions as a gnomic conclusion drawn from the aforegoing tales.

We have seen, however, that the outcome of divine therapy is not always expected, or indeed happy. For Soses of Cos, to be healed of his epilepsy was doubtless a blessing (AB 97), but his epitaph a mere 20 verses—five poems—later in the τρόποι (AB 103) exposes its ultimate futility. Miraculous cures have their limits, for as that poem's fragmentary final words seem to suggest, Soses is only mortal ("same] as you", ὁμός, ποτ]ε, ϲοῦ). That is one condition the god cannot cure.[39] Similarly for elderly Zenon (AB 100) it appeared that the gift of sight arrived with unforeseen consequences. Take care, the poem seems to suggest, what you beg from the gods; they may grant it. The same could apply to the deaf man, Asclas of Crete (AB 99), who leaves the shrine with more than he bargained for, the potentially disagreeable ability to hear "even through brick walls".

The issue here may be less one of skepticism or belief than of how one thinks about wondrous cures. One potential response to the *Iamatika* might be to suppose that they do not so much tempt one to disbelieve in the possibility of miracles, as make one question their efficacy in creating human happiness, in fulfilling one's desires: for miracles sometimes prove to be either inconvenient or useless for humans locked in the condition of mortality. As such, the cures represented in these poems become yet one more example of a far broader theme, to wit the problematic nature of divine-human interaction.

In this light, the final epigram invites a different, less staunchly affirmative, reading. The poem emphasizes moderation. μέτριον, the key adjective in this respect in verse 1, is accentuated through its placement following the bucolic diaeresis, at the other end of the line from its noun. Exemplifying a *human* stan-

---

[38] Bastianini and Gallazzi cite numerous instances of the view that health (often coupled with wealth) is the most important of goods, such as *PMG* 890, the paean of Ariphron *PMG* 813, Simonides *PMG* 604, Pindar *Olympian* 5.23, etc.

[39] Asclepius notoriously tried to raise a mortal from the dead, but was struck by Zeus' lightning for his transgression, cf. Pindar *Pythian* 3.55–58.

dard of measure, ὄλβον . . . μέτριον contrasts in an essential way with the divinity's expansive πολλὴ . . . δύναμις of verse 2. Similarly, note the ontological opposition inherent in the juxtaposition ἄρι̣ϲτο̣ϲ ἀν̣[ήρ], Ἀϲκληπιέ, v.1. In light of this emphasis, one may plausibly take μέτριον as modifying not just ὄλβον in verse 1, but as extending to ὑγί⟨ει⟩αν in verse 3.[40] This possibility is all the more appealing given how closely the poem binds together ὄλβοϲ and ὑγίεια, classing them into the single category, ἄκη, and subsuming them into the unitary image, ἀκρόπολιϲ.[41] On this interpretation, the noblest person requests not only "moderate wealth", but "*moderate* health". That is, he does not rely on the prospect of a divine cure, which—even if he were so fortunate as to receive one—might lead to unforeseen and untoward consequences. Rather he prays for what *human* methods can achieve, a more modest general fitness of body and mind which is a foundation for proper conduct. Of course the only *humanly* wrought cure in the *Iamatika* was that of Medeios, son of Lampon, in the first poem of the section (AB 95). It now appears that he was indeed an ἄριστος ἀνήρ, one of the foremost of the Ptolemaic ἄριστοι (Bing 2002b). Perhaps it is he that is meant here and implicitly exhorted to pray.[42]

I use the word "pray" advisedly here, for although this epigram is framed as a maxim, the invocation of Asclepius in verse 1 and parenthetical address to the god in verse 2 suggest that the poem is in fact an indirect prayer. Perhaps that indirection is meant to characterize the tact and moderation not just of the noble doctor Medeios, son of Lampon, but of the speaking voice itself. It tells us what an ἄριϲτοϲ ἀνήρ should do, but leaves unspoken the implication that such a pronouncement itself bespeaks an ἄριστος ἀνήρ—here obliquely requesting moderate wealth and health on its own behalf. Discreet yet authoritative, this anonymous voice may plausibly be identified as the poet's. Ending the section then with a traditional form of poetic closure, a prayer, the poet pleads for something other than a miracle, and more moderate—counsel which may be compatible with the Stoic orientation that some scholars have found in Posidippus (Gutzwiller 1998:157–162). At the close of the *Iamatika* its readers must decide if that plea retrospectively colors their response to the wonders they encountered before.

---

[40] For μέτριος two-termination, cf. *LSJ*, s.v. Or could this be simply an *anacolouthon*?

[41] In this way the epigram actualizes the traditional concept of πλουθυγίεια, which Bastianini and Gallazzi trace in their commentary *ad* verses 19–21.

[42] If that is correct, then given the wondrous nature of his cure for snakebite he may have been less ready to pray for only "moderate health", i.e. to take μέτριον as modifying ὑγί⟨ει⟩αν as well as ὄλβον— for that reading subtly undercuts his achievement. Nothing compelled him to read it thus, however: ὑγί⟨ει⟩αν can just as well stand alone.

20

'Tropoi' (Posidippus AB 102–103)

Dirk Obbink
University of Oxford

The section comprising the eight poems following col. xv 23 in P.Mil.Vogl. VIII 309 (Posidippus AB 102–109) is headed by the sub-title Τρόποι. It comes late in the collection as preserved, but it was not its final one: the blank space left after AB 109 originally contained the heading of another section, now lost, but which may have been *Erotika*.[1] If so, this would be a category of poetry that might have been expected in any self-respecting Hellenistic collection of epigrams, but which is otherwise absent in this collection represented by the Milan roll, as far as it has been preserved.

Not so the *Tropoi*. The expected content of a section sub-titled *Tropoi*, is anything but clear. The last four *Tropoi* are frustratingly fragmentary, and the second pair harbor grave uncertainties of reconstruction. The reconstruction of the first two poems of the *Tropoi*, by contrast, is at least reasonably clear in outline if not in detail. They are especially noteworthy in that they comprise the clearest examples in the collection of a set of intentionally paired and ordered successive epigrams.[2] I give here their texts as printed by AB:

(i) AB 102:

τί πρὸς ἔμ' ὧδ' ἔστητε; τί μ' οὐκ ἠάσατ' ἰαύειν,
   εἰρόμενοι τίς ἐγὼ καὶ πόθεν ἢ ποδαπός·
στείχετέ μου παρὰ σῆμα· Μενοίτιός εἰμι Φιλάρχω
   Κρής, ὀλιγορρήμων ὡς ἂν ἐπὶ ξενίης.

---

[1] AB 110, the first poem in the final section of the papyrus as preserved, begins with references to 'Spring' (εἴαρος), Ζεφυρ[, and [ὀ]κνεῖν, 'to be pressed'—thus recalling Sappho fr. 95,1–4 in Ezra Pound's famous adaptation, 'Papyrus': see Seelbach 1970:83–84.

[2] Cf. above 'Posidippus on Papyri Then and Now' (in this volume) where I argue that AB 115–116 also appeared contemporaneously in a professionally produced edition of Posidippus' epigrams; but that edition was not that of the Milan roll.

Why have you stopped here, next to me? Why haven't you let me sleep,
asking who I am, where I come from or to what country I belong?
Go past my tomb. I am Menoetius, the son of Phylarchus,
from Crete, a man of few words as you'd expect in a foreign land.

(ii) AB 103

οὐδ' ἐπερωτήσας με νόμου χάριν οὔτε πόθεν γῆς
εἰμὶ παραστείχεις οὔτε [τίς ο]ὔτε τίνων·
ἀλλὰ σύ μ' ἡσυχί[ως ἴδε κείμεν]ον, εἰμὶ δ' ἐγὼ παῖς
'Αλκαίου Cωσῆς Κῶ[ιος, ὁμός, φίλ]ε, coῦ.

In breach of custom, you didn't even ask me from where I come,
and you walk by: not even who I am, or from what family.

Come on then, take a good look at me lying here in peace: I am the son
of Alcaeus, Soses of Cos, the same sort, friend, as you.

The epigrams purport to record the speech of two dead men, each speaking
from the tomb on the same theme, each suggesting a different attitude of the
passerby toward them and their burial. The first is unfriendly and unwelcoming;
Menoetius of Crete is portrayed through his speech as a *misanthrope* or δύσκολος.
The second is similarly critical of the passerby for ignoring him, and instead
demands attention and sympathy. The second directly inverts some of the same
topics used in the first ('why are you asking who I am, from where I come or what
country I belong' in AB 102 becomes 'why didn't you ask me from where I come
. . . not even who I am, or from what family' in AB 103, both in the second line
of their respective poems)—so that the second is a more or less symmetrically
balanced, perfect reversal of the first, an inverted variation on exactly the same
theme.

But why should these epigrams have been classified under the sub-title *Tropoi*?
A glance at the way in which the Milan papyrus is structured by the sub-titles of
each section is necessary:

[LITHI]KA (20)	126 lines [cf. Orphic *L.*]
OIÔNOSKOPIKA (15)	80 lines
ANATHEMATIKA (6)	38 lines [= *AP* VI title]
[EPITUMBIA] (20)	116 lines [= *AP* VII title]
ANDRIANTOPOIIKA (9)	50 lines [= EPIDEIKTIKA in *AP*]

293

HIPP[IKA] (18)	98 lines
NAUAGIKA (6)	26 lines
IAMATIKA (7)	32 lines (but e.g. includes dedications)
TROPOI (8)	32 lines
[ ]	(?) lines (e.g. amatory/sympotic)

Since the complaints of Menoetius and Soses in AB 102–103 are in the form of funeral epigrams, we are entitled to ask why these epigrams have not been classed with the other examples under the sub-title ᾿Επιτύμβια.[3] A preliminary answer might be that the earlier section of funeral epigrams is far and away the most extensive of all the sections in the collection as preserved, comprising 20 poems in all— a number matched only by the section sub-titled [Λιθι]κά) and extending to 116 lines (exceeded again only by the [Λιθι]κά at 126 lines). A compiler wishing to maintain a degree of balance among the various thematic subsections of the collection might well have felt it proper to distribute additional epigrams of the commoner types among further, more sophisticated sub-divisions in his classification. But even if this motive is assumed,[4] we would have to explain what is distinctive about these particular epigrams that justifies them having such a separate and distinctive place and sub-title all of their own.

The notion of attitude and characterization in their respective speakers immediately suggests comparison with Theophrastus' use of the term τρόπος to designate character-types in his work *Characters*. The term appears prominently in section 1 of the preface to the work (cf. III 5) ἐθαύμασα . . . τί γὰρ δήποτε . . . συμβέβηκεν ἡμῖν οὐ τὴν αὐτὴν τάξιν τῶν τρόπων ἔχειν, 'I have long wondered why it is that we do not all have the same composition of character'. Later at XIII 3 10 Theophrastus describes the type of character who exhibits περιεργία 'over-doing-it':[5]

καὶ γυναικὸς δὲ τελευτησάσης ἐπιγράψαι ἐπὶ τὸ μνῆμα τοῦ
τε ἀνδρὸς αὐτῆς καὶ τοῦ πατρὸς καὶ τῆς μητρὸς καὶ αὐτῆς
τῆς γυναικὸς τοὔνομα καὶ ποδαπή ἐστι, καὶ προσεπιγράψαι
ὅτι οὗτοι πάντες χρηστοὶ ἦσαν.

---

[3] The title that stood before this section is lost, though there was clearly space for it in the papyrus, and its restoration here seems reasonably assured by its appearance as the sub-title to a thematically similar section in *AP* VII.

[4] See above Stephens-Obbink, 'The Manuscript' (in this volume). As argued there, the imbalance between sections evident in the Milan roll suggests that an aimed-for balance cannot be the primary explanation for the stichometric totals in the papyrus.

[5] This parallel was drawn to my attention by M. Fantuzzi.

When a woman dies, he inscribes on her tomb the names of her husband, her father and mother, and herself and place of birth, and adds that they were all of them fine and upstanding individuals.

Theophrastus' characterization of περιεργία bears comparison not only with AB 102–103, currently under discussion, but also more widely with other poems in the Milan roll. Posidippus AB 78.3–8, for example, praises Arsinoe for having as grandfather Ptolemy, as father's mother Berenike, as father king son of a king with his father's name. A similar succession occurs in AB 88.1–5, apostrophising 'my parents and I Berenike, and my mother'. The model for all these seems to have been the epigram attributed to Simonides *FGE* 26a on Archedike daughter of Hippias. This kind of hyperbolic self-encomiastic boast seems to well fit Theophrastus' description περιεργία.

Thus we might conclude that the sub-title *Tropoi* in the Milan roll designates the characters of the speakers of the epigrams of this section, together perhaps with language of emphatically characterizing or personally speaking funeral inscription: i.e. the character, τρόποι of the individuals represented as speaking in the epigrams insofar as they react to νόμοι, i.e. social conventions about how one treats a tomb, attitudes toward burial, monuments, praise of the dead, etc. It is in exactly this sense that Soses in AB 103.1 complains that the passerby (= reader) does not act in accordance with received custom, νόμου χάριν. It is worth considering whether we should attempt here to read (or emend to) νόςου χάριν, i.e. "You didn't even ask me (did I die) on account of disease, nor (did you ask me) from where I come." Spacing and the trace preserved on the papyrus,[6] however, lend slightly more support to νόμου. Reading διὰ νόςου would mean abandoning the more or less exact parallel with the second line of the preceding epigram (AB 102) and with it the inversion of topics that makes these two epigrams so fittingly paired in succession. At any rate, they would be less balanced, inverted versions of each other. In addition, νόμου χάριν is an expression that is paralleled, for example, in an epigram by Lucilius in *AP* XI 141.7–9 where a speaker, annoyed by his prosecutors, says:

πλὴν κἀμοῦ μνήσῃτι νόμου χάριν, ἢ μέγα κράξω·
"ἄλλα λέγει Μενεκλῆς, ἄλλα τὸ χορίδιον."

I beg you just to mention me for custom's sake, or I'll cry out:
"One thing says Menecles, and another says the piggie!"

---

[6] The high, rounded hook in this position is conceivably the cap of ϲ, but in light of the wide space before it, the trace conforms rather better to the scribe's characteristic similarly shaped rounded hook expected over the right leg of μ.

Another epigram by Lucilius contains the same expression, from the section 'On Gluttons' (*AP* XI 206):

οὕτω σοι πέψαι, Διονύσιε, ταῦτα γένοιτο
πάντα· νόμου δὲ χάριν δός τι καὶ ὧδε φαγεῖν·
κἀγὼ κέκλημαι, κἀμοὶ παρέθηκέ τι τούτων
γεύσασθαι Πόπλιος, κἀμὸν ἔπεστι μέρος·
εἰ μὴ λεπτὸν ἰδών με δοκεῖς κατακεῖσθαι ἄρρωστον,
εἶθ᾽ οὕτως τηρεῖς, μή σε λαθών τι φάγω.

So may you be able to digest what you're eating, Dionysus,
    the whole lot, but for custom's sake give us something to eat
    here too.
I was invited too; Publius served some of these things
    for me too to taste as well; my share is on the table too.
Unless, of course, seeing that I am thin, you think I was ill when I
    sat down,
    and so watch me in case I eat something unnoticed.

Here the speaker is complaining of his treatment at a banquet and appeals to what is customary in a bid to make the addressee feel that he is in the wrong in doing something that the vast majority of hosts would not. A similar usage of the expression reflects an association with unwritten or customary law: cf. Euripides, *Heracles* 1322:[7]

Θήβας μὲν οὖν ἔκλειπε τοῦ νόμου χάριν,
ἕπου δ᾽ ἅμ᾽ ἡμῖν πρὸς πόλισμα Παλλάδος.

Leave Thebes in compliance with the law, and follow us to Athens.

Thus in AB 103 the expression νόμου χάριν is clearly a rhetorical one, designed to make the passerby/reader feel that he needs to ingratiate the speaker. A similar appeal to custom or law is at work in Menoetius' complaint in AB 102. It warns to the passerby/reader to stay away from the tomb and not to bother it and the diseased. With this injunction may be compared the numerous inscribed imprecations on graves[8] that forbid any kind of tampering, damage, theft, or

---

[7] Cf. Athenaeus IV section 20. 6, 31. 13 Kaibel.

[8] For the most recent survey and discussion, see Dignas 2002:236–8 with references to further literature.

vandalism of the tomb, often under stated penalty, imposed either privately by the gods or publicly by the city. Such inscriptions purport to impose a kind of ἱερὸς νόμος on the passerby/reader, and in this way AB 102 could be seen as a literary adaptation in the voice of the diseased occupant of the tomb of a kind of inscription regarding burial custom which must have been encountered fairly frequently in antiquity.

Peripatetic interest in classifying of all sorts, including ethical character types is well known. Peripatetic influence in scientific matters, especially regarding logical division and classification in cataloguing, at the time of Posidippus and Callimachus is in any case to be expected, as evidenced by Callimachus' debate with the Peripatetic Praxiphanes. There may also be Theophrastean and Peripatetic influence seen elsewhere in the epigrams of the Milan roll. This is particularly apparent in the classifying function of the thematic sub-headings of the Milan roll, and in the stichometic counts that accompany these sections.[9] It is has also been argued[10] that the prognostications from birds in the section sub-titled οἰωνοσκοπικά derive from a lost prose-work by Theophrastus. If these parallels have any validity, the sub-title *Tropoi* would then designate evaluative sketches of the characteristic emotional responses of different social groups (young, old, dead, or from this or that place, etc.), a collection of 'style-markers' of defective or unusual ethical types, thus emphasizing the idea found in the philosophers (e.g. Aristotle, *NE* 9.4) that only the virtuous have real stability and cohesion of character, and that the non-virtuous are dominated by unreasonable and fluctuating desires or passions. This is an idea worked out for example in Philodemus, Horaces' *Satires* and *Epistles*, and in Virgil and Plutarch's biographies.[11] It is also well illustrated in Philodemus' Περὶ τοῦ κουφίζειν ὑπερηφανίας, *On Relieving Arrogance*, an important source which draws closely on early analyses of ethical character by Aristo (whether the Peripatetic or the Stoic is not clear).[12]

However, not all references to 'character' in philosophical literature (whether ἦθος or τρόπος) are to ethical character, i.e. 'character' with connotations of morality or in the modern sense of personality. A different use of the term τρόπος appears in the musical works of Aristoxenus (another pupil of Aristotle), where it refers to 'styles,' i.e. personal preferences of performing or appreciating music, something approximating more what we might call 'stylistic taste'. The author or

[9] On the function of the stichometry and its associations with classifying and cataloguing in the Alexandrian library, see Stephens-Obbink, 'The Manuscript' (this volume).

[10] By Sider at the Posidippus conference in Cincinnati. Contrast Baumbach-Trampedach (this volume).

[11] Cf. Gill 1994; Pelling 1990.

[12] Not currently available in a proper edition, this treatise was sufficiently important to induce J. Rusten to print select extracts from it as an appendix to his Loeb edition of Theophrastus' *Characters*. Several new editions are underway; for a sample, see Ranocchia 2001:231–263.

the Pseudo-Plutarchean treatise *On Music* XXXIII 1142e (attributed by the author to Aristoxenus) notes, for example:

> Up to the present time this sort of training and learning has never been
> supplemented with a thorough enumeration of the *tropoi*: on the
> contrary, most people learn whatever the teacher or the pupil happens
> to enjoy, while people who understand the matter criticize this unsys-
> tematic approach, as the Spartans did in the old days, and so did the
> Mantineans and Pallenians. They used to pick out just one *tropos*, or a
> very small number, which they believed to be suited to the proper
> formation of character, and practiced that sort of music alone.[13]

The exact meaning of the vague term *tropos* here is difficult to pin down. A.
Barker, for example, rejects the meanings *harmonia* (Aristoxenus, *El. Harm.*
VI 19ff), *tonos* i.e. 'pitch', 'key' (*El. Harm.* XXXVII 8ff), and settles ultimately for
'technically specifiable melodic genre'. If this is correct, in the context of classification of musical styles at any rate, the term would designate ability of a given form
to be characterized in generic terms. Applied to the epigrams of the section sub-
titled *Tropoi* in the Milan roll, the term would then be seen to designate something
like 'modes of discourse', i.e. genres, where genre not by context of performance,
composition, or dedication (for in this sense these poems would belong among the
Ἐπιτύμβια), but by a stereotyped or characterizable way of speaking. *Tropoi* in
this sense would not be divorced from the Theophrastean sense of ethical character,
but closely related to it (as it is in the context of musical styles for Aristoxenus),
being deepened and enriched by the concept of speech genres, *Tropoi*, we may
conclude, are generic 'turns' or stereotyped 'adaptations' of characterizable ways of
speaking. Callimachus, famously, in *Ep.* 27.1 uses the term τρόπος to refer to
Hesiod's and Aratus' 'mode' or 'genre' of composition.

In theory, there could be *tropoi*, 'adaptations' of this sort of any of the categories of poems represented in the collection. However, AB 104 is clearly a funeral
epigram (in which the dead man speaks), and AB 105 is likewise a funeral epigram
(the dead man is addressed); enough is preserved of the remaining AB 106–109 in
the section sub-titled *Tropoi* to show that they, like AB 102–105, were funereal in
form. In light of this fact, the *Tropoi* section seems somewhat displaced in the
collection, in that it does not immediately follow the Ἐπιτύμβια as an appendix
to them.[14]

---

[13] Barker 1984:239n213. For the Aristoxenean background see Gibson 2003:209–211, 225–244.

[14] But this would hardly be the only example of displacement in the collection: cf. AB 62 and 65, both
on the sculptor Lysippus, but which the compiler has failed to pair successively, given their identical
subject-matter.

This seems to explain the distinctive moodiness of the voices of Menoetius and Soses respectively in AB 102–103, as well as that of AB 104, on a philosopher who studied with Menedemus. This kind of characterization of voice in a funeral epigram reminds one of of the epigrams on Timon in *AP*, which have a remonstrative, crabby tone similar to that of Menoetius in AB 102.[15] In AB 103, however, the voice of Soses may strike a different note, one appealing to the reader for sympathy. This seems clear already from ἀλλὰ cύ in line 3. According to Denniston on ἀλλά (4) in commands and exhortations, it signals "a transition from arguments for action to a statement of the action required. Hence ἀλλά, in this sense, usually occurs near the end of a speech, as a clinching and final appeal . . . 'Come' or 'come now' will often get the meaning. This usage is rare in oratory, being probably too intimate in tone"[16] (and cf. καὶ cύ). Hence the expression implies a level of familiarity with the addressee that may or may not be justified, but which is invited by the speaker.

In this light we may reconsider the final words as reconstructed by the original editors: [ὁμος, φίλ]ε, cοῦ.[17] How justified are we in accepting such an extensive restoration, in light of parallels from epigrammatic poetry?[18] ὁμός is a poetic form of ὁμοῖος. See *Etym. magn.* p. 627.37 Gaisford, citing *Il.* IV 437 (οὐ γὰρ πάντων ἦεν ὁμὸς θρός οὐδ᾽ ἴα γῆρυς) as typifying the Trojans' speech. Further parallels, however, may be adduced showing it typical of Homeric poetry in which it is used to modify a variety of abstract nouns: *Il.* XIII 354 (ὁ. γένος), XXIV 57 (ὁ. τιμή), XV 209 (ὁ. νεῖκος), XIII 333, VIII 291 and Hesiod, *Theog.* 508 (ὁ. λέχος). Closer to the present passage are *IG* XIV 1721 ὁμὰ χθών and οὐ καθ᾽ ὁμὰ φρονέοντε. Compare also Callimachus fr. 1 26–27 Pf. ἑτέρων ἴχνια μὴ καθ᾽ ὁμὰ δίφρον ἐλᾶν.

A parallel[19] in epigram occurs in the *Anthologiae Graecae Appendix* 656, 8–10 (Cougny vol. III p. 200, also at e.g. *AP* XII 234,4, 2.1,314) in the last three lines of an epigram from a wife for her dead husband:

---

[15] As suggested by the original editors in their commentary (BG:229), comparing *AP* VII 313–20. But the Theophrastean and Menandrean characters ought also to have been compared.

[16] Denniston 1954:13.

[17] In the commentary the original editors also suggest [ὁμός ποτ]ε cου 'per es.', making it clear that both restorations are entirely hypothetical. I argue below that parallels support the restoration of both [ὁμοc] and [φίλ]ε.

[18] Other idiosyncrasies in this poem, as reconstructed by the editors, include ἡcυχίωc in line 3 (unparalleled: perhaps *metri gratia* for the standard ἡcυχῶc; presumably with the same valence as AB 100.1 ἥcυχον ὕπνον). R. Hunter points out to me that the expression [ἴδε κείμεν]ον restored in 3 is difficult and unparalleled.

[19] Pointed out to me, along with the Homeric parallels below, by D. Fearn.

ἀλλ' οὔτοι νόσφιν γε σέθεν ποτικείσομαι αὐτή,
ὡς πρὶν δ' ἐν ζωοῖσιν ὁμὸς δόμος ἄμμι τέτυκτο,
ὡς καὶ τεθνειῶτας ὁμὴ σορὸς ἀμφικαλύψει.

But since I will in no way like far apart from you,
since just as before in life we lived in the same house,
so in death the same urn will hide us.

As editors have noted, this is an allusion to the urn at *Il.* XXIII 91 to be shared by Achilles and Patroclus ὡς δὲ καὶ ὀστέα νῶϊν ὁμὴ σορὸς ἀμφικαλύπτοι. If ὁμός is correctly restored in AB 103.4, it could have Homeric resonances. What of the similarly restored φίλ]ε? Here another Homeric resonance may be discovered in Achilles' calling Lycaeon φίλος in the very act of killing him (*Il.* XXI 106–107):

ἀλλὰ φίλος θάνε καὶ σύ· τί ἦ ὀλοφύρεαι οὕτως;
κάτθανε καὶ Πάτροκλος, ὅ περ σέο πολλὸν ἀμείνων.

So, you die too, my friend. Why lament so?
Even Patroclus died, and he was a much greater man than you.

Commentators have suggested that Achilles calls Lycaon his friend because they are united by the common bond of mortality: so Richardson *ad loc.* (p. 61f), who notes that Achilles 'accepts Lycaon's' allusion to their earlier bond of ξενία, calling him φίλος (AB 106), and thereby suggesting a sense of sympathy which is developed in the reference to his own impending death, although at the same time there is a bitter note of irony in his use of the word "friend".[20] Similarly in AB 103, we are to understand via the Homeric resonance that the speaker is not simply being polite in addressing the passerby/reader as 'friend': he is suggesting they are the same, in that the share a deeper bond of mortality.[21]

All of this is relevant not least to the identity of the speaker. He is someone we know, not from historical sources but from the Milan roll. He is Soses of Cos, a name that has already appeared in the section sub-titled *Iamatika* in AB 97 where he is said to have been miraculously cured of epilepsy through the intervention of Asclepius: 'non si puo excludere che si tratti della medesima persona' (BG):[22]

[20] Compare Griffin 1983:55: 'Achilles kills in a passionate revenge, but not in blind ferocity. He sees his action in the perspective of human life and death as a whole, the perspective which puts slayer and slain on a level, so that it is more than a mere colloquialism that he calls Lycaon "friend" as he kills him.'

[21] This is reinforced by the use of νόμου χάριν above, suggesting how one should properly respect the dead.

[22] In AB 97 he lacks the patronymic Ἀλκαίου that he bears in AB 103, though in both he is called

As an offering for cure of his disease, Asclepius, Soses
    of Cos gives a silver chalice.[23]
His pain which lasted six years and with it the sacred disease,
    You, god, made vanish in a single night.

This poem is a plausible dedication by a man who has been cured of epilepsy
in an Asclepius sanctuary,[24] only to have his final end inevitably and ironically
recorded later in the collection in his own epitaph. As a final twist, parallel to the
miracle recorded in AB 97, AB 103 may now be read as a 'play' on the form of the
dedicatory epigram (in this sense a *tropos*), now used, instead of the marker of a
dead man, to bring the dead man back to life and let him speak, reminding the
reader of the common fate he will share.

Κῷος. I take the latter to mean that the putative context of both epigrams is not on Cos (where
    one would hardly need to be identified as a Coan), but probably in Alexandria. In any case, Ptolemaic
    connections with Cos and Coans were legion. Cf. Theocr. *Idyll* 7.
[23] With this φιάλη compare Posidippus AB Test. 4, a φιάλη in the Delian tribute lists dedicated on
    behalf of the citizens of Alexandria by an ἀρχιθέωρος named Posidippus.
[24] As suggested by A. Henrichs at the CHS Posidippus conference in Washington, D.C.

AFTERWORD

An Archaeologist's Perspective on the Milan Papyrus (P.Mil.Vogl. VIII 309)

Gail Hoffman

Boston College

When I was asked to participate in a workshop on the new Milan papyrus (P.Mil.Vogl.VIII 309) with epigrams attributed to Posidippus, I wondered how an archaeologist, who generally works in the Early Iron Age (ca. 1100–700 BCE), could possibly contribute to a discussion about Hellenistic epigrams. However, as I have come to appreciate, one of the greatest contributions of the Center for Hellenic Studies (CHS) is the way in which it fosters dialogue across traditional disciplinary boundaries. So, I dutifully attended informal evening sessions when the CHS fellows (2001–2002) gathered to read over the new poems and to discuss our initial reactions. Quite to my surprise, I found that I was intrigued by material that in all likelihood I never would have encountered in my work.[1]

Still, I worried what an archaeologist could contribute to their study. Indeed, by my estimate only four of the twelve fellows at the CHS might have claimed the Hellenistic era as their primary area of expertise. So what could the rest of us offer to a group of distinguished specialists on this period? First of all, and perhaps most importantly, we offered a spirit of collegiality in a place where scholars *do* talk across disciplinary lines, and where all, I think, benefit from the exchange. Secondly, beyond the confines of the CHS most of us would never have been invited to participate in such a workshop. I believe the broader perspective that the CHS fellows provided is rare and that it will have served to push early discussion of this exciting new material beyond borders it might otherwise not so readily have crossed. I have no doubt that the immediate future will see numerous conferences

---

[1] I must admit that nearly all of us thought on our first read through that many of these epigrams were not first rate poetry. Our opinions on this point have changed, especially as we have come to appreciate the careful crafting and arrangements of poems within their subgroups. For the uninitiated, I found Webster 1964, Bing 1988, and Gutzwiller 1998 helpful.

n the new papyrus. I do doubt whether any will actively incorporate the discipli-
ary breadth provided by the twelve fellows who were at the CHS. So, it is with
ome exhilaration and much trepidation that I offer a few comments and reflections
bout these new poems and about our workshop.

What struck me as the poems were read was how frequently a vivid visual
mage came to mind, which has also been the subject of papers by Kosmetatou and
'apalexandrou on the *Hippika*. I work in a period in which the relationship of art
nd text is not at all close. Texts rarely conjure images of "real" archaeologically
reserved objects, and conversely visual images rarely refer directly to stories known
extually.[2] Yet as I read many of these poems, they called to mind statues. For
nstance, AB 71, AB 72, or AB 76 conjured images similar to the bronze jockey
rom Artemisium, in which the expressive power of the animal galloping at break-
eck pace with his tiny jockey glancing to the side at his imagined competition
nakes palpable the tension of the race (Figure 2). Or AB 87, where the horses
hemselves speak, which calls to mind a dedication like Polyzalos' famous chario-
eer at Delphi, that would originally have included a four-horse chariot now mostly
nissing (Figure 1).[3] With the *Oiônoskopika* (AB 21–35), I was startled by the vivid-
ness of bird descriptions and even the seemingly detailed knowledge of migration
atterns. For instance, AB 22, describing the flight of cranes from Egypt to Thrace,
nd AB 23, in which the shearwater signals the presence of schools of fish, seem to
nclude real natural history. Baumbach and Trampedach discuss the structure and
neaning of this section in an illuminating exploration.

Still, for all the vivid detail of the other poems, it was the *Lithika* (AB 1–20)[4]
hat were especially striking. In these poems, the precision of description goes
eyond simply conjuring a vivid visual image to include seemingly specialized
nowledge about materials and craftsmanship—types of stone, special properties of
tones, sources of materials, even the skill of the craftsman and techniques of
roduction, as Smith has argued in his paper. For example, there is lapis lazuli
AB 5, cάπειρον), sard[5] (AB 8, cάρδιον), rock crystal (AB 13; AB 16,

---

[2] For a recent exploration of this, see Snodgrass 1998.

[3] Cf. Papalexandrou (this volume).

[4] The heading, *Lithika*, is largely restored ([λιθι]κ̣ά̣). At the workshop Stephens observed that the heading seems above the line. Frame and others wondered whether this was intended to serve as an overall title for the work as well as a subject heading for the first set of poems. Because there is damage (and repair?) to the start of the papyrus, it is an open question whether the preserved text is the actual beginning or not. It is interesting that in antiquity (though generally later than these epigrams) a genre of studies termed *Lithika* existed. These works were primarily concerned with the magical properties of stones. Plantzos 1999:10. Such works are in contrast to the largely scientific treatises of Theophrastus *On Stones* and Pliny *NH* XXXVII.

[5] The term probably refers to sard, a variety of chalcedony in layered bands of color. A paper on AB 8 was presented by Kosmetatou at the conference and is forthcoming in Kosmetatou 2003a.

κρύcταλλον ῍Αραψ), chalcedony (AB 14, ἴαcπιν), snakestone (AB 15 δράκοντοc), and perhaps beryl (AB 6, β[ηρύλλιον]).[6] The special properties o' stones are observed in the magnetic stone (AB 17) and the snakestone (AB 15) tha' hides the chariot until an impression is made.[7] There is also the wondrous ston((AB 13), that seems to reveal its image (of a Persian lion? 13.3, ὠκὺ γ[λυπτὸc λ]ὶc ὁ Πέρcηc) only after being rubbed with oil and left to dry.

The special skill of the artisan is noted in AB 15 "a marvel the craftsman did not hurt his eyes". But also in the joining of subject and material ("the use of hand and mind") in the Pegasos stone (AB 14).[8] In addition, there is the carving of the "invisible" chariot in the snakestone (AB 15), that Gutzwiller has proposed plays or an ancient belief that the snakestone could improve vision.[9] Some of the epigrams (AB 5 and AB 6 [completely conjectured]) reveal the gem carvers' names, Croniu and Timanthes,[10] as well as occasionally the owner of the stone.

These observations about the knowledge of the poet caused me to wonder about the social context of engraved gem production and use during the Hellenistic period. The materials mentioned in these epigrams are notable for their value and rarity. In particular, the large sardion cameo that is three spans round, indicates that the epigrams describe the gems of kings and royalty, not the gemstones of average citizens. The identification by name of individual carvers, while known earlier (only a few carvers' names come down from the Archaic and Classical periods),[11] is ir keeping with the Hellenistic context in which gem engravers would be employed a the royal courts to produce ruler portraits, expensive seal stones, and probably also the die for coins.[12] We also know that Hellenistic kings made collections (*dactylio-thecae*) of gemstones.[13] Perhaps we might imagine a poet sitting and chatting a lunch with a gem carver, much like philologists, philosophers, historians, and

---

[6] On some of these terms, Plantzos 1999:10, 36.

[7] This poem about the snakestone was already known from other collections (AB 15 = 20 GP). For comments, Gow 1954:197–199; GP:2 500–501. Fernández-Galiano 1987:126–129.

[8] This epigram has already received at least two comments in print. Gutzwiller 1995:385–386 and Niafas 1997.

[9] Gutzwiller 1995:387–388. Rock crystal (AB 7 and AB 16) was also known to magnify. Many rock crystal disks have been excavated and some speculate these would have been used by jeweler's as tools See Hoffman 1997:202–204. On the question of whether magnifiers were used, see Plantzos 1999:40–41.

[10] By the Hellenistic period many names of gem carvers are known, though some may be false; see Plantzos 1999:146. One of the better known from the literature (no signed work of his survives) is Pyrgoteles, who worked for Alexander the Great. Cf. Plantzos 1999:63, 60. Pliny *NH* XXXVII 8. A gem carver named Cronius is mentioned by Pliny in the same passage.

[11] Boardman 1970:17.

[12] On the question of whether gem carvers also cut coin dies, see Plantzos 1999:64–65.

[13] Pliny *NH* XXXVII 12–17.

archaeologists sit and chat at the wonderful lunches of the CHS. It could be in a context such as this, then, that a poet might learn the details of the gem carver's craft.[14] Of course, I do not mean this literally, but I think that both poet and gem carver were likely the beneficiaries of royal patronage and in such a context, their paths might have crossed.

It is also in the Hellenistic period, after all, that the *Mouseion* and Library at Alexandria are created, that poets begin to write down their works in books, and that art criticism develops new vocabulary. This is also an era when ekphrasis changes from earlier forms that can be considered largely in terms of narrative and description, examples of which can be found in Homer's *Shield of Achilles*, the pseudo-Hesiodic *Shield of Heracles* or even, Euripides' *Ion* with a description of the sculptures on the Apollo temple at Delphi.[15] It now becomes a type of ekphrasis that actively involves the viewer. Goldhill has claimed that Hellenistic ekphrasis is related to "cultural ideas about vision, reading, and the production of meaning."[16] Cosmetatou's review of the structure and meaning of the *Andriantopoiika* explores the theory behind the ecphrasis in that section (AB 62–70) arguing for its attribution to Posidippus' contemporary Samian historian Duris. There is also an imaginary place of viewing set up in some of the poems, leaving one to wonder about the possibility of collections of statues and gemstones perhaps made by Hellenistic kings, an idea that was suggested by Gutzwiller at the CHS conference.[17] Even with both an expanded understanding of ekphrasis and the expectation that real artworks are discussed, the depth of understanding of materials and technical process again seems to go beyond what has been previously described.

In terms of art criticism, I expected to find in the poems the view of an intelgentsia with links to philosophy and perhaps ideals about *phantasia*, as it was considered in the Hellenistic period,[18] but found, instead, earlier classical terms (κανών and ἀλήθεια) occurring in the *Andriantopoiika*, while in the *Lithika* the judgments on the artistry of the stones are more in the vein of what Pollitt terms "popular criticism" that is, with an emphasis on describing the realism of the art work, its miraculous qualities, and its costliness.[19] Here I wondered whether the poet was contriving to include perspectives from differing social groups, that is, the artisan in the creation of the poem and artwork, royalty in the place of viewing,

[14] Smith in this volume proposes as a source for the poet's knowledge, Theophrastus *On Stones*.
[15] Zeitlin 1994.
[16] Goldhill 1994:198.
[17] This paper is now published as Gutzwiller 2003c (*non vidi*).
[18] Hunter in follow up discussion suggested that the importance of *phantasia* has been overrated.
[19] Pollitt 1974:63–66.

materials used, and in the possibility of gemstone collections, and then, commoner in the guise of viewers commenting on the objects seen.[20]

These poems, then, somewhat unexpectedly provided many things to interes an archaeologist. Perhaps, if I had initially paid more attention to the subheading (*Lithika, Oiônoskopika, Anathematika, Epitymbia, Andriantopoiika, Hippika Nauagika, Iamatika, Tropoi*), I would not have been so surprised. After all, the describe physical objects or actions, aspects of natural history or folklore, all topic that fascinate archaeologists. It was the importance of the arrangement of indi vidual poems within these subheadings or categories and the complexity of thi structure that also turned out to be one of the fascinating themes of the worksho and its lively discussions. I would like to turn, then, to a few observations about th workshop and discussions.

Like the epigrams in the papyrus whose complex and subtle arrangement cam to be appreciated over the course of the workshop, the careful design and struc turing of the workshop papers and session, largely preserved in this volume, als became apparent over the course of the conference weekend. The arrangemen permitted even those unfamiliar with the field to educate themselves by degrees s that eventually even detailed and specialized discussions could be appreciated Papers began with background to the study of epigram (see introduction in thi volume) and details of the papyrus itself. Stephens and Obbink very ably an succinctly presented the evidence for dating, context of production (including tha it was written by a practiced professional scribe), damage and repair to the front, a well as the text written upside down on the reverse, and finally, its last use a mummy cartonnage. This presentation elicited discussion about the unusua numbering system. What does it mean, and at what point was it put on th papyrus? Both the view that it was original (Stephens) and that it was added late (Sider) were espoused. The vexing question of the marginal τоυ and its meanin also were raised, various possibilities were rehearsed without any firm conclusion being reached. Obbink's paper closing the first session in counterpoint to Stephen provided a minute analysis and commentary on a four-line epigram (AB 103) i the *Tropoi*. While the papyrologists' observations provided a refreshing perspectiv on the papyrus, observing that the text must have been produced close in time t the composition of the epigrams, one would plausibly wonder who was choosing collating, constructing this work and in what kind of social milieu. What if any would its relationship be to activities at the Library in Alexandria? The paper dealing with the papyrus itself raise what also became another theme or leit moti

---

[20] Goldhill 1994:216–223 posits a similar interpretation for the women viewers and other participan of Theocritus' *Idyll* 15.

of the workshop, that is, the social context in which and for which the papyrus was created. Nagy reminded us of the variant Homeric texts available in the third century BCE and proposed that a majority of the Homeric echoes might be drawn from the "Homerus auctus" current at the time. Sider addressed the effect of anthologists on the epigram itself, especially noting the shifting length over time. Smith observed the *Lithika* fit well in a Hellenistic context of scientific observation, proposing that Theophrastus' *On Stones* was the immediate source for the poet's specialized, accurate, and detailed knowledge of gemstones. Bing, likewise, linked the epigrams to other written documents, in this instance, noting that the *Iamatika* showed strong links to published descriptions of actual cures, such as those inscribed at Epidaurus. In discussion, we puzzled over the function of these epigrams, the reasons for a collection of cures, and wondered who would be the intended audience. Similarly, Dignas' exploration of some of the *Epitymbia* noted the unusual presence of gravestones for initiates and the preponderance of women. Again, why this selection?

It was this issue of selection and crafting of the papyrus as a whole and especially within the various subgroups to which discussion returned time and again. At the end, I think no one doubted how carefully constructed the selection of epigrams was and that much of the elegance of this work derives from a realization of this ordering and its significance. While individual epigrams alone might not seem particularly interesting, sometimes they took on striking additional characteristics and meaning when combined with neighboring poems.

The issue of structuring within the subheadings has been explored especially for the *Andriantopoiika* by Kosmetatou, the *Hippika* by Fantuzzi, and the *Oiônoskopika* by Baumbach and Trampedach. The *Oiônoskopika* were particularly fascinating as it seemed that the broad structure of the epigrams contrast *oikos* and *polis*, private with public settings, with a transitional poem bridging both placed at the center. The section closes with two mantic poems that cast the poet/reader in the role of seer. It seems almost as though these poems were designed to educate the reader in the mantic craft. This proposed interpretation of the structure is nicely supported by Henrich's analysis of the highly specialized language.[21] He observed the almost exclusive use of *phainesthai* and *idein*, two of the three necessary parts of augury, i.e. appearance and viewing. The vocabulary for the last stage, interpretation, is lacking in the text, perhaps because that is the role of the reader? The importance of the structuring within subsections came out also in Bing's paper on the *Iamatika*, though all wondered whether this could be carried further. This subject was again explored by Hunter in the *Lithika*. Even though a whole session was

---

[21] It was unfortunately not possible to include this paper in the present volume.

devoted to consideration of the *Lithika*, additional work remains to be done or their arrangement as a group.

Of course, the realization of the complex structure of many subgroup provided a strong sense of authorial or at the very least editorial hand. Although the question "is this Posidippus?" was not overtly a focus of discussion, the papers of Acosta-Hughes, Sider, and Sens sidled up to or around this question.

I have not done justice to those who tackled the literary dimensions of the poems and their place in historical developments, especially Schur on the *Lithika* and Thomas on the *Nauagika*, but perhaps as an archaeologist, I can be forgiven this blunder. These papers were especially insightful and carried analysis deeply into the poetry and its context. Let me close then, with an observation and reminder of the breadth of disciplines involved in this workshop. There were archaeologists, scholars of comparative literature and Greek religion, historians, linguists, literary critics, paleographers, papyrologists, and even philosophers. Archaeologists will find much to interest them in these poems. I hope that these general comments from "an archaeologist's perspective" as well as the other commentary and analysis of this papyrus by the CHS fellows and distinguished visiting scholars have helped to push forward the boundaries of thinking about these poems.

POSIDIPPUS CONCORDANCE

Milan Papyrus

Lithika

AB 1	I 2–5
AB 2	I 6–9
AB 3	I 10–13
AB 4	I 14–19
AB 5	I 20–23
AB 6	I 24–29
AB 7	I 30–35
AB 8	I 36–II 2
AB 9	II 3–6
AB 10	II 7–16
AB 11	II 17–22
AB 12	II 23–28
AB 13	II 29–32
AB 14	II 33–38
AB 15	II 39–III 7
AB 16	III 8–13
AB 17	III 14–19
AB 18	III 20–27
AB 19	III 28–41
AB 20	IV 1–6

Oiônoskopika

AB 21	IV 8–13
AB 22	IV 14–19
AB 23	IV 20–23
AB 24	IV 24–29
AB 25	IV 30–35
AB 26	IV 36–39

AB 27	IV 40–V 5
AB 28	V 6–11
AB 29	V 12–15
AB 30	V 16–19
AB 31	V 20–25
AB 32	V 26–31
AB 33	V 32–39
AB 34	VI 1–4
AB 35	VI 5–8

Anathematika

AB 36	VI 10–17
AB 37	VI 18–25
AB 38	VI 26–29
AB 39	VI 30–37
AB 40	VI 38–VII 2
AB 41	VII 3–8

Epitymbia

AB 42	VII 10–13
AB 43	VII 14–19
AB 44	VII 20–23
AB 45	VII 24–29
AB 46	VII 30–35
AB 47	VII 36–VIII 2
AB 48	VIII 3–6
AB 49	VIII 7–12
AB 50	VIII 13–18
AB 51	VIII 19–24

Concordance

AB 52	VIII 25–30		AB 85	XIII 23–26
AB 53	VIII 31–34		AB 86	XIII 27–30
AB 54	VIII 35–38		AB 87	XIII 31–34
AB 55	IX 1–6		AB 88	XIII 35–XIV 1
AB 56	IX 7–14			
AB 57	IX 15–22		*Nauagika*	
AB 58	IX 23–28		AB 89	XIV 3–6
AB 59	IX 29–34		AB 90	XIV 7–10
AB 60	IX 35–40		AB 91	XIV 11–14
AB 61	X 1–6		AB 92	XIV 15–18
			AB 93	XIV 19–24
Andriantopoiika			AB 94	XIV 25–28
AB 62	X 8–15			
AB 63	X 16–25		*Iamatika*	
AB 64	X 26–29		AB 95	XIV 30–37
AB 65	X 30–33		AB 96	XIV 38–XV 2
AB 66	X 34–37		AB 97	XV 3–6
AB 67	X 38–XI 5		AB 98	XV 7–10
AB 68	XI 6–11		AB 99	XV 11–14
AB 69	XI 12–15		AB 100	XV 15–18
AB 70	XI 16–19		AB 101	XV 19–22
Hippika			*Tropoi*	
AB 71	XI 20–24		AB 102	XV 24–27
AB 72	XI 25–28		AB 103	XV 28–31
AB 73	XI 29–32		AB 104	XV 32–35
AB 74	XI 33–XII 7		AB 105	XV 36–XVI 1
AB 75	XII 8–11		AB 106	XVI 2–5
AB 76	XII 12–15		AB 107	XVI 6–9
AB 77	XII 16–19		AB 108	XVI 10–13
AB 78	XII 20–33		AB 109	XVI 14–17
AB 79	XII 34–39			
AB 80	XIII 1–4		**Unidentified Section**	
AB 81	XIII 5–8		AB 110	XVI 19–22
AB 82	XIII 9–14		AB 111	XVI 23–26
AB 83	XIII 15–18		AB 112	XVI 27–28
AB 84	XIII 19–22			

"Old Posidippus"

AB 113*	*SH* 978
AB 114*	*SH* 961
AB 115	11 GP
AB 116	12 GP
AB 117	24 GP
AB 118	*SH* 705
AB 119	13 GP
AB 120	14 GP
AB 121	16 GP
AB 122	17 GP
AB 123	1 GP
AB 124	10 GP
AB 125	2 GP
AB 126*	Asclep. 34 GP
AB 127*	Asclep. 35 GP
AB 128*	Asclep. 36 GP
AB 129	3 GP
AB 130	4 GP
AB 131	21 GP

AB 132	15 GP
AB 133*	22 GP
AB 134*	Asclep. 37 GP
AB 135	5 GP
AB 136	Asclep. 38 GP
AB 137	6 GP
AB 138	7 GP
AB 139	8 GP
AB 140	9 GP
AB 141*	Asclep. 39 GP
AB 142	19 GP
AB 143º	*SH* 702
AB 144º	*SH* 701
AB 145º	*SH* 698
AB 146º	*SH* 699
AB 147º	*SH* 706
AB 148º	*SH* 700
AB 149º	*SH* 707
AB 150º	*SH* 703

Key:

* Denotes a disputed or doubly ascribed work.

º Denotes a fragment or a reference by an ancient author to a work that has not survived.

BIBLIOGRAPHY

bbenes, J. G. J. 1996. "The Doric of Theocritus. A Literary Language." In Harder, Regtuit, and Wakker 1996:1–17.

ccorinti, D. and Chuvin, P., eds. 2003. *Des Géants à Dionysos: Mélanges offerts à Francis Vian*. Hellenica 10. Alessandria.

costa-Hughes, B. 2002. *Polyeideia—The Iambi of Callimachus and the Archaic Iambic Tradition*. Berkeley.

costa-Hughes, B., and Stephens, S. A. 2001. "*Aetia* Fr. 1.5: I Told my Story like a Child." *ZPE* 136:214–216.

———. 2002. "Rereading Callimachus' *Aitia* fr 1." *CP* 97:238–55.

dams, W. L. and Borza, E. N., eds. 1982. *Philip II, Alexander the Great, and the Macedonian Heritage*. Washington, DC.

hrens, H. L. 1839–1843. *De Graecae linguae dialectis*. Göttingen.

inslie, T. and Ledbetter, B. 1980. *The Body Language of Horses*. New York.

lbino, D. 1962-1963. "La divisione in capitoli nelle opera degli antichi." Ann. Fac. Lett. Fil. Univ. Napoli 10:219-234

lbrecht, M. 1996. *The Epigrams of Posidippus of Pella*. MA Thesis. Dublin 1996.

lcock, S., Cherry, J., and Elsner, J., eds. 2001. *Pausanias: Travel and Memory in Roman Greece*. Oxford.

lgra, K., Barnes, J., Mansfeld, J., and Schofield, M., eds. 1999. *The Cambridge History of Hellenistic Philosophy*. Cambridge.

llen, T. W., ed. 1912. *Homeri Opera V (Hymns, Cycle, Fragments)*. Oxford.

———. 1931. *Homeri Ilias*. 3 vols. Oxford.

nderson, R. D., Parsons, P. J., and Nisbet, R. G. M. 1979. "Elegiacs of Gallus from Qasr Ibrim." *JRS* 69:125–155.

ndronikos, M. 1986². Ο Πλάτων και η Τέχνη. Οι Πλατωνικές απόψεις για το ωραίο και τις εικαστικές τέχνες. Athens.

Bibliography

Angiò, F. 1999. "Posidippo di Pella, l'ep. xvii Gow-Page e l'Αἰθιοπία *MF* 56:150–158.

———. 2002. "Filita di Cos in bronzo (Ermesianatte, fr. 7, 75–78 Powell-P. Mi Vogl. 309, col. X, ll 16–25." *Archiv für Papyrusforschung* 48:17–24.

Archer-Hind, R.D. and Hicks, R.D., eds. 1920. *Cambridge Composition* Cambridge.

Argentieri, L. 1998. "Epigramma e libro. Morfologia delle raccolte epigrammatich antiche premeleagree." *ZPE* 121:1–20.

Arrighetti, G. 1964. *Satiro. Vita di Euripide.* Pisa.

Asmis, E. 1999. "Epicurean Epistemology." In Algra, Barnes, Mansfeld, an Schofield 1999:260–294.

Asper, M. 2001. "Gruppen und Dichter: Zu Programmatik und Adressatenbezu bei Kallimachos." *A&A* 47:84–116.

Badian, E., ed. 1976. *Alexandre le Grand: Image et réalité.* Entretiens Fondatio Hardt 22. Genève.

Bagnall, R., Browne, G. M., Hanson, A. E., and Koenen, L., eds. 1981. *Proceedin of the Sixteenth International Congress of Papyrology.* Chico.

Barbantani, S. 1998. "Un epigramma encomiastico 'alessandrino' per Augusto (*S* 982)." *Aevum Antiquum* 11:255–344.

Barchiesi, A. 1994. "Immovable Delos: *Aeneid* 3.73–98 and the Hymns Callimachus." *CQ* 44:438–43.

———. 2000. "Rituals in Ink: Horace on the Greek Lyric Tradition." In Depe and Obbink 2000:167–182.

Barigazzi, A. 1968. "It testamento di Posidippo di Pella." *Hermes* 96:190–216.

Barker, A. 1984. *Greek Musical Writings.* Vol. I: *The Musician and his A* Cambridge.

Barker, R. 2002. *Legitimating Identities. The Self-Presentations of Rulers and Subjec* Cambridge.

Bernabé, A., ed. 1987. *Poetae epici Graeci. Testimonia et fragmenta.* Vol. I. Leipzig

Barnes, J. 1999. "Roman Aristotle." In Barnes and Griffin 1999:1–69.

314

Barnes, J. and Griffin, M. D., eds. 1999. *Philosophia Togata* II. Oxford

Bartoněk, A. 1972. *Classification of West Greek Dialects Around 350 B.C.* Prague.

Bastianini, G. 1996. "Tipologie dei rotoli e problemi di ricostruzione." *PapLup* 4:21–42

Bastianini, G. and Austin, C., eds. 2002. *Posidippi Pellaei Quae Supersunt Omnia.* Milan.

Bastianini, G. and Casanova, A., eds. 2002. *Il Papiro di Posidippo un anno dopo. Atti del convegno internazionale di studi Firenze 13–14 giugno 2002.* Florence.

Bastianini, G. and Gallazzi, C. 1993a. "Il poeta ritrovato." *Rivista Ca' de Sass* 121:28–39.

———. 1993b. *Posidippo. Epigrammi.* Milan.

Bastianini, G., and Gallazzi, C., eds. with Austin, C. 2001. *Posidippo di Pella. Epigrammi (P. Mil. Vogl. VIII 309).* Papiri dell'Università degli Studi di Milano, 8. Milan.

Baumbach, M. 2000. "'Wanderer, kommst du nach Sparta . . .' Zur Rezeption eines Simonides-Epigramms." *Poetica* 32:1–22.

———, ed. 2001. *Tradita et Inventa. Beiträge zur Rezeption der Antike.* Heidelberg.

Bearzot, C. 1992. "Πτολεμαῖος Μακεδών. Sentimento nazionale macedone e contrapposizioni etniche all'inizio del regno tolemaico." In Sordi 1992:39–53.

———. 1993. "Mantica e condotta di guerra: strategi, soldati e induvini di fronte all'interpretazione del evento 'prodigioso,'" In Sordi 1993:97–121.

Becker, A. S. 1995. *The Shield of Achilles and the Poetics of Ekphrasis.* Lanham, MD and London.

Bennett, C. 2002. "The Children of Ptolemy III and the Date of the Exedra of Thermos." *ZPE* 138:141–145.

Benveniste, E. 1932a. "Le sens du mot ΚΟΛΟΣΣΟΣ et les noms grecs de la statue." *RPhil* 58:118-135.

———. 1932b. "A propos de ΚΟΛΟΣΣΟΣ." *RPhil* 58:381.

Bernardini, P. and Bravi, L. 2002. "Note di lettura al nuovo Posidippo." *QUCC* 70:147–163.

Bibliography

Bernsdorff, H. 2002. "Anmerkungen zum neuen Poseidipp (P. Mil. Vogl. VIII 309)." *Göttinger Forum für Altertumswissenschaft* 5:11–44. http://www.gfa.d-r.de/5-02/bernsdorff.pdf.

Berve, H. 1926. *Das Alexanderreich auf prosopographischer Grundlage.* München.

Bettenworth, A. 2002. "Asclepiades XXV G.-P. (A.P. 5,181). Ein Beitrag zum sympotisch-erotischen Epigramm." In Harder, Regtuit, and Wakker 2002:27–38.

Betz, H. D. 1998, "'Der Erde Kind bin ich und des gestirnten Himmels.' Zur Lehre vom Menschen in den orphischen Goldplättchen." In Graf 1998:399–419.

Bilde, P. and Engberg-Pedersen, T., eds. 1992. *Ethnicity in Hellenistic Egypt.* Studies in Hellenistic Civilization 3. Aarhus.

Billows, R. A. 1990. *Antigonos the One-Eyed and the Creation of the Hellenistic State.* Berkeley.

Bing, P. 1988. *The Well-Read Muse: Present and Past in Callimachus and the Hellenistic Poets.* Hypomnemata 90. Göttingen.

————. 1995 "Ergänzungsspiel in the Epigrams of Callimachus." *A&A* 41:115–131.

————. 1998. "Between Literature and the Monuments." In Harder, Regtuit, and Wakker 1998:21–43.

————. 2002. "Posidippus on Stones: the First Section of the New Posidippus Papyrus (P. Mil. Vogl. VIII 309, col. I–IV 6)." APA Posidippus Panel. http://www.apaclassics.org/Publications/Posidippus/posidippus.html.

————. 2002a. "The Un-Read Muse? Inscribed Epigram and Its Readers in Antiquity." In Harder, Regtuig, and Wakker 2000:39–66.

————. 2002b. "Medeios of Olynthos, Son of Lampon, and the *Iamatika* of Posidippus." *ZPE* 140:297–300.

————. 2003. "Posidippus and the Admiral: Kallikrates of Samos in the Epigrams of the Milan Posidippus Papyrus." *GRBS* 43:243–266.

————. (forthcoming). "The Politics and Poetics of Geography in the Milan Posidippus. Section One: On Stones (P.Mil.Vogl. VIII 309, col. I–IV 6." In Gutzwiller 2004 (forthcoming).

Bingen, J. 1975. *Le monde grec. Pensée littérature histoire documents. Homages à Claire Préaux.* Bruxelles.

Blümel, W., Kramer, B., Kramer, J., and Römer, C. E., eds. 1996. *Hestia und Erigone: Vorträge und Aufsätze.* Stuttgart and Leipzig.

Boardman, J. 1970. *Greek Gems and Finger Rings. Early Bronze Age to Late Classical.* London.

Boedeker, D. and Sider, D., eds. 2001. *The New Simonides: Contexts of Praise and Desire.* New York.

Bolmarcich, S. 2002. "Hellenistic Sepulchral Epigrams on Homer," in Harder, Regtuit, and Wakker 2002:67–83.

Bonacasa, N. and di Vita, A., eds. 1984. *Alessandria e il mondo ellenistico-romano. Studi in onore di Achille Adriani.* Roma.

Borbein, A. H. 1973. "Die griechische Statue des 4. Jahrhunderts v. Chr.." *JdI* 88:43–212.

Bosworth, A. B. 1976. "Arrian and the Alexander Vulgate." In Badian 1976:1–46.

Bouché-Leclerq, A. 1879–1882. *Histoire de la Divination dans l'Antiquité,* 4 vols. Paris.

Bremer, J. M., Erp Taalman Kip, A. M. van, and Slings, S. R., eds. 1987. *Some Recently Found Greek Poems, Text and Commentary.* Mnemosyne. Supplementum 99. Leiden.

Bremmer, J. N. 1984. "Greek Maenadism Revisited," *ZPE* 55:267–286.

Bringman, K. 2000. *Geben und Nehmen. Monarchische Wohltätigkeit und Selbstdarstellung,* Frankfurt.

Brixhe C. 1993. "Le déclin du dialecte crétois: essai de phénomenologie." In Crespo, García, Ramón, and Striano 1993:37–71.

———. 1999. In Cassio 1999. Naples:66–69.

Brooklyn Museum. 1988. *Cleopatra's Egypt: Age of the Ptolemies.* New York.

Brown, J. W. 1999. "On Aesthetic Response." In Goguen 1999:144–160.

Buck, C. D. 1955. *The Greek Dialects.* Chicago.

Bibliography

Buffière, F. 1977. "Sur quelques épigrammes du livre XII de l'Anthologie." *REG* 90:95–107.

Bulloch, A., Gruen, E., Long, A. A., Stewart, A. F., eds. 1993. *Images and Ideologies. Self-definition in the Hellenistic World.* Berkeley.

Burstein, S. M. 1982. "Arsinoe II Philadelphos: A Revisionist View." In Adams and Borza 1982:197–212.

Butler, H. E. and Barber, E.A. 1933. *The Elegies of Propertius.* Oxford.

Cairns, F. 1996. In Faber, R., Seidensticker, B., eds. *Wörte, Bilder, Töne. Studien zur Antike und Antikerezeption.* Würzburg:77–88.

Cameron, A. 1980. "Poetae Novelli." *HSCP* 84:127–175.

———. 1993. *The Greek Anthology from Meleager to Planudes.* Oxford.

———. 1995. *Callimachus and His Critics.* Princeton.

Carpenter, T. H. and Faraone, C. A., eds. 1993. *Masks of Dionysus.* Ithaca.

Cartledge, P. and Spawforth, A. 1989. *Hellenistic and Roman Sparta.* London and New York.

Cassio, A. C. 1993. "Κατὰ Διάλεκτον." In Pretagostini 1993:903–1010.

———, ed. 1999. Κατὰ Διάλεκτον. Atti del III Colloquio Internazionale di Dialettologia Greca.

Celentano, M. S. 1995. "L'elogia della brevità tra retorica e letteratura. Callimaco, ep. 11 Pf. = A. P. VII. 447." *QUCC* n. s. 49:67–79.

Chamoux, F. 1975. "L'épigramme de Poseidippos sur le Phare d'Alexadrie." In Bingen 1975:214–222.

Chaniotis, A. 1998. "Willkommene Erdbeben." In Olshausen and Sonnabend 1998:404–416.

———. 2000. "Das Jenseits—eine Gegenwelt?" In Hölscher, T., ed. 2000. *Gegenwelten zu den Kulturen der Griechen und der Römer in der Antike*:159–181.

Childs, W. A. P. 1994. "Platon et les images et l'art grec du IVe siècle avant J.-C." *Révue archéologique*:33–56.

Clairmont, C. W. 1970. *Gravestone and Epigram: Greek Memorials from the Archaic and Classical Period.* Mainz am Rein.

Clarysse, W. 1992. "Some Greeks in Egypt." In Johnson 1992:51–56

———. 1998 "Ethnic Diversity and Dialect among the Greeks of Hellenistic Egypt." In Verhoogt and Vleeming 1998:1–13.

Cockle, W. E. H. 1987. *Euripides. Hypsipyle.* Rome.

Cohen, A. 1997. *The Alexander Mosaic. Stories of Victory and Defeat.* Cambridge.

Cohen, B. 1997. "Divesting the Female Breast of Clothes in Classical Sculpture." In Koloski-Ostrow and Lyons 1997:66–92.

Cole, S. G. 1980. "New Evidence for the Mysteries of Dionysos." *GRBS* 21.223–238.

———. 1984. "Life and death. A New Epigram for Dionysos." *EA* 4.37–49

———. 1991. "Dionysiac Mysteries in Phrygia in the Imperial Period." *EA* 17.41–49.

———. 1993. "Voices from beyond the grave: Dionysus and the Dead." In Carpenter and Faraone 1993:276–295.

Colin, G. 1930. *Fouilles de Delphes* III 3. *Inscriptions de la terrasse du temple et de la région nord du sanctuaire. Monuments des Messéniens, de Paul-Émile et de Prusias.* Paris.

Colvin, S. 1999. *Dialect in Aristophanes.* Oxford.

Connor, W. R. 1987. "Tribes, Festivals, and Processions: Civic Ceremonial and Political Manipulation in Archaic Greece." *JHS* 107:40–50.

Crespo, E., García Ramón, J. L., and Striano, A., eds. 1993. *Dialectologica Graeca. II Coloquio Internacional de Dialectologia Griega.* Madrid.

Criscuolo, L. and Geraci, G., eds. 1989. *Egitto e storia antica dall'ellenismo all'eta araba. Bilancio di un confronto. Atti del Colloquio Internazionale, Bologna, 31 agosto–2 settembre 1987.* Bologna.

D'Alessio, G. B., ed. 1996. *Callimaco. Inni. Epigrammi. Frammenti.* Milan.

Davies, M. ed., 1988. *Epicorum Graecorum Fragmenta.* Göttingen.

Day, J. W. 1989. "Rituals in Stone: Early Greek Grave Epigrams and Monuments." *JHS* 109:16–28.

Bibliography

de Grummond, N. T. and Ridgway, B. S., eds. 2000. *From Pergamon to Sperlonga. Sculpture and Context.* Berkeley.

Denniston, J. D. 1954. *The Greek Participle.* 2nd edition. Oxford.

Denniston, J. D. and Page, D., eds. 1957. *Aeschylus. Agamemnon.* Oxford.

Depew, M. and Obbink, D., eds. 2000. *Matrices of Genre. Authors, Canons, and Society.* Cambridge, MA.

Derrida, J. 1987. *The Truth in Painting.* Chicago 1987.

Dickey, E. 1996. *Greek Forms of Address.* Oxford.

Dickie, M. W. 1994. "Which Posidippus?" *GRBS* 35:373–383.

———. 1995a. "A New Epigram by Poseidippus on an Irritable Dead Cretan." *BASP* 32:5–12.

———. 1995b. "The Dionysiac Mysteries in Pella." *ZPE* 109:81–86.

———. 1998. "Poets as Initiates in the Mysteries: Euphorion, Philicus, and Posidippus." *A&A* 44:65–76.

Dignas, B. 2002. *Economy of the Sacred in Hellenistic and Roman Asia Minor.* Oxford.

Dillon, M. 1996. "The Importance of Oionomanteia in Greek Divination." In Dillon 1996:99–121.

Dillon, M., ed. 1996. *Religion in the Ancient World: New Themes and Approaches.* Amsterdam.

Dittenberger, W. and Purgold, K., eds. 1896. *Olympia V: Die Inschriften.* Berlin.

Dobias-Lalou, C. 1987. "Dialecte et koiné dans les inscriptions de Cyrenaïque." *Verbum* 10:29–50.

Dohrn, T. 1968. "Die Marmor-Standbilde de Daochus-Weihgeschenks in Delphi." *Antike Plastik* 8:33–53.

Donohue, A. A. 1988. *Xoana and the Origins of Greek Sculpture.* Atlanta.

———. 1995. "Winckelmann's History of Art and Polyclitus." In Moon 1995:327–353.

Dorandi, T. 1999a. *Antigone de Caryste. Fragments.* Paris.

————. 1999b. "Chronology." In Algra, Barnes, Mansfeld, and Schofield 1999:31–54.

Dougherty, C. and Kurke, L., eds. 1993. *Cultural Poetics in Archaic Greece.* Cambridge.

Dubois, L. 1995. "Une tablette de malédiction de Pella: s'agit-il du premier texte Macédonien?" *REG* 108:190–197.

Dunbar, N. 1995. *Aristophanes. Birds.* Oxford.

Ebert, J. 1972. *Griechische Epigramme auf Sieger an gymnischen und hippischen Agonen.* Berlin.

Edelstein, E. and Edelstein, L. 1998. *Asclepius. Collection and Interpretation of the Testimonies.* Baltimore.

Edelman, M. 1988. *Constructing the Political Spectacle.* Chicago.

————. 1995. *From Art to Politics. How Artistic Creations Shape Political Conceptions.* Chicago.

Edwards, C. M. 1996. "Lysippos." In Palagia and Pollitt 1996:130–153.

Eichholz, D. E., ed. 1965. *Theophrastus. De Lapidibus.* Oxford.

————, ed. 1971. *Pliny. Natural History.* Vol. X. Cambridge, MA.

El-Mosallami, A. H. S., ed. 1992. *Proceedings of the XIXth International Congress of Papyrology.* Cairo.

Elsner, J. 2001. "Structuring 'Greece': Pausanias's Periegesis as a Literary Construct." In Alcock, Cherry, and Elsner 2001:3–20.

Erbse, H., ed. 1969–1988. *Scholia Graeca in Homeri Iliadem I–VII.* Berlin.

Errington, R. M. 1976. "Alexander and the Hellenistic World." In Badian 1976:137–179.

Erskine, A., ed. 2003. *A Companion to the Hellenistic World.* Oxford.

Euben, J. P. 1990. *The Tragedy of Political Theory. The Road Not Taken.* Princeton.

Evelyn-White, H.G. 1982. *Hesiod. The Homeric Hymns and Homerica.* Cambridge, MA.

Fantuzzi, M. 1993. "Preistoria di un genere letterario: a proposito degil Inni V e VI di Callimaco." In Pretagostini 1993:III 927–946.

Bibliography

———. 2003. "La technica versificatoria del P. Mil. Vogl. VIII. 309." In Bastianini and Casanova 2002:79–97.

Fantuzzi, M. (forthcoming). "Posidippus at court." In Gutzwiller 2004 (forthcoming).

Fantuzzi, M. and Hunter, R. 2002. *Muse e Modelli. La poesia ellenistica da Alessandro Magno ad Augusto.* Rome.

Fernández-Galiano, E. 1987. *Posidipo de Pela.* Madrid.

Flach, D. 1967. *Das literarische Verhältnis von Horaz und Properz.* Giessen.

Foley, H. 1994. *The Homeric Hymn to Demeter. Translation, Commentary, and Interpretive Essays.* Princeton.

Forsmann, B. 1966. *Untersuchungen zur Sprache Pindars.* Wiesbaden.

Fowler, B. H. 1989. *The Hellenistic Aesthetic.* Madison.

Fraser, P. M. 1972. *Ptolemaic Alexandria.* 3 vols. Oxford.

Fredouille, J.-C. and Deléani, D., eds. 1997. *Titres et articulations du texte dans les œuvres antiques.* Paris.

Freyer-Schauenberg, B. 1974. *Samos* XI. Bonn.

Frischer, B. 1984. "Horace and the Monuments: A New Interpretation of the Archytas *Ode* (C.1.28)." *HSCP* 88:71–102.

Fuhrer, Th. 1992. *Die Auseinandersetzung mit den Chorlyrikern in den Epinikien des Kallimachos.* Basel.

Furley, W. D. and Bremer, J. M. 2001. *Greek Hymns.* 2 vols. Tübingen.

Gadamer, H.-G. 1989. *Truth and Method.* New York.

Garland, R. 1985. *The Greek Way of Death.* London.

———. 1995. *The Eye of the Beholder: Deformity and Disability in the Graeco-Roman World.* Ithaca/New York.

Garnsey, P. 2000. "Introduction: the Hellenistic and Roman Periods." In Rowe and Schofield 2000:404–414.

Gärtner, Th. 2002. "Zum neuen Poseidipp, col. XII 16–19: Ein Seelenverwandter der Alkibicees in hellenistischer Zeit." *ZPE* 139:32.

Gauthier, Ph. 1985. *Les cités grecques et leur bienfaiteurs.* BCH Suppl. 12. Paris.

Gerber, D. E. 1982. *Pindar's Olympian One: A Commentary.* Toronto.

Geuss, R. 2002. *History and Illusion in Politics.* Cambridge.

Giangrande, G. 1963. "Konjekturen zur Anthologia Palatina." *RM* 70:255–263.

——. 1968. "Sympotic Literature and Epigram." In *L'Épigramme Grecque.* Entretiens Fondation Hardt 14. Genève:91–174.

——. 1969. "Interpretationen hellenistischer Dichter." *Hermes* 97:440–454.

Gibson, S. 2003. *Aristoxenus of Tarentum and the Birth of Musicology.* D.Phil. thesis. University of Oxford. Oxford.

Gill, C. 1994. *The Self in Dialogue.* Oxford.

Gioure, E. 1978. Ο κρατήρας του Δερβενίου. Athens.

Girone, M. 1998. Ἰάματα: *Guarigioni miracolose di Asclepio in testi epigrafici.* Bari.

Goguen, J. A., ed. 1999. *Art and the Brain.* Special Issue of the Journal of Consciousness Studies. Controversies in Science and the Humanities 6.

——, ed. 2000. *Art and the Brain* II. Special Issue of the Journal of Consciousness Studies. Controversies in Science and the Humanities 7.

Goldhill, S. 1991. *The Poet's Voice.* Cambridge.

——. 1994. "The Naive and Knowing Eye: Ecphrasis and the Culture of Viewing in the Hellenistic World." In Goldhill and Osborne 1994:197–223.

Goldhill, S. and Osborne, R., eds. 1994. *Art and Text in Ancient Greek Culture.* Cambridge.

Gombrich, E. H. 1984. *The Story of Art.* Englewood Cliffs, NJ.

Gööck, R. 2002. *Erfindungen der Menschheit: Druck, Grafik, Musik, Foto, Film.* Blaufelden.

Gow, A. S. F. 1954. "Asclepiades and Posidippus: Notes and Queries." *CR* 68:195–200.

——. 1958. *The Greek Anthology: Sources and Ascriptions.* London.

——, ed. 1965. *Theocritus.* 2 vols. Cambridge.

Bibliography

Gow, A. S. F. and Page, D. L. 1965. *The Greek Anthology: Hellenistic Epigrams.* 2 vols. Cambridge.

———. 1968. *The Greek Anthology: The Garland of Philip.* 2 vols. Cambridge.

Graf, F. ed. 1998. *Ansichten griechischer Rituale. Geburtstags-Symposium für Walter Burkert. Castelen bei Basel 15. bis 18. März.* Basel.

Green, P. 1990. *Alexander to Actium. The Historical Evolution of the Hellenistic Age.* Berkeley.

Griffith, M. and Mastronarde, D. J., eds. 1990. *Cabinet of the Muses: Essays on Classical and Comparative Literature in Honor of Thomas G. Rosenmeyer.* Berkeley.

Griffin, J. 1983. *Homer on Life and Death.* Oxford.

Grimm, G. 1998. *Alexandria: die erste Königsstadt der hellenistischen Welt.* Mainz.

Gronewald, M. 1993. "Der neue Poseidippos und Kallimachos Epigramm 35." *ZPE* 99:28–29.

———. 2002 "Bemerkungen zum neuen Poseidippos." *ZPE* 138:1–5.

Gutzwiller, K. J. 1992. "Callimachus' *Lock of Berenice*: Fantasy, Romance, and Propaganda." *AJP* 113:359–385.

———. 1995. "Cleopatra's ring." *GRBS* 36:383–398.

———. 1996. "Vergil and the Date of the Theocritean Epigram Book." *Philologus* 140:92–99.

———. 1998. *Poetic Garlands: Hellenistic Epigrams in Context.* Berkeley.

———. 2002a. "Art's Echo: The Tradition of Hellenistic Ecphrastic Epigram." In Harder, Regtuit, and Wakker 2002:85–112.

———. 2002b. "A New Hellenistic Poetry Book." APA Posidippus Panel http://www.apaclassics.org/Publications/Posidippus/posidippus.html

———. 2003. "Posidippus and the Tradition of Ecphrastic Epigram." In *Il Papiro di Posidippo un anno dopo.* Florence.

———, ed. (forthcoming). *The New Posidippus: A Hellenistic Poetry Book.* Oxford.

Haas, V. 1994. *Geschichte der hethitischen Religion.* Handbuch der Orientalistik vol. 15. Leiden.

Habicht, C. 1969. *Altertümer von Pergamon. 8.3: Die Inschriften des Asklepieions,* Berlin.

———. 1990. "Athens and the Attalids." *Hesperia* 59:561–577.

Haegemans, K. and Kosmetatou, E. 2003. "Aratus and the Achaean Background of Polybius." In Schepens and Bollansée 2003.

Hahm, D. E. 2000. "Kings and Constitutions: Hellenistic Theories." In Rowe and Schofield 2000:457–476.

Halleaux, R. and Schamp, J., eds. 1986. *Les lapidaires Grecs.* Paris.

Halliday, W.R. 1913. *Greek Divination. A Study of its Methods and Principles.* London.

Hammond, N. G. L. and Walbank, F. W. 1988. *A History of Macedonia.* Oxford.

Harder, M.A. 1998. "Generic Games' in Callimachus' *Aetia.*" In Harder, Regtuit, and Wakker 1998:95–113.

Harder, M. A., Regtuit, R. F., and Wakker, G. K., eds. *Theocritus.* Hellenistica Groningana 2. Groningen.

———. 1998. *Genre in Hellenistic Poetry.* Hellenistica Groningana 3. Groningen.

———. 2000. *Apollonius Rhodius.* Hellenistica Groningana 4. Groningen.

———. 2002. *Hellenistic Epigram.* Hellenistica Groningana 5. Leuven.

———. (forthcoming). *Callimachus II.* Hellenistica Groningana 6. Leuven.

Hardin, J. 1996. *The Lure of Egypt: Land of the Pharaohs Revisited.* St. Petersburg, Florida.

Harrauer, H. 1981. "Epigrammincipit auf einem Papyrus aus dem 3. Jh. v. Chr. P. P. Vindob G 40611: Ein Vorbericht." In Bagnall, Browne, Hanson, and Koenen 1981:49–53.

Harris, D. 1995. *The Treasures of the Parthenon and the Erechtheion.* Oxford.

Harris, W. V. ed. (forthcoming). *Ancient Alexandria: Between Greece and Egypt, Columbia University, 10–11 October 2002.*

Harth, E. 1999. "The Emergence of Art and Language in the Human Brain." In Goguen 1999:97–115.

Bibliography

Hatzopoulos M. 2000. "'L'histoire par les noms' in Macedonia." In Hornblower and Matthews 2000:99–117.

Hauben H. 1970. *Callicrates of Samos. A Contribution to the Study of the Ptolemaic Admiralty. With a Samian Inscription published in Appendix by Günter Dunst.* Studia Hellenistica. 18. Leuven.

————. 1983. "Arsinoe II et la politique exterieure de l'Égypte." In Van 't Dack, van Dessel, and van Gucht 1983:97–127.

————. 1989. "Aspects du culte des souverains." In Criscuolo and Geraci 1989:441–467.

————. 1992. "Chronologie Macedonienne et Ptolemaique." *CdE* 67:143–171.

Hazzard, R. A. 2000. *Imagination of a Monarchy: Studies in Ptolemaic Propaganda.* Toronto.

Hebert, B. D. 1983. *Beschreibungen von Kunstwerken: Archäologischer Kommentar zu den Ekphraseis des Libanios und Nikolaos.* Graz.

Helmbold, W. C. and Cherniss, H. 1957. *Plutarch. Moralia.* Vol. 12. Cambridge, MA.

Hemingway, S. 2000. "A Technical Analysis of the Bronze Horse and Jockey Group from Artemision." In Mattusch, Brauer, and Knudsen 2000:226–234.

Henderson, J. 2000. *Aristophanes.* Vol. 3. Cambridge, MA.

Hengel, M. 1984. "Die Evangelienüberschriften." *SB Heidelberg, phil.-hist. Kl.* Bericht 3.

Henrichs, A. 1978. "Greek Maenadism from Olympias to Messalina." *HSCP* 82. 121–60

————. 1990. "Between Country and City: Cultic Dimensions of Dionysos in Athens and Attica." In Griffith and Mastronarde 1990:257–77.

————. 1993. "Response." In Bulloch, Gruen, Long, and Stewart 1993:171–195.

Henry, A. S. 1983. *Honors and Privileges in Athenian Decrees: the Principal Formulae of Athenian Honorary Decrees.* Olms.

Herrlinger, G. 1930. *Totenklage um Tiere in der antiken Dichtung.* Tübinger Beiträge 8. Stuttgart.

Herrman, P. 1998. Milet. *Die Inschriften. Band* VI 2. Berlin.

Herzog, R. 1931. *Die Wunderheilungen von Epidauros. Ein Beitrag zur Geschichte der Medizin und der Religion.* Philologus Supplementum 22. Leipzig.

Hintzen-Bohlen, B., 1990. "Die Familiengruppe. Ein Mittel zur Selbstdarstellung hellenistischer Herrscher." *JdI* 105:109–154.

————. 1992. *Herrscherrepräsentation im Hellenismus. Untersuchungen zu Weihgeschenken, Stiftungen und Ehrenmonumenten in den mutterländischen Heiligtümern, Delphi, Olympia, Delos und Dodona.* Köln/Weimar/Wien.

Hodder, I. 1991. *Reading the Past: Current Approaches to Interpretation in Archaeology.* Cambridge.

Hölkeskamp, K.-J. 1999. *Schiedsrichter, Gesetzgeber und Gesetzgebung im archaischen Griechenland.* Historia Einzelschriften vol. 131. Stuttgart.

Hoepfner, W. 1971. *Zwei Ptolemäerbauten.* AM Beiheft 1. Berlin.

————. 1989. "Zu den grossen Altären von Magnesia und Pergamon." *AA*:601–634.

————. 1996. "Der vollendete Pergamonaltar." *AA*:111–123.

Hoffman, G. L. 1997. *Imports and Immigrants: Near Eastern Contacts with Iron Age Crete.* Ann Arbor.

Hopkinson, N. 1984. *Callimachus. Hymn to Demeter.* Cambridge.

Hornblower, S. and E. Matthews, eds. 2000. *Greek Personal Names. Their Value as Evidence.* Oxford

Horrocks, G. 1997. *Greek: A History of the Language and Its Speakers.* London.

Horsfall, N. 1991. *Virgilio: l'epopea in alambicco.* Naples.

Hunter, R. 1992. "Callimachus and Heraclitus." *MD* 28:113–123.

————. 1996a. *Theocritus and the Archaeology of Greek Poetry.* Cambridge.

————. 1996b. "Mime and Mimesis: Theocritus, *Idyll* 15." In Harder, Regtuit, Wakker 1996:149–169.

————, ed. 1999. *Theocritus. A Selection.* Cambridge.

————. 2002. "Out of the Afterlife: Colin Austin and Guido Bastianini, Editors, Posidippi Pellaei quae supersunt omnia. Milan 2002." *TLS* 29 November 2002:24–25. London.

―――. 2003. *Theocritus. Encomium of Ptolemy Philadelphus.* Berkeley.

―――. (forthcoming). "Speaking in glossai: Dialect Choice and Cultural Politics in Hellenistic Poetry."

Hunter, R. and Fantuzzi, M. 2002. *Muse e Modelli. La poesia ellenistica da Alessandro Magno ad Augusto.* Rome.

Huß, W. 1975. "Die zu Ehren Ptolemaios' III. und seiner Familie errichtete Statuengruppe von Thermos (IG IX I. I2, 56)." *CdE* 50:312–320.

Hutchinson, G. O. 1998. *Hellenistic Poetry.* Oxford.

―――. 2002. "The New Posidippus and Latin poetry. " *ZPE* 138:1–10.

Huxley, G. 1992. "BHPICOC." *JHS* 112:153.

Iplikçioglu, B. 1991. *Epigraphische Forschungen in Termessos und seinem Territorium.* Wien.

Isager, J. 1991. *Pliny on Art and Society. The Elder Pliny's Chapters on the History of Art.* Odense.

Jacquemin, A. and Laroche, D. 2001. "Le monument de Daochus ou le trésor des Thessaliens." *BCH* 125:305–332.

Janko, R. 1981. "The Structure of the Homeric Hymns: A Study in Genre." *Hermes* 109:9–10.

―――. 1986. "The Shield of Heracles and the Legend of Cycnus." *CQ NS* 36:38–59.

―――. 1992. *The Iliad. A Commentary.* Vol. 4. Cambridge.

―――, ed. 2000. *Philodemus. On Poems. Book 1.* Oxford.

Jobert, B. and Muller, P. 1987. *L'État en action: politiques publiques et corporatismes.* Paris.

Johnson, H. 1992. ed. *Life in a Multi-Cultural Society: Egypt from Cambyses to Constantine and Beyond.* SAOC. 51. Chicago.

Johnson, W. A. (forthcoming). "The Posidippus Papyrus: Bookroll and Reader." in Gutzwiller 2004 (forthcoming).

Jouanna, J. 1999. *Hippocrates.* Baltimore and London.

Kaibel, G. 1878. *Epigrammata Graeca ex lapidibus conlecta.* Berlin.

Bibliography

Kant, I. 1960/1764. *Observations on the Feeling on the Beautiful and the Sublime.* Translated by J. Goldthwait. Berkeley.

Käppel, L. 1992. *Paian. Studien zur Geschichte einer Gattung.* Berlin/New York.

Kebric, R. B. 1977. *In the Shadow of Macedon: Duris of Samos.* Historia Einzelschriften 29. Wiesbaden.

Kidd, D., ed. 1997. *Aratus. Phaenomena.* Cambridge.

Kind, E. 1927. "Sotakos." *RE* 3 A1. Berlin:1211.

Kirstein, R. 2002. "Companion Pieces in the Hellenistic Epigram." In Harder, Regtuit, Wakker 2002:113–135.

Knauer, G. N. 1979. *Die Aeneis und Homer.* Hypomnemata 7. 2nd edition. Göttingen.

Koenen, L. 1993. "The Ptolemaic King as a Religious Figure." In Bulloch, Gruen, Long, and Stewart 1993:103–105.

Koerner, R. 1993. *Inschriftliche Gesetzestexte der frühen griechischen Polis.* Köln.

Koester, H., ed. 1998. *Pergamon. Citadel of the Gods.* Harrisburg.

Kokkorou-Alewras, G. 1993. "Die Entstehungszeit der naxischen Delos-Löwen und anderer Tierskulpturen der Archaik." *Antike Kunst* 36:91–102.

Koloski-Ostrow, A.O. and Lyons, C.L., eds. 1997. *Naked Truths: Women, Sexuality, and Gender in Classical Art and Archaeology.* London-New York.

Kosmetatou, E. 1993. *The Public and Political Image of the Attalids of Pergamon. Studies on Inscriptions, Coinage, and Monuments.* Dissertation. UMI. Ann Arbor.

———. 2000. "Lycophron's 'Alexandra' Reconsidered: The Attalid Connection." *Hermes* 128:32–53.

———. 2002. "The Public Image of Julia Mamaea. An Epigraphic and Numismatic Inquiry." *Latomus* 61:398–414.

———. 2003a. "The Attalids of Pergamon." In Erskine 2003:159–174.

———. 2003b. "Posidippus AB 8 and Early Ptolemaic Cameos." *ZPE* 142:35–42.

Kosmetatou, E. and Papalexandrou, N. 2003. "Size Matters: Posidippus on the Colossi." *ZPE* 143:53–58.

Bibliography

Kotsidu, H. 2000. Τιμὴ καὶ δόξα. *Ehrungen für hellenistische Herrscher in griechischen Mutterland und in Kleinasien unter besonderer Berücksichtigung der archäologischen Denkmäler.* Frankfurt.

Kozloff, A. P. and Mitten, D. G., eds. *The Gods Delight: The Human Figure in Classical Bronze.* Cleveland.

Kühner, R., Blass, F., and Gerth, B. 1983. *Ausführliche Grammatik der griechischen Sprache.* 2 Volumes (reprint). Hannover.

Kurke, L. 1993. "The Economy of Kydos." In Dougherty and Kurke 1993:141–149.

Kyrieleis, H. 1975. *Bildnisse der Ptolemäer.* Berlin.

Laks, A. and Most, G. W., eds. 1997. *Studies on the Derveni Papyrus.* Oxford.

Lapatin, K. 2001. *Chryselephantine Statuary in the Ancient Mediterranean World.* Oxford.

Lapini, W. 2002. "Osservazioni sul nuovo Posidippo (P. Mil. Vogl. VIII 309)." *Lexis* 20:35–60.

———. 2002a. "Sul nuovo Posidippo (P. Mil. Vogl. VIII 309, col. IV. 30–35)." In *ZPE* 140:13–14.

Lasserre, F. 1959. "Aux origines de l'Anthologie: I. Le papyrus P. Brit. Mus. Inv. 589 (= Pack 1121)." *RhM* 102:222–247.

Lefkowitz, M. 2002. "New Hellenistic Epigrams about Women." In *Diotima. Materials for the Study of Women and Gender in the Ancient World.* http://www.stoa.org/diotima/anthology/epigrams.shtml.

Lejeune, M. 1971. "La dédicace de Νικάνδρη et l'écriture archaïque de Naxos." *RPhil.* 45:209–215.

Lehnus, L. 2002. "Posidippean and Callimachean queries." *ZPE* 138:11–13.

Levin, S. 1970. "The Nikandre Inscription (Schwyzer 788) and the Myth of the Indo-European Long *a-." *Kadmos* 9:157–165.

Lewis, N. 1986. *Greeks in Ptolemaic Egypt.* Oxford.

LiDonnici, L. 1995. *The Epidaurian Miracle Inscriptions. Text, Translation and Commentary.* Atlanta.

Lilimbake-Akamate, M. 1989 [1992]. "Από τα νεκροταφεία της Πέλλας." Το Αρχαιολογικό Έργο στη Μακεδονία και τη Θράκη 3. Thessaloniki:91–101.

Livrea, E. 1979. "Der Liller Kallimachos und die Mausefallen." *ZPE* 34:37–42.

———. 2002. "Critica testuale ed esegesi del nuovo Posidippo," In Bastianini and Casanova 2002:61–77.

Lloyd-Jones, H. 1963. "The Seal of Posidippus" *JHS* 83:75–99. (Reprinted in Lloyd-Jones 1990:158–195).

———. 1964. "Postscript." *JHS* 184:157. (Reprinted in Lloyd-Jones 1990:194–195).

———. 1990. *Greek Comedy, Hellenistic Literature, Greek Religion, and Miscellanea: The Academic Papers of Sir Hugh Lloyd-Jones.* Oxford.

———. 1994. *Sophocles.* 3 vols. Cambridge, MA.

———. 2002. "Notes on P. Mil. Vogl. VIII 309." *ZPE* 138:6.

———. 2002a. "Two More Notes on Pap. Mil. Vogl. VIII. 309 (Poseidippos)." *ZPE* 139:33.

———. 2002b. "Posidippo di Pella. Epigrammi (P. Mil. Vogl. VIII 309); ed. Guido Bastianini e Claudio Gallazzi con la collaborazione di Colin Austin," *IJCT* (forthcoming).

———. 2003. "All by Posidippus?" In Accorinti and Chuvin 2003:277–80.

Lloyd–Jones, H., and Parsons, P., eds. 1983. *Supplementum Hellenisticum.* Berlin and New York.

Lobel, E., Roberts, C. H., and Wegener, E. P. 1941. *The Oxyrhynchus Papyri.* XVIII. London.

Loewy, E. 1885. *Inschriften griechischer Bildhauer.* Leipzig.

Ludwig, W. 1968. "Die Kunst der Variation im hellenistischen Liebesepigramm." In *L'Épigramme Greque.* Entretiens Fondation Hardt 14. Genève:297–344.

Lund, H. 1992. *Lysimachus: A Study in Early Hellenistic Kingship.* London.

Luppe, W. 1977. "Rückseitentitel auf Papyrusrollen." *ZPE* 27:89–99

Maehler, H. 1982. *Die Lieder des Bakchylides* I 2. Leiden.

Magnelli, E. 2002. *Studi su Euforione.* Quaderni dei Seminari Romani di Cultura Greca 4. Rome.

Marcadé, J. 1987, "La pélerine de l'Artémis de Nikandré." In Servais 1987:369–375.

Marinone, N. 1972. *Berenice da Callimaco a Catullo.* Bologna.

Mariotti, S. 1955 *Il* Bellum Poenicum *e l'arte di Nevio.* Rome.

Massimilla, G., ed. 1996. *Callimaco.* Aitia: *Libri primo e secondo. Introduzione, testo critico, traduzione e commento.* Pisa.

Mattusch, C. C. 1996. *Classical Bronzes. The Art and Craft of Greek and Roman Statuary.* Ithaca.

Mattusch, C. C., Brauer, A. and Knudsen, S., eds. 2000. *From the Parts to the Whole: Acta of the 13th International Bronze Congress, Held at Cambridge, Massachusetts, May 28–June 1, 1996,* vol. 1. JRA Suppl. no. 39. Portsmouth.

Mayser, E. 1906. *Grammatik der griechischen Papyri aus der Ptolemäerzeit.* Leipzig

McCartney, E.S. 1935. "Wayfaring Signs." *CP* 30:97–112.

McKeown, J. C. 1987. *Ovid. Amores.* Vol. I. Liverpool.

Meillier, C. (with Ancher, G. and Boyaval, B.) 1976. "Callimaque (P. L. 76 d, 78 abc, 82, 84, 111c). Stésichore (?) (P. L. 76 abc)." *CRIPEL* 4:255–360.

Melaerts, H., ed. 1998. *Le Culte du souverain dans l'Égypte ptolémaïque au IIIe siècle avant notre ère.* Leuven.

Merkelbach, R. 1956. "Boukoliastai. Der Wettgesang der Hirten." *RhM* 99:97–133. (Reprinted in Merkelbach 1996. *Hestia und Erigone: Vorträge und Aufsätze.* Blümel, Kramer, Kramer, and Römer 1996:129–161).

Merkelbach, R. and Stauber, J. 1998. *Steinepigramme aus dem griechischen Osten I: Die Westküste Kleinasiens von Knidos bis Ilion.* Stuttgart.

————. 2001a. *Steinepigramme aus dem griechischen Osten II: Die Nordküste Kleinasiens (Marmarameer und Pontos).* Stuttgart.

————. 2001b. *Steinepigramme aus dem griechischen Osten III: Die Ferne Osten und das Landesinnere bis zum Tauros.* Stuttgart.

———. 2002. *Steinepigramme aus dem greichischen Osten* IV: *Die Südküste Kleinasiens, Syrien und Palaestina.* Stuttgart.

Merkelbach, R. and West, M. L. 1974. "Ein Archilochos-Papyrus," *ZPE* 14:97–113.

Metropolitan Museum of Art. *Catalogue of the Collection of Casts.* New York.

Miller, F. D. 2000. "Naturalism." In Rowe, Schoffield, Harrison, and Lane 2000:320–343.

Miller-Collett, S. G. 1973. "The Philippeion and Macedonian Hellenistic Architecture." *AM* 88:189–218.

Minas, M. 1998. "Die Κανήφορος. Aspekte der ptolemäischen Dynastiekults." In Melaerts 1998:43–60.

Moles, J. 2000. "The Cynics." In Rowe and Schofield 2000:415–434.

Montanari, F. 1995. "Filologi alessandrini e poeti alessandrini. La filologia sui 'contemporanei'." *Aevum Antiquum* 8:47–63.

Moon, W. M., ed. 1995. *Polycleitos, the Doryphoros, and Tradition.* Madison.

Mooren, L., ed. 2000. *Politics, Administration, and Society in the Hellenistic and Roman World. Proceedings of the International Colloquium, Bertinoro, 19–24 July 1997.* Studia Hellenistica 36. Leuven.

Moretti, L. 1953. *Iscrizioni agonistiche greche.* Roma.

Morpurgo Davies, A. 2000. "Greek Personal Names and Linguistic Continuity." In Hornblower and Matthews 2000:15–39.

Morris, S. 1995. *Daidalos and the Origins of Greek Art.* Princeton.

Murray, A. T. 1924. *Homer. The Iliad.* 2 vols. Cambridge, MA.

———. 1919. *Homer. The Odyssey.* 2 vols. Cambridge, MA.

Nachmanson, E. 1941. *Der griechische Buchtitel.* Göteborgs Hogskolas Arsskrift 47.19. Göteborg.

Nagy, G. 1996. *Poetry as Performance: Homer and Beyond.* Cambridge.

———. 1998. "The Library of Pergamon." In Koester 1998:185–232.

———. 2001. "Éléments orphiques chez Homère." *Kernos* 14:1–9.

Bibliography

Nelson, R. S. ed. 2000. *Visuality Before and Beyond the Renaissance*. Cambridge.

Nenna, M. D. 1998. "Gemmes et pierres dans le mobilier alexandrin." In *La Gloire d'Alexandrie*. Paris.

Niafas, K. 1997. "A Poetic Gem: Posidippus on Pegasus." *Pegasus* 40:16–17.

Nisbet, R. G. and Hubbard, M. 1970. *A Commentary on Horace: Odes. Book 1*. Oxford.

———. 1978. *A Commentary on Horace: Odes. Book 2*. Oxford.

Norden, E. 1913. *Agnostos Theos*. Leipzig.

———. 1970. *P. Vergilius Maro. Aeneis Buch VI*. 5th edition. Stuttgart.

Okin, L. 1974. *Studies on Duris of Samos*. Dissertation UCLA. UMI. Ann Arbor.

Oliver, R. P. 1951. "The First Medicean MS of Tacitus and the Titulature of Ancient Books." *TAPA* 82:232–261.

Olshausen, E. and Sonnabend, H., eds. 1998. *Naturkatastrophen in der antiken Welt*. Stuttgart.

Olson, S. D. and Sens, A., eds. 2000. *Archestratos of Gela*. Oxford.

Orlandini, P. 1961 "Kresilas." *Enciclopedia dell'arte antica* 4. Rome:405–408.

Page, D. L., ed. 1942. *Select Papyri III. Literary Papyri: Poetry*. Cambridge, MA.

———, ed. 1972. *Aeschyli Septem Quae Supersunt Tragoedias*. Oxford.

———, ed. 1975. *Epigrammata Graeca*. Oxford.

D.Page, D. and Denniston, J., eds. 1957. *Aeschylus. Agamemnon*. Oxford.

Palagia, O. and Pollitt, J. J., eds. 1996. *Personal Styles in Greek Sculpture*. Cambridge.

Papalexandrou, A. 2001. "Text in Context: Eloquent Monuments and the Byzantine Beholder." *Word and Image* 17:259–283.

Papalexandrou, N. (forthcoming). *The Visual Poetics of Power: Warriors, Youths, and Tripods in Early Greece*. Cambridge, MA.

Parsons, P. J. 1977. "The Lille Stesichorus." *ZPE* 26:7–36.

Parsons, P. J. and Kassel, R. 1977. "Callimachus: *Victoria Berenices*; Nachtrag zum neuen Kallimachos." *ZPE* 25:1–50.

Paton, W.R. 1918. *The Greek Anthology*. 5 vols. Cambridge, MA.

Pearson, L. 1983. *The Lost Histories of Alexander the Great*. Chicago.

Pease, A. S., ed. 1920 and 1923. M. *Tulli Ciceronis De Divinatione libri duo*. Illinois Studies in Language and Literature 6 and 8. Illinois.

Peek, W. 1955. *Griechische Vers-Inschriften*. Berlin.

Pelling, C. B. R., ed. 1990. *Characterization and Individuality in Greek Literature*. Oxford.

Pernice, E. 1939. "Die literarischen Zeugnisse." In O. Walter, ed. *Handbuch der Archäologie*. München.

Petrain, D. 2002a. "ΠΡΕΣΒΥΣ. A note on the New Posidippus (V.6-11)." *ZPE* 140:9-12.

———. 2003. "Homer, Theocritus and the Milan Posidippus (P. Mil. Vogl. VIII 309, col. III. 28–41)." *CJ* 98:359–388.

Pfrommer, M. 1999. *Alexandria im Schatten der Pyramiden*. Mainz.

Philipp, H. 1968. *Tektonon Daidala. Die Geschichte des Kunstlers in vorplatonischer Zeit*. Berlin.

Piacenza, N. 1998. "L'Immortalità Negata: Osservazioni sull'Epigramma VII 170 dell'Antologia Palatina." *Aevum Antiquum* 345–50.

Pinner, H. L. 1958. *The World of Books in Classical Antiquity*. Leiden.

Pircher, J. 1979. *Das Lob der Frau im vorchristlichen Grabepigramm der Griechen*. Innsbrück.

Plantzos, D. 1999. *Hellenistic Engraved Gems*. Oxford.

Poland, F. 1909. *Geschichte des Griechischen Vereinwesens*. Leipzig.

Pollard, J. 1977. *Birds in Greek Life and Myth*. London.

Pollitt, J. J. 1974. *The Ancient View of Greek Art: Criticism, History, and Terminology*. Yale Publications in the History of Art, 25. New Haven, CT.

———. 1986. *Art in the Hellenistic Age*. Cambridge.

Pomeroy, S. B., ed. 2001. *Women's History and Ancient History*. Chapel Hill.

Pontani, F. 1999. "The First Word of Callimachus AITIA." *ZPE* 128:57–59.

Pouilloux, J. 1960. *Fouilles de Delphes* II. *La région nord du sanctuaire.* Paris.

Preisshofen, F. 1979. "Kunsttheorie und Kunstbetrachtung." In *Le classicisme* ‹ *Rome aux Iers siècles avant et après J.-C.* Entretiens Fondation Hardt 25 Genève:263–277.

Pretagostini, R. ed. 1993. *Tradizione e innovazione nella cultura greca da Omer‹ all'età ellenistica. Scritti in onore di Bruno Gentili.* 3 vols. Rome.

Preuner, E. 1899. *Ein delphisches Weihgeschenk.* Leipzig.

Prins, Y. 1999. *Victorian Sappho.* Princeton.

Pritchett, W.R. 1979. *The Greek State at War.* Part III: *Religion.* Berkeley.

Pulleyn, S. 1997. *Prayer in Greek Religion.* Oxford.

Quaegebeur J. 1983. *Cultes égyptiens et grecs en Égypte hellénistique. L'exploitation de sources. Egypt and the Hellenistic World.* Studia Hellenistica 27 Leuven:303–324.

———. 1988. "Cleopatra VII and the Cults of the Ptolemaic Queens." I‹ Brooklyn Museum.

———. 1998. "Documents égyptiens relatifs à Arsinoé Philadelphe." In Melaert 1998:73–108.

Radinger, C. 1895. *Meleagros von Gadara: Eine literargeschichtliche Skizz‹* Innsbruck. (Reprinted in Tarán 1987, vol. 2).

Redondo, J. (forthcoming). "Dialect Forms in Callimachus." In Harder, Regtui‹ and Wakker (forthcoming).

Ramachandran, V. S. and Hirstein, W. 1999. "The Science of Art. A Neurologica‹ Theory of Aesthetic Experience." In Goguen 1999:15–51.

Ramachandran, V. M. and Freeman, A. 2001. "Sharpening Up the 'Science of Art' An Interview with Anthony Freeman." *Journal of Consciousness Studie‹ Controversies in Science and the Humanities* 8:9–29.

Ranocchia, G. 2001. "Filodemo e il περὶ τοῦ κουφίζειν ὑπερφανίας. *Papyrologica Lupiensia* 10:231–263.

Reed, J. 1997. *Bion of Smyrna.* Cambridge.

Reitzenstein, R. 1893. *Epigramm und Skolion: Ein Beitrag zur Geschichte der alexan‹ drinischen Dichtung.* Giessen.

336

Rengakos, A. 2000. "Aristarchus and the Hellenistic Poets." *Seminari Romani di Cultura Greca* 3:325–335.

Rice, E. E. 1983. *The Grand Procession of Ptolemy Philadelphus.* Oxford.

Richardson, N. 1993. *The Iliad: A Commentary,* vol. VI. Cambridge.

Richter, G. M. A. 1956. *Catalogue of Greek and Roman Antiquities in the Dumbarton Oaks Collection.* Cambridge.

————. 1965. *The Portraits of the Greeks.* 3 vols. London.

Riedweg, C. 1998. "Initiation—Tod—Unterwelt: Beobachtungen zur Kommunikationssituation und narrativen Technik der orphisch–bakchischen Goldplättchen." In Graf 1998:359–398.

Ridgway, B. S. 1970. *The Severe Style in Greek Sculpture.* Princeton.

————. 1974. "A Story of Five Amazons." *AJA* 78:1–17.

————. 1976. "The Amazon's Belt: An Addendum to A Story of Five Amazons." *AJA* 80:82.

————. 1981. *Fifth Century Styles in Greek Sculpture.* Princeton.

————. 1989. *Hellenistic Sculpture* I. *The Styles of ca. 331–200 BC.* Madison.

————. 1993². *The Archaic Style in Greek Sculpture.* Chicago.

————. 1997. *Fourth-Century Styles in Greek Sculpture.* London.

————. 2000. *Hellenistic Sculpture* II. *The Styles of ca. 200–100 BC.* Madison.

Robertson, M. 1975. *A History of Greek Art.* London and Cambridge.

Roeder, G. 1959. *Die ägyptische Götterwelt.* Zürich and Stuttgart.

Rossi, L. 1996. "Il testamento di Posidippo e le laminette auree di Pella." *ZPE* 112: 59–65.

————. 2001. *The Epigrams Ascribed to Theocritus: A Method of Approach.* Leuven.

Roux, G. 1960. "Qu'est-ce qu'un κολοσσός? Le 'colosse' de Rhodes; Les "colosses" mentionées par Eschyle, Hérodote, Théocrite et par diverses inscriptions." *REA* 62:5–40.

Rowe, C. 2000. "The Peripatos after Aristotle." In Rowe and Schofield 2000:390–395.

Rowe, C. and Schofield, M., eds. 2000. *The Cambridge History of Greek and Roman Political Thought.* Cambridge.

Rübke, J. 2001. *Die Religion der Römer.* München.

Rumpf, A. 1967. "Xenokrates." In Pauly-Wissowa 18:1531–1532.

Rusten, J. S. 1982. *Dionysius Scytobrachion.* Papyrologica Coloniensia 101. Opladen.

Rutherford, I. 2000. "Theoria and Dar_an: Pilgrimage and Vision in Greece and India." *CQ* 50:133–145.

Rutter, N. K. and Sparkes, B. A., eds. 2000. *Word and Image in Ancient Greece.* Edinburgh.

Savalli-Lestrade, I. 1998. *Les philoi royaux dans l'Asie Mineure hellénistique.* Genève.

Schepens, G. 1998. "Geschiedschrijving als Pyrrhusoverwinning. Enkele reflecties vauit de antieke historiografie." In Tollebeek, Verbeeck, and Verschaffel 1998:89–107.

———. 2003. "Phylarchus: Polybius on Tragic Historiography." In Schepens and Bollansée 2003.

Schepens, G. and J. Bollansée, eds. *The Shadow of Polybius. Intertextuality as a Tool in Ancient Historiography.* Leuven.

Schmalzriedt, E. 1970. Περὶ φύσεως. *Zur Frühgeschichte der Buchtitel.* Munich.

Schmidt-Dounas, B. 2000. *Geschenke erhalten die Freundschaft. Politik und Selbstdarstellung im Spiegel der Monumente.* Frankfurt.

Schofield, M. 2000. "Epicurean and Stoic Political Thought." In Rowe and Schofield 2000:435–456.

Scholten, J. B. 2000. *The Politics of Plunder: Aitolians and their Koinon in the Early Hellenistic Era, 279–217 BC.* Berkeley.

Schott, P. M. 1905. *Posidippi epigrammata collecta et illustrata.* Diss. Berlin 1905.

Schröder, S. 2002. "Überlegungen zu zwei Epigrammen des neues Mailänder Papyrus." *ZPE* 139:27–29.

Schumann, Walter. 1995. *Gemstones of the World.* New York.

Schwartz, J. 1960. *Pseudo-Hesiodea.* Leiden.

Schweitzer, B. 1931. "Dea Nemesis Regina", *JdI* 46:218–220.

Scodel, R. 2003. "A Note on Posidippus 63." *ZPE* 142:44.

Seale, D. 1982. *Vision and Stagecraft in Sophocles.* Chicago.

Seelbach, W. 1970. "Ezra Pound und Sappho fr. 95 L.-P." *A&A* 16:83–84

Selden, D. 1998. "Alibis." *CA* 17.2:289–412.

Sens, A. 1997. *Theocritus. Dioscuri.* Göttingen.

———. 2002a. "An Ecphrastic Pair: Asclepiades AP 12.75 and Asclepiades or Posidippus APl 68." *CJ* 97:249–262.

———. 2002b. "The New Posidippus, Asclepiades, and Hecataeus' Philitas-Statue." APA Panel on Posidippus. http://www.apaclassics.org/Publications/Posidippus/posidippus.html.

———. 2003. "Grief Beyond Measure: Asclepiades 3 Gow-Page (AP xiii. 23) on the Troubles of Botrys." In P. Thibodeau and H. Haskell, eds. (forthcoming), *Festschrift M. Putnam.*

———. (forthcoming). "Posidippus' Statue Poems and Hellenistic Literary Criticism." In Gutzwiller 2004 (forthcoming).

Servais, J. ed. 1987. *Stemmata. Mélanges de philologie, d'histoire et d'archéologie grecques offerts à Jules Labarbe.* Bruxelles.

Severyns, A. 1928. *Le cycle épique dans l'école d'Aristarque.* Bibliothèque de la Faculté de Philosophie et Lettres de l'Université de Liège 40. Paris.

Sider, D. 1997. *The Epigrams of Philodemos.* New York.

Simon, E. and Lorenz, S. 1997. "Tydeus." *LIMC* 8. Zürich and Düsseldorf:142–145.

Simon, G. 1988. *Le Regard, l'être, et l'apparence dans l'optique de l'Antiquité.* Paris.

Skiadas, A. 1966. "Zu Poseidippos: AP 12,168. " *RM* 109:187–189.

Skinner, M. 2001. "Ladies' Day at the Art Institute: Theocritus, Herodas, and the Gendered Gaze." In Pomeroy 2001:20–47.

Snodgrass, A. M. 1998. *Homer and the Artists: Text and Picture in Early Greek Art.* Cambridge.

Solmsen, F. 1948. "Propertius and Horace." *CP* 43:105–109.

————. 1954. "The 'Gift' of Speech in Homer and Hesiod." *TAPA* 85:1–15.

Sordi, M., ed. 1992. *Autocoscienza e rappresentazione dei popoli nell'antichità.* Milan

————. 1993. *La profezia nel mondo antico.* Milano.

Spier, J. 1992. *Ancient Gems and Finger Rings.* Malibu.

Spina, L. 2000. *La forma breve del dolore. Ricerche sugli epigrammi funerari greci.* Amsterdam.

Sprigath, G. 2001. "Der Fall Xenokrates von Athen. Zu den Methoden der Antike-Rezeption in der Quellenforschung." In Baumbach 2001:407–428.

Stambolidis, N. 1982. "Καλλίμαχος 'Αλεξανδρεὺς ἀγωνοθετήσας", *AAA* 15:297–310, figs. 1–3.

Stanwick, P. E. 1999. *Egyptian Royal Sculptures of the Ptolemaic Period.* Diss. New York University. UMI, Ann Arbor.

Stears, K. 2000. "Losing the picture: change and continuity in Athenian grave monuments in the fourth and third centuries BC." In Rutter and Sparkes 2000:206–227.

Stengel, P. 1920. *Die griechischen Kultusaltertümer.* München.

Stephens, S. A. 1998. "Callimachus at Court." In Harder, Regtuit, and Wakker 1998:167–185.

————. 2000. "Writing Epic for the Ptolemaic Court. " Harder, Regtuit, and Wakker 2000:195–215.

————. 2003. *Seeing Double. Intercultural Poetics in Ptolemaic Alexandria.* Berkeley.

Stephens, S. A. and Winkler, J. J. 1995. *Ancient Greek Novels: The Fragments.* Princeton.

Stewart, A. F. 1990. *Greek Sculpture: An Exploration.* 2 Volumes. New Haven.

————. 1993. *Faces of Power. Alexander's Image and Hellenistic Politics.* Berkeley.

————. 2000. "Pergamo ara marmorea magna: On the Date, Reconstruction, and Functions of the Great Altar of Pergamon." In de Grummond and Ridgway 2000:32–57.

———. (forthcoming). "Poseidippos and the Truth in Sculpture." In Gutzwiller 2004 (forthcoming).

Strubbe, J. H. M. 1998. "Epigrams and consolation decrees for deceased youths." *AC* 67:45–75.

Svenbro, J. 1988. *Phrasikleia: anthropologie de la lecture en Grèce ancienne*. Paris.

Svoronos, J. N. 1908. *Die Münzen der Ptolemäer*. Vol. 4. Athens.

Szelest, H. 1980. "Ut faciam breviora mones epigrammata, Corde: Eine Martial-Studie." *Philologus* 124:99–108.

Tarán, S. L. 1979. *The Art of Variation in the Hellenistic Epigram*. Leiden.

———, ed. 1987. *The Greek Anthology*. 2 vols. New York/London.

Tarditi, G. 1988. "Per una lettura degli epigrammatisti greci." *Aevum Antiquum* 1:5–75.

Thomas, R. 1983. "Callimachus, the *Victoria Berenices*, and Roman Poetry," *CQ* 33:92–113. (Reprinted in Thomas, R. 1999. *Reading Virgil and His Texts*. Chicago:68–100).

———. 1988. *Virgil. Georgics*. Volume 2: Books III–IV. Cambridge.

———. 1998. "'Melodious Tears:' Sepulchral Epigram and Generic Mobility." In Harder, Regtuit, and Wakker 1998:205–223.

Thompson, D. B. 1973. *Ptolemaic Oinochoai. Portraits in Faience. Aspects of Ruler Cult*. Oxford.

Thompson, D. J. 1987. "Ptolemaios and the 'Lighthouse': Greek Culture in the Memphite Serapeum." *PCPS* 33:105–121.

———. 1988. *Memphis under the Ptolemies*. Princeton.

———. 1992a. "Language and Literacy in Early Hellenistic Egypt." In Johnson 1992:323–326.

———. 1992b. "Language and Literacy in Early Hellenistic Egypt." In Bilde and Engberg-Pedersen 1992:39–52.

———. 1992c. "Literacy in Early Ptolemaic Egypt." In El-Mosallami 1992:II 77–90.

Bibliography

———. 1993. "From Model Tools to Written Tablets: The Ptolemies in Egypt." *Journal of Juristic Papyrology* 23:149–156.

———. 2000. "Philadelphus' Procession. Dynastic Power in a Mediterranean Context." In Mooren 2000:365–388.

———. (forthcoming). "Posidippus, Poet of the Ptolemies." In Gutzwiller 2004 (forthcoming).

Thompson, D.W. 1966. *A Glossary of Greek Birds.* Hildesheim.

Threatte, L. 1980. *The Grammar of Attic Inscriptions.* vol. 1. *Phonology.* Berlin and New York.

Tod, M. N. 1954. "Letter Labels in Greek Inscriptions." *BSA* 49:1–8.

Tollebeek, J., Verbeeck, G., and Verschaffel, T., eds. 1998. *De lectuur van het verleden. Opstellen over de geschiedenis van de geschiedschrijving aangeboden aan Reginald de Schryver.* Leuven.

Tomlinson, R. A. 1983. *Epidauros.* Austin.

Tondriau, J. 1952. "Dionysus Dieu Royal." *Annuaire de l'Institute de Philologie et d'Histoire Orientales* 12:441–466.

Turner, E.G. and Parsons, P.J. 1987. *Greek Manuscripts of the Ancient World.* Second Edition. London.

Tzifopoulos, J. 1991. *Pausanias as "Stelokopas." An Epigraphical Commentary of Pausanias "Eliakon A and B".* Dissertation. Ohio State University. UMI/Ann Arbor.

Vahlen, J. 1883. "Über die Paetus-Elegie des Propertius." *Sitzungsberichten der königlichen preussischen Akademie der Wissenschaften zu Berlin* 1883.3:36–90.

Van Minnen, P. 1998. "Boorish or Bookish? Literature in Egyptian Villages in the Fayum in the Graeco-Roman Period." *Journal of Juristic Papyrology* 28:99–184.

Van 't Dack, E., van Dessel, P., and van Gucht, W., eds. 1983. *Egypt and the Hellenistic World. Proceedings of the International Colloquium Leuven, 24–26 May 1982.* Studia Hellenistica 27. Leuven.

Bibliography

Verhoogt, A. M. F. W. and Vleeming, S. P., eds. *The Two Faces of Graeco-Roman Egypt. Greek and Demotic and Greek-Demotic Texts and Studies Presented to P. W. Pestman.* Papyrologica Lugduno-Batava. XXX. Leiden.

Vernant, J.-P. 1990. *Figures, idoles, masques.* Paris.

Vollenweider, M.-L. 1984. "Portraits d'enfants en miniature de la dynastie des Ptolémées." In Bonacasa, and di Vita 1984:363–377.

Voutiras, E. 1994. "Wortkarge Söldner? Ein Interpretationsvorschlag zum neuen Poseidippos." *ZPE* 104:27–31.

——. 1998. ΔΙΟΝΥΣΟΦΩΝΤΟΣ ΓΑΜΟΙ. *Marital Life and Magic in Fourth-Century Pella.* Amsterdam.

Walbank,. F. W. 1984. "Macedonia and Greece." In *The Cambridge Ancient History* (2nd ed.) VII.1. Cambridge:221–256.

Wallace, W. and Wallace, M. 1939. "Meleager and the Soros." *TAPA* 70:191–202.

Walsh, G. B. 1991. "Callimachean Passages: The Rhetoric of Epitaph in Epigram." *Arethusa* 24:77–103.

Walter-Karydi, E. 1985. "Geneleos." *AM* 100:91–104.

Weber, M. 1976. "Die Amazonen von Ephesos." *JdI* 91:28–96.

Webster, T. B. L. 1964. *Hellenistic Poetry and Art.* London.

Weinreich, O. 1909. *Antike Heilungswunder.* Giessen. (Reprinted in Berlin 1969).

——. 1918. "Die Heimat des Epigrammatikers Poseidippos." *Hermes* 53:434–439.

Weir Smyth, H. 1922. *Aeschylus.* 2 vols. Cambridge, MA.

Wellmann, M. 1909. "Eule." *RE* 6:1064–1071.

——. 1935. "Die Stein- und Gemmenbächer der Antike." *Quellen und Studien zur Geschichte der Naturwissenschaften und der Medizin* 4.86–149.

Welsh, M. K. 1904–1905. "Honorary Statues in Ancient Greece." *BSA* 11:32–43.

West, M.L. 1966. *Hesiod. Theogony.* Oxford.

——. 1978. *Hesiod. Works and Days.* Oxford.

343

————, ed. 1998 and 2000. *Homeri Ilias* I/II. 2 vols. Stuttgart and Leipzig/München and Leipzig.

Wifstrand, A. 1926. *Studien zur griechischen Anthologie*. Diss. Lund. (Reprinted in Tarán 1987, vol. 1).

Wilamowitz-Moellendorff, U. von. 1886. *Isyllos von Epidauros*. Philologische Untersuchungen 9. Berlin.

Wilamowitz-Moellendorff, U. von. 1913. *Sappho und Simonides. Untersuchungen über griechische Lyriker*. Berlin.

————. 1931. *Der Glaube der Hellenen*. Berlin.

Williams, C. A. 2002. "Sit nequior omnibus libellis: Text, Poet, and Reader in the Epigrams of Martial." *Philologus* 146:150–171.

Winnicki J. K. 1994. "Carrying off and Bringing Home the Statues of the Gods. On an Aspect of the Religious Policy of the Ptolemies Towards the Egyptians." *Journal of Juristic Papyrology* 24:149–190.

Wißmann, J. 2002. "Hellenistic Epigrams as School-Texts in Classical Antiquity." In Harder, Regtuit, and Wakker 2002:215–230.

Wissowa, G. 1896. "Augures." *RE* II.2:2313–2344.

Zanker, G. 1998. "The Concept and Use of Genre-Marking in Hellenistic Epic and Fine Art." In Harder, Regtuit, and Wakker 1998:225–238.

Zanker, P. 1993. "The Hellenistic Grave Stelai from Smyrna: Identity and Self-image in the Polis." In Bulloch, Gruen, Long, and Stewart 1993:212–230.

Zeitlin, F. 1994. "The Artful Eye: Vision, Ecphrasis, and Spectacle in Euripidean Theatre." In Goldhill and Osborne 1994:138–196.

Zlotogorska, M. 1997. *Darstellungen von Hunden auf griechischen Grabreliefs. Von der Archaik bis in die römischen Kaiserzeit*. Hamburg.

Figure 1: Charioteer by Polyzalos. Delphi Museum. Fifth century BCE. Photo: courtesy of the Greek Archaeological Receipts Fund.

Figure 2. Artemision Horse and Jockey. Second century BCE. Athens, National Museum, Br 15177. Photo: G. Hellner. Courtesy DAI Athens 1980/59 (height of jockey 84 cm; length of horse 250 cm).

Figure 3. Emaciated man in bronze. Late Hellenistic period. Dumbarton Oaks 47.22. Photo: courtesy Dumbarton Oaks, Washington, DC. (height 11.5 cm).

Figure 4. Kenyon Cox, *Head of the Queen of Egypt*. 1888. Oil on canvas, 46.1 × 38.2 cm. 1983.31.23. Smithsonian American Art Museum, bequest of Allyn Cox. Photo: courtesy Smithsonian American Art Museum.

CONTRIBUTORS

Benjamin Acosta-Hughes is Assistant Professor of Greek and Latin at the University of Michigan. He specializes in Archaic and Hellenistic poetry, and in the translation of erotic epigram. His publications include *Polyeideia—The Iambi of Callimachus and the Archaic Iambic Tradition* (Berkeley 2002). He is currently writing a book on the Hellenistic reception of Archaic lyric.

Manuel Baumbach is Wissenschaftlicher Assistent of Greek at the University of Heidelberg. His recent work has focused on the reception of Classical literature. He is the editor of *Tradita et Inventa. Beiträge zur Rezeption der Antike* (Heidelberg 2000) and the author of *Lukian in Deutschland: eine forschungs- und rezeptionsgeschichtliche Analyse vom Humanismus bis zur* Gegenwart (Munich 2002). His articles include works on Simonidean epigram (*Poetica* 32, 2000), Hellenistic poetry, and Virgil's *Eclogues* (*Philologus* 145, 2001). He is currently preparing a commentary on Chariton's *Callirhoe*.

Peter Bing is Professor of Classics at Emory University and specializes in Archaic and Hellenistic poetry, Greek tragedy and comedy, Greek religion and myth, and Roman comedy. His publications include *The Well-Read Muse: Present and Past in Callimachus and the Hellenistic Poets* (Göttingen 1988), *Games of Venus: An Anthology of Greek and Roman Erotic Verse from Sappho to Ovid* [co-authored with R. Cohen] (New York 1991), "Ergänzungsspiel in the Epigrams of Callimachus" (A&A 41, 1995) and "Between Literature and the Monuments" in *Hellenistica Groningana III* (Groningen 1998).

Beate Dignas is Assistant Professor of History at the University of Michigan. She is interested in Hellenistic history, epigraphy, and Greek religion, and is the author of *Rom und das Perserreich. Zwei Weltmächte zwischen Konfrontation und Koexistenz* [with Engelbert Winter] (Berlin 2001) and *Economy of the Sacred in Hellenistic and Roman Asia Minor* (Oxford 2002).

Marco Fantuzzi is Professor of Greek literature at the University of Macerata and in the Graduate School of Greek and Latin philology at the University of Florence. He specializes in Hellenistic poetry, and his most important publications include an edition and commentary of the *Epitaph of Adonis* by Bion of Smyrna, a

349

monograph on the style of Apollonius Rhodius, and *Muse e modelli. La poesia ellenistica da Alessandro Magno ad Agusto* [with Richard Hunter] (Rome-Bari 2002).

Kathryn Gutzwiller is Professor of Classics at the University of Cincinnati. She specializes in Hellenistic poetry, and her publications include *Studies in the Hellenistic Epyllion* (Meisenheim am Glan 1981), *Theocritus' Pastoral Analogies: The Formation of a Genre* (Madison 1991) and *Poetic Garlands: Hellenistic Epigrams in Context* (Berkeley 1998), which won the American Philological Association's Goodwin Award of Merit in 2001. She is currently editing a volume entitled *The New Posidippus: A Hellenistic Poetry Book* and is writing a commentary on the epigrams of Meleager, both for Oxford University Press.

Gail Hoffman is Visiting Associate Professor of Classical Studies and Fine Arts at Boston College. She specializes in the artistic interconnections between the Near East and Greece during the first millennium BCE. Her publications include *Imports and Immigrants: Near Eastern Contacts with Iron Age Crete* (Michigan 1997), "Painted Ladies: Early Cycladic II Mourning Figures" (*AJA* 106, 2002), and "Defining Identities: Greek Artistic Interaction with the Near East" in *Continuity, Innovation and Cultural Contact in early 1st millennium B.C. Levantine Art*, ed. C. Uehlinger (Fribourg Switzerland, forthcoming).

Richard Hunter is Regius Professor of Greek and Fellow of Trinity College at Cambridge University. His principal interests are Hellenistic poetry, narrative literature, and the reception of Greek literature at Rome. His publications include *The Argonautica of Apollonius: Literary Studies* (Cambridge 1993), *Theocritus and the Archaeology of Greek Poetry* (Cambridge 1996), *Theocritus. A Selection. Idylls 1, 3, 4, 6, 7, 10, 11 and 13* (Cambridge 1999) and *Muse e modelli. La poesia ellenistica da Alessandro Magno ad Augusto* [with Marco Fantuzzi] (Rome-Bari 2002).

Elizabeth Kosmetatou is Fellow of the Flemish Fund for Scientific Research at the Catholic University Leuven. Her main interests are in Hellenistic history, epigraphy, and ancient politics. Her publications include "The Legend of the Hero Pergamus" (*AncSoc* 25, 1995), "Lycophron's 'Alexandra' Reconsidered: The Attalid Connection" (*Hermes* 128, 2000), "The Public Image of Julia Mamaea. An Epigraphic and Numismatic Inquiry" (*Latomus* 61, 2002), and "The Attalids of Pergamon" in *Blackwell's Hellenistic Companion* (Oxford 2003). She is currently writing a book on the Delian inventory lists.

Gregory Nagy is Francis Jones Professor of Classical Greek Literature and Professor of Comparative Literature at Harvard University and Director of the Harvard Center for Hellenic Studies in Washington, D.C. He specializes in

Homeric studies and linguistics. His publications include *The Best of the Achaeans: Concepts of the Hero in Archaic Greek Poetry* (Baltimore, 1979; second edition, 1999), which won the American Philological Association's Goodwin Award of Merit in 1982, *Homeric Questions* (Austin 1996); and *Plato's Rhapsody and Homer's Music: The Poetics of the Panathenaic Festival in Classical Athens* (Cambridge [Mass.] 2002).

Dirk Obbink is Lecturer and Fellow of Christ Church College, Oxford University. He is the Editor of the *Oxyrhynchus Papyri* and is the recipient of a MacArthur Fellowship. He specializes in Greek literature and papyrology. His publications include *Philodemus on Piety Part I: Critical Text with Commentary* (Oxford 1996), "Anoubion, Elegiacs" in *The Oxyrhynchus Papyri*, Vol. 66 (ed. N. Gonis and others, nos. 4503-7), Egypt Exploration Society (London 1999), and *Matrices of Genre. Authors, Canons and Society* [with M. Depew] (Cambridge Mass.] 2000).

Nassos Papalexandrou is Assistant Professor of Art History at the University of Texas at Austin. He specializes in Greek art and archaeology, with special emphasis on the visual culture of the early Iron Age. He is the author of *The Visual Poetics of Power: Warriors, Youths and Tripods in Early Greek Culture* (Lexington Books, forthcoming).

David Schur is Visiting Assistant Professor of Classics at Miami University, Ohio. His research has focused on ancient and modern forms of philosophical rhetoric. His publications include *The Way of Oblivion: Heraclitus and Kafka* (Cambridge [Mass.] 1998).

Alexander Sens is Professor of Classics at Georgetown University. His research has focused on late Classical and early Hellenistic poetry. His publications include *Theocritus: Dioscuri (Idyll 22): Introduction, Text, and Commentary* (Göttingen 1997), *Matro of Pitane and the Tradition of Epic Parody in the Fourth Century BCE: Text, Translation, and Commentary* [with S. Douglas Olson] (Atlanta 1999), and *Archestratos of Gela: Greek Culture and Cuisine in the Fourth Century BCE* [with S. Douglas Olson] (Oxford 2000). He is currently working on an edition of Asclepiades of Samos for Oxford University Press.

David Sider is Professor of Classics at New York University. His main interest is in Greek poetry and philosophy. His publications include *The Fragments of Anaxagoras* (Hain 1981; second edition forthcoming), *The Epigrams of Philodemus* (Oxford 1997) and *The New Simonides: Contexts of Praise and Desire* [with Deborah Boedeker] (Oxford 2001).

Contributors

Martyn Smith is a doctoral student in comparative literature at Emory University. He is interested in Greek, Arabic, and English literature and is working on a dissertation about the use of place in literary works. He is studying this year in Cairo, Egypt, on a fellowship from the Center for Arabic Study Abroad.

Susan Stephens is Professor of Classics at Stanford University. Her main interests are in papyrology, Hellenistic poetry, and Greco-Egyptian culture. She is author of *Yale Papyri in the Beinecke Rare Book and Manuscript Library* II (Yale 1985) and co-editor [with John J. Winkler] of *Ancient Greek Novels: the Fragments* (Princeton 1995). Her new work *Seeing Double: Intercultural Poetics in Ptolemaic Alexandria* has just appeared with the University of California Press (2002).

Richard Thomas is Professor of Greek and Latin and currently Chair of the Classics Department at Harvard University. He is also the current Director of the Vergilian Society. He is mainly interested in a variety of critical approaches in his work: philological, intertextual, and narratological, as well as in literary history, metrics and prose stylistics, genre studies, translation theory and practice, and the reception of Classical literature and culture, particularly as it relates to Virgil. His publications include *Lands and Peoples in Roman Poetry: The Ethnographical Tradition* (Cambridge 1982), a two-volume text and commentary on Virgil's *Georgics* (Cambridge 1988), a collection of his articles on the subject of Virgilian intertextuality, *Reading Virgil and his Texts* (Michigan 1999), and *Virgil and the Augustan Reception* (Cambridge 2001). He is currently working on a commentary on Horace's *Odes*, and a book on Augustan Poetry.

Kai Trampedach is Wissenschaftlicher Assistent at the University of Konstanz. He specializes in Greek and Roman history and philosophy. His publications include *Platon, die Akademie und die zeitgenössische Politik* (Stuttgart 1994), "Gefährliche Frauen. Zu athenischen Asebie-Prozessen im 4. Jh. v. Chr." in *Konstruktionen von Wirklichkeit. Bilder im Griechenland des 5. und 4. Jahrhunderts v. Chr.*, ed. R. von den Hoff and S. Schmidt (Stuttgart 2001), "Die Konstruktion des Heiligen Landes. Kaiser und Kirche in Palästina von Constantin bis Justinian" in *Die Levante. Beiträge zur Historisierung des Nahostkonfliktes*, ed. by M. Sommer (Freiburg i. Breisgau 2001). He is currently working on a book relating to Greek divination and Greek politics from Homer to Alexander.

INDEX OF PASSAGES CITED

A

Aelian
  De Natura Animalium I 54:277n5;
    VII 16:163n11; IX 15:277n5; X
    26:175n58; epilogue:201
  Varia Historia XII 64:241n58
Aeschines, *AP* VI 330:279n16
Aeschylus
  Agamemnon 415–419:200
  Theoroi or *Isthmiastai*
    P.Oxy. 2162:191–192
  Eumenides 213:71n26;
    488–492:138n56; 1040:82n66
  Prometheus 487:126n15
  Seven against Thebes 24–29:141
Agathias, *AP* IX 619:76n49
Alcaeus, fr. 34.1:81n66
Alcman, *PMG* 8:69; 14:69; 28:69;
    30:69; 31:69; 46:69; 59:69
Antipater Sidonius,
    7 GP (= VII 146):32;
    21 GP (= *AP* VII 164):274n34
Antipater, VII 136:32
Antipater of Thessalonica,
    IX 46:279n16
Antipater or Archias, *AP* VII 165
    (Archias XIII GP
    Garland):274n34
Anubion, P.Oxy. 4503–7:17
Apollinaris Sidonius, *Epistulae*
    IV 1:29n4

Apollodorus of Athens, *FGrHist* 244
    T 1:58n1; P.Col. inv. 5604:58n1
Apollonius Rhodius, *Argonautica*
    I 1313:103n38; III 1244:96;
    IX 1508–1512:277n5
Anthologia Palatina
    IV 2.3:119n7; IV 161:124n6
    V 147 (Archias):32
    VI 135 (= FGE 502 f.):215;
    171 (= GP adesp. 58A.1–3):77
    VII 94:261; 95:261; 96:261;
    97:261; 98:261; 99:261;
    100:261; 101:261; 102:261;
    103:261; 104:261; 105:261;
    106:261; 107:261; 108:261;
    109:261; 110:261; 111:261;
    112:261; 113:261; 114:261;
    115:261; 116:261; 117:261;
    118:261; 119:261; 120:261;
    121:261; 122:261; 123:261;
    124:261; 125:261; 126:261;
    127:261; 128:261; 129:261;
    130:261; 131:261; 132:261;
    140:32; 141:32; 143:64n16;
    191:124n6; 199:124n6;
    202:124n6; 203:124n6;
    204:124n6; 205:124n6;
    206:124n6; 210:124n6;
    230:72n33; 211:27n23;
    263:260, 265; 264:260, 265;
    265:260, 265; 266:260, 265;

Anthologia Palatina (continued)
  VII 267:260, 265; 268:260, 265;
    269:260, 265; 270:260, 265;
    271:260, 265; 272:260, 265;
    273:260, 265; 274:260, 265;
    275:260, 265; 276:260, 265;
    277:260, 265; 278:260, 265;
    279:260, 265; 282:260, 265;
    283:260, 265; 284:260, 265;
    285:260, 265; 286:260, 265;
    287:260, 265; 288:260, 265;
    289:260, 265, 272n31;
    290:260, 265, 272n31;
    291:260, 265; 292:260, 265;
    293:260, 265; 294:260, 265;
    304:27n23; 313:299n15;
    314:299n15; 315:299n15;
    316:299n15; 317:299n15;
    318:299n15; 319:299n15;
    320:299n15; 494:260n3;
    495:260n3; 496:260n3;
    497:260n3; 498:260n3;
    499:260n3; 500:260n3;
    501:260n3; 502:260n3;
    504:260n3; 505:260n3;
    550:272n31; 650:260n3;
    651:260n3; 652:260n3;
    653:260n3; 654:260n3;
    738:260n4; 739:260n3
  IX 180:243n66; 269:272n31;
    298:279n16;
    342.1 (= Parmenion 11):40;
    511:279n16; 534:148n91;
    540:34n23; 713:201; 714:201;
    715:201; 716:201; 717:201;
    718:201; 719:201; 720:201;
    721:201; 722:201; 723:201;
    724:201; 725:201; 726:201;
    727:201; 728:201; 729:201;
    IX 730:201; 731:201; 732:201;
    733:201; 734:201; 735:201;
    736:201; 737:201; 738:201;
    739:201; 740:201; 741:201;
    742:201; 793:201; 794:201;
    795:201; 796:201; 797:201;
    798:201
  XI 186:124n6
  XII 98:119; 234:299–300
  XIII 16:238; XIV 92:148n91
    Appendix: 656.8–10:299
Anthologia Planudeios 54:189n8;
    60:189n8; 81:189n8; 84:189n8;
    120:189n8; 142:189n8;
    275:189n8;
    375 (*GV* 455, 1874,7):288
Aratus, *Phaenomena* 1:95
Archelaus, *APl* 120
    (= Asclepiades 43 GP):75n46,
    76n49. *See also* Asclepiades
Archestratos of Gela, fr. 60.11 Olson-
    Sens:78–79
Aristonous, *Address to Apollo* v. 11–12
    (p. 163 Powell):82
Aristophanes
    Assembly Women 134:71n26
    Birds 323:71n26; 516:135n46;
    719–722:126n13
    Clouds 675:76n50; 726:76n50
    Frogs 1032–1035:59n2
    Lysistrata 1296:81n66
    Wasps 286:76n50; 787:71n26;
    920:76n50; 1145:76n50;
    1149:76n50; 1152:76n50;
    1350:71n26; 743:71n26
    Women at the Thesmophoria
    1148:82n66
    Fragments 202 *PCG* (= 194
    Kock):190–191n18

Aristotle
  De Anima I 3.406b:191n18
  Historia Animalium
    580a 16–19:175n58;
    607a:276–277n5
  Nicomachean Ethics 9.4:297;
    1041a:90; 1101b35:35n27
  Fragments 666:245n72
Aristoxenus, *Elementa Harmonica*
    VII 19ff.:298; XXXVII 8ff.:298
Arrian
  Anabasis I 11.2:148n92;
    I 18.6–9:148n92; III 3.6:139n58
  FGrHist 156 F 9, no.25:241n58
Asclepiades
  Epigrams 12 GP (= *AP* V 145):32;
    15 GP (= *AP* XII 46):13;
    17 GP (=*AP* XII 166):38;
    24 GP (= *AP* V 185):75n47;
    28 GP (= *AP* VII 11):80n63;
    32 GP (= *AP* IX.63):36n34;
    33 GP (= XIII 23):261;
    34 GP (= *AP* V 194 = *EG* 23):30,
    48 (*see also* Posidippus AB 126);
    35 GP (= *AP* V 202 = *EG* 24):30,
    48 (*see also* Posidippus AB 127);
    36 GP (= *AP* V 209 = *EG* 25):30,
    48 (*see also* Posidippus AB 128);
    37 GP (= *AP* XII 17 = *EG* 26):30,
    33, 48 (*see also* Posidippus AB 134);
    38 GP (= *AP* XII 77 = *EG* 27):30,
    48 (*see also* Posidippus AB 136);
    39 GP (= *APl* 68 = *EG* 28):30, 48,
    68, 75 (*see also* Posidippus AB 141);
    41 GP (= *APl* 120):75n46, 76n49
    (*see also* Archelaus)
  Fragments 78.6–7:76n48
Athenaeus, IV 141f–142:296n7;
    V 205f:240n51; VII 318d:163,

172; IX 401e:196n41;
    X 435a:244n69; XII 514f:205n67;
    XII 596c:43n4
Ausonius, *Ephemeris* 58–68:201n55

B

Bacchylides, 5.161:78; 10.1–2:82
Bion
  Adonis 58:70
  Fragments 2.15:70

C

Callignotus, 11 GP (=25 Pf.):131n36
Callimachus
  Aetia 1.1:46n15, 48n22; 1.1.5:34n23;
    1.1.29–30:35n26;
    1.13–14 Pf.:170n42;
    SH 254–269 (= *Aetia* 3 init.):2n1,
    213n5, 220n 231n21
  Epigrams 14 GP (= *Epigram* 6 Pf.
    = Athenaeus VII 318b–c):170;
    29 GP (= *AP* VII 525):48, 86n9;
    30 GP (= *AP* VII 415):48, 86n9;
    50 GP (= *AP* VII 277):92n27,
    262n10;
    51 GP (= *AP* VII 317):274n34;
    56 GP (= *AP* IX 507):298;
    63 GP (= *Epigram* 63 Pf.):131n36;
    AP VII 170 (Posidippus 21 GP;
    Καλλιμάχου C)
  Hymns 4.20:96n17; 4.199:96;
    5.89:78; 5.142:95n8; 6.91:78;
    6.127:70
  Fragments 1 26–27 Pf.:299; 110:223;
    112:95; 203:65n2–66;
    384:219n21; 400 Pf.:24;
    468 Pf.:34n23

Callimachus *(continued)*
  Iambi 6:97, 193; 6 13 Pf.:173n53;
    7:54, 193; 9:193; 13:66
Callisthenes, *FGrHist* 124, F 14
    (= Strabo XVII 1.43; Plutarch,
    Alexander 27.2):139n58; F 22a
    (= Cicero, *De Divinatione*
    I 74):146n84
Carp(h)yllides, 1 GP
    (= *AP* VII 260):89n19
Catullus, 66.52–54:223; 68:260–261;
    101:261
CEG 776:279n17; 808:280n18;
    818:280n18
Cicero
  De Divinatione I 25–26:144n75
  De Natura Deorum I 38:59n3;
    I 91:150n100
  In Verrem IV 60.135:201
Clemens Alexandrinus, I 4.26:208n87
Curtius, III 12.27:167n24;
    IV 7.15:139n58; IV 8.6:148n93;
    IV 10.1–7:148n93;
    IV 13.15:167n24;
    VIII 2.32:167n24;
    VIII511.24:167n24;
    X 10.20:241n58

D

Demosthenes, XIX 246:29n5;
    XXI 147:193–194n31
Dio, LI 16.3–5:241n58;
    LXIII 8:236n38
Diodorus, I 15.4:245n72;
    IV 71.4:245n72;
    VII 1.1–3:277n6;
    IX 76.1–3:191n18;

XV 48.1:147n89;
XV 49.4:147n89;
XVII 49.5:139n58;
XVIII 26.3–28.2–4:241n58;
XX 11.3:139n59
Diogenes Laertius, III 9.18–23:
    245n72; V 5–6.11:245n72;
    V 44:244n69; VI 37–38:284;
    VIII 3:173n50; VIII 46:206n72;
    IX 46–48:194n31
Dioscorides, 15 GP (= *AP* VI):76n49;
    33 GP (= *AP* VII 76):288n36
Duris, *FGrHist* 76:207n79, 208, 211

E

Ephorus, *FGrHist* 70 F 101:59n2
Erinna, 3 GP (= *AP* VI 352):76n48,
    188n4, 192–193
Euaenetus, 25 GP (= 56 Pf.):131n36
Etymologicum Magnum, p. 627.37:299
Euripides
  Bacchae 163ff.:182; 346–351:142n70
  Hecuba 28–30:270
  Heracles 1322:296
  Ion 184–231:194n34
  Iphigenia at Aulis 326:71n26
  PMG 755:219n20, 238
Eustathius, *Scholia ad Odysseam*
    II 190:208n87

F

FdD III 3, no.192.9f.:184n31, 282;
    III 4, no.460:234–236
Fragmente der Griechischen Historiker
    3b (Suppl.) 2,261 Anm. 6:144n77

G

Georgius Monachus,
II pp. 663–664:243n66
GV 509:180n13; 879:180n13; 969:71;
974:180n13; 1179:180n13;
1344:180n13; 1916:180n13;
2012:180n13

H

Heliodorus, *Aithiopika* V 13–14:94n2
Heraclides of Miletus,
fr. 25 Cohn *ap. Eust.* 452.20)1:78
Hermesianax of Colophon,
Powell fr. 7.75–78:196n40
Herodas, IV 11:82n66;
IV 32–34:76n48
Herodian, IV 8.9:241n58
Herodotus, I 23–24:173n52;
I 51:204n66; I 60.2–5:243n64;
I 78.84:150n98; II 53.3:59n4;
II 135:31n16; III 40–41:88, 91,
205n69; III 39–43:173n50;
III 121:173n50; VI 82:147n89;
VI 98:95n10; VII 27:205n67;
VII 37.2–3:148n93;
VIII 37.1–2:147n89;
VIII 41.2–3:147n89;
VIII 137f.:183n26
Hesiod
Theogony 91–97:154n113; 148:38;
205:52; 508:299; 826–828:151
Works and Days 826–828:123n2, 151
Hesychius, e 5483:82n68
Hippias, 86 B 6 DK:59
Homer
Iliad II 827:62n11; IV 88:62n11;
IV 437:299; V 168:62n11;
V 171:62n11; V 246:62n11;
V 302–304:104; V 795:62n11;
V 849:63; VIII 291:299; X 32:63;
X 73:63; X 274–27:140n64;
XI 101:61, 63;
XII 237–240:140n62;
XII 380–383:104;
XII 445–449:104;
XIII 45:153; XIII 62–70:153;
XIII 167–177:154;
XIII 240–294:197; XIII 333:299;
XIII 354:299;
XIII 477–486:76n51;
XV 209:299; XV 694–695:98n25;
XVIII 373–379:191n21;
XVIII 483–608:59;
XX 285–287:104; XX 484:63;
XXI 205:63; XXI 106–107:300;
XXIII 91:300;
XXIV 315f.:140n64;
XXIV 57:299;
XXIV 478–479:96; XXIV 506:96
Odyssey I 161–162:271;
II 158–159:124n6;
II 181–182:123;
III 285–296:101;
III 298–299:102;
V 388–435:270, 273n31;
VIII 167–177:154n113;
IX 65:182; IX 241–242:102;
IX 243:102; IX 247:101;
IX 305:102; IX 313:102;
IX 340:102; IX 480–482:102;
IX 537:102; X 552–560:270;
XI 51–83:270, 272, 274;
XVII 365:63; XIX 260:38;
XXIV 452:124n6

Homer *(continued)*
    Homeric Hymn
      to Apollo 70–78:101
      to Demeter 438–440:181
      to Hermes 25–55:174n56
    Nostoi FD9 Davies (= F 11 Bernabé
      = Athenaeus IX 399a):63
Horace, *Odes* I 28:261–264; IV 1:54

I

Ibycus, *Hymn to Polycrates, PMGF* S
    151–65:173n50
ID 101, line 26:205n67
IG I3 1261:198n46;
    II/III2 3829:234n32;
    III 809:236n38;
    IV2, 1, no.121:279n14,
    280–286, 289n37;
    IV2, 1, no.122:289n37;
    IV2, 1, no.123:286;
    IV2, 1, no.125:279n14, 283n27;
    V(1) 669:236n38;
    IX 12.17:240n55;
    IX.1.17, v.24:29, 184, 282;
    IX 1.1256:239n48;
    XI (2) 161, B, lines 26–27:242n63;
    XII 1.737 (= GDI 4140):79;
    XIV 1721:299
I Metr. Egypt 112 (SB 685):16
I Termessos I 22:27n22
IvP 138:206n73

L

Leonidas of Tarentum,
    10 GP (*AP* VII 648):86n9;
    11 GP (= *AP* VII 440):86n9;

64 GP (= *AP* VII 503):260n3,
    274n34;
    70 GP (= *AP* VII 163):274n34;
    75 GP (= *AP* VII 506):260n3,
    273n31
Lexeis Rhetorikai X:191n18
Lucian
    Gallus XXIV 30:202n57
    Quomodo historia conscribenda sit
    62:23n13
Lucil(l)ius, *Epigrams*
    AP XI 151.7–9:295;
    AP XI 206:296
Lucilius Iunior, *Aetna* V 592:201n55
Lysias, VII 4:71n26; XIII 76:71n26

M

Marmor Parium, FGrHist 239 F V
    11:241n58
Meleager, 12 GP (= *AP* VII 195):86n9;
    13 GP (= *AP* VII 196):86n9;
    19 GP (= *AP* XII 117):35;
    27 GP (= *AP* V 172):86n9;
    28 GP (= *AP* V 173):86n9;
    33 GP (= *AP* V 151):86n9;
    34 GP (= *AP* V 152):86n9;
    42 GP (= *AP* V 136):36;
    55 GP (= *AP* IV 1):119;
    66 GP (= *AP* XII 53):86n12;
    81 GP (= *AP* XII 52):86n12;
    130 GP (= *AP* VII 470):274n34;
    AP V 215 (Posidippus 23 GP; ἡ
    Μελεάγρου PC):30, 48, 70
Merkelbach-Stauber,
    2001a:10/03/02:180n13;
    2001b:143/07/06:180n13, 181;
    2001b16/34/24:180n15;
    2002:17/09/04:180n13;

Merkelbach-Stauber *(continued)*
  2002:18/01/22:180n13;
  2002:21/12/02:180n13;
  2002:01/19/29:180n13
Metagenes, fr. 2.1:76n50
Moretti 1953:65–66, no.27:216

O

OGIS 54:242n60; 56:240n51
Ovid
  Amores 3.1:36n34
  Ex Ponto IV 1.34:201n55
  Metamorphoses XIII 778–780:103
  Remedia Amoris 379–380:36n34
  Tristia IV 54.55–58:259

P

Pausanias, I 6.2 242n60;
  I 6.3:241n58; I 7.1:241n58; II
  5.1:168n30; II 27.3:280n20; III
  8.1:238n43; III 9.2:147n89; III
  15.1:238n43; III 15.10:168n30;
  III 23.1:168n30; V 12.5:238n43;
  VI 1.3–18.7:250n11;
  VI 13.9–10:215n12;
  VI 14.2:252n19; VI 16.3:245n72;
  IX 16:126n12, 142n71;
  IX 31:151n102; X 2.6:258;
  X 10.3:203n62; X 38.6–7:204n65
Pherecydes, fr. 43.3:76n50
Philip of Thessalonica, 1 GP *Garland*
  (*AP* IV 2):35n28, 40, 119n7;
  AP VI 203:279n16
Philo Iudaeus, II 438:236n38
Philo Byzantius Paradoxographus, *De
  Septem Orbis Spectaculis Mundi*
  14:203n61

Philostratus, *Vita Apollonii* VI 4:191n18
Pindar, *Odes*
  Isthmian 5.6:70
  Olympian 1.20–22:214–215;
    1.1.3:126n15; 1.5:78;
    1.106–111:217n17; 2.32:78;
    2.9:74n41; 5.6:70; 5.23:290n38;
    5.183–186:215; 12.8:126n15
  Pythian 1.35–38 38n40;
    3.55–58:290n39; 4.4:66n3;
    4.214:78; 12.4:81n66
  Fragments 33c4:95n10
Plato
  Apology 41a:59n2
  Cratylus 403a:288
  Euthyphro 11b–e:191
  Laws 885b:71n26; 924d:93
  Phaedrus 244b:71n26; 257c:29n5
  Republic 363a:59n2; 377d:59n2;
    612b:59n2
  Timaeus 15d:101
Plato Comicus, *AP* IX 359
  (= Posidippus 21 GP):30, 49n30
Pliny the Elder, *Natural History*
  X 3.7:163n11; XXIV 58:207;
  XXXIV 37:209n90, 211;
  XXXIV 41:203n61;
  XXXIV 52:189n10;
  XXXIV 53:198n47, 199n48;
  XXXIV 57–58:201n55, 202n57;
  XXXIV 61:208n89;
  XXXIV 75:200n52, 203n64;
  XXXIV 83:91n22, 205n68n70;
  XXXIV 85:197n42;
  XXXIV 148:168n34;
  XXXIV 156:197n42;
  XXXV 83:206n72;
  XXXV 153:204n65, 210;
  XXXVI 17:198n47;

Pliny the Elder, *Natural History (cont.)*
XXXVII 1:108; XXXVII 5:114;
XXXVII 8:87, 110, 304n10;
XXXVII 12.17:304n13;
XXXVII 53:113n23;
XXXVII 63:111; XXXVII 66:112;
XXXVII 69:111n15, 112;
XXXVII 108:168n34;
XXXVII 115:105;
XXXVII 120:108;
XXXVII 146:113n24;
XXXVII 158:113–114
Plutarch
Alcibiades 11 2:237n40; 16:194n31
Alexander 2:18n27; 2.2–3:199n50;
3.4:147n89; 4.1–7:199n49,
244n69; 4.4–5:167n22;
8.53–55:245n72; 10.1–4:245n74;
14.5:148n92; 26.5–6:148n93;
27.2:139n58; 33.3–4:164–165;
73:139n58
Dion 24.1–3:148n93
Lucullus 10:167n24
Marcus Antonius 85.5–6:246n75
Nicias 23.5 (= Philochorus,
FGrHist 328 F 135b):148n93
Themistocles 12.1:139n59
Theseus 36.1 139n58
Timoleon 12.9:147n89
Moralia, De Sollertia Animalium
975 A:138n56
Septem Sapientium Convivium
18 (160F–162B):173n50
Mulierum Virtutes 13:183n23
PMG 604:290n38; 813:290n38;
890:290n38; 934.19:82n66
Polyaenus, IV 1:183n26
Polybius, XXVII 18.2:161, 277n6;
XXIX 21.3–6:244n70

Porphyrius, *De Abstinentia*
III 5.3:123n2
Posidippus
Epithalamium for Arsinoe
P.Petrie II 49a (= *P.Lond.Lit.* 60
= AB 114 = *SH* 961):9
Milan Collection
AB 1:86n12, 97, 105n3, 118,
241n57, 303;
AB 2:86n12, 87, 97, 105n3, 110,
118, 241n57, 303;
AB 3:97, 118, 303;
AB 4:97, 118, 120–121, 164,
174n54, 241n57, 303;
AB 5:97, 105, 107, 118, 120,
241n57, 303–304;
AB 6:85, 95, 97, 105–106, 110,
118, 303–304;
AB 7:85, 86n12, 95, 97, 105,
109, 118, 303, 304n9;
AB 8:25n19, 86n12, 97,
105–106, 118, 164, 241n57, 303;
AB 9:87, 93, 97, 118 173, 205,
303;
AB 10:67, 97, 105n3, 118, 303;
AB 11:85, 88, 97, 105, 118, 303
AB 12:67, 85, 88, 97, 105, 118,
303;
AB 13:86n10, 88, 97, 105n2,
110, 118, 303–304;
AB 14:88, 97, 105, 118, 303–304
AB 15 (= Tzetzes, *Chiliades*
VII 660 = 20 GP):2, 31, 49, 50,
67–68, 71n29, 89, 97, 105–106,
114, 118, 260n4, 303–304;
AB 16:67, 86n10, 88, 97, 105,
118, 303, 304n9;
AB 17:88, 97, 105, 118, 120, 303
AB 18:88, 97, 118, 303;

Posidippus, Milan Collection *(cont.)*
AB 19:48n25, 86n12, 88, 95n5,
   96–98, 101–102, 103n42, 105n2,
   106, 109, 118, 157, 158n123, 303;
AB 20:68, 86n12, 88, 95, 95n5,
   96–98, 118, 165, 303;
AB 21:124–126, 128–129, 131,
   135–136, 137n53, 145, 152–155,
   158, 303;
AB 22:86n12, 124–126, 128, 131,
   135–136, 137n53, 152, 158, 303;
AB 23:67, 86n12, 124–126, 128,
   131, 135–136, 137n53, 146n82,
   152, 303;
AB 24:67, 124–126, 128–129,
   131, 135–136, 146, 303;
AB 25:124–126, 128, 131,
   135–136, 146, 303;
AB 26:124–126, 128–133,
   135–136, 146, 149n96, 303;
AB 27:17n2, 124–125, 128,
   132–135, 146, 154–155, 303;
AB 28:67, 124–126, 128–130,
   131n36, 132–135–136, 147, 303;
AB 29:126, 128–129, 131, 132,
   134–135–136, 147, 163, 303;
AB 30:88, 124–126, 128–129,
   132, 135–136, 147, 149, 158,
   167, 303;
AB 31:88, 124–125, 128–130,
   131–132, 135–136, 147, 149,
   155, 165, 241n57, 242, 303;
AB 32:67, 88, 124–126,
   128–129, 131–132, 135–136,
   149, 303;
AB 33:17, 88, 124–125, 126n14,
   128–130, 131n36, 132,
   135–136, 149, 158, 162, 303;

AB 34:16–17, 18, 88, 124–126,
   128, 130–131, 137, 149–150,
   152, 303;
AB 35:88, 124–126, 128–130,
   131n36, 131, 137, 149–150,
   155–156, 241n57, 303;
AB 36:17, 86n12, 88, 158,
   161–162, 165, 213;
AB 37:10n5, 52, 67–68, 86n12,
   89, 161–162, 173, 213;
AB 38:10n5, 67, 89, 161, 163, 213;
AB 39:89, 161, 163, 171, 172, 213;
AB 40:17, 67, 161, 163;
AB 42:67, 161, 163, 179, 181;
AB 43:18, 89n19, 152n108, 179,
   181;
AB 44:18, 89, 179, 182;
AB 45:67, 89, 179;
AB 46:18, 89, 179;
AB 47:73–74, 89, 179, 181;
AB 48:67, 163, 179;
AB 49:89, 179, 219;
AB 50:89, 179, 219;
AB 51:51–52, 67, 89, 179, 219;
AB 52:86n12, 88, 99, 179, 219;
AB 53:67, 89, 179, 219;
AB 54:89, 179, 219;
AB 55:51–52, 67, 89, 179, 219;
AB 56:89, 178n4, 179;
AB 57:89, 179;
AB 58:18, 68, 179;
AB 60:67, 86n12, 89, 179, 216;
AB 61:18, 86n12, 89, 179, 216;
AB 62:86n12, 90, 187n2, 188,
   193, 197–198, 200–203,
   207–208, 298n14, 305;
AB 63:67, 76, 78, 86n12, 90, 93,
   175, 187n1, 193, 196–198,
   200–201, 208, 305;

Posidippus, Milan Collection *(cont.)*
   AB 64:70–71, 75, 76n50, 79,
      86n12, 90, 191, 193, 197–199,
      201, 203, 305;
   AB 65 (P.Freib. 4 = 18 GP
      = *SH* 973 = AP XVI 119):2, 10,
      30, 49, 69, 71n25, 75, 86n12,
      89–90, 188n7, 191, 199–200,
      240, 241n57, 305, 260n4,
      298n14;
   AB 66:200–201, 208, 305;
   AB 67:86n12, 90, 205, 210, 305;
   AB 68:72, 75–77, 86n12, 90,
      202–203, 208, 305;
   AB 69:202–204, 305;
   AB 70:86n12, 90, 99, 188n7,
      205–206, 241n57, 305;
   AB 71:86n12, 91, 212, 228, 230,
      232, 239n46, 250, 303;
   AB 72:91, 212, 228, 230, 233n27,
      252–255, 303;
   AB 73:77, 91, 212, 228–230;
   AB 74:48n25, 55, 68, 71n29, 91,
      100n29, 212, 219, 223n29,
      229–230, 232n24, 233n27,
      239n46, 250–251;
   AB 75:71, 86n12, 91, 212;
   AB 76:25n19, 86n12, 91, 212,
      236, 250, 252–255, 303;
   AB 77:22n10, 78, 91, 212,
      216–218, 219n20, 236n39, 238,
      250;
   AB 78:22n10, 48n25, 74, 86n12,
      91, 100n29, 170n39, 212, 217,
      220, 231–232, 234, 236,
      250n10, 295;
   AB 79:86n12, 91, 212, 220,
      231n21, 236–237;
   AB 80:91, 212, 217n16, 220, 222;

AB 81:74, 91, 212, 220;
AB 82:86n12, 91, 212, 217n16,
   220, 231n21, 236, 239n46;
AB 83:68, 74, 86n12, 91, 212,
   216, 220, 239n46;
AB 84:86n12, 91, 212, 220,
   239n46, 250;
AB 85:72, 74, 86n12, 91, 212,
   220, 239n46, 250;
AB 86:74, 86n12, 91, 212, 220,
   236n39, 239n46, 250;
AB 87:70–71, 86n12, 91, 169,
   212, 220, 222, 238, 303;
AB 88:71–72, 91, 99, 212, 220,
   231–232, 234, 238, 295;
AB 89:68, 92, 261, 263, 271;
AB 90:51, 92, 263;
AB 91:92, 259, 263, 271;
AB 92:92, 364, 272;
AB 93:51, 92, 96, 364;
AB 94:73, 80n63, 92, 261–262,
   364;
AB 95:92, 199, 255–258, 278n8,
   279, 291;
AB 96:92, 278n10, 279, 281;
AB 97:92, 255, 278n11, 279,
   286–287, 290, 300–301;
AB 98:92, 278n11, 281;
AB 99:72n32, 92, 278n10, 279,
   281, 288, 290;
AB 100:92, 279, 281, 287, 290,
   299n18;
AB 101:92, 95, 278n8, 289–290;
AB 102:79, 92–93, 292–301;
AB 103:92–93, 306, 286n32,
   290, 292–301;
AB 104:92, 292, 298–299;
AB 105:92, 292, 298;
AB 106:92, 292, 298, 300;

Posidippus, Milan Collection *(cont.)*
AB 107:92, 292, 298;
AB 108:92, 292, 298;
AB 109:92, 162n5, 292, 298–299;
AB 110:10n5, 22n10, 162n5,
292n1;
Other Works, *SH* 706:30
On Old Age (Sphragis, Seal), AB 118
(= *P.Berol.* 14283 = *SH* 705):9n1,
10, 47–48, 59, 184n29, 185–186
Various Epigrams
AB 113 (= *SH* 978):94n2;
AB 114 (= *SH* 961):47n22;
AB 115 (= P.Louvre 7172
= *P.Firmin-Didot* = 11 GP
= Page, *GLP* 104a):9–10, 12,
19–22, 25–27, 32, 39n42, 47,
50, 67, 95, 292n2;
AB 116 (= P.Louvre 7172
= *P.Firmin-Didot* = 12 GP
= Page, *GLP* 104b
= Athenaeus VII 318d):9–10, 12,
19–22, 25–27, 32, 47, 50–51,
67, 91, 292n2;
AB 117 (= *P.Tebt.* I 3 = 24
GP):10, 12, 32, 48, 67;
AB 118 (= *P.Berol.* 14283
= *SH* 705):32–33, 67, 89, 95,
196n40;
AB 119 (= Athenaeus
VII 318d):22, 28, 30, 47, 50,
163, 171;
AB 120 (= Athenaeus X 412d
= 14 GP):30, 67;
AB 121 (= Athenaeus X 414d
= 16 GP):30;
AB 122 (= Athenaeus XIII 596c
= *SH* 699 = 17 GP):30–32,
42–45, 47, 51, 52, 67;

AB 123 (= *AP* V 134 = 1 GP):30,
54, 68;
AB 124 (= *AP* V 183 = 10 GP):30,
48n27;
AB 125 (= *AP* V 186= 2 GP):30,
49n28, 67;
AB 126:30 *(see also* Asclepiades);
AB 127:30 *(see also* Asclepiades);
AB 128:30 *(see also* Asclepiades);
AB 129 (*AP* V 211 = 3 GP):30, 67;
AB 130 (*AP* V 213 = 9 GP):30,
49n28;
AB 131 (= *AP* V 211= 3 GP):30,
32, 54, 195n37;
AB 132 (= *AP* VII 267 = 15
GP):30, 32, 49n28;
AB 133 (= *AP* V 213= 22 GP):30,
49;
AB 134:30, 34 *(see also*
Asclepiades);
AB 135 (= *AP* XII 45 = 5 GP):30,
49n28, 67;
AB 136:30 *(see also* Asclepiades);
AB 137 (= *AP* XII 98 = 6 GP):30,
33–35, 67, 119, 282;
AB 138 (= *AP* XII 120 = 7 GP):30;
AB 139 (= *AP* XII 131
= 8 GP):30, 37, 53, 65, 81;
AB 140 (= *AP* XII 168
= 9 GP):30, 35, 47n18;
AB 141:30, 68, 75 *(see also*
Asclepiades);
AB 142 (= *APl* 275 = 19 GP):30,
49, 188n7, 189n8;
AB 143 (= *SH* 702):47;
AB 144(= *SH* 701):32, 47, 61;
AB 145 (= *SH* 698
= Athenaeus XI 491c):31, 47;

Posidippus, Various Epigrams *(cont.)*
  AB 146 (= Athenaeus
    XIII 596c):31;
  AB 147:25;
  AB 148 (= *SH* 700 = Stephanus
    of Byzantium 295.3):32, 47,
    62n11, 67;
  AB 150 (= *Ad A.R.* I.1289, p.116
    Wendel = *SH* 703):29, 47
  See also Callimachus, Meleager,
    and Plato Comicus
Posidippus, *dubia*
  Elegy, Fernández-Galliano xxxvi:48
  Epigrams, Fernández-Galliano
    xxx:33, 48; xxxi:33, 48; xxxii:33, 48;
    xxxiii:33, 48; xxxiv:33, 48; xxxv:33,
    48
P.Oxy. 1643, v. 2:236n38; 3724:12
Proclus, *ad* Hesiod *Op.* 824:125n12
Procopius, *De Bello Gothico*
    IV 21:201n55
Propertius, I 1.1–4:266; III 7:260,
    264–269
Pseudo-Andocides, *Ad Alcibiadem*
    17:194n31
Pseudo-Callisthenes, I 41.4:243n66;
    III 34:241n58
Pseudo-Libanius (Nicholas Rhetor),
    Progymnasmata XXV 1–9:243n66
Pseudo-Plutarch, *On Music*
    XXXIII 1142e:298
P.Vindob. 39 (Vi^2 Allen):62n13;
    G 40611 *(incipits)*:12–13
Ptolemy I, *FGrHist* 138–139:241n58

Q

Quintilian, II 13.8:202n59

S

Sappho, *Fragments* 1:53–54, 81n66,
    96; 31:54n47; 95.1–4:292;
    127:81n66; 130 V:54
Satyrus
  Lives, P.Oxy. 1176 (= Pack 14560
    = P.Lit.Lond. 2070):194n32
  On the Demes of Alexandria,
    P.Oxy. 2465:242n60
  Fragments 2, col. 1.7–23:171n46;
    11:175n57
Scholia ad Callimachum,
    Hymn 4.11:95n10
Scholia ad Homerum,
    Iliad XI 101:62n13
Scholia ad Pindarum I, p.7.16f.:214
Florentine Scholia to Callimachus'
    Aetia, Prologue (fr. 1 Pf.
    = PSI 1219, fr. 1.1–10):46
SEG 36, 1986, no.351:146n84
Septuagint Job XXIV 6:71n26;
    XXXIV 32:71n26
Sextus Empiricus, *Adversus*
    Mathematicos VII 107:203n61
SH 903A (*Meropis*):58n1; 982:25
SIG 3 434/5:168
"Simonides," *AP* X 105:89n19;
    FGE 26a:295
Sophocles
  Antigone 601:101;
    998–1004:142n69
  Oedipus Rex 300–305:194n35;
    380–428:194n35
  Philoctetes 147:135n45
Sosibius, *FGrHist* 257a F 6:219n21
Sotades, *apud* Stobaeum
    Flor. 98.9:163n11

Stesichorus, "Lille Stesichorus"
  PMGF 22b (*P.Lille* 76):1–2n1
Strabo, *Geographica*
  XIII 1.11.42:131n38;
  XIV 1.14:202n57;
  XVII 791:22–23;
  XVII 794:241n58
Suetonius, *Augustus* 18:241n58
*Syll.*³ 1167 (= *LSAM* 30 A
  = *CIG* II 2953 = *SGDI* 5600
  = *DGE* 708
  = *IvEphesos* V 1678 A):143n72

T

TAM III, 1 no.746:27n22
Theocritus
  Epigrams
    5 GP (= *AP* VI 336):72n33;
    7 GP (=*AP* VII 658):86n9;
    8 GP (= *AP* VII 659):86n9;
    11 GP (= *AP* VII 663):72n33
  Idylls 1.9:68; 1.69:74n41;
    1.125:81n66; 2.18, 54;
    2.115:44n8; 2.151:36n35; 6:103;
    7:301 ; 7.39–41:196n41;
    7.83:43n5; 9:103; 9.54–62:104;
    11.55:96n13; 13.10:66n3;
    13.14:35n27; 13.53–54:55;
    14.6:70; 15.80–95:72n31;
    15.126:66n3; 16.76:78; 17.1:95;
    17.13–33:242–243;
    17.26–27:74n43;
    17.71–75:166n19;
    17.131–134:234n33
Theognis, 101–107:101;
  467–496:37n37
Theophrastus
  Characters III 5:294; XIII 3.10:294

On Stones I 4:111n17; I 6:106n6;
  III 18:106; IV 23:108, 111;
  IV 27:112n20; IV 37:108;
  V 28:113n23; VI 46:112n18;
  VI 37:109–110
Thucydides, VI 15.3:219;
  VI 16.1–3:218, 237n40
Timotheus, *PMG* 791 234:66n3
Tzetzes, *Chiliades* VIII 370:201n55

U

UPZ 78.28–39:24

V

Valerius Maximus, IX 12:163n11
Virgil
  Aeneid III 624:102n38;
    III 673–674:102n38;
    V 241:103n38;
    V 833–871:269–275, 274;
    V 854:274;
    VI 337–383:269–275;
    IX 490–491:271
  Georgics I 24–42:224n33;
    III 1–48:223–224; IV 211:97;
    IV 559–566:223–224
Vita Aeschyli 9:163n11
Vita Herodotea 131–140:64n16
Vitruvius, *De Architectura*
  VII, pref. 11:193n31

X

Xenophon
  Anabasis VI 1.23:139n60;
    VI 5.2:139n60, 146n84;
    VI 5.21:139n60, 146n84

Xenophon *(continued)*
  Hellenica I 3.1:147n89;
    IV 7.4:148n93; VI 4.7:147n89
  Memorabilia I 1.3:126n15;
    I 3:123n2

Z

Zenobius, III 94:241n58

INDEX

N. B.: References to specific passages, rather than general references to texts, may be found in the Index of Passages Cited.

A

Academy (Athens), 67–68, 92
Achaeans, 141
Achilles, 300
Acnonius (tetrarch of Thessaly), 235
Acropolis (Athens), 120n12, 201
Aeacus, 181–182
Aeneas, 270, 272–275
Aeschines (son of Atrometos), 279–280
Aeschylus, 141–142, 163, 174, 200, 278n8
Aetolian League, 184, 239–240
Agamemnon, 245
Agatharchus, 193
Agathon, 245n72
Agesilaus II (king of Sparta), 238
Agias, 235–236, 238
Agis II (king of Sparta), 238
Agoracritus, 198n47
Ajax, son of Oileus (Homeric hero), 153–154
Ajax, son of Telamon (Homeric hero), 32, 153–154
Alcaeus of Messene, 32
Alcamenes, 198n47, 206n71

Alcibiades, 207, 218
  Olympic victory of, 218, 237–238
Alexander III of Macedon (the Great), 69, 75, 87–88, 97, 128–131, 139, 145, 148–150, 164–168–169, 171, 174, 176, 188, 199, 226, 234, 239, 241–244, 246
  at the Ammoneion (Siwa), 241
  buried in Alexandria, 241, 246
  as Zeus Ammon, 169
Alexander (son of Ptolemy III), 239
Alexandria, 12, 23, 26, 50, 60, 73n35, 96, 166, 261
  Alexander (and *Theoi adelphoi*) cult at, 169, 207, 277
  Arsinoeion of, 168
  Eleusinia of, 181n21
  library of, 297, 305–306
  Tychaion at, 243–244
Alkmeionis (daughter of Rhodios), 182–183
Alpheos, 214
amethyst, 94n2
Amphissa, 183
Amyntas (father of Philip II), 234
Anacreon, 87, 214–215, 260

Index

Andocritus (son of Hagillus), 280n18
Antaeus, 100
anthologies, 30, 119
anthrax, 105
Antigonus Doson, 245
Antigonus Gonatas, 168
Antigonus (of Carystus), 206
Antiochus II, 213n5, 231n21
Antiphilus, 32
Anubion (horoscopic elegies), 17
Apelles, 199n49
Aphrodite, 65, 68, 81, 272
Apis bull, 16
Apollo (Phoebus), 92, 95, 115, 139,
    175, 185, 235, 257, 270
    and mantic art, 135n46
Apollonius (Ptolemaic official),
    22–23, 27
Apollonius Rhodius,151
Arabia, 87, 109–110, 121
Aratus, 95, 109, 151, 298
Archelaus (king of Macedon), 200,
    245n72
Archias, 32
Archilochus, 1, 45n12
Archytas (of Tarentum, Pythagorean),
    263
Argaeus, 183
Argead dynasty, 87–89, 129, 130n33,
    165, 171, 242
Ariadne, 223
Arion, 163, 173
Aristandros of Telmessus, 148
Aristarchus of Alexandria, 46–64, 98
Aristophanes, 125, 283n27
Aristophanes of Byzantium, 222n28
Aristotle, 26, 35n27, 245n72
Aristoxenus (Peripatetic), 297–298
Arsinoe I, 231n21, 232n24

Arsinoe II Philadelphus, 9, 89, 91, 98,
    158–159, 161–176, 213, 219n21,
    223, 232n24, 234n33, 240
    Cape Zephyrium cult of Arsinoe-
        Aphrodite, 10, 20–22, 24, 47,
        50, 89, 163, 168, 172, 208
    Arsinoe Euploia, 99, 171
    as Demeter-Isis-Tyche, 168
    other cults of, 163n10
    priestess of (*kanêphoros*), 170
    as warrior queen, 168, 171
Arsinoe III, 239
Artemis, 233
Artemisia (of Halicarnassus), 234
Artemision horse and jockey,
    254–255, 303
Artemision (Ephesus), 144
art-historical theory (in antiquity),
    187–211
Asclepiades, 5–6, 13, 30, 32–33,
    36n34, 38–40, 47–49, 68,
    75–76, 80n63, 119n8, 148n91,
    200, 256 261
Asclepieion (Athens), 120n12
Asclepieion (Corinth), 280n21
Asclepieion (Epidaurus), 278–284 ,
    289, 307
Asclepius, 92, 99, 171, 255, 276–286,
    288–291, 301
Athena, 136n49, 139n59, 169,
    243n64
    statue of, 149, 165, 167–168
Athenaeus, 31, 42, 43n4
Attalids, 206
Atticism, 206
Augustan poetry, 269–275
Augustus (Octavian), 25, 223–224, 240
Austen, Jane, 120n9
automata, 191

B

Bacchants, 182
Bacchus. *See* Dionysus
Baudelaire, 119
bereavement in epigram, 2–3
Berenice I, 91, 213, 221n26, 222, 238
Berenice Syrian or II, 68, 74, 91, 95,
    169, 175n59, 213, 217, 220–221,
    231–232, 236–237, 295
Berenice II, 164, 170, 175, 221–222,
    240
    priestess of (*athlophoros*), 170
Berenice (infant daugher of Ptolemy
    III), 239
Berisus (pseudo–homeric hero),
    32n18, 61–63
bêryllion, 105–106, 304
Billistiche (Ptolemy II's mistress), 219n21
Bacchylides, 78, 82
bird augury, 88, 123–159
    Ephesian rules on, 143–144
    Roman tradition in, 144, 148–149n94
    and spectator, 140
    symbolic value of, 138
blue chalcedony (*iaspis*), 105, 304
Boutades, 204, 210
Brontë, Charlotte, 18
bronze sculpture, 204–205
    casting of, 210

C

Calchas (seer), 142n68, 154
Calamis, 206n71
Calliades, 216n12
Callicrates of Samos, 10, 20–21, 40,
    91, 163, 171, 176, 208, 219,
    230, 239n46, 250

Callimachus, 1, 26–27, 30, 34n23,
    39, 46, 53–54, 57–58, 64, 95,
    170, 262, 298
    and Berenice II, 2, 221
    "Lille Callimachus," 11–12
Callon, 206n71
Canon, 206–207, 305
Capharaean rocks, 98, 100
carnelian (sard), 97, 105, 164, 303
Caucasus, 170
Charaxus, 42–45
Chares of Lindos (sculptor). *See*
    Colossus
Charioteer of Delphi, 230
Charmion, 246
childbirth, 132, 179–180
Chremonides (Athenian), 168
cicada, 34–35
Circe, 270
Cleanthes, 68
Cleo, 280–281
Cleopatra (daughter of Philip II), 245
Cleopatra VII (queen of Egypt), 246
Colossus (Rhodes), 47n20, 76–78, 90,
    202–203, 205
Conon, 222n28
Corinth, 214
Cos, 95
Cox, Kenyon, 247–248
crane, 175
Craterus, 19
Crates, 40n42, 261
Creon, 142
Cresilas, 71, 75–76, 79, 90, 197–198,
    204–205
Crete, 101–102, 197–199, 280n21
Croesus (king of Lydia), 245n72
Cronius, 87, 109, 304
Cyclops. *See* Polyphemus

Cynisca (queen of Sparta), 91, 169,
    238–239
Cyprus, 53, 112
Cythera, 53

D

Dactyliothecae. See gemstones:
    collecting
Daedalus, 190–191
Daochus monument (Delphi),
    234–236, 239–240
Daphne (from Dorylaion), 180n15
Darius (Persian king), 87, 165, 174n54
Darius I, 205
da Vinci, Leonardo, 247
dedicatory epigram, 48, 98. *See also*
    Milan papyrus
Deinodikes (from Naxos), 233
Deinomenes, 202n59
Deinomenes (from Naxos), 233
Delos, 95, 96n17, 120n12, 17,
    205n67, 242
Delphi, 29, 163, 175–176, 183–184,
    203n62, 219–230, 239–240,
    250n, 257, 282, 305
Demeter, 96n14, 181
Demetrius of Phalerum, 208, 244
Democritus, 112, 193
Derveni papyrus, 183
dialects, 65–83
    Aeolic, 65n2
    Attic-Ionic, 65n2; 66, 69–70, 77
    Cyrenean, 73n35, 75
    See also Posidippus: dialect in
Didymides (?), 187
Dichaearchus, 26
didactic poetry, 137, 151–156
    and *Oiônoskopika*, 137

Didymus, 61–62
Diogenes (Cynic philosopher), 284
Diomedes, 140
Dionysius Periegetes, 94
Dionysus, 184–185, 296
    triennial festivals of, 185
    See also mysteries; Posidippus: and
    mysteries
Diorcetes, 27
divination, 16–18, 24, 199
divination epigrams, 17–18. *See also*
    Posidippus: *Oiônoskopika*
Dumbarton Oaks bronze, 256–258
Doric ("West Greek"), 66–67. *See also*
    Posidippus: dialect in; Posidippus:
    transmission
Doricism. *See* Posidippus: dialect in
Doricha, 31, 42–45
Duris (of Samos), 40n42, 204,
    207–211, 305

E

eagle, 132–133, 139, 174
ecphrasis, 191, 193, 257. *See also*
    epigram: ecphrastic; Posidippus:
    Andriantopoiika
Eliot, T. S., 259, 262n10
Euboea, 97–103, 253. *See also*
    Geraestus
Eleusis, 96n14, 181
Elis, 245
Elpenor (Homeric hero), 270, 272, 274
Ephesus, 144
epigram,
    as interdisciplinary genre, 3
    complexity of, 6
    ecphrastic, 188n4, 189, 194
    evolution of, 6

epigram *(continued)*
  from stone to book, 17–19, 27,
    127, 177–178, 180n12, 186,
    194–195, 283n27
  funerary, 177–179
  intertextuality of, 127, 158n124
  monumentality as occasion for, 18
  and reader, 178–179n7, 284–286
  wit of, 40
  See also under Posidippus
Ergänzungsspiel (supplementation),
    3–4, 111, 120–121, 127–137,
    156, 159, 194–195
Eros/Erotes, 35–38, 54
Etearchus, 254
Eteocles, 141
euergetism, 227
Euhemerus, 244–245
Euhippus, 282n25
Eumenes I (ruler of Pergamon), 207n76
Eumenes II (king of Pergamon), 161n1
Euphorion, 45
Eupompus, 207, 210
Euripides, 25, 138, 237, 245n72
Eurydice (mother of Philip II), 234
Eurymachus, 124
Euthycrates, 206
Euxine, 259

F

falcon, 135, 146, 153
Familiengruppen, 225–246, 250
fishing, 128, 146

G

Galataea, 96n13, 100, 103
Gallus, Cornelius, 25

Gasr el Libia mosaic, 23
gemstones, 2, 87–88
  collecting, 88, 304
  See also individual gemstones
Geneleos group, 234, 239
Geraestus (Euboea), 96
  temple of Poseidon at, 98
Greek Anthology, 27n23, 32, 34n23,
    40, 64n16, 72n33, 77, 124n6,
    201, 215, 238, 243n66, 260n3,
    261, 265, 272n31, 279n16,
    299n15, 300
Greeks in Egypt, 45. *See also* Helleno-
    Memphites

H

Hades, 181, 274
Hagelaides, 187
Halitherses, 124
hawk, 153
Hecataeus (sculptor), 76, 90, 92,
    174–175, 196–197, 200, 205, 209
Hector (Homeric hero), 140–141
Hediste (from Demetrias-Pagasai),
    252n20
Hedylus, 5, 119n8
Hegias, 206n71
Helen (of Troy), 200
Heliodora, 68
Heliodorus, 36
Helleno-Memphites, 22–23. *See also*
    Greeks in Egypt
Hera, 52, 175, 219n21
Heracles, 29
Heraclitus, 34n23
Hermes, 174
Hermesianax (of Colophon), 31n13
Hermodikos (of Lamsakos), 283n27

Herodas, 84
Herodotus, 59
heron, 140
Hesiod, 36–38, 141, 146, 151,
    154–155, 190, 298
    didactic poetry of, 151
Hieron, 130–131, 214, 217n17
Hippocrates, 258
Homer, 36–38, 57–64, 96, 102–104,
    123, 125, 139, 145–146,
    152–155, 190, 269–270, 274
Horace, 275
Hypnos, 55

I

iaspis, 105, 112
Idomeneus (Homeric hero), 71–72,
    75–76, 79, 90, 197–198
incipits
    Oxyrynchus, 12
    Vienna, 12–13
India, 87, 170
Ion of Chius, 30n6
Isis, 244
Isthmia, 73, 163, 216n12, 250
Iulus (in Ceos), 170

K

Kleoboulos of Lindos, 64n16
kleos, 250, 255
kolossos, 187–188, 200
kyanus, 105
kydos, 169, 220–221, 224, 238

L

Labyrinth (Samian temple of Hera),
    205, 234

Lagid dynasty. *See* Ptolemies
lapis lazuli (*sapeiron*), 105, 108, 115,
    121–122, 303
Latin literature (Hellenistic back-
    ground of), 259–275
Lesbos, 31n13
Leto, 163, 175–176
Libyan asp, 276
Lincoln, Frances, 119
Lycaon, 300
Lycon, 216
Lyde, 35–37
Lyngeus, 114
lyngurium, 113n23
Lysimachus (king of Thrace), 226
"Lysimachus" (?) (son of Ptolemy III),
    239
Lysippus, 10, 69–70, 75, 90, 187–189,
    193, 195, 197, 200–202, 206n71,
    207–209, 240–241, 298n14
    Alexander statue, 90; 199
    naturalism in, 91n21
Lysistratus, 209

M

Macedonia, 170–171, 183–185
    Macedonian ruling class, 89, 232
    Dorian ancestry of Macedonians,
        74, 75n44
Magas (of Cyrene), 213, 231
Magas (son of Ptolemy III), 239
magnetic stone, 105, 111, 304
mantic art and practice, 143, 145–150
Marathon, 278n8
Mausoleion, 234
Medeios (son of Lampon), 256–257,
    277, 278n8, 291

Meleager, 6, 30, 33, 35–36, 39–40,
    47–48, 68, 84, 261, 270
Memphis (Egypt), 241
    cult of Imouthes/Asclepius at, 282
Menander, 25, 299n15
Menedemus, 299
Meriones (Homeric hero), 71, 75–76,
    90, 197–198
Menelaus (Homeric hero), 200, 270
Midas tomb, 64
Milan papyrus, *passim. See also* poetry
    books
    authorship, 4–5, 40–41, 124–125
    context, 11, 16
    corrections and errors, 11, 15, 67
    dedicatory epigrams in, 14, 98
    documentary texts of cartonnage, 12
    epigram arrangement, linkage, and
        structure, 97, 107–108, 127,
        249–250, 260, 277
    metrical constancy, 46n14, 118n3
    mythographic text on back, 11
    opening, 13, 95
    physical description of, 9–15, 306
    and reader, 130
    repairs of, 13
    scribes, 11, 13
    stichometrics, 13–15
    titles, 14n14, 98
Miletus, 53, 182–182
mimesis, 187, 189, 210
Mimnermus, 31n13, 36–37
miniaturism, 91, 205
Misenus (Virgilian hero), 270
Mnemosyne, 36–37
Molycus, 253–254
Moschus, 40n42
mother of pearl, 97, 105

Mouseion, 196, 243, 245, 305
Mozart, Wolfgang Amadeus, 40, 49
Muses, 35, 196, 221n27. *See also*
    under Posidippus
Myron, 77, 90, 201–202
    cow by, 90, 201n56, 202–203, 205,
        206n71
    Discobolus, 202
mysteries
    Dionysiac, 89, 180, 182–186
    of Eleusis, 181–182

N

Naucratis, 42, 88, 162, 170
Nefertiti, 247
Nemea, 73–74, 91, 163, 213,
    228–229, 231n21, 235–236, 250
Nemesis, 245
Nicandre base (Delos), 233, 238
Nicias, 218
Niko, 182
Nile, 42, 45
Nymphs, 54

O

Odysseus, 102, 140, 271–272, 274
Oedipus, 17
oikos, 133
Olympia, 219n21, 250, 252
Olympias (queen of Macedon), 183, 234
Olympic Games, 73–74, 91, 163,
    217n17, 229, 235
Olympus, 185
omens. *See* bird augury
Orpheus, 59, 148
Osiris, 244

P

Palinurus, 269–275
Pandaetes, 234
Pandarus (Homeric hero), 32
Parnassus, 185
Pasicles, 234
Patroclus, 300
Pausanias, 215
Pegasus, 105–106
Pella, 89, 183–185
Pentheus, 142n68
Pergamon, 206
    library of, 206n71
Periander of Corinth, 173
periodonikes, 236n38
Peripatetics, 26, 207
Persephone, 183–184
Persia, 87, 108, 112, 170
perspective (in painting), 193
Phaeacia, 271
Phalaecus, 40n42
Pharos (Alexandria), 21, 26, 47,
    49–50, 222n28
Pharsalus, 240
Phidias, 198, 206n71
Phidolas, 215
Phileia, 234
Philip II of Macedon, 17, 227, 234,
    242, 245
Philip V of Macedon, 245
Philip of Thessalonica (epigramma-
    tist), 39–40
Philetaerus (ruler of Pergamon), 207n7
Philitas of Cos, 31n13, 76, 90,
    174–175, 196–197, 200, 209
Philo, 236n38
Philodemus, 6, 12, 297
Phradmon, 198

Phrasicleia, 198
Phraxus (husband of Nicandre), 233
Phrontis, 270
Phylopidas, 74
Pindar, 72, 214, 217, 222n28, 239
Pisistratus, 243n64
Pithom stele, 168n33
Planudes, Maximus, 40, 85, 92
Plato, 245n72
Pliny (the Elder), 107, 112, 115
poetry books, 84–93, 157, 159, 186
    annotation, 25
    anthologies, 5–6, 12, 25–26, 84–85,
        91
    arrangement and publication of, 2,
        6 19, 28, 55, 84, 225
    layout, 25
    linkage between poems, 5, 86
Polemo, head of Academy, 92, 261
Polemo of Ilion, 19
Policlitus, 187, 198, 206n71. *See also*
    Canon
Polycrates, 87, 91–92, 173, 174n56,
    205
Polydamas (Homeric hero), 140
Polydorus, 271
Polyphemus (Cyclops), 96n13,
    100–104
    in Virgil, 102n38
Pompeii, 164
Poseidon, 88, 96–97, 100–101,
    153–154, 157, 171–172
    Isthmius, 192
Posidippus of Pella, *passim. See also*
    Milan papyrus
    addresses the Muses, 33–34, 68, 185
    Anathematika, 161–176
    Andriantopoiika, 187–211, 305–306
    Atticism of, 67–68

Posidippus of Pella *(continued)*
Aithiopia, 31
Asopia, 31
dialect in, 53–54, 65–83
Doric coloring in, 69–81
Epithalamium to Arsinoe, 9, 31, 47
Epitymbia, 177–186
erotic epigrams of, 49
Hippika, 212–246, 250–255, 303, 305
and Homer, 57–64, 299n19, 307
honored by Thermium, 29, 240n55
Iamatika, 255–258, 276–291, 299n18, 300–301
and inscriptions, 48, 283n27, 284
Ionic coloring in, 74, 81
On Cnidus, 30n6
language, 4–5
and Latin poetry, 5–6, 45, 120, 259–275
Lithika, 48–50, 85–89, 94–122, 303–304
meter in, 46n14
and monuments, 43–44, 188n5
and mysteries, 17–18
Nauagika, 259–275
object personification in, 44
Oiônoskopika, 16–18, 123–160, 303
"old," 4, 9–12; 16–56, 62n11, 67–69, 75, 89, 95, 119, 163, 171, 188n7, 189n8, 196n40, 282, 292n2
On Old Age (Seal, Sphragis), 9n1, 10, 32–33, 47–48, 59, 89, 184n29, 185–186
and Pathos, 54
on the Pharos, 10n5
and private life, 131–132
Progonoi epigrams, 240–241

and Sappho, 51–54
satiric epigrams, 49
Sôros, 5n12, 10, 61, 119–120
sound/word play in, 44
statue of, 34
stichometrics, 5
symposiastic epigrams of, 49
transmission, 4–5, 9, 69
Tropoi, 292–301, 306
and war, 133
Zeleia/Zelia, 32
Pothos, 35
Praxiphanes (Peripatetic), 297
Praxiteles, 206n71
Priam (Homeric hero), 32, 96
Progonoi monuments. *See Familien-gruppen*
Prometheus, 201
Propertius, 49, 260, 264–269, 275
Protesilaus (Homeric hero), 32
Proteus, 21–22, 2651n36
Ptolemaea, 236, 243, 245n74
Ptolemaus, 23–28
Ptolemies, 87, 170
queens, 2, 161, 213, 220, 223
self-definition, 5, 73–74, 161, 195, 210, 225, 227, 242
victories of, 99, 170, 213
Ptolemy I Soter, 75n44, 91, 166, 236, 239, 241–245
as an Alexander-historian, 241n58
Ptolemy II Philadelphus, 27, 91, 95, 161, 166n19, 175, 208n86, 219n21, 231n21, 232n24, 234, 236, 240–242, 246, 246, 295
Ptolemy III Euergetes I, 74n42, 91n25, 95, 169n38, 213, 220n23, 231, 232n24, 238–240
Ptolemy IV Philopator, 170, 240

Ptolemy VIII Euergetes II, 12
Publius, 296
Pyrgoteles, 87
Pyrrhus, 116
Pythagoras, 173, 206n71
Pythian Games, 73, 163, 214,
    229–230, 235–236, 250–251

R

Rhadamanthys, 181–182, 185
Rhodes, 78
Rhodope of Termessos, 27
Rhoecus, 204, 210
rock-crystal, 105, 303–4, 304n9
Rolling Stones, 120
Roman elegy, 260, 266

S

Sa'adi, 119
Salieri, Antonio, 40, 49
Samos, 173, 207, 234
Sappho, 31, 42–45, 51–54
    and Hellenistic and Latin poetry, 51
scribes, errors of, 11, 13, 19, 24–25
sea travel, 128, 146
Seleucus I, 244
Serapeum, Memphis, 9–10, 12, 16,
    19–20, 50n31
shearwater, 135, 146
shipping, 158
Simonides, 1–2n1
skênographia, 193–194
smaragdos, 105, 111–112, 116
snakestone, 105, 112–113, 116, 304
Sophocles, 30n6
Sosibius, 223
Sostratus of Cnidus, 10, 20–21, 26

Sotacus, 114–116
Sparta, 168
statuary, 2
Stephanus Byzantius, 32
Stephanus (dog), 27
Stephenson, Robert Louis, 119
Stesichorus
    "Lille Stesichorus," 1–2n1
Strabo, 22–23
Strato (of Lampsacus), 208
Styx, 272
Syria 81–82, 226

T

Tauron (dog), 27
Teisicrates, 206
Telemachus, 235, 238
Telmessos (Caria), 150
Termessos (Pisidia), 27
Thales (of Miletus), 245n72
Thanatos, 55
theater, 191–194
Thebans, 141
Thebes, 203n61
Theocritus
    Epigrams, 53, 85–86
    Idylls, 36, 39n42, 53–55, 66, 68, 70,
        74, 78, 95, 96n13, 97, 103–104,
        242–243, 301
    language of, 66–67, 74n43
Theodorus (of Samos), 91–92, 204,
    208, 210
Theophrastus
    Characters, 293–295, 298–299
    On Stones, 106-122
Thermium, 29
Thermos, 239
Thessaly, 74

Thrasybulus (of Miletus), 245n72
Thucydides, 218–219, 237n40,
   245n72
Tibullus, 49
Timotheus, 66n3
Tiresias, 142n68
touchstone, 105, 111
Triptolemus, 181n21
Trojans, 140
Tyche, 243
Tydeus, 90, 203
Tzetzes, 115

V

Venus. *See* Aphrodite
Venusgärtlein, 119
Veterans (Ptolemaic), 12
Virgil, 297
   imitates Theocritus, 85n6
visual arts (Hellenistic), 251–252, 303
vulture, 146

W

Whitman, Walt, 119

X

xanthe, 105, 109–110, 116
Xenocrates (of Athens), 206, 209
Xenombrotos, 252n19

Z

Zeno (manager), 27
Zenodotus, 40n42, 58–59, 61–63
Zephyrus, 223
Zeus, 95, 97, 139, 166, 214, 219n21,
   234, 237
   Aegiochos, 169
   Soter, 10
   statue at Olympia, 97